SOCIAL CONTROL IN CANADA
A Reader on the Social Construction of Deviance

EDITED BY
Bernard Schissel and Linda Mahood

OXFORD UNIVERSITY PRESS
Toronto   New York   Oxford
1996

To Nathan, Matthew, Lucy, and Jack

Oxford University Press
70 Wynford Drive, Don Mills, Ontario M3C 1J9

Oxford   New York
Athens   Auckland   Bangkok   Bombay
Calcutta   Cape Town   Dar es Salaam   Delhi
Florence   Hong Kong   Istanbul   Karachi
Kuala Lumpur   Madras   Madrid   Melbourne
Mexico City   Nairobi   Paris   Singapore
Taipei   Tokyo   Toronto

and associated companies in
Berlin   Ibadan

Oxford is a trade mark of Oxford University Press

Canadian Cataloguing in Publication Data

Main entry under title:

Social control in Canada: a reader on the social construction of deviance

Includes bibliographical references and index.
ISBN 0-19-540919-1

1. Deviant behaviour   2. Canada – Social conditions –
1971-   .*   3. Social control.   I. Schissel, Bernard,
1950-   .*   II. Mahood, Linda, 1960-

HM291.S63 1996   302.5'42'0971   C96-931191-5

Design: Max Gabriel Izod

1 2 3 4 — 99 98 97 96

This book is printed on permanent (acid free) paper ∞ .

Printed in Canada

Contents

List of Figures

List of Tables

Acknowledgements

This book has grown out of our experiences in teaching 'Deviance and Social Control' to undergraduates over the past decade at the University of Saskatchewan, the University of Calgary, and the University of Lethbridge. It is our effort to ameliorate this subdiscipline of sociology from the level of 'nuts, sluts, and perverts' that characterized it when we enrolled in it ourselves in the late 1970s and early 1980s. Many of our critical insights and ideas that led to the creation of this book have been shaped, in large part, by the intelligence and initiatives of the undergraduate and graduate students we have encountered in our teaching.

We would like to thank our colleagues who agreed to write contributions for this book. Their chapters have helped to create what we feel is an outstanding and groundbreaking collection of works in the field of social control in Canada, and we are grateful for their diligence and patience throughout the review and editing processes. This book has benefited from the support of colleagues at the University of Saskatchewan, the University of Guelph, and the University of Lethbridge. In particular we would like to thank Dr Patricia Chuchryk, Dr Inga Jesswein, and Diane Clark for their insights into sexual harassment at Canadian universities.

The University of Saskatchewan, through the Publications Fund and the Office of Research Services, supported the technical requirements of this work and we appreciate the support. While edited books such as this customarily contain a mix of contributions by new as well as established scholars, this reader also contains a very interesting piece by a group of Grade Eleven students from Walter Murray Collegiate in Saskatoon. We would like to thank the teachers and students for their industry and curiosity, especially Shammi Rathwell and Marshall Whelan. Also, gratitude to Kristina Shimmons for her generous and skilful work in making this book a reality.

At Oxford University Press, Valerie Ahwee undertook the editorial development of this book, and we would like to thank her and the staff at OUP for their diligence and concern. We would like to thank the anonymous reviewers for their significant and important suggestions regarding the outline and content of this book. Finally, we would like to thank Wendy and Vic for their insights, their editorial and academic expertise, and their support and patience.

B.S. and L.M.

—1—

Introduction to Deviance and Social Control

Bernard Schissel

The sociology of social control and deviance is not one coherent discipline, and most traditional books on deviance concentrate on studies of the characteristics, origins, and effects of abnormal or unconventional behaviour. This book does not take a traditional approach to deviance. The focus here is primarily on social control framed within a social constructionist perspective that is based on several assumptions. Firstly, the social construction approach argues that acceptable behavioural norms and appropriate penalties for violations of such norms are difficult to define. The degree of consensus as to what is 'normal' behaviour is, therefore, highly variable. Discussions of unconventional behaviour include conceptions of how power operates in defining and sanctioning virtuous and evil behaviour. Secondly, we assume that what constitutes deviant behaviour changes over time and across social groups and societies. As a result, the social constructionist approach is informed largely by historical studies that track changing modes of social control. This book is generally premised on the assumption that there is nothing inherently deviant, but rather that what comes to be seen as deviant is the result of socio-historical context. Thirdly, in using this approach we assume that laws and norms are not necessarily unchangeable or correct or even shared by the majority. In effect, codes of conduct are constructed by those in positions of power and are generally used to sanction the behaviours and cultures of more marginalized peoples. Lastly, when we discuss power and control and its relationship to the definition of deviance, we must acknowledge the power of words in traditional studies of deviance. The term deviance implies something negative. When deviance is defined as sin, the implication is something wicked; when defined as a medical problem, the implication is sickness; and when deviance is defined as lifestyle, the implication is deficient socialization. The sensitivity and objectivity that sociologists struggle to maintain in studying deviance must be based on the realization that research in this area of human behaviour, however important, can be misused and misrepresented to the detriment of certain people.

This relativist, social constructionist orientation stands in contradistinction to the more absolutist, consensus theories, which assume that deviance is essentially norm-violating behaviour and that the norms of conduct are consensual and, by definition, correct. An absolutist focus of control policies identifies the offender and recommends either punishment or rehabilitation. Social policy makers who are absolutist in their thinking assume that the basic problem facing society is the individual rule breaker. They advocate policy that will either deter or dissuade a violator. Quite clearly, the system of justice and punishment in our society is based on absolutist assumptions.

In this book, we focus on five social categories within which we discuss how definitions of unconventionality arise and how these definitions influence the control of certain categories of people. The five categories are law, health, sexuality, race, and education.

The historical studies in this book illustrate the relativist, social control orientation that defines abnormality based on conceptions of sin, sickness, and unconventional lifestyle, coincident with the influences of religion, science, and the law, respectively. The premodern world, for example, was characterized by an almost universally held belief that evil was rooted in sin and that the cure for evil conduct resided in religion. The Church, as a result, was the major force of social control, and as many historical accounts now tell us, millions of lives were sacrificed during the Inquisition based on the assumption that badness and evil were the devil's work.

With the Enlightenment period in Europe, science took over from religion as the keeper of knowledge of human behaviour and set the stage for modern-day understandings of deviance and crime, which developed from the natural sciences' concern with sickness and abnormality and the social sciences' concern with deviance as a rational lifestyle decision. The scientific study of deviance that has informed our contemporary formal system of social control is based on modernist precepts of rational understanding and empirical/objective research procedures. The norms of scientific inquiry that guide legal, medical, and educational practices, for example, are designed to diagnose, correct/heal, and discipline the unconventional personality. This is where the studies using the conception of lifestyle and unconventionality become enmeshed with scientific studies of sickness to define a composite deviant, one who is predisposed to abnormality and ultimately chooses abnormal conduct.

Studies that critique the scientific approach generally focus on the power that those who possess knowledge have in implementing social control policy. The work of Michel Foucault is mentioned in several places throughout this book; his work focuses on the connections between knowledge and power and on the linkages between social control and historical context (I will elaborate on this work in a later section).

In summary, this book is based not on deviance but on social control, society's tendency to identify and control the behaviour of certain types of citizens. The morality and its attendant rules that underpin this control are not givens. Instead, they change depending on historical period, social context, or socio-economic power. This view can be subsumed generally under several critical approaches incorporating conflict theories and feminist theories in contradistinction to more orthodox consensus theories, which assume that morality and the rules that proscribe behaviour are natural, universal, and unchanging. Quite clearly, then, the relationship between power and control are fundamental to this book.

This first chapter is a survey of traditional and contemporary theories of deviance and control. The classical theories tend to concentrate on traditional approaches to deviance. Most of the contemporary theories focus on the relative nature of deviance and emphasize the connections between deviance and control, more in line with the focus of this book.

In the first section of this chapter, I discuss the Enlightenment-based theories of deviance and their modern incarnations, which deal with the influences of rationality and science on detecting and controlling bad behaviour. In the second and third sections, I present traditional constructionist theories and discuss current theoretical orientations in the constructionist paradigm, respectively. These contemporary theories in the constructionist paradigm form the theoretical orientations for the chapters in this book.

CLASSICAL THEORY AND THE MODERN EXTENSIONS

The classical period embraced the scientific principles that started with Francis Bacon and formed the philosophical framework for the Enlightenment. This historical period, which saw the evolution of knowledge as religion based to knowledge based upon the principles of science and objectivity, culminated in the study of immorality as something objective and observable. Deviance, while still regarded as something absolute, was now understood as resulting from natural tendencies towards hedonism or self-preservation. The classical approaches may be thought of as the first modern approaches to the study of crime and deviance because they abandoned the metaphysical principles of religion and incorporated the logic of rational thought and scientific techniques.

Beccaria and Bentham

Classical theorists envisioned crime and deviance as the result of rational, calculated decisions by humans who are naturally predisposed to maximize pleasure and minimize pain. The principles that guide this perspective are: (a) that people are basically hedonistic, (b) that they have free will, (c) that people form a social contract with society (by birth right) whereby they agree to forego selfish pursuits to partake of and to foster the greater good of society, and (d) that punishment is an appropriate form of social control because it changes the pleasure-pain calculus, insuring that deviance and crime are minimized. These principles were articulated in the late 1700s by the Enlightenment philosopher Cesare Beccaria, who cautioned that punishment was only justified if it deterred hedonistic pursuits. Furthermore, he believed that punishment as a social control mechanism must be minimized. In other words, there should only be just enough punishment to prevent further crime. In a very 'enlightened way', classical theorists like Beccaria abhorred punishment, especially execution, and recommended the prison as the appropriate place for the minimal administration of punishment.

Jeremy Bentham, whose work provided the blueprint for the modern prison system, again used the calculus of pleasure and pain as the starting point for social reform. Bentham used mathematical models to understand and evaluate the compelling nature of deviance and the deterrent effect of punishment. He argued that money and other societal resources should be expended proportionately to the degree of the seriousness of the crime. Like Beccaria, he maintained that punishment should never exceed the degree necessary to prevent unacceptable behaviour.

Bentham's major contribution to modern systems of justice, however, was his principle of the panopticon. Classical theorists understood that prison was an ideal form of punishment because the length of sentence could be determined in days and years proportionate to the seriousness of the crime, and also because the prison provided an opportunity for the prisoner to re-evaluate the social contract and embrace a new belief in the value of conformity. The panopticon was an architectural design that fostered the principles of classical theory and social control. The architecture was based on a circular design in which prison officials occupied a central observation tower surrounded by the cells situated in a circular pattern around the tower. In short, the panopticon allowed prison officials to survey inmates and staff without being observed. The inmates and staff would conform their behaviour and would be unlikely to go astray because of the high risk of detection. The panopticon has become the architectural plan for many prison systems throughout the world. Ironically, as we will see later in this chapter, Foucault takes the concept of the panopticon to represent the omnipresent forces of social control in modern society.

Modern Classical Theory

Neoclassical theories extended the approaches of Beccaria and Bentham to include some of the principles of law that we see in modern society. For example, we account for mitigating circumstances when judging 'culpability' for criminal action. If someone commits a criminal act in self-defence, we no longer assume the person is a criminal simply by virtue of the act. As well, when we determine punishment, we now account for the offender's record and adjust the punishment on this basis; classical theory decried all forms of unequal punishment as unjust and unnecessary. Lastly, neoclassical thought maintained that free will was not uniform and that the law must account for disparities in the will to commit criminal or deviant acts. For example, the law now acknowledges that some violators may be suffering from insanity or that some criminal acts occur under duress and that the violators do not have free will in such cases.

The basis of classical theory is that it is better to prevent crime than to punish it, and that punishment is unsavoury no matter how it is administered. The modern extension of this philosophy is variously subsumed under deterrence theory, rationality theory, or social control theory. In effect, deterrence theory is one branch of social control theory that studies the various types of positive and negative sanctions that encourage normal behaviour and discourage or deter abnormal behaviour. People who commit deviant acts not only lose social rewards like job promotion and peer respect but may also suffer state-sanctioned fines or imprisonment. Deterrence theory assesses the effectiveness of official, state-administered punishment in inhibiting the individual violator (specific deterrence) and the general public (general deterrence) from engaging in a deviant act. Individuals, aware that they can be punished, take this information into account when they consciously choose to commit or refrain from a deviant act. One of the basic premises of our system of law and punishment is the principle of deterrence/cost-benefit. Of course, the questions we need to ask as sociologists of deviant behaviour is why in certain instances we punish more than necessary, and why certain categories of individuals are targeted for more severe punishment (either formal or informal) than others, even when the deviant acts they commit are similar.

For some social control theorists, however, the answer to deviant behaviour is governed by an internal logic or 'morality', the 'natural' result of internalizing the rules and norms that are shared and valued by a majority in society. The acceptance of such rules controls behaviour because people naturally experience guilt and remorse when they act in a deviant manner. Deviance results from a lack of moral socialization, a lack of conscience. The psychopath is the typical anomaly who has no morality or conscience—that is, not immoral but amoral.

Travis Hirschi (1969) typifies social control theorists who focus on morality and inner control. He focuses on the degree of bonding to conventional society as a general determinant of inner control and moral conduct. Hirschi introduced the dimensions of attachment, involvement, commitment, and belief as components of bonding and as they relate to family, education, and peer group. His theoretical model suggests a behavioural and attitudinal component to bonding, and measures elements of inner control (conscience/morality) and outer control (how people respond to social pressure and proscription). Attachment is defined in terms of attraction to parents, school, and peers. Commitment is an attitude to conventional aspirations such as occupation and education. Involvement is participation in conventional, goal-oriented activities. The belief component is an attitude towards consensual moral values, values that are perceived as generated by society as a whole, in essence, a measure of morality or conscience. For Hirschi, then, the greater the degree of bonding—as measured by the four dimensions—the less likely it will be for a youth to commit deviant acts.

Modern-day incarnations of Hirschi's work have tried to link the conservative tendencies of control theory with the critical orientations of conflict theories. Power control theory focuses on how families reproduce the gendered social class structure and how children's deviant activities are determined by the degree of parental involvement. Patriarchal family practices and structures influence the ways that boys and girls approach risk-taking behaviour. Power control theory attempts to show how power is derived from social class placement and the influence that types of parental power have on the development of deviant children (Hagan, Simpson, and Gillis 1995).

BIOLOGY AND PATHOLOGY: THEORIES OF POSITIVISM

It is impossible to explain certain types of deviant or abnormal behaviour in classical terms. Inexplicable acts, such as the crimes of serial killers or child molesters, defy logical social explanations. As such, we attempt to explain such behaviours in medical rather than criminological terms by invoking concepts of pathology or sickness. Biological or genetic explanations have persisted for hundreds of years and while the mechanisms of discovery and treatment have changed, the basic positivistic premises have remained the same: that deviant behaviour is a condition within the individual, and that people deviate not for rational reasons but for reasons connected to a disease or defect of the body or mind. As such, the positivist theories advocate correcting the condition and are perfectly suited to a medical model of cure or rehabilitation.

The Lombrosan Legacy and Social Darwinism

The earliest biological theories linked evil or abnormal behaviour with the conception of human evolution and made the assumption that evil humans were evolutionarily regressive or atavistic. The groundwork for this theorizing was laid by Charles Darwin, whose followers used the insights of the natural science concept of 'survival of the fittest' to interpret human existence. The Social Darwinists argued that the marginalized and the unacceptable were less fit than more privileged people in society, and that criminals and deviants were proliferating because society was interfering with natural selection by artificially sustaining less fit and, by their standards, less deserving people.

Cesare Lombroso (1911), an Italian physician writing in the late nineteenth century, argued that criminal behaviour was a symptom of a lower position on the evolutionary scale. Based on a comparison of a sample of inmates and a sample of Italian soldiers, Lombroso found that, relative to the soldiers, inmates were characterized by physical aberrations such as high cheekbones, protruding foreheads, eye defects, poor dentition, and malformed arms and legs. Deviants could be identified by atavistic physical characteristics. The flaws in this type of logic can be readily seen when we consider the effects that prison may have on the body, and especially when we consider that the physiological traits that Lombroso identified may be stigmatized and may prevent individuals from leading normal, productive lives or that poverty and malnutrition may produce both physical abnormalities and a need to engage in criminal activity. Lombroso's faulty logic and poor research design, coupled with subsequent research that failed to support his findings, discredited these particular types of biotheories and Lombroso's work is of only historical interest today. However, the implications of his work and the connections to Social Darwinism have led to altered versions of the biological approach, which continue to flourish.

Contemporary Biological Studies

The work of William Sheldon (1949) is one of the most noteworthy extensions of biological theories. In the 1940s, Sheldon attempted to link body type to criminal and deviant behaviour, arguing that certain body types—the ectomorph, who is skinny and fragile; the mesomorph, who is muscular, stocky, and athletic; and the endomorph, who is soft, round, and fat—are associated with temperament and behaviour. Sheldon found that an excessively high percentage of criminals, especially juvenile gang members, were mesomorphs, leading him to argue that there was a cause-and-effect relationship between physiology and behaviour. Again, faulty logic seems to be at play; it may well be that mesomorphs are more likely to be recruited to delinquent gangs, or that judges see strong, athletic boys as more of a threat than other types. Like Lombroso's theories, the supporting evidence for Sheldon's theory was weak.

The findings of later research that showed deviants were more characterized by genetic abnormalities than non-deviants created excitement in the medical and crime control communities. With the discovery of Klinefelter's syndrome in men who manifested aggressive behaviour, large (excessively tall) body types, and mental deficiencies, researchers concluded that an extra Y chromosome was the genetic marker for violent criminality (Shah and Roth 1974). Once again, the subsequent evidence has suggested that the research and the causal logic underpinning these studies may be faulty. Even if there is an association between chromosome composition and deviant tendencies, it does not suggest how or why the abnormality leads to deviance. It may be that the physical difference isolates people and restricts them from conventional society. If XYY people have lower mental capacities, for example, it may be that they find it impossible to engage in conventional social and economic activities and are driven to deviant acts. That is, the stigmatizing effects of an intolerant world may force deviant behaviour.

Despite the flaws in earlier biostudies, biological research has currently gained a new life. Current sociobiological research in alcoholism concentrates on identifying the neurological or genetic traits of people with high-risk propensities to alcoholism (Goodwin 1986; Pollock et al. 1986). As well, recent work on male predisposition to violence attempts to link evolutionary concepts, such as reproductive competition (which is characteristic of our lower primate ancestors) and status competition, with homicidal behaviour in male gangs (Wilson and Daly 1985). There is also an interest in biological phenomena in recent twin studies comparing identical (monozygotic) and fraternal (dizygotic) twins. The basic research question in these studies is the degree to which twins of different types share criminal or deviant tendencies (Mednick and Volavka 1980). The overall findings suggest a greater similarity in deviant behaviour for identical compared to non-identical twins.

Related research based on sibling comparisons and family histories has attempted to identify the genetic link to homosexuality. Much of this research is based on the assumption that the x-chromosome in gay men is genetically distinct, and that genetic material predisposing certain men to homosexuality is passed on through maternal lines. Other studies have shown an apparent tendency for homosexuality to occur more often in paternal genetic lines. Despite the ambiguity and contradictions inherent in genetic research, the search for the gay gene, the alcoholism gene, and the aggressiveness gene continues.

While biological studies are compelling and persistent, they have gained little favour in sociological research for two reasons. First, the research has failed to control for psychological and social factors that interact with biology and, secondly, the implications of such research appear to be rather frightening. The policy implications based on biological research, such as genetic engineering and selective abortions of defective foetuses, are objectionable to many people.

Psychological Theories
Psychological explanations of deviant behaviour, like biological theories, adopt a positivist approach to deviant behaviour and focus on its causes as originating within the individual. Psychological theories argue, however, that character and personality are acquired and not just inherited. For example, the psychoanalytical theories of Sigmund Freud concentrated on the improper

development of conscience. Freud maintained that personality is comprised of the id, the ego, and the superego. The id (the mostly animalistic part of the personality that leads to aggressive, self-destructive, and antisocial tendencies) conflicts with the ego (the social self) and the superego (the conscience). Deviants are those whose ego and superego are poorly developed and inadequately equipped to hold the id in check. For Freud, this impairment starts at the earliest stages of infant development and is influenced by the degree and type of parental training.

As an extension of Freudian psychoanalysis, the frustration-aggression hypothesis (Berkowitz 1969) suggests that the frustration resulting from unmet needs leads to aggressive behaviour, which may be manifested in antisocial or self-destructive behaviour. Bandura and Walters (1963) extended this explanation of aggression in a *theory of social learning*, which suggested that people learn to behave aggressively through a process called modelling, when individuals who observe the behaviour of others being rewarded are prone to regard the rewarded behaviour as acceptable. Much of this research focused on the influence that violence on television has on deviant behaviour. Simply put, if the viewer is exposed to depictions of deviance that are socially acceptable, then he or she may become insensitive to the deviance and may no longer see acts of violence as negative.

The types of vicarious conditioning that social learning theorists discussed were fundamental to the *theory of behaviourism*. Beginning with the work of B.F. Skinner (1953), behaviourism assumed that behaviour was instilled through reward and punishment, and that because behaviour is learned, bad behaviour can be unlearned. Eysenck (1977) argued that immoral behaviour is the result of improper conditioning; children never learn to associate fear and pain with bad conduct. Eysenck considered this conditioned fear as the basis of conscience. In psychological research that stressed the effect of fear and punishment on moral development, the *theory of cognitive development* focused on how moral development coincides with stages of psychological and physical maturity. For psychologists like Jean Piaget (1932) and Lawrence Kohlberg (1969), the individual is the source of 'badness'. In cognitive development theory, as in psychoanalytic theories, deviants are characterized by deficits in moral reasoning. These deficits occur at certain stages of psychic development and deviant tendencies can be rectified by redirecting the individual through the appropriate stages of development.

Psychological theories have maintained their appeal in the study and control of deviance primarily because the emphasis on the individual permits the development of a treatment program based on psychotherapy. Therapies such as behaviour modification are still used in prison to establish conformist behaviour. The main criticism of psychological theories, however, is that they ignore the relative nature of deviance; definitions and reactions to deviant behaviour depend on social power and social context. As well, psychological theories have been criticized for ignoring major forms of deviant behaviour, including violations committed by organizations (corporate crime), political crimes, and certain types of rational individual crimes such as credit card fraud. It is worth remarking, though, that some sociological theories, some of which include elements of biology and psychology, tend to consider factors other than the act and the actor.

CONSENSUS THEORIES AND THE SOCIOLOGY OF DEVIANCE

Sociological theories based on a consensus model make some prior assumptions about social behaviour that place boundaries on the theories developed from the general consensus framework. The basic assumptions are that the rules and norms by which we conduct ourselves are shared and therefore correct. Morality is a given and, as such, the basic problem facing society is that certain people fail to conform. The following sections present the major consensus theories of deviance and illustrate how the tenets of these theories have been woven into the formal mechanisms of social control in our society.

Structural Theories

Structural Functionalism. Structural functionalist theories can be traced to the works of Emile Durkheim (1964), a French sociologist writing in the late 1800s and early 1900s. For Durkheim and subsequent functionalists, the basic determinant of abnormality is lack of conformity; societies with low levels of social cohesion are typified by high rates of crime and deviance. When societies change rapidly, people are less likely to experience integration and regulation. Such societies will, as a consequence, experience high rates of unconventional behaviour. The psychological state of people in disrupted societies is *anomie* or normlessness. Anomic conditions exist when few values and norms are shared and when formal mechanisms of social control fail. According to Durkheim, suicide, while the result of several different sociopsychological forces, results mostly from lack of social integration and lack of regulation.

Durkheim also suggested in a typical functionalist manner that because deviant behaviour is endemic to all societies, it has a positive or functional role to play in the stability of society. He and subsequent functionalists argue that deviance and crime establish the boundaries of morality, strengthen community and group ties through the presence of a common enemy, provide opportunities for the release of tension resulting from rigid social norms, and provide alternative norms that may engender society's adaptation to new values. Two classical studies that illustrate this point are Kingsley Davis's study of prostitution (1937) and Kai Erikson's study of puritan society (1966). Davis views prostitution as a safety valve that protects the family by providing a sexual outlet for clients who might otherwise choose to abandon their spouses for different sexual experiences. Erikson, on the other hand, argues that public deviance and public displays of shame and punishment provide a cohesiveness by redefining morality and illustrating the consequences of violations to the moral code.

Robert Merton (1938) extended Durkheim's work by studying the social and economic forces that influence relatively vulnerable people. This contemporary body of research, labelled *anomie or strain theory*, proposes that anomic societies do not provide adequate acceptable avenues for people to achieve culturally defined and accepted goals. The discrepancy between goals and the actual means to achieve those goals creates strain, which in turn produces various illegitimate innovations for circumventing *blocked opportunity*. Merton categorized five types of responses to the strain of blocked opportunity: conformity, innovation, ritualism, retreatism, and rebellion. Conformity is the only non-deviant response and requires no further discussion. Innovation, however, involves the acceptance of shared goals, but not acceptance of the legitimate means of achievement. For example, an unsuccessful student may cheat on an exam or a fired corporate executive may decide to defraud his company. Most types of criminal behaviour fall into the category of innovation. Ritualism identifies activity wherein the means are accepted and the goals are rejected or altered. For example, Merton considered as deviant those who simply show up for work but do not accomplish as much as they can. This type of goal de-escalation is considered somewhat harmless and has received very little attention in research. On the other hand, retreatism as a response to blocked opportunity has received considerable attention in research on deviance. Retreatists reject the goals and the means of achieving it by withdrawing from society. Mental illness, substance abuse, and compulsive gambling may all be forms of retreatist behaviour, and, as we will see later in this chapter, retreatist forms of deviance are highly visible in studies on social control and deviance, even though most of these forms of deviance are likely to be victimless activities. Lastly, rebellion signifies a form of deviance much like retreatism wherein the goals and means are rejected. Rebellion, however, constitutes behaviour that advocates new forms of achievement. Merton might argue that political rebellion, for example, is born of blocked opportunity, and that revolutionary activity on university campuses in response to funding cuts or political protests of First Nations peoples in North America typify forms of rebellion in response to lack of opportunity.

Social Control Theory. Earlier in this chapter, I discussed deterrence theory, which is the contemporary extension of classical criminological theory. Deterrence theory and its parent, social control theory, are typically functionalist in their assumption that norms are generally shared and, as a result, the appropriate areas of study are the mechanisms that compel some people to violate norms and others to resist the temptations to deviate. Unlike most other consensus theories, however, social control theory assumes that norm violations are attractive and that most people are motivated to engage in deviant behaviour. Simply put, a person is a rational, self-interested being who will violate society's norms if there is an advantage in doing so. This theory concentrates on the legal, social, and personal reasons for engaging in illegal or deviant behaviour, given that such behaviour may be highly advantageous.

Sociocultural Theory. Sociocultural theories of deviant behaviour focus on how people learn deviant behaviour. Cultures and subcultures are targeted as the transmitters of deviant values. Beginning with work in the sociology department at the University of Chicago in the 1930s, a substantial body of work has focused on the relationships between environmental or spatial patterns and deviant cultures. This body of research originated with the ecological theories of crime and deviance attributed to the Chicago School of Sociology. Sociocultural theories arose in response to the 'objective' study of deviant groups in time and space. Urban settlement patterns came to be associated with pockets of deviance. *Cultural transmission theory*, otherwise known as subcultural theory, maintained that crime and deviance are concentrated in identifiable urban areas, and that abnormal behaviour is a part of the culture of certain urban areas. Unconventional values attributed primarily to inner-city subcultures are believed to be passed from generation to generation within the ecological zone. *Social disorganization theory* explains urban patterns with high deviance rates, which result in inadequately organized communities with transient populations that disrupt society. Such disruptions contribute to unstable cultural values and poorly defined mechanisms of inner and outer control.

The sociopsychological dimension of sociocultural theories, *differential association theory*, uses both social disorganization and cultural transmission theories to explain the mechanisms through which values become part of certain subcultures. Sutherland (1939), for example, argued that deviant behaviour was learned in close association with intimates and friends, and that deviant behaviour is likely if an individual is exposed to deviant influences. This theory focuses on the influence of socialization on deviance and concentrates on the process of learning and evaluating moral and immoral definitions.

CRITICAL THEORY, SOCIAL CONSTRUCTION, AND SOCIAL CONTROL

This book's critical, social constructionist approach to the study of deviance concentrates on the relationships between social and political power and the construction or definition of abnormal behaviour. It also charts the relationship between sociopolitical power and the official control of deviant behaviour. For social constructionist theorists, power is a type of currency or wealth, and its ownership gives privilege to certain people over others. Those who have power define what constitutes deviant behaviour, control discourse and language, and legitimate the definitions and the attendant methods of social control.

The approaches in this relativist mode can be subsumed under various theories, including Marxist, pluralistic conflict, knowledge/power theories, and feminism. Despite the theoretical orientation, the primary concern in this section, and in the book in general, is how social and political power gets translated into abilities to define good and bad behaviour. Such power also dictates what measures are acceptable and appropriate in controlling bad behaviour. Punishment, then, is a social institution that is fundamental to social control and is meted out or withheld on a discriminatory and preferential basis.

Conflict Theory and the Marxist Tradition

Conflict theories contrast with consensus theories by arguing that society does not necessarily share a single set of values. Conflict theory can be traced to the works of Karl Marx ([1848] 1964) and Max Weber (1947). Marx argued that social inequality is part and parcel of the capitalist economic system, that conflict between social classes is the basic social process in society, and that definitions of deviance are determined largely by the dominant class. Weber insisted that conflict can arise from sources other than class, sources such as political, organizational, and professional groups. Nonetheless, Weberian conflict theory maintains that deviance, and the corresponding mechanisms of social control, are the result of conflict and compromise.

Idealist Marxism. Conventional Marxist theories of deviance argue that social conflict exists between those who control the means of production and those who do not. Those in control constitute a ruling class, which controls relationships in areas other than the economy. This class is responsible for defining, identifying, and sanctioning what is unacceptable. Richard Quinney (1977), for example, argues that the ruling class uses the law to define as deviant certain types of activity such as prostitution and theft, while tolerating or at least minimizing the seriousness of corporate and organizational deviances, including price-fixing, safety violations, and workplace safety violations. The law, then, as determined by ruling class interests, can be selectively applied to maintain advantage for wealthy, powerful people. Chambliss (1969) has argued that we punish those people who can be tried and convicted with the least difficulty, namely, the socially and economically disadvantaged.

The two primary variants of Marxist theory, *structuralism* and *instrumentalism*, presume that ruling class interests are reflected not only in the definitions of deviance but also in the methods through which we control those who deviate. From this perspective, it is not surprising that most of those in jail are those who are from the least privileged sectors of society. Powerful people transmit their values into a system of laws, norms, and values that protects their interests. Instrumental Marxists, however, assume that the state and its laws are meant solely to protect the owners of the means of production. Structural Marxist theories, on the other hand, argue that the primary function of the state and its laws is to protect the existing productive (capitalist) system and that to do so, the state must appear to act democratically, at times putting the welfare of society ahead of the welfare of the powerful. Nonetheless, the primary functions of the state are to maintain the existing system of accumulation and to legitimate its existence through institutions like law.

Left Realism. Left realism is a relatively recent development in critical studies of crime and deviance. The perspective concentrates on social control policies in the context of 'taking crime seriously'. This adage suggests that crime and deviance operate on a behavioural and everyday level as well as on the political level. While crime and deviance, and the social control policies that result, do originate from structural inequalities that underpin disparities in deviant behaviour and judicial outcomes, society must deal with the immediate needs of those most at risk to criminal victimization and public condemnation. This concentration on victimization is based on the assumptions that much injurious deviant behaviour is largely intraclass; people are victimized by—and consequently fear—associates or people in the same social environment. As a result, the focus of research (and short-term social control policy) is to meet the immediate needs of crime victims with crime prevention and personal protection (Lowman and MacLean 1992).

Crime resides at the intersection of four realities: the offender, the victim, the state, and public opinion. This 'square of crime' perspective (Bierne and Messerschmidt 1991) suggests that social control policies that are sensitive to the economic and social disparities in society must be critical of the system that keeps offenders in prison, must be attuned to the needs of crime victims, and must be critical of ideological mechanisms—including the discourses of media, science, and politics—that control the public's understanding of deviance and crime.

Critical Theories. Like all constructionist theories, the critical theorists challenge the ideas of positivism and attempt to understand social facts as historical phenomena. One of the principal foci of the critical tradition—also referred to as the Frankfurt School—was the subtle and hidden coercion that compels even the most oppressed to believe and support the system of law and social control. And, of course, these theorists were intent on studying the real beneficiaries of the manipulation of the social control system.

Antonio Gramsci (1971) argued for an understanding of the ideological apparatuses of the state, which construct and control belief systems that give advantage to certain groups of people at the expense of others. His discussions of the concept of hegemony—a dominant world view that is so strong that people are unable to think of alternative views—suggest that the world view of the most oppressed (those living on the margins of society) is remarkably close to those who are more powerful and more affluent. For example, many marginalized or lower-class people share society's concern for law and order and for stricter measures of social control, even though they are the most oppressed by those very measures. Gramsci and others from the critical school were determined to understand the origins of hegemony as an irrational and oppressive force. The studies that emerged from this tradition concentrate on the media, education, science, and religion as cultural agencies for the dominant belief systems.

Pluralistic Conflict Theories. Pluralistic conflict theorists, like Marxist theorists, suggest that deviance and crime result from the use and abuse of power. Unlike Marxist theorists, however, pluralists see conflict and accommodation as stemming from other than economics. Status groups, as defined by Weber, may gain power and privilege because of wealth, status, political power, or occupational authority. These multidimensions of power and inequality are the bases on which groups are formed and on which privileged or powerful groups try to influence the content and application of our laws. The drama that is played out is one of constant struggle for influence.

Austin Turk (1969) argued that the law, rather than being an impartial arbiter of disputes, is a mechanism for expressing power and influence. Turk viewed status groups as dichotomized into authority and subject groups, and he maintained that conflict arises when cultural, educational, and political differences between authorities and subjects are so vast that conflict inevitably results. Ultimately in the struggle for influence, authority groups are most successful in influencing the type and direction of social control. For example, medical practitioners and researchers command a good deal of authority and respect, but they have, as well, a vested interest in insuring that certain forms of deviant behaviour are defined as medical problems in need of medical intervention or control. The security of this status group depends on the successful definition and control of certain forms of deviant behaviour, as exemplified by medicine's increasing intervention into the workplace where problems stemming from poor work environments have been redefined as individual medical problems.

Interactionist Theories

Labelling Theory. Labelling theory, although sociopsychological in nature, accepts the conflict premise that social inequality is a primary condition when studying the definition and control of abnormal behaviour. Labelling theory, however, takes the notion of social inequality and the abuse of power and searches for the process by which people come to see themselves as deviant or criminal. Central to the process of the *internalization* of deviant definitions is the argument that deviance is not naturally bad behaviour but that the deviant is one to whom the deviant label has been successfully applied. Howard Becker (1963) has suggested that 'social groups create deviance by making the rules whose infraction constitutes deviance ... deviance is not a quality of the act the person commits, but rather a consequence of the application by others of rule and sanctions to an offender' (Becker 1963:9).

Edwin Lemert (1951) expanded this perspective by suggesting that initial acts of deviant behaviour, *primary deviance*, comes from diverse sources such as biology, psychology, or social circumstance. For Lemert, however, such inconsequential and fleeting acts become important only when they are defined as abnormal. *Secondary deviance* is internalized behaviour that results in response to societal identification. As Lemert argues, 'When a person begins to employ his deviant behaviour or role based upon it as a means of defense, attack or adjustment to the overt and covert problems created by the consequent societal reaction to him, his deviation is secondary' (Lemert 1951:76). Edwin Schur (1971) has extended this argument by suggesting that the process of becoming a secondary deviant is determined by negotiation, and that some people who are so labelled successfully defend themselves against negative labels. For Schur, the power to negotiate positive labels is based on individual self-concept rather than social status or social power.

The social policy implications of labelling theory can be seen in Canada's Young Offenders Act of 1984. This legal reform stressed that the law must not contribute to the negative labelling, especially of first time young offenders, for fear that legal identification was the first step on the road to a criminal career. As a result, the act contains provisions for diverting youth from the formal justice system, and also specifies that the identities of youths must be confidential.

Ethnomethodology. The second conflict-based interactionist approach is similar in many respects to labelling theory, but makes few assumptions about social inequality and the rightness or wrongness of definitions of deviance. *Ethnomethodology*, like labelling theory, is concerned with the social construction of deviance: abnormal behaviour is neither right nor wrong, but is defined by different people in different contexts. Ethnomethodologists study how we come to create typifications (stereotypes), and how these collective images of deviance are applied in specific situations.

For example, D.L. Rosenhan (1973) and a group of research colleagues gained admission to mental hospitals as pseudopatients who claimed they heard voices. None of the pseudopatients was detected as a liar. Rosenhan reported that although they all conducted themselves normally, they were diagnosed and treated as mental patients. Rosenhan illustrated how the pseudopatients' behaviour in the hospital was interpreted by hospital staff to conform to the original diagnoses, and was further confirmed when the patients were released with their illnesses defined as 'in remission'. Such research illustrates how images of deviance, like mental illness, are shared by people in authority such as doctors, who use these predefined images to interpret and reinforce initial labels or definitions. Although ethnomethodological research in theory does not concentrate on power and inequality, much of the research stresses the effectiveness of people in authority— psychiatrists, police, and judges—in judging and typifying people of lower status. As a result, it falls under the general category of conflict theory.

Knowledge/Power: Foucault and Discourse

Discourse theorists focus on language and communication systems as fundamental forms of social construction. That is, as critical theorists, they see language and communication systems as powerful forces of social control that create systems of order and discipline. In relation to the study of deviance and social control, Michel Foucault continues to be the major discourse theorist, writing under the rubric of poststructuralism. Poststructuralist theories argue that language, and its attendant definitions of deviance and crime, are constructed according to the needs of those in power at specific historical periods. Therefore, language and knowledge systems change with changing historical exigencies. Most important, however, Foucault's major contribution is his understanding that power and knowledge cannot be separated, and that knowledge is a currency with the potential to construct definitions of good and bad according to the wishes of those who have access to the knowledge. In his study of the development of psychiatry, Foucault (1975, 1988) argues that although society gradually adopted humane practices towards the insane as a result of Enlightenment philosophies and scientific practices, a new and more insidious form of social control resulted in the incarceration and scrutiny of an increasing number of mad people. In *The Birth of the Clinic* (1975) and *Madness and Civilization* (1988), Foucault contends that the force behind this increasing social control movement was science (psychiatry) and its claim to legitimacy through its unique knowledge system and its ability to continually define new categories of sickness and deviance. In several other works, including *Discipline and Punish* (1979) and *History of Sexuality* (1980), Foucault extends the theme that as we become more 'civilized' and knowledgeable, we increase our ability to define, detect, and control an increasing number of marginalized (deviant) people. In effect, Foucault argues that we are creating an increasing number of 'docile bodies' through scientific, knowledge-based disciplines that continually define and redefine unacceptable behaviour and enforce discipline.

While Foucault's work, along with the poststructuralist tradition, have been criticized for ignoring issues of class and gender, the contributions to our understanding of the connections between knowledge and oppressive social control cannot be understated. Foucault has left an intellectual legacy that cautions us to analyse critically our positions as both researchers and intellectuals and to uncover the ulterior motives behind the language and knowledge systems that belong to only a few privileged individuals.

FEMINIST THEORIES AND THE CRITICAL TRADITION

Many of the feminist theories used to understand abnormal behaviour are similar to or derived from traditional critical theories. For example, socialist feminist approaches are based on the Marxist principle that economic position determines social placement. Similarly, liberal feminism draws on pluralistic conflict principles that recognize power differentials and the role of conflict resolution in creating social change. Feminist theories, however, depart from the more traditional critical works in emphasizing the power of patriarchy as well as the power of economic status. Traditional critical theories have been especially negligent, however, in their conceptions of how knowledge is constructed. They have typically ignored the contributions that women have made throughout history and have excluded women as the subject of study in social and historical research. Marx, for example, made very little mention of women as an oppressed group. Foucault, despite the contemporary, postmodern nature of his work, similarly ignores women and concentrates on the power of men in constructing reality. In response, feminist theorists are critical epistemologists; that is, they are concerned with and critical of how knowledge is constructed by a powerful, non-representative segment of society. In addition, these theories challenge traditional assumptions about gender, assumptions that social organization exists outside gender, and that gender is equivalent to biological sex.

Socialist Feminism

Socialist feminists argue that the power men wield over women is no less oppressive than the power that the economically advantaged have over the less advantaged. As a consequence, the forces that liberate and constrain people are economic production and biological and social reproduction. Women's deviance can be explained by their marginalized economic positions; the patriarchal values that guide behaviour emphasize a woman's role as homemaker and mother. When women step outside the boundaries of conventional behaviour, their activities are much more open to scrutiny and devaluation. Some of the chapters in this book that illustrate how women have attempted to gain control over reproduction, for example, suggest that patriarchal and economic power are closely linked to the control and valuation of reproduction and motherhood.

Liberal Feminism
Liberal feminist theories argue that woman is one of the many social categories in a plural society that competes for power, prestige, resources, and status. Liberal feminism, like pluralistic conflict theory, maintains that conflict and resolution may result in the empowerment of marginalized groups. The belief in social reform and the power of conflict to redress inequality underlie a philosophical orientation that endorses the basic premises of the existing socio-economic system.

Radical Feminism
Radical feminist approaches tend to view men and women as existing in different worlds and see the accepted gender roles and stereotypes as male constructions that marginalize and devalue women. Such theories, which are very much postmodern in their concentration on language and communication, challenge the socially constructed myths and stereotypes about gender and deconstruct our normative definitions of what constitutes appropriate gender behaviour. Deviance, for radical feminists, is a linguistic device that is part of the patriarchal system of definition and control.

Feminist Realism
The feminist realist approach draws on the basic tenets of left realism and concentrates on women's victimization and the role of conventional criminology and studies of deviance in distorting and downplaying women's victimization at the hands of batterers, especially intimates (Currie 1991). From a research perspective, the victim's experience is the central focus, and the study of deviance and crime requires a sensitivity not only to crimes against women but also to threats of violence and domination. Most important, feminist realism rejects the notion that victims are partly responsible for precipitating crime, and offers the analytical insight that because women's victimization occurs in the context of normal gender relations, it is largely hidden or ignored as inconsequential.

Feminist Theoretical Synthesis
A synthesis of feminist theories in approaching the study of deviance and social control would include several areas of investigation that challenge the way we conceive of good and bad behaviour. Firstly, social researchers need to include women's realities in their research, realities that foster the women's standpoint. Secondly, a synthesis of feminist theories would include the presumption that men and women live in different worlds, and that the

experiences of both are different and of equal importance in understanding social reality. For example, traditional studies on fear of crime assumed that many things cause people to fear for their safety, and that gender is but one of the explanatory variables. Most feminist research, on the other hand, argues that women and men live in different worlds or 'gestalts of fear', and that their realities must be analysed separately. The presumption here is that the forces that cause men to fear and alter their behaviour are different from those that cause women to fear and protect themselves. Lastly, the synthesis of feminist theories would suggest that, in the interim, women's realities must take priority over men's in the struggle to uncover a historically suppressed body of knowledge. This position, however, would include the promise that ultimately we need to conceptualize and analyse a genderless understanding of behaviour, which would focus on real harm to people or things without preferential attention to only certain individuals or cultures. An evocative example of a new historical understanding of women's reality can be seen in the National Film Board of Canada film entitled *The Burning Times*. This historical analysis of the witchcraft period during the Middle Ages in Europe presents an account described as a women's holocaust involving the loss of hundreds of thousands of lives. What makes this historical understanding unusual is that it confronts the likelihood that the Inquisition was extremely misogynistic, and that forces of patriarchy and economy resulted in the calculated, brutal, and religion-legitimated deaths of women who were educated, powerful, and threatening to the status quo.

CONCLUSION

Regardless of whatever theoretical perspective we use to study deviance, the reality is that some rules are just while others are unfair, some rules are applied without prejudice while others discriminate against the underprivileged, and certain types of deviance are more prevalent among certain categories of people than others. The chapters that follow attempt to deal with these issues from social constructionist perspectives. They confront social control and deviance from perspectives that are oriented towards understanding the discriminatory and oppressive nature of social control. They suggest how different subgroups in society come to terms with being either the victims or the agents of social control. Many of the chapters—and this is true of much postmodern research—are composites of several theories; they have practised a type of theory raiding. This is the compelling nature of contemporary research, especially as framed in a postmodern perspective: that the world is complex and multidimensional, and that many of the issues in the study of social control and deviance are best explained by drawing on a vast array of related theories. This complex theoretical nature of the study of deviance and control helps us out of the trap of theoretical nihilism (that nothing works) because it allows the social analyst to proceed when parts of a theory are untenable. The researcher does not necessarily have to reject or redraft the theory but augments it with other insights. This rethinking of the use of theory allows the researcher to be a social advocate and to suggest social policy that is progressive and practical.

The term postmodernism occurs at times throughout this text. Postmodernism, as a relatively new theoretical orientation, describes a contemporary break with traditional ways of understanding human behaviour. Modernist approaches, which originated with the Enlightenment, make assumptions about the existence of an identifiable reality and the use of the scientific/objective approach in uncovering or discovering that reality. Postmodern approaches reject the objective/scientific approach and suggest that there are many realities in existence, and that one reality need not be privileged over another. Furthermore, the approach is deconstructionist in its attempts to understand and uncover the hidden, latent, and biased messages that privilege some groups over others. Studies that criticize and unpack the scientific, empirical understandings of deviance and social control—and the languages and epistemologies of that control—are generally subsumed under the postmodern banner.

Each of the five parts in this book has an introduction explaining how the chapters fit into the social control/social construction framework and why these topics are relevant to contemporary studies of unconventional behaviour and social control. The authors approach their substantive topics from critical and/or feminist perspectives and offer rather unique approaches to the sociology of control. The chapters in this book offer a marked departure from traditional books in the area of deviance and control and it is our hope that you will find the material compelling, provocative, and profound.

FURTHER READINGS

Conrad, P., and J.W. Schneider. 1980. *Deviance and Medicalization.* St Louis: C.V. Mosby.

Deutschmann, L. 1994. *Deviance and Social Control.* Scarborough, ON: Nelson.

Downes, D., and P. Rock. 1982. *Understanding Deviance: A Guide to the Sociology of Crime and Rule Breaking.* Oxford: Clarendon Press.

Goode, E., and N. Ben-Yehuda. 1994. *Moral Panics: The Social Construction of Deviance.* Cambridge, Mass.: Blackwell.

Liska, A.E. 1987. *Perspectives on Deviance*, 2nd ed. Englewood Cliffs, NJ: Prentice-Hall.

REFERENCES

Bandura, A., and R.H. Walters. 1963. *Social Learning and Personality Development.* New York: Holt, Rinehart and Winston.

Becker, H. 1963. *Outsiders: Studies in the Sociology of Deviance.* New York: Free Press.

Berkowitz, L. 1969. *Roots of Aggression: A Re-examination of the Frustration-Aggression Hypothesis.* New York: Atherton Press.

Bierne, P., and J. Messerschmidt. 1991. *Criminology.* New York: Harcourt, Brace, Jovanovich.

Chambliss, W. 1969. *Crime and Legal Process.* New York: McGraw-Hill.

Currie, D. 1991. 'Realist Criminology, Women, and Social Transformation in Canada'. In *New Directions in Critical Criminology,* edited by B. MacLean and D. Milovanovic, 221–45. Vancouver: The Collective Press.

Davis, K. 1937. 'The Sociology of Prostitution'. *American Sociological Review* 2:744–55.

Durkheim, E. [1897] 1964. *Suicide.* Glencoe, Ill.: Free Press.

Erikson, K. 1966. *Wayward Puritans: A Study in the Sociology of Deviance.* New York: John Wiley.

Eysenck, H.J. 1977. *Crime and Personality.* London: Routledge and Kegan Paul.

Foucault, M. 1975. *The Birth of the Clinic: An Archaeology of Medical Perception.* New York: Vintage Books.

_____. 1979. *Discipline and Punish: The Birth of the Prison.* New York: Vintage Books.

_____. 1980. *The History of Sexuality: An Introduction.* New York: Vintage Books.

_____. 1988. *Madness and Civilization: A History of Insanity in the Age of Reason.* New York: Vintage Books.

Goodwin, D.W. 1986. 'Studies of Familial Alcoholism: A Growth Industry'. In *Longitudinal Research in Alcoholism,* edited by D.W. Goodwin et al., 997–1005. Boston: Kluwer Academic Publishing Group.

Gramsci, A. 1971. *Selections from the Prison Notebooks of Antonio Gramsci.* New York: International Publishers.

Hagan, J., J. Simpson, and A.R. Gillis. 1995. 'A Power-Control Theory of Gender and Delinquency'. In *Canadian Delinquency,* edited by R. Silverman and J. Creechan, 192–208. Toronto: Prentice-Hall.

Hirschi, T. 1969. *Causes of Delinquency.* Los Angeles: University of California Press.

Kohlberg, L. 1969. 'Stage and Sequence: The Cognitive-Developmental Approach'. In *Handbook of Socialization Theory and Research,* edited by D.A. Goslin, 347–480. Chicago: Rand McNally.

Lemert, E. 1951. *Social Pathology.* New York: McGraw-Hill.

Lombroso, C. 1911. *Crime: Its Causes and Remedies.* Boston: Little, Boston.

Lowman, J., and B. MacLean, eds. 1992. *Realist Criminology: Crime Control and Policing in the 1990s.* Toronto: University of Toronto Press.

Marx, K. [1848] 1964. *Selected Writings in Sociology and Social Philosophy*, edited by T.B. Bottomore and M. Rubel. Baltimore; Penguin.

Mednick, S.A., and J. Volavka. 1980. 'Biology and Crime'. In *Crime and Justice: An Annual Review of Research*, 2, edited by N. Morris and N. Tonry, 85–158. Chicago: University of Chicago Press.

Merton, R.K. 1938. 'Social Structure and Anomie'. *American Sociological Review* 3:672–82.

Piaget, J. 1932. *The Moral Judgement of the Child*. New York: Harcourt.

Pollock, V.E., et al. 1986. 'Subjective and Objective Measures of Response to Alcohol among Young Men at Risk for Alcoholism'. *Journal of Studies on Alcohol* 47:297–304.

Quinney, R. 1977. *Class, State and Crime*. New York: David McKay.

Rosenhan, D.L. 1973. 'On Being Sane in Insane Places'. *Science* 179:250–8.

Schur, E. 1971. *Labeling Deviant Behaviour*. New York: Harper and Row.

Shah, S.A., and L.H. Roth. 1974. 'Biological and Psychophysiological Factors in Criminology'. In *Handbook of Criminology*, edited by D. Glaser, 101–73. Chicago: Rand McNally.

Sheldon, W. 1949. *Varieties of Delinquent Youth: An Introduction to Constitutional Psychiatry*. New York: Harper and Row.

Skinner, B.F. 1953. *Science and Human Behaviour*. New York: MacMillan.

Sutherland, E. 1939. *Criminology*. Philadelphia: J.B. Lippincott.

Turk, A. 1969. *Criminality and the Legal Order*. Chicago: Rand McNally.

Weber, M. 1947. *The Theory of Social and Economic Organization*. New York: Free Press.

Wilson, M., and M. Daly. 1985. 'Competitiveness, Risk Taking, and Violence: The Young Male Syndrome'. *Ethology and Sociobiology* 6:59–73.

Part
I
Law and Social Control

The stated, formal function of the law is to control those people who are a threat to society, and laws are constructed to protect citizens from criminal attack. The works in this section, however, reveal that the law also has an unstated, more insidious side that stigmatizes and controls people not only for bad behaviour but also for being on the margins of society. The chapters show how power operates in the domination of relatively powerless people, and how the law can be and has been used as a vehicle for such domination.

One of the most controversial crimes that society confronts is sexual assault/rape. The central and persistent issues are whether rape is an act of violence or an act of sex and, as a result, whether it should be considered as seriously by the courts as violent assault. As you will read in Chapter 2, rape has historically been treated as a relatively minor crime to the detriment of the victim as well as to the image of women as equal to men. Hinch tackles the debates head on by describing the changes in attitudes and legal practices towards the crime of rape in Canada, and by giving the reader a concise overview of the extent, nature, and socio-economic character of sexual assault.

Hinch places the sexual assault research in the context of the various theories presented in Chapter 1. This discussion illustrates how this specific social problem is dealt with in academic literature, and how each theory either contributes to discriminatory attitudes and practices towards women or how they seek redress for historically sexist laws. This chapter is presented as an example of how the theories of social control presented in the introduction can be applied to a specific social problem. Finally, Hinch leaves us with an overview of how Canadian society currently deals with sexual assault and the pitfalls that still befall the practice of law with regard to the crime of rape.

In Chapter 3, Patricia Erickson provides historical and contemporary evidence on how Canada's political institutions have determined that certain drugs are dangerous while others are acceptable as recreational or pharmaceutical drugs. Erickson illustrates how the definition of dangerousness has much to do with the moral positions of powerful lobbyists and little to do with scientific evidence regarding danger to physical health. She shows how definitions of dangerousness were more closely tied to the social and cultural characteristics of the players involved than with the inherent medical danger the drugs presented. Throughout the chapter, Erickson suggests that dangerousness is a socially constructed category, and that those involved in the definition and legitimation of dangerousness were and are in élite political and economic positions. Their influence in the drug control debate has resulted in the control and criminalization of relatively powerless people. Her historical and contemporary analyses are laden with information that allows the reader to frame the issue of drug use and abuse in several theoretical postions typified in this book.

Chapter 4 is rather unique in terms of academic texts. This chapter addresses youth crime and justice in Canada and was written and researched by youths. It is intended to be an understanding of adolescent behaviour and control through the eyes of insiders. A Grade Eleven advanced class made this chapter its class project for the year by interviewing and studying both youths and youth justice officials. The chapter deals with youth crime and deviance and attitudes towards justice and social control. The students used demographic and socio-economic characteristics of the respondents as the foci of the study. The data collection is based on sound investigative procedures and the conclusions and speculations are based somewhat on the unique perspectives that youths as researchers bring to the study. One of the reader's tasks is to place the conclusions in a general theoretical framework. Are the interpretations less critical than the academician-based chapters in this book or do they appear to follow the same philosophical orientations? Because the research was conducted and written by youths, does it appear to be less valid than the rest of the book or are the insights relatively refreshing?

In the last chapter, Carolyn Carey presents an overview of the traditional approaches used to study women's criminality and her discussions explain how many of these perspectives have led to the oppressive and patriarchal control of marginalized women. Her work on women in prisons in Canada reminds us how academic research can be used to both control and liberate underprivileged people. The primary theoretical position in this paper is socialist feminist, and Carey illustrates how feminist approaches address issues that have been largely neglected in Canadian corrections. She concludes with a discussion of how poverty and oppression are connected, and how traditional 'legalistic' approaches to women and crime are not only ineffective but exacerbate the problem that women face in a stratified, patri-archal society. Carey's work is explicitly feminist and Marxist, but the reader will also recognize elements of the connection between power and knowl-edge that are typical of Foucauldian analyses, as well as elements of indi-vidual and cultural sensitivity that are typical of postmodern approaches to social problems.

—2—

Sexual Violence and Social Control

Ron Hinch

SEXUAL ASSAULT

This chapter reviews the sociological literature on sexual assault and is divided into four parts. The first part reviews definitions of rape and sexual assault. The second part deals with attempts to measure the extent of sexual assault. The third part reviews the major theoretical models explaining sexual assault, and the fourth part discusses methods for controlling sexual assault. In each case the focus is primarily Canadian, but data from other studies have been included where they enhance the analysis.

Definitions of Sexual Assault

Until 1983, the legal definition of rape in Canada was provided in section 143 of the Criminal Code of Canada:

> A male person commits rape when he has sexual intercourse with a female person who is not his wife,
>> a) without her consent, or
>> b) with her consent if the consent
>>> (i)   is extorted by threats or fear of bodily harm,
>>> (ii) is obtained by personating her husband, or
>>> (iii) is obtained by false and fraudulent representations
>>>   as to the nature and quality of the act.

At that time, the law also specified two other offences: indecent assault on a male, and indecent assault on a female.

Critics argued that there were several problems with these legal definitions of rape and indecent assault. First, the offences were sex-specific and thereby treated male and female victimization differently. For example, an act of rape could be perpetrated only by a man against a woman. Thus an act of homosexual rape was treated differently from an act of heterosexual rape.

Even the penalties were different. For example, the maximum penalty for an indecent assault on a male was fifteen years in prison, but for an indecent assault on a female, the maximum penalty was only five years. Similarly, the maximum penalty for homosexual rape, charged as an indecent assault on a male, was fifteen years in prison, but the maximum penalty for raping a woman was life imprisonment. The critics argued that these differences were based on unacceptable assumptions about the nature of the offences, and about the impact these had on the victims. They argued that the law assumed the outlawed behaviour was primarily sexual in nature. The critics countered that the real nature of these outlawed behaviours had more to do with demonstrations of power and domination than they had to do with sex and sexuality (see Clark and Lewis 1977).

Second, men could not be charged with raping their wives. In effect, married women surrendered their right to say no to their husbands. This angered many critics who believed that it granted married men a licence to rape their wives. (For a more detailed discussion of this issue, see either Finkelhor and Yllo 1985 or Russell 1982.)

Third, the law also required that (1) the victim had to refuse consent, and (2) the perpetrator had to intend to perform the act without the victim's consent in order for an accused to be found guilty. This meant that a man who forced sexual intercourse on a woman without her consent could not be convicted of rape if he believed that he had her consent. This is known as honest-but-mistaken belief in consent. It has been upheld by the Supreme Court of Canada as a legitimate defence in rape cases. Critics argued that this defence perpetuated the myth that women mean yes when they say no. It allowed the opportunity for some men to put the victim on trial by claiming that the victim's actions implied consent, or that women's initial protests meant they wanted to be seduced.

To deal with these concerns, the Criminal Code was amended in 1983 and again in 1992. In 1983, the offences of rape, indecent assault on a male, and indecent assault on a female were eliminated and replaced by three new offences: sexual assault, sexual assault with a weapon or causing bodily harm, and aggravated sexual assault. (For a more complete summary of these and other changes, see Hinch 1985 or Boyle 1984.) These new offences are distinguished by the level and type of violence involved. Sexual assault is the least violent form, while sexual assault with a weapon and aggravated sexual assault are the more violent offences. The new sexual assault offences are also defined in gender-neutral terms, recognizing that both males and females may be victims or offenders. Finally, the legal exemption from prosecution granted married men who raped their wives was removed.

In 1992, new limits were placed on the right of the defence to claim an honest-but-mistaken belief in consent. The accused can no longer use the honest-but-mistaken belief in consent defence if the accused's belief in consent resulted from (1) self-induced intoxication, (2) reckless or deliberate inattention to the victim's wishes, and (3) a failure to take reasonable measures to insure that consent was given.

Despite these changes, the legal definition of sexual assault continues to spark some controversy. The law has been criticized for not defining sexual assault (Jackman 1982; Landau and Lowenberger 1983; Lowenberger and Landau 1982; Ranson 1982), and for its attempt at defining gender-neutral offences (DeKeseredy and Hinch 1991; Hinch 1991). Research by Hinch (1988a, 1988b, 1991) and Ellis (1986) indicate that the police and the courts have offered wildly differing interpretations of sexual assault. In one case, a New Brunswick court ruled that unconsented touching of a woman's breasts was a common assault, not a sexual assault. In another case, an Ontario court ruled that unconsented touching of a woman's breast was sexual assault. In an attempt to resolve these problems, in 1987 the Supreme Court of Canada offered its interpretation of the legal definition of sexual assault. The Supreme Court said that sexual assault is:

> an assault... which is committed in circumstances of a sexual nature, such that the sexual integrity of the victim is violated. The test to be applied in determining whether the impugned conduct has the requisite sexual nature is an objective one: 'Viewed in the light of all the circumstances, is the sexual or carnal context of the assault visible to a reasonable observer?' (as cited in Nuttall 1989:14).

This ruling says that an assault must have a clear sexual nature before it can be termed a sexual assault.

Some critics continue to argue that this definition leaves individual police officers, as well as judges and juries, a great deal of discretion in deciding whether or not a given act is a *sexual* act 'in light of the circumstances' (Hinch 1988a, 1991). Hinch (1988a, 1988b) has shown that police decisions in applying any definition are inconsistent. Similar acts committed in similar circumstances may or may not be treated as sexual assault. Thus the subjective interpretations of individual police officers, judges, and juries may lead to different interpretations of similar circumstances.

During the summer of 1991, an Ontario woman challenged the legal definition of women's breasts as sexual objects. She was arrested for committing an indecent act when she removed her shirt and walked topless on the street. When she appeared in court, she claimed the same right as men to go shirtless in public. She was convicted, and her conviction has been upheld on appeal. Thus, as it now stands, a woman going topless in a public place can be arrested and charged with committing an indecent act. This is based on the assumption that women's breasts are sexual objects that must be covered in public.

For some people, this is as it should be. If women's breasts are culturally defined as sexual objects, then women should not be exposing their breasts in public, and men should be charged with sexual assault when touching them without consent. For other people, especially those who staged protests across Canada during the first two weeks of July 1992 in support of the Ontario woman, it may still be appropriate to charge a man with sexual assault for grabbing women's breasts without consent. Consistent with the 1987 Supreme Court ruling, if the intent of the act is sexual, then it is a criminal act. It should not be considered an indecent act for women to expose their breasts in public because the intent of this action is not sexual. This is one debate that is not likely to have a resolution that will satisfy everyone.

As for gender neutrality, some critics have been reluctant to accept either the necessity of gender neutrality, nor do they feel that the gender-neutral solution contained in the law is satisfactory. Critics who argue against the necessity of gender neutrality say that a specific legal charge of rape should have been retained (Cohen and Backhouse 1980a; DeKeseredy and Hinch 1991). At present, the law treats some rapes as equivalent to some forms of sexual assault in which the offender grabs a woman's breast or a victim's (male or female) genitals and then runs away. Even the possibility that these minor incidents of sexual assault can be processed via summary conviction procedure rather than indictment does not solve the problem. Some incidents of rape are also processed via summary conviction procedures. Prosecution as a summary offence implies a less serious crime. Reflecting the less serious nature of these procedures, trials are conducted quickly with less formality. The maximum penalty for a rape prosecuted as a sexual assault via a summary procedure is six months' imprisonment. An indictable offence implies a more serious crime. Reflecting the more serious nature of the crime, trials are usually longer and more formal. The maximum penalty for rape prosecuted as a sexual assault via an indictment is life imprisonment.

Therefore, some critics say it would be appropriate to define two separate offences: one for incidents in which penetration is involved, and one for offences in which penetration is not a factor. Boyle (1984) and Cohen and Backhouse (1980a) argue that a separate rape offence should be maintained for all heterosexual rapes. They argue that abandoning the term rape amounts to sweeping away its reality. The act of rape does not disappear by changing its name. According to Cohen and Backhouse, 'We only want rape to disappear if the crime itself goes away. In a completely nonsexist society, rape would be unthinkable. But since our culture generates rape, a peculiar overlap of violence and sex, we don't want to see that reality swept under the rug. To eliminate the word would not eliminate rape itself' (1980a:6). Hinch (1988a) adds that, for the accused, being charged and symbolically convicted of rape implies a more serious event than to be accused, charged, and convicted of sexual assault. Even though some forms of sexual assault not involving penetration are more violent than some rapes, rapes are usually more violent than most sexual assaults in which no penetration is involved.

On the other hand, DeKeseredy and Hinch (1991) argue that gender neutrality should be retained. It is possible, they say, to have a separate, gender-neutral definition of rape in the Criminal Code. They argue that rape could be defined to include any form of penetration, oral, anal, or vaginal. This would allow male and female victimization to be treated as similar events with equal seriousness. To account for the various levels of violence involved in rape, they propose three rape offences: (1) rape would constitute the offence involving the least amount of violence; (2) rape with a weapon or causing bodily harm or threats to a third party would constitute a more serious offence signifying an escalation in the level of violence; and (3) aggravated rape would signify the most violent offence. The current sexual assault categories could then be used to designate all other types of sexual assault according to the levels of violence used in their commission.

Thus the dilemma in arriving at a legal definition of either rape or sexual assault centres on deciding which type of definition is most appropriate. Is it more appropriate to have a definition based on the assumption that any unconsented sexual touching, even if the offender does not intend to do it without consent, is wrong and should be a criminal offence? Or is it more appropriate to have a definition in which the intent of both the victim and the offender must be taken into account? No matter which definition is used, there will be those who disagree.

One consequence of the proliferation of definitions of rape and sexual assault is difficulty in determining how much rape and sexual assault occurs, as well as in theorizing about rape and sexual assault. This problem is discussed in the next section.

PATTERNS OF SEXUAL ASSAULT

This section focuses on patterns of sexual assault in Canada. The first subsection deals with determining how many people are sexually assaulted. The second subsection describes the typical victim. The third subsection discusses what is known about the offender. A fourth subsection outlines the relationships between victims and offenders, and the fifth deals with the issues of lifestyle and the location of offences.

The Rate of Sexual Assault

Table 2.1 indicates the sexual assault offence rate from 1983 to 1991. However, this table measures only those events reported to and assessed by the police as founded incidents—i.e., evidence indicates that the events took place and that the events meet the legal criteria. It does not include all those events that are not reported to the police. It is well known that there are many unreported events. That is why researchers have sometimes sought information through victim surveys. These surveys ask people if they have been sexually assaulted during a given time period, usually either the previous six months or the previous year. The findings from these surveys indicate that between 60 per cent and 90 per cent of all sexual assaults are not reported to the police (CSOACY 1984; CUVS 1984; Media and Thompson 1974; Russell 1984).

TABLE 2.1

Rate Per 100,000 of Sexual Assault in Canada, 1983–91

Year	Level I Sexual Assault	Level II Sexual Assault with a Weapon	Level III Aggravated Sexual Assault	Total Sexual Assault
1983	42	3	2	46[1]
1984	54	3	2	59
1985	67	3	2	73
1986	74	4	2	81
1987	82	4	2	87
1988	91	4	1	96
1989	98	3	2	102
1990	100	3	1	105
1991	107	3	2	112

1. Numbers in this column may not equal the total of the columns to the left due to rounding.
Source: Statistics Canada, *Canadian Crime Statistics*. Catalogue 85-205, Table 2. Ottawa: Statistics Canada, 1983–91.

The CUVS (1983:7) lists the following (in descending order) as the reasons people give for not reporting these events:

1. They believe that the police couldn't do anything (52 per cent).
2. They believe that the police have negative attitudes (43 per cent).
3. Because nothing was taken, there was no reason to tell the police (33 per cent).
4. They feared revenge from the offender (33 per cent).
5. They believed it was a personal matter (33 per cent).
6. They believed the incident was too minor (26 per cent).
7. They wanted to protect the offender (16 per cent).

The CUVS also found that men were less likely than women to report incidents of personal victimization. Thus the rates shown in Table 2.1 must be read with caution.

There are, however, certain inherent problems with victim survey data. First, the definitions used in the various surveys differ. The National Population Survey (NPS) completed for the Committee on Sexual Offences Against Children and Youths (CSOACY 1984) used a very broad definition of sexual assault. Threatened acts, as well as actual acts of sexual exposure or sexual touching, were counted as sexual assaults. The CUVS survey included only acts of sexual touching. Consequently, the results of these surveys are not directly comparable.

Second, there are difficulties inherent in the research method. Victim surveys assume that respondents have accurate memories of the events being reported. Some studies, such as the CUVS, ask the respondent to report on all incidents perpetrated on them during a given time period. It is possible that some reported events did not occur within this time frame. It is also possible that some events occurring within this time frame were forgotten. In other words, faulty memories produce overestimates or underestimates that cannot be verified.

Further, the CUVS included only residents of seven urban areas: St John's, Halifax/Dartmouth, Montreal, Toronto, Winnipeg, Edmonton, and Vancouver. It is questionable that this survey offers anything more than an estimate of the rate of sexual assault in the cities surveyed. The NPS based its estimate on a random sample of the Canadian population. This seems to indicate that the NPS offers a more complete assessment of the offence rate.

In summary, it is clear that victim surveys tell us that there are many more sexual assaults than are reported to the police. They cannot tell us exactly how much higher the sexual assault rate is.

The Victim
Data relating to the sex, age, marital status, and socio-economic background are used in this section to construct a profile of the average victim. Using this data, the average victim is female, age twenty-five or under, single, and from lower socio-economic status.

Sex. Victimization surveys, as well as police statistics, tell us that female victims greatly outnumber male victims. Victim surveys like the NPS and the CUVS (1985) reveal that up to seven females are sexually assaulted for every male. By examining police records, Hinch found that female victims outnumbered male victims in Halifax by as much as nine to one (1988a:115n). Other studies of police records indicate that female victims constituted 83 per cent of victims in Hamilton (Ekos Research Associates Inc. 1988b), 96 per cent of victims in Toronto (Nuttall 1989:43), and 95 per cent of victims in Winnipeg (University of Manitoba Research Ltd 1988b). This indicates that the risk of victimization varies by sex and city of residence.

Age. There seems to be agreement that the average victim is under twenty-five, and that most victims are between the ages of sixteen and twenty-five (Clark and Lewis 1977; CSOACY 1984; CUVS 1985; Gunn and Minch 1988; Hinch 1988a, 1988b; Nuttall, 1989; University of Manitoba Research Ltd 1988b). Estimates vary, but the general pattern is for between 70 per cent and 85 per cent of victims to be in this age group. Some studies have shown an even younger average age. For example, Gunn and Minch (1988), Hinch (1988b), Ekos Research Associates Inc. (1988b), and University of Manitoba Research Ltd (1988a) report that the average age of victims in their studies was under seventeen. Sixty per cent of victims reported in Lethbridge were under fourteen (University of Manitoba Research Ltd 1988a). This latter finding is given greater credibility by victim surveys reporting that up to 80 per cent of victims were sexually assaulted for the first time before they were twenty-one (CSOACY 1984; Russell 1984). Thus older victims, those over twenty-five, account for only 15 per cent to 30 per cent of known victims (Baril et al. 1988; Clark and Lewis 1977; Gunn and Minch 1988).

Some studies have also found that the type of sexual offence committed varies with the age of the victim. For example, Baril et al. (1988) found that the older victims are more likely to be victims of serious offences like rape and/or sexual assault with a weapon, but are less likely to be victims of less serious acts of sexual touching. Younger victims, on the other hand, are more likely to be victims of less serious offences involving less violence. Compare this finding with findings showing that younger offenders are more likely to commit less serious offences (Nuttall 1989).

Marital Status. Most sexual assault victims are single (Clark and Lewis 1977; CUVS 1985; Ekos Research Associates Inc. 1988b; Gunn and Minch 1988; Nuttall 1989). Most studies, whether of police records or victim surveys, find that 20 per cent or less are married or cohabiting. Some research also shows that women who have recently separated from their spouses have a high risk of being sexually assaulted by their former husbands. For example, the CUVS (1985) found that 54 per cent of all assaults on separated women were committed by their former spouses.

Socio-Economic Background. Most victims appear to come from lower socio-economic groups (Clark and Lewis 1977; CSOACY 1984; CUVS 1983). Examination of police records reveals that 60 per cent or more of victims known to the police are from lower socio-economic groups. For example, Clark and Lewis (1977:84–5) found that at least 57 per cent of the rape victims in their study were on welfare, unemployed, prostitutes, clerical or factory workers, domestic servants, waitresses, or sales clerks. Only 7 per cent of the victims in their study were classified as professionals. Similarly, the CUVS reported that the sexual assault rates are as much as 3.5 times higher for persons with low incomes than for persons with high incomes.

Studies in both Canada and the United States indicate that residents of public housing seem to be overrepresented among victims known to the police (McCahill et al. 1979). The Metropolitan Toronto Police force survey (as cited in the CSOACY 1984:204) found that 43 per cent of child sexual assaults reported to the Toronto police involved victims who were living in public housing. It is possible that the police and other officials, including social workers, who are in contact with welfare recipients, may pay closer attention to criminal activity in these areas than they would in other neighbourhoods.

Students are another group with a high risk of being sexually assaulted. Baril et al. (1988) report that 40 per cent of victims known to the Metro CLSC Centre for Victims of Sexual Assault in Montreal and 45 per cent of victims known to Montreal police were students. The CUVS (1985) also reports that women who were students or looking for work had the highest risk of being sexually assaulted. A recent national survey of Canadian university students indicated that almost 28 per cent of female university students were victimized by some form of sexual abuse that ranged from 'unwanted sexual contact, to sexual coercion, attempted rape and rape' (DeKeseredy and Kelly 1993:148). The high rate of sexual assault among university students indicates that although most incidents reported to the police are reported by women from lower socio-economic groups, women from higher-status groups also encounter high rates of sexual assault.

The Offender
In 1971, Griffin (1971) said rape was the 'all American crime'. She argued that the typical rapist is no different from the average man. He may even be seen as more of a man than the average man. For example, Clark and Lewis (1977), summarizing research on known rapists, say that rapists show no greater tendency towards mental illness than do other men. The principle difference between rapists and other men, said Clark and Lewis, is that rapists are more aggressive, more violent, and have a greater need to dominate women. Known rapists believe they are committing acts of seduction rather than acts of violence.

This point is crucial. As Smart (1976:105–7) explains, the concept of the rapist as the average man depends on accepting certain cultural expectations of men and male sexuality. Male sexuality and aggression appear to be inextricably linked. To say that the average man and the average rapist are similar is to say that both use aggressive behaviour to pursue sexual activity. They differ only to the extent that rapists tend to be more violent in this pursuit.

When it comes to offering a description of the average offender based on existing empirical studies, the task is not so simple. Most offenders are never detected. This makes it difficult to describe the average offender. Further, it is difficult in a self-report survey to ask people to report their criminal activities, to ask respondents if they have raped or sexually assaulted someone else. Nonetheless, some studies, especially those that assess dating violence (DeKeseredy and Kelly 1993), ask people to report such activity. These studies report very high rates of dating violence among university students.

The results of such surveys, however, may not be generalizable to the rest of the population. Thus the following description should be interpreted with caution.

Sex. Most offenders are male. Even when males are the victims, police files and survey data indicate that males are usually the perpetrators. The Department of Justice (1990) reports that 99 per cent of offenders in Vancouver, 98 per cent in Lethbridge, 97 per cent in Montreal and Fredericton/Saint John (combined), and 96 per cent in Hamilton are male. Similar percentages are found in other studies using police data (Clark and Lewis 1977; Gunn and Minch 1988). When a female perpetrator is reported to the police, she is usually (but not always) reported as an accomplice to a male offender.

In reviewing the various Canadian survey data, the CSOACY (1984:215) concluded that although the various surveys offered widely differing estimates (some as high as 10 per cent), probably only 1.2 per cent of sexual assaults against children and youths in Canada are perpetrated by women. The CSOACY estimated that 3.1 per cent of offences against boys and 0.8 per cent of offences against girls are perpetrated by women. Similar findings are reported in various American studies on child sexual abuse (Russell and Finkelhor 1984; Urquiza and Capra 1990; Urquiza and Keating 1990).

Age. Offenders identified in police records are usually older than their victims. Most studies of police files indicate that the majority of offenders are under thirty (Clark and Lewis 1977; Ekos Research Associates Inc. 1988a; University of Manitoba Research Ltd 1988b). Nonetheless, some studies have reported that the average offender is some cities is over thirty. The Department of Justice (1990) reports that in Fredericton and Saint John 61 per cent of offenders were over thirty, and that 59 per cent of offenders in Vancouver were over thirty. Thus it appears that the rate varies from city to city. The Department of Justice (1990) also reports that there has been a trend since 1983 for more offenders known to the police to be over thirty.

There is also some indication that the type of sexual assault committed varies with the age of the offender. Nuttall (1989:58) reports that offenders aged twelve to eighteen were the least likely to commit acts of penetration and the most likely to be involved in other forms of sexual assault. Offenders aged twenty to twenty-nine were the most likely to commit acts of penetration and the least likely to be involved in other less serious acts of unconsented sexual touching. Recall the previous discussion of the relation between the type of offence and the age of the victim.

Marital Status. While police records do not contain information on all offenders, the majority of offenders known to the police are single. For example, Nuttall (1989:58) reports that 58 per cent of men arrested in Toronto for sexual assault (including rape) were single, 27 per cent were married, and 13 per cent were separated or divorced. Similarly, 57 per cent of offenders in Winnipeg and Vancouver were single (Ekos Research Associates Inc. 1988a; University of Manitoba Research Ltd 1988a).

Socio-economic Background. Most of the data indicating the offender's socio-economic status comes from police records. In their study of rape in Toronto, Clark and Lewis found that 'almost without exception the rapists in our study came from lower socio-economic groups' (1977:98). The University of Manitoba Research Ltd study (1988a and 1988b), the Ekos Research Associates Inc. study (1988a), and Baril et al. (1988) report similar findings. Baril et al. report that 55 per cent of sexual assault offenders were unemployed, students, retired, or on social assistance; 38 per cent were unskilled tradespeople; 9 per cent were skilled tradespeople; and only 2 per cent were professionals.

This data records only those offenders known to the police. It does not deal with the majority of offenders whose actions are not reported to the police, and who cannot be identified by either the police or their victims. Thus while the data on known offenders indicates that they come from lower socio-economic groups, it is difficult to generalize beyond the observation that most offenders known to the police are from such backgrounds.

It is also important to note the findings of a recent self-report study in which male university students were asked to report their use of force during sexual encounters. DeKeseredy and Kelly found that 11 per cent of the male students they surveyed had perpetrated some form of sexual abuse on their dating partners in the previous year. The type of abuse ranged from 'unwanted sexual contact, to sexual coercion, attempted rape and rape' (DeKeseredy and Kelly 1993:148). Based on the assumption that university students generally come from the more affluent sectors of Canadian society, this indicates that there are many more offenders from these sectors than police records show. This implies that the proportion of lower-class offenders found in police records is too high, and that lower-class offenders are disproportionately represented in these records. It is difficult to determine, however, just how unrepresentative these numbers are.

Prior Criminal Record. The available data indicates that most offenders— more than 60 per cent—known to the police have prior criminal records (Department of Justice 1990). For example, Ekos Research Associates Inc. (1988a) found that 70 per cent of offenders in Vancouver had prior records: 25 per cent had a previous record for sexual offences, and 45 per cent had committed non-sexual offences. Similarly, in Toronto, Nuttall (1989) found that 51 per cent of people arrested from 1 January 1985 to 31 December 1987 for sexual assault had prior criminal convictions. Of those with previous criminal convictions, 21 per cent had been convicted for sexual assault, and 42 per cent had been convicted for other violent crimes against a person.

However, the data upon which these studies are based are extremely limited. Not included in the data are all those offenders whose offences are not reported to the police, as well as all those offenders who the police and the victim were unable to identify. Since the majority of offenders cannot be identified, it is difficult to offer a definitive statement about the other criminal activities of offenders.

The Victim/Offender Relationship

The available data on the relationship between victim and offender is sometimes contradictory. Some studies have shown that people known to the victim outnumber strangers, while other studies show that strangers outnumber people known to the victim. For example, the NPS (CSOACY 1984) reports that only 17.8 per cent of perpetrators were strangers. The NPS was primarily concerned with detecting incidents of child sexual abuse. It is to be expected that children would have less exposure to situations in which strangers could assault them. Other studies of police records also indicate that people known to the victim outnumber strangers as offenders (Ekos Research Associates Inc. 1988b; Nuttall 1989). Ekos Research Associates Inc. (1988b) found that only 37 per cent of sexual offences were committed by strangers, while most (63 per cent) were committed by people known to the victim: 22 per cent by acquaintances, neighbours, or friends; 9 per cent by fathers; 5 per cent by step-parents; 3 per cent by spouses, ex-spouses, or common-law partners; 9 per cent by other relatives; 3 per cent by boyfriends or dates; and 12 per cent by other known people.

On the other hand, many studies of police records indicate that adult victims are more likely to be assaulted by strangers (Baril et al. 1988; Ekos Research Associates Inc. 1988a; University of Manitoba Research Ltd 1988b). Baril et al. (1988) found that 1 per cent of all sexual assaults were committed by husbands, 0.7 per cent by ex-husbands, 3 per cent by friends or former friends, 4 per cent by family members, 18 per cent by acquaintances, and 71 per cent by unknown people. In most studies, husbands account for 1 per cent or less of offenders. Even some victim surveys, such as the CUVS (1985), have found that approximately 60 per cent of offenders are strangers.

These numbers must be treated with caution. It is well known that many incidents perpetrated by persons known to the victim are not reported to the police. The CUVS (1985) found that most sexual assaults committed by people known to the victim are not reported to the police. Only 22 per cent of incidents involving family members and 36 per cent of incidents involving acquaintances are reported to the police. In contrast, 46 per cent of stranger incidents are reported to the police. Gunn and Minch (1988) comment that the closer the relationship between the victim and the offender, the less likely it is that the incident will be reported to the police.

Finally, while people known to the victim are less likely to be reported to the police, some research has shown that people known to the victim are more likely to be arrested. Nuttall (1989:26) found that 70 per cent of offenders known to the victim were arrested, while only 30 per cent of strangers were arrested. People known to the victim are more likely to be arrested because it is easier for police to identify, locate, and apprehend them.

Lifestyle and Location

Determining the typical location in which sexual assaults occur is a difficult task. Once again, victim surveys and studies of police records yield varying results. For example, the CUVS survey indicates that most sexual assaults occur in public places. Similarly, research in Montreal and Vancouver indicates that a majority of incidents reported to the police occurred outdoors (Baril et al. 1988; Ekos Research Associates Inc. 1988a). There is, however, some variation across Canada. Police records in Hamilton, Lethbridge, and Winnipeg indicate that most sexual assaults occurred indoors (Ekos Research Associates Inc. 1988b; University of Manitoba Research Ltd 1988a, 1988b).

Closer examination reveals that rapes are more likely to occur indoors, while other forms of sexual assault occur outdoors. Some police data and some victim surveys report that 55 per cent to 87 per cent of all rapes occur indoors in the victim's home, an acquaintance's home, or the offender's home (Amir 1971; Baril et al. 1988; Clark and Lewis 1977; Hindelang and Davis 1977; Media and Thompson 1974).

However, these studies deal only with urban areas. There is little specific information concerning the rate of sexual assault in rural communities. It is known that rural communities report fewer acts of personal victimization to the police. Sacco and Johnson (1990) reported that the risk of personal victimization (including acts of robbery and assault) were significantly lower in rural communities. Their data, however, do not indicate specific rates for sexual assault in rural communities because they were unable to detect a sufficient number of sexual assault cases (urban or rural) for statistical analysis.

The data also show that the probability of being sexually assaulted increases as a person's activities outside the home increase. For example, the CUVS (1985) reports that those women who 'attended the greatest number of evening activities outside the home' had the highest victimization rates. The authors of the CUVS argue that the risk of victimization, therefore, increases with the amount of time spent outside the home. This may account for high rates of victimization by strangers. Strangers are more likely to be encountered outside the home.

THEORIES OF SEXUAL ASSAULT

The following pages focus on various sociological explanations of sexual assault. The theories to be examined include control theory, interactionist theory, feminist theory, and Marxian theory. Each theory will be summarized and followed by a brief critique.

Control Theories

Control theorists argue that the deviant has not been exposed to socially acceptable behaviourial standards. A rapist or other offender has not been taught to relate to others, especially women, in a non-violent, non-aggressive manner. In some instances, he may discover that his aggressive, violent behaviour is rewarded when the targets of his aggression accede to his demands (see Cormier and Simons 1969; Groth 1979; Marshall 1973; Marshall and McKnight 1975). The rapist seeks self-gratification at the victim's expense by putting personal interests above the interests of others.

The gratification sought by rapists is not necessarily sexual. Rapists are more concerned with controlling and dominating their victims than with achieving sexual satisfaction (Gebhard et al. 1965; Groth 1979; Rada 1978). Groth (1979) says that even in gang-rape situations, the primary satisfaction is the camaraderie among the rapists. Gang rapes represent masculinity contests. The object of these contests is the sexual domination of women. On his own, or with other rapists in a gang, the rapist seeks to control the victim and to convince himself and his male peers of his masculinity. Further, many attempted rapes fail because the attacker has difficulty obtaining an erection. In other instances, the rapist may not reach orgasm. The objective is to achieve self-enhancement via the victim's degradation and humiliation.

That is not to suggest that control theorists believe that all rapists fail to experience sexual gratification through rape. Gebhard et al. (1965) and Rada (1978) argue that some rapists are sexually motivated. They rape when their efforts at persuasion fail. This type of rapist, however, is in the minority.

Critique. The rapists used as the study samples for control theorists are almost always rapists who have been caught. Given that only a small proportion of the total number of rapists come in contact with the criminal justice system, they are not necessarily representative of all rapists. Thus the theory may not be generalizable to all rapists.

Interactionist Theory

The interactionist approach to the analysis of sexual assault recognizes that people interact on the basis of shared meanings. Those shared meanings are learned through a series of interactions during which participants attempt to communicate using both verbal and non-verbal symbols: their words and actions. As long as the meanings of those symbols are shared and mutually agreed upon, relationships may be stable and free of conflict. Problems arise when meanings are not shared or when actions are interpreted differently by the participants.

For example, Klemmack and Klemmack (1976) argue that conventional gender role models provide the context within which sexual assault may occur. The concepts of femininity and masculinity contain contradictory elements. Femininity emphasizes passivity, receptiveness, and innocence, especially in relation to sexual encounters, but also encourages women to be seductive, coy, and flirtatious. Masculinity emphasizes independence, aggression, and conquest, especially conquest of women. When men and women interact in dating relationships, bringing these expectations into the interaction may present problems. Men may interpret women's passivity differently from the way women intend it. In some situations, women may not resist male sexual aggression because they fear men will become even more aggressive and more violent. Men may interpret this passivity as consent to proceed with sexual advances. The end result is that neither party has fully understood the actions of the other. In such situations, women pay the price by being sexually assaulted.

The notion of victim precipitation—meaning that the victim sets the stage for the offender's action by doing things that the offender may interpret as an indication that the victim wants him to do it—is sometimes applied to situations where men and women have misinterpreted each other's actions and words. Amir (1971) was the first to apply this concept to the study of rape, but other researchers have also contributed to its development (Ageton 1983; Curtis 1973; Gaudet 1984; Klemmack and Klemmack 1976). According to Amir (1971), 19 per cent of all rapes are victim-precipitated. Others estimate that only 4 per cent are victim-precipitated (Curtis 1973). The concept of victim precipitation means that the victims put themselves at risk by doing things, intentionally or unintentionally, that may be interpreted as deliberate risk taking by others, or as a come-on by potential attackers.

Most of the research exploring this concept has concentrated on clarifying the types of situations that may be called victim-precipitated. Amir said that victim precipitation occurs in situations 'marred by sexuality'. It results from situations in which:

1. the victim and the offender consume alcohol together prior to the rape—35 per cent of victim-precipitated rapes are of this type (Amir 1971:271)

2. the victim consumes alcohol, either alone or with others, prior to being raped—18 per cent of victim-precipitated rapes are of this type (Amir 1971:271)

3. females were hitchhiking; while a percentage is not given, Nelson and Amir (1977:288) said that the incidence of rape would be reduced 'if there were no hitchhiking females'

4. instances when the victim voluntarily goes to a man's home or invites a man to her home

5. the rapist believes, or is led to believe, that the victim has a reputation for promiscuity or for engaging in other forms of deviant behaviour; Ageton (1983) found that delinquent females were more likely than non-delinquent females to be sexually assaulted

Thus whether or not women intend their actions in these situations to be interpreted as sexual come-ons, their actions may be interpreted as such by men or by others who become aware of the event later.

To summarize, interactionists analyse rape as the result of situations in which one or both parties misunderstood the situation. Both have misinterpreted each other's actions, and may also have misunderstood how the other would react to them. These misunderstandings result from such factors as the definitions of femininity and masculinity in which femininity is defined in terms of passivity and receptiveness and masculinity is defined in terms of domination and aggression. Rape occurs when men interpret women's actions as implied consent.

Critique. While it may be true that some rapes occur as a result of misunderstood communication, it is equally true that many rapes and other sexual assaults occur when the attacker knows from the beginning that he will rape or sexually assault the victim. In almost half of all rapes reported to the police, the rapist made his intentions known at the initial contact with his victim. Therefore, these situations cannot be interpreted as misunderstood communications or as situations with ambiguous meanings.

As for the notion of victim precipitation, it has been severely criticized, even by some interactionists (see Sanders 1980) for implying that the victim is responsible for the offender's actions. It is important to note that Amir borrowed the concept of victim precipitation from Wolfgang's (1958) explanation for certain types of murder. Wolfgang used it to explain those murders in which the victim intended to provoke a specific response from the offender by behaving in ways the victim knew would elicit that response. But as Amir uses it, it also refers to actions that the victim did not intend to provoke. This extension of the concept is unwarranted.

Feminist Theories
There are several variants of feminist theory on rape and sexual assault. These include liberal feminism, radical feminism, and socialist feminism. Liberal feminism and radical feminism will be discussed in this section, while socialist feminism will be reviewed in the next section on Marxist theories. The descriptions of liberal and radical feminism offered here are adapted from those described by Boyd and Sheehy (1989).

Liberal Feminism. Liberal feminists in Canada have been primarily concerned with documenting the ways in which the law discriminates against women. They have attempted to show that the law defines rape and other forms of sexual assault in sexist ways, and this has resulted in an overconcern with the sexuality of these acts and a lack of concern for the type of violence involved. They have also tried to show how law reforms can be used to advance the cause of making the law and law enforcement less sexist.

Liberal feminists have had little difficulty in finding ways in which the law has historically favoured men. For example, prior to 1983 the law did not allow married women the legal right to charge their husbands with rape, but it was possible to charge husbands with other offences (notably assault or indecent assault). This, said the feminists, was unfair. It defined rape as only something committed by a man against a woman, and it concentrated on the sexual nature of the act—the act of vaginal penetration by a penis—rather than the violence required to perform the act. Feminists argued that the law should recognize that both men and women could sexually assault other men or women. They also argued that by replacing the gender-specific definitions of rape and the two types of indecent assault with offences that were defined primarily by the type and extent of violence used to commit the act, the law would take a major step in giving men and women legal equality. Consequently, liberal feminists supported the 1983 amendments abolishing the old definitions of rape and indecent assault, and the substitution of the new sexual assault offences. Similarly, liberal feminists argued that the rules of evidence prior to 1983 reduced the probability of both prosecution and conviction. For example, women who alleged that they were raped could be questioned about their past sexual activities with men other than the accused, and it was expected that after they were raped, women would immediately report their victimization. Liberal feminists argued that allowing women to be questioned indiscriminately about their sexual past implied that because a woman said yes in the past meant that she no longer had the right to say no. It also meant that when the victim was a disreputable woman, such as a prostitute or an alcoholic, etc., prosecutors would be less willing to prosecute for fear that the victim's social reputation would reduce the probability of conviction. Indeed, studies of juror behaviour have shown that a conviction is less likely when the victim is disreputable or engages in behaviour considered abnormal for women (see Feild and Bienen 1980).

As for the notion that women would immediately report their victimization, feminists argued that this failed to consider the variety of ways in which women might react to being raped. Some might report it to the first person they encountered, but others might prefer to tell only trusted friends or family members, even if these people were not encountered for several hours, days, weeks, or months afterwards. Still others might prefer to tell no one. In effect, the law did not consider the various ways that women reacted to being raped. It considered only the ways in which men assumed a woman would react. Finally, liberal feminists argued that the severe maximum penalty for rape, life imprisonment, was too severe, resulting in reduced convictions. They argued that juries would be unlikely to convict if they feared that the rapist would be sentenced to life in prison.

Critique. Liberal feminists have been criticized for several reasons. First they have been criticized for wanting only to remove the barriers to increased conviction rates, and not showing enough concern for eliminating rape. Critics have argued that it is somewhat simplistic to argue that increased conviction rates may lead to reducing the number of rapes. Higher conviction rates are likely to lead only to the conviction of more men from the lower socio-economic strata (the men most likely to be prosecuted), while men from higher socio-economic strata will continue to avoid prosecution because they have the social, economic, and political power to avoid prosecution (Hinch 1991; Snider 1985).

Similarly, other critics have argued that seeking gender-neutral terminology ignores the obvious gender-specific harm done by rape (Boyle 1984; Cohen and Backhouse 1980a). Rape and the threat of rape are used to limit women's social activity. It limits their freedom of movement and diminishes their personal and sexual autonomy.

Radical Feminism. The radical feminist analysis of sexual assault begins with the observation that patriarchy is the root cause of rape. Patriarchy leads to rigid gender role models in which men are assigned the dominant, active, and aggressive roles, and women are assigned the subservient, passive, and receptive roles. These gender roles are transmitted and reinforced through the institutions of patriarchy, especially the family and the law. The family encourages women to subordinate their needs, including their sexual needs, to the needs of their families. It also encourages men to assume that their economic dominance also bestows sexual dominance. The law, including law enforcement practices, makes it clear that women are men's sexual property both in and out of marriage. Within marriage, the law makes it difficult for women to resist their husbands' sexual demands. Indeed, Boyle (1981) has argued that sexual relations in marriage are inevitably non-consensual because women lack the economic and social power needed to enter into consensual relations. Outside of marriage, when women attempt to live independently of men, law enforcement practices encourage men to sexually assault these unprotected women.

With regard to their analysis of recent Canadian law reforms, radical feminists were opposed to enshrining the concept of gender neutrality. They argue that the 1983 amendments to the Criminal Code give only the appearance of granting legal equality and gender neutrality. Since women do not have the social, political, or economic power men have, there can be no equality. Cohen and Backhouse (1980a, 1980b), as well as Lowenberger and Landau (1982), add that the use of gender-neutral terms like sexual assault trivializes the gender-specific crime of rape by making it appear to be no more harmful than other types of assault, and by making it appear to be no different from minor forms of sexual assault, such as unconsented touching of the breasts.

Critique. LaFree (1989) challenges the feminist suggestion that women who engage in inappropriate gender role behaviour will usually meet with little success in having their complaints conclude with a conviction in jury trials. While LaFree agrees that it is inappropriate for juries to use the victim's behaviour to assess guilt (i.e., to blame the victim), his analysis also indicates that this is not always the case. When the major legal issues in the case centre on identification or the defendant's diminished responsibility (for example, when the victim invites the offender to her home), the data indicate that very few questions are asked about the victim's reputation or sexual history, and that juries convict on the basis of the legal issues. A second criticism concerns the implication that sexual assault laws seem to benefit only men. While there is no question that these laws and law enforcement practices function in ways that are detrimental to women, it is inaccurate to say or to imply that women receive no benefit. Even though historically the law may have defined women as men's sexual property, contemporary law nonetheless says that women are not to be sexually assaulted. Men are arrested, prosecuted, and convicted for sexual assault. While legal intervention may not occur as often as some feminists might like, it does happen. The fact that the law says that sexual assault is a criminal offence, and that some men are arrested, prosecuted, and convicted are indications that women receive some benefit, even if that benefit needs to be improved.

A third criticism centres on the feminist analysis of the law enforcement process. While feminists have frequently said that low arrest and conviction rates are the product of patriarchy, the law is differentially enforced against men from lower socio-economic groups. That is, the law is created to protect not only patriarchal interests but also class interests. By concentrating on arresting, prosecuting, and convicting men from lower socio-economic groups, the law enforcement process helps perpetuate the myth that it is lower-class men who are the threat to personal security. From our vantage point, it is necessary to analyse both the patriarchal and class nature of sexual assault law and law enforcement practices.

Marxist Theory
Two variants of Marxist analysis of rape and sexual assault are presented here: socialist feminism and the theory of structural contradictions.

Socialist Feminism. Socialist feminism attempts to understand how patriarchal and capitalist relations interact to affect the status of women in society. There are two distinct variations of socialist feminist analysis. The first, sometimes called dual systems theory, argues that patriarchy and capitalism are separate but equal systems. For example, Hartmann (1977, 1981) says that while it is improbable that patriarchy has been present in all human societies, patriarchal structures predate the emergence of capitalism. By taking advantage of both systems, men were able to continue dominating women through the family via patriarchal relations, while extending their control into the market place via control of capitalist relations.

Another variant of socialist feminism argues that it is impossible to conceptualize any mode of production that excludes the organization of gender relations (see Smith 1985). From this vantage point, the social system is not a dual system but one system. Smith writes:

> Looked at in this way, the problem of patriarchy versus class takes on a different cast. The interpersonal relations of direct dominance, between women and men, are implicated in a larger organisation of the society. Even if we see the patriarchal principal at work in each new setting, in government, business, professions, labour unions, yet that personal relation of dominance and inequality is articulated to the larger social, political and economic organisation of the society. It cannot be separated from it (1985:3–4).

As a theoretical model used to explain criminal behaviour, socialist feminism has been used to explain why men and women from different social classes commit different types of crime, and to analyse how the law functions to preserve both capitalist and patriarchal relations (see Messerschmidt 1986 and Beirne and Messerschmidt 1991).

Messerschmidt (1986; Beirne and Messerschmidt 1991) says that men in all classes commit more crime than women because men have more power and more opportunity because of their social class and patriarchal standing. The types of crime men commit vary with their social class. Men in the upper classes and managerial classes are less likely to engage in conventional crimes. They are, however, more likely to engage in corporate crime because the demand for corporate profit making is the key to success. Men from lower socio-economic positions have little or no opportunity to commit this type of crime. Their criminality is limited to more conventional crime. They encounter conditions that men from upper classes do not encounter. Periods of unemployment, lower incomes, and inferior occupations all contribute to lower-class male crime. Unemployment, low incomes, and low-paying jobs put pressure on men, especially young men, to commit crimes such as burglary and theft. Illegal activity is sometimes easier and more profitable than finding or continuing to work at low-paying or short-term jobs.

The effects of class and patriarchy also pressure men to commit violent crime. Sexual violence (such as rape and incest) and crimes of abuse (such as dating violence and wife assault) are perpetrated against women to reinforce patriarchal and class relations (see Luxton 1980:65-9). As a statement of patriarchal power, rape represents male dominance and women's subordination. As a statement of social class, women from different class positions have differential risks of being raped. The women most likely to be raped, as revealed through both official crime data and victim survey studies, are teenage women from lower socio-economic groups. Women, of course, are not the only victims of male violence. Men commit more acts of violence against other men than they do against women. Violent crime is as much a statement of masculinity and power when the victim is male as it is when the victim is female.

Critique of Socialist Feminism. A major criticism of socialist feminism, which is also applicable to radical feminism, is its failure to account for variations in patriarchy over time (Lacombe 1988). No social structure remains unchanged over time, but socialist feminists frequently treat patriarchy as unchanged and unchanging. This makes it difficult to assess how patriarchy could be eliminated.

Another criticism of socialist feminism concerns its attempted union of Marxism and radical feminism. It has been argued that this attempted merger has produced a feminist analysis that is ultimately submerged within Marxist analysis (Miles 1985). Socialist feminists are accused of reducing patriarchy to just another mechanism by which capitalism maintains control over women. Radical feminists like Eisenstein (1979) argue that capitalist exploitation of workers and men's patriarchal domination of women are not equivalent and should not be treated as such.

A Theory of Structural Contradictions. According to Chambliss and Seidman (1982), all economic systems contain contradictory elements within them. These contradictory elements create social change. In capitalist societies, the basic contradiction is the division of labour between capital and labour. This contradiction creates conflicts between capital and labour as each attempts to gain advantage over the other. For example, both labour and capital attempt to gain control over working conditions and wages. Failure to resolve conflicts over working conditions and wages could threaten the entire social structure. Consequently, it is the state's role to resolve these conflicts. However, the state's solutions can only address the conflicts. They cannot resolve the contradictions themselves. This creates a dilemma for the state. It must make the conflict, not the basic structural contradiction, appear to be the problem. It must also make its solutions appear to be the best possible solution to the conflicts. Every time the state resolves a conflict, a new conflict emerges.

Applying this model to the study of sexual assault, Hinch (1985, 1991) argues that passage of Canada's sexual assault legislation in 1983 was the result of an attempt to resolve conflicts between men and women over the definition and enforcement of the rape law as it existed prior to 1983. Hinch

(1991) argues that these reforms did little to alter the contradictions in the social and economic positions of men and women. Hence, while some sources of conflict between men and women were removed, other sources of conflict remained, and new conflicts surfaced. The state made it possible for married women to charge their husbands with sexual assault. It also gave some victims of sexual assault greater protection from character assassination in court. However, some problems remained. For example, the law did little to remove the social (as opposed to the legal) barriers that prevented married women from reporting their husbands' abusive behaviour. The social pressures on women that prevented them from reporting their husbands' abuse were unaffected by the reforms. Furthermore, some women's sexual histories could still be examined in court. The law clearly states that evidence of prior sexual contact between the accused and the complainant is admissible without restriction. Finally, the law creates some new problems. By opting for a gender-neutral definition of sexual assault, it made it possible to prosecute less serious forms of sexual assault, such as touching a breast and running away, in the same manner as a more serious form of sexual assault, such as rape. In the end, the contradictions of patriarchy and capitalism remain while men and women are still enmeshed in conflicts that lead to pressures for further legal reform.

Critique. The theory of structural contradictions fails to specify how the cycle of *conflict, resolution, conflict* can be brought to a conclusion. A central part of this thesis is that the resolution of conflicts always leaves the forces of capital in secure control, even if they must encounter new difficulties in maintaining that control. This implies that there is no way out of the cycle, that there is no way to deal with the contradictions themselves.

CONTROLLING SEXUAL ASSAULT

There is much that can be done to reduce the rate of victimization, as well as alter the way in which Canadian society deals with victims and offenders. There are changes needed in the law, in how the police and the courts deal with rape and sexual assault, and in the way victims of sexual assault are treated by the public.

Legal Changes
A number of problems with the current sexual assault laws have been identified by researchers. These problems include the retention of the honest-but-mistaken belief in consent defence and the methods of police investigation.

The Honest-but-Mistaken Defence. In 1992, the Criminal Code was amended to restrict the use of the honest-but-mistaken belief in consent defence. It cannot be used as a defence if the accused's belief in consent resulted from:

(1) self-induced intoxication, (2) reckless or deliberate inattention to the victim's wishes, and (3) a failure to take reasonable measures to insure that consent was given. Further, the law now defines consent 'as the voluntary agreement of the complainant to engage in sexual activity' (section 273.1 of the Criminal Code). Consent is not granted if it is granted by someone other than the complainant (i.e., the victim); if the complainant is incapable of giving consent; if the offender abuses his/her position of trust, power, or authority to induce the victim to perform a sexual act; or if the complainant withdraws consent to continue after initially granting consent. These restrictions make it clear that defendants cannot claim this defence and then use it as a means of attacking either the victim's reputation or character. However, critics of this defence argue that it perpetuates the myth that women don't say what they really mean.

Rape mythology has long portrayed women as not saying what they mean in sexual foreplay. Within this stereotype, women are expected to resist men's initial sexual overtures, but are also expected to give in to persistent male demands. Men are expected not to take the initial no as a final answer, and to expect that once consent is given, it cannot be withdrawn. Even though the law now offers more restrictions on the use of the honest-but-mistaken defence, it can still be argued that its continuance in its current form still perpetuates the myth that women do not mean no when they say no.

Thus critics who want to abolish this defence say it perpetuates what Clark and Lewis (1977) termed coercive sexuality. The circumstances that create a mistaken impression for the offender that consent has been given are created within the conception of male/female sexual interaction in which men are defined as conquerors and women are defined as objects to be conquered. Maintenance of this conception of male/female interaction contributes to the perpetuation of sexual assault. Even though the law now requires the offender to demonstrate that reasonable steps were taken to insure consent, the general character of sexual interaction between men and women is still essentially coercive.

However, it cannot be ignored that retention of the honest-but-mistaken defence does satisfy some people. For example, civil libertarians and some criminal lawyers argue that Canadian criminal courts cannot be effective if only the victim's intention were to be considered in criminal cases. They argue that it is a fundamental principle of Canadian criminal law that the offender must have intended to perform the act without the victim's consent in order for it to be judged a sexual assault.

It is likely, of course, that this debate will continue. It is unlikely that even the 1992 amendments will satisfy all of the critics. The attempted balance of victim and offender rights represented by the 1992 amendments may prove themselves to be problematic in time. The law does not clearly state what it means when it says that 'reasonable steps' must be taken to insure consent. It also does not clearly state what it means when it says that consent is not obtained if the complainant is incapable of giving consent. Critics of the new law claim that these clauses leave open the possibility of uneven and contradictory outcomes. Once again, similar situations may be processed differently because the law does not clearly specify what is required.

Changes in Police Processing of Sexual Assault

While there is evidence that changes are needed in the way rape and sexual assault cases are handled at all levels of the criminal justice system, concern here is focused on changes in the way the police process complaints. A major problem with police enforcement practices is the tendency to dismiss complaints from certain types of women (see Clark and Lewis 1977; Hinch 1988a, 1988b). While there is no doubt that some incidents reported to the police are false, or where there is insufficient evidence to make good court referrals, it is doubtful that all such cases are unfounded, and that the percentage of unfounded cases is as high as indicated in official statistics.

Research has also shown that the police, in conducting their investigations, use techniques and procedures that place the victim at a disadvantage. One of these procedures is the use of the polygraph test. Another is the use of medical examinations. The 1983 Criminal Code amendments abolished the requirement that corroborative evidence be established before laying a charge of sexual assault. This was done in order to acknowledge that corroborative evidence was not always available, and that the victim's account of the event, if believed, could constitute sufficient evidence for conviction. Research has shown, however, that the police and the courts remain anxious about cases where they have only the contradictory statements of the accused and the victim (Barrett and Marshall 1990; Hinch 1988a, 1988b, 1991; University of Manitoba Research Ltd 1988a). The police and Crown attorneys are reluctant to proceed with a case if they lack corroborative evidence of physical force or injury to the victim.

Consequently, as a substitute for corroborative evidence, police sometimes use the polygraph test, also known as the lie-detector test. In most instances, the police use polygraphy to determine if suspects are lying. Rape and sexual assault cases appear to be among the few cases where polygraphy is used to determine the truthfulness of victims' statements. Barrett and Marshall (1990), as well as Hinch (1988b), observe that when the police use polygraphy in rape and sexual assault cases to test the truthfulness of victim statements, their investigation is usually terminated if the victim either refuses or *fails* the test. When victims refuse or fail a polygraph test, the police frequently assume that they are lying. Thus polygraphy used in rape and sexual assault cases is a mechanism for weeding out rather than including cases for court referral.

One solution to this problem might be to ban use of polygraphy in all rape and sexual assault cases. The polygraph is a device used to determine stress when answering questions. It is well known that rape and sexual assault victims experience stress as a consequence of being assaulted. When a victim is asked to take a lie-detector test, it is a clear indication to the victim that the police believe she is lying. This only adds to the stress she is experiencing and may, therefore, distort the results of the test.

This, however, does not diminish the problem of victim credibility. Whenever it is the victim's credibility versus the offender's credibility that will determine the outcome of the case, the police and Crown attorneys are reluctant to proceed if the victim lacks credibility. As noted previously, this means that female victims with discreditable personal histories (prostitutes, known drug users, known alcoholics, women who were drinking alcohol with the accused immediately prior to being attacked, unemployed women, welfare recipients, women known to have a history of mental illness, etc.) are unlikely to see their complaints end with a court referral. This reflects not only the biases of the police and Crown attorneys but also the general public.

Similarly, medical examinations and tests used to verify allegations of penetration are also used to weed out rather than include cases for court referral (see Hinch 1988b). Although the current law does not require proof of penetration, medical tests are used to corroborate (also not needed!) the victim's allegation of penetration. When proof of penetration is not obtained through these tests, there is a tendency to end police investigations.

Police decision making is also based on their experiences in getting cases through the courts. The kinds of biases demonstrated by police in their decision making are also evident elsewhere in the criminal justice system. Gunn and Minch (1988) report that decisions of Crown prosecutors differ in no significant way from police decisions. They report that the only cases terminated by Crown prosecutors were those left unclassified by the police.

Gunn and Minch (1988) also indicate that, in addition to terminating poor cases referred to them by the police, they may either reduce charges or add charges in those cases with stronger evidence. This is done to increase the probability of conviction. The decision may be made that there is insufficient evidence for conviction on the major charge, so a reduced charge is entered. In some instances, charges may be reduced in exchange for a guilty plea from the offender. When charges are added, the Crown may still seek conviction on the major charge, but will want to have a back-up charge in case the major charge does not result in conviction. There may be sufficient evidence for a conviction on the back-up charge. Curiously, Gunn and Minch found no evidence to support the assumption that laying additional charges resulted in higher probability of conviction.

Studies of court decision making also indicate that the biases demonstrated by the police also influence court decisions (Barrett and Marshall 1990; Ellis 1986; Feild and Bienen 1980). It seems, therefore, that substantial changes are needed throughout the criminal justice system. As Gunn and Minch (1988:136–7) argue, 'The notion of breaking down the old structures and re-establishing new institutions devoid of discrimination is an overwhelming concept. Yet, it would appear that, given the imbalance of male/ female power, this idea is the only answer.'

SUMMARY

This chapter has concentrated on summarizing the criminological literature on rape and sexual assault. It has been shown that the apparently simple task of defining sexual assault or rape may influence assessments of the offence rate. If rape and sexual assault are broadly defined, then more incidents may be termed rape or sexual assault. If they are narrowly defined, fewer acts may be counted. A broad definition of sexual assault results in rates higher than those shown in Table 2.1, which does not include events that are not reported to the police. The unreported incidents include those in which the victim and offender have a close relationship, as well as those in which the victim simply does not wish to make known his or her victimization.

Regardless of the definitions, it is obvious that much needs to be done and can be done to reduce the amount of rape and sexual assault, as well as to improve victim confidence in the criminal justice system. The legal definitions of rape and sexual assault need to be changed to satisfy the need for gender-neutral terminology, as well as to reflect the seriousness of the events being defined. The law, the police, and court processing of complaints need to improve in order to reduce the tendency to blame victims. The theories of sexual assault and rape reviewed in this chapter include those concerned with demonstrating individual pathology (control theory), those concerned with understanding the nature of the interaction between the victim and the offender (interactionist theories), and those concerned with understanding how social structures such as patriarchy (feminist theories) or capitalism (Marxist theories) influence human behaviour. Each theory was shown to have its own strengths and weaknesses.

ACKNOWLEDGEMENT

I wish to thank Valerie Ahwee for her excellent work in editing this chapter. She has made me appear to be a better writer than I am. Naturally, any remaining grammatical errors, awkwardness in sentence structures, etc., are my responsibility.

FURTHER READINGS

Baril, M., M.-J. Bettz, and L. Viau. 1988. *Sexual Assault Before and After the 1983 Reform: An Evaluation of Practices in the Judicial District of Montreal, Quebec.* Ottawa: Department of Justice.

DeKeseredy, W., and R. Hinch. 1991. *Woman Abuse: Sociological Perspectives.* Toronto: Thompson Educational Publishing, Inc.

Gunn, R., and C. Minch. 1988. *Sexual Assault: The Dilemma of Disclosure, the Question of Conviction*. Winnipeg: The University of Manitoba Press.

Hunter, M., ed. 1990. *The Sexually Abused Male, Volume 1: Prevalence, Impact, and Treatment*. Toronto: Maxwell Macmillan Canada.

Messerschmidt, J.W. 1986. *Capitalism, Patriarchy, and Crime: Toward a Socialist Feminist Criminology*. Totowa, NJ: Rowman and Littlefield.

Roberts, J., and R. Mohr, eds. 1994. *Confronting Sexual Assault: A Decade of Legal and Social Change*. Toronto: University of Toronto Press.

Stanko, E.Q. 1990. *Everyday Violence: How Women and Men Experience Sexual and Physical Danger*. London: Pandora.

REFERENCES

Ageton, S.S. 1983. *Sexual Assault Among Adolescents*. Toronto: Lexington Books.

Amir, M. 1971. *Patterns of Forcible Rape*. Chicago: University of Chicago Press.

Baril, M., et al. 1988. *Sexual Assault Before and After the 1983 Reform: An Evaluation of Practices in the Judicial District of Montreal, Quebec*. Ottawa: Department of Justice.

Barrett, S., and W.L. Marshall. 1990. 'Shattering Myths: One in Four Females and One in Eight Males in Canada Are Sexually Abused'. *Saturday Night* (June):21–5.

Beirne, P., and J. Messerschmidt. 1991. *Criminology*. New York: Harcourt Brace Jovanovich.

Bill C-127 Working Group. 1982. 'Lobby Logistics: Bill C-127'. *Broadside* 3, 4 (December):4.

Boyd, S.B., and E.A. Sheehy. 1989. 'Overview'. In *Law and Society: A Critical Perspective*, edited by T.C. Caputo, M. Kennedy, C.E. Reasons, and A. Brannigan, 255–70. Toronto: Harcourt Brace Jovanovich.

Boyle, C. 1981. 'Married Women—Beyond the Pale of the Law of Rape'. *Windsor Yearbook of Access to Justice* 1:192–213.

_____. 1984. *Sexual Assault*. Toronto: Carswell Legal Publications.

Chambliss, W.J., and R. Seidman. 1982. *Law, Order and Power*. New York: Addison Wesley.

Clark, L., and D. Lewis. 1977. *Rape: The Price of Coercive Sexuality*. Toronto: Women's Press.

Cohen, L., and C. Backhouse. 1980a. 'Putting Rape in Its Place'. *Maclean's* 93, 26 (30 June):6.

_____. 1980b. 'Desexualizing Rape: Dissenting View on the Proposed Rape Amendments'. *Canadian Women Studies* 2:99–103.

Cormier, B.M., and S.P. Simons. 1969. 'The Problem of the Dangerous Sexual Offender'. *Canadian Psychiatric Association Journal* 14, no. 4:327–35.

CSOACY (Committee on Sexual Offences Against Children and Youths). 1984. *Sexual Offences Against Children*, vol. 1 and 2. Ottawa: Attorney General of Canada and National Health and Welfare.

Curtis, L. 1973. 'Victim Precipitation and Violent Crime'. *Social Problems* 21:594–605.

CUVS (Canadian Urban Victimization Survey). 1983. *Bulletin 1: Victims of Crime*. Ottawa: Solicitor General.

_____. 1984. *Bulletin 2: Reported and Unreported Crimes*. Ottawa: Solicitor General.

_____. 1985. *Bulletin 4: Female Victims of Crime*. Ottawa: Solicitor General.

DeKeseredy, W., and R. Hinch. 1991. *Woman Abuse: Sociological Perspectives*. Toronto: Thompson Educational Publishing, inc.

_____, and K. Kelly. 1993. 'The Incidence and Prevalence of Woman Abuse in Canadian University and College Dating Relationships'. *Canadian Journal of Sociology* 18, no. 2:137–59.

Department of Justice. 1990. *Sexual Assault Legislation in Canada: An Evaluation*. Ottawa: Department of Justice.

Eisenstein, Z. 1979. 'Some Notes on the Relations of Capitalist Patriarchy'. In *Capitalist Patriarchy and the Case for Socialist Feminism*, edited by Z. Eisenstein, 5–40. New York: Monthly Review Press.

Ekos Research Associates Inc. 1988a. *Report on the Treatment of Sexual Assault Cases in Vancouver, British Columbia*. Ottawa: Department of Justice.

_____. 1988b. *Report on the Treatment of Sexual Assault Cases in Hamilton, Ontario*. Ottawa: Department of Justice.

Ellis, M. 1986. 'Judicial Interpretations of the New Sexual Offences in Light of the Charter of Rights and Freedoms: An Examination of Gender-Neutrality, Discrimination and Inequality'. Unpublished ms.

Feild, H.S., and L.B. Bienen. 1980. *Jurors and Rape*. Toronto: Lexington Books.

Finkelhor, D., and K. Yllo. 1985. *License to Rape: Sexual Abuse of Wives*. New York: Holt, Rinehart and Winston.

Gaudet, M.A. 1984. 'The Victim and the Offender: A Puzzling Relationship, Part 1'. *Liaison* 10, no. 7:4–11.

Gebhard, P.H., et al. 1965. *Sex Offenders: An Analysis of Types*. New York: Harper and Row.

Griffin, S. 1971. 'Rape: The All-American Crime'. *Ramparts* 10, no. 3:26–35.

Groth, N. 1979. *Men Who Rape*. New York: Plenum Press.

Gunn, R., and C. Minch. 1988. *Sexual Assault: The Dilemma of Disclosure, the Question of Conviction*. Winnipeg: University of Manitoba Press.

Hartmann, H. 1977. 'Capitalism, Patriarchy, and Job Segregation by Sex'. In *Woman in a Man-Made World*, 2nd ed., edited by N. Glazer and

H. Youngelson Waehrer, 71–84. Chicago: Rand McNally College Publishing Company.

_____. 1985. 'The Unhappy Marriage of Marxism and Feminism'. In *Politics, Patriarchy and Practice*, edited by R. Dale et al., 191–219. Milton Keynes: Open University.

Hinch, R. 1985. 'Canada's New Sexual Assault Laws: A Step Forward for Women?' *Contemporary Crises* 9, no. 1:33–44.

_____. 1988a. 'The Enforcement of Canada's Sexual Assault Law: An Exploratory Study'. *Atlantis* 14, no. 1:109–15.

_____. 1988b. 'Inconsistencies and Contradictions in Canada's Sexual Assault Law'. *Canadian Public Policy* XIV, no. 3:282–94.

_____. 1991. 'Contradictions, Conflicts and Dilemmas in Canada's Sexual Assault Law'. In *Crimes by the State: An Introduction to State Criminality*, edited by G. Barak, 233–51. New York: State University of New York Press.

Hindelang, M., and B.J. Davis. 1977. 'Forcible Rape in the United States'. In *Forcible Rape: The Crime, the Victim and the Offender*, edited by D. Chappell, R. Geis, and G. Geis, 87–114. New York: Columbia University Press.

Jackman, N. 1982. 'Bill C-53 Law Reflects Values'. *Canadian Women's Studies* 3, no. 4.

Klemmack, S.H., and D.J. Klemmack. 1976. 'The Social Definition of Rape'. In *Sexual Assault: The Victim and the Rapist*, edited by M.H. Walker and S. Brodsky, 135–47. Toronto: Lexington Books.

Lacombe, D. 1988. *Ideology and Public Policy: The Case Against Pornography*. Toronto: Garamond Press.

LaFree, G.D. 1989. *Rape and Criminal Justice: The Social Construction of Sexual Assault*. Belmont: Wadsworth Publishing Company.

Landau, R., and L. Lowenberger. 1983. 'Rape Law Still in Crisis'. *Broadside* 4, no. 8:4.

Lowenberger, K., and R. Landau. 1982. 'A Rape by Any Other Name'. *Broadside* 3, no. 9:3.

Luxton, M. 1980. *More Than a Labour of Love: Three Generations of Women's Work in the Home*. Toronto: Women's Press.

Marshall, W.L. 1973. 'The Modification of Sexual Fantasies: A Combined Treatment Approach to the Reduction of Deviant Sexual Behaviour'. *Behavioral Research and Therapy* 11:557–64.

_____, and R.D. McKnight. 1975. 'An Integrated Program for Sexual Offenders'. *Canadian Psychiatric Association Journal* 20, no. 2:133–8.

McCahill, T.W., et al. 1979. *The Aftermath of Rape*. Toronto: Lexington Books.

Media, A., and K. Thompson. 1974. *Against Rape*. New York: Farrar, Straus and Giroux.

Messerschmidt, J.W. 1986. *Capitalism, Patriarchy, and Crime: Toward a Socialist Feminist Criminology*. Totowa, NJ: Rowman and Littlefield.

Miles, A. 1985. 'Feminism, Equality, and Liberation'. *Canadian Journal of Women and the Law*, 1, no. 1:42–68.

Nelson, S., and M. Amir. 1977. 'The Hitchhike Victim of Rape: A Research Report'. In *Forcible Rape: The Crime, the Victim and the Offender*, edited by D. Chappell, R. Geis, and G. Geis, 272–90. New York: Columbia University Press.

Nuttall, S.E. 1989. *User Report: Toronto Sexual Assault Research Study*. Ottawa: Solicitor General.

Rada, T., ed. 1978. *Clinical Aspects of the Rapist*. New York: Grune and Stratton.

Ranson, J. 1982. *Rape in Marriage*. New York: Macmillan.

_____. 1984. *Sexual Exploitation: Rape, Child Sexual Abuse and Workplace Harassment*. Beverly Hills: Sage Publications.

Russell, D., and D. Finkelhor. 1984. 'Women as Perpetrators'. In *Child Sexual Abuse: New Theory and Research* by D. Finkelhor, 171–85. New York: Free Press.

Sacco, V., and H. Johnson. 1990. *Patterns of Criminal Victimization in Canada*. Ottawa: Statistics Canada.

Sanders, W.B. 1980. *Rape and Woman's Identity*. Beverly Hills: Sage Publications.

Smart, C. 1976. *Women, Crime and Criminology: A Feminist Critique*. London: Routledge and Kegan Paul.

Smith, D. 1985. 'Women, Class and Family'. In *Women, Class, Family and the State* by V. Burstyn and D.E. Smith, 1–44. Toronto: Garamond Press.

Snider, L. 1985. 'Legal Reform and Social Control: The Dangers of Abolishing Rape'. *International Journal of Law* 13:337–56.

University of Manitoba Research Ltd. 1988a. *Report on the Impact of the 1983 Sexual Assault Legislation in Lethbridge, Alberta*. Ottawa: Department of Justice.

_____. 1988b. *Report on the Impact of the 1983 Sexual Assault Legislation in Winnipeg, Manitoba*. Ottawa: Department of Justice.

Urquiza, A.J., and M. Capra. 1990. 'The Impact of Sexual Abuse: Initial and Long-Term Effects'. In *The Sexually Abused Male, Volume 1: Prevalence, Impact, and Treatment*, edited by M. Hunter, 105–35. Toronto: Maxwell Macmillan Canada.

Wolfgang, M.E. 1958. *Patterns in Criminal Homicide*. Philadelphia: University of Pennsylvania Press.

3

The Selective Control of Drugs

Patricia Erickson

INTRODUCTION

As the twentieth century commenced, the public could choose from a broad array of legally available psychoactive substances. The growing temperance movement focused on alcohol as the root cause of most of society's problems. Opium, heroin, and cocaine were readily obtainable from the local pharmacy, and were, along with alcohol, major components of many popular and widely used patent medicines (Murray 1988). The modern tobacco cigarette, competing with pipes, cigars, and snuff, was just beginning to be marketed in quantity. Marijuana was grown primarily for the production of hemp cloth and birdseed. None of the users of the substances was regarded as sick, criminal, or seriously deviant, and extreme cases of addiction were viewed as a matter of individual misfortune or personal vice.

Soon all this changed. Forces routed drugs down various paths of social control, with varying degrees of severity of societal response. Today, the crack users are as feared and despised as the heroin 'junkie' of an earlier era. The seller of illegal 'narcotics'—that is, cannabis, opium, cocaine, or PCP (or phencyclidine)—faces a maximum sentence of life imprisonment under current Canadian law. Alcohol, which was banned briefly during the First World War, was soon re-established as society's drug of choice; now messages promoting its use compete with those for moderation. The cigarette smoker pursued his (and increasingly her) glamorous, Hollywood-endorsed habit for several decades, unimpeded except by pocketbook and hours in the day. However, current smokers confront higher prices and a barrage of no-smoking signs. Mood-modifying prescription drugs like Valium are dispensed by medical professionals as a legitimate source of relief for modern-day stresses and anxiety. For those whose tension-relieving or recreational drugs of choice are prohibited, heavy fines or jail sentences are a possible side effect of indulgence.

This chapter will address four major topics in the social construction of deviance in Canada as reflected in the varying social response to psychoactive substances. These topics are the historical development of social meanings attached to different drugs, the perceived harm of drugs and the actual extent of their use and related problems, the institutional response to drug users, and the various ways the drug users themselves concede or resist the imputation of the deviant identity.

HISTORY: A DIVERGENCE OF SOCIAL MEANINGS

The first major fork in the path of social control occurred in 1908 with the creation of the Opium Act, which was directed at Chinese labourers. Subsequent debates, concerned also with morphine and cocaine, led to the Opium and Drug Act of 1911 and the Opium and Narcotic Drug Act of 1920. Each modification of a previous statute provided harsher penalties and fewer legal protections for illicit drug users and sellers. Possession, importation, manufacture, and trafficking were not differentiated in terms of sentences available. A series of amendments in the 1920s stipulated progressively more severe penalties for all these offences and greatly extended the police's powers of search and seizure.

By 1929, mandatory minimum penalties and a maximum of seven years' imprisonment, plus whipping and hard labour, were in effect. In 1922, police officers received the right to search, without a warrant, any place except a dwelling in which they suspected illicit drugs were concealed. Police powers to search dwellings were expanded further in 1929 through a measure called the writ of assistance. The writ was issued to a particular officer, rather than in relation to a specific search in limited circumstances, as would be the case in the normal, judicially approved, search warrant procedure. Until 1985, the designated officer could:

> aided and assisted by such person or persons as he may require, at any time enter and search any dwelling house within Canada in which he reasonably believes there is a narcotic and search any person found in such a place and as he deems necessary, break open any door, window lock, fastener, floor, wall, ceiling, compartment, plumbing fixture, box container or any thing (Narcotic Control Act, RSC 1970, s. 10(4)).

These penalties and unusually broad police powers set the stage for defining as criminals all those involved with illegal narcotics, including the physicians who supplied them.

This pattern, with some modification, has persisted up to the present. The dominance of the criminalization approach to 'narcotics' (including cannabis, so defined without debate in 1923) is attributable to two principal factors (Giffen, Endicott, and Lambert 1991). The first is that opium use was associated with Asians, a negatively stereotyped racial group, as well as unconventional, low-status Whites. The creation of the 'dope fiend' mythology encouraged a moral crusade against narcotic addiction, one that demanded harshly punitive measures. Any pharmacological distinction between different drugs, as long as they originated from exotic, far-away places, was irrelevant to the mythology. Soon-to-be Prime Minister MacKenzie King was skilful in mobilizing this cultural antagonism on behalf of political interest groups who wanted to prevent further Asian immigration. During this early period, Canadian representatives played a prominent role in the international movement among Western nations to criminalize the use and distribution of narcotics through various conferences and treaties.

The second factor in the persistence and expansion of criminalization is the power base established by the centralized drug bureaucracy during the formative period of Canadian narcotic law. The Division of Narcotic Control in the national Department of Health, in conjunction with the federal enforcers and the federal prosecutors, gained a virtual monopoly over drug policies during the crucial early years. The Canadian medical profession, only weakly organized at the time, was easily intimidated and provided little advocacy for a medical approach to addiction; indeed ninety-one physicians were prosecuted in the 1920s for prescribing opiates (Giffen, Endicott, and Lambert 1991:324). The formidable early chiefs of the Division of Narcotic Control, Cowan and Sharman, coordinated reports from police and prosecutors concerning their expressed need for greater powers, met regularly with politicians and top civil servants, and saw to it that legislative support was forthcoming (Giffen, Endicott, and Lambert 1991). The bureaucratic partnership of social control agents remained virtually unchallenged until the 1950s when the treatment issue gained prominence and was further assailed by the marijuana controversy that erupted in the late 1960s.

For alcohol consumers, the first serious control efforts took a different path. Early temperance efforts focused on local jurisdictions, with some success in rural areas in Ontario and the Maritimes (Smart and Ogborne 1986). A national referendum on prohibition in 1898, held under the authority of the Canada Temperance Act of 1879, received approval in all provinces except Quebec, but with only 44 per cent turnout of voters. With an eye for trouble, Prime Minister Wilfred Laurier refused to implement the ban, and temperance organizations had to wait until the First World War. Then national prohibition was imposed in all provinces, only to be defeated by 1929 in postwar votes everywhere except Prince Edward Island, which held out until 1948.

Alcohol prohibition in Canada never amounted to a total ban on buying and drinking alcohol. Rather, alcoholic beverages containing no more than 2.5 per cent of ethanol were allowed, alcohol was available by prescription, and production for export was permitted (Smart and Ogborne 1986). Canadians made fortunes supplying the 'dryer' American market. Manufacturers and distributors, not consumers, were the targets of enforcement within Canada. Thus users of alcohol never had a criminal identification like that already associated with illicit drug users in this era. At the same time, the medical or 'disease' model of alcoholism was beginning to gain some currency (Blackwell 1988). This set the stage for the expansion of the treatment approach in the 1950s and 1960s, and the definition of the alcoholic as 'sick' rather than bad, contagious, and morally suspect.

Cigarettes became the object of a short-lived prohibitionist campaign in 1908. Despite debates in the House of Commons describing nicotine as the 'narcotic poison of tobacco' with the capability of 'impairing health, arresting development [and] weakening intellectual power', members of Parliament nevertheless failed to pass any legislation other than that forbidding sale to those under sixteen years of age, but also approved a bill protecting domestic tobacco producers and manufacturers from foreign competition (Giffen, Endicott, and Lambert 1991:50). For the ensuing decades, the tobacco industry freely marketed and promoted its product, officially *not* a drug, and by 1980 Canada had one of the highest levels of per capita consumption of cigarettes in the world.

Also in contrast to the Chinese opium situation in these early years was the growing influence of vested interests in the fledgling pharmaceutical industry (Murray 1988). The Proprietary and Patent Medicine Act of 1908, intended explicitly 'to safeguard the public interest without committing injustice to the business interests' contained weak restrictions and penalties. The act required only that the ingredients of any medicine had to be listed on the bottle. Cocaine and 'excessive' amounts of alcohol were forbidden, but opium and morphine were not, and even heroin could be included in the miracle cures in 'safe' amounts. The maximum penalty for infractions was $100, compared to $1,000 and/or three years' imprisonment under the Opium Act of the same year (Giffen, Endicott, and Lambert 1991:50). Although stricter requirements were later imposed, the principle that the production of 'medicine' was in the control of legitimate manufacturers was established.

It is evident that the first decades of this century were extremely important in establishing historical dividing lines between licit and illicit drugs. This led to very different social definitions of their acceptability and appropriate controls. The system of complete prohibition that was established for 'narcotics' suppressed all legitimate availability and provided severe criminal penalties for a variety of offences involving importation, cultivation, trafficking, and possession. In contrast, regulatory schemes permitted controlled access to many other substances. Licit drugs were subject to varying limits on conditions of sale, to certain standards for the quality of the product, and to professional guidelines for medical prescription. Violations of regulatory statutes were subject to milder penalties such as fines or loss of licences.

Alcohol, after Canada's brief fling with partial 'prohibition', was clearly differentiated from medicines and re-established as a socially approved, recreational beverage. Physicians eventually gained more control of prescribing an ever-increasing array of pharmaceuticals produced by a global industry. Almost no controls over tobacco products existed. The label 'drug user' was a highly negative one, synonymous with *illicit* use of 'narcotics', when the 1960s ushered in a new era of psychoactive drug use.

DANGERS REAL AND IMAGINARY: USE AND ABUSE IN CULTURAL CONTEXT

It is a truism to point out that virtually all human societies (except the traditional Inuit) have indulged in some form of mind-altering substance use with indigenous plants (McKenna 1992). It is also accurate to state that in no society where drug use was subject to cultural rituals and restrictions has destructive use been the norm (Heath 1992). Individuals and societies find ways of avoiding serious harm by using informal social controls (Maloff et al. 1979). These include rules for appropriate use generated in social interaction between friends, family, and peers. The modern, rapid diffusion of new, more potent drugs into societies lacking a traditional cultural context for their appropriate use has led to some harmful patterns of use. When identified as a threat, these help to spawn an overreliance on more repressive, external, formal controls (Black 1989; Peyrot 1984).

Official and popular assessments of the harm caused by alcohol and other drugs differ from culture to culture and also shift within a particular culture over even relatively short time periods. This establishes an important principle about understanding drug problems: they are not simply inherent in the pharmacology of the substance but rather emerge in the interaction between the drug, the user, and the social and physical environment (Heath 1992; Zinberg and Shaffer 1990). In other words, there are no 'bad' (or 'good') drugs, but rather more or less harmful consequences, depending on how the drug is used and who is using it. The designation of a pejorative label is largely arbitrary. Drug 'abuse' is in the eye of the beholder, reflecting a socially constructed reality. A new prohibition or 'war on drugs' is imposed on those who conform to the stereotype of the evil, dangerous, often foreign, users and pushers (Duster 1970; Musto 1973). Such approaches may have little to do with an objective reality that recognizes a continuum of drug use/misuse, regardless of the drug's legal status (Goode 1990; Jensen and Gerber 1993; Jenson, Gerber, and Babcock 1991).

Reviews of the pharmacological properties of drugs, including their short- and long-term effects and addictive capacity, are available in a number of sources (Alexander 1990; Boyd 1991; Fehr 1988a, 1988b; Jacobs and Fehr 1987). For sociological analysis, the concern is the perception of drug effects—their imputed properties—as a basis for social stigma and punitive social control. These perceptions are important because many of the intensely moralistic judgements about narcotics are based on conceptions of the physiological consequences of the drugs (Duster 1970:29).

Cannabis was portrayed in the 1930s as leading to 'reefer madness' then, in an about-face in the 1970s, to the 'amotivational syndrome'. Beginning to be valued as a relaxant and euphoriant by some in the 'counterculture', its scientific reputation was also briefly rehabilitated by various national commissions that concluded that the adverse consequences of cannabis had been exaggerated. Then a counter-reaction in the 1980s attributed anew both physical and mental damage to marijuana (Erickson 1985). Such a reaction was hardly surprising, given the enormous resources that were invested in animal studies to establish any possible harms of cannabis, rather than any assessment of benefits of safer dosages for human users (Fehr and Kalant 1983). The research effort petered out quickly once the wave of decriminalization ended (Negrete 1988). This has meant that we have very little knowledge about the long-term effects of cannabis use in relation to varying amounts and frequency of intake (Smart 1993). The image of cannabis as a dangerous narcotic has persisted despite scientific opinion that like alcohol, tobacco, or any other pharmacologically active agent, cannabis can produce detrimental effects if enough is taken, and can be used in sufficiently low amounts so that no detriment results (Kalant 1982).

The drugs subject to the most persistent demonizing mythology have been the opiates, particularly heroin. An unrivalled analgesic (painkiller), the most deleterious effects of chronic opiate use are severe constipation and reduced libido (Jacobs and Fehr 1987). Throughout most of this century, medical and scientific commentators have agreed that opiates are not otherwise significantly damaging to the minds and bodies of regular users (Brecher 1972:21-7). A recent quote from Nobel prizewinner, Solomon Snyder, expresses this perspective: 'opiate addiction in and of itself is not physically dangerous. Ingesting opiate extracts by mouth is safer than injecting morphine, but if dosage is reasonably well controlled, even opiates by injection are not inherently dangerous' (Snyder 1989:38).

The undeniable poor health and degraded lives of 'street' opiate addicts are rather attributable to the damaging, deprived, and marginal lifestyle generated by the prohibition itself (Alexander 1990; Chein et al. 1964; Lindesmith 1965; Stephenson et al. 1956). The major risks of opiate injection are related to the unknown potency and impurity of the drug, the possible contamination of needles with hepatitis and HIV, and unsafe injecting practices. In addition, involvement in the criminal black market with its inherent violence in order to obtain opiates at inflated prices generates further individual and social costs (Boyd 1991; Faupel 1991; Johnson et al. 1985). The image of the opiate user as a hopelessly passive misfit has nevertheless been challenged by evidence that many lead very demanding lives in their job of 'hustling', many fluctuate in their usage patterns according to availability, and many stabilize in relatively productive lives (Blackwell 1983; Johnson et al. 1985; Preble and Casey 1969; Rosenbaum 1981).

Cocaine and, more recently, crack have been the latest 'headliners' in the drug crisis industry (Reinarman and Levine 1989). Cocaine, like amphetamine, is a powerful stimulant that acts on the central nervous system to create short-term feelings of euphoria, energy, and well-being. Since the lethal dose in unknown, its potentially deadly effects are unpredictable (Smart and Anglin 1987). Repeated heavy use can lead to a well-documented phenomenon known as cocaine psychosis, marked by paranoia and 'formication' (i.e., the sensation of insects crawling under the skin (Jacobs and Fehr 1987). Clearly, cocaine use is not without risks.

Cocaine has gone through extreme cycles of popularity in which it has been portrayed as a benign, non-addictive tonic and as the most powerfully addictive drug on earth (Akers 1991; Erickson et al. 1987; Murray 1987). The confusion about cocaine's addictive potential is attributable in part to the absence of a clear-cut physical withdrawal syndrome after the cessation of regular use. This confusion is also attributable to a behavioural pattern of compulsive, socially destructive use by a small proportion of those who try cocaine (Erickson and Alexander 1989). The contrast between cocaine and heroin, which can produce an extremely unpleasant though not life-threatening withdrawal syndrome, is captured by William S. Burroughs in *Naked Lunch*:

> You can smell it going in, clean and cold in your nose and throat then a rush of pure pleasure right through the brain lighting up those C[ocaine] connections. Ten minutes later you want another shot, you will walk across town for another shot. But if you can't score for C, you eat, sleep and forget about it (Burroughs 1959:19).

The currently dominant notion of cocaine's powerful addictive quality is a considerable overstatement: between 5 per cent and 10 per cent of those who ever try cocaine will use it weekly or more often; most users will not continue, and the majority of those who do will use it infrequently. Of the more frequent users (weekly or more often), about one-tenth to one-quarter will develop uncontrolled use patterns at some time (Erickson and Alexander 1989; Erickson et al. 1987; Waldorf, Reinarman, and Murphy 1991). Even crack use, when studied outside of treatment settings, is not necessarily compulsive (Cheung, Erickson, and Landau 1991). The natural history of the recent crack epidemic in the United States has been described as differing little from that of previous (drug) epidemics (Fagin and Chin 1989:606). Cocaine use patterns, then, span a continuum. Although persistent uncontrolled use is the outcome for a small minority, many more users stop for periods of time, maintain moderate use, stop completely, or regain control over their cocaine use (Erickson 1993).

Since all psychoactive drugs have the potential for harm, the selection of particular drugs for harsh repression is a social process that has little relationship to objective evidence. During the alternating waves of panic and indifference (Giffen, Endicott, and Lambert 1991) that have marked this century's response to illicit drugs, Canada's most deadly drugs were quietly gaining ground. Tobacco and alcohol are currently used, respectively, by about 32 per cent and 78 per cent of the population aged fifteen years and older, according to a national survey conducted in 1989 (Health and Welfare Canada 1992). For tobacco, this represents a decline from peak levels of consumption in 1966 when 82 per cent of Canadians smoked. While the proportion of alcohol drinkers has remained quite stable, per capita consumption of alcohol has declined slightly in the 1980s to about 11 L of absolute alcohol by 1989. Of course, these more widely used legal drugs generate substantial government revenue. Nevertheless, an estimated 15,000 people now die annually in Canada from alcohol-related causes and 35,000 from tobacco-related causes (Boyd 1991). Nor are medically prescribed drugs immune from excessive or inappropriate use. In contrast, the deaths attributable each year to all the illicit drugs combined number in the hundreds; these occur among the approximately 7 per cent to 10 per cent of Canadians who are cannabis users, 1.4 per cent who are cocaine users, and the much less than 1 per cent who regularly inject opiates (Boyd 1991; Health and Welfare Canada 1992). Such figures are the basis for the conclusion that the drugs carrying the greatest health and safety risks are not, in fact, illegal (Addiction Research Foundation 1987–8:10).

INSTITUTIONAL RESPONSE: THE PERSISTENCE OF CRIMINALIZATION

A reliance on strict enforcement and punishment has traditionally been Canada's primary strategy for the control of illicit drugs. The upsurge in drug use, especially marijuana and hashish, by otherwise normal, middle-class youth in the 1960s precipitated the questioning and some selective penalty modification of the dominant policy (Erickson 1980). Before 1969, limited sentencing options in the Narcotic Control Act meant that half of all cannabis possession offenders were imprisoned. The courts were overloaded with several thousand of this new breed of 'cannabis criminals'. The federal government's initial response to the public controversy was to provide a 'fine only' sentencing opinion in the Narcotic Control Act in 1969, and to appoint the Royal Commission of Inquiry into the Non-medical Use of Drugs, the Le Dain Commission (Erickson and Smart 1988).

During the 1970s, cannabis was at centre-stage in an unprecedented public debate over illicit drug policy. Although the government did not act on the findings of the Le Dain majority report recommending the decriminalization of cannabis possession, it did provide the new sentencing alternative of a discharge (which still imposes a criminal record) in a Criminal Code amendment in 1972. Judges were quick to utilize the fine and discharge options; a lower proportion of possession offenders were imprisoned. The rapid increase in the number of convictions, however, resulted in greater *numbers* of these cannabis offenders actually being incarcerated than in the 1960s (Erickson 1980:22). During this decade, annual arrests and convictions for cannabis climbed dramatically, numbering about 41,000 convictions in 1980, over 90 per cent of them for possession. In contrast, convictions for each of heroin, cocaine, LSD, and other drugs did not exceed 1,000 in any given year (Erickson and Cheung 1992).

Despite ongoing controversy over the appropriate social response to cannabis and Prime Minister Trudeau's remark to students in 1977 that 'if you have a joint and you're smoking it for your private pleasure, you shouldn't be hassled', no other significant legal changes occurred (Erickson 1992:247). A proposal to move cannabis into the less restrictive but still criminal statute, the Food and Drugs Act, surfaced several times, but never progressed through Parliament. Despite increasing numbers of young people subjected to criminalization, a combination of the decline in sentence severity for cannabis possession, the low-visibility of police enforcement activity, and the greater efficiency of the courts in processing these offenders helped to defuse the earlier pressure for meaningful law reform (Erickson 1982; Erickson and Murray 1986). By the beginning of the 1980s, cannabis users and society had, it appeared, learned to live with prohibition (Erickson 1989).

As the 1980s advanced, most forms of illicit drug use declined, arrests for cannabis decreased while those for cocaine gradually increased, and heroin convictions remained low. Cannabis use had become normalized to some extent. It is difficult to continue regarding as seriously deviant a behaviour that has been engaged in by over 4.5 million Canadians, or about one-quarter of the adult population (Health and Welfare Canada 1992). The passage of the Charter of Rights and Freedoms in 1982 resulted in the removal of some of the procedural disadvantages accruing to suspected drug users and sellers (Erickson 1992). It seemed possible that illicit drug use would gradually wane in importance and like other previously criminalized acts (e.g., abortion and homosexuality) would follow the cycle of diminished social concern, less enforcement, minimal intervention, and greater tolerance (Glaser 1985).

This trend was reversed, like those before it, with the emergence of a new drug of concern, cocaine. Panic again dominated the cycle of response. Despite evidence that use levels in Canada were one-fifth or one-quarter of those in the United States, Canadian perceptions of their cocaine 'problem' tended to be shaped by the extreme views presented in the American media (Erickson et al. 1994). Within two days of President Reagan's declaration in 1986 that 'Drugs are menacing our society, there is no moral middle ground', Prime Minister Mulroney departed from a prepared speech to warn that 'Drug abuse has become an epidemic that undermines our economic as well as our social fabric' (Erickson 1992:248). Levels of cocaine use in the 1985 national survey indicated that less than 1 per cent of adults had used cocaine in the previous year (Erickson et al. 1987). The only trend data available in the 1980s from the Ontario surveys showed that cocaine use was declining among students and was stable among adults (Adlaf and Smart 1991; Adlaf, Smart, and Canale 1991). As a senior health official commented about this rediscovery of Canada's drug crisis, 'When [the Prime Minister] made that statement, then we had to make it a problem' (Erickson 1992:248).

The result was the resurgence of criminalization, fuelled both by the concerns about cocaine and crack emanating from the United States, and by the direction of additional resources into enforcement as part of Canada's new 'drug strategy' launched in 1987 (Erickson 1992). Cocaine charges went up by a factor of ten in the 1980s, seizures of cocaine increased markedly, and cocaine products became the avowed target of antidrug activity (Erickson and Cheung 1992). The proportion of cocaine possession offenders who were jailed rose from 19 per cent in 1980 to 29 per cent in 1989. The proportion of inmates incarcerated federally from all narcotic offences went up from 9 per cent to 14 per cent between 1986 and 1989.

During this same period, the Royal Canadian Mounted Police's investigation of suspected traffickers in cocaine or cannabis increasingly focused on small-scale dealers (Royal Canadian Mounted Police 1990). For example, the proportion of traffickers investigated for the smallest amount of drug tripled for both cocaine and cannabis, while those pursued for the largest amounts actually declined (Erickson 1992). Cannabis possession offenders were also caught up in this slipstream of antidrug activity, and the decline in charges halted in 1986 and stabilized at about 28,000 yearly for the rest of the decade. Thus during a period of declining illicit dug use, the overall drug crime rate (i.e., recorded drug law offences per 100,000 population) actually climbed from 221.9 in 1986 to 258.9 in 1989 (Erickson 1992). The United States might have been waging a drug war, but Canada, it appeared, was waging a drug strategy.

How has the perception of an emerging crack problem in Canada been portrayed as a basis for an intensification of criminalization? There were no seizures of crack before 1986, but once it began to appear, the Canadian media and police reports alerted the public to the arrival of a 'crack epidemic'. The *Toronto Star* informed its readers that this drug was a 'one-way ticket to hell for the user' (1989a) and that crack posed 'the greatest threat to society over the past fifteen years' (1989b). Crack use quickly reached 'crisis proportions', according to the *Globe and Mail*, and was being used by a 'very, very paranoid, psychotic group' (1989). A deadly plague of drugs was described by *Maclean's* to be infesting Toronto and other Canadian cities. In 1987, the Royal Canadian Mounted Police reported that crack comprised a very modest proportion of all cocaine seizures in Canada, and in 1989 it reported that the 'use of crack is not widespread in Canada at the point' (Royal Canadian Mounted Police 1989:42). The same report, however, also referred to the greatly increased number of seizures, especially in Toronto, and referred to crack as 'almost instantly addictive'. In combination with local news stories and police reports of a growing crime problem linked to crack, it is not surprising that the public perceived a growing 'crack menace' (Cheung and Erickson forthcoming).

While there was considerable evidence that cocaine and crack misuse were responsible for a substantial increase in drug-related problems in the United States in the middle to late 1980s (Goode 1990), this situation was not reflected to nearly the same extent in Canada (Erickson et al. 1994). As noted earlier, Canadian surveys showed stable or declining use at fairly low levels in adult and student populations during this period. It was therefore possible to answer no to the question of a major crack epidemic (Smart 1988). A study of crack users in Toronto dispelled some of the myths about crack's 'instantly addictive' property and the lack of control purportedly displayed by all those exposed to this form of cocaine (Cheung, Erickson, and Landau 1991). Some indicators of cocaine problems, such as treatment admissions and drug-related deaths, did show some increase during the latter part of the 1980s, but levelled off by the end of the decade (Single et al. 1992). Such trends in problem indicators also likely reflect the greater purity and lower price of the cocaine that was available on the street, where the price had dropped from $100,000 in 1981 to $34,000 per kilogram in 1989 (Erickson and Cheung 1992). Despite the relatively minor nature of the problem in Canada, sufficient public concern was generated to revive a call for tougher action against drug users and sellers.

The intensified criminal justice response to illicit drugs in the 1980s continued a well-established tradition, aided and abetted by the influx of additional resources to enforcement in Canada's Drug Strategy. Since recorded offences for activities like drug use and sale depend on proactive police discovery, a growing drug crime rate in part reflects this deployment rather than any real increase in actual deviant behaviour (Hagan 1991). Thus the police have been able to demonstrate and maintain a high level of productivity in overall investigations, seizures, arrests, and charges during a period of decreased illicit drug use. This occurred despite the avowed purpose of the new strategy, which was to balance enforcement with prevention and treatment and take Canada's drug policy in a new, less punitive direction (Erickson 1992).

In sum, after a wave of repression that accompanied the upsurge in illicit drug use in the 1960s, Canada appeared to be less wedded to its traditional responses for a brief period in the early 1980s. This shift of emphasis was marked by decreases in drug use, reductions in cannabis arrests and convictions, less severe sentences, various proposals for law reform, increased protection of the rights of drug offenders, and greater social tolerance of drug use. Then, fuelled by the latest American antidrug crusade and Canada's local version of the cocaine scare, the pendulum swung back from about 1987 onwards. The resurgence of criminalization was characterized by an increase in drug charges, especially for cocaine, more investigations of small-scale traffickers, severe sentences, and several other measures that have not been presented due to space limitations. These include new state powers of seizure and forfeiture of assets of those arrested on drug charges, the military's involvement in interdiction efforts, banning of drug paraphernalia, expansion of workplace drug testing, and proposals to limit the parole eligibility of convicted drug traffickers (Erickson 1992). Canada's institutions of social control of illicit drugs, i.e., repressive laws, broad police powers, highly discretionary criminal justice procedures, and substantial community support for punitive measures, have remained ascendant and impeded fundamental change in drug policy.

RESISTANCE OR CAPITULATION: THE DEVIANT STRIKES BACK?

Norwegian criminologist, Nils Christie, has called illicit drug users the 'easy enemy': poor, often sick, and powerless. Some Canadian research is relevant to this question: to what extent have drug users been the helpless targets of narcotic laws, and to what extent have they resisted and reshaped the current policies? The evidence suggests that drug users have not been a viable political force in Canada, but have often personally resisted the stigmatization of a deviant identity and supported others in doing so. In the wake of the AIDS epidemic, injection drug users have become better organized around public health issues in Europe and Australia, and this may influence future directions in Canada.

Historically, it is clear that Chinese opium smokers had little power to resist increasingly harsh penalties, including deportation, once prohibition was in place (Giffen, Endicott, and Lambert 1991). Before that, Chinese merchants had sought recompense from Mackenzie King for the destruction of their opium stocks in the anti-Asiatic riot of 1907 in Vancouver. This marked the last legitimacy of the narcotic drug dealer in this century. Canadian heroin addicts, few in number and marginalized, have expressed an almost fatalistic view of the hardships of their lives on the street (Stoddart 1988, 1991). The revolving cycle of arrest and imprisonment, the search for a 'fix', has changed little since Stephenson and colleagues first reported in 1956. Recently, however, a small group of opiate users called a press conference in Toronto to protest the shortage of methadone maintenance places in the province. Users were also represented at a harm reduction conference held in the city in 1994.

The cannabis controversy of the early 1970s led to a far more open political debate than had occurred previously (e.g., in the punishment versus treatment controversy of the 1950s). Drug users themselves testified before the Le Dain Commission (Erickson and Smart 1988). Many different interest groups were involved—the medical and legal professions, social service workers, and treatment representatives—to challenge the bureaucratic hegemony of the social control agents (Giffen and Lambert 1988). At several points, change in the drug laws seemed imminent. In the end, however, no significant alteration to the dominant social policy occurred.

A Toronto sample of ninety-five first-time offenders for cannabis possession were interviewed in depth at the time of their sentencing and again one year later (Erickson 1980). Their responses indicated a wide variety of reactions to the experience of being caught and officially labelled a 'cannabis criminal'. Some reported humiliating or frightening experiences at the hands of the police; for others, the processing was routine, even good-natured. For many, the arrest and the waiting period before going to court provoked anxiety that their employer, family, or others might learn about the charge. Others arrived at court with several friends or parents in attendance to show support. Nearly all (about 95 per cent) did not consider themselves as criminals after their court appearance, and thought that peers shared that perception. Most were fairly long-term, regular cannabis users who had no intention of changing their behaviour, and indeed had not one year later. A replication study several years later found little change in offenders' attitudes and experiences of criminalization, but these criminalized users were more confident that employers would be unlikely to learn of their record (Erickson and Murray 1986). The stigma attached to becoming a criminal for cannabis use seemed to decrease progressively for these deviants, resembling a state of *de facto* decriminalization despite the lack of legal change.

Interviews with experienced drug users who are in the community rather than in prison or treatment institutions consistently reveal the 'normalcy' of their behaviour to themselves and their friends (Erickson 1980; Erickson et al. 1994). Drug use is rarely the focal point of their lives, but is an important part of their recreational activities. Considerable effort and planning are devoted to acquiring drugs for special occasions such as birthdays or parties. Concern about health risks, rather than fear of apprehension, is more likely to influence users to cut down their intake or cease use (Cheung, Erickson, and Landau 1991; Erickson 1989; Erickson and Murray 1989).

A sample of long-term cannabis users (average duration was thirteen years) had no trouble maintaining a regular source of supply and were far from unanimous in their support for more liberal legal availability (Erickson 1989). The support by a minority for continued penalties for trafficking to those who would sell cannabis to a new generation of youthful users helps to explain the lack of coherent political lobbying for drug law reform. As Mugford (1990) has noted with regard to similar findings in Australia, it also illustrates the persistence of the antidrug ideology.

Thus Canadian drug users have had little success in actively resisting the operation of public policy that declares them to be criminals. The policy objective has been to suppress all use rather than to reduce the harmful consequences of use. Those who are officially criminalized are only the tip of the iceberg of several million current or former illicit drug users. Shared knowledge and experience of both the risks and benefits of drug use in informal social control networks can reduce harmful effects (Erickson 1993). Fears about the transmission of the AIDS virus among injection drug users has helped to orient a more public health approach towards the consequences of drug use (Smart 1993). Perhaps the 'shadow line' (Gomme 1993)—that vague boundary between the official, highly deviant, criminalized world of illicit drug users and the reality of casual, widespread use of illicit substances by the younger mainstream of the population—will continue to be blurred until a more rational public policy emerges. The Le Dain Commission envisioned a gradual withdrawal of criminal sanctions as they were replaced by more effective, less costly forms of social control (Commission of Inquiry into the Non-Medical Use of Drugs 1972, 1973).

CONCLUSION

The future of the social construction of drug problems in Canadian society may reflect more stigmatization of the currently legal drugs, alcohol and tobacco. Canada has some of the strictest antismoking laws in the world. It has also instituted a number of checks on the availability of alcohol and mounted antidrinking/driving and moderate drinking campaigns. The neo-temperance ideology, which has strong roots in English Canada (Levine 1992), relies on external controls to reinforce the internal controls. These are seen as essential to check drug-induced intoxication. In cultures where the loss of self-control is not so negatively valued, temperance ideology has never had widespread support. Thus, for example, Quebec has always expressed a different alcohol culture, and also has a much lower rate of cannabis criminalization than other provinces (Moreau 1988). Even if punitive responses to illicit drugs are relaxed again in the future, and convergence develops in policy approaches to all psychoactive substances, it is difficult to envision a major change without a concomitant shift in the social evaluation of the acceptability of losing self-control. In Canada, such behaviour is the basis for being viewed as deviant.

NOTES

The view expressed in this chapter are mine and do not necessarily reflect those of the Addiction Research Foundation.

I wish to thank Benedikt Fischer and Gordon Walsh for their helpful comments.

FURTHER READINGS

Alexander, B. 1990. *Peaceful Measures: Canada's Way Out of the War on Drugs*. Toronto: University of Toronto Press.
Blackwell, J.C., and P.G. Erickson, eds. 1987. *Illicit Drugs in Canada: A Risky Business*. Toronto: Nelson Canada.
Boyd, N. 1991. *High Society: Legal and Illegal Drugs in Canada*. Toronto: Key Porter Books.
Erickson, P.G, et al. 1994. *The Steel Drug: Cocaine and Crack in Perspective*, 2nd ed. New York: Macmillan.
Giffen, P.J., S. Endicott, and S. Lambert. 1991. *Panic and Indifference: The Politics of Canada's Drug Laws*. Ottawa: The Canadian Centre on Substance Abuse.
Mitchell, C.N., ed. 1991. 'Drug Issues: A Canadian Perspective'. *Journal of Drug Issues* 21:1–197.
Smart, R.G., and A.C. Ogborne. 1986. *Northern Spirits: Drinking in Canada Then and Now*. Toronto: Addiction Research Foundation Books.

REFERENCES

Addiction Research Foundation. 1987–8. *Annual Report*. Toronto: Addiction Research Foundation.
Adlaf, E.M., and R.G. Smart. 1991. 'Drug Use Among Adolescent Students in Canada and Ontario: The Past, Present and Future'. *Journal of Drug Issues* 21:59–72.
_____, R.G. Smart, and M.D. Canale. 1991. *Drug Use Among Ontario Adults 1977–1991*. Toronto: Addiction Research Foundation.
Akers, R.L. 1991. 'Addiction: The Troublesome Concept'. *Journal of Drug Issues* 21:777–92.
Alexander, B. 1990. *Peaceful Measures: Canada's Way Out of the War on Drugs*. Toronto: University of Toronto Press.
Black, D. 1989. *Sociological Justice*. New York: Oxford University Press.
Blackwell, J.C. 1983. 'Drifting, Controlling, and Overcoming: Opiate Users Who Avoid Becoming Chronically Independent'. *Journal of Drug Issues* 13:219–35.
_____. 1988. 'Sin, Sickness, or Social Problem? The Concept of Drug Dependence'. In *Illicit Drugs in Canada: A Risky Business*, edited by J.C. Blackwell and P.G. Erickson, 158–74. Toronto: Nelson Canada.
Boyd, N. 1991. *High Society: Legal and Illegal Drugs in Canada*. Toronto: Key Porter Books.
Brecher, E.M., et al. 1972. *Licit and Illicit Drugs*. Mount Vernon: Consumers Union.
Burroughs, W.A. 1959. *Naked Lunch*. New York: Grove Weidenfeld.

Chein, I., et al. 1964. *The Road to H: Narcotics, Delinquency and Social Policy*. New York: Basic Books.

Cheung, Y.W., and P.G. Erickson. Forthcoming. 'Crack Use in Canada: A Distant American Cousin'. In *Crack in Context: Myths, Realities and Social Policy*, edited by C. Reinarman and H.G. Levine.

_____, P.G. Erickson, and T.C. Landau. 1991. 'Experience of Crack Use: Findings from a Community-Based Sample in Toronto'. *Journal of Drug Issues* 21:121–40.

Commission of Inquiry into the Non-Medical Use of Drugs. 1972. *Cannabis*. Ottawa: Information Canada.

_____. 1973. *Final Report*. Ottawa: Information Canada.

Duster, T. 1970. *The Legislation of Morality*. New York: Free Press.

Erickson, P.G. 1980. *Cannabis Criminals: The Social Effects of Punishment on Drug Users*. Toronto: ARF Books.

_____. 1981. 'Questioning the Conventional Wisdom: A Comment on the Marijuana Arrest Studies'. *Journal of Drug Issues* 11:389–97.

_____. 1985. 'Cannabis Law Reform: An Unfinished Era'. *Psychotropes* 2:96–8.

_____. 1989. 'Living with Prohibition: Regular Cannabis Users, Legal Sanctions, and Informal Controls'. *The International Journal of Addictions* 24:175–88.

_____. 1992. 'Recent Trends in Canadian Drug Policy: The Decline and Resurgence of Prohibitionism'. *Daedalus* 121:239–67.

_____. 1993. 'The Prospects of Harm Reduction for Psychostimulants'. In *Psychoactive Drugs and Harm Reduction: From Faith to Science*, edited by N. Heather et al., 184–210. London: Whurr.

_____, and B. Alexander. 1989. 'Cocaine and Addictive Liability'. *Social Pharmacology* 3:249–70.

_____, and Y.W. Cheung. 1992. 'Drug Crime and Legal Control: Lessons from the Canadian Experience'. *Contemporary Drug Problems* 19:247–77.

_____, and G.F. Murray. 1986. 'Cannabis Criminals Revisited'. *British Journal of Addiction* 81:81–5.

_____, and G.F. Murray. 1989. 'The Undeterred Cocaine User: Intention to Quit and Its Relationship to Perceived Legal and Health Threats'. *Contemporary Drug Problems* 16:141–56.

_____, and R.G. Smart. 1988. 'The Le Dain Commission Recommendations'. In *Illicit Drugs in Canada: A Risky Business*, edited by J.C. Blackwell and P.G. Erickson, 336-44. Toronto: Nelson Canada.

_____, et al. 1987. *The Steel Drug: Cocaine in Perspective*. Lexington: D.C. Heath and Company.

_____, et al. 1994. *The Steel Drug: Cocaine and Crack in Perspective*, 2nd ed. New York: Macmillan.

Fagin, J., and K.L. Chin. 1989. 'Initiation into Crack and Cocaine: A Tale of Two Epidemics'. *Contemporary Drug Problems* 16:579-618.

Faupel, C.E. 1991. *Shooting Dope: Career Patterns of Hard Core Heroin Users*. Gainesville: University of Florida Press.

Fehr, K. 1988a. 'Making Connections: Drugs, Mind, and Body'. In *Illicit Drugs in Canada: A Risky Business*, edited by J.C. Blackwell and P.G. Erickson, 5–27. Toronto: Nelson Canada.

_____. 1988b. 'The Dealer's Choice: An Introduction to Street Drugs'. In *Illicit Drugs in Canada: A Risky Business*, edited by J.C. Blackwell and P.G. Erickson, 28–50. Toronto: Nelson Canada.

_____, and H. Kalant. 1983. *Cannabis and Health Hazards: Proceedings of an ARF/WHO Scientific Meeting on Adverse Health and Behavioral Consequences of Cannabis*. Toronto: Addiction Research Foundation.

Giffen, P.G., and S. Lambert. 1988. 'What Happened on the Way to Law Reform'. In *Illicit Drugs in Canada: A Risky Business*, edited by J.C. Blackwell and P.G. Erickson, 345–69. Toronto: Nelson Canada.

_____, S. Endicott, and S. Lambert. 1991. *Panic and Indifference: The Politics of Canada's Drug Laws*. Ottawa: Canadian Centre on Substance Abuse.

Glaser, D. 1985. 'The Criminal Law's Nemesis: Drug Control'. *American Bar Foundation Research Journal*, 619–26.

Globe and Mail (Toronto). 1989. 'Crack Use Near Epidemic Toronto Police Warn' (11 February).

Gomme, I.M. 1993. *The Shadow Line: Deviance and Crime in Canada*. Toronto: Harcourt Brace Jovanovich.

Goode, E. 1990. 'The American Drug Panic of the 1980s: Social Construction or Objective Threat?'. *The International Journal of the Addictions* 25:1083–98.

Hagan, J. 1991. *The Disreputable Pleasures: Crime and Deviance in Canada*, 3rd ed. Toronto: McGraw-Hill Ryerson.

Health and Welfare Canada. 1992. *Alcohol and Other Drug Use by Canadians: A National Alcohol and Other Drug Survey (1989): Technical Report*. Prepared by E. Eliany et al. Ottawa: Minister of Supply and Services Canada.

Heath, D.B. 1992. 'U.S. Drug Control Policy: A Cultural Perspective'. *Daedalus* 121:269–91.

Jacobs, M.R., and K. Fehr. 1987. *Drugs and Drug Abuse: A Reference Text*, 2nd ed. Toronto: Addiction Research Foundation.

Jensen, E.L., and J. Gerber. 1993. 'State Efforts to Construct a Social Problem: The 1986 War on Drugs in Canada'. *Canadian Journal of Sociology* 18, no. 4:453–62.

_____, J. Gerber, and G.M. Babcock. 1991. 'The New War on Drugs: Grass Roots Movement or Political Construction?' *Journal of Drug Issues* 21:651–67.

Johnson, D.B., et al. 1985. *Taking Care of Business: The Economics of Crime by Heroin Abusers*. Lexington: Lexington Books.

Kalant, H. 1982. 'Commentary on the Home Office Report on the Effects of Cannabis Use'. *British Journal of Addiction* 77:341–5.

Levine, H.G. 1992. 'Temperance Cultures: Concerns About Alcohol Problems in Nordic and English-Speaking Cultures'. In *The Nature of Alcohol and Drug-Related Problems*, edited by G. Edwards and M. Lader, 15–36. London: Oxford University Press.

Lindesmith, A. 1965. *The Addict and the Law*. Bloomington: Indiana University Press.

Maclean's. 1989. 'A Deadly Plague of Drugs' (3 April).

Maloff, D., et al. 1979. 'Informal Social Controls and Their Influence on Substance Use'. *Journal of Drug Issues* 9:161–84.

McKenna, T. 1992. *Food of the Gods*. New York: Bantam Books.

Moreau, J.A.E. 1988. 'Appendix A: Selected Statistics on Convictions for Illicit Drug Use in Canada'. In *Illicit Drugs in Canada: A Risky Business*, edited by J.C. Blackwell and P.G. Erickson, 449–55. Toronto: Nelson Canada.

Mugford, S.K. 1990. 'Drug Policy and Criminal Consequences: The Australian Experience'. Paper presented at the annual meeting of the American Society of Criminology, Baltimore, Maryland.

Murray, G.F. 1987. 'Cocaine Use in an Era of Social Reform: The Natural History of a Social Problem in Canada'. *Canadian Journal of Law and Society* 2:29–43.

_____. 1988. 'The Road to Regulation: Patent Medicines in Canada in Historical Perspective'. In *Illicit Drugs in Canada: A Risky Business*, edited by J.C. Blackwell and P.G. Erickson, 72–87. Toronto: Nelson Canada.

Musto, D.F. 1973. *The American Disease: Origins of Narcotic Control*. New Haven: Yale University Press.

Negrete, J.C. 1988. 'What Happened to the Cannabis Debate?' *British Journal of Addiction* 83:354–72.

Peyrot, M. 1984. 'Cycles of Social Problem Development: The Case of Drug Abuse'. *The Sociological Quarterly* 25:83–95.

Prebel, E., and J.J. Casey. 1969. 'Taking Care of Business: The Heroin User's Life on the Streets'. *The International Journal of Addictions* 4:1–24.

Royal Canadian Mounted Police. 1987. *National Drug Intelligence Estimates 1986/1987*. Ottawa: Minister of Supply and Services Canada.

_____. 1988. *National Drug Intelligence Estimates 1987/1988*. Ottawa: Minister of Supply and Services Canada.

_____. 1989. *National Drug Intelligence Estimates 1988/1989*. Ottawa: Minister of Supply and Services Canada.

_____. 1990. *National Drug Intelligence Estimates 1989/1990*. Ottawa: Minister of Supply and Services Canada.

Reinarman, C., and H.G. Levine. 1989. 'The Crack Attack: Media and Politics in America's Latest Drug Scare'. In *Images of Issues: Current*

Perspectives on Social Problems, edited by J. Best, 115–37. New York: Aldine DeGruyter.

Rosenbaum, M. 1981. *Women on Heroin*. New Brunswick: Rutgers University Press.

Single, E., et al. 1992. 'Policy Developments in Canada'. In *Drug Problems in Society: Dimensions and Perspectives*, edited by J. White, 63–72. Parkside: Drug and Alcohol Services Council.

Smart, R.G. 1988. 'Crack Cocaine Use in Canada: A New Epidemic?' *American Journal of Epidemiology* 127:135–17.

_____. 1993. 'What Are the Rules of Thumb of Avoiding Problem Drug Use?' *Addiction* 88:179–81.

_____, and L. Anglin. 1987. 'Do We Know the Lethal Dose of Cocaine?' *Journal of Forensic Sciences* 32:303–12.

_____, and A.C. Ogborne. 1986. *Northern Spirits: Drinking in Canada Then and Now*. Toronto: ARF Books.

Snyder, S. 1989. *Brainstorming: The Science and Politics of Opiate Research*. Cambridge: Harvard University Press.

Stephenson, G.H., et al. 1956. 'Drug Addiction in British Columbia'. Unpublished ms, University of British Columbia.

Stoddart, K. 1988. 'The Enforcement of Narcotics Violations in a Canadian City: Heroin Users' Perspectives on the Production of Official Statistics'. In *Illicit Drugs in Canada: A Risky Business*, edited by J.C. Blackwell and P.G. Erickson, 244–62. Toronto: Nelson Canada.

_____. 1991. 'It's Easier for the Bulls Now: Official Statistics and Social Change in a Canadian Heroin-Using Community'. *Journal of Drug Issues* 21:83–103.

Toronto Star. 1989a. 'Aroused Public Needed to Fight Drugs Mayor Says' (16 June).

_____. 1989b. 'New Group Joins Fight to Curb Cocaine Trade' (24 February).

Waldorf, D., C. Reinarman, and S. Murphy. *Cocaine Changes: The Experience of Using and Quitting*. Philadelphia: Temple University Press.

Zinberg, N.E., and H.J. Shaffer. 1990. 'Essential Factors of a Rational Policy on Intoxicant Use?' *Journal of Drug Issues* 20:619–27.

——4——

Youth Misconduct: Deviance and Social Control

Grade Eleven Advanced Class
Walter Murray Collegiate
Saskatoon, Saskatchewan

INTRODUCTION

The Grade Eleven Advanced Program at Walter Murray Collegiate Institute includes a credit called Advanced Research. Each student researches and presents a topic of particular interest. In the latter half of 1993, a group of thirteen students took on a project of a different nature: to write a chapter on the attitudes teenagers have about deviance for a textbook on social deviance. Starting with their assumptions, the students then read, researched, interviewed, and reflected on the topic, approaching it from the position of privilege. Indeed these students are a privileged group, coming from middle- to upper-middle class backgrounds where education is highly valued.

The group was comprised of six boys and seven girls from various ethnic and cultural backgrounds, including East Indian, Chinese, and American. Philosophically and politically, their views ranged from relatively well-developed ideologies to unconscious, 'understood' family-inculcated values and ideas. Their views were just as widely divergent along the political spectrum, ranging from those of active socialists (one a card-carrying member of a political party) to die-hard, free-enterprise conservatives. Other prominent factors in their ideologies were feminism, religion, and environmental awareness and concern. At various times, the advancement of and reaction to these major concepts (subjects) caused much discussion. Certainly, there was a wide and active involvement in both the arts and athletics. Nearly every student in the class was involved in some form of extracurricular activity, including student government at Walter Murray. Although the differences outweigh the similarities within the group, one interesting factor does emerge: when the survey was conducted, all the students came from intact family units, most with both parents working.

They tackled the project energetically; it was clear that they would all have strong opinions on the topic as well as on the methodology used for research. In the journals they kept on the project, they reflected on their assumptions and preconceptions about youth deviance, first defining it for themselves, and then speculating on the causes and factors influencing it. They read and discussed literature about the different definitions of deviance and the inherent assumptions underlying each. Following this, they were ready to research.

A brainstorming session followed, during which the students listed all they wanted to know. With help from Dr Bernard Schissel, they were able to decide on a survey questionnaire for students as their major source of data. They decided on three urban and three rural high schools, which covered the range of socio-economic and cultural mixes. (One rural school later reneged, leaving only two rural schools.)

The construction of the questionnaire proved to be a challenge. With assistance from an academic who has expertise in questionnaire construction, the students edited their instrument down to ninety well-worded items. Once during this process, a longer survey was field-tested to check for any wording or ambiguity problems. Finally, after much heated debate, the final questionnaire was administered to approximately 550 students from the five high schools. This questionnaire comprised the larger portion of their data.

A second source of data was a panel discussion set up by the Walter Murray Collegiate Institute social studies department on the topic of youth deviance. The panel members were two lawyers (one from Public Legal Aid), one police officer, one social worker, a sociologist, and a director of a youth detention centre. The students posed questions to the panel about causes of youth deviance, the backgrounds of the offenders, the Young Offenders Act, and their own feelings about youth deviance. They later had individual interviews with panel members.

The analysis of the data focused on the following factors: urban/rural, gender, age, socio-economics, race, grades, and family background of the survey respondents. These are the seven sections included in this chapter, written using the 'voice' of the students themselves.

RURAL VERSUS URBAN GEOGRAPHIC AREA

We began our research about rural and urban deviance thinking that there would be more acts of deviance committed by urban youths because there would be more opportunities for them to commit crimes. We felt that rural communities would be less accepting of misconduct, and that a greater variety of actions would be considered deviant. We thought that rural teenagers would commit deviant acts because there would not be as many police officers to restrict their actions. We thought that deviant acts would be more common in the city schools, and that these students would have a broader range of acceptable actions. One social worker we talked to said that all teenagers can be deviant, but urban youths have more opportunities and deviant actions are more likely to occur in cities than in rural settings.

We were interested in finding out how the two groups of youths made decisions about their own deviant actions and those of others. We wanted to learn how deviance would be responded to by the penal system and by teenagers. We only dealt with information where the difference in response was greater than 5 per cent because we were very interested in differences in attitudes. We decided that a variation of less than 5 per cent would not be able to support any conclusion of different attitudes. We noted some difference in the attitudes about deviance and deviant behaviour. Rural and urban teenagers had different acceptance levels for socially deviant actions within their age group.

Thirty per cent of rural teenagers surveyed thought that it was acceptable for teens to use illegal drugs. We found that the urban acceptance level was slightly higher, with 38 per cent of our urban respondents stating that illegal drug use was acceptable. The attitudes about prank calls were startingly divided. Thirty-eight per cent of the rural students thought that making prank phone calls was acceptable. However, only 23 per cent of the urban students found this action acceptable. Fifty-one per cent of the rural students thought that skipping school was acceptable, compared to the 38 per cent of urban students who thought so. These statistics show that urban students are more tolerant than rural students of actions that would directly affect only the person doing them. They are less tolerant of deviant actions committed against another group.

We asked the students which would most likely happen to them: physical assault, vandalism of personal property, someone breaking into their home, or receiving prank phone calls. Fifty-four per cent of the rural students said prank phone calls, 23 per cent said vandalism, 15 per cent said physical assault, and 6 per cent said it would be more likely that someone would break into their home. Of the urban students surveyed, 44 per cent chose prank phone calls, 24 per cent chose physical assault, 17 per cent chose vandalism, and 13 per cent said it would be more likely that someone would break into their home. We can see that besides a significant difference in percentage, the overall trends were also varied. Rural students thought that they would be more likely to have property vandalized than be physically assaulted. This was opposite to the urban response.

We also asked our survey respondents how afraid they were of being sexually assaulted by a stranger. Twenty per cent of the rural students said 'very much', while 21 per cent of the urban group responded similarly. The majority of rural teens (40 per cent) were 'a little afraid', while only 32 per cent of the urban teens were. Thirty-five per cent of the rural teens were 'not afraid at all', while the majority of urban teens (47 per cent) were not afraid either. The statistics regarding sexual assault by an acquaintance showed less than a 5 per cent difference between the two groups, with the urban students slightly more afraid than their rural counterparts of this happening to them.

The use of alcohol is very similar for teenagers living in both rural and urban environments. Fourteen per cent of both groups said that they drank whenever given the chance. Forty-two per cent of the rural students, as compared to the slightly higher 45 per cent of the urban students, drink with their friends or at parties. Twenty-four per cent of the rural students and only 17 per cent of the urban students said that they never drink. From these percentages, we could say that drinking seems slightly more common in the cities, but many teenagers will drink no matter where they are.

We found that there were some very distinct differences in the attitudes of urban teenagers and rural teenagers concerning sexual issues. Three-quarters of the urban students thought that sex before marriage was accept-able, while only 63 per cent of the rural teenagers thought so. Fifty-two per cent of the urban teens, as compared to 45 per cent of the rural teens, thought that abortion is acceptable for today's teenagers. However, 31 per cent of urban youths and 19 per cent of the rural youths knew someone who had had an abortion. It seems that the more exposure people have to issues such as abortion, the more accepting they are about them.

Thirty per cent of the urban respondents thought it was acceptable for teenagers to have multiple sex partners. Twenty-five per cent of the rural group thought this was acceptable. We asked our survey respondents if they agreed that a guy who has sex with a consenting drunk girl is raping her. Thirty per cent of the urban teenagers and 35 per cent of the rural teenagers agreed. Forty-five per cent of urban students and 36 per cent of rural stu-dents disagreed with this statement.

Ninety per cent of urban teenagers thought that sexual harassment is unacceptable. However, only 75 per cent of the rural teenagers thought so. Only a small portion of both groups (4 per cent of the urban teenagers and 5 per cent of the rural teenagers) thought that it is the woman's fault if she is sexually harassed.

We were very surprised with our survey results regarding stalking. In the urban areas, only 22 per cent of teenagers knew someone close to them who had stalked another person. This statistic was much higher in the rural areas, where 48 per cent of the students knew that someone close to them had stalked someone else. We thought that the statistic for rural areas would be lower because everyone knows everyone else in small towns. However, the large difference might be attributed to a variation in the definition of stalk-ing. Still, it is frightening to think that many people cannot trust people they have known their whole life.

From these results, we concluded that urban students were more tolerant than the rural students of some types of deviance. These were mostly actions that would not directly affect anyone except the person committing them.

On the other hand, the deviant acts that were more common in the rural areas were the kind where there was an obvious victim.

Rural and urban students had varying opinions and views on racial matters. Fifteen per cent of the rural youths and 6 per cent of urban youths thought that teenage immigrants were less law-abiding than teenagers born in Canada. In our survey, we asked which racial group, if any, was the most likely to commit various deviant actions. The categories we provided were: Asian, Black, Native, White, or All Racial Groups Equal. It was interesting to see that the trends in responses were the same for both the rural and urban samples. For all three actions (drug abuse, alcohol abuse, and vandalism), the most common choice was All Racial Groups Equal. However, if a specific racial group was chosen as a response, both the rural and urban teenagers chose Native.

Fifty-three per cent of rural teens and 64 per cent of urban teens believed that all races are equal in their likelihood to use drugs. Thirty-three per cent of rural teens and 20 per cent of urban teens thought that Natives are most likely to use drugs. Fifty-seven per cent of the rural teens and 65 per cent of the urban teens thought that all races were equal in their likelihood to drink alcohol. Thirty-five per cent of the rural teens and 25 per cent of the urban teens thought that Natives are the most likely to drink alcohol. Fifty-seven per cent of rural students and 67 per cent of urban students thought that all races are equal in their likelihood to vandalize. Thirty-five per cent of rural teens and 20 per cent of urban teens said that they thought Natives are most likely to vandalize. Although the trends are similar in the rural and urban areas, the urban students tended to believe more than the rural students that all racial groups are equal in their likelihood to commit deviant acts.

We also found differences between urban and rural attitudes in perceptions of the police and justice systems. Forty-seven per cent of rural students and 63 per cent of the urban students thought that the police pick on teenagers. We might account for this remarkable difference in the fact that there are more police in cities than there are in rural areas. Urban teenagers would therefore have more contact with the police force and other authority figures who attempt to limit their actions. There were some difference in attitudes about how young offenders should be treated. Forty-five per cent of the rural students and 32 per cent of urban teenagers thought that young offenders should be tried as adults. Twenty-five per cent of the rural youths and 36 per cent of urban youths felt that young offenders should be counselled. One-quarter of each group thought that young offenders should be jailed in juvenile hall.

The majority of teenagers (over 60 per cent of each group) thought that the justice system should focus on preventing crime. Nineteen per cent of rural youths and 27 per cent of urban youths believe that it should focus on rehabilitation. Fourteen per cent of rural youths and only 10 per cent of urban youths believe that the justice system should focus on punishment for crimes. We can therefore assume that urban teenagers, more so than rural youths, thought that the police and the justice system are too harsh when dealing with teenagers.

The experts whom we interviewed revealed that there was systemic racism in the justice system. The survey respondents also echoed this sentiment; 45 per cent of the rural students and 55 per cent of the urban students thought that a court would favour a White person over a Native person. Fifty-one per cent of the rural teenagers and 59 per cent of the urban teenagers thought that the court system would favour a rich person over a poor person. However, in both scenarios, over 30 per cent of all teenagers thought that the court system was unbiased.

We have shown that there were a few significant differences in teenagers' attitudes, depending on where they live. We have concluded that urban teenagers seemed to put more importance on individual decisions than their rural counterparts. The urban teenagers did not appreciate the intervention of the police or justice system. They felt themselves capable of deciding how to live their lives. Therefore, they were more tolerant of deviant actions that would only affect the person doing them. However, urban teenagers were less tolerant and more fearful of deviant actions where someone was victimized. They felt that victims were having decisions made for them.

GENDER AND DEVIANCE

When a norm is defined by society, then anything that is different is considered deviant. At the beginning of this project, we thought that males were more deviant than females. Regardless of sexual equality, we were of the opinion that males are generally larger and stronger than females, less intellectual, and more physically aggressive. Males would tend to look for permanent, physical solutions to their dilemmas because negotiation and mediation are too slow for them. Males seem to be more daring and adventurous than females because males prefer physical actions with tangible results. Thus we concluded that males would be more prone to committing deviant acts in a wider range of categories. We argued that males would be more likely to commit crimes such as vandalism, breaking and entering, armed robbery, and various kinds of assaults.

While we felt that males were adventurous and action-oriented, we felt that females were more cautious and passive. Since we believed that females were more intellectual than males, we also thought that females generally would have some purpose or motive behind the crimes they committed. We thought that females would avoid senseless acts of violence and vandalism, preferring instead to commit low-profile crimes for personal gain. For example, we thought that the typical female delinquent would cheat on exams, or dub CDs and cassette tapes, or shoplift.

Finally, we hypothesized that the sexes were equally inclined to abuse substances such as drugs and alcohol, although the abuse would be for different reasons. Males, because of a superiority complex and 'macho male egos', would abuse substances to be popular or to maintain their image as a result of peer pressure. Females would tend to be more emotional than males and would therefore be more susceptible to low self-esteem and depression, which would tend to lead to drug and alcohol abuse.

The results of our survey have shown that the majority of our respondents also felt that males had a more daring and violent nature than females. Eighty per cent of males and 69 per cent of females surveyed believe that men were more likely to commit acts of vandalism, and 76 per cent of males and 69 per cent of females thought that males are more liable to break and enter. As well, 57 per cent of males and 37 per cent of females thought that males were more likely to steal, and in fact 80 per cent of males and 64 per cent of females had actually stolen. Those results from our survey all confirmed our belief that males would be more likely to (and did) commit senseless acts of deviance. The percentages regarding vandalism also indicate that males were more likely to commit acts of deviance with no clear purpose or motive. Finally, the high percentage of females that had actually stolen indicates that personal gain was a factor in female deviance. As for cheating on exams, 73 per cent of both sexes had done so before.

When asked about the severity of crime that will most likely affect them, the majority of both sexes surveyed believed that they were more likely to receive a prank phone call than be physically assaulted, have their property vandalized, or have someone break into their home. Twenty out of the 254 (8 per cent) males surveyed believed that date rape is acceptable behaviour for today's teenagers, while only seven of the 258 (3 per cent) females surveyed believed the same thing; 52 per cent of males and 37 per cent of females believed that a guy who was having sex with a consenting drunk girl was not raping her; and 7 per cent of males and 2 per cent of females thought that sexual harassment was acceptable behaviour. All three results seem to indicate that males have fewer qualms about forced intercourse; perhaps this is a reflection of the more physical nature of males. When the respondents were asked about consenting sexual intercourse, 11 per cent of males and 5 per cent of females said that they approved of teenage prostitution. Once again, this could be another possible indication that males have a more physical nature than females.

The survey also showed that 76 per cent of males and 69 per cent of females thought that premarital sex was all right, while 37 per cent of males and 17 per cent of females believed that having multiple sex partners was acceptable; both statistics contradicted our hypothesis that females were more promiscuous than males, and once more demonstrated that males have a more liberal attitude towards premarital sex.

As we had suspected, high percentages of male and female youths had been drunk at least once (78 per cent and 71 per cent respectively), and both males and females believed that both sexes were equally likely to drink alcohol. Forty-nine per cent of males and 43 per cent of females surveyed had used illegal drugs, once again proving that the sexes are nearly equal in substance abuse. Finally, when asked which sex was more likely to use drugs, an overwhelming 45 per cent of males and 52 per cent of females believed that both males and females were just as likely to use illegal drugs, once again confirming that both sexes are likely to abuse substances.

According to a recent report, violent offences are much more likely to involve males (81 per cent) than females (19 per cent), although the proportion of female violence seems to be increasing (Statistics Canada, *Youth Court Statistics 1992–93*, Ottawa, Dec. 1993). The percentage increase in the number of charges for violent crimes committed by young women in recent years has been much greater than that committed by young men. While percentages for both sexes have been rising, they are rising much faster for young women. Researchers note that historically, violent behaviour by young women has been viewed as unacceptable and has been more likely to result in charges against the women, whereas men who committed the same acts might go unpunished (Saskatoon Police Department).

While researchers admit that males are generally more violent than females, they also hypothesize that the motivation for using violence frequently differs for young women and young men. Women who use violence against men are most commonly motivated by self-defence, or as a pre-emptive strike after a verbal or other type of threat. In one recent study, it was found that young women who have been aggressive against other young women were victims of childhood sexual assault. Young men who use violence against women have had motives linked to a variety of factors, including power, control, and access to sex. Young men's use of violence against other men is linked predominately to society's recognition that violence is a legitimate and often necessary form of dominance (Saskatoon Police Department).

The Saskatoon police force realizes that young male and female offenders have different motivations for the deviant acts they commit, but that does not mean that one sex is more easily apprehended than the other. Officers moving into a situation that requires the use of force do so with great caution, regardless of the gender of their opponent. A well-placed kick from anyone, male or female, will be equally effective in taking down the officer.

Most police officers maintain that they do not discriminate between the gender of their opponents and that they do not give preferential treatment to one or the other.

We conducted a follow-up interview with the police officer who represented the Saskatoon Police Department on the panel. We asked him questions to help us distinguish the different tendencies in deviance between males and females. His responses were worded in a politically correct manner that we felt were also slightly evasive. For example, whenever we asked a question that required him to distinguish between the sexes—for example, if one sex was more deviant than the other, or if there were typical crimes that were more commonly committed by one sex or the other—he answered that each person was unique and that everything differed from case to case without any clear trends. We realize that this was the only appropriate response he could have given because the views he presented were those of the Saskatoon Police Department and not his personal views, and the Saskatoon Police Department is interested in treating everyone equally, regardless of their sex.

When it comes to deviance, there are clearly many differences between the sexes. Researchers argue that delinquent young women are influenced by their environment, such as their family background, their social condition, or their relationships with the people close to them. Young women are provoked into doing deviant acts, which is their way of lashing out at a society that has aggravated them (Saskatoon Police Department). However, the cause of deviance in young men seems to be more complicated. Our results suggest that the source of male deviant behaviour can be found in their egos. Males seem to be very sensitive about their image and reputation. They appear to be more willing to stretch the limits of acceptable behaviour if it means gaining a higher social standing among their peers. The infamous 'male ego' may be responsible for the adventurous nature that males demonstrate more so than females. Finally, the violent nature of males may be explained by looking at human history. Throughout our mainly male-dominated history, many of the greater disputes have often been solved by using brute force. Perhaps today's male youths are influenced by the forceful resolutions of yesterday's problems, and perhaps they really do regard physical force as a way of solving their problems. These are but a few of the many conclusions that could explain increasing trends in senseless, physical deviant acts among the male youth population.

AGE

Before the survey, we felt that age would indeed have an effect on deviance. We felt and still feel that education has a direct effect on deviance, and that younger teens would be less deviant and commit less severe offences than older teens, perhaps because society has begun to regard deviant youths not as bad apples but as teenagers with problems. This has been carried over into the educational system in the form of new curriculum involving programs that attempt to provide direction for younger teens before a small problem becomes much greater.

The age differences in the survey respondents were small; the youngest person was about thirteen and the oldest was around nineteen. As a result, we did not see many clear differences in the answers of older teens compared to those of younger teens. If we had surveyed a larger age group (i.e., thirteen to twenty-five years old), the differences in the responses would have been more evident. With a larger age group, those surveyed would not be restricted to high school students; there would be respondents from a greater variety of backgrounds, for example, high school students, university students, high school drop-outs, or full-time labourers.

In questions related to alcohol abuse, we thought that the older age groups would find underage drinking acceptable more so than their younger counterparts. This may be because older students are closer to the legal drinking age than the younger teens, and they may feel that a thirteen-year-old drinking is committing a much greater crime than an eighteen-year-old. Finances may also enter into the equation, as older teens are more likely to have a steady income, allowing them to support such a habit.

On the topic of underage drinking, the most interesting results pertained to the question asking if the legal drinking age was too high. Forty per cent of older respondents (eighteen and older) agreed with this, while 54 per cent of sixteen-year-olds and 45 per cent of those aged fourteen and under agreed. We think this indicates that all teenagers are drinking with little regard for the law.

One question in the survey asked if teenagers drink at parties because their friends encourage them. We had attributed a lot of substance abuse to peer pressure, and felt that most of the respondents would answer yes to this question. On the contrary, all age groups disagreed quite strongly, particularly those in our age group (sixteen years old), of whom only 38 per cent attributed the cause of drinking to peer pressure.

For the question 'Do you consider drug use acceptable?' 28 per cent of the youngest age category answered yes, as did 42 per cent of fifteen-year-olds, 53 per cent of sixteen-year-olds, 36 per cent of seventeen-year-olds, and 48 per cent of eighteen-year-olds and older. Generally speaking, the percentage of teens who found drug use acceptable increased as their ages increased. Perhaps younger teens are exposed to very little drug use and as they grow older, they see a greater amount of drug use around them and are therefore more open to it.

Responses to the question asking if teenagers who shoplift are doing it for fun showed a slight trend related to age, as 35 per cent of the youngest respondents agreed, and 53 per cent of the oldest agreed. There was also a definite trend in a question regarding sexual promiscuity. Forty-nine per cent of teens fourteen and under agreed that girls under sixteen who have sex have low moral standards, while only 28 per cent of sixteen-year-olds and 33 per cent of the oldest teens surveyed thought so. Again, this could be because younger teens may not yet be wise to the ways of the world. As they mature through high school, they become aware of how much this sort of activity takes place.

When our respondents were asked if they considered sex before marriage acceptable, 67 per cent of the fourteen-year-olds, 76 per cent of sixteen-year-olds, and an overwhelming 91 per cent of the oldest age group said yes. Of the 508 respondents, 400 or 79 per cent found premarital sex acceptable. Our respondents generally think that fifteen years of age is too young to be having sex, but that it is not necessary to wait until marriage.

For a more controversial subject (because it is not illegal and debatable as to whether or not it is immoral), we asked teenagers if they considered abortion acceptable. We had varied responses within each age group, with very definite results. In the fourteen and under category, 45 per cent said yes; in the fifteen-year-old category, an incredible 94 per cent said no; while 94 per cent of sixteen-year-olds said yes. Of the seventeen-year-olds, 51 per cent thought abortion was acceptable, as did 54 per cent of eighteen-year-olds. We do not know why these results were so skewed. On the topic of prostitution, the overwhelming response was that it was not an acceptable form of deviance. Only a small percentage of each group found it acceptable.

We also asked them which of a variety of offences was most likely to happen to them. Of the 112 fifteen-year-olds surveyed, 24 per cent thought that they were most likely to be physically assaulted, 14 per cent felt that vandalism of their personal property was most likely, 9 per cent answered break and enter, and 53 per cent felt that they were most likely to be the victim of a prank phone call. This age group generally showed the results of all of the age groups surveyed. We were not surprised to find that prank calls was the most frequent answer in every age group, as it is a minor form of deviance, but we were surprised to find that over 23 per cent in each age group (excluding those fourteen and under) felt that physical assault is most likely to happen to them.

We interviewed a lawyer with the Saskatoon legal aid clinic. He believed that age had an effect on delinquency. It has been his experience that certain small crimes often lead to more serious crimes. He found that older teens seem to commit more frequent and more violent offences, reinforcing what we have found through our survey. He also talked about age and the amount of alcohol that teens drink. Alcohol abuse is the direct cause of many forms of deviance and crime. When teenagers first drink, they can tolerate only a small amount of alcohol, so the situation will not get completely out of hand. As teens continue to drink, they are able to consume more and, as a result, become drunk. The more inebriated teens are, the more out of control they will be, and the more likely they will commit crimes.

In conclusion, we found that while some deviant acts were affected by age, the difference between fourteen and eighteen years of age did not appear to be very great. There were some questions that showed a big difference between the age groups, but there were many more that did not. However, we feel that age should be taken into consideration when studying deviance, and we argue that society should detect problems in youths early on and take preventive measures while they are still young in order to avoid greater problems later.

SOCIO-ECONOMIC STATUS

We researched how people's economic backgrounds determine what kinds of crimes they will commit and for what reasons. Our beliefs about socio-economic status and youth deviance did not always concur with research results. We thought that poor youths committed the overwhelming majority of crimes such as stealing because they had to, and that violent crimes were committed by poorer youths because they were forced into those situations, or because they did not have good role models.

Research results showed that it is true that youths from low-income backgrounds do not always have good role models, but this does not explain the high rate of property crimes and vandalism that youths from high-income brackets commit. When youths commit crimes, they do so for different reasons. Some will commit them for economic reasons, and some will commit them for other reasons. It is more likely for young people from low-income brackets to commit violent crimes because of the economic and social conditions that they live in. The economics of a person's life will affect his or her social and living conditions and ultimately his or her beliefs and values. Our assumptions about the kinds of crimes youths commit were valid, but our reasoning for their antisocial activity was not always well considered.

Our survey asked what income bracket the individual was from and other questions of an economic nature. The respondents were from five different income brackets: (1) under $12,000 annually, (2) between $12,000 and $25,000, (3) between $26,000 and $35,000, (4) between $36,000 and $50,000, and (5) $50,000 and up.

The first result worth noting was that more wealthy individuals than poorer ones thought shoplifting was unacceptable behaviour. About 12 per cent from the top two income brackets thought that shoplifting was acceptable compared to about 24 per cent from the lowest income bracket. The second result was that a much higher percentage of teens in the highest income bracket think that teenagers shoplift for fun. This was quite an eye-opening result because it seemed to re-establish the theory that wealthier individuals steal for reasons that are not related to their economic background. Another interesting result was that in the lowest income bracket, more respondents thought that women and men were equally likely to steal, as opposed to respondents in the other income brackets, the majority of whom thought men were more likely than women to steal. This was interesting because perhaps it shows that more low-income women steal or, more significantly, perhaps there are more women than men in the low-income bracket.

We asked respondents whether they thought a rich person or a poor person would be favoured in court if they were charged with similar offences. Nobody in the lowest income bracket believed that the court system would favour the poor person. The majority of people in that bracket believed that the rich person would be favoured. There was some variation in the middle income brackets, but most still believed that the rich person would be favoured. In the highest income bracket, the majority believed that the court would favour the rich person, but there was a higher percentage in this group than in the other income brackets who believed the poor person would be favoured. This result shows that youths in general think that the court system favours the rich person, which concurs with the opinion of the lawyer on our panel, who believed that the rich person can afford better legal representation and is therefore favoured in court.

Youths commit deviant acts for many reasons. How does the economic status of a person affect the kind of crimes he or she will commit? From our interview with the lawyer, we learned many things about how young offenders from different income brackets are treated in court. A person's economic status does indeed affect what kind of crimes he or she will commit. A young offender from the low-income bracket was more likely to commit a crime because of his or her economic background, while a young person from a high-income bracket would tend to commit a crime for other reasons. The lawyer regarded property crimes, for example, as crimes of privilege. In general, shoplifting or even stealing are crimes committed by both groups, but for very different reasons. For example, young offenders will steal because they need certain things to survive; they were raised in such a way that the values they learned did not include obeying the law. If someone from a high-income bracket steals, it will be because he or she wants something, but may not necessarily need it. The lawyer believes that youths from a high-income bracket tend to steal because often they are simply bored or enjoy the thrill of stealing. This is not to say that poor people will not commit crimes for these reasons, but certainly they will also steal because they have to. In the panel discussion, the lawyer said that a rich youth will steal simply because he or she is mad or tired of authority and chooses to lash out by committing vandalism or shoplifting. The lawyer also believed that the court system itself was not racially or sexually prejudiced, but that such things as legal representation tend to privilege the wealthy. A person who cannot afford an expensive lawyer will not fare well in court, as compared to a person who can. This is why he feels that a change must be made to somehow balance the inequities in legal representation.

It was difficult to determine from the research exactly why people from high- and low-income brackets would commit crimes. It was even difficult to determine if a crime was committed for reasons related to a person's economic background. We realized that people from low-income brackets probably commit crimes for economic reasons. Their reasons for stealing are different from those of richer individuals much of the time. We saw how people tended to view individuals from different incomes who committed crimes, and we saw that the beliefs of the wealthy individual did not always coincide with the beliefs of the poor individual. People from different income brackets commit some crimes for the same reasons, but they also commit crimes for many different reasons.

RACE

We were interested in finding out how many respondents had actually done things that were considered 'deviant'. We thought that Whites believed teenage immigrants were less law-abiding than teenage non-immigrants. We thought Native youths would think White people would be favoured in the courts. We also thought that the majority of White teens would think that Natives and other minority groups would be more likely to use drugs, drink alcohol, vandalize, and attempt suicide. We assumed that most people with a low income and a low academic standing would be the ones most likely to use drugs and drink alcohol. We thought that White people would be more likely to use drugs and that Natives would be the most likely to drink alcohol.

In the survey we chose to focus on the perceptions teens have about race and the effects race has on deviance. Three hundred and fifty-nine Whites, fifty Natives, nineteen Asians, six Blacks, and sixty-one Other (people who were a race not listed above) comprised the 521 respondents.

We did not find any race to be particularly racist against another race. When asked which race was most likely to (a) use drugs, (b) drink alcohol, (c) vandalize, (d) commit a break and enter, and (e) attempt suicide, most of the respondents replied with an 'All Groups Equal' answer. Only fifteen White people out of 359 answered 'Natives' to all five acts of deviance. We especially found it interesting that the Natives believed an equal number of Natives and Whites attempt suicide. Nineteen per cent of Natives thought Natives were most likely to attempt suicide, while another 19 per cent of Natives thought that more Whites would. Fifteen per cent of all people surveyed thought Natives were most likely to attempt suicide, while the same percentage thought Whites would. Most people did not think that any one race would be more likely to attempt suicide. We also found it interesting that 17 per cent of Natives surveyed believed that Natives were more likely than Whites to use drugs. Sixteen per cent of Natives answered that Whites were most likely to use drugs. Another surprise was that 31 per cent of all Natives surveyed believed that Natives drink alcohol more than any other race. Only 5 per cent of Natives thought that Whites were most likely to drink alcohol. Of all people surveyed, 27 per cent thought Natives drink more, while only 7 per cent thought that Whites did.

We were surprised to find that many people of all races answered 'Don't Know' when asked if they thought teenage immigrants were less law-abiding than teens born in Canada. We assumed that everyone would have an opinion. Obviously this was not the case.

For the question regarding the justice and court system, 62 per cent of the Natives surveyed thought a White person would be favoured in court, and 54 per cent of Whites believed that Whites would be favoured. As much as we would like to believe that our justice system is entirely fair, obviously there are many youths who believed that the courts are prejudiced against certain races. This conflicts with the answer the sociologist whom we interviewed gave us. We asked him if he felt Native people thought that Whites received special treatment in the justice system and he did not think so. Survey results showed that 62 per cent of Natives felt that Whites would be favoured.

We also asked the sociologist if he thought that White youths thought Natives committed more deviant acts than Whites. He did not think so, yet our survey results show that 23 per cent of Whites thought Natives used drugs more than any other race, compared to the 9 per cent who thought Whites used drugs more.

In response to the questions concerning vandalism and alcohol abuse, 23 per cent of Whites thought that Natives vandalize more, and 26 per cent of Whites thought that Natives drank more. This was compared to the 6 per cent of Whites who thought that Whites vandalized more, and 7 per cent of Whites who thought that Whites abuse alcohol more. The sociologist did not think that society has many prejudices or stereotypes, but our results show the opposite. We found that youths think many stereotypes exist in society and in the justice system.

We believe that race is not publicly accepted as a factor in deviance, and therefore people are less willing to talk about it. If they do talk about it, they may be considered politically incorrect. We think this is what happened when we talked to the sociologist. We had the impression that the sociologist was holding back his own opinions for fear they may be considered politically incorrect. We thought the answers he gave us were the ones he felt were right to say, ones that were politically correct. As for the survey results, we feel that perhaps race is not a direct factor affecting deviance, but that there are obviously many stereotypes about how different races may commit more crimes than others.

FAMILY BACKGROUND

We thought that family background could be a major factor in the criminal deviance of youths. We knew that divorce and separation of parents can be very hard on children and can provoke negative behaviour. We also knew that neglect and abuse can ruin a young person's self-confidence and self-esteem, and lead her or him towards a more deviant path. We thought that parents' attitudes would be very important in forming young people's ideas about deviance. The criminality of parents should definitely have an effect on children and if someone sees crime committed on a regular basis, she or he could regard it as normal and acceptable. Poverty is one reason for crime, and we knew that youths from poorer backgrounds would be more likely to deviate in order to make up for what could not be provided for them.

The survey supported most of our original ideas and added a few more, but it was not the main source of information or learning for our part of the project. Our cross-tabulations dealt mainly with people from broken homes or those who no longer lived at home. We wanted to find out what effects broken homes could have on children, and we wanted to see if the lack of guidance and rules had an effect on the ideas of those youths living on their own. (Broken homes include divorced, separated, and a single parent who never married.)

We found that a surprisingly high percentage of people from broken homes had been or knew someone who had been physically abused, and a large percentage of these respondents had divorced parents. Another surprising result was that of the twenty-seven people who thought that date rape was acceptable, ten of them came from divorced families.

Many of the survey questions dealt with people's attitudes towards sex, and we were hoping to find some connections between these attitudes and family backgrounds. Unfortunately, the results were inconclusive for many of the questions, and few patterns could be found. What we did find was that 35 per cent of people from broken homes thought that having multiple sex partners was acceptable, while only 17 per cent of people from two-parent families agreed with this statement. We also found that youths whose parents had never been married had the highest percentage of people who thought that sex before marriage was acceptable. These answers validated our assumptions that parents' attitudes and values influenced their children and determined how their children will act and think.

Alcohol abuse by youths is a deviant act and can lead to more serious deviant acts. When teens go out drinking, trouble is bound to happen, such as fighting, vandalism, or theft. Alcohol alters their behaviour and clouds their judgement. Drunk teens do not always act like themselves and often participate in activities that they would not usually do. They become more violent and more willing to take unnecessary risks. We found that 12 per cent of youths who live alone, compared to 18 per cent of youths who live at home, never drink alcoholic beverages. We also found that 18 per cent of youths who live alone, compared to 15 per cent of youths who live at home, drink alcohol whenever they have the chance. These percentages were very close, which surprised us because we thought that the lack of parental rules and consequences would affect the attitudes towards and opportunities for the consumption and abuse of alcohol.

The panel discussion provided us with one very important piece of information. Many of the youths who go through the justice system and lead very deviant lives have absolutely horrific family backgrounds. Their experiences are so strange and terrible that most of us could not comprehend them. These backgrounds drive them towards deviant paths. The lack of guidance and caring sends them out on the street and gives them the opportunity to try out different crimes.

We interviewed a social worker employed by the provincial division of social services. It was his view that the family definitely plays a very important role in youth deviance. The common factor among the majority of youths who commit criminally delinquent acts is a significant event in their families, such as divorce, neglect, or abuse. The social worker gave us several such examples. One young boy was in trouble with the police 174 times before the age of twelve. When he was fourteen, he was still continually in trouble with the law for various offences. People were ready to give up on him and were so disgusted by his behaviour that they could not see the point in trying to help him. When talking to the boy, it was discovered that when he was nine years old, he attended a party with his father. At this party it was his father's job to 'mark' eight people in attendance. By 'mark', he meant that his father had to hurt or scar eight prostitutes who were not obeying their pimps. The boy carried eight steak knives and walked behind his father, while his father took a knife, cut the designated person, handed the bloody knife back to his son, and took a clean one. It was obvious that the boy's behaviour was not entirely his fault and stemmed from childhood exposure to violence and most likely abuse and possible neglect. After that kind of childhood, how could any youth not be messed up?

There is no 'typical' family background for all youths who commit deviant acts. The family backgrounds are varied, yet there are some types of families that put the youth at greater risk. The criminality of a parent or parents, such as drug or alcohol abuse, plays a major role in youth deviance since children learn much of their behaviours from their parents. One girl the social worker was working with was addicted to 'sniffers', substances such as paint thinner and Lysol spray. Many of her offences happened when she was high on these 'sniffers', and it was revealed that she often did these 'sniffers' around the kitchen table with her mother and siblings.

Another major factor is parents who do not have any productive parenting techniques. This means that there are no rules or no consequences when the rules are broken, so youths do not learn responsibility or accountability. If they are allowed to do whatever they want at home, why not in society too? Neglect is a bad parenting technique. One youth who was a client of Youth Services came from such a home. On the surface, his family seemed quite ordinary, but a visit to their house proved otherwise. The boy was mildly mentally disabled and had been getting into a lot of trouble recently at school and with the police. Youth Services spoke with his parents to find out what might be bothering the boy. When the social worker arrived, the inside of the house was filthy. It looked like it had not been cleaned in years because there was garbage, old food, and dirty dishes piled up in the corners, and the floor was covered with dog faeces. The youth had a problem with wetting his bed. Originally he slept on a mattress on the floor, but he had soaked that so many times that his father threw it out and told him to sleep on the floor. He eventually soaked the entire carpet with urine, and the floorboards beneath it began to rot. The fact that this youth was so neglected definitely contributed to his deviant behaviour. It may have been his way of trying to get attention from his father.

Many people will disagree that youths from broken homes are at a higher risk than those from traditional, two-parent families for deviant behaviour, especially during adolescence. Adolescence is a difficult period in one's life. Young people try to establish autonomy. With the added stress of a broken home, life becomes more difficult. Youths may try to deflect their parents' problems by acting out. They will try to stop their parents from fighting by putting the focus on themselves through delinquent acts, self-harm, or both.

When dealing with young offenders, their family background must be looked into and dealt with. When trying to decrease youth deviance, we should deal with it at the roots—the family.

GRADES

We initially assumed that as a youth's grades went up, the tendency to act deviantly would be reduced. We thought that alcohol consumption would be fairly even throughout the grade levels, and that drug use would be greater in the lower grade groups. These assumptions were based mainly on the people we know or know of. We assumed that the acceptance of violent crimes would go down as the grades went up for both boys and girls. The results of the cross-tabulations yielded some interesting information, but we were not really surprised. We cross-tabulated grades with sex and three groups of deviant behaviour: (1) substance deviance, (2) non-violent deviance, and (3) violent deviance.

Substance Deviance

The survey results generally showed that as school grades went down, the tendency to be deviant increased. It also showed that girls tend to do better in school; 49 per cent of all girls surveyed had an over 80 per cent average, while only 30 per cent of boys did. Twice as many males as females surveyed were getting falling grades. As for substance abuse, more girls than boys have gotten drunk and have used illegal drugs. Four girls with a 60 per cent to 70 per cent average drank the most, and thirty-one out of thirty-two girls (or 91 per cent) answered yes to that question. In general, the students (male or female) with a 60 per cent to 70 per cent average had been drunk the most, with 92 per cent of them answering the question positively. Surprisingly, the percentage of respondents who drank were just over 50 per cent of the students with an A average; the percentage rose to 74 per cent for the boys and 77 per cent for the girls with a 70 per cent to 80 per cent average. The percentage for students with averages of 60 per cent to 70 per cent was the highest. From here, the percentages began to drop. Thirty-one out of thirty-five (88 per cent) students with a D (50 per cent to 60 per cent) average said that they drank. The percentages of students who drank then dropped with the grades; 77 per cent of students whose marks were below fifty had been drunk. However, due to the small numbers of students in this category, this percentage may not be totally accurate.

Students getting 60 per cent to 70 per cent marks in school feel in the middle; they are not known for being 'smart' or for being 'too cool to be smart', so they may try to get recognition by being 'bad'. We think different grade groups drink for different reasons. Those who get A's may drink because they are stressed or because they do not want to be seen as 'a smart person with no life'. However, they may have the lowest percentage for drinking because they are too busy with school and school-related activities, or because they are worried about the future consequences of their actions. Perhaps they do not care about what others think because they know that they have bright futures and many people with lower grades do not. It makes them feel better than the others. As grades begin to go down, youths start to worry and their drinking increases.

As for drug use, as the grades of those surveyed went down, their use of drugs went up. The trend and percentages for male and female respondents were very similar. Thirty-one per cent of all students with an over 80 per cent average admitted to using illegal drugs; this number increased by 17 per cent as the grade average dropped 10 per cent. For the first two grade groups, the percentage of boys using drugs was slightly higher than the percentage of girls. However, for the last three grade groups, the girls were slightly ahead of the boys. Fifty-nine per cent of students with a C average use illegal drugs. This rose to 71 per cent among students with a 50 per cent to 60 per cent average. Eight of nine (89 per cent) students with falling grades said that they used illegal drugs. We think that this is not so much the grades affecting the behaviour as it is the behaviour affecting the grades.

Non-violent Deviance

With regard to non-violent deviance like theft and cheating, survey results showed that in all categories but one, more males than females have stolen. The trends for boys and girls concerning cheating in school or school-related projects were a little different. Girls with a 50 per cent to 60 per cent average ranked higher than boys with the same averages when asked if they have ever stolen or cheated. As for cheating in school, the girls were more guilty than the boys in all but the 80 per cent-plus group where both were the same. The percentage of male students who cheated increased with a decrease in grades. The percentages went from 67 per cent (forty-seven out of seventy-three) for males with an over 80 per cent average to 83 per cent (five out of six) for males getting failing (below 50 per cent) grades. The trend was slightly different for females. The percentages increased by 10 per cent between those with A averages and those with B averages; the percentage then dropped from 77 per cent to 69 per cent for the girls with a 60 per cent to 70 per cent average. It increased again for those getting marks between 50 per cent and 60 per cent (eleven out of thirteen girls) and again for three out of three girls getting marks below 50 per cent. We think girls cheat more than boys because it is less acceptable for girls to do poorly in school than it is for boys. Students who are not doing well in school are more willing to get higher marks by cheating. Perhaps those doing well got there by doing things themselves and take pride in it. Besides, why cheat when you could probably do a better job on your own?

Stealing appears to be more common among boys than girls, usually by 10 per cent to 15 per cent more. Seventy-one per cent of boys with an 80 per cent-plus average have stolen something, while only 55 per cent of girls with the same average have stolen. Theft rises for males as their marks go down: 77 per cent for those with a B average, 90 per cent for those with a C average. It also increases by 11 per cent for girls with a B average to 78 per cent for girls with a C average, and to 92 per cent (twelve out of thirteen) for girls with a D average. Of the students with a D average, 6 per cent more girls than boys said that they stole. Of the students with marks under 50 per cent, nine out of nine were guilty of theft. Males are more pressured to be cool and macho than girls, who are pressured to be beautiful. This may be why males steal more in the different grade groups. Some are trying to shake the 'geeky, smart person' image that students with an 80 per cent-plus average are often given. Perhaps failing students steal because if they cannot get recognition for being smart, they will get it for being deviant.

Violent Deviance

For violent crimes like rape and physical assault more boys than girls said that these were acceptable. For the question dealing with date rape, only four girls said that it was acceptable. One of 109 girls getting A's, two of 100 girls getting B's, and one of thirty-two girls earning C grades said that date rape was acceptable behaviour. No females receiving grades under 60 per cent agreed. We cannot explain why the four girls with marks over 60 per cent thought that date rape is acceptable. The results for the boys were quite different, as one would guess: 8.2 per cent of males with over 80 per cent averages found rape acceptable. For the next grade group, 7.1 per cent also thought it was acceptable, and in the 60 per cent to 70 per cent average group, the percentage rose back to 8.1 per cent. However, of all boys getting grades between 50 per cent and 60 per cent, only one out of the twenty-two agreed, but one-third of the boys with failing grades felt that date rape was acceptable.

The trends in physical violence among boys and girls are different; the boys have slightly higher percentages for most categories. Of the girls with an over 80 per cent average, 1.8 per cent of the 80 per cent said that physical assault was acceptable. As the average went down by 10 per cent, the percentage of those who agreed increased to 7 per cent, only to fall to 3 per cent in girls with a C average. Two of the thirteen girls with a 50 per cent to 60 per cent average believed that physical assault was acceptable behaviour, which was roughly proportionate to what the boys with the same averages said. No girls with a below 50 per cent average agreed.

Eleven per cent of boys in the highest grade group said that physical violence was acceptable; this fell to 3.6 per cent in the next grade group. Violence was acceptable behaviour to 19.4 per cent of males with a 60 per cent to 70 per cent average, and then fell to 14 per cent among boys with a D average. In the lowest grade group, five out of six boys felt physical assault was acceptable.

From our panel discussions and interviews with professionals about youth deviance, we found out how school performance is related to youth deviance, and that the amount of deviance increases as school performance worsens due to boredom. Youths act deviantly for lack of something to do. Chances are that a good student will be involved with schoolwork and school-related activities, and will have less time to be bored and will therefore be less likely to commit deviant actions.

We think that how students feel about school will affect their behaviour. If they think that school is important, they are likely concerned about their future and what will happen after high school. This type of attitude will result in good grades. However, if students do not care about school or their future, they will concentrate on having as much fun as they can in the present. They will not concentrate on school at all and will find some other way to occupy their time. Also, if a student does well in school, we can probably assume that she or he listens to what is going on. With this comes an understanding of handling problems verbally instead of physically and that there are reasons for the norms set in our society.

CONCLUSIONS

The questionnaire, while not perfect, was nonetheless a tremendous effort for these teenagers. The results are factual and the conclusions speculative. These students are not ordinary teens, regardless of their attempts to be. They are privileged economically, academically, and come from intact families. Yet they are kids, so the insights are 'from the inside' so to speak.

The process of formulating questions and then refining them was arduous, extremely well thought out, and in the end resulted in a genuine common document. The administration of the questionnaire was uniform and consistent, and the data was computer scored. The survey data was not minutely scrutinized by adult workers in the field, but the students did validate their findings by discussing the general trends of the survey with these experts.

Over the course of this survey project, we noticed changes in the students. Originally, they were quick to be judgemental and had to make an effort to work as a group. They were very strong in their beliefs, but not particularly strong in understanding the contradictions. They could see each other's views, but did not necessarily condone or accept them. However, the survey forced them to examine their own views and assumptions, and, in light of the data, caused them to reflect again.

They were also forced to think about and interact with a variety of students from different backgrounds and circumstances. Stereotypes were shattered in more than one instance, and the experiences, although brief, gave rise to valuable discussion. Two such examples were the disbelief over the insolent attitudes and behaviours that the survey teachers and researching students encountered from students at a predominantly White, upper-middle class school, and the initial fear and misgivings of entering a mixed but mainly Aboriginal inner-city high school, where the students demonstrated politeness, respect, and decent behaviour and cooperation.

As teachers involved in this study, we found this to be a fascinating if at times exasperating experience. Coordinating the efforts of students and attempting to stabilize many variables in order to make the administration of the questionnaire as reliable and valid as possible was never easy. Our thanks are offered wholeheartedly to the staff and students of the participating schools, to the principal of Walter Murray Collegiate, and to the University of Saskatchewan professors from the Department of Education Curriculum and the Department of Sociology, all of whom cooperated. Our greatest thanks go to a group of very strong-willed individual students who, in the end, pulled together.

—5—

Punishment and Control of Women in Prisons: The Punishment of Privation

Carolyn Carey

Federally sentenced women in Canada have a history of savage treatment and outright neglect (Adelberg and Currie 1987b; Cooper 1987). Since the development of the prison system, women have been tucked away in institutions that were geared to meet the interests of male prisoners. Inside the Prison for Women at Kingston, for example, strategies of correctional management were developed in a White male context, leaving the specific needs of the women unfulfilled, in conditions 'unfit for bears much less women' (Sub-Committee of the Penitentiary System in Canada 1977). The closure of the Prison for Women was affirmed in 1990 following the suicides of four Aboriginal female inmates. Although federally sentenced women continue to be housed in the Kingston prison, a four-year, $50-million development to create five regional women-directed facilities has been implemented by the Solicitor General. These new facilities represent a proposed paradigm shift from a correctional philosophy (designed with men in mind) to an approach characterized by holistic healing and empowerment that is sensitive to the specific needs of women in conflict with the law. It is important to realize that women who commit acts defined as criminal are generally victims of poverty, abuse, and dysfunctional families. *What You Said: A Report Back to All Federal Women on the 1989 Survey of Your Views* shows that 68 per cent of women prisoners have been physically abused and 53 per cent have been sexually abused. Eighty per cent of the entire female prison population indicate some form of abuse in the past. Abuse is more common among those of lower social/economic status and contributes to the continual problem of the status of women (Duffy and Mandell 1994). Most often these women commit non-violent property crimes, an indication of the correlation between 'criminality' and women's lower social and economic status. These life situations are characteristic of the gender and racial discrimination experienced by most women.

This chapter has two main goals. The first is to describe how women's treatment in federal prisons and how traditional criminological theories about women and crime have contributed to the social control of women. The second is to assess whether the new regional facilities for women represent a paradigm shift in female corrections; that is, whether this new system is based on a new belief system about women. My main position is that a theory of crime and crime prevention and control must begin with an understanding of women's historical position in society, a position that has been characterized by subservience and exploitation.

POSITIVIST CRIMINOLOGY AND CONSENSUS THEORIES OF FEMALE CRIMINALITY

Many legal researchers and correctional officials explain the paternalistic and neglectful treatment of federally sentenced women throughout history as the result of the smaller numbers of women relative to men in Canadian corrections (Cooper 1987; Curtis 1985). Cooper writes, 'because of their small numbers and insignificance attached to their crimes, women offenders have been housed wherever and in whatever manner suited the needs of the larger male offender population' (1987:127). Traditional theories concerning women's biological, psychological, or sociological nature, supported historically by criminological inquiry, have justified the treatment of female offenders (Cooper 1987; Currie 1986; Smart 1976). For decades women prisoners were defined as evolutionary or socially regressive anomalies who were uncharacteristic of the stereotypical nurturing female and were subject to traditional 'reproductive' labour in the interest of men.

The 'classical' work of Lombroso and Ferrero, *The Female Offender* (1895), represents the first 'scientific' inquiry regarding women and crime. Using a biological determinist perspective, Lombroso and Ferrero define criminality as a pathology originating in the biological make-up of individuals. Central to their thesis is the notion of atavism, which they use to suggest that criminals are genetically deficient and evolutionarily regressive. Atavists are identifiable through certain physical features that indicate genetic deficiency. An individual is defined as a born criminal if four or more of these features are evident. According to Lombroso and Ferrero, these features are rarely found among women criminals because women are less evolved than men. This did not suggest that women are therefore more likely to be criminal; rather, they argue that women's biologically determined nature is antithetical to crime. Because of the woman's lower genetic form, however, she makes up for her lower crime rate in the cruelty and vileness of her crimes:

> ... when a morbid activity of the psychical centres intensifies the bad qualities of women, and induces them to seek relief in evil deeds; when piety and maternal sentiments are wanting, and in their place are strong passions and intensely erotic tendencies, much muscular strength and a superior intelli-

gence for the conception and execution of evil, it is clear that the innocuous semi criminal present in the normal woman must be transformed into a born criminal more terrible than any man (Lombroso and Ferrero 1895:151).

Although Lombroso and Ferrero's biological explanations are largely discredited, parallels still exist in more recent works. Cowie, Cowie, and Slater's work, *Delinquency in Girls* (1968) argues that female crime requires a biological explanation, whereas delinquency in boys requires a socio-economic explanation. The authors include social and environmental causal factors that predispose boys to delinquency. In contrast, biological factors are thought to be more important than crimogenic environmental factors with young women: 'delinquent girls more often than boys have other forms of impaired physical health; they are noticed to be oversized, lumpish, uncouth and graceless, with a raised incidence of minor physical defects' (Cowie, Cowie, and Slater 1968:166, 167).

Dalton (1978) and Pollak (1979) also provide biological explanations for female delinquency. In her study of imprisoned women, Dalton claims that a relationship exists between the criminality of women and women's menstrual cycles. She found that 57 per cent of her sample committed offences during menstruation or the immediate pre- and postmenstrual hormonal disturbances (Dalton 1978, cited in Currie 1986). Pollak similarly argues that women are more likely to commit crime during hormonal changes, especially during pregnancy and menopause (Pollak 1979, cited in Currie 1986). Dalton and Pollak's theories have been criticized for predicting a higher crime rate for women than is empirically verifiable or intuitively plausible. Campbell (1981), for example, writes that '"hormonal" explanations predict that a woman is at risk to commit crime seventy-five percent of her life' (1981:47, cited in Currie 1986:233).

Role theory moves away from solely biological explanations, offering the more 'liberal' notion that individual pathologies are induced by society and can, therefore, be modified by society. Although role theorists consider sociological factors such as inequality of opportunity, they utilize concepts such as diverse socialization as causally related to criminal behaviour. Inadequate socialization becomes an individual pathology that can be cured through resocialization.

An example of contemporary role theory is found in the work of Hoffman-Bustamente (1973). He argues that boys are encouraged to be aggressive and are allowed more freedom than girls. Girls are supervised more closely and encouraged to be passive and non-violent. He concludes that on the basis of this diverse socialization, women have a lower crime rate than men and, in keeping with their auxiliary role, commit crimes only in supplementary roles or as associates of male criminals. Criminal activity in women is an anomaly caused by poor socialization.

Freda Adler, in her work *Sisters in Crime* (1975), also suggests that differential crime rates between men and women are due to different socialization processes. She suggests that the women's liberation movement has allowed women to challenge traditional sex role stereotypes and to participate in legitimate and illegitimate activities that were once restricted. An obvious problem in Adler's work is that she attributes female 'criminality' to an increase in the 'masculine' qualities of female behaviour, but fails to explain why males assume these criminal roles. The most essential critique, however, is that Adler's theory, and role theory in general, fail to discuss the structural origins of differential sex roles in society (Currie 1986; Smart 1976). By attributing sex role differences as an explanatory variable of crime rather than as a variable that in itself needs to be explained, role theory tends to accentuate the differences between men and women.

More recent liberal feminists and critical theorists refute positivistic explanations and argue that the problem of women and crime must be located in its socio-economic and gendered life contexts. Women who come into conflict with the criminal justice system are victims of their gendered life situations both inside and outside of the prison. Critical theorists find that the majority of imprisoned women are generally young, unskilled, poor, and Native; many have drug and/or alcohol addictions and many have been victims of sexual or physical abuse. The liberal account posits a causal relationship between women's social and economic position and 'criminalization', but, unlike critical Marxist theories and socialist feminism, it does not directly address the underlying ways in which class, gender, or racial oppression produces the socio-economic situation of these women. The focus is on the individual rather than on the political economic structures that produce gendered oppression. In efforts to promote the elimination of female oppression, liberal feminists tend to argue for individualized notions of female 'criminality'.

In general, biological, psychological, and sociological positivistic theories fail to question diverse and discriminatory sex roles and the historical definitions of what constitutes criminal behaviour. By using 'criminality'—either natural or socialized—as an explanatory variable for crime, these positivist theories help legitimate social control policies for deviating individuals. By labelling female criminality as a biological, psychological, or social pathology, science has the power to define what is normal or healthy for the population.

My argument, then, is that theories emphasizing individual pathologies have historically acted as a formal mechanism of control over imprisoned women by (1) labelling women offenders as pathological, (2) justifying traditional stereotypical images of men and women as normal, and (3) denying that women's criminal actions may be justified responses to poverty and victimization. Most important, each of these theoretical positions is produced within a historical context and reproduces, and scientifically legitimates, ideological (belief system) and structural (socio-economic and political) processes.

The most important criticisms of (liberal feminism) biological/psychological correctionalist theories are similar to those that were directed at the theories of liberal pluralism and the contradictions of 'liberal democracy'. For example, how can we understand capitalist societies' social inequalities between the sexes, classes, and races in the context of formal political equality as proposed by the principles of democracy (Brickley and Comack 1986). Similarly, although law may be applied evenly, economic and social inequalities between citizens affect the way that different people adapt, reject, and avoid the standards set by state agents—police, judiciary, etc. (Caputo et al. 1989).

CRITICAL CRIMINOLOGY, FEMINIST THEORY, AND LEGAL STUDIES

Detailing the work of critical criminologists has been the subject of entire academic volumes. At the risk of offering what Schwartz and DeKeseredy (1991) call a 'reductionist caricature' of critical and radical criminologists, I take the lead of the new left realist criminologists and discuss the major themes under one heading: 'idealist criminology'. Idealist criminologists refute individual positivistic explanations of crime and argue that real reductions in the crime rate will be achieved through the elimination of capitalist oppression rather than through reforms to the criminal justice system. Idealist criminologists ask how the state criminalizes people and provide a substantial critique of the correctionist theories that have neglected the political dimension of crime, including why certain acts and individuals are criminalized and others are not. Following the historical materialist method of Marx and Engels (1939), traditional Marxism believes that a criminal is a victim of the inequality of material-based class relations, and that the poor and the underclasses are the primary targets of the crime control system. Women who become criminal offenders are often lumped into the same category as men in the subordinate classes.

From this left idealist position, laws are based on standards of 'equity' and 'universality' in order to satisfy and mystify the dominated classes. The legal system supports formal equality, while structural inequalities prevent substantive equality before the law. As Anatole France quips, 'The law in all its majestic impartiality forbids rich and poor alike to sleep under bridges, to beg in the streets and steal bread' (quoted in Hunt 1976:184, cited in Brickley and Comack 1986:20). The belief that the law transcends class, racial, and sexual divisions and provides equality for everyone is essential in legitimating the capitalist system of production. Because the political processes are always being shaped to insure the maintenance and reproduction of the capitalist system (Ratner, McMullan, and Burtch 1987), substantive inequalities must continue. Laws based on equality serve only to convince people that the system is working fairly for everyone. As a result, the 'idealist criminologies' do not allow for the possibility of legislative reforms by the state, the legal sphere, or any other institution to reduce substantive inequalities between classes, races, or sexes.

'Idealist' criminology is criticized especially by left realist criminologists for its inability to provide viable alternatives to the real social disorganization that results from capitalist oppression (Lea and Young 1984). By reducing all oppression to class domination, Marxist criminology has failed to provide comprehensive information on the problems caused by the activities of the state. As Lea and Young (1984) demonstrate, crime, whether working class or white-collar class, is likely to be levelled against those who are economically and socially vulnerable. Left realism argues that the working classes are victims of crime from all directions.

The left realist perspective argues more optimistically that measures such as welfare, social service, and the right to organized union activity show the organized power of different classes in creating contradictory pressures that the state must address. Left realism offers a practical political agenda based on the premise that emancipatory gains may result from the democratic state apparatus: 'there is an implication that reform is politically feasible and that the state is an arena of class struggle, because it is an important agency facilitating the material power of capital and because it opens up a space for potential social justice reform' (McMullan 1987:248).

Feminist writing has stressed the importance of left realists' work on the victimization of women in criminology (Carlen 1992a, 1992b). Women's experiences as victims of crime and violence are taken seriously. In the same breath, however, feminists argue that the realists' call for decreased state control and minimized police activities may contradict the need for women to be kept safe (Schwartz and DeKeseredy 1991). Also, realists do not take prisoners' and lawbreakers' experience as seriously as the experience of the victims, and feminists argue that no political agenda can successfully reduce crime without an agenda informed by the 'criminal's' standpoint (Carlen 1992b). This need to understand the perspective of the lawbreaker justifies qualitative investigations about women's (and men's) experiences surrounding their crimes and their experience of the state's response:

> ... taking seriously women's views of their lawbreaking might lead to: political demands for a diminution of the oppressive conditions in which much of women's lawbreaking is committed; the democratic construction of feasible interventionary programs in relation to the drug taking, thieving, and other crimes that often cause misery to women other than the offender, as well as aggravating the existing problems of the woman lawbreaker herself; and the democratic management of housing and other schemes for women in trouble (Carlen 1992b:212).

Finally, feminist writing criticizes left realists, who in a rather conventional, conservative manner argue that economic conditions and class status may cause criminal activity, but that because some individuals who live in deplorable conditions do not commit crime, then most lawbreakers choose criminal lifestyles and must take responsibility for those choices. Carlen points out that while people do make choices around their actions, they 'do so under conditions not of their own choosing' (1992b:214). Social and economic conditions greatly affect people by constraining and limiting their choices.

The most important critique of the left realist perspective for this thesis is its partial return to individualistic explanations for criminal behaviour (Carlen 1992b). For women and crime, this theoretically backward step denies that the problem of the status of women and problems of social justice contribute to criminal activity. Carlen states: 'a refusal to abandon the space of politics should not also entail an abandonment of a principled theoretical commitment to calling into question all already known explanations of crime, including those developed under the auspices of socialism, feminism, and/or left realism' (1992b:214). The following section introduces the socialist feminist position on the problem of women's treatment in the criminal justice system and illustrates how the history of federally sentenced women is best informed by this critical feminist criminology.

SOCIALIST FEMINISM, CRIME, AND CRIMINAL JUSTICE POLITICS

Socialist feminists argue that women's criminal activity is a reflection of the failure of some women to abide by existing class and gender norms (including motherhood, matrimony, and domesticity). In a study of thirty-nine imprisoned women in the British legal system, Carlen writes, 'the 39 women had in the main committed crime because in addition to experiencing poverty and an excess of welfare regulation, they had also sensed that such poverty and welfare regulation violated some of the most fundamental liberal political discourses concerning welfare rights and the rights of private citizens' (1988:13, 14).

Carlen, like many socialist feminists, argue that women in conflict with the law generally do not have the resources to challenge oppressive gender roles. Either by choice or circumstance, some women are led to difficult life situations characterized by abuse, poverty, and victimization. Criminal behaviour, in this context, becomes a survival mechanism and an indirect response to oppressive gender roles.

Women who do not follow traditional reproductive and economically dependent roles are especially subject to formal and informal patriarchal collective mechanisms of control through the state. These women are primarily working-class women who do not enjoy the same economic advantages as their male counterparts (Currie 1986; Dahl and Snare 1978). The rising female crime rate is thus partially the result of more women entering the workforce and/or the feminization of poverty and child support.

Prisons offer women few opportunities either to challenge or overcome racial, sexual, or class barriers. As Carlen writes, 'In so far as prisons debilitate, women's prisons feed off their own product. But it is an indictment of (British) society at the end of the twentieth century, and not of the penal system itself when women tell me that they will go out to a world that has even less to offer them than prison' (Carlen 1988:163).

Socialist feminists argue therefore that the first step towards decreasing crimes of necessity lies in equality and the elimination of female dependence on men, possibly through job equality and 'community orientated types of provision for families' (Carlen 1988:161). The elimination of female dependency must be coupled with an analysis of class inequality that accompanies gender inequality. It is here that socialist feminism differs from liberalism. Socialist feminists critique capitalist labour, including 'legal mechanisms, both patriarchal and bourgeoisie liberal, which over time reinforce women's sole responsibility for unpaid domestic and reproductive labour, making them vulnerable to economic dependence and exploitation both within and beyond family roles' (Currie 1986:242).

Overall, the socialist feminist analysis provides a model to contextualize rehabilitation as part of changing patriarchal systems of domination. Socialist feminists such as Carlen emphasize the academic need for an understanding of: (1) the historical dialectical relationship between the law and the social structure; (2) the class, sex, and race differentials in crime rates; and (3) the importance of constructing a feminist jurisprudence that may empirically document how women's and men's experiences differ and how these differences influence and are influenced by the criminal justice system (Carlen 1992a, 1992b). Political efforts need to address the short-term pragmatic strategies that may insure that formal control mechanisms (policing, the courts) are non-discriminatory and that women's oppression is reduced. At the same time, long-term democratic ideals of equality and legality are paramount.

This type of feminist analysis demands that female federal corrections be understood in the context of changing patriarchal relations. The following sections ask how the corrections system has defined female offenders and whether these definitions are discriminatory and controlling or liberating.

A CONTEXTUAL HISTORY OF FEDERAL CORRECTIONS FOR WOMEN

Feminists argue that industrialization created a new form of patriarchal relations. Ursel (1986) argues that patriarchal roles changed from the familial to the social in which control shifted from individual fathers and husbands to the state. She suggests that women's control of production and reproduction were limited by restricting women's access to a means of livelihood. When women married, they became dependent on the support of the patriarchal family. Women's self-sufficiency was restricted by labour laws and family and welfare legislation. Currie argues that the very structure of capitalist society entailed the necessity of a sexual division of labour that 'foster(ed) sexist ideologies' (1986:237). While changes in formal laws, such as family law, symbolized the decline of familial patriarchy by restricting the control husbands had legally to control their wives, a sexual division of labour was entrenched by the capitalist system which restricted the role of women and symbolized instead a 'public paternalism of the state' (Currie 1986:241). From this perspective, the treatment of women inside the Kingston prison for men in early Canadian corrections is an additional mechanism that maintained patriarchal ideologies that distinguished men's and women's gender roles—women being primarily reproducers and men being primarily producers.

THE SPECIAL SITUATION OF WOMEN

Since the opening of the Kingston prison in 1835, federal women prisoners have been housed inside a facility built for men's needs. Originally they were kept away from the male prisoners in a temporary location, above the 'mess table of the male convicts' (Cooper 1987:129). In 1846, when the number of women increased to twenty-six (Cooper 1987), the warden had them moved, complaining that they were housed in an area needed for the men to dine. The new cells were 'eight feet four inches long, seven feet six inches high and thirty inches wide' (Journals of the Legislative Assembly, 1843, cited in Cooper 1987:131) and described as small, dirty, uncomfortable locations that were infested with bugs (Brown Commission 1848-9, cited in Cooper 1987). Public criticism of the treatment of female offenders in male penal institutions (which included such things as inadequate facilities, whipping or flogging and other corporal punishments) resulted in the establishment of a separate unit for women inside the penitentiary. Recommendations for sending women back to their own provinces were made one year later and were based on criticisms regarding the inadequate size and barbaric conditions ('Report of the Royal Commission on Penitentiaries', 1914, cited in Curtis et al. 1985). Twenty years after this date, a federal prison for women (P4W) was opened in Kingston.

The secondary status of women in the Kingston Penitentiary is evident in historical documents about federal corrections, especially from matrons' reports. Except for one paragraph in each matron's report stating that discipline is satisfactory and work is completed for the male convicts, women are generally not mentioned at all. Overall, historical documents inside P4W indicate no evidence of correctional planning specific to the needs of the women. Women's care was considered secondary to men's, with women moved into uncomfortable quarters for the convenience of the male inmates.

The overall neglect of women inside the Kingston prison for men—mostly by omission—echoes the nineteenth-century assumptions about woman's lesser importance in the changing economic environment. I argue that such omission tends to reinforce the acceptance of existing assumptions about female offenders. Female offenders were regarded as deviants partly because they did not conform to Victorian expectations of women's maternal and wifely roles.

Prison programs for women have generally been based on assumptions about the innate nature of women. Early government documents summarized the correctional philosophy of the day for all criminals despite gender: 'the source of conduct including criminal conduct is to be sought for in the material substance of the being, in an undeveloped, dormant diseased nerve tissue' (Minister of Justice 1914, 1912/13–1919/20:18–19). While the notion of atavism was predominant for men and women, women were regarded by some corrections officials as worse than men because of their extreme departure from the proper maternal role designated for females outside of the prison. The 'Report of the Superintendent of Penitentiaries' (1864) stated: 'a few of the worst female convicts are absolutely more turbulent than those of the male sex, and I may with great safety state the "cats" (whips) would make a very wholesome change with some of the worthless of them and not by any means endanger their health' (cited in Cooper 1987:130). In 1920, the parole board wrote that Ontario women prisoners are immoral and subnormal: '... I might add that the board would rather deal with men's cases any day than the women's, and only sees women as a matter of duty and justice to them' (Lavell 1948, cited in Cooper 1987:136). Prison officials may have been aware that poverty played a role in women's crime, but this view was overridden by assumptions about women's 'natural moral character'.

Every penitentiary report from 1868 to 1934 in which women were mentioned reflected assumptions about their biological or psychological character. Even the reports that were written in the interest of the female offenders contained biodeterminist views. In the 'Report of the Director of the Penitentiary', the matron, who was in charge of the welfare of the female prisoners, labelled the women as 'lazy and worthless characters' who must be isolated in proper cells for their work to be 'extracted from them' (Directors of Penitentiaries 1868:22). Nickle's 1921 report, which resulted in better immediate conditions for the female offenders was also based on sexist assumptions. Nickle defined women offenders as sexually 'aberrant': 'and my attention was called to one instance of this group of cases where a sedative had to be given to soothe desire' (cited in Cooper 1987:135).

From the few available assessments of women in correctional reports, it is evident that until the late 1800s women were viewed as predominantly 'abnormal, lazy and sick', and as evolutionarily regressive because of their failure to meet societal expectations of a woman's proper role and conduct. By the beginning of the nineteenth century, the focus moved to sexual behaviour and aggressiveness. The most important point is that from the opening of the Kingston Penitentiary in 1835 to the beginning of the building of the Prison for Women in 1921, the dominant discourse explaining female criminality centred around biological and psychological explanations for women's abnormal and criminal behaviour and the connection to inappropriate gender conduct and roles.

These assumptions about gender roles were not uncommon during the early twentieth century. The correctional reports echo Lombroso and Ferrero's (1895) criminological writing, which suggested that women's lower evolutionary form made female criminals more cruel and vile than male criminals. Beginning in 1865, early medical textbooks were based on similar biological views about women. The textbooks discussed the 'conservation of energy' principle, which argued that living organisms have a limited amount of energy and must therefore use it wisely. For women, both physical and intellectual activities were forbidden so as to preserve energy for their 'primary bodily function-procreation' (Currie 1986:240). The medical professional views were subsequently taken up by the Labour Commission in 1890. The commission suggested that women's reproductive capacity meant that work environments must consider their natural physical state as delicate and vulnerable: 'medical testimony proves conclusively that girls, when approaching womanhood, cannot be employed at severe or long continued work without a serious danger to their health, and the evil effects may follow them throughout their lives' (cited in Ursel 1986:163).

I argue in this chapter that as a result of the official labelling of women prisoners as 'abnormal' for going against 'natural' maternal instincts, the state justified women's reproductive role as a primary function. This justification is less subtly maintained by restricting labour and by involving women prisoners in tasks defined as reproductive. Women's work in the prison included domestic duties that helped ease the lives of the male inmates, not to mention the prison system itself, which would have had to pay for these services. From 1868 to 1918, penitentiary reports cite the labour of the female inmates as household cleaning, washing, ironing, cooking, nursing, knitting, and sewing for the male inmates. Restrictive labour legislation and the subsequent control of women's economic power thus circumscribed women's appropriate activity.

THE CHANGING ROLE OF PATRIARCHY AND THE PRISON FOR WOMEN

The evolution of advanced capitalism and the change from private to corporate finance has entailed a change in the role of women. Socialist feminists argue that with the move to advanced capitalism in Canada, the reproductive labour of women has been gradually converted into wage labour, engendering more surplus value. Because advanced capitalism demands that labour be legally autonomous from capital, formal laws announcing the 'equality of free labour' became necessary. The ideologies of capitalism, based on equality before the law, however, are directly contradictory to the ideologies of patriarchy, based on the natural inequalities between the sexes. Socialist feminists argue that this contradiction engenders a consciousness of female oppression that results, in part, in the reform of the legal system's move away from patriarchy (Currie 1986). For example, discriminatory 'protective legislation' that restricts employment and promotion in paid labour for women has been gradually removed. Ursel argues that the state abandoned legislation that restricted using female labour in capitalist production between the postwar years from 1948 to 1968 (Ursel 1992). She also suggests that at the end of this period, some of the old patriarchal structures were dismantled with new legislative measures such as the 'legalization of birth control, liberalized divorce and abortion statutes' (Ursel 1992:291).

Despite many legislative changes that reflect the pressure on the state to address inequality issues for women—for example, affirmative action programs, pay equity, and employment equity legislation—(Findley 1990, cited in Ursel 1992), the impact of legislation is considerably reduced when other changes such as equality in wages, household labour, and reproductive rights are not addressed. Many working women make at most 63 per cent of what men make and are in low-skilled, low-wage employment with little room for advancement. Women continue to work mostly in 'clerical, service, sales, medicine and health, and teaching' (Duffy and Mandell 1994). Limited child care, pornographic images of women, violence against women, moralizing debates on reproductive rights, and feminization of poverty issues (Currie 1992) exacerbate women's dependence on men and reinforce patriarchal notions. Socialist feminists argue that formal equality that fails to consider the actual differences and experiences of men and women in society—double day, unequal pay and opportunity, abuse, and discrimination—are apt to oppress the most vulnerable groups even further.

Although the federal Prison for Women was designed with women in mind, the correctional paradigm continued to be designed for White men. I argue that just as legislative changes concerning women's employment have not been liberating when women have continued to have full-time responsibility for children, so correctional changes have not been liberating when women continue to be removed from their children and are denied adequate living conditions appropriate to their gender. Denying that there are real differences between the life situations of female and male offenders further oppresses women as the more vulnerable gender group. When the life situations of the women who come into conflict with the law are characterized by abuse, poverty, racism, and sexism, treatment that fails to deal with these 'status of women' issues reinforces patriarchal control over women and is unlikely to deal effectively with the problem of female crime.

P4W 'Unfit For Bears Much Less Women'

The federal Prison for Women was completed in January 1934. The conditions inside the prison, however, were not much better than when women resided in the male prison across the road. The contrast between the Prison for Women and the other prisons in Canada was first noted in 1938 by the Archambault Commission. After investigating all prisons in Canada, the commission argued that the conditions and treatment of female offenders were inferior to those of men and that the prison for women must be closed: '[The Prison for Women] remained similar in appearance to the men's facility with a 16 foot wall surrounding the prison, with 10 feet of woven wire and barbed wire placed on top' (cited in Cooper 1987:137). The report added that there were no windows, no recreational facility, and no programs for education.

The criticisms of P4W and recommendations for decentralized imprisonment were repeated in 1956 when the government appointed another royal commission. Since then, at least thirteen government studies, investigations, and private sector reports have reiterated the need for decentralized facilities and the closure of the Kingston Prison for Women.

The most serious problem for women in P4W was the centralized location of the prison. Women offenders were taken away from their communities and support systems. While some women were from the central provinces, most were sent '500 to 3,000 miles' away from their homes. Only sixty out of 130 women inside P4W in 1990 were from communities in Ontario (Correctional Services Canada 1990:74). Access to Kingston was very difficult as well as costly for visitors, leaving many families unable to visit. Furthermore, released women were geographically stranded after completing their sentences. Many of the women could not even afford to call home (Sub-Committee of the Penitentiary System in Canada 1977).

Although a centralized location was the dominant concern that led to the proposed closure of P4W, other criticisms included the lack of proper educational, recreational, and therapeutic programs and the intermixing of security classifications. The correctional system had rationalized the failure to separate maximum, medium, or minimum security offenders with the low rate of imprisonment for women and the increased cost of separate facilities. This situation not only implied that minimum-risk offenders were subjected to more security than was necessary (Correctional Services Canada 1990; Standing Committee on Justice and Solicitor General 1988; Sub-Committee of the Penitentiary System in Canada 1977), but also that maximum-security offenders were often placed in additional segregated units (Cooper 1986; Correctional Services Canada 1990). This resulted in worse conditions than those already noted for both classifications of inmates.

In P4W, counselling and therapeutic services were minimal and were developed based on a correctional philosophy for male offenders. The *Report on Self-Injurious Behaviour in the Kingston Prison for Women* (Heney 1990) reported that 98 per cent of the prison population and 93 per cent of the correctional staff thought the counselling services were inadequate. The prisoners suffered physical, sexual, and emotional abuse, and services failed to address their immediate psychosocial/medical needs. The correctionalist alternative to counselling and empowerment was a policy of isolation as punishment and behaviour modification. The prison's rules and regulations, which limited prisoners' movements and interactions, especially the rules of solitary confinement, created environments that women offenders identified as disempowering (Heney 1990). Isolation and segregation quite clearly exacerbated crisis and trauma.

The historical data about vocational and educational training for women in corrections reveal a corrections philosophy based on traditional gender role stereotypes that restricted employment choices for women. Employment and training programs within prison are still primarily 'cleaning, laundry, hairdressing, cooking, sewing and clerical work' (Elliot and Morris 1987:154; Jackson 1988:292). Non-traditional options such as 'carpentry, auto-mechanics and microfilming' exist within the men's prisons, but are available to very few women (Elliot and Morris 1987:154).

Aboriginal women are doubly oppressed in a system designed primarily for White men, although Correctional Service Canada has begun recently to address Aboriginal cultural needs. When the special needs of Aboriginal women are mentioned—even within commission reports—their specific cultural concerns are neglected in favour of a context that examines the needs of all federally sentenced women (Correctional Service Canada 1990). As a result, services pertaining to the cultural and psychological needs of Aboriginal women were almost non-existent until recently. Aboriginal women had access to mainstream psychological services, but these services lacked cultural awareness and were not readily available (Heney 1990). Similarly, the cultural needs of francophone women were ignored as there were no French language programs.

The suicides of four Aboriginal women are evidence of the personal pain experienced by female prisoners at the Prison for Women. Suicides have been called a form of liberation (*Star Phoenix* 1991a) and an escape from the pain. The amount of media attention focused on the suicides has been tremendous. The tragedies have focused national attention on the plight of federally sentenced women.

Feminists and legal historians have thoroughly documented the correlation between women's poverty, abuse, victimization, and crime. Unfortunately, P4W has, at the same time, historically ignored differences in the crime rates between women and men and has failed to address the underlying reasons why women come into conflict with the law. As a result, the rhetoric of reform at P4W transformed sociopolitical problems into moral-

istic or individual pathologies. The historical evidence illustrates how federally sentenced women were imprisoned in conditions that supported definitions of womanhood, which contributed to the continued patriarchal control
of women under capitalism, and which fostered roles for women that made
their criminal activity more understandable.

CREATING CHOICES

This final section explores whether the growing body of knowledge about
federally sentenced women, directed at changing women's life situations, is
of the same talk or if it has the potential for change. The central question is
whether the new regional federal facilities, which are based on suggestions
from progressive theories and research programs, will eliminate the patriarchal characteristics of P4W and challenge traditional sex role stereotypes.

The decentralized locations for federally sentenced women are praised by
the Federal Task Force on Women Offenders as a humanitarian response to
the oppressive treatment characteristic of the Kingston Prison for Women.
The centralized prison has been replaced with five smaller regional facilities
located in 'Halifax, Montreal, Central/Southwestern Ontario, Edmonton,
Maple Creek, Saskatchewan, a unique Aboriginal accommodation option,
and the lower mainland of British Columbia' (Correctional Service Canada
1990). The advantages are obvious. Federal women prisoners will be closer
to their homes, communities, and regional support services. The facilities
will be homelike and/or will provide resources to facilitate either live-in
arrangements for children or allowance for close contact. A healing lodge in
Maple Creek will be run for and possibly by Aboriginal women, with culturally sensitive services and contact with Aboriginal elders and staff.

The proposed programs for women inside the regional and healing centres address the need for increased choices as a requirement for women,
the importance of child care and empowerment, and healing as defined by the
women. One of the most important changes of the 1990 task force is that, in
principle, women and Aboriginal people will be given a voice of their own in
corrections. The task force argues that the philosophy of corrections must
change from male-oriented to 'women-based'. Replacing the White male
system with a women-directed approach accounts for the differences between women's and men's experiences. This is a first step towards recognizing the problems of poverty, abuse, and victimization that women face.

Another immediate benefit is that the facilities will offer counselling and
programs according to the needs of non-Aboriginal and Aboriginal female
inmates. The task force insists that women cannot 'fit' into the existing programs designed by correctional staff but rather should identify their own needs
and subsequently have them fulfilled. The task force proposes a 'resources'

approach (Correctional Service Canada 1990:102) in which programming responds to the 'multi-faceted, inner-related nature of women's experience' (Correctional Service Canada 1990:103). The regional women's facilities, healing lodge, and community release strategies all emphasize individual 'healing' and 'wellness'. They offer programming according to women's needs, including addiction, childhood sexual/physical/emotional abuse, domestic abuse, spirituality, independent living, self-reliance, and positive interaction.

The focus is on individual assessments, the needs of the women, and healing. The programming will emphasize holistic measures. Implicit in this policy is a movement away from classification of the women in generalized categories towards a better understanding of women's needs and experiences. In support of self-determination and esteem, the task force maintains the emphasis of staffing shift from security to support. The holistic approach emphasizes self-sufficiency, not dependency.

The recommended training and vocational facilities also illustrate a movement away from limited traditional gender roles. The vocational and educational training emphasizes women's independence outside of the criminal justice and patriarchal family systems. Each program is designed to increase women's choices when they reintegrate into their communities, a step that may increase women's abilities to take advantage of some of their formal 'equality'.

Aboriginal-directed programs also offer increased choices for Aboriginal women. The twofold discrimination against Aboriginal women led the task force to conclude that an 'Aboriginal justice system within the context of self-government' is the best solution (Correctional Service Canada 1990:118). Because of the long-term nature of this task, members of the task force have instead adopted an approach that has attempted to understand the Aboriginal perspective.

The socialist feminist perspective regards female crime as the product of oppressive class and gender relations and argues that the elimination of criminal behaviour rests in structural changes and not in treatment in prison. The analysis in this chapter suggests that the task force recommendations have the potential to alter conditions inside the criminal justice system, conditions that have historically defended and reinforced traditional gender roles. From the socialist feminist perspective, the task force report advocates measures that increase life choices for women and help break the apparatuses that control women. Recognizing the problems of poverty, abuse, and victimization of female offenders, and supporting greater choices through counselling, education, and vocational training that pertains to individual needs promote empowerment and choice.

The task force's recommendations have the potential to be progressive only if they do not lose sight of the formal and informal mechanisms that maintain patriarchal control over women. If social policy broadens employment opportunities for women by creating access to jobs that were generally limited, correcting unfair wages, and remembering the long-term political agenda of reducing gender inequities, measures such as the task force's proposals can provide the groundwork for broader change. If correctionalist policy loses track of the larger political agenda, the short-term measures for women will fail to solve the larger problem of the status of women and, in effect, may exacerbate the problem through the co-optation of law reform. For example, the regional facilities are now called 'prisons' by the Canadian Association of Elizabeth Fry Societies, which withdrew from the task force when implementation strategies failed to include concerns of federally sentenced women.

On the basis of my research, I conclude that the task force reform represents a substantial paradigm shift in female federal corrections and follows the socialist feminist agenda to offer women increased choices and to reduce patriarchal control. The optimistic position is that law reform will work towards crime prevention by redressing gender, class, and race inequities and by addressing what acts are criminalized. This long-term agenda will not be realized, however, unless a feminist jurisprudence continues to be responsible for the design and implementation of federal corrections for women.

CONCLUSION

As mentioned at the outset, female offenders' backgrounds are characterized by poverty, abuse, and dysfunctional families. Because the criminal acts of women are the result of problems stemming from their unequal socio-economic and gender statuses, the long-term solution to the problem of women in prisons is in communities where inequality between sexes, races, and classes is eliminated. I have attempted to demonstrate that federal corrections in Canada are antithetical to the enhancement of women's status and therefore fail to deal with the problem of most female crime. Preventive community measures to eliminate abuse and poverty, and the gradual breakdown of sexist and racist practices and ideologies, present a socialist feminist political agenda for real justice. The task force report recommendations have the potential to improve situations of female offenders, particularly in response to the barbaric conditions at the Prison for Women. Regionalization, however, must be accompanied by a commitment to the eventual abolition of prisons and the reduction of lawbreaking behaviour by women by reducing inequalities that make crime understandable.

This chapter has sought to uncover the patriarchal definitions of womanhood inherent in the federal prison and the correctional system of Canada. I have suggested that the traditional correctional paradigm and theories about women and crime are part of the historical social control of women through

(1) their failure to challenge oppressive patriarchal norms; (2) labelling women pathological or abnormal for not following traditional roles for women; and (3) defining women's role as primarily reproductive. The next challenge is to identify other formal and informal mechanisms that reinforce patriarchal definitions of womanhood, including women's responsibility for unpaid reproductive tasks, and economic exploitation within familial roles and in the workforce. Part of this challenge includes an assessment of the regional correctional facilities for women to insure that the new model represents a paradigm shift from a White male correctional model to a woman-centred treatment approach predicated on increasing women's choices in the economic and social realms.

FURTHER READINGS

Carlen, P. 1992a. 'Women, Crime, Feminism and Realism'. In *Realism Criminology: Crime Control and Policing in the 1990s*, edited by J. Lowman and B.D. MacLean, 203–20. Toronto: University of Toronto Press.

_____. 1992b. 'Criminal Women and Criminal Justice: The Limits to, and Potential of, Feminist and Left Realism Perspectives'. In *Issues in Realist Criminology*, edited by R. Matthews and J. Young, 51–69. London: Sage Publications.

Faith, K. 1993. *Unruly Women: The Politics of Confinement and Resistance*. Vancouver: Press Gang.

LaPrairie, C. 1993. 'Aboriginal Women and Crime in Canada: Identifying the Issues'. In *Women in Conflict with the Law: Women and the Canadian Justice System*, edited by E. Adelberg and C. Currie, 235–44. Vancouver: Press Gang.

Shaw, M. 1993. 'Reforming Federal Women's Imprisonment'. In *Women in Conflict with the Law: Women and the Canadian Justice System*, edited by E. Adelberg and C. Currie, 50–68. Vancouver: Press Gang.

REFERENCES

Adelberg, E., and C. Currie. 1987a. 'In Their Own Words'. In *Too Few to Count: Canadian Women in Conflict with the Law*. Vancouver: Press Gang.

_____. 1987b. *Too Few to Count: Canadian Women in Conflict with the Law*. Vancouver: Press Gang.

Adler, F. 1975. *Sisters in Crime*. New York: McGraw-Hill.

Armstrong, S. 1991. 'P4W: Lockup = Breakdown: A Formula for Despair at the Prison for Women'. In *Homemakers* (September):12–30.

Black, D. 1992. 'Women's Report' (Spring). Ottawa: House of Commons.

Boyd, S., and E. Sheehy. 1986. 'Canadian Feminist Perspectives on Law:

Summary and Bibliography'. Presented to ECCLS Conference Theory and Practice: Feminist Perspectives on Law, 3–5 April.

Brickey, S., and E. Comack. 1986. *The Social Basis of Law: Critical Readings in the Sociology of Law*. Toronto: Garamond Press.

Canadian Advisory Council on the Status of Women. 1979. *Ten Years Later*. Ottawa: Canadian Advisory Council on the Status of Women.

Canadian Association of Elizabeth Fry Societies. 1978. *Brief on the Female Offender*. Ottawa: Canadian Association of Elizabeth Fry Societies.

_____. 1988. *Sentencing in Context: Revealing the Realities of Women in Conflict with the Law*. Ottawa: Canadian Association of Elizabeth Fry Societies.

Canadian Committee on Corrections. 1969. *Report of the Canadian Committee on Corrections* (Quimet Report). Ottawa: Queen's Printer.

Canadian Corrections Association. 1968. *Brief on the Woman Offender*. Ottawa: Canadian Corrections Association.

Canadian Corrections Service. 1978. *Progress Report on the Federal Female Offender Program*. Ottawa: Canadian Corrections Service.

Canadian Federation of University Women. 1978. *Brief on the Woman Offender*. Montreal: Canadian Federation of University Women.

Caputo, T.C., et al., eds. 1989. *Law and Society: A Critical Perspective*. Toronto: Harcourt Brace Jovanovich.

Carlen, P. 1983. *Women's Imprisonment: A Study in Social Control*. London, Boston, Melbourne, and Henley: Routledge and Kegan Paul.

_____. 1988. *Women, Crime and Poverty*. Milton Keynes, UK/Philadelphia: Open University Press.

_____. 1990. *Alternatives to Women's Imprisonment*. Buckingham, UK: Open University Press.

_____. 1992a. 'Criminal Women and Criminal Justice; The Limits to, and Potential of, Feminist and Left Realist Perspectives'. In *Issues in Realist Criminology*, edited by R. Matthews and J. Young, 51–69. London: Sage Publications.

_____. 1992b. 'Women, Crime, Feminism, and Realism'. In *Realist Criminology: Crime Control and Policing in the 1990s*, edited by J. Lowman and B.D. MacLean, 203–20. Toronto: University of Toronto Press.

Civil Liberties Association of Canada. 1978. *Brief to the Solicitor General*. Ottawa: Civil Liberties Association of Canada.

Coles, D. 1979. *Nova Scotia Corrections: An Historical Perspective*. Halifax: Communications Project in Criminal Justice, Correctional Services Division.

Comack, E. 1987. 'Theorizing on the Canadian State and Social Formation'. In *State Control: Criminal Justice Politics in Canada*, edited by R.S. Ratner and J.L. McMullan, 225–40. Vancouver: University of British Columbia Press.

Committee Appointed to Inquire into the Principles and Procedures
    Followed in the Remission Service of the Department of Justice of
    Canada. 1956. *Report of the Committee Appointed to Inquire into the
    Principles and Procedures Followed in the Remission Service of the
    Department of Justice of Canada* (Fateux Report). Ottawa: Supply and
    Services.
Cooper, S. 1987. 'The Evolution of the Federal Women's Prison'. In
    Too Few to Count: Canadian Women in Conflict with the Law, edited by
    E. Adelberg and C. Currie, 127–45. Vancouver: Press Gang.
Correctional Service Canada. 1990. *Creating Choices: The Report of the Task
    Force on Federally Sentenced Women*. Ottawa: Correctional Service
    Canada.
Cowie, J., V. Cowie, and E. Slater. 1968. *Delinquency in Girls*. New York:
    Humanities Press Inc.
Currie, D. 1986. 'Female Criminality: A Crisis in Feminist Theory'. In
    The Political Economy of Crime, edited by B. MacLean, 232–46. Toronto:
    Prentice-Hall.
_____. 1992. 'Abortion Law Reform: A Pendulum That Swings One Way'.
    In *Rethinking the Administration of Justice*, edited by D. Currie and
    B. MacLean, 60–85. Halifax: Fernwood Publishing.
_____, and B. MacLean, eds. 1992. *Rethinking the Administration of Justice*.
    Halifax: Fernwood Publishing.
Curtis, D., et al. 1985. *Kingston Penitentiary: The First Hundred and Fifty
    Years: 1835–1985*. Ottawa: Canadian Government Publishing Centre,
    Supply and Services Canada.
Dahl, T., and A. Snare. 1978. 'The Coercion of Privacy: A Feminist
    Perspective'. In *Women, Sexuality and Social Control*, edited by B. Smart
    and C. Smart. London: Routledge and Kegan Paul.
Dalton, K. 1978. 'Menstruation and Crime'. In *Crime in Society*, edited by
    L.D. Savitz and N. Johnston, 259–62. New York: John Wiley.
Delphy, C. 1977. *The Main Enemy*. London: Women's Research and
    Resources Centre.
Department of Justice. 1956. *The Committee Appointed to Inquire into the
    Principles and Procedures Followed in the Remission Service of the Department
    of Justice of Canada* (Fateux Committee). Ottawa: Minister of Supply and
    Services.
Department of the Secretary State of Canada. 1988. *Convention on the
    Elimination of All Forms of Discrimination Against Women*. Ottawa:
    Minister of Supply and Services.
Directors of Penitentiaries. 1870–3. 'Annual Report of the Directors of
    Penitentiaries of the Dominion of Canada for the Years 1868, 1870,
    1871, 1872' in *Sessional Papers no. 5, 27, 60, 75*. Ottawa: I.B. Taylor.

Duffy, A., and N. Mandell. 1994. 'The Widening Gap: Social Inequality and Poverty'. In *Canadian Society: Understanding and Surviving in the 1990s*, edited by D. Glenday and A. Duffy, 49–85. Toronto: McClelland and Stewart.

Eisenstein, Z. 1979. *Capitalist Patriarchy and the Case for Socialist Feminism*. New York: Monthly Review Press.

Ekstedt, J.W., and C.T. Griffiths. 1988. *Corrections in Canada: Policy and Practice*, 2nd ed. Toronto and Vancouver: Butterworths.

Elliot, L., and R. Morris. 1987. 'Behind Prison Doors'. In *Too Few to Count: Canadian Women in Conflict with the Law*, edited by E. Adelberg and C. Currie, 145–61. Vancouver: Press Gang.

Flemming, D., and K. Pate. 1992. 'News Release', (18 June).

Gavigan, S. 1987. 'Women's Crime: New Perspectives and Old Theories'. In *Too Few to Count: Canadian Women in Conflict with the Law*, edited by E. Adelberg and C. Currie, 23–46. Vancouver: Press Gang.

Globe and Mail. 1990a. 'Close Women's Penitentiary, Government Task Force Urges' (21 April):A4.

————. 1990b. 'Women Charge Discrimination at Prison' (23 June):A4.

Gregory, J. 1986. 'Sex, Class and Crime: Towards a Non-Sexist Criminology'. In *The Political Economy of Crime*, edited by B. MacLean, 317–35. Toronto: Prentice-Hall.

Heney, J.H. 1990. *Report on Self-Injurious Behavior in the Kingston Prison for Women*, rev. Ottawa: Correctional Service of Canada.

Hoffman-Bustamente, D. 1973. 'The Nature of Female Criminality'. In *Issues in Criminology* no. 2 (Fall).

House of Assembly. 1833–9. *Journals of the House of Assembly*.

Inspector of Charitable Institutions. 1884–1912. 'Inspector of Charitable Institutions Annual Reports'. In *Ontario Sessional Papers, 1884–1912*. Ottawa: Inspector of Charitable Institutions.

Inspectors of Penitentiaries. 1912/13–1919/20. 'Annual Report of the Inspectors of Penitentiaries for the Fiscal Year 1912–1918. In *Office of the Inspectors of Penitentiaries Report*. Ottawa: Printer to the King's Most Excellent Majesty.

Jackson, M. 1988. *Justice Behind the Walls*. Ottawa: Canadian Bar Association.

Johnson, H. 1987. 'Getting the Facts Straight: A Statistical Overview'. In *Too Few to Count: Canadian Women in Conflict with the Law*, edited by E. Adelberg and C. Currie, 11–22. Vancouver: Press Gang.

Joint Committee to Study Alternatives for the Housing of the Federal Female Offender. 1978. *Report of the Joint Committee to Study Alternatives for the Housing of the Federal Female Offender* (Chinnery Report). Ottawa: Department of Justice.

Justice and Solicitor General. 1988. *Taking Responsibility: Report of the Standing Committee on Justice and Solicitor General on Its Review of Sentencing, Conditional Release and Related Aspects of Corrections*. Ottawa: Second Session of the Thirty-third Parliament, August.

Kendall, K. 1988. 'Women and Mental Illness: Directions for Feminist Inquiry'. In *From the Margins to the Centre*, edited by D. Currie, 95–120. Saskatoon: College of Graduate Studies and Research Studies, Women's Studies Research Unit, University of Saskatchewan.

Kinsey, R., J. Lea, and J. Young. 1986. *Losing the Fight Against Crime*. London: Blackwell.

Labatt, M. 1990. 'Violence Against Women: An Epidemic and National Disgrace'. In *Newsletter: Federation of Women Teachers Associations of Ontario* 9, no. 3 (December 1990/January 1991):2–9.

Lavell, A. 1948. 'The History of Prisons of Upper Canada'. Mimeograph. Kingston: Queen's University.

Lea, J., and J. Young. 1984. *What Is to Be Done About Law and Order?* Harmondsworth: Penguin.

Legislative Assembly. 1840–9. *Journals of the Legislative Assembly*. Toronto: Clarkson W. James, Printer to the King's Most Excellent Majesty.

_____. 1849. *Journals of the Legislative Assembly*, Appendix BBBBB. Toronto: Clarkson W. James, Printer to the King's Most Excellent Majesty.

Leonard, E. 1982. *Women, Crime and Society: A Critique of Theoretical Criminology*. New York: Longman.

Lombroso, C., and W. Ferrero. 1895. *The Female Offender*. London: T. Fisher Unwin.

Lowman, J., and B.D. MacLean. 1992. 'Introduction: Left Realism, Crime Control, and Policing in the 1990s'. In *Realist Criminology: Crime Control and Policing in the 1990s*, edited by J. Lowman and B.D. MacLean, 3–29. Toronto: University of Toronto Press.

_____. 1992. *Realist Criminology: Crime Control and Policing in the 1990s*. Toronto: University of Toronto Press.

MacLean, B.D. 1986. *The Political Economy of Crime*. Toronto: Prentice-Hall.

Mannheim, H. 1979. 'The Sex Factor: Female Delinquency'. In *The Criminology of Deviant Women*, edited by F. Adler and R.J. Simon. Boston: Houghton Mifflin.

Marx, K. 1906. *Capital: A Critique of Political Economy*, edited by F. Engles. New York: Random House Inc.

_____, and F. Engels. 1939. *The German Ideology*. New York: International Publishers.

McMullan, J.L. 1987. 'Epilogue: Law, Justice, and the State'. In *State Control: Criminal Justice Politics in Canada*, edited by R.S. Ratner and

J.L. McMullan, 243–53. Vancouver: University of British Columbia Press.

Minister of Justice. 1877, 1878, 1880, 1882, 1887. 'Report of the Minister of Justice as to Penitentiaries in Canada for the Year Ended 1876, 1877, 1879, 1881, 1886'. In *Sessional Papers no. 4, 12, 15, 17*. Ottawa: Maden, Roger and Co.

_____. 1914, 1912/13–1919/20. *Minister of Justice as to Penitentiaries of Canada for the Fiscal Year Ended March 31, 1914, 1912/13–1919/20*.

Ministry of the Solicitor General. 1976. *Report of the National Advisory Committee on the Female Offender*. Ottawa: Solicitor General.

_____. 1978. *Report of the National Planning Committee on the Female Offender*, (Needham Report). Ottawa: Solicitor General.

_____. 1990. 'New Release: Notes for a Statement by the Solicitor General of Canada. The Honourable Pierre H. Cadieux at the News Conference Announcing the Government's Response to the Task Force on Federally Sentenced Women' (26 September). Ottawa: Solicitor General.

Mitchell, J. 1984. *Women: The Longest Revolution: Essays in Feminism, Literature and Psychoanalysis*. London: Virago Press.

Murray, L. 1989. *Prison Social Worker: Prison for Women Report*. Kingston: Kingston Penitentiary.

Office of the Commissioner of Penitentiaries. 1947/8–1950/1. 'Annual Report of the Commissioner of the Penitentiaries for the Fiscal Year Ended 1952–1956'. In *Office of the Commissioner of Penitentiaries Report*. Ottawa: Printer to the King's Most Excellent Majesty.

_____. 1951/2–1955/6. 'Annual Report of the Commissioner of the Penitentiaries for the Fiscal Year Ended 1952–1956'. In *Office of the Commissioner of the Penitentiaries Report*. Ottawa: Queen's Printer and Controller of Stationery.

_____. 1956/7–1959/60. 'Annual Report of the Commissioner of the Penitentiaries for the Fiscal Year Ended 1957–1970'. In *Office of the Commissioner of Penitentiaries Report*. Ottawa: Queen's Printer and Controller of Stationery.

_____. 1960/1–1964/5. 'Annual Report of the Commissioner of the Penitentiaries for the Fiscal Year Ended 1961-1965'. In *Office of the Commissioner of Penitentiaries Report*. Ottawa: Kingston Penitentiary.

_____. 1967. *Annual Report of the Commissioner of Penitentiaries for the Fiscal Year Ended March 31, 1967*. Ottawa: Queen's Printer and Controller of Stationery.

Office of the Inspectors of Penitentiaries. 1909/10–1911/12. 'Report of the Minister of Justice as to Penitentiaries of Canada for the Fiscal Year Ended 1910–1912'. In *Office of the Inspectors of Penitentiaries Report*. Ottawa: Printer to the King's Most Excellent Majesty.

Pollak, O. 1961. *The Criminality of Women*. New York: A.S. Barnes.

_____. 1979. 'The Masked Character of Female Crime'. In *The Criminology of Deviant Women*, edited by F. Adler and R.J. Simon. Boston: Houghton Mifflin.

Prince Albert Herald. 1990a. 'Dad Tells of Finding Daughter Dead in Kingston Penitentiary' (14 March):3.

_____. 1990b. 'Three Prisoner Suicides at Kingston in the Past Year and All Three Were Native Women from Saskatchewan' (March).

_____. 1990c. 'Local Native Woman Kills Self in Kingston' (17 September):1.

_____. 1990d. 'P.A. Woman's Suicide Sorrows Fellow Prisoners, Kingston Jail Staff' (18 September):3.

Ratner, R.S., and J.L. McMullen. 1987. *State Control: Criminal Justice Politics in Canada*. Vancouver: University of British Columbia Press.

_____, J.L. McMullen, and B.E. Burtch. 1987. 'The Problem of Relative Autonomy and Criminal Justice in the Canadian State'. In *State Control: Criminal Justice Politics in Canada*, edited by R.S. Ratner and J.L. McMullen, 85–125. Vancouver: University of British Columbia Press.

Report on the State and Management of the Female Prison. 1921.

Royal Commission of Labour and Capital. 1889. Ottawa: Royal Commission of Labor and Capital.

Royal Commission on Penitentiaries. 1914. *Report of the Royal Commission on Penitentiaries, Sessional Paper no. 252*. Ottawa: Royal Commission on Penitentiaries.

Royal Commission on the Status of Women. 1970. *Report of the Royal Commission on the Status of Women*. Ottawa: Information Canada.

Royal Commission to Inquire and Then Report Upon the Conduct, Economy, Discipline and Management of the Provincial Penitentiary. 1849. *Report of the Royal Commission to Inquire and Then Report on the Conduct, Economy, Discipline and Management of the Provincial Penitentiary* (Brown Report). Ottawa: King's Printer.

Royal Commission to Investigate the Penal System of Canada. 1938. *Report of the Royal Commission to Investigate the Penal System of Canada* (Archambault Report). Ottawa: Printer to the King's Most Excellent Majesty.

Schwartz, M., and W.S. DeKeseredy. 1991. 'Left Realist Criminology: Strengths, Weaknesses and the Feminist Critique'. *Crime, Law and Social Change* 1, no. 15 (January):51–72.

Shaw, M. 1989. *The Federal Female Offender: Report on a Preliminary Study*. Ottawa: Solicitor General.

_____. 1990. *What You Said: A Report Back to All Federal Women on the 1989 Survey of Your Views*. Under contract to the Secretariat of the Ministry of the Solicitor General and the Survey Team.

_____, and K. Rogers. 1990. *Survey of Federally Sentenced Women: Report to the Task Force on the Prison Survey, Final Report*. Ottawa: Solicitor General of Canada.

_____, et al. 1989. 'Survey of Federally Sentenced Women'. Prepared under contract for the Ministry of the Solicitor General, Ottawa.

Smart, C. 1976. *Women, Crime and Criminology: A Feminist Critique*. London, Henley, and Boston: Routledge and Kegan Paul.

Socialist Worker. 1991. 'Racist Horror at Kingston Pen—Inmates Fight Back' (March):1.

Standing Committee on Justice and Solicitor General. 1988. *Report on the Standing Committee on Justice and Solicitor General on Its Review of Sentencing, Conditional Release and Related Aspects of Corrections*. Ottawa: Standing Committee on Justice and Solicitor General.

Star Phoenix. 1991a. 'Dying to Get Out of P4W: In Kingston's Prison for Women Some Natives Find Death a Form for Liberation' (23 March):'Prism', 1–2.

_____. 1991b. 'Life and Death in P4W: Victims Couldn't Cope with Despair' (23 March):'Prism', 2.

_____. 1991c. 'Woman Hanged Self in Cell, Coroner's Inquest Told' (13 June):A18.

Statistics Canada. 1990. 'Women in the Justice System'. In *Women in Canada: A Statistical Report*, 2nd ed., (February), Cat. 89–503E. Ottawa: Statistics Canada.

Status of Women Canada. 1987. *Fact Sheets: Nairobi Forward-Looking Strategies for the Advancement of Women: Issues and the Canadian Situation*. Ottawa: Status of Women Canada.

_____. 1992. *Women's Report*. Ottawa: Status of Women Canada.

Sub-Committee on the Penitentiary System in Canada. 1977. *Report to Parliament by the Sub-Committee on the Penitentiary System in Canada* (Parliamentary Report). Ottawa: Supply and Services.

Sugar, F., and L. Fox. 1990. 'Survey of Federally Sentenced Aboriginal Women in the Community'. Prepared on behalf of the Native Women's Association of Canada for submission to the Task Force on Federally Sentenced Women. Ottawa: Native Women's Association of Canada.

Superintendent of Penitentiaries. 1912/13–1919/20. 'Annual Report of the Superintendent of Penitentiaries for the Fiscal Year Ended 1919–1920'. In *Office of the Inspectors of Penitentiaries Report*. Ottawa: Printer to the King's Most Excellent Majesty.

_____. 1926/7–1935/6. 'Annual Report of the Superintendent of Penitentiaries for the Fiscal Year Ended 1927–1936'. In *Office of the Superintendent of Penitentiaries Report*. Ottawa: Printer to the King's Most Excellent Majesty.

_____. 1936/7–1945/6. 'Annual Report of the Superintendent of Penitentiaries for the Fiscal Year Ended 1937–1946'. In *Office of the Superinten-*

dent of Penitentiaries Report. Ottawa: Printer to the King's Most Excellent
   Majesty.
Taylor, I., P. Walton, and J. Young. 1973. The New Criminology: For a Social
   Theory of Deviance. London: Routledge and Kegan Paul.
_____, P. Walton, and J. Young. 1975. Critical Criminology. London:
   Routledge and Kegan Paul.
Thomas, W. 1967. The Unadjusted Girl. New York: Harper and Row.
Toronto Star. 1988. 'Jail Conditions to Blame for Suicide, Inmate Says'
   (8 December):A26.
Ursel, J. 1986. 'The State and the Maintenance of Patriarchy: A Case Study
   of Family, Labour and Welfare Legislation in Canada'. In Family,
   Economy and State: The Social Reproduction Process under Capitalism, edited
   by J. Dickinson and B. Russell, 150–91. Toronto: Garamond Press.
_____. 1992. Private Lives, Public Policy: 100 Years of State Intervention in the
   Family. Toronto: Women's Press.
Wine, S. 1992. A Motherhood Issue: The Impact of Criminal Justice System
   Involvement on Women and Their Children. Prepared on contract for the
   Corrections Branch, Ministry of the Solicitor General of Canada.
   Ottawa: Ministry of the Solicitor General.
Winnipeg Free Press. 1988. 'Tensions at Women's Prison Blamed for
   Convict's Suicide' (8 December).
Women for Justice. 1980. Brief to the Canadian Human Rights Commission.
   Ottawa: Women for Justice.

Part II

Health and Social Control

The chapters in this section of the book deal with medicine and its relationship to social control. As such, they address how conventional medical practice has come to define what constitutes disease on the basis of more than physical criteria. What these chapters reveal, then, are historical and contemporary examples of how the institution of medicine, by focusing on the individual body as the source of sickness, has employed socio-economic and political characteristics in the definition of health and well-being. In effect, the chapters illustrate how medicine has acted as a powerful force for the status quo and has had very little impact in changing the social and political nature of society.

In Chapter 6, Kathleen Kendall argues that the medical model of disease, which places the source of sickness within the individual body or mind, has structured the evolution of our modern-day concept of madness as sickness. The author traces the history of madness from Greek and Roman times to contemporary Canadian psychiatric practice. In so doing, she illustrates how science and its professional affiliations have competed for the right to administer and ultimately control peoples who are identifiable more so because of their sociocultural characteristics than because of their madness. She concludes that the ever-widening power of medical science has resulted in a society in which more and more forms of human conduct are seen as deviant and in need of some form of control. Her final arguments expose the controlling and perilous potential of knowledge and the possibilities that exist to resist the coercive domination of medical science. As this chapter unfolds, you will recognize the decidedly critical perspective that underlies the author's arguments and how more specific critical theories like Foucauldianism and several feminist theories inform the arguments.

In Chapter 7, Maticka-Tyndale and Bicher provide a comprehensive study of how conventional medicine has appropriated knowledge and control of women's physiology. The authors provide historical evidence that suggests that over time, medicine has seized much of the knowledge and therapy that is associated with reproduction and child care and has essentially constructed pregnancy and childbirth to be 'medical conditions' worthy of highly invasive intervention. The authors then extend the discussion to include mental health and the typical gendered medical approach to emotional distress. The final discussions in the chapter include a theoretical overview of psychiatry as an agent of social control and the authors place this social control argument in the context of gender and the medical construction and treatment of emotional distress. As with Kendall's chapter, the authors take a critical, social constructionist approach to social control, medicine, and gender and the reader will notice implicit references to feminist theories, to Foucault, and to postmodernism.

The last chapter in this section follows in the critical/feminist orientation of the previous chapters. Deborah Findlay presents a compelling argument that medicine has been influential in constructing the image of the typical healthy female body that is not only rare and all but impossible to achieve, but also medically and socially dangerous. Women's efforts to aspire to this publicized image result in illnesses such as eating disorders and in falling victim to potentially dangerous medical interventions that are intended to alter body shape. She presents a theoretically composite position that includes feminist, Marxist, and Foucauldian perspectives and the reader is challenged to discover and critique this theoretical position. Findlay concludes her chapter with a program for combatting the socially, psychically, and physically dangerous nature of medical practice and its influence on body appearance norms.

—6—

Mental Illness—Tales of Madness: From the Asylum to 'Oprah'

Kathleen Kendall

INTRODUCTION

Stories about the evolution of psychiatry generally have happy endings. The mad are depicted as 'damsels in distress', victimized by the cruelty and ignorance of the community and the villainy of the asylum keepers. Psychiatrists are portrayed as 'knights in shining armour' who rescue the mad from the clutches of barbarism and combat ignorance through the forces of good: science, medicine, rationality, and humanitarianism. With the progression of knowledge, technology, and therapy, everyone lives happily ever after.

The story in this chapter is, however, a rather cautionary tale. It is woven together by many different themes: professional struggle for money, power, and prestige; changing theories of madness and numerous cures; people in search of purposeful meaning or answers to misery and despair; reform and resistance. The common thread is an insistent focus upon individual people for the cause, prevention, and treatment of madness to the exclusion of social, political, and economic factors. In this process of individualization, the political becomes reduced to the personal and structural sources of oppression are neglected and masked. The medical or disease model that underlies this practice has continually expanded and now encompasses virtually all aspects of our personal and social lives. This model is applied in very visible and exclusionary ways (as with the asylum), but can also be found in less obvious places, such as on television talk shows like 'Oprah'. Yet, even as the psychiatric net extends over us, we fail to recognize its hold. This is partially because therapeutic language disguises invasion, coercion, and control as 'help' and camouflages power relationships with claims of scientific neutrality. In this way, deviants are controlled 'for their own good' (allowing the public conscience to be assuaged), while the non-deviant are controlled as they voluntarily search for personal growth and fulfilment. Thus, under the mantle of psychiatry, social control operates through a myriad of means, including scapegoating individuals for social injustices, promoting individual rather than political analyses, and defining and enforcing acceptable behaviour.

In the contemporary Western world, symptoms of madness are generally understood to be expressions of disease within individual bodies or psyches. However, this medical model of madness has not always been the predominant explanation in the West and other cultures hold different beliefs regarding the origins of and remedy for madness. Conceptualizations of madness are always socially and historically specific and therefore we cannot assume their truth nor naturalness. Rather, we can look behind representations of madness for what they may reveal about the political and social context within which they are constructed. The ascendancy and expansion of the notion that madness is illness did not occur by evolutionary progress nor by chance.

The following overview describes and analyses changing conceptions of madness in the West, with an emphasis upon Canadian history. Professional contests over the definition and organization of madness is central to this history, and the use of professional power to manage marginalized populations reflects the racism, sexism, classism, and heterosexism within Canadian society. Some of the most visible examples of professional abuses of power include gynaecological operations on female asylum patients, the eugenics movement, and CIA involvement in sensory-drug experiments performed upon unsuspecting mental patients. The history of madness further reveals how such abuses can be confronted, challenged, and resisted as illustrated by the antipsychiatrists and the psychiatric inmates' liberation movements. Finally, the story of madness is indicative of the various manifestations of social control.

GREEK AND ROMAN MODELS OF MADNESS

Bennett Simon (1978) describes how many of the ideas within contemporary Western psychiatry are rooted within classical Greece. For example, Plato wrote about dream interpretation and unconscious motivation, which later became central to Freudian theory. Socrates also spoke of unconscious processes (Fernando 1991). However, historians have traditionally focused upon Hippocrates, the 'father of medicine', as central to the development of modern Western psychiatry. Hippocrates maintained that disease could be understood by natural rather than supernatural or cosmological explanations. Both somatic symptoms and madness were regarded as diseases and were explained by the humoral theory. This theory held that the body contained four humours: yellow bile, black bile, blood, and phlegm, and that diseases resulted from an imbalance in these humours. Madness was regarded as a consequence of humoral excess. Hippocrates identified melancholia, mania, epilepsy, and paranoia as the results of distinctive humoral imbalances (Zilboorg in Conrad and Schneider 1992:40). When treatments were applied, they were directed towards readjusting the humours. Interventions included a range of physical and psychotherapeutic remedies: rest, massage, bleeding, baths, recreation, mental exercises, purges, and beatings (Conrad and Schneider 1992; Rosen 1968). Roman medicine, with its emphasis upon empirical methods, further developed Greek knowledge. However, in Greece and subsequently in Rome, both supernatural and medical explanations of madness were followed: the former generally by the masses, and the latter by the intelligentsia and upper classes. Medical treatment for the mad was relatively rare in ancient Greece and Rome (Conrad and Schneider 1992; Rosen 1968).

THE MIDDLE AGES AND THE THEOLOGICAL MODEL OF MADNESS

As Conrad and Schneider (1992) write, the fall of the Roman empire led to a return to supernatural and mythological beliefs. While medieval physicians continued to extend the medical conception of madness, the dominant understanding was a theological one, informed by the Christian Church. The Church was very powerful throughout this period, and its reach extended into all aspects of human affairs. Seen through the theological lens, madness was defined as a punishment for sin, and exorcism was often the prescribed cure. A preoccupation with sin, evil, and the devil, which emerged during this time, reached its pinnacle from the fourteenth until the seventeenth century with devastating consequences. Numerous people accused of being witches were persecuted and killed during the Inquisition and organized witch-hunts. Many contemporary orthodox explanations regard those who were defined as witches as, in fact, the undiagnosed mad. Even as early as 1563, a physician, Johann Wyer, argued that those accused of practising witchcraft were suffering from a mental disease rather than being inherently evil or possessed by the devil. The witchhunts ended partly because physicians insisted that behaviour deemed demonic was actually illness. The humanitarianism and enlightenment of those early physicians is said to have fostered psychiatry, which then replaced the brutality and ignorance of the inquisitors (Conrad and Schneider 1992; Rosen 1968). This interpretation is disputed by Thomas Szasz (1970), who argues that psychiatry is an extension of, rather than an alternative to, the Inquisition. Szasz regards both the Inquisition and psychiatry as instruments of social control, each designed to protect the social order by creating scapegoats and eradicating dissent. Feminists have taken this argument further by claiming that most of those accused of witchcraft were powerful women—often healers and midwives—who posed a challenge to male power and privilege (Ussher 1991).

MADNESS AS MENTAL ILLNESS

As with other aspects of Graeco-Roman art and science, medicine was revived during the Renaissance. However, until the early nineteenth century, physician involvement with the mad was minimal (Conrad and Schneider 1992). Prior to the seventeenth century, the mad were very visible; they were either in the care of their families, or were allowed to roam the countryside or sailed along the waterways in 'ships of fools'. The public was familiar with the mad, and were involved in open discussions and debates about madness (Foucault 1965).

In the middle of the seventeenth century, with the developing capitalist order, a very different approach was taken towards the mad. Foucault (1965) refers to this period as the 'great confinement' because it marks the beginning of exclusionary responses to the mad. In 1656, the Hôpital Général opened in Paris to house the mad and other marginalized people, such as the idle, the poor, and the unemployed. Approximately 1 per cent of the city's population were confined. The Hôpital Général and similar establishments were created not for treatment but primarily as means of coping with the poor. Those confined within the institutions were subjected to hard physical labour and lived under brutal conditions, yet such treatment was considered appropriate because the imprisoned were thought to be devoid of reason. As reason was understood to be that which separated humans from other living creatures, those lacking in reason were regarded as having lost their humanity, and were therefore regarded and treated as animals. Poverty, despair, idleness, and madness were all interpreted as symptoms of unreason. In this way, the poor, desperate, idle, and mad became defined as non-human and, as such, it made sense for them to be taken out of mainstream society (Foucault 1965; Ingleby 1983).

The institutions provided important functions for the new capitalist system. Confinement prevented uprisings against the emerging order (those protesting could be defined as mad); insured a steady supply of workers (those not working could be considered idle); and instilled within the population the values necessary for a productive workforce (such as hard work and discipline) (Conrad and Schneider 1992; Foucault 1965; Scull 1979).

Gradually the mad were separated from the rest of the confined because they were seen as disruptive to institutional order and control. This eventually led to the establishment of numerous private madhouses throughout England in the eighteenth century. These houses were typically owned and run by physicians, even though at the time they did not possess any special knowledge about madness, nor could they offer any remedy for its cure. Physicians were attracted by the lucrative nature of their involvement with the madhouses (Scull 1979). In England in 1774, a physician's certificate was mandatory for committal to a madhouse. Prior to this time, all that was required was a magistrate's judgement (Conrad and Schneider 1992). Within the houses, the mad lived in very harsh conditions that included physical restraints and violence.

In the early nineteenth century, a reform movement emerged that called for a coordinated system of public asylums and their inspection. Conventional accounts of this campaign regard it as a humanitarian enterprise exemplified by Philippe Pinel in France and William Tuke in England. Both of these men sought to replace the physical brutality and constraint within the asylums with 'moral treatment'. In general, those advocating moral treatment contended that through kindness and gentle coercion, the values associated with disciplined labour could be instilled in the mad, and once the mad acquired this work ethic, they could then become productive members of society. Whereas the previous paradigm regarded the mad as non-human and therefore incapable of rationality, the reformers viewed the mad as lacking in self-discipline and therefore capable of change through resocialization. In England the reformers' goals for the creation of publicly financed and controlled asylums were codified into law in 1845 (Ingleby 1983; Scull 1979).

Scull (1979) views the reform movement as inspired by the economy—the rise of wage labour in particular—rather than motivated by compassion. He argues that the new public asylums and the moral treatment philosophy provided certain advantages to the bourgeois entrepreneurs and industrialists. The madhouses were questioned as the horrible conditions within them were made public, yet it was still necessary to segregate non-working people from the rest of society for the following reasons. First, it deterred those capable of working from malingering, it provided an opportunity to instil the necessary work ethos into the confined, and it was more efficient than domestic relief. However, as the mad were a threat to institutional order and control, they had to be separated from others who were confined. With its emphasis upon caring and compassion, the moral treatment model helped to counter claims of abuse and thus prevent enforced closure of madhouses on the grounds of cruelty. The benign appearance of the new model was also much more acceptable to the families of potential inmates. Second, the moral treatment philosophy provided legitimation for segregating the mad because a 'cure' (good work habits) could be promised. Third, the work ethos that was necessary to the capitalist system was further perpetuated. Finally, the management of institutions was much more effective through psychological rather than physical means. This emphasis upon psychological control mirrored developments elsewhere in the developing capitalist system (Ingleby 1983).

During this period, physicians began to dominate the treatment of madness. Scull (1979) analyses this achievement within the context of professionalism. As outlined by Freidson (1970), the ability to establish professional status requires monopoly over a particular set of services, acquiring authority over qualifications and training, and possessing unique knowledge and skills. Physicians began this process of professionalism with the expansion of the asylum system. The segregation of the mad into madhouses and asylums created the opportunity for an occupational group to claim expertise over their care and treatment. Physicians were already involved in managing the madhouses, but the increasing number of asylums following the reformers' demands provided greater scope for involvement. However, the philosophy of moral treatment did not readily reconcile with medicine. As with the custodial model before it, physicians could not demonstrate that their methods had any therapeutic value other than the provision of care for physical afflictions. They therefore argued that both physical and moral treatments were necessary for recovery, and because only physicians held legitimate authority over medical treatment, it was logical that they should also govern or, at the very least, supervise moral treatment (Scull 1989).

A series of parliamentary acts were passed in England between 1816 and 1845 to insure that physicians had legal authority over the regulation of madhouses and asylums. That the physicians were able to convince Parliament to grant them such power was not because they possessed unique knowledge or a cure but because they were able to organize and lobby effectively. Although there was little medical justification, physicians' dominance insured that madness became equated with illness. Thus despite any evidence to support a medical interpretation, the medical model of madness became public policy. In this sense, physicians made the treatment of madness their domain and this control has since consolidated and expanded (Conrad and Schneider 1992; Scull 1989).

While physicians were guaranteeing their privileged position within the madhouses and public asylums, the moral treatment regime soon disappeared. For economic reasons, the asylums were built to hold a large population. The large number of confined people under the care of a small, unskilled staff made moral treatment unfeasible. The harsh conditions against which the moral treatment reformers campaigned once again became standard (Conrad and Schneider 1992).

CANADIAN ASYLUMS

In accordance with British provisions for the creation of public asylums, in 1839 the Upper Canada legislative assembly authorized the construction of an asylum in Toronto. However, it was not until 1850 that a permanent building was completed. Over the next thirty years a network of public asylums was quickly established. Similar to British reforms, various Canadian legislation mandated physician involvement at several levels. For example, all asylums had to be inspected by a board of justices and at least one physician (Warsh 1989). Committal required a medical certificate or a lieutenant-governor's warrant. For a medical certificate to be issued, two or three physicians had to agree on a diagnosis of insanity following independent examinations. The warrant procedure was a legal imperative that allowed the imprisonment of people considered dangerous until they were medically examined. Following a medical examination, if a person was diagnosed as insane, he or she would be committed to an asylum when there was a vacancy. People under a lieutenant-governor's warrant were given priority over certificate cases for admittance into an asylum because of their perceived danger. Consequently, families frequently declared a person as dangerous in order to insure committal through the warrant system (Mitchinson 1991:303).

Physicians' dominance over asylums was further consolidated by the fact that superintendents were practising physicians. Despite the extent of physician involvement, there was no medically based explanation for madness, nor was there any medical treatment available within the asylums. Canadian asylums followed the same general patterns as asylums in Britain: the replacement of physical restraint and punishment with moral treatment, which was followed by overcrowding, understaffing, a chronic population, and deteriorating facilities (Mitchinson 1991; Warsh 1989:4).

Moral treatment was implemented in the second half of the nineteenth century in Canada. While not eliminating mechanical restraint, the introduction of moral treatment reduced the use of physical bonds. Restraint was much more commonly used on women than men. There is little evidence to indicate that women were more violent than men, but they were considered to be more unmanageable. This perceived unmanageability may have stemmed from the very limited nature of activities and work available to women to keep them occupied. Work and recreation were segregated by sex, and women were disadvantaged in both areas (Mitchinson 1991).

Having defined work as therapy, the moral treatment philosophy emphasized that the essential value of work lay in its potential for instilling discipline and good work habits in the mad. A willingness to work and good work performance were thus interpreted as signs of recovery. Men's work typically involved outdoor labour (i.e., cleaning the stables, gardening, painting, etc.), while women's work was more limited and domestic in nature (i.e., sewing, sweeping, dishwashing, etc.) (Mitchinson 1991:327). Although the therapeutic value of the work undertaken is dubious, it is clear that such work benefited the maintenance of asylums through guaranteed cheap and efficient labour (Mitchinson 1991).

If women's work did not provide them with the opportunity to be outdoors, neither did the recreation offered to them. While men could play cricket or ball and engage in other outdoor activities, women were expected to carry out their recreation indoors. Even when indoors, women were disadvantaged by limited activities and less leisure time for amusement. Since men's work was outdoors, it usually ended daily with the setting sun, and was often cancelled due to poor weather conditions. Women's work, however, was not generally influenced by the outdoor environment and therefore continued rain or shine, day and night. This left women with little time for recreation or leisure (Mitchinson 1991).

Despite the concrete changes associated with the partial removal of constraint and the introduction of work therapy, the functioning of asylums remained primarily custodial, providing the basics of food, clothing, and shelter (Mitchinson 1991). While physicians were the gatekeepers and guardians of asylums, they could still not claim any special knowledge regarding the care and treatment of the mad. Furthermore, staff were usually untrained attendants rather than trained nurses. As Mitchinson (1991:323) writes, 'If judged by their conditions of work, the care provided by the attendants must have been minimal.' Medical dominance over the mad was consolidated with the introduction of physical treatments. If madness was caused by physical disease and therefore required somatic intervention, asylum physicians could finally legitimate their involvement and integrate themselves into the mainstream of medicine.

SOMATIC TREATMENTS

Inspired by advances in somatic medicine, psychiatrists (asylum physicians) began to look for physiological explanations of madness. In the last decades of the nineteenth century, advances in bacteriorology provided medicine with a scientific basis. Anaesthesia and antisepsis allowed great progress to be made in surgery. Koch and Pasteur's 'germ theory of disease' maintained that disease could be caused by introducing a single specific factor—a pathogenic micro-organism—into a healthy body. Following that, it was assumed that all diseases have a specific cause that can be discovered by examining the body's biochemical and physiological functioning while ignoring the social, psychological, and behavioural dimensions of disease. The notion that diseases evolve from a specific physical cause is the basis of the medical model guiding contemporary medical practice (Dubos 1959; Kelman 1977). The medical model and the new methods of laboratory science enabled physicians to legitimate their medical practices because they could claim to hold special curative knowledge and ability.

General paresis provided the first direct application of the medical model to madness. General paresis was said to be a kind of madness caused by neurological deterioration in third-stage syphilis. With this link between madness and physiology, physicians could rationalize their involvement in the asylums and thereafter madness became equated with mental illness. It was believed that if a physical cause was found for one form of madness, modern medicine would eventually find a cause for all of them (Conrad and Schneider 1992).

Once the medical model was applied to madness, psychiatrists engaged in numerous somatic cures, such as leeching and crude electrical treatments. Within the asylum, one of the more frequent interventions was gynaecological surgery. While such surgery was not uncommon outside of the asylum, those inside provided physicians with a captive clientele who could be operated upon without consent. During the nineteenth century, female reproduction became defined as inherently pathological. The female life cycle, linked to reproduction, was regarded as fraught with biological crises during which periods of insanity arose. Women's madness was thought to be cured by surgical removal of the cervix, ovaries, and clitoris (Mitchinson 1991; Ussher 1991).

Gynaecological surgery became central to the treatment of women housed in Canadian asylums. In the London asylum, for example, superintendent Richard Maurice Bucke and his surgeon in charge, A.T. Hobbs, instituted gynaecological surgery as a fairly common form of treatment. Prior to surgery, Hobbs would perform pelvic examinations. If a woman resisted, she would be anaesthetized and the examination would take place while she was unconscious. Such examinations led Bucke and Hobbs to conclude that 96 per cent of the women inside the London asylum in 1896 suffered from diseased ovaries, uterus, or both (Mitchinson 1991:336). In a 1898 report, Hobbs concluded 'that perhaps one-sixth if not one-fourth of all the women in asylums for insane are there because of the special infirmities of their sex and the disasters and penalties of their lives as wives and mothers' (cited in Mitchinson 1991:336). A vast array of surgeries, such as abdominal hysterectomy and curettage, were carried out (Mitchinson 1991). According to a 1896 report, 107 different surgical procedures were conducted on forty-seven women (Mitchinson 1991:336). Bucke and Hobbs enthusiastically promoted gynaecological surgeries in Canadian medical journals, and boasted a recovery rate of 51 per cent among the female mad due to the curative powers of surgical intervention (Mitchinson 1991:338).

The medicalization of women's reproduction provided physicians who worked inside and outside the asylum with an opportunity to widen their domain and eliminate competition (Ehrenreich and English 1973). For psychiatrists in particular, it provided legitimacy for their control over the mad. Physicians were not as concerned with linking men's madness to their sexuality, except for the belief that masturbation was a common cause of male madness. While females were generally thought to have little sexual feeling, the male sex drive was perceived as strong, potentially harmful, and difficult to control. Mitchinson (1991:111) describes various methods designed to stop male masturbation. One device, designed to fit over the penis, consisted of a leather ring with metallic points. If the penis were erect, the pressure would create a great deal of pain. Other measures documented in America included circumcision, castration, and the application of plaster over the genitals.

Physicians continued to search for somatic causes of mental illness. In the 1930s, this quest led physicians to invent three types of shock treatments (insulin-coma, metrazol-convulsion, and electroconvulsive shock) and psychosurgery. As Valenstein (1986:45) states, theoretical attempts describing the treatments' rationale were so vague that it was difficult to take them seriously. Also, the adverse effects of these interventions were often severe and sometimes fatal. Nevertheless, each therapy was applied enthusiastically soon after discovery, and both the medical profession and the press avidly promoted the treatments. Their use was quite widespread throughout the 1940s and 1950s, but only electroconvulsive shock therapy continues to be applied to any great extent today (Valenstein 1986).

Insulin-coma therapy used insulin injections to induce hypoglycaemia, including convulsions and coma. It was invented in 1929 by Manfred Sakel, a Viennese physician who noticed apparent improvement in a drug-addicted patient following a coma that resulted from an accidental overdose of insulin. Initially Sakel advocated the use of insulin-coma for the treatment of drug addictions, but later recommended that it be applied to the treatment of schizophrenia. Over the subsequent two decades, insulin-coma therapy was used quite frequently on those diagnosed as schizophrenic (Valenstein 1986).

The metrazol-convulsion shock treatment was also used extensively as a cure for schizophrenia. Reported in 1935 by Ladislas von Meduna at the University of Budapest, metrazol-convulsion shock functioned in a similar fashion to insulin-coma, but involved the injection of metrazol rather than insulin. It also received wide recognition and application (Valenstein 1986).

Electroconvulsive shock, the third major convulsive therapy, was introduced by two Italian physicians, Ugo Cerletti and Lucio Bini, in 1938. This procedure involves attaching electrodes to a person's head. Electrical currents travel to the brain for a few seconds. The patient undergoes a fierce convulsion, loses consciousness, and has memory loss upon awakening (Conrad and Schneider 1992). The treatment is typically applied three times a week for up to ten sessions, and is used for a wide variety of symptoms (Breggin 1991). Despite its controversial nature, electroconvulsive shock continues to be widely used today, including in Canada, where it is estimated that 8,000 to 10,000 people undergo this treatment yearly (Burstow and Weitz 1988:317). Women are reported to receive electroconvulsive shock almost twice as often as men (Fine 1985; Smith and Richman 1984).

Psychosurgery uses various techniques to destroy brain tissue. This method was first introduced by neurosurgeon, Egas Moniz, in Portugal in 1935 when he drilled two holes into a patient's skull and injected absolute alcohol into the frontal lobes of the brain, thus destroying nerve cells. Moniz soon altered the technique. Instead of injecting alcohol, he used an instrument much like an apple corer to crush the nerve fibres of the brain. The operation was named prefrontal leucotomy (also known as lobotomy or prefrontal lobotomy) and spread rapidly throughout the world. In 1949, Moniz received the Nobel Prize in physiology and medicine for his discovery (Valenstein 1986).

Walter Freeman, an American neuropathologist and neuropsychiatrist, is regarded as the person most responsible for the wide adoption of psychosurgery. He performed numerous psychosurgeries throughout North America, including the transorbital lobotomy in which an instrument resembling an ice-pick was inserted through the eye socket behind the eyeball and into the frontal lobe of the brain (Valenstein 1986). The extent to which psychosurgical operations were carried out in Canada is not known, partly because of poor record keeping. However, psychosurgery is still legal and is performed in Canada, the United States, England, and elsewhere (Burstow and Weitz 1988).

Despite theoretical inadequacies and the adverse consequences of shock and psychosurgery, physicians were able to use these procedures to attain expert status in the treatment of madness. As physicians were the only ones legally qualified to perform surgery, they could claim a monopoly on the medical treatment of madness.

THE TALKING CURE

This medical monopoly over madness appeared to be challenged with the advent of Sigmund Freud's talking cure (psychoanalysis). Freud believed that the repression of internal impulses, such as sex and aggression, created mental symptoms, such as hysteria and other neurotic disorders. These impulses were thought to be suppressed by sociocultural forces (often parents) and then repressed into the unconscious. The cure for this psychogenic explanation of madness was a series of conversations between patient and analyst, during which the patient would talk about whatever came to mind, thus reliving and resolving past conflict within a safe environment. Rather than competing with the medical model, however, psychoanalysis was grafted onto it (Conrad and Schneider 1992).

Freud originally trained as a physician-neurologist and moved gradually from a somatically based theory of madness towards an intrapsychic one. It is perhaps therefore not surprising that elements of the medical model were infused within his framework: people were regarded as *patients* who had *illnesses* that *experts* attempted to *cure* (Conrad and Schneider 1992:53). Furthermore, as with physical therapies, the diagnosis and cure occurred in a consulting room while the patient lay in a supine position. With the focus on the patient, the explanation for madness was still very individualistic (Conrad and Schneider 1992:53). Today, the connection to medicine is further evidenced in the fact that to become trained in psychoanalysis, one typically must be a medical doctor. Also, while other professionals as well as non-professionals practise psychotherapy, Canadian government health insurance plans cover only medically trained professionals for the administration of this treatment (Burstow and Weitz 1988).

In the early decades of the twentieth century, somatic treatments were still dominant—psychoanalysis was limited to the treatment of less extreme symptoms of madness, and its application within the asylums was impractical given the large number of confined people and the small number of untrained staff, yet because of the way psychoanalysis merged with the medical model, it extended rather than replaced the notion that madness equalled illness. As will be discussed later in this chapter, Freud's discovery allowed for the growth and diversification of the disease model of madness by creating the conditions under which all kinds of deviant and conforming behaviours could be classified as diseases and therefore subjected to psychiatric-medical control (Conrad and Schneider 1992).

THE EUGENICS MOVEMENT

In Canada physicians further extended their reach during the first half of the twentieth century through the eugenics movement. The core philosophy of this movement was a belief that the human race could be improved through controlled breeding. Racist, classist, and xenophobic, many physicians and other professionals who advocated this movement supported and campaigned for policies and practices to prevent particular groups from reproducing. The eugenicists argued that the feeble-minded, the insane, and the criminal were to blame for most of society's problems and that their deviance was hereditary. Policies aimed at sterilization, immigration controls, sex instruction, intelligence testing, and birth control were all introduced in efforts to prevent 'race suicide' (McLaren 1990).

Physicians were the leading eugenics reformers, claiming that social problems were, in fact, medical ones, and that they could be contained by medical interventions. As McLaren (1990) writes, physicians were at least partially motivated by professional gains through their involvements. Driven by anti-immigrant sentiment, the eugenicists argued that the increasing numbers of people from other lands were not only creating massive social decay but that they were also lowering the fertility of Anglo-Saxon nationals by forcing them to limit their own family size in order to pay taxes that supported the immigrants. It was feared that the Anglo-Saxon race would be eventually overtaken by the 'genetically impaired' immigrants (McLaren 1990).

To support their arguments, reformers gathered nationwide 'scientific evidence' by examining files and conducting surveys within asylums, penitentiaries, orphanages, rescue homes, and other institutions. They claimed the results indicated that immigrants were greatly overrepresented among the deviant. For example, the United Farm Women of Alberta stated that in 1927, 75 per cent of provincial mental patients were immigrants (McLaren 1990:64). Armed with this information, the eugenicists demanded tighter restrictions at border crossings. Canada's first Immigration Act, enacted in 1869, contained provisions prohibiting the entry of 'idiots' and 'lunatics' into Canada, and a system of inspection has been implemented ever since (McLaren 1990). Nonetheless, it was felt that the controls were too lenient and eventually restrictions were introduced. While the eugenicists claimed victory for the large-scale closing of Canadian borders to the mentally ill following the election of the Conservative government in 1930, McLaren (1990) argues that the restrictions were more a consequence of the depression than a result of reformist pressures. Nonetheless, Canadian immigration policy and practice remained racist.

The Canadian National Committee for Mental Hygiene (CNCMH), a self-appointed body of experts who advised the government and business on mental health issues, declared that most deviants were driven to their actions through mental illness, an inherited disease, not because of social inequalities or adverse environmental conditions (McLaren 1990:110). The efforts of the CNCMH and other reform groups led to the passage of sterilization acts in Alberta and British Columbia. In 1928, the Sexual Sterilization Act in Alberta stated that 'mental defectives could, on the recommendation of a Eugenics Board and with the consent of the patient or guardian, be subject to sterilization' (McLaren 1990:100). By 1937, approximately 400 operations were performed, yet it was felt that more extreme measures were necessary, so the consent provision was removed. The act was enforced until 1971 and, until that time, 4,725 cases of sterilization were proposed and 2,822 were approved (McLaren 1990:159). As McLaren (1990:159–60) argues, the act was almost used solely to control marginalized populations: women comprised 64 per cent of those sterilized, 60 per cent were under twenty-five, most were unskilled or unemployed and single, and many were eastern Europeans. The racist application of these measures is clearly demonstrated by the fact that in the final years of the sterilization act, Indian and Métis people accounted for over 25 per cent of those sterilized, although they comprised only 2.5 per cent of Alberta's population (McLaren 1990:160).

British Columbia's sterilization law was passed in 1933, the same year that the Nazis began their racial hygiene campaigns in Germany. The act permitted the sterilization of anyone in a provincial institution who was diagnosed as retarded or mentally ill by a eugenics board comprised of a judge, social worker, and psychiatrist. The act remained in effect until 1971;

it is unknown how many people were sterilized during its existence. Although Ontario did not pass any sterilization laws, it was discovered in 1978 that hundreds of such operations were performed every year (McLaren 1990:169). The eugenics campaign was not a fringe movement but headed by prominent people in medicine, psychiatry, public health, social work, and genetics. Their actions reflected the racism, sexism, classism, and xenophobia of the time, and led to Draconian government policies against marginalized people. The reformers' actions were also self-serving because by claiming to possess expert knowledge, they made themselves indispensable and created new spheres of influence (McLaren 1990).

Physicians expanded and diversified their position and power through their involvements in gynaecological surgery, shock treatments, psychosurgery, psychoanalysis, and the eugenics movement. None of these was guided by concrete scientific rationale, most were cruelly invasive and used against marginalized sectors of society, and yet all received broad support and were widely implemented. Furthermore, physicians spread the medical model of madness into new realms, transforming more and more social problems and behaviours into diseases and creating new scapegoats. This process intensified the individuation of social problems by perpetuating individual rather than political analysis and change. Psychiatry could now safely move out of the asylum without losing its *raison d'être*.

COMMUNITY PSYCHIATRY AND PSYCHOTROPIC DRUGS

Following the Second World War, psychiatry successfully defined madness as mental illness and began to move out of the asylum and into the community. This transformation involved the swift depopulation of asylums and their closure, a rapid increase in general hospital psychiatric units, and the extensive development of community-based facilities (Dickinson and Andre 1988). Scull (1979) maintains that this shift was the result of cost-cutting measures arising from a 'fiscal crisis' as well a means to increase social control under advanced capitalism. However, as Dickinson and Andre (1988) argue, empirical evidence indicates that total state expenditures did not decrease. Rather, they contend that the creation of community psychiatry marked the beginning of a bifurcation process in which two distinct but related forms of psychiatric practice simultaneously expanded: 'the hospital-based private-sector psychiatric services system' and the 'mental health clinic-based, public sector psychiatric services system increasingly dominated by non-medically trained professionals such as psychologists and social workers' (Dickinson and Andre 1988:295). The authors argue that this process is rooted in the fact that mental illnesses are regarded as both biological and social/psychological (psychoanalytic) in nature. This ambiguity allows for treatment to occur in hospital and outside of hospital, enabling a wide range of professionals to compete for control over mental illness. Although professionals such as social workers and psychologists are not medically trained, they adhere to the individualistic and disease-based foundation of the medical model, as illustrated through their embrace and endorsement of the mental health concept (Dickinson and Andre 1988).

Cohen (1985) sees this bifurcation process as a means of establishing exclusionary and inclusionary forms of social control. Exclusionary forms include measures that isolate individuals from the rest of society, such as psychiatric wards, mental hospitals, and prisons. These institutions represent the hard side of control, and are used against the more recalcitrant members of society. The soft side of control is maintained through inclusionary means and appears to be expanding indefinitely. It is less visible and more encompassing because it involves mostly psychological management and is often voluntary. Examples of inclusionary social control measures are behaviour modification, self-actualizing therapies, transactional analysis, and self-help groups. Central to both the soft and the hard side of control is the disease model, which individualizes social problems as personal illnesses and therefore diverts attention from political understandings and actions.

Some writers maintain that community psychiatry occurred with the invention of psychotropic or mood-altering drugs because they rendered the asylum obsolete (Andre and Dickinson 1988). Primarily affecting a person's mind, these drugs produce symptom-'free' behaviour and manageable patients. Introduced in 1952, chlorpromazine was the first of these drugs, followed by numerous other psychotropics. Following aggressive advertising campaigns, mood-altering drugs were widely prescribed throughout North America and Europe, and their use superseded all other forms of treatment for mental illness. Because physicians had achieved a legal monopoly over the prescription of drugs, their involvement with mental illness was further consolidated with the introduction of psychotropics (Swazey 1974).

The prevalence of psychotropic drugs is shown in 1977 Saskatchewan data, which reveal that 20 per cent of drug plan beneficiaries received prescriptions for mood modifiers (Saskatchewan Health Joint Committee on Drug Utilization 1978). Mood modifiers also comprised the greatest proportion (almost 24 per cent) of all drugs dispensed in the province (Harding 1986). It has been estimated that between 67–72 per cent of all psychotropic drug prescriptions go to women (Harding 1986; Stephenson and Walker 1980). Lexchin (1984) argues that aggressive marketing strategies help to create a pattern of high prescription drug usage. Breggin (1991) catalogues numerous serious adverse reactions to these drugs, including tardive dyskinesia, a neurological disorder that causes uncontrollable movement of the voluntary muscles.

The invention of mood modifiers is thought to have revolutionized the treatment of mental illness by facilitating treatment of the mentally ill in the community rather than in the hospital. However, as discussed earlier, there are other contributing factors to the decline of asylums. Whatever the reason for the creation of community psychiatry, the consequence was an expansion and diversification of the medical model of madness and thus more penetrative and expansive mechanisms of social control.

CANADIAN PSYCHIATRY AND THE CIA

Psychiatry's potential for social control is illustrated by a real life Orwellian nightmare. During the late 1950s and early 1960s, a series of experiments were carried out by the late Ewen Cameron in the Allen Memorial Institute in Montreal. Cameron was president of the American Psychiatric Association (1953) and was also the first president of the World Psychiatric Association. A world-renowned and respected psychiatrist, he was also chairman of the psychiatry department at McGill University and director of the Allen Memorial Institute (Breggin 1991; Frank 1978).

While funded by the CIA, Cameron conducted brainwashing experiments on unsuspecting patients. He called his experiments 'depatterning' as they were designed to remove a person's memory and reprogram the patient. The treatments involved twice-daily applications of six electroconvulsive shocks, one after another. On average, thirty to forty shocks were administered. Cameron also subjected patients to psychic driving, in which hypnotic messages were repeated continuously for as long as sixteen hours; he also administered high doses of various mind-altering drugs, including LSD. The results were devastating as patients lost their memories, suffered severe brain damage, and were essentially infantilized (Marks 1980).

Masson (1990) contends that such abuses are common, indeed intrinsic to psychiatry. He describes numerous examples of physical, sexual, and emotional abuses incurred by patients while undergoing psychotherapy, often with well-recognized and well-regarded therapists. A 1991 Ontario task force on patient sexual abuse received 303 reports of such abuse (likely a conservative estimate) and described such psychological consequences as fear, depression, panic, intense anxiety, suicidal behaviour, self-mutilation, and damage to personal relationships (Independent Task Force on Sexual Abuse of Patients 1991).

THE ANTIPSYCHIATRY AND EX-PATIENT MOVEMENTS

During the 1960s, radical mental health professionals, patients, and ex-patients challenged psychiatry by publicizing psychiatric abuses, critiquing psychiatric theories and treatment, and offering alternatives. The antipsychiatrists included ex-psychiatrists and professionals, such as Thomas Szasz, R.D. Laing, and Thomas Scheff. Together they deconstructed psychiatry by writing about the issues in this chapter and thus exposed its political nature.

More recently, feminists have demonstrated how misogyny pervades psychiatry (see, for example, Ussher 1991), while others have uncovered the racist and Western imperialist roots of psychiatry (see, for example, Fernando 1991), as well as the heterosexism embedded within it (see, for example, Blackbridge and Gilhooly 1985). While antipsychiatrists, feminists, and others demonstrated psychiatry's oppression and effectiveness as a form of social control, they did not offer any real remedy to those in despair and misery. As Ussher (1991:214) writes, emotional pain is real, and while deconstruction is theoretically useful, it does not offer comfort to those looking for immediate relief.

Psychiatric patients themselves established concrete alternatives. During the 1970s, the psychiatric inmates' liberation movement began. The movement published literature that exposed psychiatric abuses and documented personal stories, held conferences, organized demonstrations, formed consciousness-raising groups, and created client-controlled services (Burstow and Weitz 1988). In Canada, successful psychiatric inmate and ex-inmate initiatives include Toronto's On Our Own, an ex-inmate group that published the quarterly magazine, *Phoenix Rising*, described as 'the voice of the psychiatrized'; and the Vancouver Mental Patients Association, which operated a drop-in centre as well as five cooperative residences, and produced the newsletter, 'In a Nutshell' (Chamberlin 1988). In 1991, Bonnie Burstow and Don Weitz published the book, *Shrink Resistant*, which documents a number of Canadian 'mental patient' experiences and includes a directory of psychiatric inmate liberation organizations.

Despite the challenges to psychiatry from the antipsychiatrists and the psychiatric inmates' liberation movement, psychiatry has continued to grow and many of the groups and organizations that were initially designed to counter psychiatry have become co-opted by it (Chamberlin 1988). The success of the self-help movement throughout North America is another example of psychiatric expansion.

SELF-HELP GROUPS

A new vocabulary has evolved over the last decade. Words like 'codependency', 'recovery', 'dysfunctional', and 'inner child' have become commonplace. They are part of the specialized language of self-help, a growing movement comprised of books, groups, and television talk shows all promoting the medical model of madness. While the self-help movement is potentially subversive, the underlying message of self-help is that we are all sick and that our sickness is self-imposed. We are completely responsible for our diseases and can recover only by admitting our illness and then surrendering our will to a higher power. We can be addicted to just about everything: sex, work, drugs, food, and relationships. Almost every part of our lives is diseased and if we do not believe it, then we are in denial. The cause of illness is always internal, requiring a 'revolution from within' instead of social and political transformation (Kaminer 1992).

Many Canadians voluntarily attend self-help groups, read self-help books, and watch 'Oprah' as well as other television talk shows. While we are not simply passive recipients of these activities, their message of individual cause and cure touches every aspect of our lives. Within the self-help movement, we may become disconnected from the rest of the world as we are self-absorbed in our own recovery, and social injustice loses meaning because degrees of injustice are denied. As Kaminer (1992) writes, the political implications of a vast movement encouraging people to surrender their will to a higher power are frightening. As the psychiatric net claims more territory, the political becomes further reduced to the personal and social control takes a firmer hold.

CONCLUSION

The story of madness is one of professional extension and diversification. It demonstrates how, despite the lack of concrete evidence and the likelihood of harm, professional theories can shape public policy and justify the most intrusive of treatments. It exposes the sexism, racism, classism, and hetero-sexism intrinsic within professions and the broader society. It challenges the notion that madness is mental illness by showing how interpretations of madness have changed across time, and how the meaning of madness is constructed by social, political, and economic forces. The story of madness further shows how power relationships can be masked through language and claims to scientific objectivity. Deviants can be controlled by treating them as scapegoats, disguising coercion as help, or simply by advocating the merits and necessity of control; and the non-deviant walk into the control net as they voluntarily enter therapy, swallow medication, and immerse themselves in self-help books, groups, and television. The possibility of challenging social control was demonstrated by the antipsychiatry movement, feminists, and the psychiatric inmates' liberation movement. Perhaps the moral of the story is the need to resist the forces that individualize social problems by turning them into personal sicknesses and issues.

FURTHER READINGS

Burstow, B., and D. Weitz. 1988. *Shrink Resistant: The Struggle Against Psychiatry in Canada*. Vancouver: New Star Books.

Fernando, S. 1991. *Mental Health, Race and Culture*. London: MIND.

Ussher, J. 1991. *Women's Madness: Misogyny or Mental Illness?* New York: Harvester Wheatsheaf.

Valenstein, E. 1986. *Great and Desperate Cures: The Rise and Decline of*

Psychosurgery and Other Radical Treatments for Mental Illness. New York: Basic Books.

REFERENCES

Blackbridge, P., and S. Gilhooly. 1985. *Still Sane*. Vancouver: Press Gang.
Breggin, P. 1991. *Toxic Psychiatry*. New York: St Martin's Press.
Burstow, B., and D. Weitz. 1988. *Shrink Resistant: The Struggle Against Psychiatry in Canada*. Vancouver: New Star Books.
Chamberlin, J. 1988. *On Our Own*. London: MIND.
Cohen, S. 1985. *Visions of Social Control*. Cambridge: Polity Press.
Conrad, P., and J.W. Schneider. 1992. *Deviance and Medicalization: From Badness to Sickness*, expanded ed. Philadelphia: Temple University Press.
Dickinson, H.D., and G. Andre. 'Community Psychiatry: The Institutional Transformation of Psychiatric Practice'. In *Sociology of Health and Health Care in Canada*, edited by B.S. Bolaria and H.D. Dickinson, 295–308. Toronto: Harcourt, Brace Jovanovich.
Dubos, R. 1959. *The Mirage of Health*. London: Allen & Unwin.
Ehrenreich, B., and D. English. 1973. *Witches, Midwives and Nurses*. Old Westbury, NY: Feminist Press.
Fernando, S. 1991. *Mental Health, Race and Culture*. London: MIND.
Fine, P. 1985. 'Women and Shock Treatment'. *Phoenix Rising* 5, no. 1:54–6.
Foucault, M. 1965. *Madness and Civilization*. New York: Random House.
Frank, L. 1978. *The History of Shock Treatment*. San Francisco: Leonard Roy Frank.
Freidson, E. 1970. *Profession of Medicine*. New York: Dodd, Mead.
Harding, J. 1986. 'Mood-Modifiers and Elderly Women in Canada: The Medicalization of Poverty'. In *Adverse Effects: Women and the Pharmaceutical Industry*, edited by K. McDonnell, 51–86. Toronto: The Women's Press.
Independent Task Force on Sexual Abuse of Patients. 1991. *The Final Report*. Toronto: College of Physicians and Surgeons of Ontario.
Ingleby, D. 1983. 'Mental Health and Social Order'. In *Social Control and the State*, edited by S. Cohen and A. Scull, 141–88. Oxford: Martin Robinson.
Kaminer, W. 1992. *I'm Dysfunctional, You're Dysfunctional*. Reading: Addison-Wesley Publishing Company.
Kelman, S. 1977. 'The Social Nature of the Definition Problem in Health. *International Journal of Health Services* 5:625–41.
Lexchin, J. 1984. *The Real Pushers*. Vancouver: New Star Books.
Marks, J. 1980. *The Search for the Manchurian Candidate: The CIA and Control*. New York: McGraw-Hill.
Masson, J. 1990. *Against Therapy*. London: Fontana Paperbacks.
McLaren, A. 1990. *Our Own Master Race: Eugenics in Canada, 1885–1945*. Toronto: McClelland and Stewart.

Mitchinson, W. 1991. *The Nature of Their Bodies: Women and Their Doctors in Victorian Canada*. Toronto: University of Toronto Press.

Rosen, G. 1968. *Madness in Society*. New York: Harper & Row.

Saskatchewan Health Joint Committee on Drug Utilization. 1978. *Utilization of Mood-Modifying Drugs*, Report no. 1–4. Regina: Saskatchewan Health Joint Committee on Drug Utilization.

Scull, A. 1979. *Museums of Madness: The Social Organization of Insanity in Nineteenth-Century England*. Middlesex: Penguin Books.

_____. 1984. *Decarceration, Community Treatment and the Deviant: A Radical View*, 2nd ed. Cambridge: Polity Press.

_____. 1989. *Social Order/Mental Disorder: Anglo-American Psychiatry in Historical Perspective*. Berkeley: University of California Press.

Simon, B. 1978. *Mind and Madness in Ancient Greece: The Classical Roots of Modern Psychiatry*. London: Cornell University Press.

Smith, E., and A. Richman. 1984. 'Electroconvulsive Therapy: A Canadian Perspective'. *Canadian Journal of Psychiatry* 29:693–9.

Stephenson, P., and G. Walker. 1980. 'Psychotropic Drugs and Women'. *Bioethics Quarterly* 2, no. 1:20–38.

Swazey, J. 1974. *Chloropromazine in Psychiatry: A Study of Therapeutic Intervention*. Cambridge: MIT Press.

Szasz, T. 1970. *The Manufacture of Madness*. New York: Harper & Row.

Ussher, J. 1991. *Women's Madness: Misogyny or Mental Illness?* New York: Harvester Wheatsheaf.

Valenstein, E. 1986. *Great and Desperate Cures: The Rise and Decline of Psychosurgery and Other Radical Treatments for Mental Illness*. New York: Basic Books.

Warsh, C.K. 1989. *Moments of Unreason: The Practice of Canadian Psychiatry and the Homewood Retreat, 1883–1923*. Montreal and Kingston: McGill-Queen's University Press.

—7—

The Impact of Medicalization on Women

Eleanor Maticka-Tyndale
and
Marilyn Bicher

THE IMPACT OF MEDICALIZATION ON WOMEN

Catherine Reissman describes medicalization as having two central components: (1) ascribing a medical meaning to a wide variety of human experiences and conditions, and (2) using medical means to eliminate or control those experiences that are deemed problematic (Reissman 1983). Once human experience is categorized as a medical problem, medicine has the authority to define the problem, set its boundaries, specify its course and causes, and prescribe a treatment. In essence, the experience comes under the *control* of medicine and the medical model, with the medical approach reified as the *only* appropriate approach. In this chapter, we focus on the medicalization of women's lives. We place medicalization within its sociocultural and historical contexts and examine its consequences for women's lives.

Women's lives and experiences have been medicalized more so than men's. This is obvious when we consider Canadian statistics on contact between individuals and medicine. More women than men consult doctors. Women are hospitalized more often than men. Women spend more days in hospital than men, even when hospitalizations associated with childbirth are excluded (Trypuc 1988). This applies not only to physical illnesses but also mental illnesses (Statistics Canada 1991), even though epidemiological research clearly demonstrates that there is no sex difference in the overall prevalence of mental disorder (Myers et al. 1984; Robins et al. 1984).

Barbara Ehrenreich and Dierdre English were among the early feminist scholars to examine the process of medicalization of women's lives (Ehrenreich and English 1973a, 1973b). Their analysis was rooted in a conspiracy theory in which the emerging male medical establishment aggressively wrested control of women's health issues from women healers and midwives. Medicalization caused a shift away from women using a gynocentric, working with nature model towards a masculinist, control over and intervention in the natural processes model. The consequences for women's health have been predominantly negative.

More recent work by feminist historians has gone beyond this model to uncover a far more complex web of factors in the medicalization of women's lives. Central to these more recent analyses is the recognition of the role women played by actively supporting medicalization as a way to gain control over the natural processes that frequently threatened their health and lives. At times this brought women in direct conflict with husbands, religious advisers, and male physicians who *opposed* women's desire to intervene in nature.[1] Class differences were as central to this process as sex differences.

The desire for control over their own lives, as well as the differences between women in different classes, recur in the lives of contemporary women and their relationships to the institution of medicine. To understand medicalization today and its effects on women's lives, we must first understand the process of medicalization.

THE PROCESS OF MEDICALIZATION

The dominant perception of women at the beginning of the nineteenth century was that they were controlled by their reproductive systems. There was some truth to this belief. In 1800, married women in the United States gave birth to an average of 7.04 children (Leavitt 1984c:141). Many women's lives were a perpetual cycle of pregnancies, which compounded the effects of poor diet and overwork to weaken their overall health and damage reproductive organs and the pelvic region. In this sense, women's biology was their destiny, but the perception extended beyond pregnancy, childbirth, and even physical health to all areas of ability and activity. Any and all of women's physical and emotional abilities (and disabilities) were considered to be related to their reproductive systems. Their appropriate roles and functions revolved around child-bearing and child-rearing. They were considered emotionally and physically unsuited to pursue higher education or careers, both of which were believed to be dangerous for women. Motherhood, on the other hand, was regarded as essential to a woman's mental and emotional health. Women were seen as closer to their natural state than men, and it was necessary, for their own health and well-being, to keep them that way (various articles in Leavitt 1984a).

Lower-class and rural women were believed to be closer to nature than wealthy urban women. The former were sturdier, appeared to have fewer emotional and physical problems, and were able to sustain repeated pregnancies and births with fewer difficulties than wealthier women. The greater fragility of urban and particularly of wealthier women was blamed on their movement away from their natural state. Wealthier women were considered to be more prone to difficulties in pregnancy and birth, headaches, consumption, pelvic disorders, nervous disorders, languishing, feebleness, cantankerousness, hysteria, and melancholia. To be 'sickly' was appropriately feminine. Women of the wealthier classes retreated to their chambers and beds on numerous occasions, particularly during pregnancy and after childbirth. Lower-class women did not have the luxury to be ill or sickly because they did not have household help. Often they were the household help for wealthier women. Among the lower classes, women as well as men worked. In hindsight, the diseases of the wealthy have been related to their inactive and monotonous lifestyles, while those of the lower classes have been related to poor diet, lack of sanitation, and overwork. The former were treated by a variety of practitioners, while the latter, primarily as a result of poverty, went untreated or received informal treatment.

From the late 1700s to the present, women went from consulting primarily women on 'women's problems' to consulting male general practitioners and eventually two primary groups of specialists: obstetrician-gynaecologists and psychiatrists. In this century there has been another shift from care at home to care in a hospital. The changes can be traced to at least three forces: women's desire for survival and good health, the development of medical knowledge and techniques, and the exclusion of women from obtaining the latter. Until Medicare was introduced in Canada, the change widened the gap between the health care received by the wealthy and that received by the poor, as well as that between urban and rural dwellers. Rural and poor women had few choices; they received whatever care was available at low or no cost.

Women's Desire for Survival

Until the early 1900s, women experienced childbirth in the company of women friends and relatives and often with the assistance of a midwife. The potential pain, injury, deformity, and even death have been central to the medicalization of pregnancy and childbirth in North America. Though birthing was a women's affair, men were called on when a midwife's abilities were insufficient to deliver the child (Donegan 1984; Scholten 1984). Until the end of the 1700s, the call for a male physician or barber-surgeon to assist meant the death of the child, and potentially also of the mother. Because of the social nature of labour and birth, every woman had witnessed death in childbirth and knew many who had not delivered a live child (Leavitt and Walton 1984; Wertz and Wertz 1979).

Training in Medicine

Standardization in medical training did not occur until the twentieth century. Without standardization, virtually anyone could use the title 'doctor'. The American Medical Association estimates that between 1765 and 1905, over 800 medical schools were founded in the United States, most with a profit motive (Wertz and Wertz 1979). Training rarely required more than two years, and frequently lasted only a few months. Schools ranged from those that trained 'regular' doctors in primarily European methods of allopathic medicine to alternative schools, which focused on more homeopathic approaches and trained a variety of 'irregular' doctors. Women were generally not trained because few families were willing to invest in educating daughters who had little or no income-earning potential. Though some alternative schools taught midwifery, the skill was most often passed among women and learned through experience.

Knowledge of human anatomy and of bodily and mental processes was poor. As a result, the primary difference between the variously trained practitioners was in the techniques they used rather than in their results. 'Regular' doctors were trained in the use of more interventionist techniques (cauterization, surgery, leeching, instruments), while 'irregular' doctors and midwives relied more on herbal medications, injections, and manipulations (Donegan 1984; Wertz and Wertz 1979). Some early doctors broke with the interventionist techniques to prescribe cures and treatments based on more natural approaches, such as rest and water cures (Morantz 1984; Wood 1984).

Regular Doctors Move into Birthing
Doctors began to move into birthing rooms with the introduction of forceps in the late 1700s. Forceps made it possible for physicians to assist in difficult deliveries without the loss of life of mother or child. Increasingly, wealthy urban women called on physicians to attend their birthing, together with midwives and other birth attendants (Scholten 1984; Wertz and Wertz 1979). As physicians gained the confidence and trust of women during childbirth, they were consulted for an ever wider range of female complaints (headaches, nerves, moods, abdominal pains), problems on which women had formerly consulted only other women (Scholten 1984).

The presence of male doctors during labour and childbirth meant the norms of modesty that regulated male-female interaction came to influence the birthing process. Women no longer delivered their babies while sitting or squatting on a birthing stool, as they had when only women were in attendance. They now lay on their backs totally draped or covered (a practice that continues today). The midwife's frequent visual checks and use of massage and manual manipulation were *not* part of the men's practice because these were considered improper forms of contact between men and women. Labouring women were draped, and male doctors were forbidden to look at the vaginal area. Doctors delivered babies by feel alone, even when forceps were used.

While regular doctors continued to focus primarily on the management of childbirth, women began to advocate for painless childbirth. This was made possible with the introduction of anaesthesia, which was first used during a delivery in 1847. The active role played by wealthier women in obtaining painless childbirth is seen in the campaign for the introduction of scopolamine (Leavitt 1984c), a drug used in Europe to produce a semiconscious state referred to as twilight sleep. Scopolamine was first used on this continent in 1914 (Garner and Tessler 1989). North American doctors were reluctant to use it in part because they resented the interference of women in determining their practice, and in part because they feared the dangers of the drug (Leavitt 1984c). Influential women of the time formed a national association to pressure for the use of scopolamine (Leavitt 1984c:177). The scopolamine campaign was part of the changing view of childbirth from an experience to be endured to one in which women could choose various ways to manage their births and, in particular, to reduce their pain. The use of anaesthesia was among the forces that accelerated the move of childbirth from the home to the hospital.

Professionalization of Medicine and the Exclusion of Women

By the mid-1800s, doctors in Canada and the United States had formed medical associations to act as gatekeepers and moral entrepreneurs. As gatekeepers they controlled who could practise medicine. As moral entrepreneurs, they made decisions about the most appropriate procedures and treatments. Despite over 200 years of regular doctors' gradual involvement in birthing, in 1910 50 per cent of births in the United States were still attended by midwives. Competition between doctors and midwives intensified. Modesty and availability were on the side of midwives (Donegan 1984). Many people felt it was improper to have a man in attendance during childbirth, regardless of his qualifications. Besides, there were not enough doctors to attend to all women, and not all women could afford to pay.

Those who supported the role of midwives set up training facilities to teach midwives the new techniques. Most doctors, however, moved to discredit midwives as untrained and ignorant. It was not possible to train them adequately, doctors claimed. Women's fears were played on. Childbirth was portrayed as a perilous event and doctors, with their instruments and training, were essential aids to insure women's safety. 'Lying-in' hospitals, based on the British model, were established to provide proper care for lower-class women in labour. These women received a physician's care for little or no cost in exchange for providing doctors and students with experience from which they could better learn about childbirth (Kobrin 1984; Wertz and Wertz 1979).

In the early 1900s, the American Medical Association asked Abraham Flexner to evaluate American and Canadian medical schools, and assess their programs for scientific quality and rigour. Only Harvard, Johns Hopkins, and Western Reserve in the United States, and the University of Toronto and McGill University in Canada met the established criteria of excellence (Clarke 1990). Few of the existing schools and *none* of those established for alternative or homeopathic training or midwifery met the standards set by Flexner. Some schools were able to upgrade their programs to meet the standards. However, the alternative schools and those for training midwives were based on a totally different model of training and were forced to close. The North American approach differed quite profoundly from that in Europe, where professionalization and quality control led to the creation of government-sponsored schools for training midwives.

In North America, training was privately run, controlled by the American Medical Association. Following the reforms resulting from Flexner's report, training in midwifery was not available separate from training in medicine. In the attempt to eliminate 'quacks', only *one* form of medical practice was allowed in North America (Fisher 1988:137). In the aftermath of the Flexner report, medical schools began to stress medical specialization (e.g., obstetrics, psychiatry) and to lobby for legislation to restrict medical practice to only those trained in accredited facilities. Obstetrical specialists stressed the pathological nature of childbirth, the need for *specialist* supervision, and the availability of a full range of technology and pharmaceuticals (e.g., anaesthetics) in a hospital setting. In their search for the best care, wealthier women moved their births from home to hospitals in increasing numbers and chose specialists for their care. By the 1950s, virtually all births in North America occurred in hospitals under the supervision of physicians (Wertz and Wertz 1979).

Medicalization of Childbirth

In the move from home to hospital, childbirth lost its social nature. Women no longer attended to friends and relatives giving birth. The labouring woman was now delivered, free of pain, under the exclusive control of trained physicians (Leavitt 1984c). Women's fear of death and their desire for pain-free childbirth in the context of the cultural beliefs of the day, as well as the evolving structure of medicine, resulted in their loss of control over the birthing process and its transformation from a natural to a pathological, medically managed process.

A medically managed birth may be characterized as:

> physician attended and professionally managed with an orientation towards medical technology and pharmacological methods of pain relief. Concomitantly, a woman who enters the hospital is treated as a patient when she is admitted, decision-making power and responsibility for her state pass from her to the hospital personnel and the physician in charge (Jordan 1983:33).

Today, medically managed births are likely to include use of episiotomies, forceps, anaesthetic, foetal heart monitors, various medications to control pain and/or speed contractions, and other interventions. Though our trust in medicine makes us view most of these as necessary, many studies of births that are assisted by trained midwives and that involve fewer of these interventions indicate that outcomes are as good as births supervised by physicians (Burtch 1988; Pinchus et al. 1984). Members of the Canadian Medical Association argue today, as they did at the turn of the century, that physician-attended births in a hospital are safer, and that because one never knows when complications will occur, women who are giving birth *should* be under constant surveillance. Many physicians claim that the reduced infant and maternal mortality rate in Canada is due largely to medical advances and intervention. However, in Holland where 70 per cent of all births occur at home, the infant mortality rate is lower than that in Canada (Edginton 1989). Edginton (1989), in his review of data on infant health and mortality, claims that the worldwide drop in infant mortality can be credited to improved nutrition, clean water, improved sanitary conditions, proper housing, and the availability of birth control, as well as appropriate medical care.

MEDICALLY MANAGED PREGNANCY

In Canada today, Medicare has virtually eliminated the gap between classes in prenatal and childbirth care, though there are still differences between rural and urban areas in the facilities available. Though most pregnancies and births proceed without complications or difficulties, prenatal care focuses on identifying any potential difficulty. Pregnancy is consequently treated as an illness, with most pregnant women receiving prenatal care from a specialist and almost all pregnant women subjected to a series of tests. Women in high-risk groups (approximately 5 to 10 per cent of the population) have benefited from advanced medical and technological testing. The *standardization* of tests as part of regular prenatal care, however, exposes *all* women to their iatrogenic effects (undesired, negative consequences). The most common tests that pregnant women are encouraged to undergo include ultrasound, amniocentesis, and chorionic villi sampling (cvs).

Prenatal Tests
An ultrasound is considered a non-invasive procedure. A jellylike substance is placed on the abdomen and a transducer is moved back and forth over the pregnant woman's abdomen. High-frequency sound waves are transmitted into the woman's womb. These sound waves produce echoes that are transformed into electronic signals and converted into pictures. Today in Canada, almost all pregnant women have at least one ultrasound. The test assesses the development of the foetus, foetal abnormalities, foetal position, the position of the placenta, and may also establish the sex of the foetus. There is no known short-term biological iatrogenic effect, but long-term effects of this test are still unknown. Laboratory experiments in the 1970s indicated that

ultrasound contributed to foetal abnormalities in animal studies. Chromosomal and other abnormalities were found in human cell studies (Patychuck
1985).

Amniocentesis is an invasive test that must be done by a highly skilled
technician or physician. A long needle is inserted through the abdominal
wall into the womb to withdraw amniotic fluid. The test is usually done
around the sixteenth week of pregnancy and results are known between the
eighteenth and twentieth week of pregnancy. It can identify certain chromosomal abnormalities and metabolic disorders, as well as the sex of the foetus.
Amniocentesis is usually recommended for pregnant women who are over
thirty-five because it is believed there is a greater risk of chromosomal
abnormalities. There is a possibility of injury to the foetus and a one in 400
to 450 chance of miscarriage.

Chorionic villi sampling is another invasive procedure in which a mal-
leable catheter is inserted through the vagina and cervix to remove pieces of
threadlike tissue from the outermost layer of the amniotic sac. This test can
also assess chromosomal defects, a number of diseases, and the sex of the
foetus. It is usually done around the ninth week of pregnancy. The risk of
biological iatrogenic effects is higher and the effects are more serious with
CVS than with amniocentesis. New studies indicate the increased possibility
of babies being born with limb deformities (*Newsweek*, 22 June 1992). Also,
the miscarriage rate is twice as high with CVS than it is with amniocentesis.
Consequently, CVS is only used when very early detection of problems is
considered necessary.

If a problem in foetal development is anticipated, testing during pregnancy is reasonable and generally warranted. However, these tests lead to increased costs, potential increased risk as a result of the test itself, and further
medicalization of pregnancy. Such testing therefore raises a number of issues.
What are the full range of iatrogenic effects? What are the costs and benefits of
each test? Whose interests are served? What medical and psychosocial support
is provided? Are these tests necessary for all pregnant women?

Testing is used to detect foetal abnormalities. Some abnormalities can be
corrected while the foetus is in the womb; however, there is little knowledge
about the potential maternal risk of such procedures, and such correction is
still in the very rudimentary stages. If an abnormality is detected, most often
a woman's choices are limited to carrying the baby to term while aware of
the abnormality, or aborting. With the exception of CVS, tests that are likely
to indicate the presence of foetal abnormalities provide results in the second
trimester of pregnancy, exposing women to the higher risks of second trimester abortions.

Cultural and Social Iatrogenesis

The social control function of medicine is seen most clearly in the social and
cultural iatrogenic effects of testing during pregnancy. Testing creates and

defines a 'norm' of what is considered a healthy baby. If a pregnant woman refuses any of the recommended tests and then has a baby with health problems that could have been identified during pregnancy, the woman assumes responsibility and may blame herself. Pregnant women are pressured to accept recommendations to be tested in order to avoid possible feelings of guilt or of being judged as irresponsible. However, if a test indicates a problem, there are but two choices available: to abort or carry to term. If a woman chooses to carry to term, she does so knowing she consciously willed an 'abnormal' child to be born. She also knows there may be additional costs in raising her child since the child will often require special services, therapies, equipment, or education. If she chooses abortion, she is choosing to abort a wanted child. The choice may well be one based on her economic ability. Women have had abortions throughout history, but the health status of the foetus was never known, and therefore was not the influencing factor.

Today we live in a society in which abortion as an option is often difficult to get, particularly for rural and poor women, or its choice is questioned, yet inadequate support is provided to families who have children with health problems, and tight economic times threaten what assistance and service are provided. An example is the Alberta government's announcement in July 1992 that it would no longer cover full corrective and restorative dental work for children born with cleft palate. This reduction in services will leave families of cleft-palate children with costs as high as $10,000 to $20,000 for dental corrections alone, not considering the additional emotional and economic costs directly and indirectly related to raising a child who was born with a cleft palate. Clearly, a class difference will result in the treatment available to these children and potentially in the choices that pregnant women make. Are we promoting a subtle message that only healthy babies will be accepted in our society?

MEDICALLY MANAGED CHILDBIRTH

In the United States, 50 per cent of children were born at home at the beginning of this century (Leavitt 1984b). Today in Canada and the United States, almost all women have their babies in the hospital. Births are attended by physicians (usually obstetricians) and nurses. As of 1993, three Canadian provinces (British Columbia, Ontario, and Quebec) were working towards formal recognition of midwives. The care of a midwife, however, is still available to only a few women. With physician care, women are subject to a wide range of technological interventions that obstetricians promote to expedite the delivery process and ease childbirth. The use of these interventions has had a cascade effect. The consequence or iatrogenic effects of using one intervention necessitates the use of a succession of others (Klein et al. 1986).

Cascade Effect

In response to pressures that began since the earliest childbirth hospitalizations, some hospitals have now established birthing rooms. These rooms are meant to resemble a home bedroom and are supposed to provide an atmosphere of comfort and warmth. Unfortunately, most women, whether in a birthing room or not, are still subject to technological interventions. Women continue to give birth while lying on their backs, now with legs up in stirrups. Though this position is no longer likely to be chosen for the sake of modesty, it is a legacy of earlier times and is maintained because it makes the observation of the birthing and the use of interventions during the birth process easier for the doctor. This position, however, makes it more difficult for a woman to deliver her baby.

Once a woman is admitted to the case room or birthing room, she is likely to be attached to a foetal heart monitor. There are two types of monitors used to assess the baby's health status during labour. One is an external monitor, which uses ultrasound to track the baby's heartbeat and the strength of the contractions. The other is an internal monitor, which can only be used once the membranes are ruptured. The external monitor is not as invasive as the internal one. It is placed on the abdomen and held in place with two belts. The internal monitor, although more invasive, is considered more accurate. A recording machine is connected to an electronic lead screwed into the baby's scalp. Use of the foetal heart monitor was initiated in the United States, Germany, and Uruguay in 1960 to monitor high-risk births. This technology has gone from occasional to common use and is now part of almost all hospital birth procedures (Kunisch 1989).

Drugs are usually administered during labour to regulate the speed of contractions and reduce pain. The drugs administered for these two purposes, however, are commonly counterproductive. Drugs for pain reduction *slow* labour, necessitating the use of additional drugs to speed labour. Both forms of medication are usually administered intravenously. Being attached to a foetal heart monitor and an intravenous tube requires a woman to remain immobile and lie on her back. Immobility contributes to slow labour. The longer the labour lasts, however, the more fatigued a woman becomes, necessitating further interventions to 'assist' her as she becomes less able to birth her own child. The cascade effect is clearly evident here.

The final intervention that almost all women are subjected to is an episiotomy, an incision to enlarge the vagina in order to facilitate childbirth and reduce the likelihood of a vaginal tear. This is the most frequently performed surgical procedure in the Western world. In Canada, approximately 80 per cent of women who give birth are likely to have an episiotomy (Klein et al. 1992). The traditional approaches to birthing that are common in midwife-assisted births included delivering a child while squatting or in some other position that aided the birth process. Midwives commonly massaged the vaginal area and applied ointments to encourage dilation and reduce the likelihood of vaginal tears. Though vaginal tears still occurred, they were the exception rather than the rule.

Many obstetricians believe that an episiotomy can reduce urinary incontinence and pain during sexual intercourse following childbirth. The validity of this belief was checked in a study by Sleep and Grant (1987) in West Berkshire, England, and replicated in a Montreal study (Klein et al. 1992). Physicians' beliefs regarding urinary incontinence or dyspareunia (painful coitus) were not borne out either in the short term (ten days to three months following childbirth) nor the long term (three years following birth). Women who did not have episiotomies were, however, more likely to resume sexual intercourse within one month of childbirth. These findings, and those of Klein's most recent study (Klein et al. 1994), have led to the recommendation that episiotomies should no longer be considered routine.

Caesarean Section
The final and ultimate intervention is a Caesarean section, the surgical removal of the child. In North America there has been a marked rise in Caesarean section deliveries. In the United States, the Caesarean section rate was 5.55 per cent of hospital births in 1970 and rose to 24.7 per cent by 1988. In Canada, the rate rose from 5.8 to 19.5 over the same period (Nair 1992). Though lower infant and maternal mortality rates are used to explain and justify Caesarean sections, Japan, which has a rate one-third that of Canada, has a lower infant mortality rate (Nair 1992). According to the World Health Organization, rates higher than 15 per cent of hospital deliveries should be questioned.

In Canada, Caesarean section rates vary from province to province, and within each province they vary from hospital to hospital. In 1988–9, Newfoundland had the highest Caesarean section rate at 23.3 per cent of hospital births; British Columbia had the second highest at 22.2 per cent; Manitoba had the lowest rate at 15.5 per cent. The rates in the other provinces in 1988–9 were as follows: Alberta, 17.1 per cent; Saskatchewan, 17.4 per cent; Prince Edward island, 18.1 per cent; Quebec, 19.0 per cent; Nova Scotia, 19.9 per cent; Ontario, 20.3 per cent; New Brunswick, 20.8 per cent (Nair 1992).

In an attempt to insure safety and eliminate pain, women actively participated in the medicalization of childbirth. While medicalization has helped women who have difficulty carrying a baby to term or delivering a child without assistance, it has also acted as a form of social control over women and removed them from a position of control over their own birthing. Medical intervention and advanced technology have interfered with women's ability to adequately understand their reproductive system. Some women have lost confidence in giving birth without medical assistance. Medicine has established the norm: for pregnancy, for birthing, and for what constitutes a 'healthy' child. Women have been socialized to trust the medical profession, making it difficult for them to question their doctors. Often when women *do* attempt to minimize medical intervention during pregnancy and childbirth, they are dissuaded from doing so.

EMOTIONAL DISTRESS

Profound sadness, emptiness, fear, guilt; a sense of helplessness, that something terrible is wrong and nothing can be done to make it right; difficulty in sleeping, concentrating, or focusing thoughts; an absence of interest in work or leisure activities; irritability, 'crabbiness', jumpiness; physical aches and pains, such as headaches, backaches, indigestion, constipation, or joint pains; profound fatigue on the one hand or agitated pacing and movement on the other; worry, anxiety; a sense of impending doom and no way of avoiding or changing it. These have been variously referred to as symptoms of malaise, demoralization, nervous disorder, melancholia, or depression. Whatever the terminology, what is described above is emotional distress. Research repeatedly demonstrates that whether we consider general emotional distress or the specific distress associated with a psychiatric diagnosis of depression, whether we consider those in their teens or those in their fifties or older, women far outnumber men (Kavanagh 1992; Myers et al. 1984; Robins et al. 1984). Historical records further demonstrate that such distress has been a part of women's lives for a long time. In fact, the development of psychoanalysis in the last century addressed almost exclusively the emotional distress of women. Where do women turn with their distress? What do they do? Why is there a gender difference?

Dealing with Distress

How women deal with distress is influenced by the type of resources they have available, and by the responses of those close to them and those they encounter in their search for an explanation and relief. Some women consider these symptoms as 'their lot in life' and seek no help, while others seek help but don't know how or where to go.

In emotional distress, there are no visible wounds, no fever, no elevated blood counts, no objective indicators that these are signs of illness. The symptoms often appear to others as mere laziness, lack of motivation, crankiness, unreasonableness, or as 'not trying'. In the past, only wealthy women obtained medical help for their distress. Poor women only received medical attention when their distress was so extreme that they endangered themselves or others. They were then hospitalized in public wards for the insane. Wealthy women were tended to by private physicians and analysts. The dominant theory through most of psychiatry's history has ascribed women's symptoms, in great part, to their reproductive functions. Confinement and care were usually provided at home or in private sanatoriums. Rest cures, with total bed rest and isolation from all stimulation or outside contact over several months, were commonly prescribed (Wood 1984).

Women have sought counsel for distress throughout history. In the past this may have been from religious or spiritual counsellors, midwives, or friends and relatives. Today doctors, social workers, and psychologists have joined this list. Medicare in Canada and private medical insurance in the United States have made physicians a resource that is free and available to the vast majority of Canadians and to those Americans with insurance. American studies demonstrate that only a small fraction of those in emotional distress seek medical care (Travis 1988). Whether this is true in Canada, or to what degree Medicare may have changed this, is not known. D'Arcy and Fritz, in their research on the impact of Medicare, found an increase in the use of medical services for the treatment of emotional distress and depression when universal medical insurance was introduced (D'Arcy and Fritz 1979).

General Practitioners and Emotional Distress

The family physician is usually the first to be consulted for emotional distress. More women than men turn to their family physician for relief from distress (Cooperstock 1979; D'Arcy and Schmitz 1979). Women turn to doctors in part because medical care is free, but also because, with medicalization, we have come to regard the family physician as someone to whom we can bring a variety of problems and complaints. Evidence from a recent Calgary study suggests that men may be more likely to turn to alcohol. It is only when symptoms are particularly severe that medicine intervenes, most typically when men are brought to the emergency room of an acute-care hospital (Maticka-Tyndale, Wright, and Coleman 1993).

During the meeting between the doctor and patient, symptoms receive a label, their cause an explanation, and a treatment is prescribed. Stewart Page's research in Ontario suggests that gender stereotyping is common and has a profound impact on how women and men are perceived by mental health practitioners (Page 1987). His work is corroborated by that of Ruth Cooperstock in Vancouver, who found that when men and women brought the same complaints, the family physician was more likely to see these as indicators of emotional problems in women and of physical problems in men (Cooperstock 1978). Doctors viewed these symptoms, much as they did in the past, as the result of stresses in women's lives (Gabe and Lipschitz-Phillips 1984; Penfold and Walker 1983). Those stresses have been elaborated in a 1987 report of the Canadian Mental Health Association, *Women and Mental Health in Canada: Strategies for Change*. Briefly, the very structures of work, family, and community that deny women autonomy place women in inequitable situations and relationships, overburden them with responsibility, expose them to abuse, and require them to adapt their own lives and needs to mesh with those of others. These are not specific and unusual stresses, as sought in epidemiological studies, but persistent conditions and environments that are an ever-present reality in the lives of women. They comprise an oppressive and mentally unhealthy environment for women and make them more susceptible than men to distress.

Women rarely go to their doctors complaining of the oppression in their lives. Instead, they have internalized the individualistic, medical model and identify their 'problem' as intrapsychic in origin, i.e., as something wrong with *them* (Gabe and Lipschitz-Phillips 1984). They search for relief of symptoms, often specifically requesting tranquillizers (Cooperstock 1979; Cooperstock and Lennard 1979; Gabe and Lipschitz-Phillips 1984). Physicians are neither trained to address the social conditions causing women's distress, nor are they encouraged to be informed of community resources available to women (Travis 1988). Often, in fact, there is tension between doctors and community or self-help groups. Tranquillizers, most often benzodiazepines (e.g., Valium), with their relatively immediate effect, are the common treatment. Tranquillizers ease anxiety, stress, and agitation. They make an untenable situation at home, work, or in the community tolerable. Women describe tranquillizers as their 'lifeline', as the 'stand-by' that helps them get through (Cooperstock 1979; Gabe and Lipschitz-Phillips 1984). But their biological iatrogenic effect is to exacerbate feelings of helplessness and hopelessness and a low, sad mood—the depressive symptoms of distress. They cause drowsiness, reduced motor coordination, slowed reflexes, and addiction if the dosage and duration of use are not carefully monitored (Travis 1988). As benzodiazepines decrease anxiety, they also erode awareness of the oppressive life circumstances that produced the distress. Among the social and cultural iatrogenic effects is that the oppression continues and women become less aware of any other way of dealing with their response to it. Women can easily become emotionally dependent on these drugs at the same time as they are becoming physically addicted to them.

Psychiatric Care for Emotional Distress

Psychiatric care is probably required if the family physician's care does not alleviate symptoms, if they become worse (in both cases this may be related to the use of tranquillizers), if it appears that suicide is a possibility, or if children are not being adequately cared for. At times this is not merely a referral but an involuntary commitment to hospitalization as a psychiatric patient. There are criteria and conditions governed by federal and provincial mental health legislation for committing people who are deemed a danger to themselves or to others. In a review of psychiatric commitments in Ontario, Page found that men were most likely to be committed when they exhibited passive, depressive, anxious behaviour, while women were committed when they showed aggressive, antisocial behaviour. The behaviours indicative of danger to self or others are those that violate our prescribed gender roles (Page 1985).

Labelling theory (Penfold and Walker 1983; Scheff 1974) alerts us to the realization that people who are seen by a psychiatrist are considered by others and by themselves as mentally ill. Such a label is not viewed neutrally in our society. It has a myriad of social consequences, among them job and housing discrimination, possible grounds for divorce, denial of custody or even access to one's children. Considering Page's work, we are *labelled* mentally ill when we diverge from gender role prescriptions (Page 1987).

The Biopsychosocial Model

Contemporary psychiatry views mental disorder from within the context of a biopsychosocial model. Disorders are caused not by one but by an interplay between all three dimensions of this model. *Biological* factors establish propensities or inherent strengths or weaknesses (potentially inherited), or are the body's response to certain experiences (e.g., the release of adrenalin in response to fear). *Psychological* factors influence how we respond to life experiences and whether they will produce more or less stress, fear, or anxiety. Finally, we live in a *social* environment that, for example, places certain demands and stresses on us, facilitates or impedes our access to needed resources, and creates the situation to which we respond biologically or psychologically. Psychosocial *adaptation* (as opposed to *mal*adaptation or illness) is the conscious and unconscious acceptance and incorporation of the existing social order and one's location in that order into one's self-perception and roles.

The symptoms listed at the beginning of this section closely approximate those of various depressive disorders listed in the *Diagnostic and Statistical Manual of Mental Disorders* (American Psychiatric Association 1987). Depression is the 'common cold' of psychiatry, with epidemiological studies estimating that 20 per cent of women and 10 per cent of men will show symptoms of depression at some time in their lives (Kaplan and Sadock 1988:289). There are many different categories of depressive disorder, with the primary distinctions between types based on the duration and severity of symptoms. Depression may last a few weeks or many years, and symptoms range in severity to the point where they make it impossible for an individual to function at all. Depression is typically either cyclical, recurring in 50 to 85 per cent of cases (Keller 1988:201), or chronic and resistant to therapy. From a biopsychosocial perspective, in biologically and psychologically susceptible individuals, social stressors are likely to produce distress and depression, with the specific symptoms the result of certain biological processes.

Minimization of Social Factors

Though social factors figure prominently in depression, the emphasis in psychiatric training and practice is almost exclusively on the biological and psychological components. In a series published by the American Psychiatric Association, the vast majority of chapters in the volume on depression focus on biological factors, with occasional reference to psychological ones (Frances and Hales 1988). There is no exploration of the social factors that are implicated in depression.

Psychiatry carries a legacy of the view of women as emotionally tied to their reproductive functions. Debates continue about whether depression specific to menstrual cycle (late luteal phase dysphoric disorder or LLPDD) or menopause (involutional melancholia) are appropriate diagnostic categories with biological bases. These debates continue despite research that demonstrates neither a gender-distinct biological basis nor even a defensible association between menstruation or menopause and depressive symptomatology apart from their social bases (McFarlane et al. 1988; McKinlay et al. 1987; Stoppard 1992).

The focus on the individual as opposed to the social is also apparent in the way in which psychiatry captures the three dimensions of the biopsychosocial model in its diagnostic schema. The DSMIII-R, the newest diagnostic approach in psychiatry, captures these in a five-axis system (American Psychiatric Association 1987). The specifics of an individual's unique social situation are reduced to a single number that indicates the severity of all social stressors combined. The *individual* is disordered, not the society or social system in which he or she lives.

Hospital Treatment for Depression

Psychiatric treatment may be on an in- or out-patient basis. Canadian statistics indicate that in 1988–9, women were hospitalized as in-patients for treatment of depressive disorders just over 32,000 times and men just over 16,500 times (Statistics Canada 1991). Whether as in- or out-patients, women typically remain under psychiatric care longer than men (Cooperstock 1978, 1979; Maticka-Tyndale, Wright, and Coleman 1993).

In-patient care is used when symptoms are severe and/or there is a possibility of suicide. Patients are physically removed from their environment and relieved of day-to-day responsibilities and tasks. Careful supervision of the patient and of any treatments is possible under these conditions. The most commonly used in-patient treatments for depression are, in order, antidepressant medications, psychotherapy, and electroconvulsive therapy (ECT). In out-patient or private care, patients are treated while they continue to live in the community. Patients receiving out-patient care have less severe symptoms and are judged able to remain in their homes and communities. Treatment strategies vary, but various talk or psychotherapies are generally most prominent. The goal of the talk therapies is to improve a patient's ability to cope with stressful and distressing situations and to understand better the factors that are producing distress.

Antidepressants are powerful though slow-working drugs that act on the centres of the brain that cause the symptoms of depression. They only work in some forms of depression, most often those that are severe and cyclical, which are referred to as major depressive episodes. The chronic, persistent depression referred to as dysthymia is not responsive to antidepressant therapy. Antidepressants relieve symptoms, but do not 'cure' depression. This is evident in the recurrence of depression in the majority of individuals and the need to continue medication long after symptoms have remitted to guard against relapse. For those who view depression as biologically based, antidepressants are a logical choice. They correct the chemical imbalance in the brain much as insulin corrects imbalance in diabetics.

ECT may be used for patients whose symptoms do not respond to antidepressant treatment, or for whom there is some risk associated with their use. ECT is an electrical shock sent to certain portions of the brain, causing the body to respond with a *grand mal* seizure. Of all the treatments for depression, ECT produces the highest rate of success and most rapid relief of depressive symptoms, but its history has been highly controversial. This is in large part because of the injuries caused by the seizures in early ECT procedures, the side effects of the treatment, the concern with potential brain damage, and the potential for misuse of the treatment. Reviews of ECT use prior to the 1950s provide evidence that it *was* at times used more to control unruly and difficult patients than for therapeutic treatment (Rose and Pincus 1988:431–4). Its use is now quite stringently controlled with precise guidelines, regular reporting procedures for monitoring its use, and much refined, safer, and reduced application. However, there are still three major documented side effects: acute confusion that generally lasts less than an hour, but has the potential for lasting several days; loss of short-term memory and the ability to form new memories, which lasts for varying lengths of time; and spontaneous seizures that may recur days, weeks, or years following treatment (Sachs and Gellenberg 1988). Because of these effects and the concerns with potential *mis*use both from in and outside psychiatry, the use of ECT has drastically reduced since the 1950s. There are active debates over whether this therapy is now being unnecessarily withheld from patients who could benefit from its use, or whether its use is *ever* justifiable, given the side effects (Rose and Pincus 1988).

A Calgary study found a distinctive gender difference in women's and men's experiences with psychiatric care. Women were usually referred to psychiatrists by their family physicians. They remained in care until they were considered ready to terminate treatment. Men usually came to hospital emergency rooms with severe symptoms and no history of prior medical care. They were also more likely to show signs of alcohol abuse. Men were more likely than women to be admitted for in-patient care and to be involuntarily committed to care. Their stays were shorter, as men frequently terminated care against their physician's advice. Women, in their search for relief, have willingly submitted themselves to medical treatment and have internalized a medical view of their 'condition'. Men, on the other hand, resist medical treatment (Maticka-Tyndale, Wright, and Colemen 1993; Wright et al. 1990).

The goal of treatment is to return a patient to daily life and responsibilities, symptom-free or with reduced symptoms. Since depression may be chronic or cyclical, it is not uncommon for individuals to find themselves in a cycle of symptom-treatment-relief-symptom-treatment-relief, which keeps their attention focused on medications, the possibility of repeated treatment, and the idea that ultimately they *themselves* are disordered. The question becomes whether the cyclical or chronic natures of the different depressive disorders are related to the treatment of symptoms alone while leaving their social causes intact. Thus, while social conditions that precipitate distress and depression are left unchanged, patients (predominantly women) are treated and returned to the same social conditions, hopefully better able to cope. They are encouraged to be vigilant to the possibility that the symptoms may recur—evidence that *they* have not adequately coped. Thus the victim is blamed and kept vigilant, and the status quo is maintained.

Psychiatry as Social Control

Psychiatry's unique position of treating behaviours, emotions, and thought patterns has left it open to accusation that it functions primarily as an agent of social control, insuring that people follow socially prescribed norms. This view of psychiatry was initially an outgrowth of the work of Thomas Szasz, himself a psychiatrist (Szasz 1974), and labelling theory in sociology and social psychology (Scheff 1974). Both describe a control that is direct and overt. To Szasz, psychiatry's primary function is to control unwanted, bothersome, or socially undesirable behaviours. This control comes through labelling those people who show these behaviours as sick and subjecting them to incarceration in mental institutions, physical confinement and restraints, and by modifying behaviour through the use of surgery, chemical or electric shock, or medication. Labelling theorists have taken much the same perspective as Szasz, but also address the control that continues after patients leave the hospital. This results from the stigmatization associated with the label 'mentally ill' or 'mental patient', even when these are preceded by the word 'former'.

The recent changes made by psychiatry in *what* are considered mental disorders (e.g., homosexuality and menopausal depression have been removed from the compendium of psychiatric disorders) have certainly contributed to the scepticism regarding psychiatry's role in *enforcing* social norms as compared to *treating* illness. In addition, reviews of the use of the most invasive therapies, among them surgery and chemical and electric shock treatment, have led to the recognition that, at times, these *have been* used primarily for control rather than treatment (Rose and Pincus 1988:431–4). Thus when we consider the history of psychiatry, it is clear that it *has* been an agent of direct social control.

Since the 1960s, two phenomena have reduced (though not eliminated) the direct social control function of psychiatry. The first is the development of active patients' advocacy groups that highlighted psychiatric practices and pressured governmental and medical agencies to insure accountability. The second is change within psychiatry itself, moving it closer to a model that recognizes and celebrates diversity in human experience rather than its older, conformity-based view of healthy behaviour. Direct social control continues, however, as is seen in the interaction between psychiatry and the law. Commitment of a patient to psychiatric care is a legal process in which a patient may be held against his or her will. Court defences of innocence due to insanity involve the testimony of a pyschiatrist and essentially state that a person cannot be held responsible for his or her actions. Of interest is the potential use of diagnoses such as LLPDD in such defences (Kendall 1992).

Social control, however, is most insidious in its indirect, covert form. Psychiatry in particular and medicine in general *do* act as agents of indirect social control. Indirect control is exercised through psychiatry's role as the sole or primary authority on mental health and illness. As the authority, the biological, individually focused psychiatric model dominates. It influences social policies, legislation, research, development of prevention and treatment programs, and funding. For the individual, psychiatry's authority influences the way distress is perceived, to what its cause is ascribed, and the types of cures or treatments that are sought and demanded. Emotional distress is medicalized and decontextualized. Physician and patient alike focus on the individual while ignoring the social context. Distress is seen and treated as an individual pathology. The goal of treatment is to return the individual to the very environment that produced the distress. In this way, treatment of depression constitutes social control. It keeps women in their place, 'fixing' them when that place breaks them down, and returning them to that proper place. As Penfold and Walker state in their introduction to *Women and the Psychiatric Paradox*: 'if women's reactions to oppression can be explained in terms of individual pathology, or as a function of feminine psychology, the objective facts of oppression are obscured and need not be changed' (1983:vi).

It is not so much that medicine and psychiatry treat only the individual, for individuals in distress frequently search for and need relief from their symptoms, but that as a society we have placed problems that are socially caused exclusively into the domain of medicine. We mandate *only* medicine (in part through Medicare) to treat the distressed person, who is usually a woman. The consequence is that the treatment is most likely to be based on a biological model of depression, one that places the cause and solution within the individual and virtually ignores the social concomitants. We mandate no one to 'treat' the social conditions that cause the distress. In this way we have medicalized distress and made medicine an institution of social control.

CONCLUSIONS

Today, as in the past, many problems are only legitimized once they are identified as medical. This has been the case with premenstrual tension, wife abuse, pain in childbirth, emotional distress, and depression. Women's problems are often ignored until they have been moved into the medical domain. Women have actively sought to insure their own survival and well-being by gaining medical attention for their problems, but the consequence of their successes are mixed. On the positive side, medicalization has given these problems legitimacy and 'treatment'; this is seen in childbirth and depression. On the negative side, they are controlled in their definition and treatment by medical practitioners and their problems are individualized. The methodologies and treatments used are highly interventionist, have a wide range of biological, cultural, and social iatrogenic effects, and frequently create a cascade effect of escalating interventions. Women are in a paradoxical situation.

Women are not passive victims of this paradox today, any more than they were in the past. Women are entering medical schools in record numbers. Professionals and lay-women alike have actively participated in bringing about change in medical practice and providing alternative choices. The goal of their advocacy has been to insure that the gains are maintained while the iatrogenic effects are minimized, and that autonomy and diversity rather than social control and conformity are the norms. This is seen, for example, in women's advocacy and lobbying for the recognition of trained midwives as valid pregnancy and birth counsellors and caregivers who work in collaboration with the medical establishment, as in many European countries. The expansion of nurses' roles to address health enhancement and maintenance and the social factors associated with health and illness—areas that medical doctors generally ignore—is another example. Women have established self-help groups and worked with professional women to establish women's clinics and health centres for treating physical and mental health and illness. These clinics and health centres use more holistic approaches that recognize women's unique position in society and their unique social and medical needs. Though there has often been a tension between the medical community and self-help groups, that tension may be replaced by greater collaboration in the future. Federal agencies and some provincial ministries have begun to recognize the role of self-help organizations in meeting mental health needs. The recent CMHA report, *Mental Health for Canadians: Striking a Balance* (1988), presented a progressive vision of mental health needs and ways to meet those needs. Self-help and community organizations figured prominently in this vision. In New Brunswick and Quebec, self-help organizations are funded by the province, legitimizing their role in improving mental health (Mcnaughton 1992). Women's presses have published materials on women's health. Women's shelters and crisis counselling centres have been established to work with and for women who are experiencing the most oppressive conditions. Finally, women and women's groups actively lobby for legislative change to address the oppressive and inequitable conditions under which women live.

In understanding that medical knowledge is just one type of knowledge, women are taking back responsibility and control over their own lives. Increasingly women are combining their rediscovered expertise with that of medicine in a more collaborative model of health enhancement and disease treatment.

ACKNOWLEDGEMENTS

Many thanks to Shirley Pettifer, Donna Cherniak, Janet Wright, and Lynn Meadows for comments on earlier drafts.

NOTE

1. Judith Leavitt's edited volume, *Women and Health in America*, provides an excellent collection of articles by feminist historians who have examined various areas of the process of medicalization in women's lives. Catherine Reissman's article, 'Women and Medicalization: A New Perspective', carries this historical work into the present with a brief look at medicalization of pregnancy, weight, aging, and mental health.

FURTHER READINGS

Bolaria, B.S., and R. Bolaria. 1994. *Women, Medicine and Health*. Halifax: Fernwood Publishing; Saskatoon: Social Research Unit.

Burtch, B. 1994. *Trials of Labour: The Re-emergence of Midwifery*. Montreal: McGill-Queen's University Press.

Currie, D.H., and V. Raoul, eds. 1992. *Anatomy of Gender: Women's Struggle for the Body*. Ottawa: Carleton University Press.

Laurence, L., and B. Weinhouse. 1994. *Outrageous Practices: The Alarming Truth About How Medicine Mistreats Women*. New York: Fawcett Columbine.
Miller, L., and D. Findlay. 1994. 'Through Medical Eyes: The Medicalization of Women's Bodies and Women's Lives'. In *Health, Illness, and Health Care in Canada*, 2nd ed., edited by B.S. Bolaria and H.D. Dickinson, 276–306. Toronto: Harcourt Brace & Co.

REFERENCES

American Psychiatric Association. 1987. *Diagnostic and Statistical Manual of Mental Disorders*. Washington, DC: American Psychiatric Association.
Burtch, B.E. 1988. 'Midwifery and the State: The New Midwifery in Canada'. In *Gender and Society Creating a Canadian Women's Sociology*, edited by A.T. McLaren, 349–71. Toronto: Copp Clark Pitman.
CMHA (Canadian Mental Health Association). 1988. *Mental Health for Canadians: Striking a Balance*. Toronto: Canadian Mental Health Association.
Clarke, J.N. 1990. *Health, Illness and Medicine in Canada*. Toronto: McClelland and Stewart.
Cooperstock, R. 1978. 'Sex Differences in Psychotropic Drug Use'. *Social Science & Medicine* 12:179–86.
———. 1979. 'A Review of Women's Psychotropic Drug Use'. *Canadian Journal of Psychiatry* 24:29–34.
———, and H.L. Lennard. 1979. 'Some Social Meanings of Tranquillizer Use'. *Sociology of Health and Illness* 1:331–47.
D'Arcy, C., and W. Fritz. 1979. 'A Mental Health System in Transition: Profiles of Change'. *Canadian Journal of Psychiatry* 24:121–31.
———, and J.A. Schmitz. 1979. 'Sex Differences in the Utilization of Health Services for Psychiatric Problems in Saskatchewan'. *Canadian Journal of Psychiatry* 24:19–27.
Donegan, J. 1984. '"Safe Delivered," But by Whom? Midwives and Men-Midwives in Early America'. In *Women and Health in America*, edited by J.W. Leavitt, 302–17. Madison: University of Wisconsin Press.
Edginton, B. 1989. *Health, Disease and Medicine in Canada: A Sociological Perspective*. Toronto: Butterworths Canada Ltd.
Ehrenreich, B., and D. English. 1973a. *Complaints and Disorders: The Sexual Politics of Sickness*. Old Westbury, NY: Feminist Press.
———. 1973b. *Witches, Midwives and Nurses*. Old Westbury, NY: Feminist Press.
———. 1979. *For Her Own Good: 150 Years of the Experts' Advice to Women*. New York: Anchor Books.
Fisher, S. 1988. *In the Patient's Best Interest: Women and the Politics of Medical Decisions*. New Brunswick, NJ: Rutgers University Press.

Frances, A., and R. Hales, eds. 1988. *Review of Psychiatry*, vol. 7. Washington, DC: American Psychiatric Press Inc.

Gabe, J., and S. Lipschitz-Phillips. 1984. 'Tranquillisers as Social Control?' *Sociological Review* 32:524–46.

Garner, L.C., and R.C. Tessler. 1989. 'Technology in Childbirth: Effects on Postpartum Moods'. In *Healing Technologies: Feminist Perspectives*, edited by K.S. Ratcliff, 119–34. Ann Arbor: University of Michigan Press.

Jordan, B. 1983. *Birth in Four Cultures: A Crosscultural Investigation of Childbirth in Yucatan, Holland, Sweden and the United States*. Montreal: Eden Press.

Kaplan, H., and B. Sadock. 1988. *Synopsis of Psychiatry: Behavioral Sciences, Clinical Psychiatry*, 5th ed. Baltimore: Williams and Wilkins.

Kavanagh, J. 1992. 'Juggling a Family, Career, a Big Concern'. *Calgary Herald*, 17 July.

Keller, M. 1988. 'Foreword to Section II'. In *Review of Psychiatry*, vol. 7, edited by A.J. Frances and R.E. Hales, 147–8. Washington, DC: American Psychiatric Press Inc.

Kendall, K. 1992. 'Sexual Difference and the Law: Premenstrual Syndrome as Legal Defense'. In *Anatomy of Gender: Women's Struggle for the Body*, edited by D.H. Currie and V. Raoul, 130–46. Ottawa: Carleton University Press.

Klein, M., et al. 1986. *Controverse obstétricales et les soins maternels*. Quebec: Minister of Health and Social Services.

_____, et al. 1992. 'Does Episiotomy Prevent Perianal Trauma and Pelvic Flow Relaxation?' *Online Journal of Current Clinical Trials*, Document #10, vol. 1, 1 July.

_____, et al. 1994. 'Relationship of Episiotomy to Perineal Trauma and Morbidity, Sexual Function, and Pelvic Floor Relaxation'. *American Journal of Obstetrics and Gynecology* 171:591–8.

Kobrin, F.E. 1984. 'The American Midwife Controversy: A Crisis of Professionalization'. In *Women and Health in America: Historical Readings*, edited by J.W. Leavitt, 318–26.

Kunisch, J. 1989. 'Electronic Fetal Monitors: Marketing Forces and the Resulting Controversy'. In *Healing Technologies: Feminist Perspectives* edited by K.S. Ratcliff, 41–60. Ann Arbor: University of Michigan Press.

Leavitt, J.W., ed. 1984a. *Women and Health in America: Historical Readings*. Madison: University of Wisconsin Press.

_____. 1984b. 'Women and Health in America: An Overview'. In *Women and Health in America: Historical Readings*, edited by J.W. Leavitt, 3–8. Madison: University of Wisconsin Press.

_____. 1984c. 'Birthing and Anaesthesia: The Debate over Twilight Sleep'. In *Women and Health in America: Historical Readings*, edited by J.W. Leavitt, 175–84. Madison: University of Wisconsin Press.

_____, and W. Walton. 1984. '"Down to Death's Door": Women's Perceptions of Childbirth in America'. In *Women and Health in America: Historical Readings*, edited by J.W. Leavitt, 155–65. Madison: University of Wisconsin Press.

Maticka-Tyndale, E., J. Wright, and M. Coleman. 1993. 'Gender Specific Profile of Depressive Disorder in a General Hospital Population'. Paper presented at the meetings of the Canadian Psychiatric Association, Winnipeg, Manitoba.

McFarlane, J., et al. 1988. 'Women versus Men and Menstrual versus Other Cycles'. *Psychology of Women Quarterly* 12:201–23.

McKinlay, J.B., et al. 1987. 'The Relative Contributions of Endocrine Changes and Social Circumstances to Depression in Mid-Aged Women'. *Journal of Health and Social Behavior* 28:345–63.

Mcnaughton, E. 1992. 'Canadian Mental Health Policy: The Emergent Picture'. *Canada's Mental Health* 40:3–10.

Morantz, R.M. 1984. 'The Perils of Feminist History'. In *Women and Health in America: Historical Readings*, edited by J.W. Leavitt, 239–45. Madison: University of Wisconsin Press.

Myers, J.K., et al. 1984. 'Six-Month Prevalence of Psychiatric Disorders in Three Communities'. *Archives of General Psychiatry* 41:959–67.

Nair, C. 1992. 'Trends in Caesarean Section Deliveries in Canada'. *Health Reports* 3, 3:203–18.

Page, S. 1985. 'Commitment Decisions and Similarity of Symptomatology to Sex Role Stereotypes'. *Ontario Psychologist* 17:4–7.

_____. 1987. 'On Gender Roles and Perception of Maladjustment'. *Canadian Psychology/Psychologie Canadienne* 28:53–9.

Patychuck, D. 1985. 'Ultrasound: The First Wave'. *Healthsharing: A Canadian Women's Health Quarterly* 6:25–8.

Penfold, P.S., and G.A. Walker. 1983. *Women and the Psychiatric Paradox*. Montreal: Eden Press.

Pinchus, J., and N. Swenson. 1984. 'Pregnancy'. In *The New Our Bodies, Ourselves: A Book by and for Women*, edited by the Boston Women's Health Collective, 401–34. New York: A Touchstone Book.

Reissman, C.K. 1983. 'Women and Medicalization: A New Perspective'. *Social Policy* 14:3–18.

Robins, L.N., et al. 1984. 'Lifetime Prevalence of Specific Psychiatric Disorders in Three Sites'. *Archives General Psychiatry* 41:949–58.

Rose, R., and H.A. Pincus. 1988. 'Foreword to Section IV'. In *Review of Psychiatry*, vol. 7, edited by A. Frances and R. Hales, 431–5. Washington, DC: American Psychiatric Press.

Sachs, G.S., and A.J. Gellenberg. 1988. 'Adverse Effects of Electroconvulsive Therapy'. In *Review of Psychiatry*, vol. 7, edited by A. Frances and R. Hales, 498-512. Washington, DC: American Psychiatric Press Inc.

Scheff, T. 1974. 'The Labelling Theory of Mental Illness'. *American Sociological Review* 39:444–52.

Scholten, C.M. 1984. '"On the Importance of the Obstetrick Act": Changing Customs of Childbirth in America, 1760–1825'. In *Women and Health in America*, edited by J.W. Leavitt, 142–54. Madison: University of Wisconsin Press.

Shea, M.T., I. Elkin, and R.M.A. Hirschfeld. 1988. 'Psychotherapeutic Treatment of Depression'. In *Review of Psychiatry*, vol. 7, edited by A. Frances and R. Hales, 235–55. Washington, DC: American Psychiatric Press Inc.

Sleep, J., and A. Grant. 1987. 'West Berkshire Perineal Management Trial: Three Year Follow-up'. *British Medical Journal* 295:749–51.

Statistics Canada. 1991. 'Mental Health Statistics 1988–1989'. *Health Report Supplement 3* 3, no. 2.

Stoppard, J.M. 1992. 'A Suitable Case of Treatment? Premenstrual Syndrome and the Medicalization of Women's Bodies'. In *Anatomy of Gender: Women's Struggle for the Body*, edited by D.H. Currie and V. Raoul, 119–29. Ottawa: Carleton University Press.

Szasz, T. 1974. *The Myth of Mental Illness*, rev. ed. New York: Harper and Row.

Travis, C.B. 1988. *Women and Health Psychology: Mental Health Issues*. Hillsdale, NJ: Lawrence Erlbaum Associates Publishers.

Trypuc, J.M. 1988. 'Women's Health'. In *Sociology of Health Care in Canada*, edited by B.S. Bolaria and H.D. Dickinson, 154–66. Toronto: Harcourt, Brace Jovanovich.

Wertz, R.W., and D.C. Wertz. 1979. *Lying-In: A History of Childbirth in America*. New York: Schocken Books.

Women and Mental Health Committee. 1987. *Women and Mental Health in Canada: Strategies for Change*. Toronto: Canadian Mental Health Association.

Wood, A.D. 1984. '"The Fashionable Diseases": Women's Complaints and Their Treatment in Nineteenth-Century America'. In *Women and Health in America: Historical Readings*, edited by J.W. Leavitt, 222–37. Madison: University of Wisconsin Press.

Wright, J., et al. 1990. 'Gender Blind or Gender Bias'. Paper presented at the Abe Littman Psychiatric Research Conference, Calgary, Alberta.

—8—

The Body Perfect:
Appearance Norms, Medical Control, and Women

Deborah Findlay

'We may not have a cure for every disease, alas, but there's no reason we can't have a disease for every cure', writes Barbara Ehrenreich (1992:56). Modern medicine, in this view, not only treats disease but identifies and produces it. Medicine is frequently a form of social control, monitoring and defining what constitutes women's deviations from supposedly 'normal' feminine appearances. Our bodies are controlled through a strict dichotomization of sex and gender (Findlay 1993a, 1993b, 1995). The norms for masculinity and femininity often exaggerate the differences between men and women, cajoling and coercing them to adhere to socially produced appearances. Of course, the norms vary for women of different social classes, races, and ethnic backgrounds. Non-White women and working-class women are often treated as outside the dominant norms as defined by White culture. They are compelled to adhere to devaluating stereotypical images of their class or race. Black women, for example, are represented in the media as the exotic 'Other'. As one woman commented, 'Especially for Black women ... you are never good enough' (Chapkis 1986:48–9, 53–8, 190, 193; hooks 1992:17–18). Nevertheless, the emphasis on their difference from men is especially troublesome for many women because they face greater stigmatization based upon appearance and because the maintenance of particular appearances is actually the prescription for *behaviours* (Wolf 1991:14). Appearance norms thus restrict women more than men and limit their life chances more narrowly.

In this chapter, I explore these issues and examine the ongoing struggle between medicine and women over the right to define and deviate from appearance norms. I begin by studying why women are the prime targets of appearance norms and why they are subjected to medical control of their bodies. Then I investigate current ideals of bodily appearance for women, the type of 'bodywork' that women do to adhere to such norms, the historical development of these appearance norms, and the role of medicine in producing and sustaining the effects of appearance norms on women. I focus on obesity, related eating disorders, and the body-sculpting practices of cosmetic surgery. The chapter concludes by analysing women's resistance to medicalized appearance norms.

APPEARANCE NORMS, DEVIANCE, AND WOMEN'S BODIES

Medicine has long conceptualized women's bodies as irrational, closer to nature than to culture, and deviant from the cultural norms of male bodies. These and other social attitudes have been and continue to be a rationale for claiming the 'natural' inferiority of women and for keeping 'women in their place' (Currie and Raoul 1992:2, 4, 6, 9; Schur 1984:8). The medical regulation of appearance norms is simply the latest form of control over women and their bodies in that it defines bodily processes as disorders and/or diseases (Conrad and Schneider 1980; Findlay and Miller 1994; Riessman 1983:5, 15; Wolf 1991:10–11). Women are thus considered doubly deviant, first from the norm of maleness, and second from the medically approved appearance and behaviour norms. The penalties for not adhering to these norms are great: stigma, shame, guilt, moral anxiety, personal doubt, social rejection, and isolation (Schur 1984:3, 4, 7, 8).

The contemporary appearance norms in many Western societies are for women to have slim, well-toned, muscular bodies that do not reveal flab or bulges. They are expected to create such bodies, and to hone them by diet, dress, make-up, hairstyle, and cosmetic surgery. While men also have to abide by appearance norms, women are the primary targets for compliance since they are more commonly and strongly associated with beauty and decoration. Men may easily deviate from the norms of male appearance, for example, by developing a legitimate 'pot-belly' and acquiring acceptable grey hair after a certain age. Slight girth is a sign of affluence and despite the body-building movement, there is still a wide variety among celebrated adult male body images. Women have less leeway and are more often censured for bodily changes that accompany the aging process. They are subjected to antiaging skin products that prevent bumps, eliminate blemishes, and smooth out wrinkles. Women are much more likely to be medically scrutinized for shortcomings.

Women receive normative images of the feminine body through the media and medicine. Norms for the female body in magazines and movies have shifted away from a voluptuous, curvaceous figure to a body shape with few curves. Gone is the old Rubenesque ideal of pleasant plumpness, even though the weight of average females has increased. The current ideals tend to emphasize young, White, middle-class, slim, and fit images. Metaphorically, today's ideal favours a female body that is tightly controlled and takes up little space, limiting the social territory that women can command. It emphasizes a hairless, adolescent, sexually immature, and powerless body that denies adult female sexuality. Self-denial of other desires is very much part of this contemporary norm (Coward 1985:41, 44–5; Garner et al. 1980:483–4, 489–90). The media and advertising industries, for example, promote their products by suggesting that success and beauty will belong to every woman if she diets properly or purchases the latest stay-slim formulas. The medical profession, for its part, advocates a thin build over a heavy one, thus reinforcing the dominant norms. Consequently, women equate the attainment of normative appearance with social mobility. Moreover, women's experiences reveal a link between thin bodies and material success. Obesity seems to occur more commonly among working-class women, while slimness, infinite dieting, anorexia, and bulimia correlate with higher socio-economic standing (Garner et al. 1980:490). A recent study published in *The New England Journal of Medicine* confirms that there are plenty of social imperatives for being thin. It found that overweight women were 20 per cent less likely to marry and 10 per cent more likely to live in poverty (Nemeth 1994:46).

The social labelling of women of different classes and races, however, is a complex process. The class of the person or group doing the labelling plays an important part in the evaluation of women. Middle- and upper-class women may deviate less from the appearance norms because they have more economic and social resources to attain the ideal, so more may be expected of them. Obesity among middle-class women is therefore condemned more harshly even though it is working-class women who demonstrate a higher rate of obesity and are judged more intrinsically deviant. A similar process applies to women of colour. The appearance norms that are prescribed tend to be White norms, and women of colour find themselves largely excluded from cultural representations of the ideal. While this is racist, it also reduces the expectation that they conform to certain body ideals. Similarly, participating in a subculture (e.g., female athletes) may deflect deviant definitions and lessen stigma normally attached to bodily appearance (Dawson 1990). So the social control of women's bodies is not simple, unidimensional, or uniform; it is a complex process that is more or less restrictive, depending upon ethnicity, race, class, and age.

While the social control of women varies in form and degree, all women face the task of 'keeping up appearances' because beauty has been a major source of esteem and status (Orbach 1979:iii, xv). Men, in contrast, face fewer demands to maintain a body ideal because their status relies more upon career achievement, power, and money than upon physical attractiveness (Wolf 1991:12). While both sexes care about their looks, for women 'looks' have become necessary, with an exaggerated and unambiguous sense of female appearance being promoted by both the wider society and by women themselves. Statistics Canada reports that 37 per cent of normal-weight women and 8 per cent of underweight women still want to shed pounds (Nemeth 1994:46).

Such appearance norms accentuate and bifurcate the dominant versions of femininity and masculinity (Coward 1985:230–1; Epstein and Straub 1991:20–1). Women's bodies are overexposed and made more visible than men's. They are visual objects to others and to themselves (Schur 1984:68). Male bodies, in contrast, are often taken for granted. Men avoid much scrutiny, while controlling the body ideal for women. '[M]en have left themselves out of the picture because a body defined is a body controlled' (Coward 1985:229). No longer are women taught 'how to be a lady'; the rules of acceptable femininity are now normalized indirectly in visual images and in medical prescriptions (Bordo 1989:17). Rarely are women criticized for adhering to the appearance norms, and even more rarely are the appearance norms themselves questioned. Women, of course, are rebuked privately and publicly when they go 'too far' and develop anorexia, or submit to poorly done stomach stapling or cosmetic surgery. The commentary on daytime television talk shows, for example, focuses on the extremes and the sensational, rendering the rule-breakers as 'nuts', 'freaks', or 'perverts'. This allows 'average' women to consider themselves 'normal', and to miss the link between their 'normal' efforts at dieting and body management and the women who go beyond the bounds (Bordo 1990:85). In reality, all women are subjected to appearance norms, all women are encouraged to monitor their bodies, and all women are potentially deviant.

Because women's 'success' is often evaluated in terms of their looks, 'bodywork' is prioritized, while other features are downplayed. Adornment, of course, does have a long history and its use does not belittle the wearer, but when a model is done over with cosmetics and photography techniques, so much so that the imaginary is presented as the real thing, then the ideal is 'deeply suspect' (Schur 1984:68–9). As Bordo (1989) notes, in managing their bodies, women pursue an 'unattainable norm'. Consistent exposure to impossible images of ideal beauty conveys a sense of perpetual 'deficiency' to ordinary women. Women no longer find themselves intrinsically interesting and are made to feel inadequate or ugly. They are told by media experts, advertisers, family, friends, and the medical profession that dress, cosmetics, 'bodywork', and surgery will repair their shortcomings and 'deviance' (Wolf 1991:272). They are encouraged to focus their energy and money on bodily appearance, to the detriment of their intellect, career, and income-earning potential (Schur 1984:68; Wolf 1991:14, 16, 84).

'Martyrs to their appearance' and 'slaves of that impossible master, perfection', many women discover that bodywork requires time, energy, and money to shop, consume, and learn the tools of the trade to achieve the right look or undergo the latest cosmetic surgery procedure (Rodin 1992:60).

Bodywork demands a knowledge of calorie counting and food preparation, as well as the willpower to diet amidst the constant temptation of so-called bad food and drink. It results in enormous external regulation and subjection to 'exacting and normalizing disciplines of diet, makeup, and dress' (Bordo 1989:14). The effort required is often exhausting and painful, while many of these routines and rituals lower self-esteem and promote insecurity. At bottom, the focus on *self*-modification, and *self*-improvement is a 'durable and flexible strategy of social control' over women (Bordo 1989:14). Nor is this a matter of free choice. Underlying the appearance of choice is the reality of no choice. Appearance norms, it seems, pressure and coerce women to adhere to body norms, especially if they want to be heard and valorized in our society. In some instances, women are compelled to comply with appearance norms as a requirement of their job. For example, diet and fashion-consciousness are crucial elements for success in the airline industry, modelling, business, and many of the professions. The emphasis on body-management practices continues to affect women's life choices well after they have entered the workplace (Schur 1984:66; Wolf 1991:14, 16, 272–3).

What is the role of the medical profession in creating and reproducing these norms? Well, to start with, the discourses surrounding women's bodies are now mainly medical ones, espoused in terms of cures and diseases. Medical semantics have taken the form of critiquing fad diets, promoting new recipes to achieve the healthy, beautiful body, and monitoring the self as well as the body (Coward 1985:21; Outram 1989:45; Spitzack 1990:11). In the words of the World Health Organization, health is *total* well-being, not just the absence of disease (Zola 1975:83–7). Health is seen less and less as a choice and more and more as a problem that requires 'control, discipline, denial, and will-power' (Edgley and Brissett 1990:259). Consider the middle-class jogging and aerobics movements, and dieting, health foods, and antismoking campaigns in which people are exhorted to monitor themselves and others. The idea that anyone '*can* be healthy given the proper combination of diet, exercise, and life-style, has been translated into an ethic that everyone *should* be' (Edgley and Brissett 1990:259). Being overweight, for example, results in stigma. The overweight person's appearance is said to reveal her 'true' character, and she is set apart and branded deviant. Her size is referred to as disease, rectified not by prayer but by health regimes. The old emphasis on asceticism in morals is now an asceticism of the body ... a 'health fascism' (Edgley and Brissett 1990:260). Good health is defined as normality, while disease is equated with disorder and deviance (Edgley and Brissett 1990:260).

The equation of appearance with health is also part and parcel of the medical discourse. According to the American Medical Association, a preoccupation with beauty is the same as a preoccupation with health (Spitzack 1990; Wolf 1991:227). This identification makes women's bodies the property of society and places new demands on women. The exhortations to good health are 'exhortations to take control of your life' and to work 'at becoming sexually attractive' (Coward 1985:21). The main message is 'you might not be able to look like a model, but you certainly should try'. Women can feel better and invigorate and energize their way to a beautiful body by eating healthy, high-fibre foods, by drinking lots of water, and by strenuous physical exercise. The healthy body is one that has an improved appearance. As Coward (1985:23–3) puts it, the ideology is '[f]eel better and you'll look better'. Clear skin and fit bodies are a reality if only women have 'the will-power to change' (Coward 1985:24) their lifestyles.

Women are also allocated a key role in the expanding medical theatre of the body. They frequently monitor others' bodies and regularly assess conformity to or deviation from the norm. We commonly hear mothers tell daughters that they are 'getting a little flabby in the thighs', or hear sisters chide one another to 'lose that extra five pounds'. Often this seemingly constant surveillance of other women's bodies conveys moral censure for gender transgressions. 'Something really should be done about the hair on your upper lip' (common to many dark-haired women) 'because it is ruining family photos'! Adhering to gendered body prescriptions, however, produces not only an artificial and controlled body but also an unhealthy one. Attempts at hair removal often cause severe irritation or scarring of the skin. Dieting, when a woman is minimally overweight, can lead to malnutrition, hypoglycaemia, fatigue, and further health problems. Hypoglycaemia, for example, can lead to heart attacks, while poor nutrition that accompanies dieting can produce calcium deficiency and brittle bones in later life. Many of these cures, offered by medicine and promoted by the media, are 'invariably tangled up with the narcissistic construction of women as objects for "the look"' (Coward 1985:25). In turn, this emphasis may itself be a factor in causing women's illness. Hence, the cause is presented as the solution, leaving women's actual health problems unsolved (Coward 1985:25).

Social concern with women's status and mobility also contributes to the regulation of women and their bodies. As Wolf (1991:184) notes, when women came *en masse* into male spheres in the 1970s and 1980s, the cultural ideal for female bodies reflected 'an urgent social expedient that would make women's bodies into the prisons that their homes no longer were'. One check on male anxiety was for women to conform to male norms in the workplace. Through cultivating the slim and straight 'male' look and dressing with shoulder pads, ties, and long jackets, women were seen as less of a threat to men's domination in the public sphere (Bordo 1990:104–5). Consider the professions and the business world, where women often wore a suit (traditionally male garb) but added to it a traditional feminine touch (i.e., a piece of jewellery or a scarf) that was non-threatening. Of course, since their initial inroads into the business world, women have moved away from conformity to a male dress code and adopted more 'feminine' preferences in dress. Now they are able to take more licence because they have gained a foothold in traditionally male spheres. At the same time, adopting the 'accoutrements of the white, male world may be experienced as empowerment by women themselves'. The androgynous, slim female body is a norm that many women perceive as enabling, since it is associated with qualities like 'detachment, self-containment, self-mastery, [and] control', which are highly valued in our culture (Bordo 1990:105). How did these body norms emerge? What role did medicine play in their development?

To start, the emergence of a capitalist economy and workplace created a need for bodies to be closely monitored and disciplined. Unlike feudal relations, which were governed by barter, exchange, and extraction of rent from a primarily agricultural labour force, capitalism entailed a mode of production aimed primarily at the accumulation of surplus extracted directly from the labour process. Towns and cities were established, and an urban way of life evolved. Commerce and industry organized work according to tasks, timetables, and rules. The factory replaced the farm, and the clock (not the seasons) determined the rhythms of the workday. In an increasingly money-based economy, the direct supervision of labour was important and necessary. Profits flowed more easily to those owners who regulated their workforces. To that end, workers had to be disciplined by wages and schedules. They had to learn how to work long hours in a factory and not be guided by their own bodily needs and desires. The control of the body and nature, by mind and culture, was crucial to both the regulation of labour and to the accumulation of capital (Turner 1984:261–6). As Weber (1958) notes, the control of instincts and the delay of gratification, as advocated by the Protestant work ethic, was fundamental to the development of capitalist social relations. Sexual desires, work, leisure, and eating were increasingly ordered and regulated by money. Capitalism, however, required not only the constant production of goods but also the consumption of products. Consumerism continuously reintroduces new 'needs' to be satisfied. As our producer-selves, we are expected to repress desires, including physical ones, yet as our consumer-selves we are expected to indulge (Bordo 1990:96). There is a contradiction between the demand to 'eat less' and the demand to 'consume more' (O'Neill 1985:104–5). Food consumption, for example, while necessary for productivity could, if excessive, become a threat to people's health and a 'problem' for capital, so it requires considerable deviance management (Bordo 1990:94). Not surprisingly, the expectations that people both repress and consume fall heavily on women because their desires are the most socially threatening and because they do the bulk of societal consuming.

One societal mechanism that regulates the desire for food is the 'medical gaze' (Turner 1984). The 'medical gaze' symbolizes medicine's control over our bodies as part of culture. It isolates and reveals deviations from the normal and the expected, exhorting individuals to tame their desires by 'spiritual combat with themselves' (Bordo 1990:96). Expurgation has been replaced with self-mastery and the best way to succeed is to dominate your body with your will. For example, no longer does an excessively large, rotund stomach mark high social status and bourgeois success, as it did in the past. By the twentieth century, the ideal body form was lean and straight. As Bordo (1990:94) puts it, 'slender wives became the showpieces of their husbands' success'. The toned, fit, and slender body was increasingly thought to indicate a person of middle-class status, while obesity indicated working-class laziness and lack of discipline. The ability of the middle class to conquer their bodies and to manage their desires is said to represent their ability to manage corporations and to become upwardly mobile (Bordo 1990:94–5).

Medicine incorporates similar social judgements about what is desirable and successful. Its classifications of 'diseases' include social norms. Those falling into the categories of 'disease' were stigmatized as deviants by the medical profession, who gained the power to label and who took over from nurses, midwives, and homeopathic doctors in the administration of health. As medicine was 'professionalized' in the nineteenth century, it specialized and expanded its markets and clientele, replacing traditional forms of knowledge. It widened its sphere of influence by defining more and more life conditions as health matters. Medicine increased its social power and acquired the right to intervene by controlling the training of medical students, by regulating the demand for doctors (thus insuring high status and income for members of the profession), and by obtaining the legal sanction of the state, thereby forbidding others to practise medicine and effectively acquiring a monopoly (Findlay 1993a, 1993b; Freidson 1970; Torrance 1987:15; Turner 1987:140).

In addition, medicine's prerogative to officially, legally, and legitimately define and treat deviance from social norms was bolstered by its alliance with science. Until the twentieth century, many medical practitioners thought that the art of healing, including good bedside manner and an interpersonal knowledge of the patient, was more important than extensive scientific knowledge. Eventually, medicine linked itself closely with science and the universities; and '[t]he spread of scientific and techno-rational procedures ... latched onto a new terrain, the body of individuals and the body of populations' (Ludmerer 1985:107, 231; Turner 1984:160). Medicine repackaged its knowledge to the public as 'science' and strengthened its claims over knowledge and practice by defining them as objective and technical. Scientific medicine is now thought to possess objective, bias-free solutions to social problems, and is relied upon to 'interpret the benefits of disinterested science for the social good' (Fisher 1988:134; Morantz-Sanchez 1985:280–1; Rothman 1989).

As Conrad and Schneider (1980:36) note, '[t]he medical profession domi-nates the organization of health care and has a virtual monopoly over any-thing that is defined as an illness or a "medical" treatment'.

The spirit of medical expertise has recently expanded into new markets like substance abuse and the 'beauty business'. What were once considered 'normal' conditions, such as obesity, drinking, and wrinkles, are now points of intervention for medicine (Fisher 1988:141; Wolf 1991). Anorexia and obesity, for example, exist largely in relation to a norm of slenderness. The new markets concentrate disproportionately on women and their bodies. In this sense, physicians define the normality and deviance of women's appear-ance, and standardize medical versions of normality and pathology. Medi-cine not only reflects social notions of how women should look, it also *creates* and *produces* social views of women's appearance. When we take for granted that women should be a particular weight or body shape, we are often accepting medical values and judgements as the only 'truth' about women's bodies. Let us examine more carefully medicine's power by considering eating disorders and obesity, as well as cosmetic surgery.

CONTROLLING WOMEN'S HUNGER

In the late twentieth century, an obsession with appearance and particularly with body weight came to characterize many Western societies. As Nemeth (1994:45) puts it, 'it is a uniquely late-twentieth-century ritual, this noon-hour work-out, and the temple is any health club in any Canadian city'. The middle and upper classes now frequently report on their struggles to reduce body fat to a minimum. Devotees diet, 'sweat and pant for healthy hearts and lungs, for flat stomachs', firm biceps, and 'chiselled pectorals' (Nemeth 1994:45). Such asceticism and denial of bodily hunger existed earlier, but it was not widespread and it was more a matter of the religious practice of denying the appetites (Bordo 1990:83; Turner 1984:165–70). But as the state became interested and involved in the productivity of its working citi-zens, the religious and moral approach to diet was replaced by a scientific, technical reliance on the medicine of calorie counting and nutrition. Indi-viduals were taught to police themselves, and those who did not or could not monitor themselves were induced to do so by coercive measures (Elias 1978; Foucault 1979).

Medicine creates and recreates these self-monitoring norms for women by designating deviance from the body weight norms as diseases. Medical definitions of body weight are actually deviations around a social standard of the 'best' weight (Schwartz 1990:189, 223). Obesity is now viewed as a woman's body 'out of control'. The current discourse about obesity revolves around its health risks, as supposedly 'an attractive body ... signifies a healthy attitude' (Spitzack 1990:2), but it is not ultimately for health reasons that obesity is stigmatized in our society. In fact, for women, there is little or no relation between obesity and poor health. In reality, the norm is about the immorality of female fat and that is a public, not a medical or private, issue. Thinness and hunger are not personal prerogatives but concessions demanded by the wider society concerned with women's power and freedom (Wolf 1991:186–7). Obese individuals, then, are judged for social reasons. Their character is stigmatized. They are marked as 'abnormal', 'lazy', 'weak-willed', and 'unruly'. Unable to control their bodies, they are identified as untrustworthy and unable to succeed. Culture has lost the war to the abhorrent ravages of the flesh (Orbach 1979:4; Schur 1984:71; Spitzack 1990:2).

Interestingly, the social meaning of obesity is quite different to particular individuals or to groups of women. Obesity, for some women, represents a form of rebellion against social conformity, a refusal to be 'normal' and 'play by the rules' (Bordo 1990:100). Fat is a way of rejecting restrictive gender norms that advocate an ideal of self-denial and powerlessness for women (Schur 1984:73–4). When the obese express contentment with their weight and appearance, and say that they have no wish to diet, they are met with incredulity, denial, and anger. The outright hostility directed at the obese is a response to what is perceived as a rebellion against the social demand for normalcy. Only if they indicate that they are 'trying' to be normal are they responded to sympathetically (Bordo 1990:100–1). The meaning of changes in women's body ideals (from the voluptuous to the slim), however, contains the seeds of other rebellions. For many women, the new body form conveys a positive emancipation from domestic life centred around child-bearing and child-rearing. For others, as noted earlier, it allows favourable association with the most highly valued traits of our culture: control, self-mastery, strength, objectivity, and empowerment. The slender body image, then, conveys multiple symbolic meanings and resistances, and politicizes body reduction as a site of struggle for women (Bordo 1990:103–5; Spitzack 1990:4).

A key player in that struggle is the medical profession. How does medicine direct and shape women's efforts to achieve the perfect body? Why is it that some women develop anorexia nervosa (self-starvation) or bulimia (binging and purging)? Treating and labelling eating disorders are primarily in the hands of medical practitioners in therapeutic settings. They define eating disorders as medical problems and treat symptoms as part of an individual's pathology (Currie 1988:199). Yet as one physician acknowledges, 'it is normal for women in our society to feel uncomfortable with their bodies' (Dawson 1990:87). Most middle-class women have a 'compulsive fear of and fixation upon food' that can be defined as an eating problem, making most women 'mental anorexics' (Wolf 1991:183). One study found that individuals on low-calorie diets exhibited symptoms of semistarvation. They were obsessive about food and food-related objects, and developed depression, hysteria, and psychosis. They lost energy and alertness, and could not function at work. The dieters eventually developed uncontrollable hunger and binged on large quantities of food. In a manner similar to famine survivors, they continuously hoarded and hid food, even though they later had an abundance of it (Wolf 1991:194–5). The effects of semistarvation are common to low-calorie diets, yet we hear little from medical practitioners about the health risks of extended dieting. It is difficult to know where 'normal' dieting ends and deviant dieting starts. Ironically, since medicine is in large measure part of a social control solution, there is no critique of the existing norms or categories in their approach to eating disorders. Medicalization perpetuated the very problem it seeks to eradicate because it does not explore why the roots of the eating disorders exist in the body norms in the first place (Findlay and Miller 1994).

Let us look more carefully at eating disorders, the medical knowledge and social control of such 'deviance', and the meaning of eating disorders for women. Clinical records indicate that anorexia is not a new phenomenon in Canadian society. It was documented as early as the 1860s. It usually begins with dieting and appears typically in female adolescents, the age group most susceptible to peer pressure to be slim and attractive (Turner 1984:183; 1987:106). Eating disorders are serious conditions; 5 to 15 per cent of those hospitalized from anorexia die, while 40 to 50 per cent never recover completely (Wolf 1991:182). There are numerous and extensive effects on the body, including hypothermia, edema, hypotension, impaired heartbeat, lanugo (excessive growth of body hair), infertility, and death. Bulimia leads to tooth erosion, electrolyte imbalance, dehydration, and abnormalities of the heart (Wolf 1991:183).

Traditional psychoanalytic approaches argued that anorexia was a denial of femininity. This interpretation focused on the individual and emphasized the role of 'dysfunctional families' for women. The mother-daughter and father-daughter relationships were examined in detail and high middle-class familial expectations were thought to be contributing factors to anorexia (Currie 1988:204–6). By starving, women rejected their own physical characteristics, retarded their menstrual periods, and created a boylike body. Deviance lay with the individual and their families, not with the social norms for women, but this explanation cannot account for why eating disorders have lasted so long. Nor can it account for why such disorders seem to have predominated in one class and racial group, but have now spread from the White middle class to other social classes and races (Boskind-Lodahl 1976:343–6; Orbach 1979:167; Székely 1988:18; Wolf 1991:183).

More recent theories consider social relations and view anorexia as an exaggerated version of femininity—a manifestation of women's sense of powerlessness. Anorexia, in this view, is a symbolic 'hunger strike', a protest against the social conditions in which women live. It is a desperate response to the traditional pressure on women to be desirable as sexual objects (Currie

1988:207–8; Székely, 1988:19). Anorexia is closely related to the fact that women are increasingly faced with contradictory social expectations. They are expected to be domestic providers and to maintain a feminine appearance, yet they are simultaneously urged to achieve in the public sphere (Orbach 1978:167; Székely 1988:24; Turner 1984:196, 1987:106; Wolf 1991:211). This creates a double bind for women who must be passive at home, but competitive and assertive in the workplace. Young women, beginning to develop an identity, are initially valued for their appearance, but as adults, they are considered vain, obsessive, and 'dumb' if they spend too much time and energy on it (Chernin 1985; Dawson 1990; Shute 1993; Turner 1987:107). These contradictory demands are impossible for women to fulfil. Masculine and feminine traits may not be added to each other easily, as they are often considered mutually exclusive. Anorexia is an attempt to achieve precisely a blended, androgynous self (Bordo 1989:18–20).

Women are also expected to manage the contradiction between dietary management/slimness and consumerism. This dual emphasis on ascetic control and consumer indulgence is symbolized by bulimia. The bulimic's purges are an expression of the asceticism of production, while her binges are a form of capitalist consumerism (Bordo 1990:97, 99). Women gain control over their social situation by controlling their bodies and mastering them, by denying the body's desires and transcending the flesh, and by achieving a sense of moral superiority (Turner 1984:184, 193; 1987:104, 107).

While eating disorders may appear as 'out of control' deviance to the medical profession, these disorders may mean the opposite to women—the ultimate means of order. Anorexics, for example, see parts of their bodies, especially the stomach, as fat that needs to be contained (Wolf 1991:183). As one woman put it, 'My body can turn on me at any moment; it as an out-of-control mass of flesh' (Bordo 1989:18, 1990:89). Food restrictions and the denial of hunger allow women to experience self-esteem and admiration in a society in which they feel excluded, and to reject the curvaceous female body shape, which has been linked with social vulnerability, sexual abuse, and incompetence. Unable to control the patriarchal social contexts, they try to control their bodies. Another woman describes having anorexia as 'like living in a fake world. When you're not eating you feel like you're running away from whatever it is and staying ahead of the game. Like drugs, it is a different way to cope' (Webb 1994:50). Anorexia, then, is an 'empowered protest' even if it is unheard and counterproductive (Bordo 1990:20; Wolf 1991:198–9). It is a 'normative obsession', but one in which female behaviour and obedience is the essence of the obsession, not women's beauty (Bordo 1990:20; Wolf 1991:187).

For women, eating disorders are ways of managing contradictory social demands for normality. They begin as sane responses (rather than diseases) to an insane reality (Wolf 1991:198). Indeed, some studies suggest that the

exaggerated conformity of the anorexic's body reflects a general social nar-
cissism centred around an ethic of 'consumer sexuality'. This ethic promotes
a thin, socially attractive body through the use of diets and exercise programs, body-building and aerobics. But the sense of controlled consumption
developed by extreme dieting and exercising regimes is a chimera because
the body dominates the self more and more, and conduct gradually becomes
obsessed with only food, dieting, and medical control (Turner 1984:184–5,
199, 203). Anorexia is a paradoxical protest; it resists the social conditions
and lack of voice for women, but it does so couched in the silent body
language of femininity.

Unfortunately, the medical conceptualization of eating disorders downplays
the social context and emphasizes the separation of healthy, 'normal' women
from pathological, sick ones. That division is premised on interpretations of
inappropriate body weight that emphasize personal inadequacies (e.g., low
self-esteem, depression) and not medical definitions of body weight. As Székely
(1988:18–9, 174–6) observes, medicalization obscures that fact that the dieting practices of women with anorexia do not differ markedly from those of
other women in this same social context. Medicalization is also pervasive.
The cultural fear of fat has spread from adults to children and even to
foetuses. The belief that fat cells in a foetus lead to adult obesity has already
caused medical restrictions on women's weight gain during pregnancy and
greater medical control over pregnant women's bodies in prenatal care
(Schwartz 1990:251, 269, 296–7).

Women are placed in increasingly contradictory positions. While the
current body norms emphasize slimness, medical research shows that repeated weight loss and gain is more hazardous than living as an overweight
person (Hill 1990:114). While obese people face higher risks of heart disease
and diabetes, dieting results in hypoglycaemia (which may lead to death),
ketosis (an acidic condition that produces sticky blood), osteoporosis, gout,
and increased cholesterol and triglyceride levels, with the attendant risk of
cardiovascular disease (Douglas 1987a:19, 1987b:10). A recent heart study
done by the National Institute of Health in the United States found that
'people whose bodyweight fluctuates have as great a risk of cardiovascular
disease and coronary heart disease as people who are consistently obese'
(Nemeth 1994:48).

Not surprisingly, these arguments have given rise to a new antidiet discourse wherein women are advised to abandon 'the battle of the bulge'.
They are counselled to become less preoccupied with food and weight and
to throw away their scales and calorie counters. Rather, they are urged to
exercise more and tone body parts. Advertisers are hyping this antidiet twist
in the norms for women. Beer ads, for example, beat out a new message—
women should not work on improving themselves; instead, they should relax
and enjoy themselves. Medical practitioners are also reducing the emphasis

on diets and warning of bodily battle fatigue. Women may find this antidiet approach refreshing. They need not view themselves as failures for not living up to an unattainable cultural norm of female appearance. Of course, women who don't diet may still be labelled deviant because they reject the social norms for women. As one psychologist notes, 'If you take a piece of cake', others will still respond with 'You're not having cake are you? You're going to get fat if you eat that.' It's unbelievable what people feel they are allowed to say about other people's weight. It's an open target' (Turner 1991:E1, E6). Notwithstanding the effects of shaming, women at least have a weapon of resistance against such monitoring—they can cite the long list of negative health risks associated with dieting.

Although this antidiet discourse for the 'modern' woman is being sold by media, advertisers, the fitness industry, and health care practitioners, an even closer monitoring of bodies is on the agenda. Women are exhorted to trim tummies, hip bulges, all cellulite, and soft or loose areas even on an otherwise thin body. The language used to describe this is militaristic. Fat must be 'burned', tummies 'busted', abdomens 'blasted', and flab 'attacked' and 'destroyed' (Bordo 1990:90). Cher's recent video, for example, speaks of 'trying to continuously burn your body' in order to achieve a tightly regimented body—'Buns of Steel', as the video advertises it (Bordo 1990:90; Nichols 1991).

If battle is one semantic rationale, freedom is another powerful language of the politics of the body. Health monitoring and self-regulation are often framed in terms of autonomy and progress, which makes the discourse seductive for women. Jane Fonda, for instance, describes her approach to bodywork as enhancing and emancipatory. She claims she resists and challenges the feminine ideal of slimness, freeing women for that ideal, revolutionizing their lives, and bringing them success and power. Well-being and good health are now imbedded in a 'rhetoric of appreciation'. Health is determined visually, through a woman's self-perception and through others' perceptions of her. Liberated women are defined as those who participate in women's health promotion and who develop healthy mental attitudes, as evinced by the attractive body. Those who deviate are encouraged to confess their dietary lapses and save themselves by more and more exercise so as to regain the status of 'normal' women. The paradox of this discourse is that in promising women individuality, natural beauty, and freedom, it in fact makes them rely on experts, reduces their individuality, and produces a highly *unnatural* appearance.

Ironically, the new health discourse that promotes strong, muscled, and toned bodies for women also reproduces a restrictive feminine ideal based on traditional gender norms. Women may *feel* more powerful when shaping their bodies to approximate the muscular male body type, but this is a valorization based on the traditional *dualism* of gender. It suggests that women are moving to the male side and away from the female norm. We see this most strikingly in the development of female athleticism, which challenges the traditional norms of feminine appearance, and in the promotion of 'power look' body-building in which women now cultivate the 'hulk-like, triangular shape' (Bordo 1989:24) of male body-builders. As Bordo (1989:24) notes, this development 'is no less determined by a hierarchical, dualistic construction of gender than was the traditional "feminine" norm that tyrannized female body-builders ... for years'.

The muscled female body, however, is for now too deviant and dangerous for wholesale social acceptance. Both the anorexic body and the muscled body are on a continuum, battling soft and excess flesh through self-policing and medical monitoring, but this battle for freedom through bodywork is paradoxical. Social control also becomes self-control through self-monitoring and scientifically managing food through denial and restraint (Spitzack 1990:30). Women are advised to turn away from experts and to internalize the control of their own deviance. Furthermore, the promotion of exercise programs to trim and contain body parts overlaps with the antidiet discourse. Both recommend their approaches to 'liberated' women in health terms, implying that women who don't comply don't care about their health. Both find negligent behaviour incomprehensible and deviant. Yet with antidieting, traditional self-examination is attached to traditional versions of femininity. Bodywork is individualized and introspective, in effect rejecting the question of social standards. Eating disorders, in this view, are not food problems but quests for inner self-worth. A major contradiction in the weight loss/fitness discourse and in some antidiet tracts is that women are encouraged to become physically less in order to become personally more wholesome (Spitzack 1990:1–10). They are told that to achieve permanent weight loss and slenderness (which is still a goal of many antidiet programs), they have to become less compulsive about food and become non-dieters first and foremost. The rationale is that everything and nothing must change for the individual woman in order to achieve a thin body. Diets are portrayed as repressing the individuality of each woman, while antidieting draws on the expression of individualism to frame its discourse. Orbach's (1979:xv, 23) antidiet approach, for example, recommends that the obese use self-regulation to accept the self and give up the struggle to attain the norms of femininity. She still promotes the thin body ideal, but it will be achieved, she says, by self-work, self-surveillance, and self-acceptance. Susan Powter, the newly slim author of *Stop the Insanity* (twenty-five weeks on the *New York Times* best-seller list), 'indicts the diet and exercise industries' even as she offers her own 'advice on how to get fit' and achieve the ideal appearance (Nemeth 1994:45).

Much of the fitness industry remains focused on women's appearance norms, which is a traditional feminine preoccupation, and women are still enjoined to scrutinize their bodies for deviance from the firm, slim, athletic look (Spitzack 1990:30; Székely 1988:191). Medicine bolsters this self-policing by directly disciplining women's bodies, and its equation of health with beauty (Wolf 1991:227). An attractive appearance is linked to emotional health, well-being, and a beautiful mind (Synnott 1989:632). With bodywork and beauty now a prescription for good health, there is 'health fascism' afoot (Edgley and Brissett 1990:259). As one high school student remarked, friends will not say '"You're fat." But they might say "Look at that girl, she's so big." I look and I think "What are they saying about me?"' (Nemeth 1994:47). This fosters a societywide morality play in which each of us monitors the health of others, while overall monitoring is done by the health experts (Outram 1989:45; Spitzack 1990:3–4, 9, 33).

In the end, this is an unsatisfactory solution for women, for conformity to the ideals of beauty and thinness is still the outcome. All the blame for eating disorders and obesity is placed on the individual in each of the medical, antidiet, or fitness approaches. This does not take us very far. The solutions promoted are psychological and personal. Medical contexts and wider social relations are ignored, yet doctors gain professionally from the diet industry, medicalizing obesity as illness and addiction, and corporations benefit economically by promoting both the diet industry and the antidiet approaches (Spitzack 1990:11–29). Women, however, find their bodies marketed as commodities and regulated by the new, improved health police.

SCULPTING WOMEN'S BODIES

I have argued that the beauty/health complex is deeply implicated in the enhancement and enforcement of appearance norms. Another means of realizing appearance ideals is to 'go under the knife' for face-lifts, liposuctions, and breast reductions or augmentations. Cosmetic surgery brings us the 'designer body' and is a reminder of how far our 'disgust with bodily bulges has gone' (Bordo 1990:90). As a director of Cosmetic Surgery Hospital remarked, 'I have a scalpel and I'm creating a surgery of happiness' (Nemeth 1994:49). Liposuction, for example, sucks out the unwanted bulges of people of *normal* weight; it is not recommended for the obese. It is a quick fix on the road to the perfect body when all else fails. Body shape and size, it seems, need not be constrained by genetics; they can be overcome by skilful surgery and will-power. Consider the case of Laura, forty-two, who runs a small marketing business. She has had extensive body contouring done, including liposuction of her waist, stomach, thighs, buttocks, calves, and ankles. 'Before the cosmetic sculpting, she was a size ten above the waist and a size fourteen below; now she is a straight size ten', and considers herself more socially acceptable. Now she says, 'I feel better about myself. I'm not so self-conscious' (Nemeth 1994:49). However, cosmetic surgery is costly. It is rarely covered by health insurance, and so is affordable only to middle- and upper-class women. The financial costs prohibit obese, working-class women from having plastic surgery.

Women account for about 85 per cent of the 65,000 cosmetic surgery patients in Canada, and in the United States, plastic surgeons estimate that about 25 per cent of their business is now comprised of teenagers. Asian teenagers, for example, are having their eyelids reshaped, and some Black youths, à la Michael Jackson, are having their noses narrowed and lips thinned. The social ideal seems to be the White, middle-class appearance norm. As one plastic surgeon pointed out, 'Esthetic surgery has become a commodity.' Parents are pushing it, wanting their adolescent children to have a new stereo, the latest fashions, and a new nose. Men, too, are pursuing the wonders of cosmetic surgery. Through new chest (pectoral) muscles, nose jobs, cheek implants, penile enlargements, testicular implants, liposuction, eyelid surgery, and silicone calf augmentations, they now account for about 15 per cent of cosmetic surgery operations in Canada (Taylor 1992:D5). While some physicians decry these trends, others claim that surgery will help bolster a patient's self-esteem and save on later medical and psychiatric bills. As one doctor mused, 'Our society is becoming more image conscious. People want to improve their bodies, thereby improving their inner selves.' Some women hate 'what they see in the mirror', but plastic surgery gives them back what they lost and they are 'ecstatic' (Nemeth 1994:49). However, there are medical risks. Silicone implants can trigger autoimmune diseases such as arthritis and scleroderma, and implants inserted under muscles may rupture, especially if they are subjected to high stress levels. For teenage girls, the hazards may be even greater. Many have unrealistic expectations, hoping that altered appearance outcomes will solve personal and psychiatric problems. Once changed, the surgery is irreversible and the disappointment may last a lifetime (Alexander 1990:A10).

A common medical route to 'the look of the modern woman' is through breast implants, but experience with the Même and other silicone implants reveal that women are sacrificing their health and their lives for appearance's sake. The health hazards include permanent immune system damage, connective tissue diseases, cancers due to leakage of the silicone gel, severe infections, decreased visibility of breast cancer in mammography, and further surgery. For these reasons, many Canadian and American women sued the Dow Corning Corporation, a major implant manufacturer. One US jury found that the company 'acted with fraud, malice and oppression' (Chisholm 1992:42) because it did not disclose information on the safety risks of implants. Harms were suspected as far back as 1971, yet the warnings of employees and scientists about the cancer risks of silicone gel were ignored or suppressed. As one scientist observed to Dow Corning, 'Without this testing, I think we have excessive personal and corporate liability exposure'

(Chisholm 1992:42–3; *Globe and Mail* 1992b:A1; Jenish 1992:38–41). Profits were put ahead of health until costs of covering lawsuits, 'the cost of doing business', finally outweighed the profits from sales.

Federal governments in Canada and the United States eventually imposed temporary bans on the use of silicone breast implants. In Canada, an independent panel has already recommended that the use of silicone implants be restricted to women over forty and to those awaiting reconstructive surgery following a mastectomy. They also urged the creation of an information phone line and a national registry of breast implant recipients. More controversially, they argued that women receiving silicone implants should sign an informed consent form. This measure protects physicians and corporations from lawsuits, while not really affording much protection to women (McIntosh 1992).

The Canadian Medical Association compiled a report on the Même breast implant and concluded that high cancer risks are speculative and that the removal of implants is unwarranted. Those in the medical profession, who stood to lose their market and their income, pressured the federal government to lift the moratorium, claiming it was based on 'anecdotal reports' and 'uninformed hysteria' (*Globe and Mail* 1992b:A1, A6) rather than on scientific data. In a news conference, called to counter the negative publicity around breast implants, the past president of the Canadian Association of Plastic Surgeons maintained that doctors were not more concerned about their incomes than about women's health (*Globe and Mail* 1992b:A1, A6). But Pierre Blais, a scientist with the Department of Health and Welfare, questions the Canadian Medical Association's arguments. He states that the basic issue is not whether implants increase the risk of getting breast cancer, but what happens when a woman with an implant gets breast cancer. Blais believes that the Même implant speeds up the spread of cancer, and makes it especially difficult to detect or remove the cancer because it is hidden by the implant. He asserts that the findings of the Canadian Medical Association report are biased, given the make-up of the panel. Only two panel members were familiar with plastic surgery and both were at one time associated with Surgitek, the company that manufactured the Même implant. Furthermore, the funding for the report came from a government department that was implicated in the distribution of the implants in the first place. Surgitek eventually withdrew its product from the market to deal with the lawsuits; Health and Welfare Canada denies that there were or are any serious health risks associated with the implant; and Pierre Blais was fired from his position with Health and Welfare Canada.

Women's organizations like Je Sais/I Know, which is a national network of women with breast implants, also protested the Canadian Medical Association's findings and the government's denial of wrongdoing. They argued that the Canadian government has been trying to protect itself from liability rather than conducting needed research on implants and their effects. They have raised several important questions. Why was the implant not tested thoroughly before being given to women? What other health risks are associated with implants? Why has women's health been jeopardized by corporations and the medical profession, and ignored and covered up by governments (Williams 1991:5)? As with the Dalkon Shield (an intra-uterine contraceptive device that caused death, sterilization, and injury to women) and the administration of the hormone DES to women, which caused rare forms of cancer and high infertility rates among offspring, it is difficult not to conclude that health risks were deliberately suppressed by pharmaceutical companies and many physicians. As Emily Martin observes, 'they never tested the implant in breast tissue'. Nor did they act on 'decades of complaints from women'. Products for women were 'not as well-scrutinized as products for men' (quoted in Foreman 1992:D1–5; Smith 1992). The imperative to 'do no harm' was not and is not strictly followed in the marketing of drugs and medical devices for women. As one journalist sums up, 'the pursuit of profit' is the driving motive behind a network of manufacturers, doctors, and health regulators, which places their interests first and those of women second (Olive 1992; Turner 1992b).

We see this money motive most clearly in the discovery of 'new diseases', which create new medical markets. You probably did not know it, but there is a 'new disease' sweeping the country: micromastia—yes, small breasts. Since we all know women who fall short in the mammary department, there must be by now an epidemic of micromastia. Not to worry; apparently it is not fatal. Those hobbling around untreated carry the 'plague's dread symbol—the A-cup bra'. But if they want, they can be cured by the insertion of the breast implant—medical science's solution to the large breast appearance norm in North American culture. One can only wonder what new diseases will emerge next as rationales for plastic surgeons' activities (Ehrenreich 1992:56).

Fortunately, the medical profession is not a uniform group with one set of interests. Plastic surgeons may support breast implants, but rheumatologists who have seen the serious illnesses created by the implants are more wary (Turner 1992a:K1, K7). They are supporting women in their lawsuits, and promoting women's health interests.

But what constitutes women's best interests is complex. Some women oppose the social ideal of appearance norms as well as their 'normalizing' function. Women's rationales for breast implants often typify that function, especially when women assert that their 'boyfriends love the implants', 'they look good in a bathing suit', and 'the implants make them look normal' (Smith 1992). Yet at the same time as there is opposition to the ideal, other women want the right to decide in matters regarding their own bodies. Those who have elected to have implants resent health organizations pushing for a ban. They argue that they are not passive victims; with the right information about risk, they can decide for themselves. Still, other women have had mastectomies that they feel are disfiguring. They are uncomfortable without reconstructive surgery (Olive 1992; Smith 1992). Finally, other women have suffered at the hands of the surgeon and want redress for their pain and humiliation.

There is no single uniform 'women's' position on this issue. There are multiple sites of resistance to the abuses of the medical profession and corporate capital, as well as to the neglect of governments, but one thing is certain. The problem will not disappear until the norms for women's appearance are addressed and changed. Women's breasts have been fetishized as an erogenous zone and separated from their function in mothering. It is not surprising that women with small breasts may feel self-conscious about their bodies. One woman explained, 'When you're going to buy a $600 dress and it's perfect except for the breasts, that's when you feel confronted with it—this dress would be perfect if I had normal breasts' (Underwood 1992:45). Women who don't have the socially designated breast size may also experience low self-esteem in relationships with their partners. If they don't 'measure up', they don't feel attractive and they may easily feel unloved. Plastic surgeons acknowledge the power of the ideal image of feminine appearance. One doctor reports that the current ideal is 'a physical peculiarity, encompassing a slim body shape with large breasts. Everyone tries to live up to that image and if you don't it's a problem' (Underwood 1992:44–5). This ideal, however, is a physiological impossibility, yet the medical profession continues to support the cultural ideal of women's appearance by medicalizing the bigger-is-better syndrome (Nemeth 1994:47). In the early 1980s, plastic surgeons launched a public relations campaign, claiming that small breasts were really a 'deformity' and that if the 'disease' is unaddressed, it may result in a 'total lack of well-being' (Turner 1992a:K7). Unfortunately, this kind of medical hysteria will not change the cultural ideal. Until society broadens 'its definition of female beauty beyond bra size, the bigger-the-better ethic will remain a plastic surgeon's dream' and a woman's nightmare (Underwood 1992:45).

RESISTANCE AND STRUGGLE

I have stressed some of the detrimental effects of appearance norms for women: the normalization of their bodies, self-monitoring and psychological surveillance, unhealthy competitions for self-esteem and for the social approval of others, overemphasis on bodywork, and an uncritical acceptance of the social basis of appearance norms (Coward 1985:25; Wolf 1991:14, 16). For example, defining anorexia in medical terms (psychoanalytic and psychological) individualizes the issue and makes it difficult to expose the social foundations of the appearance norms. I have noted that the social discourse that encourages bodywork in the name of health, betterment, and freedom is difficult to question. But can women reconstitute the more positive potential of body consciousness and health movements? The meaning of appearance and bodywork for many women may differ from the intentions of medicine and the definitions of society. Women do at times turn the obsession with female beauty and bodies to their own ends, redefining what constitutes normal appearance and what is labelled deviant. Just as there are various institutions that have the power to define feminine norms (medicine, media, government, and so on), there are also many ways in which women resist that power (for example, through eating disorders, alternative health organizations, and new social movements).

We need to recognize that appearance norms are problematic because they restrict and exclude. If we are to lessen the influence of beauty norms over women and increase their range of choices, then we need to legitimate a variety of body shapes. Can women deconstruct the ideal of the perfect body? Can they overcome the mechanical formulations of their bodies as machines? A body, it must be remembered, cannot be redesigned as a 'perfect, self-sufficient machine'. A person does not *have* a body, one *is* a body, and that includes appearance, internal physical parts, and mind/soul (Shute 1993:230). Can women as a group demonstrate that methods like anorexia are inappropriate means of solving life problems?

This overemphasis on appearance and its medicalization requires a new politicization of health care. One way that women can resist medicalization is to demedicalize the body and challenge power relations between doctors and patients. More patients' rights to medical knowledge and to control in decision making can counterbalance physicians' ability to define issues medically rather than socially (de Swaan 1990:71; Fox 1990:410). However, because the root problem is the 'beauty myth', medical solutions are not sufficient answers. Eating disorders need to be politicized by exposing the social expectations inherent in images of women. The Canadian Advertising Foundation has guidelines about sex and gender stereotyping, which say that women and men 'of a variety of ages, backgrounds, and appearances' should be portrayed (*Globe and Mail* 1992a:A12). Developing various images of women in advertising is one strategy that could increase women's self-esteem and body confidence. Indeed, boycotting products that are advertised in poor taste may send a clear economic message to corporations that sexist and racist images of women will not be tolerated. When the White, affluent ideal is no longer profitable, or less profitable, then appearance norms will likely change (Chapkis 1986:41–2).

Eating disorders are also symbolic forms of resistance that meet the needs of young women for control, influence, status, and power, but they are paradoxical and self-destructive. Perhaps acknowledging women's economic and social needs at the outset can lead to a new and less harmful political solution (Wolf 1991:274–9, 281). Recognizing the *structure* of social inequality creates awareness of the ways in which women's avenues to status and power are limited. This might fortify women's challenge to the appearance norms that cause eating disorders. It might lessen dependency on the cosmetic surgery industry, drugs, and diets, and allow women to set their own agendas and normative boundaries (Dawson 1990:95; Shute 1992:227).

The intolerance and stigmatization of obesity must also be questioned. The predominant health discourse supports the endless and mindless dieting that harms women's bodies, suppresses their needs, and causes eating disorders (Wolf 1991:196). Some women resist this appearance norm and its effects by creating organizations like Hersize, the Living Large Club, the Ample Opportunity Group, the National Association to Advance Fat Acceptance, and the More to Love Dating Service, all of which battle fat phobia. These organizations urge people to 'picket diet or weight-loss surgery establishments, feed the hungry, and enjoy a hearty meal'! They also encourage exercise and fitness. As one woman put it, 'I lift weights, I do aerobics, I'm in very good shape. Not for a fat lady—I'm in good shape period' (Hill 1990:115; Nemeth 1994:45, 48). Other women struggle against the negative effects of appearance norms through education. Parents learn to enhance their children's self-esteem and security by teaching them that individual bodies and appearances may vary and that all are equally desirable (*Globe and Mail* 1992b:A12). Consumer groups recognize that medicine and the media have used symbolism and rhetoric to promote a false relationship between a slim body, empowerment, and freedom. Toronto's Eating Disorder Information Centre runs television advertisements criticizing society's preoccupation with thinness and warning consumers about the dangers of yo-yo dieting (Nemeth 1994:46). Other groups advocate that fashions should be designed and sold for the larger woman and that larger and older fashion models should be used.

More and more women are realizing that their bodies are 'sites of struggle' that must work 'in the service of resistance to gender domination, not in the service of "docility" and gender normalization' (Bordo 1989:15, 28). Women are seeing through the media and advertising images and discovering that the 'new woman' or the 'career woman' plays on the courage and freedom that women want, but often repackages them in appearance norms. They are sceptical and critical of the way in which 'body resistance gets turned into an extension of existing gendered power relations' (Bordo 1989:15, 28; Schur 1984:79; Wolf 1991:77–8, 282). Consider the Bay's marketing strategy for women who, in their words, are 'above average'. The Bay acknowledges the current regard for fat acceptance and for greater diversity in body sizes. They believe 'that every woman no matter what her size, wants to look her very best'. Their discourse links the large woman with career needs, offering 'exclusive career dressing'. But the meaning of this marketing is ambiguous or, even worse, disingenuous. The new trend may benefit the manufacturers who have expanded their clothing market to yet another group of women. The segregation of larger clothing sizes, nevertheless, carries the connotation that these are not 'normal' sizes but deviations from the norm of small, slim women (Schur 1984:80). So offering more choices need not challenge the ground rules and women are well cautioned to be wary of advertisers bearing new appearance norms.

One way to transform the cultural image of women's appearance is to reform advertising to include natural female beauty, but this strategy must be used with caution, for it can also be turned against women. For this reason, and because advertising sells by lowering people's self-esteem, some women believe that new images can best be created by women as part of a female subculture. Women's magazines, for example, should reject articles promoting unhealthy dieting. They should provide more informative articles on what women need to know rather than on what they should look like. They should print pictures of women naturally and not airbrush them, since that eradicates women's truth and identity (Wolf 1991:83).

The experience of women from non-dominant cultures may also be helpful in resisting pervasive appearance norms. Since the appearance norms are largely White and middle class, women who are outside the dominant discourse have insight into struggling against the worst of consumer society. They are forced to create their own images to counter those that equate success and beauty with white skin. As bell hooks suggests, 'it is only as we collectively change the way we look at ourselves and the world that we can change how we are seen' (1992:6). This means seeing oneself positively while, at the same time, resisting the negating and denigrating effects of media-sponsored appearance norms. As one woman of colour put it, 'As I discovered my own power, I lost the longing for blue eyes'...'There is real power to be found in recognizing your own beauty' (Chapkis 1986:12, 70, 174–5; hooks 1992:4–6, 13, 18–20). Not surprisingly, many cultures actively discourage women's excessive concern with appearance. They resist consumer culture because it displays women as objects, diminishes their role as mothers, and devalues their gender-based skills and intelligence. Many East Indian women, for example, consider consumerism to be oppressive and reject the meanings it gives to women's bodies. They suggest to their daughters that they need only a few saris and a good skirt and blouse in their wardrobes (Dawson 1990:62).

Such resistance, in part or in whole, may increase women's self-esteem and control over their bodies. Worrying less about their outward appearances may actually clarify who they are. Women then might blame themselves less when they don't meet the social expectations of female beauty or when others attempt to use the beauty myth against them. As Gloria Steinem

(1993) recently observed, 'the revolution within' has to connect women's self-esteem to social changes on a societal level. Both sexes need to concentrate less on appearance norms and more on relative strengths and talents (Rodin 1992:60; Wolf 1991:275, 288–9). We might begin by examining genuine needs rather than pursuing the illusions of physical appearance, particularly since our physical selves are not 'infinitely plastic' (Rodin 1992:60). Varying routines and adding new interests 'will help broaden our horizons so that how we look is not the sum of what we are' (Rodin 1992:60), but such changes will not come about easily. They require, in turn, changes in media images, medical attitudes and practices, and a strong resolve from women and men.

FURTHER READINGS

Bordo, S. 1990. 'Reading the Slender Body'. In *Body/Politics: Women and the Discourses of Science*, edited by M. Jacobus et al., 83–112.

Edgley, C., and D. Brissett. 1990. 'Health Nazis and the Cult of the Perfect Body: Some Polemical Observations'. *Symbolic Interaction* 13, no. 2:257–79.

Spitzack, C. 1990. *Confessing Excess: Women and the Politics of Body Reduction*. Albany: State University of New York Press.

Székely, É. 1988. *Never Too Thin*. Toronto: The Women's Press.

Turner, B.S. 1984. *The Body and Society*. Oxford: Basil Blackwell.

Wolf, N. 1991. *The Beauty Myth*. Toronto: Vintage Books.

REFERENCES

Alexander, S. 1990. 'Teens' Cosmetic Surgery Fad Causes Dismay among Experts'. *Globe and Mail* (25 September):A10.

_____. 1992. 'Breast Implants Spurred Complaints for Decades'. *Globe and Mail* (11 February):A1–A2.

Bordo, S. 1989. 'The Body and Reproduction of Femininity: A Feminist Appropriation of Foucault'. In *Gender/Body/Knowledge*, edited by A.M. Jagger and S.R. Bordo, 13–33. New Brunswick: Rutgers University Press.

_____. 1990. 'Reading the Slender Body'. In *Body/Politics: Women and the Discourses of Science*, edited by M. Jacobus et al., 83–112. New York: Routledge.

Boskind-Lodahl, M. 1976. 'Cinderella's Stepsisters: A Feminist Perspective on Anorexia Nervosa and Bulimia'. *Signs* 2, no. 2:342–56.

Chapkis, W. 1986. *Beauty Secrets, Women and the Politics of Appearance*. London: The Women's Press.

Chernin, K. 1985. *The Hungry Self: Women, Eating, and Identity*. New York: Harper and Row.

Chisholm, P. 1992. 'Anatomy of a Nightmare'. *Maclean's* (9 March):42–3.

Conrad, P., and J.W. Schneider. 1980. *Deviance and Medicalization: From Badness to Sickness.* St Louis: C.V. Moseby.

Coward, R. 1985. *Female Desires: How They Are Sought, Bought and Packaged.* New York: Grove Weidenfeld.

Currie, D. 1988. 'Starvation Amidst Abundance: Female Adolescents and Anorexia'. In *Sociology of Health Care in Canada,* edited by B.S. Bolaria and H.D. Dickinson, 198–215. Toronto: Harcourt Brace Jovanovich.

Currie, D.H., and V. Raoul, eds. 1992. *Anatomy of Gender: Women's Struggle for the Body.* Ottawa: Carleton University Press.

Dawson, J. 1990. *How Do I Look?* London: Virago Press.

de Swaan, A. 1990. *The Management of Normality: Critical Essays in Health and Welfare.* London: Routledge.

Donzelot, J. 1979. *The Policing of Families.* New York: Pantheon Books.

Douglas, H. 1987a. 'Fat Wimmin Breaking the Mold', Part I. *Vitality* 9, no. 2–3:18–19.

_____. 1987b. 'Fat Wimmin Breaking the Mold', Part II. *Vitality* 9, no. 3:8–10.

Edgley, C., and D. Brissett. 1990. 'Health Nazis and the Cult of the Perfect Body: Some Polemical Observations'. *Symbolic Interaction* 13, no. 2:257–79.

Ehrenreich, B. 1992. 'Stamping Out a Dread Scourge'. *Time* (17 February):56.

Elias, N. 1978. *The History of Manners.* New York: Urizen Books.

Epstein, J., and K. Straub, eds. 1991. *Body Guards: The Cultural Politics of Gender Ambiguity.* New York: Routledge, Chapman and Hall.

Findlay, D. 1993a. 'The Medical Gaze: Medical Models, Power, and Women's Health'. *Atlantis* 18, no. 1–2:104–24.

_____. 1993b. 'The Good, the Normal and the Healthy: The Social Construction of Medical Knowledge about Women'. *Canadian Journal of Sociology* 18, no. 2:115–35.

_____. 1995. 'Discovering Sex: Medical Science, Feminism and Inter-sexuality'. *The Canadian Review of Sociology and Anthropology* 32, no. 1 (February):25–52.

_____, and L.J. Miller. 1994. 'Through Medical Eyes: The Medicalization of Women's Bodies and Women's Lives'. In *Health, Illness, and Health Care in Canada,* edited by B.S. Bolaria and H.D. Dickinson, 276–306. Toronto: Harcourt Brace Jovanovich.

Fisher, S. 1988. *In the Patient's Best Interest: Women and the Politics of Medical Decisions.* New Brunswick: Rutgers University Press.

Foreman, J. 1992. 'The Sordid Saga of Breast Implant Surgery'. *Toronto Star* (25 January):D1, D5.

Foucault, M. 1979. *Discipline and Punish: The Birth of the Prison.* New York: Vintage.

Fox, R.C. 1990. 'The Medicalization and Demedicalization of American Society'. In *The Sociology of Health and Illness: Critical Perspectives*, 3rd ed., edited by P. Conrad and R. Kern, 390–4. New York: St Martin's Press.

Freidson, E. 1970. *Professional Dominance: The Social Structure of Medical Care*. New York: Aldine.

Garner, D.M., et al. 1980. 'Cultural Expectations of Thinness in Women'. *Psychological Reports* 47:483–91.

Globe and Mail. 1992a. 'Struggling against the Beauty Myth' (17 February):A12.

_____. 1992b. 'U.S. Panel Recommends Restriction of Silicone-Gel Breast Implants' (21 February):A1, A6.

Hill, C.L. 1990. Review of 'Fat Oppression and Psychotherapy: A Feminist Perspective', by L.S. Brown and E.D. Rothblum. *Atlantis* 15, no. 2:114–15.

hooks, b. 1992. *Black Looks, Race and Representation*. Toronto: Between the Lines.

Jenish, D. 1992. 'Beauty and the Breast'. *Maclean's* (9 March):38–41.

Ludmerer, K.M. 1985. *Learning to Heal: The Development of American Medical Education*. New York: Basic Books.

McIntosh, G. 1992. 'Ottawa Extends Moratorium on Breast Implants'. *The Gazette* (18 April).

Morantz-Sanchez, R.M. 1985. *Sympathy with Science: Women Physicians in American Medicine*. Oxford: Oxford University Press.

Nemeth, M. 1994. 'Body Obsession'. *Maclean's* 107, no. 18 (2 May):44–9.

Nichols, P.M. 1991. 'Cher's Fresh Angle'. *Globe and Mail* (November).

Olive, D. 1992. 'Strange What a Bad Record Companies Have in Marketing Medical Products for Women'. *Globe and Mail* (25 January).

O'Neill, J. 1985. *Five Bodies: The Human Shape of Modern Society*. Ithaca: Cornell University Press.

Orbach, S. 1979. *Fat Is a Feminist Issue*. New York: Berkley Books.

Outram, D. 1989. *The Body and the French Revolution: Sex, Class and Political Culture*. New Haven: Yale University Press.

Riessman, C.K. 1983. 'Women and Medicalization: A New Perspective'. *Social Policy* 14, no. 5 (Summer):3–18.

Rodin, J. 1992. 'Body Mania'. *Psychology Today* (January/February):56–60.

Rothman, B.K. 1989. 'Women, Health and Medicine'. In *Women: A Feminist Perspective*, 4th ed., edited by J. Freeman, 76–86. Mountainview: Mayfield Publishing.

Schur, E.M. 1984. *Labeling Women Deviant: Gender, Stigma, and Social Control*. Philadelphia: Temple University Press.

Schwartz, H. 1990. *Never Satisfied: A Cultural History of Diets, Fantasies and Fat*. New York: Anchor Books.

Shute, J. 1993. *Life-Size*. London: Mandarin.

Smith, L. 1992. 'Feminist Fury: Breast-Implant Issue Enrages Some Women'. *The Gazette* (22 February).

Spitzack, C. 1990. *Confessing Excess: Women and the Politics of Body Reduction*. Albany: State University of New York Press.

Steinem, G. 1993. *Revolution from Within*. Boston: Little, Brown and Company.

Synnott, T. 1989. 'Truth and Goodness, Mirrors and Masks—Part I: A Sociology of Beauty and the Face'. *The British Journal of Sociology* 40, no. 4:607–36.

Székely, É. 1988. *Never Too Thin*. Toronto: The Women's Press.

Taylor, P. 1992. 'After Silicone'. *Globe and Mail* (7 March):D5.

Torrance, G.M. 1987. 'Socio-historical Overview'. In *Health and Canadian Society*, 2nd ed., edited by D. Coburn et al., 6–32. Toronto: Fitzhenry and Whiteside.

Turner, B.S. 1984. *The Body and Society*. Oxford: Basil Blackwell.

_____. 1987. *Medical Power and Social Knowledge*. London: Sage Publications.

Turner, J. 1991. 'Getting Out of the Diet Rut'. *Toronto Star* (19 December):E1, E6.

_____. 1992a. 'Living with Implants'. *Toronto Star* (8 February):K1, K7.

_____. 1992b. 'Many Implant Issues Are Still Unresolved'. *Toronto Star* (8 February).

Underwood, N. 1992. 'Is Bigger Better?' *Maclean's* (9 March):44–5.

Webb, A. 1994. 'The Starvation Demons'. *Maclean's* 107, no. 18 (2 May):50.

Weber, M. 1958. *The Protestant Ethic and the Spirit of Capitalism*. New York: Charles Scribner's Sons.

Williams, M. 1991. 'Même Implants "Safe"?' *Healthsharing* (Fall):5.

Wolf, N. 1991. *The Beauty Myth*. Toronto: Vintage Books.

Zola, I.K. 1975. 'In the Name of Health and Illness: On Some Socio-Political Consequences of Medical Influence'. *Social Science and Medicine* 9:83–7.

Part
III
Sexuality and Social Control

'The time has come to think about sex', Gayle Rubin has argued. She claims that while some people may regard sexuality as a trivial topic, 'a frivolous diversion from the more critical problems of poverty, war, disease, racism, famine, or nuclear annihilation', history has demonstrated that it is precisely at times such as these that 'people are likely to become dangerously crazy about sexuality'. Disputes over sexual conduct and the scapegoating of erotic minorities 'often become the vehicles for displacing social anxieties ... Consequently, sexuality should be treated with special respect in times of great social stress' (Rubin 1989:267). One of the most important dimensions of the social construction of deviance, then, is an examination of the symbolic weight that modern industrial societies like Canada attach to sexual values, sexual conduct, and the mechanisms by which sexuality is controlled by such institutions as religion, law, the family, and social policy. This section will examine how people are labelled as deviant on the basis of their sexuality. We will also examine the differential scrutiny of women and men by social control agencies and the criteria on which sexuality and gender intersect to form categories of deviance.

Canada has had laws prohibiting prostitution-related activities since the 1750s. In Chapter 9, 'The Regulation of Prostitution: Setting the Morality Trap', Fran Shaver argues that the growth in the number and type of sex laws and their subsequent retargeting of who and what is 'problematic' about prostitution has gone full circle from social nuisance, to social purist, to social nuisance. Recently, gender-neutral language was embodied in the Criminal Code. However, the actual (operational) definition of prostitution and the decision to prosecute those involved are based on social characteristics that range from the sex, race, and class of the offender to the social context of the act in question. The social and legal discourse surrounding the criminalization of prostitution falls into four clearly distinct periods.

Taken as a whole, these data demonstrate that political and social forces are at work in constructing what is reprehensible or deviant about prostitution.

Sex in the 1990s is a contested terrain upon which modern sexual debates are continually being fought. In 'Constructing Sexuality in the AIDS Era', Barry Adam argues that contemporary debates over AIDS offer us a key to revealing the clash of regulatory agencies and popular movements, the roles of governments and commerce, and the actions of judges and journalists over sexual issues. What sex means in Canada has been negotiated and redefined through a series of recent critical events: royal commissions on child abuse and prostitution, the collapse of the abortion law in the courts and in Parliament, the continuing regime of censorship of sexual imagery, the struggle for sexual orientation and domestic partners' rights, reform of age-of-consent laws, and public responses to the AIDS crisis. Understanding the ongoing revaluations of different sexualities as 'progressive' and 'emancipatory', or as 'criminal' and deviant, means sorting through the government agencies, moral entrepreneurs, capitalists, social movements, and image producers who populate the contemporary historical stage.

In 'Deconstructing Spousal Violence: A Socialist Feminist Perspective', Kathy Storrie and Nancy Poon shift the focus from 'illicit' sexual practices to the so-called 'normal' state for mature, healthy adults—that is, heterosexual 'marriage'. Through their feminist critique of programs for men who batter, Storrie and Poon explore a range of complicated issues regarding domestic violence, most specifically the assumptions made by 'experts' about the causes of domestic violence. These 'experts' frequently place the blame on the other family members and not the batterer. This article provides some important insights into the ways in which societal institutions replicate the domestic victimization of women and children in Canadian society.

REFERENCE

Rubin, G. 1984. 'Thinking Sex'. In *Pleasure and Danger: Exploring Female Sexuality*, edited by C. Vance, 267–319. London: Pandora.

——9——

The Regulation of Prostitution:
Setting the Morality Trap

Frances M. Shaver

INTRODUCTION

Canada has had laws prohibiting prostitution-related activities for well over
200 years. One of the earliest—which made the status of being a prostitute
or streetwalker an offence—was contained in the Nova Scotia Act of 1759. It
was clearly directed against women. More complex provisions designed to
protect females in general from the wiles of the procurer, pimp, and brothel
keeper were introduced at Confederation. These were extended and strengthened in the decades that followed with the most recent amendments appear-
ing in the last ten years. They provided that prostitution and exploitation
could be practised by a person of either sex, extended and strengthened the
prohibitions against street prostitution, and increased penalties against those
exploiting juveniles.

This growth in the number and type of provisions and their subsequent
retargeting of who and what is 'problematic' did not happen in response to
changes in the way prostitution is practised; for the most part, it has remained the same. What changed was the way people—both individually and
collectively—identify what is harmful about prostitution.

In illustration, I show that the social and legal discourse surrounding the
criminalization of prostitution falls into four clearly distinct periods. I then
examine the disparities between law in theory and law in practice within
each historical period. Finally, I consider the deficiencies of both theory and
practice in relation to the realities of contemporary prostitution. Taken as a
whole, these data demonstrate that political and social forces are at work in
constructing what is reprehensible or deviant about prostitution. These factors are not necessarily inherent in the act or practice itself. I begin with an
examination of prevailing definitions and theories.

PREVAILING DEFINITIONS AND THEORIES OF PROSTITUTION

In the last ten years, legal definitions of prostitution in Canada have become gender neutral. They no longer define the prostitute as a woman, or imply that prostitution is limited to the selling of sexual services. As a consequence, the male prostitute and the male buyer now fall within the purview of the law.

Social definitions have failed to keep pace with the current legal ones. Most dictionaries define a prostitute as 'a woman who has promiscuous sexual intercourse for payment', and prostitution as 'the act, practice or profession of offering the body for sexual relations for money'.[1] Similar definitions are advocated by the students in my sexuality classes. They are somewhat more open-minded regarding the sex of the prostitute (mentioning both men and women), but of the 200 students polled over the last three years, the majority (58–69 per cent) focused on the seller when defining prostitution. A third or so of the definitions (29–37 per cent) indicated that prostitution involved both a buyer and seller. Only a small minority (7–15 per cent) defined prostitution simply as the buying of sexual services.

Non-monetary sexual bargaining falls outside the purview of the law as well as outside most social definitions. The vast majority of my students (85–93 per cent) limited their definition of prostitution to monetary sexual bargaining; so do the majority of Canadians. In a national opinion poll conducted for the Department of Justice in 1984, 90 per cent agreed that prostitution involved the exchange of sex for money. A somewhat smaller proportion of the respondents (57 per cent) supported the definition of prostitution as the exchange of sexual services for gains other than money.[2] Interestingly, women are more likely than men to consider non-monetary sexual bargaining as prostitution (Fraser et al. 1985:396). These definitions legitimate female prostitutes as targets of control and reinforce the notion that it is the individual actor rather than the act of prostitution that is deviant.

Similar themes occur in the sociological research on prostitution. There are four basic theoretical traditions: sociopsychological, functionalist, feminist, and sociology of work. All reflect a normative preoccupation with the deviance of prostitution and most of the theorizing that is done traces not the causes of prostitution but the etiology of the female prostitute. The actor rather than the act becomes identified as the legitimate focus of control, especially within the first two traditions. In the latter two, the legitimization of what is to be controlled shifts slightly to include the practice of prostitution and the conditions that reproduce and maintain it, but both still retain traces of covert moralism.

The most pervasive sociological approach to prostitution is the social-psychological one. Entry into prostitution is seen as a consequence of family dysfunction, undersocialization, or different socialization. The first two explanations, grounded for the most part in a consensus model, attempt to explain how individual actors come to violate norms and values we are assumed to share in common. Specific theories—developed to explain rule-breaking behaviour of this type (anomie, neutralization theory, and control theory)—are evident in several prostitution studies.[3] The latter approach explains entry as a consequence of socially learned differences (differential socialization). It is grounded in a pluralist or class-stratified model of society and centres on how certain behaviours (acts) come to be valued or devalued within different groups. For example, it is argued that the poor and undereducated are more likely to be drawn into the supply side of the prostitution trade because they are more likely, given their reference group, to see it as a viable option. Although this approach draws attention to the broader social and economic structures in which prostitution is located, most of the theorizing focuses on the entry patterns of prostitutes rather than the institution of prostitution. Labelling theory and the group conflict theories are the most common examples of this tradition and traces of these theories are evident in studies by Winslow and Winslow (1974:240–2) and Akers (1977).

Until the 1970s, the theorizing about the institution of prostitution was primarily developed within a functionalist perspective. Kingsley Davis (1937), for example, traced its existence and persistence to the double standard of social sexual expectations for men and women: 'bad girls' are needed in order to meet the needs of the stronger innate sex drive of men while maintaining the institution of the family. In this context, the deviance of prostitution serves as a source of social stability. Davis portrayed the male customer as a victim of his uncontrollable sex drive on the one hand and, on the other, as immune from sanctions because of the important social functions he provides (Lowman 1992:59). Such a portrayal legitimates the persistence of prostitution as well as the disparate social and legal response to the female prostitute and the male customer.

Functionalist and social-psychology perspectives on prostitution are both based on differences between male and female sexuality: the former in biology and the latter in socialization. In addition, they both legitimate rather than question the inequitable social and legal response to the female prostitute and the male customer. At the core of contemporary feminist theorizing about prostitution is a direct challenge to these allegations: gender differences in sexuality are located in the wider structures of social (i.e., male) power.[4] For feminist theory, prostitutes are segregated from the business of prostitution, and the commonly held view of prostitutes as 'bad girls' is challenged by providing clear evidence that they are women struggling to maintain their socio-economic independence in a male-dominated world. In doing so, however, many feminist theorists simply denounce prostitution in particular and sex work in general as dangerous, degrading, and entirely undesirable as a profession. There is much evidence of this tendency in the work of Canadian feminists (CACSW 1984a; Fraser et al. 1985; House of Commons 1982; NAC 1984). The few who go on to evaluate the validity of these denouncements do so philosophically rather than empirically (e.g., Brock 1985–6; Overall 1992; Shaver 1988; Shrage 1989). Prostitutes are seen as other than deviant, but not so the practice of prostitution.[5]

The fourth approach to prostitution stands out from the rest because it is grounded in a sociology of work perspective. It focuses on the differences between deviant and respectable careers and the consequences this may have for individuals' work and non-work lives. The potential here for empirically evaluating the conditions of prostitution is high. However, research focusing on career entry or the actions and experiences of the career deviant (e.g., Laner 1974; Perkins and Bennett 1985) is much more in evidence than studies analysing career management and departure, the organizational structure within which the deviant behaviour occurs, or the broader social and economic structures within which prostitution operates (e.g., Heyl 1979; McLeod 1982; Romenesko and Miller 1989; Visano 1987).

It will become evident in the following discussion that these social definitions and theories are grounded in nineteenth-century notions of social evil (McLaren 1986) and passive female sexuality (Edwards 1981:22). To a very large extent they also carry over into the way in which Canadian prostitution laws are enforced. The feminist challenge to the former and the call to empirically evaluate the latter have largely fallen on deaf ears.

HISTORICAL VARIATIONS IN DIALECTIC AND LEGISLATIVE CONCERNS[6]

Although the buying and selling of sex (prostitution *per se*) has never been illegal in Canada, various activities relating to the exchange have always been prohibited. Currently, three classes of prostitution-related activities are criminalized: (1) procuring and living on the avails of prostitution, (2) bawdy-house offences, and (3) communicating in a public place for the purpose of buying or selling sexual services. This was not always the case—the focus of concern and the individuals targeted have changed substantially over the last 230 years. In comparison to substance criminalization—which first occurred just over eighty years ago in 1908 (Boyd 1991:141)—the criminalization of prostitution has had a relatively long and varied history. It can be divided into four clearly distinct periods: pre-Confederation (1759–1867), Victorian (mid-nineteenth-century–1920), post-Victorian (1920–72), and contemporary (1972–92).[7]

Pre-Confederation

Before Confederation, legislation controlling prostitution was in the form of vagrancy laws proscribing both street and brothel prostitution. As mentioned earlier, the earliest prohibition was contained in the Nova Scotia Act of 1759. It made the status of being a prostitute or streetwalker an offence. Disruptive or annoying behaviour was not a prerequisite to detention and once the status was established, conviction would follow more or less automatically. According to McLaren, both prostitutes and those who ran or frequented common bawdy-houses were dubbed vagrants. They were seen as 'social nuisances to be penalized and controlled when public concern or outrage needed to be dispelled. The purposes of the law were to get prostitutes off the streets when necessary, and to alleviate the land use conflicts and problems of public disorder associated with the operation of brothels' (McLaren 1986:127).

McLaren demonstrates that during this period, the state of Canadian law relating to prostitution and the protection of women and children from vice reflected the values of a society 'in which the desirability or efficacy of the state's intervention to condemn or control sexual errancy was not readily conceded. Where intervention was undertaken, the legal expedients served purely pragmatic ends' (McLaren 1986:126). Others (Backhouse 1985; Edwards 1981; Walkowitz 1980) also demonstrate that the law during this period reflected a system in which women's virtue was valued in proprietary terms and protected only where their men's assets or lineage were in jeopardy. During this earliest period of Canadian history, the targets of prostitution legislation were clearly the prostitutes and those running and frequenting bawdy-houses.

Victorian

After Confederation, and in response to the concerns of British reformers and their Canadian counterparts, the focus of legislative concern began to change and the statutes against exploiters were introduced, extended, and strengthened. Although the links between the initiatives of reformers and the development of national policy has not been explored in detail, McLaren argues that the national temperance, women's rights, and church organizations created and maintained a climate in which the evils of White slavery were very much in the public domain (1986:149). The objectives of the reformers were to abolish the 'social evil' by punishing the exploiters and rescuing women and children from sexual exploitation in general and White slavery in particular.

In 1867, the new federal government enacted provisions prohibiting the defilement of women under the age of twenty-one (CACSW 1984b:131). In 1869, the existing vagrancy provisions in the criminal law were consolidated and expanded to embrace males who were living on the avails of prostitution (McLaren 1986:131). The penalties were increased in 1874 and in 1886, the bawdy-house provisions were re-enacted. Canada's Criminal Code was finalized in 1892. The vagrancy provisions outlawing streetwalking and bawdy-houses in vogue at the time (and essentially no different from the provisions adopted in 1759) were incorporated; an additional offence was included in the nuisance part of the Criminal Code prescribing up to one year in prison for the operation of a bawdy-house, and new statutes were adopted proscribing the procurement of women for unlawful carnal connection (CACSW 1984b:131; McLaren 1986:136). 'Provision was also made for the securing of a search warrant where there was reason to suspect the harbouring of a woman or girl inveigled or enticed into a house of ill fame or assignation' (McLaren 1986:136).

Over the next twenty-eight years, the legislation relating to procuring and living on the avails of prostitution continued to be refined. The penalty for procuring women increased from a maximum of two years to five in 1909, and to a maximum of ten years in 1920. The penalty was expanded to include whipping on second and subsequent convictions in 1913. The definition of procuring was expanded to include everyone who 'on the arrival of any women or girl in Canada, directs her to any common bawdy house', or who 'for the purposes of gain, exercises control, direction or influence over the movements of any women or girl in such a manner as to show that he is aiding, abetting or compelling her prostitution with any person or generally'. At the same time, men charged with living on the avails of prostitution were subjected to a reverse onus clause that required them to satisfy the court that they had other means of support (CACSW 1984b:132).

The bawdy-house provisions were refined during the same period, although much less extensively than the provisions for procuring. The definition was amended in 1907 to include 'a house, set of rooms or place of any kind kept for the purposes of prostitution or occupied or resorted to by one or more persons for such purpose'. It was amended again in 1917 to embrace establishments kept for acts of indecency.[8] Penalties were increased: in 1913 habitual frequenting was no longer a prerequisite for conviction and in 1915 penalties were increased (CACSW 1984b:133).

Prostitution was also shaped by sharp racial conflicts between Native peoples and White settlers and between Asians and Whites. Valverde (1991:86-7) argues that these conflicts interacted with the gender divisions in each racial group to create severe problems for women of colour. In the case of Native women, it was 'the "civilizing influence" of white women settlers' that brought about their lower status and encouraged their ghettoization in prostitution' (Valverde 1991:86). In the case of Asian women, it was the Canadian government's measures to curtail Chinese immigration by making it difficult for families to immigrate that encouraged the semiclandestine importation of Chinese women to be prostitutes to the male Chinese community (Valverde 1991:87). In each case the alarm was sounded: Canadian churches ritually denounced the 'traffic' in Indian women (Valverde 1991:86), and women's organizations called on the government to allow those Chinese labourers already in Canada to bring their wives into the country (Valverde 1991:87).

All these interests were reflected in the social and legal policies of the era: the exploiters were identified as men who were to be punished, and the women and children as victims who were in need of rescue. Nevertheless, legislation penalizing prostitutes—especially non-White, working-class prostitutes—was maintained.

Post-Victorian

The social purity movement waned in the 1920s and the sex trade thrived for fifty years with little public comment (Lowman 1991:122). There were no changes to the procuring and street prostitution sections and only minor changes to the bawdy-house section. The latter took place in 1947 when the maximum sentence for keepers and inmates of bawdy-houses was increased to three years and a new offence added: everyone knowingly transporting another to a bawdy-house became liable.

Contemporary

When public debate was rekindled in the late 1970s and early 1980s, it was prompted not by the 'White slave trade' or the international traffic in women but by growing concern about the increased visibility of street prostitution in residential neighbourhoods. The rhetoric used during this period shifted into a less moralistic, more neutral expression of concern. The rationale for the suppression of prostitution recaptured the social nuisance concerns of the pre-Confederation era. Citizens' groups, portraying prostitution as either an insidious source of neighbourhood decay or as a public nuisance in residential areas, lobbied municipal, provincial, and federal politicians to enact more effective laws to control street prostitution (Fraser et al. 1985; Lowman 1991:127; Shaver 1984:54–6). The solutions most groups advocated were simply aimed at strengthening the soliciting section of the Criminal Code.

In opposition to the limited concerns of this movement, prostitutes' rights organizations, civil libertarians, a variety of feminists' groups, and the Fraser Committee[9] argued for much broader legal and social reform. In large part, their concerns duplicated those manifested by the nineteenth-century abolitionists. They called for the penalization of those profiteering from the prostitution of others, and a full array of social reforms to eradicate the objective conditions that force people into prostitution. In addition, they called for the amendment of bawdy-house legislation, thus making it possible for a prostitute to work without being subject to criminal offence (Fraser et al. 1985; Shaver 1984). Although it is given much less priority, the rhetoric around prostitution as either a potential or actual public nuisance prevails here as well. Many twentieth-century abolitionists concede that residents have a right to live in peace, but are highly critical of the measures advocated (Shaver 1985:500). Others are less critical, arguing that some measures limiting street prostitution must be retained in criminal law (CACSW 1984a; Fraser et al. 1985).

The prostitution legislation enacted during this period changed the wording of the Criminal Code in four areas. First, street prostitution ceased to be a status offence. The vagrancy provision was repealed and replaced by a soliciting law in 1972 and then by a communicating offence in 1985. In the process, the legal understanding of the offensive behaviour prerequisite to detention was expanded to include communicating and even 'attempting to communicate' for the purpose of prostitution. Second, the liability for engaging in prostitution was extended to men, both as prostitutes and as purchasers. A definitional amendment in 1983 provided that prostitute meant 'a person of either sex engaging in prostitution' and the new communicating section clearly included customers. It stated that every person communicating for the purposes of engaging in prostitution *or of obtaining the sexual services of a prostitute* is liable. Thirdly, the protection of women under the procuring offence now extended to both men and women, and persons of either sex can be charged with procuring and living on the avails. Fourth, customers of juvenile prostitutes and pimps who engage youths were singled out for more severe sentences in 1988.

In spite of these latter two amendments, the major focus of discourse during this current period has been the nuisance of street prostitution to law-abiding citizens. The legislation was revised mainly in response to the public outcry of several lobbying groups (municipalities, concerned residents, and police). The latter group was concerned with the pragmatics of enforcing the existing law and the former two with the 'cleaning up of the streets'. The major targets identified were the street prostitutes and their customers.

DISPARITIES IN THEORY AND PRACTICE

Overall, a hierarchy is reflected in both social rhetoric and formal law. Some acts are commonly constructed as serious offences (procuring, living on the avails of prostitution, and operating a bawdy-house) and others as less serious (transporting individuals to a common bawdy-house, being an inmate or frequenter of a bawdy-house, and soliciting or communicating for the purposes of prostitution in a public place). Men are variously constructed as more evil than women (as was the case during the Victorian era), or as equally liable (as is the case with respect to contemporary concerns about street prostitution). Interestingly, a different hierarchy is reflected in the manner in which the law in each period is enforced: a much more limited set of individuals and acts are actually prosecuted. Surprisingly, the disparities are greatest when public scrutiny is the most prolific—during the Victorian and contemporary periods.

Pre-Confederation
From all accounts, enforcement during pre-Confederation was sporadic and capricious. Prostitution was likely to be tolerated in port cities such as Halifax (Fingard, cited in McLaren 1986:127) and on the western frontier (Gray 1971), where there was a large surplus male population, and repressed when it was seen as a direct threat to respectable members of the population. Regardless of where and when the laws were enforced, however, the focus of attention was female prostitutes, whether operating on the streets or out of residences or rooms (Gray 1971; McLaren 1986). Customers of street prostitutes and frequenters of bawdy-houses were rarely harassed, but since the former fell outside the purview of the law and the latter were exempt because of their 'uncontrollable sexual drive' and the 'important social functions they provided', this is not surprising.

Victorian
Although the legal policies adopted during the Victorian period strengthened and extended the laws against exploiters, McLaren (1986) illustrates convincingly that the laws penalizing prostitutes were the most often enforced. Between 1887 and 1897—the years immediately before and after the enactment of the Criminal Code—little appears to have happened: there were no entries for either defilement or procurement, nor for the nuisance offence of keeping a bawdy-house. Convictions for the vagrancy offences of keeping, frequenting, or being an inmate of a bawdy-house increased, but there was no decisive upward trend in response to the pressure to abolish the social evil (McLaren 1986:142). What does become evident after 1895—the first year a gender breakdown of the annual conviction rates for the bawdy-house offences is available—is that a much greater number of convictions were registered against women than men: in 1895, there were 278 convictions against women and 182 against men. The gender breakdown in 1896 was 439 to 224, and in 1897 it was 519 to 336 (cf., Table 9.1).

The conviction rates for bawdy-house offences increased after 1900. The average annual rate of conviction between 1901 and 1910 was 1,741 and increased to 3,868 between 1911 and 1917. However, as can be seen in Table 9.1, the convictions of females continue to significantly outnumber those of males: between 1901 and 1910, 73 per cent of those convicted on bawdy-house offences were female, while only 27 per cent were male. The corresponding figures for the years 1911–16 show some closing of the gap, but the differential is still significant with 65 per cent of the convictions accruing to women and only 35 per cent to men.

TABLE 9.1

Average Conviction Rates for Bawdy-house Offences in Canada by Gender and Year, 1895–1916

Year	Female		Male	
1895	278	(60%)	182	(40%)
1896	439	(66%)	224	(34%)
1897	519	(59%)	336	(38%)
1901–10	1,403	(73%)	517	(27%)
1911–16	2,455	(65%)	1,329	(35%)

Source: J.P.S. McLaren, 'Chasing the Social Evil: Moral Fervour and the Evolution of Canada's Prostitution Laws, 1867–1917', *Canadian Journal of Law and Society* 1:125–65.

Since the criminal law statistics of the period do not allow for a more discriminating comparison of male and female convictions, McLaren examines the statistics in particular cities. Here again he finds that females came off worse, particularly in charges of keeping bawdy-houses:

> In Toronto for the period 1907 to 1917, charges against females consistently outnumbered those against males by a ratio of 2.3 to 1.0 ... In Vancouver a preliminary survey of the Prisoners Record Books for the period 1912–1915 shows that over 80 percent of those charged were females operating solo or in tandem out of single rooms (McLaren 1986:151).

In 1911, when convictions for procuring became numerous enough to warrant reporting, the figures were very small—the annual rate never exceeded more than sixty-six convictions for all of Canada. It 'vacillated between eleven and sixteen a year between 1911 and 1914; it then jumped to 66 in 1915, fell to 34 in 1916 and rose again to 52 in 1917' (McLaren 1986:150). These figures are insignificant in comparison to the fervour over the extent of the White slave trade. The determination to punish exploiters and rescue women and children did not carry over into practice. What did carry over was the criminalization of women selling sexual services.

Post-Victorian
The public outcry against the social evil of prostitution may have waned in the 1920s, but not so prostitution or the enforcement patterns in evidence with respect to gender. Prostitution continued to flourish as a predominately female crime. In Toronto, for example, 'between 1913 and 1937, an average of 182 women were charged annually with vagrancy ... probably most of them [female] prostitutes, while an average of 177 were charged with bawdy house offenses'. In contrast there were only ninety prosecutions for procuring during the entire twenty-five-year period (Lowman 1991:122).

TABLE 9.2

Convictions for Prostitution Offences in Canada by Gender and Selected Years, 1920–70

Year	Bawdy-house* (Summary)		Bawdy-house** (Indictable)		Procuring (Indictable)	
	Female	Male	Female	Male	Female	Male
1920	1,289	1,709				
1925	1,311	2,242				
1930	1,649	2,078	781	142	4	34
1935	1,481	1,193	1,513	141	8	55
1940	41	18	3,887	151	15	39
1945	–	802	488	74	3	12
1950	–	586	134	83	6	33
1955	143	463	137	65	4	24
1960	226	301	102	36	11	40
1965	172	220	160	31	7	41
1970	35	89	69	24	2	39

Source: Statistics Canada, *Statistics of Criminal and Other Offenses*, Catalogue No. 85-201 (Ottawa: Statistics Canada, 1920–70).

* Includes summary convictions for frequenters and inmates.
** Includes indictable convictions received by keepers and inmates from 1930–55 and keepers from 1960–70.

At the national level, two sets of statistics related to bawdy-house offences are available. One reflects the summary convictions of frequenters and inmates, and the other the indictable convictions related to keeping and being an inmate. Both conviction rates remained in the 1,000s throughout the 1920s and 1930s, but dropped rapidly after the Second World War (cf., Table 9.2). Lowman (1991:122) argues that this overall decline reflected a change in the nature of prostitution (the off-street trade became more decentralized after the Second World War) rather than a change in policing practices. Police practices also persisted with respect to the enforcement patterns regarding the more serious (indictable) bawdy-house offences; convictions of females outnumber those of males throughout the period. Only with respect to the less serious bawdy-house offences do convictions of men outnumber those of women. The national conviction rates for procurement remained very small throughout this period, never exceeding more than sixty-three convictions in any one year. As in the previous period, most convictions of this type accrue to males.

Contemporary

When prostitution moved back into the public domain in the 1970s and 1980s, the increased public scrutiny was not accompanied by changes in enforcement patterns. In 1972, when the soliciting law was enacted, the words 'every person' were not universally interpreted in a gender-neutral manner. Judicial pronouncements on whether the soliciting law applied to both women and men, prostitutes and customers were many and varied and took place in the Supreme Court of Canada as well as in the Appeal Courts of BC and Ontario.[10] Further, even in those jurisdictions that endorsed a gender-neutral interpretation, it was rarely so enforced.[11]

The communicating section was meticulously designed to be non-sexist in nature and to criminalize both prostitutes and customers. At first glance, it appears to have fared much better than the soliciting section: the enforcement patterns in evidence nationally indicate that the communicating section did significantly change the proportion of women and men charged (cf., Table 9.3). Up to 1977, when the soliciting law was in place and actively being applied, many more females than males were charged: at its worst, the average ratio is almost seven females to every male; at its best, it is 3.4 females to every male. After 1985, when the communicating section was introduced, the proportions are much closer to parity (1.1 women to 1.0 men), indicating a huge increase in communicating charges involving customers, at least at the aggregate level.

Nevertheless, a closer look at the city-based data sets gathered for the Department of Justice during the three years following the enactment of the communicating section tells a different story. First, male prostitutes were underrepresented in the charge statistics in several cities. In Calgary, where 18 per cent of the prostitutes identified in head counts were male, only 12 per cent of prostitution charges involved males. In Toronto an estimated 5 per cent of the prostitution charges involved males, but about 25 per cent of the prostitutes counted were men. In Halifax the figures were 11 per cent and 33 per cent respectively, and in Vancouver they were 8 per cent and 10 per cent. Montreal was the exception; a slightly higher percentage of males were charged than appeared in the head counts (Department of Justice 1989:42–4).[12]

Second, more prostitutes than customers were charged in nine of the ten Canadian cities studied. The law was most equally applied in Toronto and London, where about one-half of the charges laid involved customers. In Winnipeg, Niagara Falls, Montreal, and Quebec, however, only between 30–40 per cent involved customers, and in Vancouver, Calgary, and Halifax, customers represented 25 per cent or fewer of the charges laid (Department of Justice 1989:Table 3, 41–2). In addition, there is evidence that the sentences against prostitutes were more severe than those received by custom-

Table 9.3

Adults Charged with Prostitution Offences in Canada by Gender and Year, 1974–91

	Bawdy-house		Procuring		Other*	
Year	Female	Male	Female	Male	Female	Male
1974	416	295	81	66	1,885	269
1975	620	378	33	62	1,719	256
1976	543	544	17	54	1,478	303
1977	639	526	15	52	1,273	380
1978	478	265	21	56	368	644
1979	428	209	20	57	473	125
1980	421	247	18	60	521	262
1981	471	681	3	32	377	270
1982	266	125	34	76	127	56
1983	470	200	31	72	70	59
1984	507	336	22	88	18	37
1985	473	241	24	84	69	60
1986	440	316	67	111	3,356	2,512
1987	407	372	103	208	4,428	4,760
1988	373	214	162	130	4,910	4,835
1989	345	255	22	137	4,910	4,019
1990	314	168	52	125	5,157	4,651
1991	339	211	58	158	5,199	4,706

*Includes soliciting and transporting up to and including 1985, and communicating and transporting after 1985. A small number of charges relating to living on the avails are included with both the soliciting and communicating charges.

Source: Statistics Canada, *Canadian Crime Statistics*, Catalogue No. 85-205 (Ottawa: Statistics Canada, 1974–91).

ers (Department of Justice 1989:Table 10, 60). Even when the prior record of the accused was controlled, first-offender prostitutes received more severe sentences than first-offender customers in Vancouver and Toronto, although this phenomenon did not appear to take place in Montreal (Department of Justice 1989:Table 11, 61).

Third, enforcement patterns differentiate between customers—some appear to be more at risk than others. Data from Vancouver indicate that the weight of the law falls primarily on lower-class men: eighty-three (91 per cent) of the ninety-one men charged under the communicating section came from the generally lower-class east side of Vancouver (Lowman 1990:69–72).

Such patterns are more in line with the double sexual standard condoned by Victorian moralists than with the sentiments of the recent lobbyists, who claimed to be arguing that customers and prostitutes are equally responsible for the problems of street prostitution.[13]

Overall, these enforcement patterns, as well as those in evidence nationally (cf., Table 9.3), indicate (1) that the control of street prostitution is the most pressing issue[14] and (2) that except for procuring, prostitution is a predominately female crime.[15]

DEFICIENCIES OF THEORY AND PRACTICE IN RELATION TO REALITY

The rhetoric of the Victorian reformers and contemporary theorists conceals a great many assumptions about the realities of prostitution. In this section, I identify the assumptions and then draw on a number of empirical studies about prostitution and recent writings by sex workers in order to assess their validity.

Victorian

Overall, the assumptions behind the rhetoric of the Victorian reformers and legislators labelled prostitutes as fallen women, presented them as 'passive, sexually innocent victims', and described exploiters as White slavers: 'sinister, shadowy figures who were in the business of seducing or abducting girls and women to serve in establishments from which there was no easy means of escape' (Gorham cited in McLaren 1986:138). McLaren (1986:137–9) illustrates the deficiency of these images on all three counts. First, economic and social forces, not social immorality, lead women and young girls into prostitution. Second, working-class females are far from being sexually passive. 'Typically, they were individuals who had been toughened by the realities and demands of working class life, and who were well aware of what they were doing and why' (McLaren 1986:138). As to the identity of the exploiters, they were most often men and women of the same background and social circumstances as the prostitutes. More seriously, McLaren argues that the reformers and legislators ignored their own logic: the 'draconian body of law against exploiters', which was mobilized during the period and which penalized prostitutes, was *added* to the existing law rather than replacing it (McLaren 1986:139).

Contemporary

Our assumptions concerning prostitutes and prostitution today are somewhat different but no less deficient. First, the monetary focus of the social and legal definitions of prostitution misrepresent the extent of the problem by suggesting that it is the commercialization of sex that dehumanizes prostitution. I have reasoned elsewhere that it is not the exchange of money that dehumanizes sex. Non-commercial sexual relations are also characterized by brevity, impersonality, or a lack of mutual affection, and blatant sexual bargaining goes on in singles clubs, in the back seats of cars, in the office, and in marriage (Shaver 1988).

Sweeping generalizations about the inferiority of commercial sex combined with the strong tendency to disregard the fact of male prostitution means that important gender differences among street prostitutes regarding the way they manage sexual relations with their clients are overlooked. A comparison of studies on male and female prostitution suggests that these differences may be considerable. Women are more careful to point out that the service they provide is very limited—a hand job, a blow-job, straight sex (coitus), or half-and-half (a combination of fellatio and coitus)—and the majority insist on using condoms. Their objective is to complete the sexual transaction within twenty to thirty minutes at most. The more personal touches—kissing, hugging, hand-holding, prolonged eye contact, the touching and stroking of breasts—are rarely a part of their repertoire. Male hustlers, on the other hand, tend to engage in and enjoy a greater variety of services than do female prostitutes and negotiate lengthier time periods (McLeod 1982; Perkins and Bennett 1985; Visano 1987).

Studies of off-street prostitution indicate that there may be even greater diversity in the management and expression of commercial sexuality. Stein, who studied hundreds of client/call-girl relationships, found that their sexual practices included a sizeable proportion of experimentation and fantasy enactment (Stein 1974:93) and a variety of other non-coital sexual practices (e.g., tongue kissing, petting, and cunnilingus (Stein 1974:94) rarely practised by street prostitutes. The point is that there is a good deal of variety in sexual relations and the potential for inferior or abhorrent sex exists within both commercial and non-commercial settings. Focusing on the exchange of cash for sex as the distasteful factor tends to distort and deflect attention away from the more basic problem.

Secondly, disregard for gender differences may also lead to faulty conclusions about the source of the dangers involved in sex work. While I do not want to downplay the risks taken by those involved in prostitution—especially street prostitution—gender variations in the experience of the hazards indicate that they are not necessarily linked to the commoditization of sex. Male hustlers run less risk from on-the-job hazards than do either women or transgender prostitutes. They report fewer rapes and fewer beatings than either of the other two groups and are less likely to be arrested for prostitution-related offenses (Perkins and Bennett 1985:238–41). When they are assaulted, it is more likely to be related to their alleged homosexuality than to their involvement in sex work (Perkins and Bennett 1985:240).

Alcohol use is lower with women than men, but women appear to depend more on opiates (Perkins and Bennett 1985:241–2). Gender differences prevail with respect to the pimp factor as well—the most often cited source of violence and abuse. Our experience in the field, and that reported by others (Forbes 1977; Fraser et al. 1985:379; Lowman 1985:35–6; Perkins and Bennett 1985), indicates that pimps are rarely (if ever) involved in homosexual prostitution. Such findings suggest that the dangers are gender-based rather than work-based.

Thirdly, there is some evidence to suggest that the dangers currently associated with female prostitution may be exaggerated. Women are more at risk than men, but there appears to be a great deal of variation in the degree of exploitation and violence they experience. This is especially true with respect to the pimp factor. While it is unlikely to be as low as the police reports imply (cf., Table 9.3), it is also unlikely to be as high as the public believes,[16] or as abusive as implied in some feminist theorizing. Several studies indicate that not all prostitutes are pimped in the traditional sense. Prostitutes distinguish between the pimp as lover and the pimp as business manager (Fraser et al. 1985; Jaget 1980; Layton 1975; McLeod 1982) and are adamant about the qualitative difference between the two (Lowman 1985:36). The law, however, makes no distinction: 'everyone who lives wholly or in part on the avails of prostitution of another person' is defined as a pimp. Although such legislation violates an accused's constitutional right to be presumed innocent until proven guilty, it was recently upheld by the Supreme Court of Canada. Mr Justice Peter Cory, writing for the majority of Supreme Court judges, said pimps are 'parasites' who cruelly threaten, exploit, and abuse (often physically) prostitutes who are a 'particularly vulnerable segment of society'.

General claims such at this obscure the nature and source of the exploitation. They also serve to hide the extent to which all women in our society, not just female prostitutes, are vulnerable to male violence. Battered prostitutes need protection, just as battered wives do, and before either will bring charges against their abusers, they need to feel safe from future attacks and reprisals. Appropriate legislation must therefore differentiate between friend and parasite, as well as create conditions under which a woman is either willing to bring charges against an accused, or to stand up in court as a witness (Matthews 1986:207).

Concern regarding the remaining occupational dangers may also be misplaced since most prostitutes have developed procedures to minimize them. Prostitutes have regular medical check-ups, examine their customers for STD symptoms, and require them to use condoms (Fraser et al. 1985; James 1977; Layton 1975; McLeod 1982; Perkins and Bennett 1985:244; Prus and Irini 1980). They do not accept customers indiscriminately and usually develop techniques to avoid many of the potentially dangerous ones. Dans La Rue in Montreal, POWER in Vancouver, and Maggie's in Toronto distribute 'Bad Trick Sheets' describing and identifying the characteristics of dangerous customers.[17] On being harassed by a potential customer, it is a simple matter for the prostitute to say 'No' or 'I'm not working tonight' (a ploy I often used when approached by a client during my fieldwork). If this does not work, the situation often requires nothing more than a shout to a co-worker down the street: 'Hey Jan! This here jerk thinks he can get a blow-job for $25!' The customer invariably responds by moving in the opposite direction.

Risks increase once a prostitute is alone with a customer, but research suggests that protective routines have been developed: female prostitutes often work in pairs, noting when and with whom the other leaves and timing her return; licence plates are remembered; desk clerks are tipped and in return are expected to keep an eye on the time and an ear out for the sounds of violence (Fraser et al. 1985; McLeod 1982; Prus and Irini 1980).

Finally, although contemporary theorists and policy makers are to be applauded for recognizing the social and economic forces that lead women and girls into prostitution, most give little or no credibility to the claim some prostitutes make that this is their profession of choice (Bell 1987; Delacost and Alexander 1978; Pheterson 1989). The tendency to see prostitutes as victims of social, economic, and sexual inequality, or of their own false consciousness, is still very much a part of the dominant ideology. In contrast, studies that view prostitutes in the context of their profession (rather than their deviance) do not describe them as victims of male power or as the passive partners in the interaction. Authors of such studies argue that the prostitute sets the price, chooses the client, and has the last say as to when, how, and even if sex takes place (Jennes 1992; McLeod 1982; Perkins and Bennett 1985; Stein 1974).

CONCLUSION

Prostitution has long been treated as a deviant activity. Nonetheless, our views of who and what are deviant are socially constructed and subject to change. Variations in perception are evident in different historical periods. In Canada, although the objective properties and conditions of prostitution changed only slightly, the rhetoric surrounding it moved full circle from social nuisance, to social purist, to social nuisance. Variations in the perception of harm also occur with respect to the perceiver's point of reference. Residents speak of the deterioration of their neighbourhoods, feminists of the objective conditions that lead women into prostitution, and sex workers of being denied the right to work without being subject to criminal offence. Interestingly, it is the voices of those most directly involved—the sex workers—that have the least impact on the social construction of prostitution. If we were to listen more closely to them, we would hear them say, as they did in 1985 when writing the World Charter for Prostitutes' Rights, that 'prostitution *per se* (i.e., commercial sex) must be decriminalized and existing laws against fraud, coercion, violence, child abuse, rape and racism should be enforced both inside and outside the context of prostitution. [Prostitution must be recognized] as a legitimate work decision for adults, be it a decision based on choice or necessity' (Pheterson 1989:34).

Disparities between theory and practice are another indication of the extent to which prostitution is a social construction: only certain categories of people and certain acts are singled out for prosecution. These disparities provide a clear demonstration of the extent to which prostitution is constructed and maintained as a gender-specific crime. In spite of the large variation in legislative concerns expressed by the Victorian moralists and their contemporary counterparts, there are few differences, if any, in the way in which the laws within each historical period were enforced. The actual definitions of prostitution and prostitute reflected in the decision to prosecute indicate that female prostitutes engaged in street prostitution are singled out over male prostitutes, male customers, and pimps and procurers as offenders.

Another indication of the extent of the social construction of prostitution is reflected in the 'knowledge' we share about prostitution. Most of this knowledge is shaped and reproduced through our own misconceptions and value judgements rather than by the realities of prostitution and the commercialization of sexual services. Police, courtroom statistics, and sociological theorists suggest that most prostitutes are young, female, and poor, but the actual social distribution is likely to be less bleak. Higher-status, older, and more affluent female prostitutes who work off the street are unlikely to be the subject of police surveillance and are therefore underrepresented; so are male prostitutes. The social characteristics of customers and 'pimps' are likely to be more varied as well. Wealthier customers are underrepresented, and sweeping generalizations about abuse and exploitation by pimps and customers seem to be exaggerated.

These variations suggest that political and social forces are at work in constructing what is reprehensible or deviant about prostitution. It is not inherent in the practice or act itself. As with most social problems, what is seen as 'problematic' is a product of human enterprise and subject to considerable diversity. Individually and collectively, we are all variously involved in the making, shaping, and maintaining of prostitution as a gender-specific crime.

NOTES

The research for this paper is supported in part by grants from Social Sciences and Humanities Research Council, Fonds pour la Formation de Chercheurs et l'Aide à la Recherche, and Concordia University. I would like to thank Bill Reimer for his comments on earlier versions of this paper.

Thanks are due as well to my research assistants, Sheryl Dubois and Jane LeBrun, for their help in compiling the data for the tables.

1. These definitions were taken from the 1972 *Larousse Illustrated International Dictionary*. The revised and updated 1987 version provides the same two definitions.
2. This may be an overestimation of the thinking along these lines. The respondents in the opinion poll were asked whether they agreed with the non-monetary definition. The students in my classes designed their own definitions and fewer than 15 per cent included non-monetary sexual bargaining.
3. For example, Drew and Drake (1969) and Lloyd (1972) focus on the dysfunctional family; James (1977) on anomie; and Hirschi (1969), Greenwald (1970), Alder (1972), and Gray (1973) on social control.
4. This separates them from their Victorian counterparts, who accepted the notion of passive female sexuality (Edwards 1981; Walkowitz 1980).
5. The varieties of feminist perspectives on prostitution are least evident in their analysis of how it is structured and maintained and most evident in their assessment of what is problematic about it and how to 'cure' it (cf., Brock 1984; Overall 1992).
6. These arguments and the supporting data are presented in more detail in Shaver (1994b).
7. The first three periods overlap those documented by Susan Edwards (1981) in her study of female sexuality and the law. The year 1972 was selected as the point of departure for the most contemporary period because this is when 'Vag C' (the most recent prostitution-related vagrancy offence) was repealed and replaced by a soliciting law: 'Every person who solicits any person in a public place for the purpose of prostitution is guilty of an offence punishable on summary conviction.'
8. Bathhouses used by homosexuals for 'promiscuous' sexual activity fall under this new provision even though the sexual activity is rarely (if ever) exchanged for money.
9. The Special Committee on Pornography and Prostitution (the Fraser Committee) was appointed in 1984. Its mandate was to describe pornography, adult prostitution, and the laws regulating them in Canada; to review prostitution law in selected countries; to hold public hearings, and to recommend solutions to the various problems identified.
10. There was also much discussion regarding the meaning of the term 'solicits'. The dialogue focused on the actions that constituted soliciting. It is not gender-related and therefore is irrelevant to this discourse. For a brief discussion of the decisions taken on this issue, see CACSW (1984b:20–3) and Fraser et al. (1985:419–26).

222 SOCIAL CONTROL IN CANADA

11. The sexist enforcement of the soliciting provision has been well documented (CACSW 1984b; Fraser et al. 1985; House of Commons 1982; Lowman 1990; Ridington and Findlay 1981).

12. Interestingly, Toronto data show that there are no significant differences in rates of detention and sentencing of male and female prostitutes once arrested (Carrington and Moyer 1991:8–12).

13. Some of the discrimination in enforcement strategies may be structural, particularly with respect to the communicating section. For example, charges against 'communicators' are most often laid using 'decoys'— undercover police officers posing as customers or prostitutes. However, since vice squads are made up predominantly of men, most of the undercover work is done by male officers posing as customers. Female officers are used, but to a much lesser extent since it usually means bringing them in from another division. A further problem with female officers posing as prostitutes is that they are more likely to be recognized on the street than male officers posing as customers (Department of Justice 1989).

14. This should come as no surprise. A study of media coverage of prostitution between 1978–83 indicates that control issues received the most sustained coverage in the 970 articles sampled. Broader issues, such as the consequences of prostitution, the working conditions of those involved, and the definition of prostitution, were rarely covered (Kosmos 1984:Table 6, 30). The study also shows that the majority (41 per cent) of the 1,560 recorded comments came from those involved with the enforcement of the law (police, lawyers, and judges). Politicians were the source of 24 per cent of the comments. Those most directly involved (prostitutes, customers, and pimps) had a voice in only 12 per cent of the comments—equal coverage was given to journalists and other concerned groups (Kosmos 1984:Table 8, 33).

15. For evidence and arguments that challenge the accuracy of this construction, see Shaver (1994a).

16. Sixty per cent of the respondents surveyed for the Department of Justice maintain that organized crime is a major factor in the business, and that most prostitutes have pimps (Fraser et al. 1985:397).

17. Dans La Rue is an organization serving street kids. Maggie's (the Toronto Prostitutes' Community Service Project) produces 'Bad Trick Sheets' and 'Bad Call Sheets', runs the Prostitutes' Safe Sex Project, and operates a resource centre for sex workers. It is an offshoot of CORP (the Canadian Organization for the Rights of Prostitutes). POWER stands for Prostitutes and Other Women for Equal Rights.

FURTHER READINGS

Bell, L., ed. 1987. *Good Girls/Bad Girls: Sex Trade Workers and Feminists Face to Face*. Toronto: Women's Press.

Fraser, P., et al. 1985. *Pornography and Prostitution in Canada*, vol. II. Report of the Special Committee on Pornography and Prostitution. Ottawa: Minister of Supply and Services Canada.

Jennes, V. 1993. *Making It Work: The Prostitutes' Rights Movement in Perspective*. Hawthorne: Aldine de Gruyter.

McClintock, A., ed. 1993. *Social Text* 37 (Winter). A special edition exploring the sex trade.

McGinnis, J.D. 1994. 'Whores and Worthies: Feminism and Prostitution'. *Canadian Journal of Law and Society* 9, no. 1:105–22.

Overall, C. 1992. 'What's Wrong with Prostitution? Evaluating Sex Work'. *Signs: Journal of Women in Culture and Society* 17, no. 4:705–24.

Pheterson, G., ed. 1989. *A Vindication of the Rights of Whores*. Seattle: The Seal Press.

Shaver, F.M. 1985. 'Prostitution: A Critical Analysis of Three Policy Approaches'. *Canadian Public Policy* XI, no. 3:493–503.

REFERENCES

Akers, R. 1977. *Deviant Behaviour: A Social Learning Approach*. Belmont: Wadsworth.

Alder, P. 1972. 'On Becoming a Prostitute'. In *Criminal Life*, edited by D. Peterson and M. Truzzi. Englewood Cliffs: Prentice-Hall.

Backhouse, C. 1985. 'Nineteenth-Century Canadian Prostitution Law: Reflection of a Discriminatory Society'. *Social History* 53:387–423.

Bell, L., ed. 1987. *Good Girls/Bad Girls: Sex Trade Workers and Feminists Face to Face*. Toronto: Women's Press.

Boyd, N. 1991. 'Legal and Illegal Drug Use in Canada'. In *Canadian Criminology: Perspectives on Crime in Canada*, edited by M.A. Jackson and C.T. Griffiths, 135–52. Toronto: Harcourt Brace Jovanovich.

Brock, D. 1984. 'Feminist Perspectives on Prostitution: Addressing the Canadian Dilemma'. Unpublished MA dissertation, Department of Sociology and Anthropology, Carleton University.

_____. 1985–6. 'Beyond Images: Hookers and Feminists'. *Broadside* 7, no. 6:8–9.

_____, and J. Stephen. 1987–8. 'Which We Is Who?' *Broadside* 9, no. 3.

CACSW (Canadian Advisory Council on the Status of Women). 1984a. 'On Pornography and Prostitution'. A brief presented to the Special Committee on Pornography and Prostitution. Ottawa: Canadian Advisory Council on the Status of Women.

_____. 1984b. *Prostitution in Canada*. Ottawa: Canadian Advisory Council on the Status of Women.

Carrington, P.J., and S. Moyer. 1991. 'A Comparison of the Treatment of Prostitutes and Their Customers by the Police and Courts in Toronto,

1986–87'. Paper presented at the Canadian Sociology and Anthropology Association Annual Meeting.

Davis, K. 1937. 'The Sociology of Prostitution'. *American Sociological Review* (October):744–55.

Delacost, F., and P. Alexander. 1978. *Sex Work: Writings by Women in the Sex Industry*. Pittsburgh: Cleis Press.

Department of Justice. 1989. *Street Prostitution: Assessing the Law Synthesis Report*. Ottawa: Department of Justice.

Drew, D., and J. Drake. 1969. *Boys for Sale*. New York: Brown.

Edwards, S. 1981. *Female Sexuality and the Law*. Oxford: Martin Robertson.

Forbes, G.A. 1977. *Street Prostitution in Vancouver's West End*. Vancouver: Vancouver Police Department.

Fraser, P., et al. 1985. *Pornography and Prostitution in Canada*, vol. II. Report of the Special Committee on Pornography and Prostitution. Ottawa: Minister of Supply and Services Canada.

Gray, D. 1973. 'Turning Out: A Study of Teenage Prostitution'. *Urban Life and Culture* 1, no. 4:401–26.

Gray, J.H. 1971. *Red Lights on the Prairies*. Toronto: Macmillan.

Greenwald, H. 1970. *The Elegant Prostitute*. New York: Ballantine.

Heyl, B.S. 1979. *The Madam as Entrepreneur: Career Management in House Prostitution*. New Brunswick, NJ: Transaction Books.

Hirschi, T. 1969. 'The Professional Prostitute'. *Berkeley Journal of Sociology* 7:37–41.

House of Commons. 1982. 'Minutes of Proceedings and Evidence of the Standing Committee on Justice and Legal Affairs', issues no. 86, 90, and 91, including submissions from the National Action Committee on the Status of Women, the National Association of Women and the Law, the Canadian Association of Elizabeth Fry Societies, and the Vancouver Coalition for Non-sexist Criminal Code (May and June).

Jaget, C., ed. 1980. *Prostitutes: Our Life*. Bristol, UK: Falling Wall Press.

James, J. 1977. 'Prostitutes and Prostitution'. In *Deviants: Voluntary Actors in a Hostile World*, edited by E. Sagarin and F. Montanio, 368–428. New York: General Learning Press.

Jennes, V. 1990. 'From Sex as Sin to Sex as Work'. *Social Problems* 37, no. 3:403–20.

Kosmos, M. 1984. *Working Papers on Pornography and Prostitution, Report #3: Canadian Newspapers' Coverage of Pornography and Prostitution, 1978–1983*. Ottawa: Department of Justice.

Laner, M. 1974. 'Prostitution as an Illegal Vocation: A Sociological Overview'. In *Deviant Behaviour: Occupational and Organizational Bases*, edited by C. Bryant, 406–18. Chicago: Rand McNally.

Layton, M. 1975. *Prostitution in Vancouver (1973–75) Official and Unofficial Reports*. Vancouver: Vancouver Police Commission.

Lloyd, R. 1972. *For Money of Love: Boy Prostitution in America*. New York: Ballantine.

Lowman, J. 1985. 'Prostitution in Canada'. *Resources for Feminist Research* 13, no. 4:35–7.

_____. 1990. 'Notions of Formal Equality Before the Law: The Experience of Street Prostitutes and Their Customers'. *The Journal of Human Justice* 1, no. 2:55–76.

_____. 1991. 'Prostitution in Canada'. In *Canadian Criminology: Perspectives on Crime in Canada*, edited by M.A. Jackson and C.T. Griffiths, 113–34. Toronto: Harcourt Brace Jovanovich.

_____. 1992. 'Street Prostitution'. In *Deviance: Conformity and Control in Canadian Society*, edited by V.F. Sacco, 49–94. Toronto: Prentice-Hall.

Matthews, R. 1986. 'Beyond Wolfenden? Prostitution, Politics and the Law'. In *Confronting Crime*, edited by R. Matthews and J. Young, 188–210. London: Sage.

McLaren, J.P.S. 1986. 'Chasing the Social Evil: Moral Fervour and the Evolution of Canada's Prostitution Laws, 1867–1917'. *Canadian Journal of Law and Society* 1:125–65.

McLeod, E. 1982. *Working Women: Prostitution Now*. London: Croom Ltd.

NAC (National Action Committee on the Status of Women). 1984. 'Prostitution'. A brief presented to the Special Committee on Pornography and Prostitution.

Overall, C. 1992. 'What's Wrong with Prostitution? Evaluating Sex Work'. *Signs: Journal of Women in Culture and Society* 17, no. 4:705–24.

Perkins, R., and G. Bennett. 1985. *Being a Prostitute*. Sydney: George Allen and Unwin.

Pheterson, G., ed. 1989. *A Vindication of the Rights of Whores*. Seattle: The Seal Press.

Prus, R., and S. Irini. 1980. *Hookers, Rounders and Desk Clerks*. Toronto: Gage.

Ridington, J., and B. Findlay. 1981. *Pornography and Prostitution*. Vancouver: Vancouver Status of Women.

Romenesko, K., and E.M. Miller. 1989. 'The Second Step in Double Jeopardy: Appropriating the Labor of Female Street Hustlers'. *Crime and Delinquency* 35, no. 1:109–35.

Shaver, F.M. 1984. 'The Prostitution Debate'. In *Prostitution in Canada*, edited by Canadian Advisory Council on the Status of Women, 53–72. Ottawa: Canadian Advisory Council on the Status of Women.

_____. 1985. 'Prostitution: A Critical Analysis of Three Policy Approaches'. *Canadian Public Policy* XI, no. 3:493–503.

_____. 1988. 'A Critique of the Feminist Charges Against Prostitution'. *Atlantis* 4, no. 1:82–9.

_____. 1994a. 'Prostitution: A Female Crime?' In *In Conflict with the Law:*

Women and the Canadian Justice System, edited by E. Adelberg and
C. Currie, 153-73. Vancouver: Press Gang.
_____. 1994b. 'The Regulation of Prostitution: Avoiding the Morality
Traps'. *Canadian Journal of Law and Society* 9, no. 1:123–45.
Shrage, L. 1989. 'Should Feminists Oppose Prostitution?' *Ethics* 99:347–61.
Stein, M. 1974. *Lovers, Friends, Slaves*. New York: Berkeley Medallion.
Valverde, M. 1991. *The Age of Light, Soap, and Water: Moral Reform in
English Canada, 1885–1925*. Toronto: McClelland and Stewart.
Visano, L.A. 1987. *This Idle Trade: Occupational Patterns of Male Prostitution*.
Concord, ON: VitaSana Books.
Walkowitz, J.R. 1980. *Prostitution in Victorian Society: Women, Class and the
State*. Cambridge: Cambridge University Press.
Winslow, R., and V. Winslow. 1974. *Deviant Reality*. Boston: Allyn and
Bacon.

—10—

Constructing Sexuality in the AIDS Era

Barry Adam

Not so long ago, an article on Canadian sexuality might have adopted the reigning scientific view of the day: that sex is a fundamentally natural, biological phenomenon common to human beings as a species, and clearly demarcated by boundaries separating the normal from the deviant.[1] Various versions of this naturalist view have tended to assume that family relationships have been basically the same throughout history, that love and romance are a natural and primary part of family formation, or that the same set of sexual activities is normative, and others abnormal, in different societies. AIDS (acquired immune deficiency syndrome), which was only identified for the first time in the medical literature in 1981, has been one of many elements that has helped overturn this view by throwing into relief the various struggles and conflicts that have marked the recent history of sexuality in Canada. Today it is difficult to claim that there is any national 'community standard of tolerance' defining a single set of sexual norms, despite the insistence of Canadian courts who wish there were. Rather, sex in the 1980s and 1990s is a contested terrain upon which modern sexual discourses are being continually rewritten. Contemporary debates over AIDS offer us a key to revealing the clash of regulatory agencies and popular movements, the roles of governments and commerce, and the actions of judges and journalists over sexual issues. What sex means in Canada has been negotiated and redefined through a series of recent critical events: royal commissions on child abuse and prostitution, the collapse of the abortion law in the courts and in Parliament, the continuing regime of censorship of sexual imagery, the struggle for sexual orientation and domestic partners' rights, reform of age-of-consent laws, and public responses to the AIDS crisis. Understanding the ongoing revaluations of different sexualities as 'progressive' and 'emancipatory', or as 'criminal' and 'deviant', means sorting through the government agencies, moral entrepreneurs, capitalists, social movements, and image producers who populate the contemporary historical stage.

Sex and Power

The contemporary 'flashpoints' of abortion, censorship, sex abuse, gay and lesbian rights, and AIDS, which define much of the arena of debates over sexuality in Canada, emerge from a lengthy history of social change. Trends in sexuality have been shaped by changes in larger socio-economic forces, though at first glance such considerations may seem remote and unconnected. Yet the development of modern ideas about romantic love, family size, or sexual conduct are bound together with changes in authority relations among family members, control over the production and distribution of goods in the larger society, and policies enforced by church and state. Confrontations over the sex issues of today inherit deeply rooted contests over these fundamental problems and often function as symbolic indicators of the rise or decline of entire cultural systems and groups.

Modern capitalist societies such as Canada continue to wrestle with cultural legacies that prescribe a moral system rooted in traditional agrarian cultures. Historical and anthropological studies of settled agrarian societies at their height typically reveal societies where the fate and well-being of their members largely depend upon access to and control of land. Kinship rules regulate the holding and transfer of land in a manner (often in contrast to foraging societies) that guarantees the dominance of elder males over women, children, and sometimes other household members and possessions (see Blumberg 1978; O'Kelly and Carney 1986). These relations of authority, vested in what Paige and Paige (1981) call 'strong fraternal interest groups', are most often associated with heightened male control over the reproductive potential of 'their' women, high valuation and enforcement of female virginity, and dependence of young males upon their male lineage elders. The moral system consistent with this sociologic is one that demands the subordination of women and children to the patrilineage in the interests of concentrating the means of production and reproduction in the hands of the strong fraternal interest group. This kind of agrarian experience is the foundation of the religious and legal traditions of Judaeo-Christian societies and is conserved most vigorously today in the conservative Christian churches and Orthodox Judaism.

The reorganization of Western societies along capitalist lines, from the fifteenth century to the modern day, has fundamentally shifted the relations of production and distribution and thus the avenues to wealth, status, and power (see Wallerstein 1976–89). In modern capitalist societies, wage labour provides an income to wage-earners independent of family, thereby undermining the power of kin ties to determine the well-being of family members who work outside the home. In precapitalist societies, kinship obligations and the ways of making a living are typically bound together so that one can scarcely be separated from the other, but in capitalist societies, home and work become increasingly separated spheres of life, thereby changing the meaning and development of each.

With their mass entry into the labour market in the twentieth century, women became able to acquire resources that men had long taken for granted. With increased economic power, women could challenge their traditional subordination to patriarchal relations and mobilize into a movement to secure their gains and opportunities at work. Similarly, as parental authority devolved into the hands of prospective marital partners themselves, the expression of both heterosexual and homosexual attraction became increasingly possible, and people became more able to live together as they pleased using their own money and disregarding the pressure of parents and tradition (see Adam 1985).

The reality today is that the idealized image of two parents living together with their children in one household has become a *family of nostalgia* that describes only a minority of Canadian households. Everyone else lives in reconstituted families (following divorce), in more than one household, single-parent families, gay and lesbian families, or alone or in groups.

Whether Canadians *should* live this way is the substance of current debates. Many of the current confrontations stem from the larger stakes underlying the issues at hand. 'Progressives' seek to overcome the older systems, encouraging people's liberation from the strictures and subordination inherent in the traditional order. For them, freedom is constantly threatened by the bulwark of law, custom, and religion, which institutionalizes traditional hierarchies and folkways through a hegemonic regime of ideological and police powers. 'Reactionaries' lament the loss of a familiar and comfortable social code and decry the new 'anarchy' and 'permissiveness' as criminal, sinful, or pathological. For them, the good and the normal represent fragile accomplishments now under siege and in need of defence. Both conservative and liberalizing forces move within a larger historical context that presents often unanticipated dilemmas and possibilities in the arena of sex, bonding, and intimacy. These changing historical conditions give shape to the discursive and practical responses that make up the public debate.

Among the most visible of progressive forces have been the women's movement and the gay and lesbian movement. Both movements have been fundamentally concerned with increasing the options that people have in their personal, family, and work lives, seeking to break the hold that gender has had on determining 'appropriate' behaviours and social expectations. Activists have sought to disrupt the symbolic associations that have dominated social codes in Western societies where:

Female = emotional/nurturant = passive/dependent =
        in the home = subordinate to male authority
Male   = rational/controlling = active/independent = in
        the public sphere = authoritative

Progressive movements have aimed to free people to combine these elements in innovative ways. They advocate letting women determine for themselves when to become sexual or to bear children; letting men become involved with taking care of children; and letting young people and people of
the same sex have loving relationships and live in households of their own if
they wish. To make this possible, feminists have worked for social services
for 'refugees' from male power by creating rape crisis centres and shelters
for battered women. They have worked, earlier in this century, for the right
to use contraception and later for the right to determine pregnancy and
abortion for themselves, an issue that strikes at the heart of the traditional
prerogative of husbands and fathers to control the fertility of women. In a
1969 law reform, the Canadian state handed over the power to approve
abortions to committees of three physicians who were to certify that a proposed abortion was necessary to prevent endangerment of the life or health
of the patient. An abortion rights movement, which organized in 1970,
succeeded, in a series of court cases centring around Dr Henry Morgentaler,
in having the law struck down by the Supreme Court in 1988 as an unconsti-
tutional interference with a woman's right to 'life, liberty and security of the
person' (Day and Persky 1988:13).

Gay and lesbian activists have similarly pressed for the inclusion of 'sexual
orientation' in human rights codes, the recognition of gay and lesbian relationships, the construction of autonomous women's cultural forms, and the
humanization of relations among men now so beset by competitive and
hierarchical divisions (Adam 1995).

The opposition to these trends has tended to come from people fearful of
the effects of disrupting traditional family arrangements. For traditionalists,
rising rates of divorce and abortion in recent decades are signs of a moral
crisis connected with a 'decline of the family'. Their solution is *not* to allow
people to seek alternative domestic arrangements but to reinforce the patriarchal system. While feminists see the problems arising from the subordination of women in the traditional family system, conservatives see problems
arising from too much 'permissiveness' and too little 'discipline'. For them,
sexual 'promiscuity' and delinquency result from loosening the traditional
folkways that have governed sexual conduct.

These opposing perspectives are frequently associated with different abilities to take advantage of the options promised by change. Antifeminist women,
such as the supporters of organizations like REAL Women (Steuter 1992),
have tended to look upon the employment options advocated by feminism as
little more than abandonment in a heartless labour market. Women's entry
into wage labour, they have feared, would also relieve men of their obliga-

tion to support wives and children. Sociological research on the proponents and opponents of the abortion rights in the United States has shown that *opponents* more often include women who are White, rural, and housewives without advanced education (and thus limited job prospects), with more than three children, and with strong church participation. *Proponents*, on the other hand, are more often women who are urban, 'educated, affluent liberal professionals' (Luker 1984:194–8; see Conover and Gray 1983:111). The new options for women, for which feminists advocate, may appear alternately as inviting or fearsome, depending upon social location.

Negotiating and redefining the boundaries of the acceptable and respectable in sexuality in Canada has been the outcome of many decades of conflicting social forces. Just as most Western societies went through centuries of bloody conflict over which religion to establish as the single state-recognized orthodox church before resolving the issue by allowing for freedom of conscience and religious pluralism, so today a struggle continues over disestablishing the monogamous, patriarchal, heterosexual family as the 'one true' household arrangement in favour of permitting a variety of forms.

GAY AND LESBIAN RIGHTS

The recent history of conflicts over the recognition of gay and lesbian rights has shown fundamental shifts since the Second World War. Canada was not immune to the repressive wave of McCarthyism, which swept through the United States in the early 1950s, targeting 'Communists' and 'homosexuals' for persecution (Adam 1993). The Royal Commission on Criminal Sexual Psychopaths, which met from 1954–8, ignored the one lone voice raised against the antihomosexual campaign (Kinsman 1987:127) and the RCMP operated a probe well into the 1960s, which resulted in the dismissal of many gay people from the federal civil service, the National Film Board, and the CBC (Sawatsky 1980). 'Respectable' magazines suppressed any discussion of gay and lesbian issues; only the scandal tabloids would report on homosexuality, but then almost always as crime or spectacle.

In 1964, the Association for Social Knowledge formed in Vancouver as Canada's first public gay and lesbian organization. By 1970, in a period marked by the rise of civil rights and student and women's movements, gay liberation groups sprang up across the country. The movement's first march on Ottawa articulated several basic demands: abolition of the gross indecency law; uniform age of consent; protection through human rights codes; equal rights for same-sex couples; destruction of police files; the right to serve in the armed forces; and an end to discrimination in immigration, employment, custody and adoption, and housing (Jackson and Persky 1982:217–20).

The euphoria of the movements for social change in the 1960s and early 1970s abated in the face of reorganized state opposition (see Adam 1995).

From the mid-1970s to the mid-1980s, conservatives launched new offensives to roll back the gains made by the women's and gay and lesbian movements. In the late 1970s as pro-life, anti-ERA,[2] antipornography, and antigay movements mobilized across the United States and Canada, police raids in Montreal and Toronto netted several hundred gay men who subsequently had to endure many years of courtroom prosecution for the crime of being 'found-in a common bawdy-house' for having been in a gay establishment.

The 1982 constitution added 'sex' to the list of protected categories in its human rights provisions following a last-minute, nationwide campaign by the women's movement; 'sexual orientation' was voted down by the Liberal and Conservative parliamentarians of the day. Quebec, however, had already extended human rights coverage to lesbians and gay men in 1977 following the victory of the Parti Québécois, and in 1986, Ontario followed when the Liberal minority government adopted an initiative made by the NDP. The following year, NDP governments in Manitoba and the Yukon did the same. By 1993, seven of the ten provinces had adopted the amendment;[3] the federal government followed in 1996 after a Supreme Court decision that read 'sexual orientation' into Section 15 of the constitution.

The struggle for the recognition of same-sex couples remains the unresolved issue of the 1990s. Two cases ultimately worked their way to the Supreme Court. In the first launched in 1988, the pioneering gay activist, Jim Egan, then sixty-five, went to court to win his partner of thirty-nine years, John Nesbit, the spousal allowance available to heterosexual couples under the Canada Pension Plan. The second begun in 1989, involved Brian Mossop's appeal to the Canadian Human Rights Commission when his employer, the federal government, refused to allow him a day off to attend the funeral of his lover's father. In both cases, the Supreme Court ruled against equal treatment of same-sex couples. The overall approach of the courts to gay and lesbian families has typically been punitive, subjecting parents to such onerous rules as not being allowed to be involved in any public organization in support of their rights; not being allowed to live with someone of the same sex or to share a bedroom; or not being allowed to have their child stay overnight (Eaton 1990; Ryder 1990). Of course, the struggle continues and in 1992, the Ontario government acquiesced to a ruling of its human rights commission, which struck the words 'of the opposite sex' from the definition of 'spouse' by extending domestic partners' rights to its own employees. Lower court rulings and union contracts continued to build the rights of same-sex partners in other jurisdictions.

CONSTRUCTING AIDS

Into this complex of historical trends and social movements there appeared a new, deadly disease in 1981. Unlike, say, leukemia or diabetes, which generally escape moral or political implications, from the beginning AIDS became embroiled in the controversies surrounding the future of sexuality and family. Like contraception in the early years of the twentieth century and abortion in later years, AIDS immediately raised the question of who controls whose bodies. In the early twentieth century, conservatives feared that contraception challenged the moral regulation exerted by church and state by allowing the escape of sex from family control, the release of women from the obligations of motherhood, and the disengagement of men from the responsibilities of family support. It 'let sex "leak away" from the family to youth and to people who might stay unmarried, become "loose" or "bad" women, or prefer homosexual relationships' (Adam 1992:309). In the 1980s, AIDS was to become a cause for the political right wing to 'return' to the ethic of monogamy or celibacy; for the left, the issue was letting people know how to have sex in an epidemic. An AIDS awareness movement, pioneered in gay communities, pointed out that sex remains possible and that AIDS is avoidable through the simple technology of placing a barrier between oneself and the blood, semen, or vaginal fluids of another person. Like contraception, safer sex separates sex from 'its consequences', enabling people to make informed sexual decisions without the supervision of churches and governments.

These opposing social constructions of the meanings of AIDS have become deeply embedded in contemporary accounts and images. Public school systems have generally adopted a policy of introducing AIDS education by recommending celibacy and monogamy to young people, while allowing safer sex as a poor third choice. Roman Catholic school systems, at least at the official level, continue to suppress the safer sex alternative altogether. The mass media have typically engaged in a process of presuming their readers and viewers to be patriotic families in opposition to the 'disposable constituencies' of the HIV-infected (Watney 1989:69; 1987). People with HIV disease remain 'bound, gagged and hidden away behind antiseptic screens and curtains of AIDS commentary', Simon Watney (1989:70) observes. The resulting not-so-covert message underlying this ideological system has remained: respectable people don't get AIDS. For people living with AIDS, their families and friends, the message received is to tread carefully because employers and police have a licence to express their contempt through dismissal and prosecution. Nor are these apprehensions unrealistic; there are egregious examples from a number of American cities of seropositive people convicted of attempted murder for allegedly biting prison officials, many fired outright at a time of greatest need in their lives (see Adam and Sears 1996), and a ban on seropositive foreigners (including Canadians) from even visiting the United States. In Ottawa, Halifax, Calgary, and St John's, people with HIV disease have been jailed on the grounds that others have been or may have been exposed through their blood donations or sexual activities.

Not everyone succumbs to the punitive approach. Social science research shows that people who are most punitive towards people with AIDS are the same people who are the most homophobic, which, in turn, indexes the characteristics of the sexual conservatives discussed earlier (see Clift and Stears 1989; Nelkin 1987; Triplet and Sugarman 1987). Still, the message that only 'other' people get AIDS is pervasive. Eleanor Maticka-Tyndale's (1992) research on Montreal students shows that high levels of knowledge about HIV transmission can often be combined with widespread denial of personal vulnerability. Safer sex is thereby ignored because the respondents practise only 'regular sex'—nothing homosexual; they 'trust' their partners not to endanger them; they think they can spot a risky partner due to (usually, 'her') 'sleazy reputation'; or careful partner selection will suffice (see also Chapman and Hodgson 1988). By constructing AIDS as a disease of the 'other', many convince themselves that they need not practise safer sex, yet it is precisely this failure to take precautions that creates the most favourable conditions for continued HIV transmission.

SEX AND THE STATE

There is some warrant for seeing these antilabelling tendencies as processes of *democratization*. For feminists, gay and lesbian activists, and AIDS workers, much of their struggle has been to 'deregulate' sexuality, placing the freedom and responsibility for sexual decision making in the hands of all citizens. Feminists have sought the right to be the primary agents of their own sexual and reproductive potential without the control or management of the state, patriarchy, or their delegates in the form of clergy or professionals. Lesbian and gay activists have created space for people to express same-sex affectional and erotic bonding free from the priests, psychiatrists, and judges who would stigmatize it as sin, sickness, or crime. The AIDS awareness movement has aimed to provide the information and techniques necessary to allow people to act sexually while minimizing the risk of infection without demanding that everyone choose between monogamy or celibacy. Still, these have not been simply antistate movements arguing, as did Pierre Trudeau, that 'the state has no place in the bedrooms of the nation'. At times, theirs has also been a plea for state protection not unlike the claim made by movements for people of colour and Aboriginal peoples. Human rights protection, labour law legislation, domestic partners' recognition, and funding for AIDS research have been part of an agenda to make the state respond to citizens who have been too often marginalized or excluded from consideration. Sometimes the choice between these strategies has raised new, more vexing problems, as in the cases of the depiction of sexual images and the sexuality of young people.

For many feminists, so much pornography seems little more than hate propaganda directed against women with its mix of violence and sexuality and its depiction of women as no more than objects for male consumption.

In 1977, a chapter of Women Against Violence Against Women formed in Toronto, dedicated to curbing this cultural affirmation of male dominance (Lacombe 1988:47). Yet in Canada, there was already no lack of state and corporate institutions engaged in the control and suppression of sexual imagery. Most representations of sexuality pass through three or four separate screening processes before Canadians are permitted a look for themselves. Canada Customs imposes a set of administrative criteria and maintains a compendium of banned books that limit various forms of sexual explicitness. Provincial film review boards 'classify' movies and videos, restricting some to adult audiences, issuing warnings, and, in some instances, cutting or suppressing them altogether. An Ontario Advisory Committee reviews most periodicals distributed in the nation, advising publishers about which pictures, texts, or magazine issues violate Canadian 'standards of tolerance'. Though these are non-binding recommendations, most publishers comply with them. Finally, material that has passed these hurdles remains subject to prosecution under federal obscenity statutes.

Given this array of established social control agencies, the attack on pornography was quickly able to attract many well-established institutional allies, unlike many other feminist concerns. The antipornography initiative provoked division among activists concerning the appropriate definition of the problem and the strategies employed to 'solve' it. Some feminists and gay activists opposed the enlistment of existing state institutions in the control of sexual representation, arguing instead that pornography was better critiqued through the generation of a humanized erotica produced from women's and gay/lesbian perspectives (see Burstyn 1985). But caught in the censors' nets in the 1980s have been such films as the National Film Board antipornography epic, *Not a Love Story*, a picaresque portrait of German gay life called *Taxi zum Klo*, several paintings from art galleries, and Marian Engel's novel, *Bear*, about Aboriginal mythology, which included reference to sex with a bear. These and not the 'mainstream' machista epics of the *Terminator*, *Basic Instinct*, the *Rambo* series, or 'hard-core' heterosexual images suffered police seizures and banning orders in recent years. Gay and lesbian bookstores in the three largest cities have endured decades of repeated Customs seizures, police visits, and court appearances for daring to stock books that mention anal sex or admit to a sexual experience by someone under the age of eighteen (Adam 1995).

In British Columbia, antipornography feminists set up a BC Periodicals Review Board at the invitation of entrepreneur, Jim Pattison, and with space provided by the Social Credit government of the day. In the words of a founding member, such groups as the Canadian Civil Liberties Association, which are 'known to have extreme opinions are not invited to nominate members' to the board (Ridington 1989:11). Operating since the mid-1980s, the British Columbia Periodicals Review Board takes additional cuts from magazines, many of which have already been censored by the Ontario Committee. In 1987–8, it suppressed 8 per cent of the periodicals it saw, mutilated a further 22 per cent, and banned three times as many gay periodicals as 'mainstream' magazines (Ridington 1989:9–10). In the words of the board chairperson, gay magazines that Canada Customs had already screened, showed 'signs of extensive editing. At first pages were deleted, then blank spaces and "black spots" became common. The plots of stories became impossible to follow because complete sections were blanked out' (Ridington 1989:13). No gay person was invited to serve on the BC Periodicals Review Board.

In 1992, the Supreme Court of Canada rendered a new interpretation of obscenity law in the Butler case, co-opting feminist language that 'the portrayal of persons being subjected to degrading or dehumanizing sexual treatment results in harm, particularly to women and therefore to society as a whole'. Characteristically, the first target of a police raid following the court's decision was Toronto's Glad Day Bookstore for selling *Bad Attitude*, a journal of erotica produced by and for lesbians. Once again, the application of censorship never failed to uphold traditional patriarchal and antigay standards while ignoring the glorification of (heterosexual) male power in sexual images and texts.

Pornography is not the only instance of the role of the state in moral regulation, labelling deviance, and the subvention of one form of sexual interaction against another. The federal government appointed royal commissions in the 1980s on prostitution (see Shaver, this volume) and child sexual abuse. Public concern, fed by frequent media reports, about the sexual exploitation of children led the Badgley Commission to diagnose the problem in terms of more law reform, policing, and judicial intervention. Critics pointed out that this state definition of the problem left several other possibilities untouched. Even though social science research and the courts have increased awareness of the extent of violence against women and children within families, this report on the abuse of children had little to say about its roots in the patriarchal family system. Though 'overwhelmingly, those who sexually assault or otherwise sexually abuse and/or exploit children, youths and others are male', the state had nothing to say about how sexual abuse was consistent with the way in which 'males learn to link their sexuality with power, authority and violence in order to become "real men," competent to exercise the control the system extends to them' (Clark 1986:96, 99; see also Kaufman 1987). As well, enforcement of age-of-consent laws in order to 'protect' young people from sexual predation at the same time suppressed their own sexuality under the label of 'abuse'. Kinsman and Brock (1986:124) note that the root of the problem might be addressed if 'young people [were] empowered to say "no" to sexual and other forms of abuse, including the ability to lay assault or other criminal charges against adults, including parents'. Yet these kinds of structural reforms, which would challenge relations of domination, whether in face-to-face relations or institutional forms, were the least likely to receive serious public consideration. Democratizing critiques and recommendations again and again were assimilated into (rather than influential in dismantling) the predominant forms of power relations.

RECONSTRUCTING SEXUALITY

While the state is a critically important force in social negotiations over sexuality, it is not alone. Not to be forgotten are the commercial ventures that shape sex as a commodity to be marketed for profit. While the pornography industry is one business contributing to our ideas of sexual attractiveness and technique, other capitalist enterprises are more pervasive. Sex has become a ubiquitous means for advertisers to glamorize a wide range of products to improve the profit margins of beer and car companies. As sex has come to seem more treacherous in the AIDS era, new entrepreneurs have offered us that uniquely postmodern form of sexuality, the sex-talk phone line. While the pornography producers create sex with *representations* of bodies, the sex lines offer, for a fee, *sex without bodies*. Furthermore, while feminists have critiqued the objectification of women in sexual imagery, capitalists have responded with a new equality of representation—sexually objectified male bodies in advertising and male strippers in bars. Such are the ironies of history with its unintended consequences arising from earlier conflicts in which neither side gets what it thought it was working for.

Much of the attention of feminist and gay/lesbian organizations remains focused on dealing with the concrete, everyday effects of subordination, which very often takes the form of overt violence. The 1989 Montreal massacre, in which fourteen female engineering students were murdered by an overtly misogynist assassin, coalesced the ongoing violence against women into a potent national symbol. This incident was only the most visible event in the larger field of everyday, 'routine' physical and sexual assault directed towards women. Similarly, the ongoing, persistent regime of violence against lesbians and gay men results in an occasional media incident, as in the 1985 murder of a Toronto librarian by teenage males. When these cases come to court, gay victims typically suffer the fate accorded to female sexual assault victims: the ensuing legal circus develops a voyeuristic obsession with the lives of the victims while excusing the actions of heterosexual, male perpetrators. As well, murderers have made good use of the 'homosexual panic' defence in courts by claiming that their actions were justified because the victim made a sexual advance to them. While this argument rarely works for female victims of male attackers, it worked in 1986 to acquit Gerald Moore, the murderer of Ralph Fredsburg in Windsor, and there are a number of similar incidents.

For the new social movements in the sexual sphere, there remains a compelling agenda of overcoming the structural subordination that has consigned women, young people, and sexual minorities to the margins of political discourse. In 1990, a Toronto group calling itself Queer Nation sought to bring together, in the category 'queer', not only lesbians and gay men but everyone stigmatized for unorthodox sexual practices, be they punks, boy-lovers, leather folk, HIV-positive people, or others. Though this idea has yet to develop fully, it is a step towards challenging the patriarchal hegemony, which guarantees heterosexual men overwhelming predominance in positions of power and which glorifies their 'right' to exert violence over women, gay people, and racial minorities, whether in the street or in a variety of cultural forms from blockbuster movies to television news broadcasts.

We remain in the midst of a historical process of disengagement from agrarian, patriarchal family forms. This process opens new possibilities for revisioning the ways in which people can relate to each other intimately and erotically. This is the challenge in the struggles over sexuality in Canada today.

NOTES

I would like to thank Alan Sears, Christina Simmons, Janice Drakich, and Jacqueline Murray for their helpful comments on this chapter.

1. See Weeks (1981, 1985) on the history of sexology in the twentieth century.
2. A movement dedicated to defeating the Equal Rights Amendment to the US constitution, which would have forbidden discrimination on the basis of sex. The movement succeeded in having the amendment fall two states short of the two-thirds ratification necessary to amend the constitution.
3. Only Alberta, Prince Edward Island, and Newfoundland continued to hold out by not including 'sexual orientation' in their human rights legislation.

FURTHER READINGS

Adam, B. 1995. *The Rise of a Gay and Lesbian Movement*, 2nd ed. New York: Twayne.
Kinsman, G. 1987. *The Regulation of Desire*. Montreal: Black Rose.
Lacombe, D. 1988. *Ideology and Public Policy*. Toronto: Garamond.
Miller, J. 1992. *Fluid Exchanges*. Toronto: University of Toronto Press.
Stone, S. 1990. *Lesbians in Canada*. Toronto: Between the Lines.
Weeks, J. 1985. *Sexuality and Its Discontents*. London: Routledge and Kegan Paul.

REFERENCES

Adam, B.D. 1985. 'Structural Foundations of the Gay World'. *Comparative Studies in Society and History* 27, no. 4:658.

_____. 1992. 'The State, Public Policy, and AIDS Discourse'. In *Fluid Exchanges*, edited by J. Miller, 305–20. Toronto: University of Toronto Press.

_____. 1993. 'Winning Rights and Freedoms in Canada'. In *The Third Pink Book*, edited by A. Hendriks, R. Tielman, and E. van der Veen. Buffalo: Prometheus.

_____. 1995. *The Rise of a Gay and Lesbian Movement*, 2nd ed. New York: Twayne.

_____, and A. Sears. 1996. *Experiencing HIV*. New York: Columbia University Press.

Blumberg, R.L. 1978. *Stratification*. Dubuque, IA: William Brown.

Brock, D., and G. Kinsman. 1986. 'Patriarchal Relations Ignored'. In *Regulating Sex*, edited by J. Lowman et al., 107–26. Burnaby: School of Criminology, Simon Fraser University.

Burstyn, V. 1985. *Women Against Censorship*. Vancouver: Douglas & McIntyre.

Chapman, S., and J. Hodgson. 1988. 'Showers in Raincoats'. *Community Health Studies* 12:97–105.

Clark, L. 1986. 'Boys Will Be Boys'. In *Regulating Sex*, edited by J. Lowman et al., 93–106. Burnaby: School of Criminology, Simon Fraser University.

Clift, S., and D. Stears. 1989. 'Undergraduates' Beliefs and Attitudes About AIDS'. In *AIDS: Social Representations, Social Practices*, edited by P. Aggleton, G. Hart, and P. Davies, 39–63. London: Falmer.

Conover, P., and V. Gray. 1983. *Feminism and the New Right*. New York: Praeger.

Day, S., and S. Persky. 1988. *The Supreme Court of Canada Decision on Abortion*. Vancouver: New Star.

Eaton, M. 1990. 'Lesbians and the Law'. In *Lesbians in Canada*, edited by S. Stone, 109–32. Toronto: Between the Lines.

Jackson, E., and S. Persky. 1982. *Flaunting It!* Vancouver: New Star.

Kaufman, M. 1987. *Beyond Patriarchy*. Toronto: Oxford University Press.

Kinsman, G. 1987. *The Regulation of Desire*. Montreal: Black Rose.

Lacombe, D. 1988. *Ideology and Public Policy*. Toronto: Garamond.

Luker, K. 1984. *Abortion and the Politics of Motherhood*. Los Angeles: University of California Press.

Maticka-Tyndale, E. 1992. 'Social Construction of HIV Transmission and Prevention Among Heterosexual Young Adults'. *Social Problems* 39, no. 3:238–52.

Nelkin, D. 1987. 'AIDS and the Social Sciences'. *Reviews of Infectious Diseases* 9:980.

O'Kelly, C., and L. Carney. 1986. *Women and Men in Society*. Belmont, CA: Wadsworth.

Paige, P., and J. Paige. 1981. *The Politics of Reproductive Ritual*. Los Angeles: University of California Press.

Ridington, J. 1989. *Confronting Pornography*. Ottawa: Canadian Research Institute for the Advancement of Women.

Ryder, B. 1990. 'Equality Rights and Sexual Orientation'. *Canadian Journal of Family Law* 9, no. 1:39–97.

Sawatsky, J. 1980. *Men in the Shadows*. Toronto: Doubleday.

Steuter, E. 1992. 'Women Against Feminism'. *Canadian Review of Sociology and Anthropology* 29, no. 3:288–306.

Triplet, R., and D. Sugarman. 1987. 'Reactions to AIDS Victims'. *Personality and Social Psychology Bulletin* 13:265–74.

Wallerstein, I. 1976–89. *The Modern World-System*, vol. 1–3. San Diego: Academic Press.

Watney, S. 1987. *Policing Desire*. London: Comedia.

_____. 1989. 'The Subject of AIDS'. In *AIDS: Social Representations, Social Practices*, edited by P. Aggleton, G. Hart, and P. Davies, 64–73. London: Falmer.

Weeks, J. 1981. *Sex, Politics and Society*. London: Longman.

_____. 1985. *Sexuality and Its Discontents*. London: Routledge and Kegan Paul.

—11—

Deconstructing Spousal Violence:
A Socialist Feminist Perspective

Kathy Storrie and Nancy Poon

INTRODUCTION

Programs for men who abuse their female intimate partners have a wide range of theoretical frameworks and a resulting variety of objectives, strategies, and techniques. Useful reviews of this diversity have been done by a number of scholars (Bersani and Chen 1988; Frankel-Howard 1989; Gondolf 1988; Stark and Flitcraft 1988). Not surprisingly, the field resounds with debates and controversies that can create some rather unproductive factionalism, especially when, in Yllo's words, 'the many sides stop talking and listening to one another' (1988:29).

A complete review of this complex situation will not be attempted here, but instead the focus will be on some of the crucial issues that arise from feminist (in contrast to non-feminist) approaches, and also from differing feminist perspectives. These will include questions of epistemology and method, and the implications of state involvement in services for battering men.

EPISTEMOLOGY AND METHOD

When one considers the complexities inherent in the behaviour that has been given a variety of labels such as 'battering', 'abuse', and 'violence', the question of epistemology assumes considerable importance. Feminist scholars have joined others with other orientations, such as Kuhn (1962), Barnes (1974), Feyeraband (1975), and Bloor (1977), in analysing ways in which scientific knowledge is moulded by its particular social and political context. Feminists of varying philosophies (radical, socialist, etc.) have produced a literature critical of science that is too voluminous to recapitulate here (see Harding 1986, 1989; Keller 1982, 1985; Longino 1989; Millman and Kanter

1975; Stanley and Wise 1983). This work, however, provides the context for our comments.

Although these scholars have developed a number of feminist epistemologies such as 'feminist empiricism', the 'feminist standpoint', and 'feminist postmodernism' (Harding 1986), a common and central issue in all of them is a critique of objectivity as conceptualized and practised in mainstream science. In the positivist paradigm, typical of this science, the relation between the knower and the known is one of distance and separation whereby the knower is constituted as subject and the known as object. This distancing supposedly insures that the knower will be value neutral, emotionally detached, immune to the effects of his or her social characteristics and position, and hence 'objective'.

It is important to note that making 'objective' synonymous with 'unemotional' and 'uninvolved' has the effect of rendering suspect and 'unscientific' any work that implies political action or social change. Mainstream academics have been known to criticize feminist literature for being biased and political and to imply or even to claim that their own work is non-political and hence 'objective' (see, for example, Neidig 1984 and the response of Pence et al. 1984). Feminists locate the historical roots of this objectifying and distancing stance in the male monopoly of science, and in the way masculinity has been socially constructed, with its stress on domination and autonomy. Furthermore, these feminists argue that the gendered character of positivist science has existed from the very beginning of Western science (Bleier 1984; Keller 1978; Rich 1979).

Smith's (1974, 1979, and 1990) work is useful in understanding this process of organizing knowledge. She points out that knowledge in preliterate, kinship-based societies is created directly from experience and is thus accessible and accountable to all knowers in a given community. But in class societies, it is the work of the intelligentsia to detach ideas from their grounding and origin in real people and their life activity, and to translate them into abstract concepts suitable for discourses that are then used to govern society. Thus ideological practices are developed by which dominant groups shape the lives of subordinate groups and systematically exclude their perspectives and experiences from mainstream knowledge. In patriarchal, capitalist societies, the realities of women's everyday lives undergo these processes of abstraction and are thus distorted, masked, and disguised 'through relations of ruling' (Smith 1987:3). In this way, Smith argues that a rupture is created between the daily lives of women on the one hand and, on the other, the dominant discourses that until recently have been almost exclusively the domain of men in mainstream academic and professional capacities. Furthermore, the impersonal language of these discourses renders invisible the specific interests and perspectives of the author(s) but does not eliminate their influence, nor the fact that power is thereby being exercised. The result is that women find themselves alienated from official knowledge and indeed from many aspects of their lives through these ruling relations. The many consequences of androcentric knowledge have been documented by feminist scholars through extensive critiques of all disciplines (see Dubois et al. 1985; Eichler 1985; Franklin et al. 1981; Spender 1981).

In contrast to the objectifying practices typical of positivist scholarship, strategies advocated by many feminists include an emphasis on 'reflexivity' and a standpoint research strategy. 'Reflexivity' refers to a consistent consciousness of self when constructing any discourse. Such feminist scholars would agree with Piaget's statement that

> Objectivity consists in ... fully realising the countless intrusions of the self in everyday thought and the countless illusions which result ... Realism, on the contrary, consists in ignoring the existence of self and thence regarding one's own perspective as immediately objective and absolute. Realism is thus anthropocentric illusion, finality—in short, all those illusions which teem in the history of science. So long as thought has not become conscious of self, it is prey to perpetual confusions between objective and subjective, between the real and the ostensible (Piaget 1972:34).

Feminist scholars argue that it is this lack of self-consciousness that lies at the root of androcentric biases in academic discourses, so that masculine experience and perspectives have been taken to constitute the universal.

The standpoint strategy involves taking up women's perspectives and treating them as subjects and not objects (Rose 1983). Such a strategy can also be justified on the grounds that subordinated groups are necessarily familiar with the relations that constrain and disadvantage them, while those who benefit from such inequality usually remain blind to its essential features and the labour that sustains their privileges.[1]

One way in which a feminist inquiry can tap into the female familiarity with oppressive relations is to treat the everyday world of women as problematic. This method not only makes visible the character and organization of the everyday world, but because this world is not fully comprehensible within its own scope, it also identifies the organizing 'social relations which are not fully apparent in it [this world] nor contained by it' (Smith 1987:92). The concept of the problematic means that one focuses on properties of the everyday world in an effort to elicit 'questions that may not have been posed or a set of puzzles that do not yet exist in the form of puzzles but are "latent" in the actualities of the experienced world' (Smith 1987:91).

When one studies the experiences of abused women, one encounters a number of puzzles. One example is the discrepancy between women's primary accounts of their partners' coercive behaviour on the one hand, and these men's legitimations of their own actions on the other. These women regard their partners' behaviour as intimidating at the very least, and, in the case of physical injury, as destructive, dangerous, and intentional. But that reality is continuously presented to them by the men and by others as something else, such as a normal and indeed justifiable reaction to the women's 'provocative' behaviour and/or the men's loss of control, i.e., as unintentional (Adams 1988a, 1988b; Adams and McCormick 1982; Ptacek 1988). In this and in many other ways, the everyday world of abused women have a continuously invalidating character that is not necessarily obvious to them or to others who also occupy that world. Indeed, typically such women internalize and reproduce the rationalizations of their abusers, and unless they become free of their partners' ideological and physical control, they continue to blame and denigrate themselves (Dobash and Dobash 1979; Dutton 1988; Martin 1976; Okun 1986; Walker 1979).

Furthermore, there is considerable evidence indicating that if abused women encounter social service agencies and the criminal justice system, they often find that social workers, psychologists, psychiatrists, lawyers, judges, and others, including those working directly with batterers, accept the abusers' interpretations at face value (Gondolf 1985; Ptacek 1988). Thus the experiences of abused women in their homes are invalidated institutionally and, in this way, the abused undergo a double victimization (Edwards 1989; MacLeod 1987; Pahl 1985). We argue that the abusers' accounts and the academic and professional explanations for male domestic violence are so similar that they constitute parallel ideological practices; both insure that male dominance is sustained at both the individual and institutional levels. This situation will be explored further in this chapter.

FEMINIST APPROACHES TO MALE DOMESTIC ABUSE

Although feminists differ in important ways in their perspectives on male domestic violence (as Bograd 1988 and others have pointed out) all adopt a strategy, whether implicit or explicit, that constitutes battered women as subjects whose accounts are to be listened to and taken seriously. Furthermore, this work is avowedly done for women and their advancement (see Smith 1979). In the language of the everyday world paradigm, feminists begin with accounts of abused women and then examine how the female experience of male domestic abuse is organized by social relations that are immanent in but external to such relations. Since abused women are obviously being victimized, this feminist method inevitably focuses on the behaviour of the assaultive men and asks why these men violate their intimate partners in these ways.

Feminists conceptualize the answer essentially in terms of power and control at the micro level (Stets 1989) and at the macro level (Dobash and Dobash 1981; Schecter 1982). In other words, they place male abuse in a sociopolitical context. The domestic abuse of women is viewed as stemming from historical economic and social relations that create gender, i.e., definitions of masculinity and femininity.[2] Central to the type of masculinity found in male-dominated societies is a pervasive system of male privilege. Central to such societies' definitions of femininity are processes of subordination and dependency by which the system of male privilege is sustained and legitimated (Kaufman 1987; Kimmel 1987). Feminists thus see male violence as multidimensional and as part of a continuum of 'policing' of women by men as a group. Such practices of social control include sexist jokes and sexist language, pornography, sexual harassment, rape, and sexual abuse of children (Kelly 1988b). The abuse of wives at the personal level and male dominance at the institutional level are seen as mutually reinforcing. In fact, for centuries, major institutions such as the church and the state gave husbands the legal right to inflict corporal punishment on their wives (Dobash and Dobash 1979; Klein 1982; Nadelhaft 1987; Pleck 1979). This legal right was only eliminated through the arduous struggles of nineteenth-century feminists, but the removal of the relevant statutes did not abolish either the abuse by husbands or the 'the reluctance of the church and state to breach in any way what was thought of as "the sanctity of marriage" through effective intervention' (Anglican Church 1987:20).

Feminist definitions of male abusive behaviour vary and are strongly debated (Edleson et al. 1985; Walker 1990). It is important to conceptualize such behaviour so as to include at least two aspects: a distinction between actual violence and the threat of violence and its multifaceted character involving economic, sexual, and psychological coercive controls. Several definitions in the literature collapse the difference between overt and potential violence. Adams (1988a:5), for example, claims that, 'Violence is any act that causes the victim to do something she does not want to do or causes her to be afraid.' This results in the category of intimidation becoming redundant, but its retention as a separate category can be justified—the consequences of a threat may be just as serious as the act itself, and abusive men need to be convinced of that fact. The concept of cruelty seems to capture all these dimensions and another that does so is that of 'terrorizing', meaning the kind of terror that hostages experience at the hands of those that take them: 'the most damaging and unbearable aspect of being a battered woman seems to be life in an environment where terror reigns' (Edleson et al. 1985:231; Graham et al. 1988; Ptacek 1988). For our purposes, we will use the term abuse to mean patterns of cruelty, coercive controls, and terrorizing tactics that include intimidation of various types and actual physical force. This seems a more reasonable approach than extending the term 'battering' to include not only physical and sexual assault but psychological coercion and the destruction of property and pets (Ganley 1981:8–16; MacLeod 1987:6).

Socialist feminist perspectives tend to stress the materialist aspects of male abuse more so than other feminist approaches. Men's coercive actions are viewed as tantamount to extortion rackets whereby men can obtain from their female partners all kinds of domestic labour/sexual services, emotional care, housework, child care, etc., exactly when, where, and how they want them (Anglican Church 1987; Luxton 1980). In other words, abusive men do gain material benefits from their coercive actions. We do not assume that this extortion process is necessarily a conscious or a deliberately planned strategy: the dynamics involved may be inchoate and may serve different emotional needs felt by these men. This point is made in order to avoid seeming to conflate motivations and consequences—an error that Liddle (1989) argues is often made in feminist literature on male violence. Nevertheless, evidence from abusive men themselves suggests that they hold an exaggerated form of the traditional belief that men have the authority to demand services from their wives (Long 1987) and that, in fact, they are more dependent on their wives than are non-abusive men (Adams 1989; Dutton 1988; Gondolf 1985). But, typically, abusive men remain oblivious to this dependence, to the effects of their belief systems, and to the many benefits they obtain through their coercive behaviour. Furthermore, as Kurz (1989:502) points out, 'Batterers either have a set of explanations by which they deny their abusive behaviour or a set of expectations by which they legitimize their violent behaviour' (Adams and McCormick 1982; Ptacek 1988). Gondolf (1985:6) agrees: 'Batterers are ... characterized by their extensive denial, objectification of women, predilection for rigid control and overinflated sense of privilege.' One of the crucial issues, then, is the extent to which counsellors hold such men accountable for their actions. Another question of obvious significance is whether or not counsellors link the 'overinflated sense of privilege' typical of male abusers to the institutional support for the general system of male privilege and dominance.

Another theme evident in socialist feminist literature concerns the interaction between gender and class relations so that masculinity 'scripts' vary according to social class and social location (Connell 1987; Hartmann 1981; Livingstone and Luxton 1989; Messner 1989; Sargent 1981; Staples 1978; Tolson 1977). This issue, however, is only rarely addressed in feminist literature on male abuse (Schwartz 1988) and even less so in programs for abusive men. Yet one assumes that workers in such programs would encounter differences in the masculine subjectivities of their clients that might suggest the relevance of class and ethnicity to abusive behaviour.

NON-FEMINIST APPROACHES TO MALE DOMESTIC ABUSE

As one would expect, non-feminist approaches to male abuse do not begin with the experience of abused women and thus the stance is, in general, an objectifying one. Unlike feminists, such researchers do not make explicit their values and do not usually comment on their particular interests. These, however, can often be discerned with careful critical scrutiny. Occasionally, the agenda is clear: for example, Geffner et al. (1988:115) state openly that the name of their program for reducing family violence [sic] is the 'Family Preservation Project'.

Male abuse is conceptualized in terms of the traditional positivist mode in which the everyday experiences of people disappear under the grid of a predetermined conceptual scheme (Kelly 1988a). Consequently, the focus of this type of work is not directly on the abusive male but on some other factors such as individual psychopathology in the abuser, or in the victim, or in both (Snell et al. 1964), or a dysfunction in the family (Deschner 1984; Neidig 1984). Not surprisingly, male abuse is rarely named as such but rather is subsumed under rubrics like 'couples in violent relationships', 'spousal abuse', 'violent-prone families', 'abusive couples', 'dysfunctional relation-ships', or 'mutual combat' (Geffner et al. 1988; Neidig and Friedman 1984; Straus 1976; Straus and Gelles 1986; Straus et al. 1980; Weitzman and Dreen 1982), or even reversed into 'the battered husband syndrome' (Steinmetz 1977-8 and see criticisms of this concept by Pleck et al. 1977–8 and Pagelow 1985).

Such conceptualizations have been critically scrutinized and convincingly argued as practices of social control (Berk et al. 1988; Stark and Flitcraft 1988). In the context of our discussion, they also constitute examples of the ideological practices inherent in the positivist paradigm. A further issue is how the work of academics and professionals becomes connected with the interests of the state. A brief discussion of the emergence of programs for abusive men will illustrate this process.

THE RISE OF PROGRAMS FOR ABUSIVE MEN

These programs were first developed in the United States in the mid-1970s and began in Canada in the early 1980s where they number at least 130 (National Clearinghouse on Family Violence 1988). They arose primarily as a result of the preceding decade of activism by the women's movement, which in turn led to the battered-women's movement. When shelters and other services for victims were established, feminist women began to urge men to deal with other men who were perpetrating this abuse. The first programs in the United States, such as Emerge in Boston, were developed by collectives of men who labelled themselves 'pro-feminist' and saw them-selves as directly accountable to battered women and shelter workers (Adams and McCormick 1982). However, this grass-roots phase of both the bat-tered-women's movement and pro-feminist programs for abusive men was rather quickly superseded by the state's involvement in community cor-rections services, mental health clinics, psychiatric institutes, and state-supported voluntary organizations, such as family service bureaus. The consequences of state intervention into male abuse are vigorously debated by feminist scholars and practitioners.

Morgan (1981, 1985), for example, identifies processes of bureaucratization, professionalization, and individualization: the management of what the state defines as a social problem is fragmented by involving various bureaucracies and by abstracting it from its social context. Political demands, such as those of the battered-women's movement, are transformed into social problems, which are then identified as individual private pathologies rather than public issues. These individualizing tendencies are further accentuated by the work of professional élites and their reliance on mainstream science. Another aspect of these 'relations of ruling' involves agencies' development of 'treatment' strategies, thus medicalizing both victims and abusers (Stark and Frazier 1979).

The state uses social problems and human needs as entry points for increasing social control. In the case of abused women, grass-roots feminist efforts to empower women through community-oriented actions have been undermined by such tactics as the redirection of state funding into direct services (Davis 1988; Walker 1990). In the case of abusive men, pro-feminist programs are very much in the minority, and in the case of both women and men, we have seen what Foucault (1975) has identified as 'heightened surveillance' and Cohen (1985) has labelled as 'net widening'. As a result, feminists, like other critics of state intervention, face major dilemmas when considering policy recommendations for the elimination of male terrorizing in the home (DeKeseredy and Schwartz, forthcoming; Edwards 1989). For example, given the state's long-standing reluctance to acknowledge the lethal aspect of abusive behaviour, one can understand why feminists call for more effective protection for abused women through increased criminalization of abusers. But the demands for such policies raise some difficult questions. For example, will invoking harsher penalties for domestic abuse via retributive criminal justice really serve the best interests of abused women in the long run, quite apart from those of the men involved? Such questions need to be located within a general debate about penal policy (Gregory 1986).

ISSUES AND THEMES IN PROGRAMS FOR ABUSIVE MEN

Given the discussion of ideological practices, a socialist feminist critique of programs for abusive men would include such issues as: (1) the type of explanations offered for the abuse, (2) the allocation of responsibility, (3) the goals and mode of intervention, (4) the safety and rights of the abused women and accountability to such women through some organizational relationship with shelters and abused women's services and, (5) whether or not societal and institutional changes are advocated with counsellors taking activist roles. The last three points need to be clarified.

Mode of intervention refers to the counselling format (either individual or group oriented), and whether counsellors adopt a (supposedly) clinical neutral stance (Snell et al. 1964) or a proactive one that challenges the sexist expectations and controlling behaviours of abusive men (Adams 1988b). It is crucial in intervention that the safety of the female partners is insured since there are many ways in which these women may be further victimized or endangered through their men's involvement in programs. For example, men may, in the group process, gain new coping skills that might enhance their intimidation of their wives (Adams 1988a, 1988b; Ganley 1987; Hart 1988a). Moreover, because there is a real possibility of counsellors colluding with their clients, safeguards need to be built in by making programs directly accountable to shelters and battered-women's services (Hart 1988a, 1988b; Sinclair 1989). We will focus primarily on the issue of explanation and the goals of intervention.

The most common theoretical frameworks used by non-feminist practitioners dealing with abusive men include psychodynamic, social learning, cognitive and family systems theories. Each of these frameworks locates the origins of male cruelty within some form of psychological pathology. Each is individualistic in that it does not include a focus on the general institutional supports for male privilege and male dominance. Psychodynamic perspectives assume that the husband or wife or both have certain traits that make them prone to a 'violent relationship'. In the case of the husband, factors frequently cited include personality disorders, e.g., sadism, paranoia, or pathological dependence (Browning 1984; Faulk 1974; Shainess 1977), and underlying processes such as impaired ego functioning, low self-esteem, poor impulse control, and feelings of inadequacy. While such psychological explanations may be partially correct, focusing on such factors as the sole cause of violence is misleading and dangerous (Adams 1988b). The explanations ignore both the effects of the men's abuse on their partners and the structures that condone and legitimate coercive and controlling behaviour. Furthermore, counsellors using these perspectives tend to show little concern for the safety of the abused women, or a sense of accountability to battered women in general.

The cognitive social learning perspective appears to be the most commonly used framework in programs for abusive men (Correctional Service of Canada 1988). It assumes that changing cognitions can produce changes in behaviour and feelings, and that violence is socially learned and therefore can be unlearned (Gondolf 1985; Saunders 1988). Furthermore, it also assumes that abusive men suffer from deficits in social and interpersonal skills (Dutton 1988; Gondolf and Russell 1986). Among the goals of counsellors using this approach is a cognitive restructuring of the clients. Techniques include enhancement of interpersonal skills and anger management skills. These methods have been criticized by feminists on a number of grounds.

For example, the presence and use of interpersonal skills have been found to be often situation-specific. That is, men in general (and particularly abusive men) are much more likely to demonstrate listening and assertion (as opposed to aggression) when interacting with co-workers and other male peers than with their wives (Adams 1988a:190–1). In other words, when relating with their wives, these men choose to replace their cooperative skills with controlling skills. The fact that non-feminist counsellors overlook this important point constitutes yet another effect of male-centred knowledge.

Anger management techniques focus on the environmental cues and physiological signs of arousal that can precede the anger and rage typical of abusers. A number of shortcomings have been identified with some of these techniques:

1. The focus is on the wife's alleged provocations, thus implicating her as an accomplice in the violence.

2. Little account is taken of the premeditated syndrome of terror associated with physical abuse.

3. Excuses are provided for the abuse, much as alcohol or stress are cited as excuses by abusive men.

4. Men are encouraged to ignore other feelings, such as hurt or helplessness.

5. Batterers can claim that they are 'cured' in an effort to lure their wives back—in other words, as a 'quick fix'.

6. No attempt is made to confront the structural inequalities that lie at the root of male abuse, but instead the behaviour is individualized and psychologized (Adams 1988a, 1988b; Gondolf and Russell 1986).

Although social learning theory can be useful, unless it is accompanied by feminist insights and values, this cognitive behavioural approach can merely produce 'non-violent terrorists' (Gondolf and Russell 1986), i.e., men whose control and coercion becomes less physical but no less degrading and destructive. Nevertheless, stopping or reducing the number of physical assaults may constitute 'success' from the point of view of agents in the criminal justice system since psychological abuse is not necessarily a crime. For example, while threatening an assault is a criminal offence, constant verbal criticism and other forms of degradation are not. From a feminist point of view and, one would hope, from a societal point of view, producing even more skilled psychological abusers is hardly a happy outcome of programs for abusive men. In no way does such a result challenge the system of male privilege on which female subordination is built. Furthermore, if programs do not deal with the systematic psychological coercion practised by their clients, then such men are unlikely to learn how to emotionally nurture themselves or anyone else (Gondolf 1985; Long 1987; Sinclair 1989).

The family systems or interaction approaches may include social learning concepts, but they focus on the transactional dynamics within the family, so that the origins of male terrorism and cruelty are seen as the result of a breakdown in marital communication. Abusive behaviour is essentially viewed as 'an interpersonal transaction' (Neidig 1984:469). In this way, responsibility for the abuse is allocated equally to the wife and the husband. The behaviour of each 'can be thought of a both a cause and an effect depending on how the interactional sequence is punctuated' (Neidig 1984:469). The mode of intervention is usually conjoint therapy with the 'abusive couple' meeting with a counsellor, one of whose functions is to help the wife to identify the ways in which she contributes to her husband's violent treatment of her (Deschner 1984; Neidig and Friedman 1984). As one person in the 'violent couple', the wife is expected to learn how to control her husband's behaviour. Countering these arguments of mutual responsibility, Pence et al. point out that: 'One of the people telling the story, regardless of how it is punctuated, has a black eye, a cut lip, a swollen face or smashed teeth and the other does not. It is political to ignore that the gender of the person injured is almost always female' (1984:478).

Although family systems therapists may invoke concepts like 'stereotyped views of sex roles', challenging male privilege and power forms no part of their practice, based as it is on systems paradigm in which structured inequality simply does not fit. Inevitably, concerns about the safety of the women involved in conjoint therapy may appear muted at best and completely discounted at worst. For example, Geffner et al. (1988:117) suggest that counsellors should help 'a woman and man to negotiate the level of violence that ... [is] acceptable to each individual ...' Furthermore, the contradictions inherent in trying to apply this perspective to situations of male violence are apparent when these authors also state: 'Violence, however, is never an acceptable option' (Geffner et al. 1988:119). Nevertheless, there are practitioners using the systems approach who do concede that conjoint therapy should never be used as the first and only intervention and have developed several criteria for its use (Harris and Sinclair 1981; Margolin et al. 1988).

PARALLEL IDEOLOGICAL PRACTICES OF ABUSERS AND MAINSTREAM DISCOURSES

As a further comment on non-feminist approaches, the similarities between abusers' accounts and academics' and practitioners' explanations of abusive behaviour will be explored briefly. Abusive men use two types of accounts to neutralize socially disapproved actions: excuses and justifications. Ptacek (1988:141) defines excuses as 'those accounts in which the abuser denies full responsibility for his actions', and justifications as 'those accounts in which the batterer may accept some responsibility but denies or trivializes the wrongness of his violence'. One common excuse is loss of control. Abusive men frequently attribute their violence to a build-up of frustration resulting in loss of control, yet in most cases their assaults are very selectively targeted and confined to family members, particularly their female partners. The second most common excuse is that of victim-blaming. The abusers' wives are consistently presented as provoking the men, commonly through their verbal responses, which the men seem to view as equivalent to physical aggression (Ptacek 1988). The justifications include denial of injury through, for example, minimizing the physical and psychological damage they have inflicted. One abuser quoted by Ptacek stated, 'I never beat my wife. I responded physically to her' (1988:146). Abusers also justify their actions by accusing their wives of failing to be 'good wives' (Bograd 1983).

When one examines discourses that deal with male domestic cruelty, one finds that poor impulse control is a frequently cited factor in intrapsychic approaches. It is also one of the bases of the anger management techniques used in the cognitive and social learning perspectives. Furthermore, victim-blaming permeates non-feminist discourses. For example, wives are often described as masochistic in psychological explanations; other adjectives include aggressive, masculine, frigid, controlling, and castrating (Snell et al. 1964). As we have already indicated, family systems theory and practice inevitably implicate the wife in the husband's abusive behaviour. Furthermore, those practitioners who engage in conjoint therapy while the men are still violent and psychologically coercive use denial practices that are very similar to those of their abusive clients. These include minimizing the injury and danger to the abused women and blaming the victim. In other words, these professionals, through their theory and practice, are implicated in relations of ruling. They incorporate the abusers' excuses and rationalizations into their discourses, legitimating them as 'scientific truth' and thus they collude in male dominance and male abuse of women. Moreover, a full circle has emerged in which concepts in non-feminist discourses such as 'dysfunctional families' are being cited as part of the repertoire of excuses by 'unregenerate' batterers who have been in family systems programs.[3]

CONCLUSION

The focus of this chapter has been on issues of 'knowing' and the way male cruelty and coercion have been conceptualized and explained by academic and professional discourses, particularly in terms of feminist and non-feminist frameworks. A comprehensive analysis of what this feminist critique might imply for the criminal justice system is beyond the scope of the discussion here. But since courts are referring or ordering numbers of domestically violent men to a variety of programs across North America, it seems clear that judges, corrections workers, and others have or should have an interest in the kinds of issues we have raised. For example, as we have argued, non-feminist discourses fail to confront the batterer directly with his criminal behaviour or they give ambiguous messages about the nature of his responsibility, e.g., that responsibility is shared by his intimate partner. But such a position, at the very least, runs counter to the legal tradition of holding individuals responsible for their behaviour. As Pence et al. point out, such a tradition 'should be applied to criminal assaults within families. Certainly no other crime committed by a husband whether it be arson, theft or drunk driving is seen as the responsibility of other family members' (1984:479).

However, academic and professional discourses and counselling practices are obviously not the only sources of collusion with abusive men. Victim-blaming and various forms of denial, such as trivializing the injuries sustained by abused women, have been documented as widespread in the criminal justice system itself (MacLeod 1987; Pahl 1985; Pence 1988; Ptacek 1988). The ways in which all societal institutions replicate the domestic victimization of women have been stressed in this chapter. It follows that programs for abusive men should not be seen as a panacea in and of themselves. Given what Pence (1988:24) and Sinclair (1989) have called community collusion, what is needed is community confrontation. This would involve a thorough and sophisticated intervention and prevention strategy that would include coordinating police and human service agencies' responses to domestic assault cases. The general goal would be to create 'a community that holds [abusive men] fully accountable for their use of violence' (Pence 1988:39). An example of such policies can be found in the Domestic Abuse Intervention Project in Duluth, Minnesota (Pence 1988). A number of similar policies have been advocated elsewhere (Currie 1988; Sinclair 1989). However, we as academics also have to be accountable for our part in creating knowledge that can be used either as an instrument for disguising and condoning inequalities, or for confronting and helping to change systemic injustices. Pence summarizes this transforming possibility:

> As a community, our ability to successfully intervene with a batterer is directly tied to our understanding of him as a manifestation of a part of all of us. He mirrors the worst in our culture. He is changed by our responding not in collusion with him, not by seeing him as different from us or as mentally ill, but by acknowledging the need for our own personal and institutional transformation to be a part of his (1988:50).

NOTES

1. The origins of a feminist standpoint approach can be found in Hegel's discussion of the master/slave relationship and its elaboration in the works of Marx, Engels, and Lukacs (Harding 1986:26).
2. For historical accounts of male abuse in the nineteenth century, see Bauer and Ritt 1983; Cobbe 1878; Nadelhaft 1987; Pleck 1979.
3. Personal communication from formerly abused women.

FURTHER READINGS

Adams, D. 1998. 'Treatment Models for Men Who Batter: A Profeminist Analysis'. In *Feminist Perspectives on Wife Abuse*, edited by K. Yllo and M. Bograd, 76–99. Beverly Hills: Sage.
Anglican Church of Canada. 1987. *Violence Against Women*, Toronto: Anglican Book Centre.
Bauer, C., and L. Ritt. 1983. '"A Husband Is a Beating Animal': Frances Power Cobbe Confronts the Wife Abuse Problem in Victorian England'. *International Women's Studies* 6, no. 2:99–118.
Deschner Jeanne, et al. 1994. 'Services for Men Who Batter: Implications for Programs and Policy'. *Family Relations* 33, no. 2:217–33.
Gondolf, E. 1988. *Research on Men Who Batter; An Overview, Bibliography and Resource Guide*. Bradenton, FL: Human Services Institute Inc.
Ptacek, J. 1988. 'Why Do Men Batter Their Wives?' In *Feminist Perspectives on Wife Abuse*, edited by K. Yllo and M. Bograd, 133–57. Beverly Hills: Sage.

REFERENCES

Adams, D. 1988a. 'Feminist-Based Interventions for Battering Men'. In *Treating Men Who Batter: Theory, Practice and Programs*, edited by P.L. Caesar and L.K. Hamberger, 3–23. New York: Springer.
_____. 1988b. 'Treatment Models for Men Who Batter: A Profeminist Analysis'. In *Feminist Perspectives on Wife Abuse*, edited by K. Yllo and M. Bograd, 176–99. Beverly Hills: Sage.
_____. 1989. 'Stages of Anti-Sexist Awareness and Change for Men Who Batter'. In *Family Violence: Emerging Issues of a National Crisis*, edited by L. Dickstein and C. Nadelson, 63–97. Washington, DC: APPI Press.
_____, and A.J. McCormick. 1982. 'Men Unlearning Violence: A Group Approach Based on the Collective Model'. In *The Abusive Partner*, edited by M. Roy, 170–97. New York: Van Nostrand Reinhold.
Anglican Church of Canada. 1987. *Violence Against Women*. Toronto: Anglican Book Centre.
Barnes, B. 1974. *Scientific Knowledge and Sociological Theory*. London: Routledge and Kegan Paul.
Bauer, C., and L. Ritt. 1983. '"A Husband Is a Beating Animal" Frances Power Cobbe Confronts the Wife Abuse Problem in Victorian England'. *International Journal of Women's Studies* 6, no. 2:99–118.
Berk, R.A., et al. 1988. 'Mutual Combat and Other Family Violence Myths'. In *The Dark Side of Families: Current Family Violence Research*, edited by D. Finkelhor et al., 197–212. Beverly Hills: Sage.
Bersani, C.A., and H.T. Chen. 1988. 'Sociological Perspectives in Family Violence'. In *Handbook of Family Violence*, edited by V.B. Van Hasselt et al., 57–86. New York: Plenum Press.

Bleier, R. 1984. *Science and Gender*. Elmsford, NY: Pergamon.

Bloor, D. 1977. *Knowledge and Social Imagery*. London: Routledge and Kegan Paul.

Bograd, M. 1983. 'Domestic Violence: Perceptions of Battered Women, Abusive Men, and Non-Violent Men and Women'. PhD dissertation, University of Chicago.

_____. 1988. 'Feminist Perspectives on Wife Abuse: An Introduction'. In *Feminist Perspectives on Wife Abuse*, edited by K. Yllo and M. Bograd, 11–26. Beverly Hills: Sage.

Browning, J. 1984. *Stopping the Violence: Canadian Programs for Assaultive Men*. Ottawa: National Clearinghouse on Family Violence, Health and Welfare Canada.

Cobbe, F.P. 1878. 'Wife Torture in England'. *The Contemporary Review* 32:55–87.

Cohen, S. 1985. *Visions of Social Control: Crime, Punishment and Classification*. New York: Polity Press.

Connell, R.W. 1987. *Gender and Power*. Stanford, CA: Stanford University Press.

Correctional Service Canada. 1988. *Breaking the Cycle of Family Violence*. Ottawa: Correctional Service Canada.

Currie, D.W. 1988. *The Abusive Husband: An Approach to Intervention*. Ottawa: National Clearinghouse on Family Violence, Health and Welfare Canada.

Davis, N. 1988. 'Battered Women: Implications for Social Control'. *Contemporary Crises* 12, no. 4:345–72.

DeKeseredy, W., and M. Schwartz. Forthcoming. 'British Left Realism on the Abuse of Women: A Critical Appraisal'. In *Criminology as Peacemaking*, edited by R. Quinney and H. Pepinsky. Bloomington: Indiana University Press.

Deschner, J. 1984. *The Hitting Habit: Anger Control for Battering Couples*. New York: Free Press.

Dobash, R.E., and R.P. Dobash. 1979. *Violence Against Wives: A Case Against the Patriarchy*. New York: Free Press.

Dobash, R.P., and R.E. Dobash. 1981. 'Community Response to Violence Against Wives: Charivari, Abstract Justice and Patriarchy'. *Social Problems* 28, no. 5:563–81.

Dubois, E., et al. 1985. *Feminist Scholarship: Kindling in the Groves of Academe*. Chicago: University of Chicago Press.

Dutton, D. 1988. *The Domestic Assault of Women*. Boston: Allyn and Bacon.

Edleson, J., et al. 1985. 'Men Who Batter Women: A Critical Review of the Evidence'. *Journal of Family Issues* 6, no. 2:229–47.

Edwards, S. 1989. *Policing Domestic Violence*. Beverly Hills: Sage.

Eichler, M. 1985. 'And the Work Never Ends: Feminist Contributions'. *Canadian Review of Sociology and Anthropology* 22:619–44.

Faulk, M. 1974. 'Men Who Assault Their Wives'. *Medicine, Science and Law* 14:180–3.

Feyeraband, P. 1975. *Against Method*. London: New Left Books.

Foucault, M. 1975. *Naissance de la Clinique*. New York: Vintage Books.

Frankel-Howard, D. 1989. *Family Violence: A Review of Theoretical and Clinical Literature*. Ottawa: Minister of National Health and Welfare Policy, Communications and Information Branch, Health and Welfare Canada.

Franklin, U., et al. 1981. *Knowledge Reconsidered: A Feminist Overview*. Ottawa: Canadian Research Institute for the Advancement of Women.

Ganley, A. 1987. 'Perpetrators of Domestic Violence: An Overview of Counseling the Court Mandated Client'. In *Domestic Violence on Trial: Psychological and Legal Dimensions of Family Violence*, edited by D. Sonkin. New York: Springer.

_____. 1981. *Court Mandated Counselling for Men Who Batter*. Washington, DC: Center for Women's Policy Studies.

Geffner, R., et al. 1988. 'A Psychoeducational Conjoint Approach to Reducing Family Violence'. In *Treating Men Who Batter: Theory, Practice and Programs*, edited by P.L. Caesar and L.K. Hamberger, 103–33. New York: Springer.

Gondolf, E. 1985. 'Anger and Oppression in Men Who Batter: Empirical and Feminist Perspectives and Their Implications for Research'. *Victimology* 10, no. 1-4:311–24.

_____. 1988. *Research on Men Who Batter: An Overview, Bibliography and Resource Guide*. Bradenton, FL: Human Services Institute Inc.

_____, and D. Russell. 1986. 'The Case Against Anger Control Treatment Programs for Batterers'. *Response to the Victimization of Women and Children* 9, no. 3:2–5.

Graham, D., et al. 1988. 'Survivors of Terror: Battered Women, Hostages and the Stockholm Syndrome'. In *Feminist Perspectives on Wife Abuse*, edited by K. Yllo and M. Bograd, 217–33. Beverly Hills: Sage.

Gregory, J. 1986. 'Sex, Class and Crime: Towards a Non-sexist Criminology'. In *Confronting Crime*, edited by R. Matthews and J. Young, 53–71. Beverly Hills: Sage.

Harding, S. 1989. 'How the Women's Movement Benefits Science: Two Views'. *Women's Studies International Forum* 12, no. 3:271–83.

_____. 1986. *The Science Question in Feminism*. Ithaca: Cornell University Press.

Harris, S., and D. Sinclair. 1981. 'Domestic Violence Project: A Comprehensive Model for Intervention into the Issue of Domestic Violence'. Family Service Association of Metropolitan Toronto. Unpublished paper.

Hart, B. 1988a. 'Beyond "the Duty to Warn": A Therapist's "Duty to Protect" Battered Women and Children'. In *Feminist Perspectives on Wife Abuse*, edited by K. Yllo and M. Bograd, 234–48. Beverly Hills: Sage.

———. 1988b. *Safety for Women: Monitoring Batterers' Programs*. Harrisburg, PA: Pennsylvanian Coalition Against Domestic Violence.

Hartmann, H. 1981. 'The Family as Locus of Gender, Class and Political Struggle: The Example of Housework'. *Signs* 6:37–86.

Hartsock, N. 1983. 'The Feminist Standpoint: Developing the Ground for Specifically Feminist Historical Materialism'. In *Discovering Reality*, edited by S. Harding and M. Hintikka. Dordrecht, Holland, Boston, and London: D. Reidel.

Kaufman, M., ed. 1987. *Beyond Patriarchy: Essays by Men on Pleasure, Power and Change*. Toronto: Oxford University Press.

Keller, E.F. 1978. 'Gender and Science'. *Psychoanalysis and Contemporary Thought* 1, no. 4:409–33.

———. 1982. 'Feminism and Science'. *Signs* 7, no. 3:588–602.

———. 1985. *Reflections on Gender and Science*. New Haven: Yale University Press.

Kelly, L. 1988a. 'How Women Define Their Experiences of Violence'. In *Feminist Perspectives on Wife Abuse*, edited by K. Yllo and M. Bograd, 234–48. Beverly Hills: Sage.

———. 1988b. *Surviving Sexual Violence*. Minneapolis: University of Minneapolis Press.

Kimmel, M.S., ed. 1987. *Changing Men: New Directions in Research on Men and Masculinity*. Newbury Park, CA: Sage.

Klein, D. 1982. 'The Dark Side of Marriage: Battered Wives and the Domination of Women'. In *Judge, Lawyer, Victim, Thief*, edited by N. Rafter and E. Stanko, 83–107. Boston: Northeastern University Press.

Kuhn, T. 1962. *The Structure of Scientific Revolutions*. Chicago: University of Chicago Press.

Kurz, D. 1989. 'Social Science Perspectives on Wife Abuse: Current Debates and Future Directions'. *Gender and Society* 3, no. 4:489–505.

Liddle, A.M. 1989. 'Feminist Contributions to an Understanding of Violence Against Women—Three Steps Forward, Two Steps Back'. *Canadian Review of Sociology and Anthropology* 6, no. 5:759–75.

Livingstone, D., and M. Luxton. 1989. 'Gender Consciousness at Work: Modifications of the Male Breadwinner Norm Among Steelworkers and Their Spouses'. *Canadian Review of Sociology and Anthropology* 26, no. 2:240–75.

Long, D. 1987. 'Working With Men Who Batter'. In *Handbook of Counseling and Psychotherapy With Men*, edited by M. Scher et al., 305–20. Beverly Hills: Sage.

Longino, H.E. 1989. 'Feminist Critiques of Rationality: Critiques of Science or Philosophy of Science?' *Women's Studies International Forum* 12, no. 3:261–9.

Luxton, M. 1980. *More Than a Labour of Love: Three Generations of Women's Work in the Home.* Toronto: Women's Press.

MacLeod, L. 1987. *Battered But Not Beaten ... Preventing Wife Battering in Canada.* Ottawa: Canadian Advisory Council on the Status of Women.

Margolin, G., et al. 1988. 'Wife Battering'. In *Handbook of Family Violence*, edited by V.B. Van Hasselt et al., 89–117. New York: Plenum Press.

Martin, D. 1976. *Battered Wives.* New York: Pocket Books.

Messner, M. 1989. 'Masculinities and Athletic Careers'. *Gender and Society* 3, no. 1:71–88.

Millman, M., and R. Kanter, eds. 1975. *Another Voice.* New York: Vintage Books.

Morgan, P. 1981. 'From Battered Wife to Program Client: The State's Shaping of Social Problems'. *Kapitalstate: Working Papers on the Capitalist State* 9:17–39.

_____. 1985. 'Constructing Images of Deviance: A Look at State Intervention into the Problem of Wife-Battery'. In *Marital Violence*, edited by N. Johnson, 60–75. London: Routledge and Kegan Paul.

Nadelhaft, J. 1987. 'Wife Torture: A Known Phenomenon in Nineteenth-Century America'. *Journal of American Culture* 10, no. 3:39–59.

National Clearinghouse on Family Violence. 1988. *Canadian Treatment Programs for Men Who Batter.* Ottawa: National Clearinghouse on Family Violence, Family Violence Prevention Division.

Neidig, P.H. 1984. 'Women's Shelters, Men's Collectives and Other Issues in the Field of Spouse Abuse'. *Victimology* 9, no. 3–4:464–76.

_____, and D.H. Friedman. 1984. *Spouse Abuse: A Treatment Program for Couples.* Champaign, IL: Research Press Company.

Okun, L. 1986. *Woman Abuse: Facts Replacing Myths.* Albany: State University of New York.

Pagelow, M. 1985. 'The "Battered Husband Syndrome" Social Problem or Much Ado About Little?' In *Marital Violence*, edited by N. Johnson, 172–95. London: Routledge and Kegan Paul.

Pahl, J., ed. 1985. *Private Violence and Public Policy.* London: Routledge and Kegan Paul.

Pence, E. 1988. 'Batterer Programs: Shifting from Community Collusion to Community Confrontation'. In *Treating Men Who Batter: Theory, Practice and Programs*, edited by P.L. Caesar and L.K. Hamberger, 24–49. New York: Springer.

_____, et al. 1984. 'Response to Peter Neidig's Article: Women's Shelters, Men's Collectives and Other Issues in the Field of Spouse Abuse'. *Victimology* 9, no. 3–4:477–82.

Piaget, J. 1972. *The Child's Conception of the World.* Totowa, NJ: Littlefield, Adams.

Pleck, E. 1979. 'Wife-Beating in Nineteenth-Century America'. *Victimology* 4, no. 1:60–74.

———, et al. 1977–8. 'Comment and Reply: The Battered Data Syndrome: A Comment of Steinmetz's Article'. *Victimology* 2, no. 3–4:680–3.

Ptacek, J. 1988. 'Why Do Men Batter Their Wives?' In *Feminist Perspectives on Wife Abuse,* edited by K. Yllo and M. Bograd, 133–57. Beverly Hills: Sage.

Rich, A. 1979. *On Lies, Secrets and Silence.* New York: W.W. Norton.

Rose, H. 1983. 'Hand, Brain and Heart: A Feminist Epistemology for the Natural Sciences'. *Signs* 9, no. 1:73–90.

Sargent, L. 1981. *Women and Revolution: A Discussion of the Unhappy Marriage of Marxism and Feminism.* Montreal: Black Rose Books.

Saunders, D.G. 1988. 'Wife Abuse, Husband Abuse or Mutual Combat? A Feminist Perspective on the Empirical Findings'. In *Feminist Perspectives on Wife Abuse,* edited by K. Yllo and M. Bograd. Beverly Hills: Sage.

Schecter, S. 1982. *Women and Male Violence: The Visions and Struggles of the Battered Women's Movement.* Boston: South End Press.

Schwartz, M. 1988. 'Ain't Got No Class: Universal Risk Theories of Battering'. *Contemporary Crises* 12:373–92.

Shainess, N. 1977. 'Psychological Aspects of Wifebeating'. In *Battered Women: A Psycho-Sociological Study of Domestic Violence,* edited by M. Roy, 111–19. New York: Van Nostrand Reinhold.

Sinclair, H. 1989. *Prospectus for the Accountable/Advocacy Intervention Programs for Batterers.* San Rafael, CA: Manalive.

Smith, D. 1974. 'A Sociology for Women'. In *The Prism of Sex: Essays in the Sociology of Knowledge,* edited by J.A. Sherman and E. Tuchman, 135–54. Madison: University of Wisconsin Press.

———. 1979. 'The Ideology Practice of Sociology'. *Catalyst* 8, no. 2:39–54.

———. 1987. *The Everyday World as Problematic: A Feminist Sociology.* Toronto: University of Toronto Press.

———. 1990. *The Conceptual Practices of Power: A Feminist Sociology of Knowledge.* Toronto: University of Toronto Press.

Snell, J., et al. 1964. 'The Wifebeater's Wife: A Study of Family Interaction'. *Archives of General Psychiatry* 11:107–13.

Spender, D., ed. 1981. *Men's Studies Modified: The Impact of Feminism.* Oxford, Toronto, and New York: Pergamon.

Stanley, L., and S. Wise. 1983. *Breaking Out: Feminist Consciousness and Feminist Research.* London: Routledge and Kegan Paul.

Staples, R. 1978. 'Masculinity and Race: The Dual Dilemma of Black Men'. *Journal of Social Issues* 34:169–83.

Stark, E., and A. Flitcraft. 1983. 'Social Knowledge, Social Policy and the Abuse of Women: The Case Against Patriarchal Benevolence'. In *The Dark Side of Families: Current Family Violence Research*, edited by D. Finkelhor et al. Beverly Hills: Sage.

_____. 1988. 'Violence Among Intimates: An Epidemiological Review'. In *Handbook of Family Violence*, edited by V.B. Hasselt et al., 330–48. New York: Plenum Press.

_____, and W. Frazier. 1979. 'Medicine and Patriarchal Violence: The Social Construction of a Private Event'. *International Journal of Health Services* 9, no. 3:461–94.

Steinmetz, S. 1977–8. 'The Battered Husband Syndrome'. *Victimology* 2, no. 3-4:499–509.

Stets, J. 1989. *Domestic Violence and Control*. London: Springer-Verlag.

Straus, MA. 1976. 'Sexual Inequality, Cultural Norms and Wife-Beating'. *Victimology* 1, no.5:4–76.

_____, et al. 1980. *Behind Closed Doors: Violence in the American Home*. Garden City, NY: Doubleday.

Straus, M.A., and R.J. Gelles. 1986. 'Societal Change and Change in Family Violence from 1975 to 1985 as Revealed by Two National Surveys'. *Journal of Marriage and the Family* 48, no. 3:465–79.

Tolson, A. 1977. *The Limits of Masculinity*. London: Tavistock.

Walker, G.A. 1990. *Family Violence and the Women's Movement: The Conceptual Politics of Struggle*. Toronto: University of Toronto Press.

Walker, L. 1979. *The Battered Woman*. New York: Harper and Row.

Weitzman, J., and K. Dreen. 1982. 'Wife Beating: A View of the Marital Dyad'. *Social Casework: Journal of Contemporary Social Work* 259–65.

Yllo, K. 1988. 'Political and Methodological Debates in Wife Abuse Research'. In *Feminist Perspectives on Wife Abuse*, edited by K. Yllo and M. Bograd, 28–50. Beverly Hills: Sage.

Part
IV
Race and Social Control

This section will explore the issues surrounding race and ethnicity and how these social dimensions, in certain political and institutional contexts, come to be seen as more or less acceptable. In virtually all arenas of social control, race or ethnicity appears as one of the criteria for disparities in treatment. The discussions will address the historical and contemporary nature of racism/ethnocentrism and its relation to the social construction of deviance. In a Canadian context, the central issues for our discussions involve the historical disenfranchisement of Aboriginal Canadians and the historical and contemporary nature of immigration in the evolution of the modern Canadian state.

In 'Social Control and the Historical Construction of "Race"', Vic Satzewich and Li Zong argue that racial categories are defined by and used to advantage certain groups of people in their quest for social and economic supremacy in Canada. Their chapter illustrates how racial categories, as social constructions, are imbued with evaluative components, and become important 'master statuses' that affect social interaction. They then develop this social constructionist argument in the context of theories of social control, concentrating specifically on rational choice theory and a theoretical synthesis based on political economy approaches. Lastly, they argue, using examples from Canadian history, how the concept of 'other' or 'outsider' has come to be defined in racial terms and how such conceptions have evolved from political and economic interests.

In 'Native Canadian Deviance and the Social Control of Race', Jim Frideres places the historical and contemporary problems facing Aboriginal Canadians in a social organization/social control context. Frideres uses the main theoretical positions presented in Chapter 1 to familiarize the reader with the current approaches that academics use to understand why Aboriginal societies have deteriorated economically, socially, and culturally. He concludes by providing a cultural deterioration/social disorganization explanation that draws on several theoretical perspectives, and it is the challenge for the reader to locate Frideres's perspective in the various theories that inform this book specifically and social research in general. The reader will find a wealth of information in this chapter and will discover that the author's overall perspective, while framed in a social control perspective, departs somewhat from the more critical perspectives that inform the works in this book.

Expressions of youthful discontent have been a common feature of Western culture since the end of the Second World War. Unlike British, German, and American youths, until very recently adolescents in English-Canadian society have not demonstrated collective forms of social disruption, violence, and criminality that warranted intense public, police, and media scrutiny evident in other modern capitalist societies. In Chapter 14, 'Youth Culture, Racism, and Alienation: The Control of Youth', Tom Fleming explores the phenomena of collective forms of youth violence in activities such as swarming, runs, wildings, and membership in gangs. He suggests that in order to understand fully the cultural significance of these forms of youthful protest, disaffiliation, alienation, and rebellion, we must examine the overall political and economic dissent in our society, and this means paying specific attention to the issue of race and racism within the Canadian context as a predeterminant of youth alienation and rebellion.

Social Control and the Historical Construction of 'Race'

Vic Satzewich and Li Zong

Sociology is ethnocentric if its practitioners operate with the folk categories of their own societies. They need to examine the categories in which they organize their observations and discard any definitions which are culture bound (Banton 1983:388).

In North America, various European states' desire for economic and military gain brought people from different parts of the world into physical proximity and resulted in a number of what Michael Banton (1983) calls 'contact situations'. The ensuing nature of these contact situations varied in part on the differing material interests of groups involved and in part on the relative power of those groups. Initial European interest in Canada was merchant capitalist in nature. Within the fur trade, Europeans entered into complex military and exchange relationships with the indigenous population. Following the decline of the fur trade, the indigenous population of Canada came to be defined as surplus, indeed as an obstacle, to the needs of the emergent system of industrial capitalism and yeoman farming. But at the same time that the indigenous population was disinherited and placed onto reserves in the middle of the nineteenth century, employers in Canada, acting through the Canadian state, began an ambitious program of recruiting workers from outside the state in order to fuel the process of capital accumulation and state formation. Throughout Canada's history as a settler capitalist society, the language of 'race' has been central to social and political discourse about the nation and the character of intergroup relations. In the context of these various contact situations, the Canadian case provides an ideal opportunity to examine how groups of people were defined as 'others', how 'racial' boundaries are created, and the links between 'racial' categorization and the social construction of deviant populations.

There are several parts to this chapter. We begin by first arguing that instead of seeing 'race' as something that people possess as an objective characteristic, which then has consequences for social interaction and social practices, 'race' should be seen as a socially constructed label. Put differently, in Howard Becker's (1963:32–3) terms, 'race' is a 'master status' that is socially created, which tends to override other statuses, and which affects the nature of social interaction. Second, we examine two sociological traditions—rational choice theory and theories stemming from the framework of political economy—to try to understand theoretically the links between the construction of 'race' as a master status and the process of social control. Third, using the cases of French-English relations, Aboriginal peoples, and immigrants, we examine how various 'others' have been defined in racial terms. We suggest that 'race' was used to define particular groups of people as 'others' and as 'deviant', and that these definitions of deviant populations were rooted in wider political and economic contexts associated with state formation and economic exploitation.

'RACE' AND THE SOCIAL CONSTRUCTION OF A MASTER STATUS

Within the sociological and anthropological literature, the category of 'race' has been defined in two different ways. The first, which has been termed a 'primordial definition' by Mason (1986:7–9) and which corresponds to much common sense usage, conceptualizes 'race' as an objective characteristic of groups of people stemming from observable physical or genetic differences. Reflecting this primordial definition, M.G. Smith (1986:189), an anthropologist interested in the study of plural societies in Africa, argues that 'races are biological divisions of mankind differentiated by gross phenotypical [physical] features which are hereditary, polygenic, highly resistant to environmental influences, distinctive and of doubtful adaptive value'. In explaining his position, Smith likens human 'races' to breeds of dogs or cattle. Different human races are the human equivalent of Doberman pinscher, Chihuahua, and German Shepherd dogs, or of Holstein, Angus, or Friesian cattle. Indeed, for Smith, breeds of animals are akin to varieties of 'races' of humans (Smith 1986:189). In other words, while of the same species, human 'races' are seen to be real, biologically based groups of people who are inherently different and who engage in certain types of social relations that can be called 'race relations'.

Primordial definitions of 'race' have been described by Montagu (1964) as 'man's most dangerous myth', and have been criticized on a number of grounds. Following the Second World War, the United Nations Scientific, Educational and Cultural Organization (UNESCO) sponsored a series of conferences on 'race' and racism where the aim was to scientifically discredit Nazi biological doctrines in particular and the primordial definition of 'race' more generally (Montagu 1972). The arguments that were put forward at the conferences (1950, 1951, 1964, 1967), and indeed since then by biologists, population geneticists, anthropologists, and sociologists are complex and shall not be reviewed in detail here (but see Miles 1982; Montagu 1972; Rose et al. 1984). Two points, however, are important to note. First, the amount of genetic variation within groups is as great or greater than that between groups. Second, it is as irrational to use skin colour as a marker of 'race' difference as it is to use foot size, length of index finger, or lines on the palm of a hand: that is, there is no logical, scientific reason to choose one or more physical differences over any other as the markers of 'race' difference.

Problems with primordial definitions of 'race' have led to reconceptualizations of 'race' as a socially constructed label. The alternative to the primordial view sees 'race' not as a biological reality, in the sense that it is an objective division within the human species, but as a social construct. Thus while physical and genetic differences do exist between people, these are not 'racial' differences; 'race' is simply the label used to describe these differences. This means that for sociologists, the main conceptual problems in the study of 'race' are how and why the 'race' label is applied to certain groups of people and to certain forms of difference, and how and why certain forms of social relations are defined as 'race relations'. In other words, the main issues for the constructionist view are how and why group boundaries have been defined in 'racial' terms, and the social significance of those boundaries (see, for example, Goldberg 1990; Miles 1989).

However, even if there is now widespread agreement that 'race' is a label, there is no such agreement on the criteria for constructing 'racial' statuses and boundaries, and the social meaning of those boundary-creating processes.

Miles (1989) argues for an analytical distinction between the concepts of racialization and racism. Racialization refers to 'those instances where social relations between people have been structured by the signification of human biological characteristics in such a way as to define and construct differentiated social collectivities' (Miles 1989:75). For Miles, the crucial element in racialization is the creation and delineation of group boundaries on the basis of physical or genetic criteria. But, in addition, racialization also refers to those situations in which the term 'race' is used specifically to define groups and group boundaries. There are two important implications of this definition. First, a process of racialization can occur even in the specific absence of the term 'race'. For example, when people refer to 'Blacks' and 'Whites', they are referring to a certain physical characteristic (skin colour). Even though the discourse may not contain references to the term 'race', there is nevertheless a process of signification of physical difference that counts as racialization. Alternatively, a process of racialization can occur when the term 'race' is used to label particular groups, even though those groups may not be defined as possessing distinctive physical or genetic criteria. That is, while particular groups may be called 'races' and while certain social relationships may be characterized as 'race relations', it is possible that those groups and their interrelations may be defined culturally rather than biologically or somatically.

Racialization is distinguished from racism. According to Miles, racism is an ideology with the following representational content:

> ... first, its signification of some biological characteristic(s) as the criterion by which a collectivity may be identified. In this way, the collectivity is represented as having a *natural, unchanging* origin and status, and therefore as being *inherently* different. In other words, a process of racialization must be occurring. Second, the group so identified must be attributed with additional, negatively evaluated characteristics and/or must be represented as inducing negative consequences for any other. Those characteristics may be either biological or cultural. Thus, all the people considered to make up a natural, biological collectivity are represented as possessing a range of (negatively evaluated) biological and/or cultural criteria (Miles 1989:79, our emphasis).

One useful way to think about the distinction between racialization and racism is in the context of the so-called 'Black' and 'Red power' movements in North America. These movements, which aim to represent the interests of persons of Afro-American and Aboriginal origin respectively, are clearly engaged in racialization to the extent that social significance is attached to skin colour. Historically, the 'race' label has been externally imposed on groups of people, but more recently it has also become a way in which colonized groups have come to define their own identities. This is not necessarily a *racist* process because there is no negative evaluation of differences in skin colour. Indeed, the aim of these organizations is empowerment, and the presentation of positive images of the collectivity is a mode of resistance to racism and ethnocentrism (Miles 1993).

In formulating his definition of racism, however, Miles tends to ignore the second form of racialization. That is, racism is defined in such a way as to rule out as racist those negative evaluations of groups who are defined as 'racial' groups but whose 'racialness' is defined in terms of culture, lineage, or history, and where non-biological characteristics are negatively evaluated. This leads Anthias (1992) to conclude that his definition of racism is too narrow. In limiting the definition of racism to an ideology that negatively evaluates characteristics regarded as fixed and permanent, it rules out the possibility of labelling as racist those ideas that negatively evaluate differences in culture, language, and religion. In many cases, these characteristics are regarded as changeable (i.e., that they are not 'naturally' occurring or 'inherent' characteristics), but they are nevertheless negatively evaluated and used to rationalize the differential treatment of groups. Thus the definition of racism needs to be broadened to include those negative evaluations of groups who are defined as 'racial', but also where the 'racial' difference is constructed in non-biological terms.

It is precisely in the context of the distinction between racism and racialization, and the negative evaluations of cultural rather than biological difference that led Barker (1981) to conclude that a 'new racism' has emerged. According to Barker, this new racism consists of the belief that 'Human nature is such that it is natural to form a bounded community, a nation, aware of its differences from other nations. They are not better or worse. But feelings of antagonism will be aroused if outsiders are admitted' (1981:21). Barker's new racism, then, consists of the belief that there are naturally occurring subdivisions of the human population ('races' of people) who normally constitute themselves into nations, and who prefer to maintain exclusive group boundaries. In this context, it is cultural and national *difference*, not biological and cultural *inferiority*, that tends to be seen as the source of social antagonisms and as grounds for various kinds of exclusions. We suggest that historically, there is nothing 'new' about the 'new racism' and that in the case of Canada, both the discourse of difference and the discourse of inferiority have characterized racist thinking and have provided the basis for the formation of deviant 'racial' master statuses.

THE SOCIAL SIGNIFICANCE OF 'RACE'

Even though many now agree that 'race' should be seen as a socially constructed label, there is little agreement on its social significance. In this section, we critically assess two sociological approaches to understanding why 'racial' boundaries are constructed, and why 'race' became a master status. In particular, two approaches are examined: rational choice theory and theories stemming from a broadly defined political economy approach. In doing so we argue that the connection between the two approaches is the centrality of the concept of social control in explaining the application of the 'race' label onto groups of people.

Michael Banton, one of the main representatives of rational choice theory, makes an initial distinction between scientific and folk conceptions of 'race'. According to Banton, racism refers to a historically specific and limited set of ideas developed in the realm of science. It is 'the [scientific] doctrine that a man's behavior is determined by stable inherited characteristics deriving from separate racial stocks having distinct attributes and usually considered to stand to one another in relations of superiority and inferiority' (1970:18). According to this definition, the first racist was an Edinburgh anatomist named Robert Knox, who wrote *The Races of Men* in 1850 (Banton 1970:19, 25). It was Knox's contention that differences in physical make-up determined cultural differences, and that 'race' was the major determinant of the different levels of cultural and historical development of groups of people (Miles 1982:12). While the theory of racial typology developed in different ways following Knox's publication, the most extreme version of racist thinking occurred in Nazi Germany, where theories of biological inferiority/superiority were used to justify the extermination of 6 million Jewish people during the Second World War.

This doctrine has been scientifically discredited, particularly in the aftermath of the Second World War (see Barkan 1992). For Banton, this means that as a scientific doctrine, 'racism is dead'. Within this framework, racism was an error committed by scientists who were honestly trying to come to terms with and explain the diversity of human populations that European colonialism had brought together. But even though he argues that racism is dead, Banton still feels a theory of 'race' and ethnic relations is necessary because a variety of folk or non-scientific conceptions of 'race' continue to be present and have an impact on social relationships.

In his analysis of folk conceptions of 'race', Banton puts forward a rational choice theory of 'race' and ethnic relations. According to Banton (1983:104), there are two main presuppositions of rational choice theory: (1) individuals act to obtain maximum net advantage, and (2) actions at one moment of time influence and restrict the alternatives between which individuals will have to choose on subsequent occasions. Building on these assumptions, rational choice theory argues that: (1) individuals utilize physical and cultural differences to create groups and categories by inclusion and exclusion; (2) ethnic groups result from inclusive and racial categories from exclusive processes; (3) when groups interact, processes of change affect their boundaries in ways determined by the form and intensity of competition, and in particular, when people compete as individuals, this tends to dissolve the boundaries that define the groups, whereas when they compete as groups, this reinforces those boundaries (Banton 1983:104).

Banton's definition emphasizes that group boundaries are created to regulate and control competition. Ethnic boundaries occur when a group defines itself as a distinct collectivity with a common language, heritage, or nationality, whereas racial boundaries arise when one group wishes to exclude members of another group from access to membership in the group and limit access to resources. He uses examples from a number of different contexts to highlight different aspects of his argument. With respect to the issue of assimilation and resistance to assimilation, he argues that in order for a minority to resist assimilation and remain distinctive, it must offer rewards to the children born to group members so that when they become adults they will identify socially with the group. Rewards, like access to occupations or sanctioned marriages, must exceed the costs of foregoing their distinctiveness. In this way, it is much easier for a minority group to maintain an ethnic identity when it holds a monopoly over a specific occupation since it can reward successive generations for making endogamous marriages and thereby, at least with respect to marriage, resist assimilation (Banton 1980:487–9). What this means in terms of social control, then, is that boundaries are created to control competition or the distribution of valued resources.

Even though Marx made passing references to slavery and more systematic reference to British colonialism in India, he never developed a theory of 'race' in his analysis of the capitalist mode of production. The theorization of 'race' and racism has been left to subsequent thinkers working within his general framework. Three strands of thought are noted here. First, one of the initial formulations of the problem of 'race' and racism within the framework of political economy came from Oliver Cromwell Cox. Cox was interested in demonstrating, among other things, that racism was a feature of the development of capitalism. Cox argued that 'race prejudice' is 'an attitudinal justification for an easy exploitation of some race ... [It] is the social attitudinal concomitant of the racial-exploitative practice of a ruling class in a capitalistic society' (Cox 1970:47). Ideas about the biological superiority of some groups and the inferiority of other groups were self-servingly created by capitalists in order to allocate groups of people with particular phenotypical features to particular positions within production relations, to justify their unequal treatment within those relations, and to divide and conquer the working class. In this way, racism is an ideology created by capitalists in the context of colonization and slavery to control and justify the exploitation of a racially defined working class.

This argument has been developed further by, among others, Nikolinakos (1973) and Castles and Kosack (1973). They argue that racism is an ideology whose origins lay in the material interests of capitalists. The ideology consists of a belief in the genetic inferiority of certain groups and has been used in a number of contexts, including postwar Europe, to assign migrant workers to low-paid, undesirable jobs, and then to justify their unequal treatment and superexploitation. Thus the creation of racialized boundaries in Europe entailed the definition of certain groups of workers from the Caribbean, Asia, North Africa, and southern Europe as inherently deviant, and emerged out of capitalists' efforts to disorganize, confuse, and hence control the working class in capitalist societies.

The second strand of thought within the framework of political economy is the theory of the split labour market. According to split labour market theorists (Bonacich 1979:38), the first approach is overly functionalist as the existence of racism is explained in terms of the results it has supposedly achieved. That is, 'to know that something led to a certain result in no way shows how that result was achieved, nor even that the result was intended' (Bonacich 1979:39). It also assumes that the working class is an empty vessel that can be pumped full of false ideas about the world.

Split labour market theorists argue instead that 'racial' boundaries emerge in the context of class struggle. According to Bonacich (1979), for historical reasons unconnected to biology, non-European peoples were often cheap labourers within the emergent system of merchant and industrial capitalism. Conversely, and again for reasons not related to biology, the labour power of European workers has historically been more costly. Since capitalists are interested in the maximization of profit, and since one of the ways that this can be achieved is by lowering the costs of labour power, one of the tendencies of capitalist production is for employers to try to replace higher-priced with lower-priced workers. Higher-priced workers, threatened with potential displacement by lower-priced ones, attempt to control the nature of the competition they face in the labour market. Group boundaries are formed, then, around superficial physical traits, and struggles emerge to limit capital's access to cheap labour. Thus legal codes, like the system of apartheid in South Africa, are interpreted as the result of working-class agitation and action, and were created to control the ability of lower-priced workers to compete for jobs. When a low-wage group is excluded from competing with the high-wage group for jobs or material rewards, then a split labour market emerges. Thus racism is not so much a false idea that is created by capitalists to confuse the working class but a reflection of larger class conflicts and attempts by more powerful factions of the working class to limit the ability of lower-priced workers to compete in the labour market.

The third strand of thought within the framework of political economy has rejected the idea that racism and racialized group boundaries are created for the same reasons at all time and in all places. They have suggested that the development of a theory of 'race' is misguided because of the diversity of ways in which the term is used to describe groups and intergroup relations, and because the meaning of 'race' is constantly changing. This has led to the view that what exists is not so much racism but a range of *racisms* (Husband 1982). One of the arguments within this framework is similar to the split labour market theory as the focus is on working-class racism. The issue here has been how the category of 'race' has been used by members of the working class in capitalist societies to interpret and explain the particular contradictions they face (Hall 1978; Phizacklea and Miles 1980). Another line of thinking has examined the link between 'race' and nation. In an effort to understand the process of state formation and reproduction, a process that is central to the maintenance of the capitalist world economy more generally (Wallerstein 1983), some have argued that race can become a basis upon which a group defines itself as a people and hence a self-governing collectivity (Anthias and Yuval-Davis 1992). Thus contrary to Banton, racialization can be both an inclusive and an exclusive process. When it is used inclusively, it is used by groups to define themselves and their 'nation', and when it is used exclusively, it is used to define others as deviant or different and as a means to control physical and symbolic entry to the nation state via immigration controls and differential access to citizenship rights.

The connecting thread to these various political economy approaches is that racialization entails a process of simultaneously defining certain groups as 'other', as different from the 'self', and consequently as inherently deviant. Thus the creation of racialized master statuses occurs largely in the context of attempts to subordinate groups of people, whether it is in the labour market, within immigration policies, politically, or within civil society more generally. In Anthias and Yuval-Davis's (1992:2) view, the analysis of racisms involves understanding the 'modes of exclusion, inferiorization, subordination and exploitation that present specific and different characters in different social and historical contexts'.

In the remainder of this chapter, we examine three cases of racialization in Canada before the Second World War. We demonstrate that the application of the 'race' label to particular groups of people did not carry the same implications or social significance in each case. While the common element of 'race' thinking is to demarcate group boundaries, the criteria used and the meaning of those boundary-creating processes varied situationally and on the basis of the interests of those who were creating and defining those boundaries.

FRENCH-ENGLISH RELATIONS AS 'RACE RELATIONS'

During the sixteenth century, numerous European countries had a merchant capitalist interest in the resources that were 'discovered' on the land and in waters that now make up Canada. By the middle of the eighteenth century, France controlled much of the land that is now Quebec, while England controlled much of the Maritimes and small portions of what is now the province of Ontario. The transfer of control over 'New France' to England in 1763 marked the beginning of an intensive national struggle that has yet to be resolved. Throughout much of the nineteenth century and the first two decades of the twentieth century, the struggle between people of French and English origin was regularly characterized as a 'racial' struggle.

For two of the most notable early outsiders, Lord Durham and Andre Siegfried, who commented on and 'studied' French-English relations, the language of 'race' was central to their analysis of what was regarded as a specifically 'Canadian problem'. In his report on the rebellions of 1837, for example, Lord Durham outlined his understanding of Canadian reality in the following terms:

> I expected to find a contest between a government and a people: I found two nations warring in the bosom of a single state: I found a struggle, not of principles, but of *races*; and I perceived that it would be idle to attempt any amelioration of laws or institutions, until we could first succeed in terminating the deadly animosity that now separates the inhabitants of Lower Canada into the hostile divisions of French and English (Durham 1963:22–3, our emphasis).

He argued that many of the political problems in Lower Canada were specifically based on 'race' difference. In further explaining the nature of the problem, though, Durham did not argue that it was simply a matter of the incompatibility of two equal but different 'races'. Instead, he defined members of the 'French race' as a deviant subculture within North America. 'The French Canadians ... are but the remains of an ancient colonization and are and ever must be isolated in the midst of an Anglo Saxon world' (Durham 1963:215).

He went on to attribute a number of negatively evaluated characteristics to them. Durham was particularly harsh in his analysis of French-Canadian peasant life. He describe *habitant* farms as 'worn-out and slovenly', and in a manner consistent with later English Social Darwinist thinking, Durham argued that the seigneurial system established during the French regime in Canada, and which remained intact for nearly a century of British rule, had produced a population that was distinctly inferior:

> It need not surprise us, that under such circumstances, a *race* of men habituated to incessant labour of a rude and unskilled agriculture, habitually fond of social enjoyments, congregated together in rural communities ... [that] they remained the same uninstructed, inactive, unprogressive people (Durham 1963:27, our emphasis).

This characterization of the 'French race' was coupled with another common racist stereotype, namely the possession of a childlike character: 'They are mild and kindly, frugal and industrious and honest, very sociable, cheerful and hospitable, and distinguished for a courtesy and real politeness, which pervades every class of society' (Durham 1963:28). Despite these quaintly redeeming qualities, Durham knew of 'no national distinctions marking and continuing a more hopeless inferiority' (Durham 1963:215–16).

This was in sharp contrast to the numerous virtues he attributed to the English. The 'English race ... [with] their own superior energy, skill and capital ... have developed the resources of the country; they have constructed or improved its means of communication; they have created its internal and foreign commerce' (Durham 1963:22). With 'the decided superiority of intelligence on their side', Durham regarded the English 'race' as responsible for all of the progress in British North America. Durham's vision was to see the French 'race' amalgamate with the English.

Andre Siegfried, another 'outsider' who commented on French-English relations in Canada nearly seventy years after Durham, also defined the Canadian problem as a 'racial' problem. Reminiscent of Lord Durham, the opening line of Siegfried's *The Race Question in Canada* stated that 'In the first place, and above all, it is a racial problem' (Siegfried 1966:14). Siegfried, who was French, Protestant, and anticlerical (Underhill 1966:3) did not, however, go on to attribute negative and positive characteristics to each group. He described in considerable detail differences in characters of the two 'races', but regarded the problem not so much in terms of the inferiority or superiority of one or the other group but as a matter of *difference* in itself.

Siegfried (1966:15) described the main differences between the two 'races' in terms of religion, customs, habits, and group psychology, with the former 'at the root of all Canadian differences and divisions'. He also argued, though, that while Confederation had forced an 'artificial unity' of the two 'races', the greatest threat to both 'races' actually came from the United States.

The language of 'race' was also incorporated into French-Canadian nationalist thinking during the late eighteenth and early nineteenth centuries.[1] Nationalist thinkers defined the French people in racial terms, and thus the process of racialization was inclusive rather than exclusive. It was used as a means by which French Canadians defined themselves, their unique virtues, and their unique status within North America; it was not a marker of deviance and inferiority. 'Race' was used by nationalist thinkers to signify a master status of relatively permanent difference, and this difference justified the continued distinctiveness of their institutions and ways of life. But even though the language of 'race' was central to the conception of the French nation, the term 'race' was used in differing ways with differing implications.

For some, 'race' was defined in terms of a religious mission similar to a calling. Monsignor L.-A. Paquet, in his 1902 'Sermon on the Vocation of the French Race in America' delivered at the Diamond Jubilee of the Saint-Jean Baptiste-Society, stated that 'the Maker of All Things has created different races with varied tastes and aptitudes; ... within the hierarchy of societies and empires, he has assigned to each one of the races a distinct role of its own' (Paquet 1969:153). Thus Paquet defined 'races' as being religious in origin, and in a fashion reminiscent of the Calvinist definition of the calling described by Weber, each 'race' had its role to play in society. He argued that some 'races' were meant to be farmers, while others were meant to be industrial workers, merchants, conquerors, or apostles. He suggested that members of the French 'race' were destined to the latter vocation. Their role was that of a social priesthood: their 'mission is less to handle capital than to stimulate ideas; less to light the furnaces of factories than to maintain and spread the glowing fires of religion and thought, and to help them cast their light into the distance' (Paquet 1969:154).

Other nationalists used more secular definitions of 'race', but nevertheless retained the sense that the French 'race' in North America had an important role to play in the development of Canadian society. Henri Bourassa, the French-Canadian nationalist, politician, and journalist, repeatedly described the French and English as distinct 'races', each with their own language and religion. 'Race' was used by Bourassa in a number of ways, reflecting a sense in which it was sometimes a phenomenon based on biology and sometimes on lineage. Reflecting a biological basis for 'race' difference, Bourassa argued that 'Race instinct is, like all natural instincts, a powerful means of individual and social action; but, like other instincts, it must be checked and tempered by reason' (Bourassa 1969:124). In that same context, however, he also argued that while he did not wish 'to stifle in my compatriots the call of our blood', he urged that they should not forget the responsibilities to themselves, and those responsibilities laid onto them by their 'history and present situation'.

But if for some 'race' was the main marker of difference between the French and English in Canada, for others 'race' was what made the French and English populations similar. In 1944, Abbé Arthur Maheax, a professor of history at Laval University in Montreal, argued that 'the Norman blood, at least, is a real link between our two groups' (cited in Berger 1966:13). In some cases, these links of 'blood' were reinforced by climatic conditions in Canada. In 1891, F.B. Cumberland, vice-president of the National Club of Toronto, argued that 'nature is welding together into Unity and by this very similarity of climate creating in Canada a homogeneous Race, sturdy in frame, stable in character, which will be to America what their forefathers, the Northmen of old, were to the continent of Europe' (cited in Berger 1966:13).

Since the 1960s, the language of 'race' has declined in importance in describing relations between the French and English populations of Canada. Quebec nationalists conceive of themselves not so much as a distinct 'race' but as a nation. The nation now takes on an inclusive character, where the distinctiveness of Quebec society is now emphasized, defined in terms of culture and language.

In the context of our earlier discussion, there are two issues that are of interest about the early characterization of French-English relations as 'race relations'. First, the characterization of that struggle as 'racial' highlights the contested nature of and fluid meaning attributed to 'race'. Generally, physical markers and signifiers were not used to describe these populations, but rather difference tended to be constructed around linguistic, cultural, and religious characteristics; these differences were nonetheless termed 'racial'. Second, this characterization highlights the interrelationship between 'race' and nation. 'Race' was used by both French-Canadian and 'English'-Canadian nationalists to create master statuses for both themselves and 'others'.

THE SOCIAL CONSTRUCTION OF ABORIGINAL RELATIONS

If there was a deracialization of French-English relations during the course of the twentieth century, the same cannot be said of relations between Aboriginal and non-Aboriginal peoples. According to some social and historical analysts (see Frideres 1993), an ideology of racism was developed by European colonizers soon after initial contact with Aboriginal peoples, and this ideology was used to justify the appropriation of Aboriginal land and the exploitation of Aboriginal labour power. While racism certainly has been central to the history of internal colonialism in Canada, in this section we suggest that this formulation is silent on the changes in the way that Aboriginal peoples and Aboriginal/non-Aboriginal relationships have been racialized at different stages of the colonization process.

For more than 200 years after the arrival of Europeans in Canada, Aboriginal peoples were central to the economic and social reproduction of merchant capitalism via their roles in extracting furs from the environment, in commodity circulation, and in providing commodities to sustain traders at Hudson's Bay Company posts (Ray 1974). They were also of value for military purposes and formed various alliances with different European groups to consolidate control over the lands that now make up North America.

During the fur trade period (which, depending on the region under consideration, extended into the early part of the twentieth century), the process of racialization was not a simple construction of Aboriginal peoples as genetically inferior so that their land and labour power could be exploited. Instead, racialization involved complex negative and positive evaluations of Aboriginal difference, and there does not appear to have been consensus among Europeans that Aboriginal peoples were biologically or genetically different from, let alone inferior to, Europeans. Certainly, the historical record is replete with negative references to Aboriginal peoples and their religious and cultural practices. On the West Coast, missionaries were instrumental in problematizing the potlatch as a pagan, non-Christian practice that reflected primitiveness and cultural inferiority. In *The Jesuit Relations and Allied Documents* (Mealing 1963), Indians were described as *sauvages*, and were attributed with a number of negative characteristics, particularly in relation to religious practices.

But for many years the differences between Aboriginal and non-Aboriginal peoples were not necessarily regard as fixed and unchanging. In *The Jesuit Relations*, French missionaries in the seventeenth century thought that Aboriginal peoples' differences in appearance were due to environmental conditions and not necessarily biologically based. In a letter to his superiors in France in 1632, Father Paul Le Jeune stated that 'Their natural color is like that of those French beggars who are half-roasted in the Sun, and I have no doubt that the Savages would be very white if they were well covered.' He went on to suggest that 'Mind is not lacking among the Savages, but education and instruction' (cited in Mealing 1963:18, 19). The sense that environment rather than biology was the source of differences between Aboriginal and non-Aboriginal peoples is confirmed more generally by Vaughan (1982). He argues that in seventeenth- and eighteenth-century America, the predominant explanation for Aboriginal peoples' particular skin colour was that they were 'white' skinned, but through influences of the environment, their skin became tawny in colour. Skin colour was therefore seen as environmentally determined, and the differences between the two groups were accordingly understood in cultural, not biological and genetic, terms.

Similarly, despite certain negative evaluations of Aboriginal peoples, when Europeans referred to Aboriginal peoples during the fur trade, only rarely did they refer to them as a single 'race' or a homogeneous, biologically based collectivity. Most references to Aboriginal peoples were made to specific linguistic or cultural groups. Hudson's Bay Company and Northwest Company traders, as well as others who were involved in extensive dealings with Aboriginal peoples, were as cognizant of the differences as they were of the similarities between groups. In what later became western Canada, fur traders repeatedly noted differences between, among others, Cree, Assiniboine, Mandan, Ojibway, Chipewyan, Gros Ventre, and Blackfoot. These groups were defined and socially evaluated in terms of their geographical location, their ability to deliver different types of commodities to posts, the condition of those commodities, the types of commodities they traded for, and their particular skills or talents. Each group was usually attributed with a combination of both positive and negative traits. For example, La Vérendrye, a Northwest Company fur trader, described the Mandan as 'the most skillful in dressing leather, and they work very delicately in hair and feathers; the Assiniboine cannot do work of the same kind. They are sharp traders, and clean the Assiniboine out of everything they have in the way of guns, powder, ball, kettles, axes, knives and awls' (cited in Ray 1974:88).

What appears to have been important in the fur trade was the role that particular groups played within the division of labour. This division of labour involved military-type tasks in protecting hunting territories and transportation routes, extracting furs from the environment and processing and transporting them to posts, and supplying 'country food' to European posts. While there were important elements of a racialized division of labour in the fur trade, particularly in relation to restricted Aboriginal access to wage labour positions around the trading posts (Bourgeault 1988:48), it is also the case that different bands were assigned different roles in the trade and consequently had different degrees of power and influence. Linguistic, cultural, and kinship divisions played an important role in shaping the roles of particular bands in the fur trade and, in that context, the particular position within this division of labour they occupied tended to affect how they were evaluated and defined.

Arguably, the important shift in the racialization of Aboriginal peoples occurred in the middle of the nineteenth century during the decline of the fur trade and a corresponding reduction in the military importance of Indians. This was coupled with the increased importance of other merchant capitalist-based activities as well as the emergence of industrial capitalist and agrarian interests. Both processes helped constitute Aboriginal peoples as a relative surplus population, a population that was surplus to requirements for production. Aboriginal peoples were no longer central to the process of economic production; indeed, they and their way of life now constituted an obstacle to the process of capitalist development via commercial agriculture and industrialization. Aboriginal peoples increasingly became defined as a problem population that required careful stewardship. This resulted in a shift in the process of racialization in the latter part of the nineteenth century. Reflecting a process outlined earlier by Banton, Aboriginal peoples came to be defined increasingly in racially exclusive terms as a homogenous collectivity, and there were far fewer references to specific linguistic or cultural groups. This shift is evident in the quantitative increase in state legislation directed towards the collectivity and the manner in which this legislation was framed. Legislation reflected less of a concern over particular groups, and became more focused on the category of 'Indian'.

Despite the emergence of a homogeneous category of 'Indian', the definition of an Indian for legal purposes in the Indian Act of 1876 was based on a combination of patriarchally defined lineage, 'blood', and social acceptance. The use of lines of descent as the basis for the legal definition of Indian until the 1980s created situations in which Indian women who married non-Indian men (and their children) were no longer defined as Indians, at least in terms of the Indian Act, while non-Indian women married to Indian men (and their children) were defined as 'Indian' for administrative purposes.

The definition of an Indian in terms of a line of descent was coupled with the notion that it was nevertheless possible for Indian people to change. Almost every instance of postfur trade legislation affecting Indian peoples contained reference to the process of 'enfranchisement'. For the state, enfranchisement meant the termination of the special status of Indian peoples and their acquisition of full Canadian citizenship rights. The policy of enfranchisement, which was pursued with varying degrees of intensity over the years, was premised on the assumption that with careful guidance, Indian peoples could be resocialized, transformed into something else, and indeed take on what were seen as the rights and duties of citizenship. Even those instances of legislation that reflected blatantly racist ideas about Indian peoples assumed that the 'problem' was not biological or genetic *per se* but cultural. For example, the 1857 Act for the Gradual Civilization of the Indian Tribes in the Canadas, specified that the Indian commissioners could examine:

> any Indian male over twenty-one and not over forty years of age, desirous of availing himself of this Act, although he be not able to read and write or instructed in the usual branches of school education; and if they shall find him able to speak readily either the English or French language, of sober and industrious habits, free from debt and sufficiently intelligent to be capable of managing his own affairs ... he shall thereupon be enfranchised (cited in Leslie and Macguire 1979:27).

Even Duncan Campbell Scott's infamous statement before the Committee to Examine Bill 14, which became an amendment to the Indian Act that allowed for compulsory enfranchisement of Indian peoples, and which is often interpreted today as the quintessential expression of racism against Aboriginal peoples, reflected a cultural rather than biological conception of Indian difference. Scott, the superintendent general of Indian Affairs, stated that

> I want to get rid of the Indian problem. I do not think as a matter of fact, that this country ought to continuously protect a class of people *who are able* to stand alone ... Our objective is to continue until there is not a single Indian in Canada that has not been absorbed into the body politic; and there is no Indian question, and no Indian department and that is the whole object of this Bill (cited in Titley 1986:50, our emphasis).

Scott's conception of the solution to the 'Indian problem' was not the physical annihilation of Indians, which was the 'final' solution adopted by the Nazi's during the Second World War in a circumstance where the 'other' was defined as biologically inferior. Notwithstanding the genocide of the Beothuks in Newfoundland, the aim of British (and later Canadian) policy was never really physical extermination of the Indian population. Instead, despite extremely uncomplimentary and indeed racist views held about Indian peoples and their capabilities, Scott along with many of his Department of Indian Affairs colleagues, seemed confident that with guidance from the state, Indian peoples were capable of social, cultural, and religious change: in other words, they were capable of becoming ideal-typical 'Europeans'.

Thus while defined as a deviant other, as 'racially' different from the dominant population, and as inferior, this supposed inferiority was not regarded as a fixed and unchanging characteristic of their essential nature. In a perceptive observation about the United States, but which nevertheless also appears to be applicable to the Canadian case, Vaughan argues that had Indian peoples been universally defined as innately different and innately inferior, 'missionary activity would have languished or expired everywhere ... [and] most Indians would have been enslaved or exterminated' (Vaughan 1982:949). The aim of Canadian state policy was to transform Indian peoples culturally, although this has been defined quite correctly as a process of cultural genocide. Aboriginal peoples were accorded a racialized 'master status', but this status was seen as only temporary.

IMMIGRATION AND 'RACE MAKING'

In the absence of an adequate supply of subjects from within Canada to feed the interrelated processes of capital accumulation and state formation, Canada has historically had to rely on immigrants. Since immigrants have been needed not only as a source of labour but also as a source of future citizens of a nation state characterized by the existence of 'free' institutions, answers to questions about who should be let in, and the conditions under which they should be allowed to remain, have been fundamental to the historical development of Canada. This also engendered vigorous political and ideological debates about the character of certain groups of people and their respective abilities to contribute as future workers and citizens to the formation of a nation state. The terminology used in debates about immigrants has changed over the years. Until the mid-1960s, the terms of the debate were framed, in part, by both racialization and racism. The mid-1960s witnessed what some might call a 'deracialization' of immigration control in Canada (Hawkins 1988), but arguably, issues of 'race' remain just below the surface of current concerns about immigration.

Since Confederation in 1867, if not before, the language of 'race' was central to how immigrants were constructed and evaluated. The term 'race' was applied to both potential and actual immigrants, and was used to demarcate groups that most would now not normally consider as 'racially' different from one another. Groups that we would now consider as ethnic groups or nationalities were widely seen as separate 'races': English, Scottish, Italian, Russian, and Scandinavian peoples, for example, were each regarded as separate 'racial stock' with their own unique characteristics, capacities, and abilities. In other words, many Canadians possessed a clear racialized hierarchy of desirability in relation to the admittance of immigrants to Canada. The discourse of 'race' tended to transcend the particular political leanings of individuals or groups. Conservatives and 'progressives' alike applied the term 'race' without question to groups of people, and while there were differences of opinion as to which specific groups were inferior and which specific traits were particularly problematic, there was nevertheless an underlying paradigmatic agreement that groups could be hierarchically ranked, and that if care were not taken in properly managing immigration, negative consequences would ensue for the Canadian nation.

Despite a basic level of agreement that 'races' of people existed and that immigrant groups could be ranked in a hierarchy of inferiority and superiority, there were differing points of view on the origins of those differences and whether they could be overcome. For some, the source of the 'race' difference was clearly conceived in biological terms. Usually, but not always, those groups that were defined as incapable of change possessed a skin colour that was considered 'non-White'. In J.S. Woodsworth's view, the only group that appeared to be biologically incapable of change were 'Orientals'. 'They have their own virtues and vices; their own moral standards and religious beliefs. The Orientals cannot be assimilated' (Woodsworth 1972:155). Mackenzie King, in a different context, argued in 1908 that East Indians were

not suited to this country, that accustomed as many of them are to the conditions of a tropical climate, and possessing manners and customs so unlike our own people, their *inability* to readily adapt themselves to surroundings entirely different could not do other than entail an amount of privation and suffering which renders a discontinuance of such immigration most desirable in the interests of the Indians themselves (cited in Bolaria and Li 1988:171).

As noted earlier, climate was often seen in Canada as a key component of character and 'race' formation. As noted previously, during the early part of the twentieth century, some 'Canadian' nationalists saw the essential difference between 'races' in climatic terms. During the turn of the century, many thought that climate had a determinate impact on character; that character could not be changed, even by long exposure to different conditions. Thus 'northern races' were attributed with a range of positive qualities ranging from an inherent capacity for self-government, hard work, thrift, and stoicism. On the other hand, 'southern races' were attributed with a range of negative traits, including effeminacy, indolence, and laziness.

However, this was not necessarily the most prevalent view. Many of the most virulent racists viewed the inferiority of different immigrant groups in terms of their history and culture, and not solely, or even exclusively, in terms of their biology. The prevalence of a 'softer' racism directed against immigrant 'others' was rooted, in part, in material necessity. A shortage of workers and citizens in Canada meant that racial boundaries had to be defined less rigidly. The predominance of a stronger, biologically based form of racism would have resulted in widespead exclusion of many potential immigrants, which would have had harmful consequences for various employers in Canada (Castles and Miller 1993:227). In many cases, class position was seen to override 'race' in the evaluation of the potential contribution of individuals and groups to the formation and reproduction of Canadian society. Thus in some cases, class position could make up for the disadvantages of 'race', while in other cases, class position could nullify the advantages of 'race'.

J.S. Woodsworth, one of the founders of the Co-operative Commonwealth Federation and a political 'progressive' on many issues, held views that were not substantially different from his more conservative colleagues in their assessments of the capacities of certain groups. Woodsworth's book *Strangers Within Our Gates* was, in part, a plea for tolerance and understanding of the plight of immigrants to Canada in the early part of this century. However, it also contained considerable discussion of the characteristics of different 'races' and assessments of their ability to contribute to the Canadian nation. His characterizations of 'racial' groups were laced with both positive and negative stereotypes. Swedish and Norwegian men were described as 'big, brawny, broad-shouldered, fair-haired giants', and women as 'pretty, healthy, clear-featured and rosy-cheeked, with great masses of golden hair ... Accustomed to the rigors of a northern climate, clean-blooded, thrifty, ambitious and hard-working, they will be certain of success in this pioneer country, where the strong, not the weak, are wanted' (Woodsworth 1972:74, 77). Germans were 'easily assimilated' and 'are among the best immigrants' (Woodsworth 1972:84). 'The most intelligent and progressive of the Slavic races are the Czechs or Bohemians' (Woodsworth 1972:108).

Other groups, however, were described in less positive terms. 'Bulgarians from Macedonia' were the largest of the 'various races from far Eastern Europe'. In Woodsworth's terms, 'they are a simple, sluggish people, who have been oppressed and down-trodden for ages; therefore, it can scarcely be expected that they can land in this country, and at once fall in with our peculiar ways, and understand or appreciate our institutions' (Woodsworth 1972:122). 'Centuries of poverty and oppression have, to some extent, animalized ... [the 'Galician', or Ukrainian]. Drunk, he is quarrelsome and dangerous. The flowers of courtesy and refinement are not abundant in the first generation of immigrants. But he is a patient and industrious workman. He is ambitious. He is eager to become Canadianized' (Woodsworth 1972:112).

What is notable about Woodsworth's evaluations is that the 'racial' inferiority of negatively defined European groups was attributed not to their biological make-up but to their unique historical and cultural circumstances. Their 'inferiority' was seen to lie, in part, in their peasant-class origins: for centuries they lived in rural areas under oppressive conditions that had a determinant impact on their character. With a change of circumstances, it was even possible in Woodsworth's eyes for Galicians (Ukrainians) to overcome the influence of those circumstances and become 'Canadian'.

In a few cases, peasant origins were described and evaluated in positive terms. Clifford Sifton, one of the architects behind the settlement of the Canadian West via the aggressive recruitment of both eastern and western European immigrants at the turn of the century, made a direct link between the process of racialization and labour reproduction (a process in which certain groups were assigned to positions in the division of labour because of their supposed 'racial' characteristics) in his retrospective comment on his role in recruiting Ukrainian immigrants for prairie settlement. In sounding like he was describing cattle, Sifton commented in 1923 that 'I think a stalwart peasant in a sheepskin coat, born on the soil, whose forefathers have been farmers for ten generations, with a stout wife and half a dozen children is good quality' (cited in Lehr 1991:38).

Even those who were more politically conservative than Woodsworth, and who were vehemently opposed to the establishment of bloc settlements on the prairies by immigrants from eastern Europe, were opposed on cultural and not biological grounds. Government officials regarded bloc settlement as an administratively convenient and inexpensive way to settle parts of the West. However, an editorial in the *Winnipeg Telegram*, the conservative rival of the liberal *Free Press*, for example, stated that

> The Government is making a great mistake in establishing these exclusively foreign colonies. The proper policy is to mix the foreigners up with the rest of the population as much as possible. It is only in that way that they will be assimilated. The colony system tends to perpetuate their own language and peculiar customs. It prevents their observation of improved methods of cultivation and keeps them out of touch with British institutions and ideas (cited in Lehr 1991:39).

Critics of the system felt that the physical concentration, particularly of eastern European immigrants in certain rural areas, would result in the formation of ethnic 'colonies'. The problem with these colonies was that they made it more difficult for the newcomers to assimilate into Canadian society and uphold British traditions and institutions. Thus the 'problem' with those groups was not that they were unable to change to take up the rights and duties of Canadian citizens, but that circumstances of their settlement needed to be carefully controlled in order for them to change.

These historical-cultural definitions of 'racial' inferiority were also applied to groups that were thought of as 'non-White'. The discourse of the British Columbia branch of the Knights of Labour, one of the main working-class organizations in the province that aggressively pressured the federal and provincial governments to restrict the flow of Chinese workers to Canada in the 1880s and 1890s, further highlights the contradictory and highly ambiguous meaning of 'race'. While attributing Chinese labourers who were living and working in the province with what became the gamut of standard negative characteristics, they nevertheless argued that these characteristics were the result of historical conditions and not biology:

> Chinese labour is confessedly of a low, degraded and servile type ... their standard of living is reduced to the lowest possible point, and being without family ties, or any of those institutions which are essential to the existence and progress of our civilization, they are enabled to not only live but to grow on wages far below the lowest minimum at which we can possibly exist. They are thus fitted to become all too dangerous competitors in the labour market, while their docile servility, *the natural outcome of centuries of grinding poverty and humble submission to a most oppressive form of government*, renders them doubly dangerous as the willing tools whereby grasping and tyrannical employers grind down all labour to the lowest living point (Royal Commission 1885:156, our emphasis).

For the Knights of Labour, then, the 'problem' was not biological but historical: for historical reasons related to their peasant origins, Chinese people could live and work on wages that were below the wages White people received and this made them better competitors within a capitalist labour market.

Even though certain groups of people were defined racially, it is also the case that class background could override the disadvantages of 'race'. Earlier this century, members of the Chinese working class were subject to various forms of racism, exclusionary practices, and discriminatory treatment in

Canada. They were required to pay a head tax upon entry to the country from 1885 to 1923, they faced legal restrictions on entry into certain occupations and professions, and legal restrictions on their political and civil rights. At the same time, however, members of the Chinese merchant class tended to be evaluated positively and were not subject to the same treatment as their working-class countrymen. One of the commissioners at the 1885 Royal Commission on Chinese Immigration noted that 'It is universally admitted that the merchants are honorable and capable men, of high credit and of great commercial advantage to the community; and these would not only be welcomed but would be desirable' (Royal Commission 1885:cxxxii). Merchants and their families, then, were not only exempted from paying the head tax upon arrival but were also exempted from the Chinese Immigration Act of 1923 that otherwise outlawed Chinese immigration to Canada until 1947.

One albeit indirect measure of the relative esteem in which Chinese (and Japanese) merchants were held by the federal government is that in the aftermath of the 1907 Vancouver 'riots', in which the property of a number of Chinese merchants was damaged by Whites, the federal government established a royal commission to investigate the merchants' losses with the aim of providing compensation. Neither the federal nor the provincial government felt compelled to establish commissions of inquiry to investigate the extent of damage inflicted on members of the Chinese working class during nearly two decades of racist attacks and violence in the province.

'Race', then, was not an attribute that was of equal importance or significance for members of different social classes. For those groups whose 'racial' origin was otherwise a positive attribute, class origin could also bring individuals down in rank and counteract the otherwise positive benefits of 'race'. For example, J.S. Woodsworth was generally pleased with the performance of British immigrants: 'the Scotch, Irish and Welsh have done well' (Woodsworth 1972:46). However, 'the greater number of failures have been among the English. This is due partly to a national characteristic which is at once a strength and a weakness—lack of adaptability.' However, reflecting certain Social Darwinist assumptions about the nature of the working class, he argued that 'the trouble has been largely with the *class* of immigrants who have come to Canada ... Canada has needed farmers and labourers ... [but] England has sent us largely the failures of the cities' (Woodsworth 1972:46). Many were, in Woodsworth's terms, 'the culls from English factories and shops'.

CONCLUSION: THE NEW RACISM?

According to Barker (1981) and Anthias and Yuval-Davis (1992), a 'new racism' has emerged in the 1970s and replaced the 'old', biological inferiority type of arguments about groups of people. According to Barker (1981), there are two central components of this new racism. One component consists of the argument that no 'race' is biologically superior or inferior to another, but that 'races' are naturally different from one another and it is the simple 'fact' of difference that causes social conflict and social unrest and is therefore grounds for exclusion. The second component is the belief that cultural and not biological difference is the source of conflict and tension. One of the conclusions of this paper is that the distinction between the old and new racism is more apparent than real.

Through our analysis of the social construction of 'race' in Canada and an attendant examination of some of the institutional practices that have sought to control racially defined groups of people, this chapter has argued that there is not a radical disjunction between so-called new racism and the old racism of the late nineteenth and early twentieth centuries. Contrary to Barker, this chapter suggests that in Canada groups defined as 'races' have only rarely been defined as fixed biological types incapable of change. Instead, most commentators on the 'race' question in Canada have conceived of 'races' in a contradictory way, with culture as one of the main identifying criteria. A central component of the process of racialization as it occurred in Canada was that 'race' was a master status that was nevertheless capable of being changed. This meant that the 'problem' was not so much conceived in terms of biology but in cultural, social, and historical differences between groups. Canadian racialization was premised on the belief that it was possible to assimilate or resocialize groups of people into a 'Canadian' way of life.

The racialization of the Indian population of Canada is interesting when one compares it to other processes of racialization, particularly those associated with immigration. For various reasons, it was politically unacceptable for either the British or later the Canadian state to pursue a policy of physical genocide. In the absence of an option to exclude Indian peoples from living in Canada, the only other option was to exclude them from the imagined community of the Canadian nation until such time as they could become 'civilized'. In other words, in the absence of a political will to annihilate Indian peoples, the only other option was to define them as capable of change. Physical exclusion was, however, possible for immigrants. This meant that racial boundaries were defined in a more fixed, permanent, and negative way for certain groups of immigrants.

Note

1. The various forms of nationalism in Quebec are complicated and shall not be discussed in detail here.

Further Readings

Bolaria, B.S., and P. Li. 1988. *Racial Oppression in Canada*, 2nd ed. Toronto: Garamond Press.

Miles, R. 1993. *Racism After 'Race Relations'*. London: Routledge.
Rex, J., and D. Mason, eds. 1986. *Theories of Race and Ethnic Relations*. Cambridge: Cambridge University Press.
Small, S. 1994. *Racialized Barriers: The Black Experience in the United States and England in the 1980s*. New York: Routledge.
Woodsworth, J.S. 1972. *Strangers Within Our Gates*. Toronto: University of Toronto Press.

REFERENCES

Anderson, B. 1983. *Imagined Communities: Reflections on the Origin and Spread of Nationalism*. London: Verso.
Anthias, F. 1992. 'Connecting "Race" and Ethnic Phenomena'. *Sociology* 26:421–38.
_____, and N. Yuval-Davis. 1992. *Racialized Boundaries: Race, Nation, Gender, Colour and Class and the Anti-Racist Struggle*. London: Routledge.
Banton, M. 1970. 'The Concept of Racism'. In *Race and Racialism*, edited by S. Zubaida, 17–34. London: Tavistock.
_____. 1980. 'Ethnic Groups and the Theory of Rational Choice'. In *Sociological Theories: Race and Colonialism*, edited by UNESCO, 475–99. Paris: UNESCO.
_____. 1983. *Racial and Ethnic Competition*. Cambridge: Cambridge University Press.
Barkan, E. 1992. *The Retreat of Scientific Racism*. Cambridge: Cambridge University Press.
Barker, M. 1981. *The New Racism*. London: Junction Books.
Becker, H. 1963. *Outsiders: Studies in the Sociology of Deviance*. New York: Macmillan.
Berger, C. 1966. 'The True North Strong and Free'. In *Nationalism in Canada*, edited by P. Russell, 3–26. Toronto: McGraw-Hill.
Bolaria, S., and P. Li. 1988. *Racial Oppression in Canada*. Toronto: Garamond Press.
Bonacich, E. 1979. 'The Past, Present, and Future of Split Labor Market Theory'. *Research in Race and Ethnic Relations* 1:17–64.
Bourassa, H. 1969. 'The French Language and the Future of Our Race'. In *French-Canadian Nationalism*, edited by R. Cook, 132–47. Toronto: University of Toronto Press.
Bourgeault, R. 1988. 'Race and Class under Mercantilism: Indigenous People in Nineteenth-Century Canada'. In *Racial Oppression in Canada*, edited by S. Bolaria and P. Li, 41–70. Toronto: Garamond Press.
Castles, S., and G. Kosack. 1973. *Immigrant Workers and Class Structure in Western Europe*. Oxford: Oxford University Press.
Castles, S., and M. Miller. 1993. *The Age of Migration*. London: MacMillan.
Cox, O.C. 1970. *Caste, Class and Race*. New York: Monthly Review Press.

Durham, J.G. 1963. *The Durham Report*. Toronto: McClelland and Stewart.

England, R. 1929. *The Central European Immigrant in Canada*. Toronto: Macmillan.

Frideres, J. 1993. *Native Peoples in Canada*. Toronto: Prentice-Hall.

Goldberg, D. 1990. 'The Social Formation of Racist Discourse'. In *Anatomy of Racism*, edited by D. Goldberg, 295–318. Minneapolis: University of Minnesota Press.

Hall, S. 1978. 'Racism and Reaction'. In *Five Views of Multi-Racial Britain*, edited by Commission for Racial Equality, 23–35. London: Commission for Racial Equality.

Hawkins, R. 1988. *Canada and Immigration: Public Policy and Public Concern*, 2nd ed. Montreal: McGill-Queen's University Press.

Hechter, M. 1986. 'Rational Choice Theory and the Study of Race and Ethnic Relations'. In *Theories of Race and Ethnic Relations*, edited by D. Mason and J. Rex, 264–79. Cambridge: Cambridge University Press.

Husband, C. 1982. 'British Racisms: The Construction of Racial Ideologies'. In *'Race' in Britain: Continuity and Change*, edited by C. Husband. London: Hutchinson.

Knowles, V. 1992. *Strangers at Our Gates: Canadian Immigration and Immigration Policy, 1540–1990*. Toronto: Dundurn Press.

Lehr, J. 1991. 'Peopling the Prairies with Ukrainians'. In *Canada's Ukrainians: Negotiating an Identity*, edited by L. Luciuk and S. Hrynuik, 30–52. Toronto: University of Toronto Press.

Leslie, J., and R. Macguire. 1979. *The Historical Development of the Indian Act*. Ottawa: Department of Indian and Northern Affairs Canada.

Mason, D. 1986. 'Controversies and Continuities in Race and Ethnic Relations Theory'. In *Theories of Race and Ethnic Relations*, edited by D. Mason and J. Rex, 1–19. Cambridge: Cambridge University Press.

Mealing, S. 1963. *The Jesuit Relations and Allied Documents: A Selection*. Toronto: McClelland and Stewart.

Miles, R. 1982. *Racism and Migrant Labour*. London: Routledge.

_____. 1989. *Racism*. London: Tavistock.

_____. 1993. *After 'Race Relations'*. London: Routledge.

Montagu, A. 1964. *Man's Most Dangerous Myth*. New York: World Publishers.

_____. 1972. *Statement on Race*. New York: Oxford University Press.

Nikolinakos, M. 1973. 'Notes on an Economic Theory of Racism'. *Race* 14:365–81.

Paquet, L.-A. 1969. 'Sermon on the Vocation of the French Race in Canada'. In *French-Canadian Nationalism*, edited by R. Cook, 152–60. Toronto: University of Toronto Press.

Phizacklea, A., and R. Miles. 1980. *Labour and Racism*. London: Routledge.

Porter, J. 1965. *The Vertical Mosaic*. Toronto: University of Toronto Press.

Ray, A. 1974. *Indians in the Fur Trade*. Toronto: University of Toronto Press.

Rose, S., et al. 1984. *Not in Our Genes: Biology, Ideology and Human Nature*. Harmondsworth: Penguin.

Royal Commission. 1885. *Report of the Royal Commission on Chinese Immigration*. Ottawa: King's Printer.

Satzewich, V. 1991. *Racism and the Incorporation of Foreign Labour: Farm Labour Migration to Canada Since 1945*. London: Routledge.

Siegfried, A. 1966. *The Race Question in Canada*. Toronto: McClelland and Stewart.

Smith, M.G. 1986. 'Pluralism, Race and Ethnicity in Selected African Countries'. In *Theories of Race and Ethnic Relations*, edited by D. Mason and J. Rex, 187–225. Cambridge: Cambridge University Press.

Solomos, J. 1986. 'Varieties of Marxist Conceptions of "Race", Class and the State: A Critical Analysis'. In *Theories of Race and Ethnic Relations*, edited by D. Mason and J. Rex, 84–109. Cambridge: Cambridge University Press.

Statutes of Canada. 1876. *An Act to Amend and Consolidate the Laws Respecting Indians*, s.c. 1876, c. 18 (39 Victoria).

Titley, B. 1986. *A Narrow Vision: Duncan Campbell Scott and the Administration of Indian Affairs in Canada*. Vancouver: University of British Columbia Press.

Underhill, F. 1966. 'Introduction'. In *The Race Question in Canada*, edited by A. Siegfried, 1–13. Toronto: McClelland and Stewart.

Vaughan, A. 1982. 'From White Man to Redskin: Changing Anglo-American Perceptions of the American Indian'. *American Historical Review* 87:917–53.

Wallerstein, I. 1983. *Historical Capitalism*. London: Verso.

Woodsworth, J. 1972. *Strangers Within Our Gates*. Toronto: University of Toronto Press.

—13—

Native Canadian Deviance and the Social Control of Race

Jim Frideres

INTRODUCTION

The linkage between community structure and deviance has long been noted. Durkheim (1933) discussed both the ideas of normality and functions of deviance in society. He argued that in all societies, a certain proportion of the population would engage in deviant acts and, furthermore, that this component would remain stable over time and across cultures. In short, Durkheim argued that deviance was a necessary component of society and was functional to the maintenance of that society. The elaboration of this causal structure has been further explicated by more recent researchers. For example, Erickson (1966:4) noted that 'The deviant individual violates rules of conduct which the rest of the community holds in high respect and when these people come together to express their outrage ... they develop a tighter bond of solidarity than existed earlier.' The underlying logic of such a claim is that when a deviant act is committed in the community, the residents rally to combat the deviant act, which in turn enhances the solidarity of the group and strengthens the moral boundaries of the community. Stinchcombe (1968), following the above, claims that a feedback loop of the causal model produces a positive impact upon the community. That is, the deviant act brings the community together through an attempt to deal with the deviant action, which requires community social action, which in turn leads to an increased solidarity or cohesiveness of the community. This enhanced solidarity reduces the likelihood that more deviance will be committed in the near future.

Most social scientists assume that some deviant behaviour in society is functional as it defines the boundaries of acceptable behaviour in the community. Breton (1991) argues that social cleavages and opposition, instead of being indicators of destruction of a community, can be viewed as essential ingredients of a viable community. Nevertheless, those individuals who transgress the social boundaries of the community are defined as deviant and are dealt with in some fashion. In order to deal with these transgressions, the community develops cohesiveness and solidarity in order to confront the deviant individual(s). Consequently, most communities have evidence of deviant behaviour. It is also agreed that excessive amounts of deviance and for continuous periods of time are dysfunctional for a community. The dysfunctionality is at several levels of analysis: (1) the individual, e.g., self-concept, identity, self-esteem, fear; (2) the level of the interaction, e.g., relationships between individuals in a variety of settings—family, work, school—through such activities as violence, marital separation, lack of bonding; and (3) the structural level, e.g., inability to establish economic activities, lack of jobs, lack of community.

As we scan the Canadian social landscape, we find one group in society that shows evidence of extreme and excessive deviant behaviour—Native[1] communities. In these communities, the number of deviant activities are extremely high and have existed for some time, sometimes extending beyond a generation. However, it is also true that historically, deviance was not a salient attribute of Native communities. What, then, has happened to produce such inordinate levels of deviant behaviour today? What is unique about the Native community that has produced such behaviour? What ecological changes have taken place in the socio-economic environment that has led a community to engage in deviant activities in a number of social spheres? Why hasn't the community become cohesive and dealt with the deviants?

Our goal is to provide an explanation for the high rate of deviant behaviour in Native communities. We will couch our explanation within a historical framework as it is important to appreciate fully that the behaviour observable in Native communities today is a result of both historical and contemporary factors. We also take a structural approach in developing our explanation. Our analysis of Native deviance reveals why an individual initiates and continues to engage in deviant behaviour over time. Again, using Durkheim's conceptualization, we will argue that deviant acts are not a function of personality traits or flaws in the biological make-up of an individual but is based upon a behavioural strategy used by normal individuals attempting to maximize their chances of meeting their needs, whatever they are. In short, we will show how Native deviant behaviour is an evolution of behavioural strategies that have developed over time and have spread through the Native population as a culturally mediated process (Vila and Cohen 1993). As Cohen and Machalek (1988) point out, a focus on evolutionary process shows how populations change over time, providing an explanation for both how and why it changes. They argue that the social organization of a community has an impact on the opportunity structure, which in turn determines the behavioural strategies or options utilized by the members of the community. We also introduce the concept of compliance ideology as a crucial factor in community evolution, which now evinces high rates of deviant behaviour. Overall, our task is to provide a micro-macro link in explaining the deviant behaviour in Native communities. However, before we propose our theoretical explanation, we first provide a comparison of behaviours between Native and non-Native communities throughout Canada.

A COMPARATIVE PERSPECTIVE

Deviant behaviour in Native communities has become commonplace, whether or not it is officially 'criminal' behaviour or other less formal types of socially deviant acts. Whenever there are violations of formal norms, they are bureaucratically noted and all levels of government keep statistics on acts that violate the formal laws of Canadian society. For example, we can surmise from Table 13.1 that Native peoples engage in or are defined as engaging in deviant acts at a much higher rate than non-Natives from comparable communities nearby. These statistics reveal that Native peoples are much more likely to spend time in jail than non-Natives. For Natives, there is over an 80 per cent probability that they will spend some time in jail at some point in their lives. In the Prairie regions of Canada, Aboriginal men comprise 34 per cent of the total federal inmate population. In Saskatchewan, Aboriginal men make up two-thirds of the provincial jail population, while Aboriginal women make up 85 per cent of the inmate population. Nearly 70 per cent of youths in custody are Native. The inequity continues as people are processed through the legal system. Few Natives plead not guilty, fewer Natives are represented by legal counsel, more Natives are found guilty, Natives tend to serve longer sentences in the jails, and Natives are more likely to be refused bail or parole than non-Natives. This list goes on revealing inequities that Natives experience in the formal legal system. One might argue that legal statistics are partially a result of the definition of crime and the legal system that enforces it. However, when we review other types of behaviour, we find the same kinds of disparities between Natives and non-Natives.

Rates of substance abuse are nearly ten times higher in Native communities than in nearby communities. Sexual abuse and other types of violence, e.g., personal, family, are five to six times the rate of nearby non-Native communities. One of the most disturbing mortality data is the high rate of suicides among Native Canadians. Figure 13.1 reveals the suicide rate for Indians, Inuit, and the total Canadian population. It shows that while the suicide rate for the Canadian population has remained stable for a number of years, Native rates are double those figures and increasing. Figure 13.2 reveals the comparative rates of violent deaths. It shows that the number of violent deaths of Natives is between three and four times the national rate. These figures reveal a continuing historical trend confirming that violent

TABLE 13.1

Per cent of Native Admissions to Jails by Year and Province

	1985–6		1986–7		1987–8		1988–9		1989–90	
	P[1]	F[1]	P	F	P	F	P	F	P	F
Newfoundland/ Labrador	4	1	5	1	4	4	5	6	4	2
Prince Edward Island	4	–	3	7	3	–	3	6	3	–
Nova Scotia	4	1	4	3	4	1	5	1	4	1
New Brunswick	4	3	4	2	4	2	4	2	5	5
Quebec	–	–	2	1	–	–	2	2	2	1
Ontario	9	2	9	4	9	4	10	5	8	5
Saskatchewan	64	61	64	56	66	51	65	52	66	54
Manitoba	54	34	56	39	55	36	44	35	47	40
Alberta	10	22	10	20	11	22	11	11	11	23
British Columbia	16	13	18	14	19	12	18	17	19	14
Yukon	57	33	60	33	60	54	63	50	65	44
Northwest Territories	85	76	90	73	88	63	88	96	88	75
Canada (Total)	20	10	18	10	22	11	19	13	18	11

1. P = Provincial jail, F = Federal jail

Source: Canadian Centre for Justice Statistics, *Adult Correctional Services in Canada, 1985–90*, Preliminary Data Report (Ottawa: Statistics Canada, 1992).

deaths have been more common in the Native population than in the Canadian population. Whether the abuse was perpetrated by Natives or outsiders living in the community, few Native residents have escaped from abuse in one form or another. Fewer than 30 per cent of Native young people complete their secondary education. Chronic unemployment is characteristic of these communities, with rates of 70–80 per cent as the average. Perceived from the dominant society's perspective, other forms of activities, much higher than the national average, also give evidence of deviant behaviour, e.g., family separation, child abandonment, residing on skid row, urbanization, and high rates of infectious diseases, such as TB and AIDS. Figures 13.3 and 13.4 show two additional social factors that reveal substantial differences between Natives and non-Natives. Less than 1 per cent of Canadian children are under the care of welfare authorities, while for Natives the percentage is four times. Crowding statistics (Figure 13.4) show that the quality of living conditions has decreased for Natives while increasing for non-Natives.

Figure 13.1

Suicides Per 100,000 Population: Status Indians, Inuit, and All Canadians, 1981–6

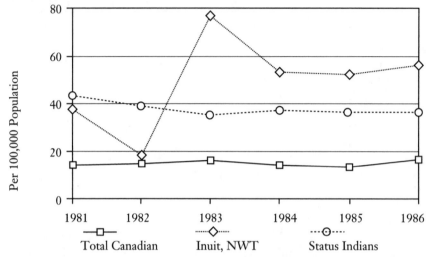

Source: N. Nagey, G. Larcque, and C. McBride, *Highlights of Aboriginal Conditions, 1981–2001* (Ottawa: Indian and Northern Affairs, Ministry of Supply and Services, 1989):7.

Figure 13.2

Violent Deaths Per 100,000 Population: Status Indians, Inuit, and All Canadians, 1981–6

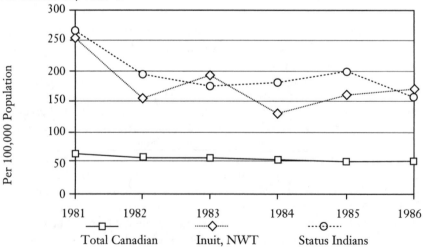

Source: N. Nagey, G. Larcque, and C. McBride, *Highlights of Aboriginal Conditions, 1981–2001* (Ottawa: Indian and Northern Affairs, Ministry of Supply and Services, 1989):8.

Figure 13.3

Children in Care: Indians on Reserve and All Canadians, 1981–7

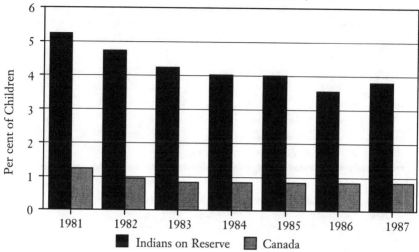

Source: N. Nagey, G. Larcque, and C. McBride, *Highlights of Aboriginal Conditions, 1981–2001* (Ottawa: Indian and Northern Affairs, Ministry of Supply and Services, 1989):17.

Figure 13.4

Crowded Dwellings: Aboriginals and All Canadians, 1981, 1986

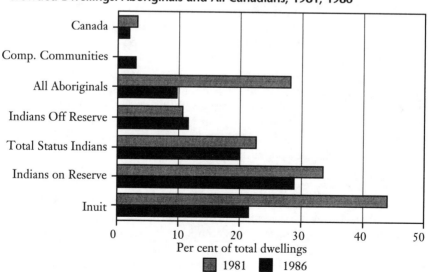

Source: N. Nagey, G. Larcque, and C. McBride, *Highlights of Aboriginal Conditions, 1981–2001* (Ottawa: Indian and Northern Affairs, Ministry of Supply and Services, 1989):13.

The data in Figure 13.4 also shows that the percentage of crowded Native dwellings is eleven times that in nearby non-Native communities. Finally, Native peoples in Canada have not mastered the social skills required to enter the modern economy, e.g., education, language, and conformity, and are viewed as deviants by those who come into contact with them. In the end, it is difficult to identify any social, economic, or health activity that does not reveal stark differences between the Native population and the remainder of the Canadian population. In almost all cases, one would be forced to conclude that Natives are unable to participate fully in society because of the deviant behaviour they demonstrate.

The actual incidents and rates of deviant behaviour in Native communities vary as one moves from region to region, even though they are almost always higher than nearby non-Native communities. Whether or not the deviant behaviour is demonstrated by juveniles, young men, or middle-aged women, the rate is much higher than that of any comparable group. Only in the elderly do many forms of social behaviour become comparable to the rest of Canada.

DEVIANT BEHAVIOUR

The concept of deviance has always been recognized in Native communities. However, Native communities traditionally focused on conformity rather than deviance.[2] Most Native communities preferred a state of affairs that was 'balanced' and that reflected a harmonious interdependence between the individual and the community. Individual behaviours were viewed as to whether or not they contributed to the welfare of the group. In short, the interests of the individual were subordinate to that of the group. Any action not conforming to this value, from the Native perspective, would be defined as deviant. As Nielsen (1992) points out, attempts to deal with deviants in Native communities were based upon informal social control mechanisms that became progressively harsher, depending upon the circumstances. Black (1976) argues that traditionally, Natives lived in a world he calls 'communal anarchy'. Nevertheless, proper behaviour in traditional Native communities was determined by natural laws that did not distinguish, as in the dominant society, between the sacred and the secular (Chapman et al. 1991).

Native and non-Native worlds vary in a number of ways in how the world is viewed, including deviance and the reaction to it. Illustrative of these differences is the definition of crime. Traditional Native societies had no division of behaviour into criminal versus non-criminal. Instead, they viewed behaviour as serving or not serving community needs, and it fell on a flexible continua of 'wrongdoing'. Traditionally, the elders were the sources of information and provided the basis for decision making in the community. They determined whether or not specific behaviours should be defined as deviant. However, this traditional structure and system of dealing with wrong-doings has been suppressed over time. Furthermore, as Keon-Cohen (1982) points out, most Native peoples have lost their interest in traditional Native law and now consider it inappropriate in the modern world. The past century of coercive tutelage implemented by the federal government (Dyck 1991) has reduced the importance and influence of traditional culture to a minimum and produced considerable social disorganization within Native communities. At the same time, many Natives also feel that the dominant system of law is inappropriate, that it discriminates against Natives. This has posed a dilemma for Natives, for if values are imposed upon them without grass-roots support, they are not likely to obey the rules (Law Reform Commission of Canada 1991). At the same time, much of the traditional law has disappeared from Native communities. Nevertheless, the use of coercion by the dominant group has elicited overt Native support of values deemed important by the dominant society, and over time it has diminished the traditional values of Natives. As a result, many Natives find themselves in a marginal position, forced to accept a foreign legal and social system, yet are unwilling to legitimize the imposed structure.

As noted earlier, Native social control mechanisms were based upon community standards. Many Natives have suggested that traditional forms of law and social control be reinstated within Native communities. However, over the past century, Canadians (including Natives) have been given greater liberty to engage in non-conforming behaviour and to carry out deviant acts. Given that there is less and less community control over people's behaviour in Canada over the recent past, can the process be reversed, either in or outside of Native communities? If community control were to be re-established, the personal liberty and autonomy that now exist would be eroded (Merry 1982). It is unlikely that the dominant society would accept such restrictions on personal rights. It is also unlikely that Native communities would revert to a communal system of social control (Native Counselling Services of Alberta 1982), although it is likely that some communities might find this acceptable if they could work out an arrangement under the rubric of self-government.[3] Ponting (1993:92) notes that an Aboriginal justice system has been investigated by a number of royal commissions over the past thirty years. He points out that on the basis of past experience, 'taking control over justice can result in community conflicts surfacing in the domain of the administration of justice, whereas earlier they had been absent or confined to other institutional spheres such as the family'. Moreover, the extent of current social disorganization in Native communities will also be problematic in reintroducing and implementing traditional values supported by appropriate institutional spheres. Finally, the introduction of traditional methods of social control would mean that such methods would have to be realigned with other modern institutional structures, such as transportation, media, and educational institutions. This shows that all institutions within a cultural system are interrelated and changes in one institutional order will have impacts upon others. Whenever one institutional order is revised, there will be compensatory changes in other institutions and their networks with the social structure.

THEORIES OF DEVIANCE

As we review the incidence of deviant behaviour for Native peoples, we ask why. One answer might be that there are good people and bad people and Natives are the bad people and non-Natives are the good. While this explanation was used prior to the eighteenth century, today most people do not accept this explanation. Given that a considerable number of non-Native people engage in deviant behaviour, this explanation is lacking. More recently, people have argued for biological explanations for deviant behaviour. A variety of studies focusing on genetic, chromosome, endocrine, and brain factors tried to isolate the causes of deviant behaviour (Lynch and Groves 1989). Conceding lack of supporting evidence, other researchers began to focus on psychological attributes of individuals as the cause of deviance. Theories of personality, moral development, or mental illness have been the basis for many studies.

Early theorists attempting to explain Natives' high rates of deviant behaviour focused on the individual as the source of their 'cause'. Early explanations centred on the idea that Aboriginals were not human and thus not subject to the laws of human society, hence their deviant ways. Later, as Aboriginals were accepted as part of the human race, religious explanations were provided for understanding their behaviour.[4] This was followed by a belief that the genetic attributes of Native peoples caused them to engage in deviant acts. For example, it has been argued that Natives have a physiological condition that causes deviant behaviour when they consume alcohol. As a result of such a theoretical perspective, proponents of the individual model of behaviour insist that Natives are the cause of their current peripheral and impoverished condition, as well as for their deviant behaviour. These individual perspectives ignore the historical influences on Natives, as well as the structural factors that impinge upon their way of life. Instead of looking at Natives as holding the 'secret' for locating the cause of deviant behaviour, we must begin to look at the structural conditions in which Native peoples operate, both yesterday and today,[5] and we must look at the evolutionary changes that have taken place in a Native community. Today strain, interactionism, conflict control theories, and social organization theories have been posited in the search for causes of deviant behaviour. These more recent theoretical perspectives look at the structure and context in which people operate as the key to understanding why they engage in deviant

behaviour. In addition, these more recent theories take into account historical influences that are still operating.[6] In summary, these more contemporary theoretical perspectives are concerned about the structural conditions in
which people live and how these structures impinge upon their behaviour.

Conflict Theory, Natives and History, Domination and European Hegemony

As Europeans arrived in Canada in the mid-seventeenth century, there was a
considerable exchange of technology. Natives shared their intimate knowledge of the land with immigrants, and immigrants imparted their developed
industrial technology and the artefacts they produced with the Natives. Both
groups negotiated and bargained with the other to gain additional knowledge about their environment and how to adapt to it. However, by the late
nineteenth century, the increasing number of immigrant settlers, the development of agricultural activities, and capitalist developments began to disrupt traditional Native life. There was competition for scarce land-based
resources and scarce commodities. For example, Native peoples were prohibited from homesteading land. Nevertheless, they tried to negotiate their
entrance into the 'new society' primarily through treaties, but their inability
to exercise influence resulted in a lack of success. Because of the dominance
of European trade and technology, Natives were soon pushed aside in order
for the new technology to define and determine the immigrants' actions.
The 'bigger is better' and 'more is marvellous' values were the ideological
underpinnings that drove the settlers to develop land and make a new home
for themselves and their families. A series of legislative acts were passed in
the late nineteenth century that prevented the sale of agricultural products
grown on land set aside for Natives unless it was in accordance with government regulations. Capitalist and entrepreneurial ideology became the basis
upon which decisions were made; meritocracy was the basis for forging
ahead.

In the course of fulfilling their manifest destiny to become the masters of
the universe, Euro-Canadians experienced many obstacles. Problems were
summarily dealt with, sometimes on the basis of moral or philosophical
arguments, but other times on the basis of practical, day-to-day decisions. As
nations expanded their control over areas previously uninhabited by other
Christian peoples, Natives were not viewed as 'humans' but as infidels or
simply part of the larger animal world. As such, rules and regulations applicable to other humans were not viewed as relevant or appropriate to Natives. While we find these views extreme today, it must be remembered that
these attitudes were commonplace and widely accepted just a few years ago.
It is important to understand fully that these were the structural conditions
in which non-Natives and Natives operated less than a generation ago. Natives did not receive the right to vote in federal elections until 1960, and in

some provinces were not eligible to vote in provincial elections until 1965 (Alberta) and 1969 (Quebec). Original legislation specifically forbade Natives from voting. Later, there were no explicit statements in the existing legislation denying Native peoples from voting, but the property qualifications effectively excluded the vast majority of them, i.e., the electoral statutes essentially linked the franchise to ownership in fee simple of land with a specified minimum value (Moss and Gardner-O'Toole 1991:3). This denial of the franchise also meant that Natives were ineligible to serve on juries and school boards.[7]

Until recently, Natives have always represented a small population surrounded by an institutional structure, language, and ideology that is completely foreign to them. Nor did Natives have a chance to 'try on' the new ideology, to modify it to fit their traditional way of life, and then revise it as their culture underwent the normal slow pace of change. Instead, they were subjected to the ideology of the dominant culture and enjoined to take on its cultural attributes. The enforcement was relentless. Beginning with the 1869 Act for the Gradual Enfranchisement of Indians, the federal government determined the social and political structure of Native communities. When Natives rejected the new culture, or when the rate of Natives' cultural assimilation was not fast enough, the dominant group intervened and used any means at their disposal to hasten the process. Laws were passed, actions were taken that would, it was believed, promote the loss of the old culture and facilitate the assimilation process. The process did not allow Natives to construct a new ethos to give meaning to new experiences and social contexts. In the end, it was assumed that the Native population, or at least the Native culture, would be phased out of existence and Natives would take on the cultural attributes of the dominant society.[8]

Nevertheless, there was a dialectic in the dominant culture. On the one hand, Natives had to become more like non-Natives. Actions had to be taken to persuade, force, or otherwise coerce them to take on the attributes of the larger dominant society. When they resisted, new actions were needed to bring about the transformation. On the other hand, Christian ideology dictated that outright killing of the indigenous population was unacceptable, particularly if the action was not provoked. Some ideology had to be created to legitimize the actions of government officials by which they could handle recalcitrant Natives. The solution lay in redefining the issue so that Natives themselves were the cause of the problem! As such, the concern could be redirected, and members of the dominant society only had to find out why Natives were resisting assimilation, why they were not taking on the values and mores of the dominant society. What was wrong with them? What were the individual attributes or societal attributes of Native culture that led them to resist taking on the 'new' ways? Why were they resisting the dominant society's helpful actions against their traditional culture?[9] As a result, the subsequent action of non-Natives towards Natives emerged out of a search for an answer to these questions.

Native culture had many attributes that did not fit into the dominant culture. Natives were defined as socialists (communists) and thus led a communal life that was the antithesis of capitalism. Natives were pagans and thus unable to accept the Christian views of reality.[10] Natives were nomadic and thus resisted the sedentary life of agriculturalists. Natives were predisposed to live off the land, hunting and trapping, and were thus unable to hold office jobs. The list goes on. All of the explanations are from the dominant group perspective and focus on Native culture as the explanation for their continued resistance to the larger dominant ideology and socio-economic culture. The actions taken by government (at all levels), as well as by groups dealing with Natives, accepted this view of reality and based their actions and reactions on the premise that the problem with Natives was to be found in their culture. For example, the implementation of the antipotlatch laws[11] was based on the belief that the potlatches (sharing of wealth) were the antithesis of capitalism and the Protestant ethic. Therefore, such cultural practices had to be destroyed. Hence, the strategy was to find the key to the Native culture that would unlock the secrets to their rejection of the dominant culture and/or resistance to accepting the dominant culture. In the meantime, dealing with Natives was frustrating and expensive. Natives seem to accept some new cultural attributes, but resisted others. The reason for this seemingly inconsistent behaviour was unclear to the dominant culture. One way of dealing with Natives was to create isolated reserves for them where they could be moved and forgotten about. With nominal care and cost, the population would remain out of the way of 'progress' and if all went right, they would disappear. In the meantime, if the key to their cultural resistance could be found, Natives would be contained in small ethnic enclaves that were easy to deal with and properly assimilated. Only in the past decade has this ideological perspective been challenged.

As Dyck (1991) has so eloquently pointed out, the settlers had a compulsion to transform Native peoples into civilized individuals, and this has been a central focus of colonization. The dominant society has an interest in the way Natives and their communities behave, how they perceive themselves, and where they fit into Canadian society. Dyck argues that the government of Canada has implemented, over the years, a coercive tutelage of Indians, which has stymied the development capacities of an entire people. The dominant society has intervened in the identity formation of Native peoples, defined the importance of Native culture, and evaluated their place in society. For example, the establishment of a capitalistic trade system was instrumental in breaking up the folk community and bringing about a personal network consisting of impersonal relations. The influence and control was based upon the premise that Europeans were morally and culturally superior to Aboriginals. The result was the creation of Natives as a pariah group, a distinctive hereditary social group lacking autonomous political organization, characterized by political and social disprivilege and a far-reaching distinctiveness in economic functioning (Zenner 1991). This historical process as well as the institutional structures put in place by the dominant group has produced the deviant behaviour and existing social disorganization now so prevalent in Native communities.

Symbolic Interaction: Compliance and Behaviour

Social life is possible through a consensus on the meaning of various symbols that people experience. Certainly the precise meaning of these symbols may vary, but the general meaning for most residents within that community is accepted. Culture is the beliefs, values, and definitions that make up that consensus. In short, a common cultural definition regarding a host of actions and structures allows for a common standard to become the collective standard. As Wilson (1992:11) says, 'every collectivity has a set of orientations that are used by its members in authority contexts to make choices, resolve dilemmas, and accept particular resolutions as valid'. In the present analysis, two very different institutional arrangements, representing two very different cultures, have distinct perspectives about the meaning of different symbols and do not share a collective standard, yet one of the groups has the power to enforce its definition upon the other.

The institutional arrangements put in place by each culture allow the collective to achieve the goals from its social and religious ethos. The arrangements are functional in that they constrain people's behaviour in achieving those public goals and allow for an efficiency otherwise not achievable. Moral and ethical guidelines are established by which people in the society are to follow and expect others to follow. These rules inform the members of society as to which behaviours are acceptable or unacceptable in carrying out their roles within society. This provides social stability, which allows for the socialization process to proceed in a predictable fashion. This process allows for orderly governance procedures within the community.

Control then becomes a central issue in the conduct of individual behaviour as does the issue of who exercises that control. Leaders of the society, however defined, are given the right to exercise control and are afforded the legitimacy that goes with authority. Those in positions of authority thus coordinate the activities of society and exercise power in an attempt to maximize the goal attainment of the central values of their society. Those in authority are also in a position to determine who is a deviant, e.g., they can criminalize activities that violate the accepted rules of behaviour. This boundary-setting mechanism sets the limits and the strategies by which individuals can operate to carry out their goals. Sometimes monitoring agencies are established to insure that behaviour of members of the society conform to the accepted rules. If social stability is to be achieved, (1) the rules must be seen as reasonable, (2) the enforcement procedures seen as fair; and (3) the general public accepts that those in authority have the right to create, maintain, and enforce the rules. Most people believe that the rules are reasonable and serve a common end. As Wilson (1992) points out, the extent of institutional efficiency depends upon the perceived legitimacy of the institutional arrangements.

Through the socialization process, agents are designated to insure that subsequent generations accept the rules, the methods of enforcement, and the legitimacy of the rules and of those who implement the rules. Those who uphold these beliefs may be selected as the new leaders of society and are granted the right to enforce the existing standards. These beliefs and values that accompany the behaviour support unique institutional arrangements that allow people to achieve their goals efficiently in a stable society. These beliefs and values constitute an ideology, and Wilson (1992:19) concludes that it is an economizing device that incorporates a world view that legitimizes the existing order and provides a framework for a consensus on the general purposes of community life. As such, an ideology is a judgement, it does not have to be supported by empirical or objective evidence.

When applied to the legitimacy of those in authority positions, this constellation of values and linked behaviour can be considered a 'compliance ideology'. In other words, the acceptance of the moral order, the ethos, is based upon support of the existing institutional arrangements. There is also a belief that if the existing structure is not supported, individual and community goals will not be achieved and the system will degenerate into instability and chaos. The establishment of a compliance ideology allows the system to operate unimpeded. Large segments of the population accept and support the existing institutional arrangements, allowing for the mobilization of people to attain goals, establishing boundaries of unacceptable behaviour, and channelling activities towards achieving institutional goals. The acceptance of the ideology also allows various institutions to coordinate and integrate their activities.

Social Organization Theory and Native Communities

People do not act in isolation. They obtain membership in various organizations and institutions as they grow up. As such, it is important to understand the impact of structural conditions on people as they carry out their daily routines. At the most intimate level is the family organization, i.e., primary group. At a more abstract level is the community, e.g., secondary groups, in which the individual lives. Both have substantial impact upon the individual.[12] Focusing on community structure, Shaw and McKay (1929) argued that there were three structural factors that have an impact upon community social organization: low income, ethnic diversity, and residential mobility. In turn, low community organization accounted for high rates of deviant behaviour. Suttles (1968) has, using an ethnographic approach, also tested this linkage and found supporting evidence. More recently, Heitgerd and Bursik (1992) carried out empirical work in this area, which supports this hypothesis.

Blau and Blau (1982) empirically demonstrated that socio-economic inequality increases the rate of deviance, e.g., violence. They concluded that inequality is the root cause of both social disorganization and deviant (criminal) acts. Inequality increases individual alienation and undermines social cohesion. In the end, they argue that it is inequality, not poverty, that causes deviant behaviour. Rainwater (1970) argues that economic marginality leads to tense and conflicting role relationships, which increases marital instability and ultimately leads to a matrifocal family structure that reduces the solidarity of a community. Communities experiencing inequality suffer from disorganization and segregated family structures that encourage higher rates for deviance, e.g., crime and delinquency (Steffensmeier et al. 1989).

The community is a complex system of institutions comprised of both formal and informal networks, family connections, and an ongoing socialization process. This network links individuals and groups to one another. Our first group affiliations are with primary groups, which represent strong emotional ties. Primary groups are important in forming and maintaining an integrated sense of self. Communities are also composed of secondary groups, which are characterized by impersonal relations and carry out goal-oriented activities. Thus people operate within the two different types of groups. If people are able to maintain a good standing in their membership for both types of groups, both the individual and the group prosper. However, if there is a lack of structure that does not allow the groups to form, or if the individual is prevented from participating in the groups, social disorganization results (Tagaki and Platt 1978).

Aboriginal societies, like other cultural systems, have had and still have specific structural constraints on people's behaviour. In the case of Native communities, traditional organizational structures as well as concepts of self differ considerably from those of the dominant group. For example, as Chapman et al. (1991) point out, the concept of Aboriginal self is based upon the teachings of the Circle (sometimes called the Medicine Wheel). This conceptualization encompasses the theology, philosophy, and psychology of Native life.[13] This presumed that behaviour was based upon the knowledge that all things in life are related and are governed by natural or cosmic laws. Within this Native cosmology, there are four fundamental values in traditional Native culture that influence an individual's behaviour: kindness, honesty, sharing, and strength. Organizationally in Native social structure, unlike the larger dominant society, there is a de-emphasis on hierarchy. The Aboriginal cultural values of equality, patience, and respect are not values accepted in the dominant society as part of the organizational ethos. Nevertheless, these organizational structures are embedded in both the primary and secondary groups of the traditional Native community. A break in the linkage of these structures produces social disruption in the Native community.

Social disorganization is a community's inability to achieve the linkage identified above, an inability to achieve the goals and objectives of the individuals and the community, as well as difficulty in maintaining effective social controls (Sampson and Groves 1989). If the community is not able to solve community problems or effectively engage in social control, the community will have high levels of disorganization, which results in high rates of deviant behaviour. On the other hand, highly cohesive communities can control their residents and have low levels of deviance. Skogan (1986) also notes that when residents form local ties, they are better able to control individual behaviour, develop internalization mechanisms, and thus guard against individuals being subjected to deviant acts. This is related to Krohn's (1986) theory of network density, which suggests that when community residents are interconnected with each other, control is high and deviant activity is low. As noted earlier, there are several factors that produce the differing levels of social organization. Let us take each in turn.

Socio-economic status has long been a correlate of deviant behaviour. Low community income reflects the residents' inability to use resources to combat deviant behaviour. Weak organizational structures will also be evident in these communities since residents are unable to organize effectively. There is no doubt that Natives occupy the lowest rungs of our stratified society. Native peoples have the lowest income, the lowest rates of labour force participation, and hold occupations with the lowest prestige.

Residential mobility is also an important factor in levels of deviant activity. High levels of residential mobility effectively stop integration of newcomers. After a while, all social integration is removed, and an entirely anomic society remains. Furthermore, kinship and friendship bonds are unable to develop and create social organization within the community. Since the 1950s, Native peoples have had very high rates of sojourning—temporary movement—between Native communities and the urban environs. *Family disruption* decreases the extent of social control exerted by the family. Families (nuclear and/or extended) that are stable and have less conflict are able to channel resources towards family members. Thus they will be able to have some control over individuals in the family organization. Native families are characterized by relatively high levels of social disorganization, especially with the rapid increase in the number of female-headed, single-parent families. As such, these families lack male role models with legitimate jobs, leaving open the possibility that children will be socialized by others in the community, including individuals engaging in deviant acts.[14] *Urbanization of*

Figure 13.5
Potential Causes of Deviant Behaviour and Their Relationship

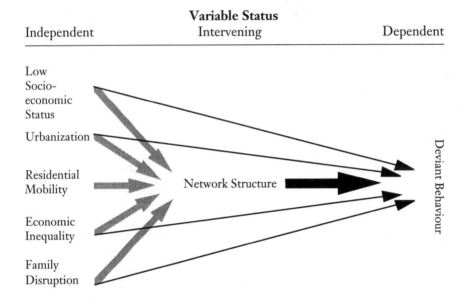

Native communities is also an important factor in the level of deviant activities. Those communities that are more urbanized have less control over the residents and reduce the extent of family and local network control. These factors produce a systemic community structure, which is related to deviant activity. Figure 13.5 identifies the variables and their relationships.

Given this perspective, one might be tempted to suggest that Native communities have many of the attributes of highly cohesive communities. They are linked by extensive kinship networks, they share common problems, speak a common language, and have many other similar cultural attributes. Then why is the Native community characterized by a high level of social disorganization? We will soon see that the structural arrangements of the various institutions both within and outside the Native community have the determining influence upon the actions of its residents and the community organization. These structural arrangements far outweigh the impact of cultural variables in the cause of deviant behaviour.

Social Control and Social Strain

How does a society insure that the younger generation conforms to social norms and values so as to insure the society's continued existence?[15] To facilitate the process, there must be institutional structures that motivate the younger generation to assume adult roles and responsibilities. Social control theory focuses on the bonds of the individual to his or her society (Merton 1938). When these bonds are weakened or broken, people tend to take up deviant behaviour. Four dimensions of bonding are relevant to this analysis. The first is attachment, which refers to the affective ties an individual has with others in his or her community. If an individual is sensitive to others' feelings, then this will constrain his or her behaviours. Those lacking such ties will not feel the constraints. Since attachment may vary from time to time, the lack of attachment may be the structural conditions that precipitate the deviant act. The second dimension is commitment. Commitment is the process by which an individual invests time and energy into a certain activity. To engage in deviant action places the commitment at risk. A third dimension centres on the idea of involvement. Non-deviant activities, e.g., a job or school, keep people busy and less likely to engage in deviant activities. Finally, the belief dimension is also involved in one's behaviour. If one believes in the values, morality, and legitimacy of the dominant law, it will constrain one's behaviour. These bonds are powerful structural psychological influences. A loss of these bonds places the individual in an anomic condition with little concern about social control.

The formation of bonds is most problematic since research demonstrates that most deviant behaviour peaks at adolescence. In addition, young people, who are trying to establish and test their self-identities, are likely to respond to short-term, situationally induced desires to obtain valued goods, which increases the probability of their engaging in deviant activities. Also, we find that people barred from choosing any legitimate avenues for achieving socially valued goals are not deterred by social and legal costs (Bailey 1970). In other words, if you don't have a job, you won't have to worry about getting fired if you engage in a criminal act and get caught. On the other hand, graduating, getting married, finding a job, or going to a postsecondary educational institution all increase the social integration and orientation to conventional society; increasing individuals' social costs will diminish their opportunities for committing deviant acts (Matsueda 1992). These examples illustrate a structure that allows young people to enter the labour market and participate in the educational system with some expectation that they will benefit from their participation. However, not all segments of our society, such as Native peoples, have equitable access to this. As a result, they are not able to develop positive self-esteem, find themselves subject to social control mechanisms that do not fit their lifestyle, and are unable to socialize, which will allow them to take over the values and norms of the older generation. For example, Cohen (1955) points out that schools are dominated by a middle-class measuring rod, which sets up certain standards: sophistication, good appearance, selling oneself, controlling aggression, respect for authority, and deferred gratification. If young adults are to become successful in today's urban economy, they have to emulate those attributes. For those students who do not complete their education, these expectations cannot be realized. In fact, many students from lower socio-economic strata may find that even though they possess the educational skills required to participate in a technical society, they do not have the social skills to retain the position.[16] This example clearly demonstrates that people are driven by social structural forces, not just cultural values, when engaging in behaviour.

Social skills involve individuals internalizing positive self-images. Previous research has suggested that self-esteem is an important mediator variable between parental socialization and deviant behaviour. In order to achieve positive self-esteem, three mechanisms are required: reflected appraisals, social comparison, and self-attribution. People develop conceptualizations about themselves from others' actions towards them over time. Social comparison allows the individual to evaluate and judge his or her self-esteem by comparing with other people over time and in a variety of social contexts. Finally, people make inferences about their self-esteem on the basis of others' overt actions. Structures that prevent someone from participating fully in the organizational structures of his or her society strike at the heart of developing a positive self-image.

Focusing on social control, we are concerned with the mechanisms by which formal and informal groups direct the actions of their members. Early in the process of socialization, each inexperienced person learns how to take the role of the other—first the specific, then the generalized. These include the norms, rules, and expectations attached to the various roles and positions in society. In the end, if proper socialization does not take place, individuals representing the new generation will not accept the mores and laws of the older generation, nor will the new generation be able to sustain positive self-concepts, which in turn will lead to a lack of social control.

Strain Theory: Blocked Opportunity and Native Peoples

All societies have values and norms that are used by their members to make decisions regarding their behaviour. These values and norms govern both the internal relational patterns as well as those that extend beyond the domestic boundaries. As Wilson points out:

> In achieving their stated ends, institutions set constraints on behaviour. On the one hand, such restrictions are general and apply to the membership as a whole: on the other hand, they are specific in terms of a person's role in the institution's division of labour. It is the incumbents of leadership positions who are responsible for enforcing constraints, specifying incentives and disincentives, and devising rules that will promote institutional efficiency. By surrounding power with a halo of legitimacy, leaders are able to uphold moral and ethical guidelines for cooperative endeavour that reduce the costs of enforcing compliance (Wilson 1992:13).

Human aspirations are boundless and people cannot always have what they want. They need to be persuaded to accept what they receive. The norms of the various institutions within a culture govern the behaviour of people in that society. These rules provide standard information for people so that they can decide how to act, how to behave in order to achieve their goals, and what the rewards and punishments are for specific behaviours. When social cohesion breaks down within a community, it loses its traditional social control mechanism and eventually suffers from a high rate of deviant behaviour, e.g., crime. Lack of similarity in values and norms leads to lack of social cohesion, which leads to deviance. If people are not persuaded to accept the community norms and values, society becomes anomic, moral guidelines become unclear, and social control breaks down as people begin to engage in deviant behaviour.

People operate in situations where they must decide how they will behave. At the same time, communities are structured so that they provide their members with legitimate and/or illegitimate opportunities (Kobrin 1951). This means that people must choose between engaging in legitimate or illegitimate actions, e.g., productive or deviant, to obtain their goals. However, just because people in a community have access to illegitimate opportunities, it does not necessarily mean they will commit deviant acts. Furthermore, people can only participate in certain behaviours if they have access to the means to do so (Cullen 1984). For example, Natives seldom engage in white-collar crime, mainly because they are not in a position that allows them to control money or decision making. Figure 13.6 illustrates the relationship between illegitimate and legitimate actions and the dilemma facing each individual as he or she decides upon a behavioural option. In cell one, the individual has equal access to both legitimate and illegitimate activities. That is, he or she can engage in either deviant or non-deviant behaviour to achieve goals or objectives. The choice is fraught with conflict as the individual struggles to make a decision The final decision will be based upon a variety of contextual factors, based upon the social costs and rewards, including both short- and long-term gains, that will result in choosing one of the two alternatives. This analysis combines both the structures in which people operate as well as the behavioural strategies they must decide on in carrying out their everyday activities. Those choosing to engage in illegitimate acts under such circumstances will be defined as more serious deviants (and receive more severe punishments) than other cases (cells 2 and 4) since it is assumed that they have chosen to reject the legitimate opportunities of society.[17]

Those who are denied access to legitimate activities but have access to illegitimate activities (cell 2) will engage in deviant behaviour as their only choice in their attempt to achieve their goals. On the other hand, people who have access to legitimate activities but do not have access to illegitimate

FIGURE 13.6

Individual Decisions and Actions

Legitimate Activity

		Accessibility	No Accessibility
Illegitimate Activity	Accessibility	Opportunist (Deviant)	Impulsive (Deviant)
	No Accessibility	Model Citizen	Welfare, Dependent (Deviant)

actions (cell 3) will take on activities accepted by the dominant society and will be defined as productive 'model citizens', emulating the attributes of success as defined in the larger society. Finally, those who are denied access to both illegitimate and legitimate avenues of action will become 'welfare state dependants'. While they do not overtly engage in defined deviant behaviour, this kind of behaviour will also be defined as deviant by the larger society.[18]

Over time, the structure imposed upon Native peoples has led them to deal with their immediate and mostly hostile social environment in a unique fashion. Unable to counteract the structural forces impinging upon them, Natives have chosen behavioural strategies that have produced what are now called deviant behaviours. Over time, Natives have developed these behavioural strategies and passed them on to other members of the community as reliable, workable strategies. The initial selection of the behavioural strategy is based upon the level of perceived potential success. Subsequent assessment takes place once the behavioural strategies have been exercised. Successful actions will be continued and promoted by other members of the community; those that are unsuccessful will be dropped from people's behavioural repertoire. Further complicating this process is the pay-off rate. In other words, success may be limited, but when it is successful, there are considerable gains. Hence, certain behavioural strategies only need to be used sparingly and within circumscribed contexts. Thus certain kinds of deviant behaviour are not utilized in a uniform manner. As Natives use behavioural strategies defined as deviant and that impinge upon non-Natives, there will be counter-responses as well as 'moral outrage' reactions. These will affect the pay-off rates for Natives and generally promote new and innovative forms of deviance.

The matrix outlined in Figure 13.6 becomes even more complex when one realizes that what is defined as legitimate and illegitimate behaviour will vary as one moves from Native culture to the dominant culture. In both cultures there will be some common definitions, but in cases where Natives engage in behaviour not sanctioned by the larger society, the dominant culture will be in the position to define the behaviour as deviant and specify the causal agent, e.g., cultural or individual defects. This underlying principle also reflects the uncommon matrix of costs and rewards that people in the two cultures must weigh in choosing how to behave. Finally, the dominant society is generally unwilling to accept responsibility for the choices available to Native peoples. There is a pervasive belief that people are wholly responsible for their choices.

Each culture establishes its own behavioural codes and norms. When divergent cultures come into contact, conflict may result. This conflict is exacerbated when the cultural codes of one culture are enshrined in the formal laws of the society, while the other culture is not protected. When this happens, the minority culture must either alter its culture and behaviours or risk punitive action by the dominant group. This conceptualization illustrates how non-cultural factors, e.g., economic, affect the power to define and enforce social norms of all kinds.

NATIVES IN CANADIAN SOCIETY

The extreme social disorganization now so evident in Native communities has a long history. With the colonization of Canada, Natives were forced to choose between entering the modern economy without support from the government or remaining isolated in the rural hinterland. Those who chose the first alternative quickly found that there were few support structures for them to draw upon, and most of the Natives who tried to integrate into the dominant society's institutional structures were unable to succeed in making the transition. Their subsequent choices were to exist outside the formal structures of the polity (sometimes to achieve the status of middleman minorities, e.g., Métis) or return to the isolated rural Native communities. Not until the late 1960s were there infrastructural supports that Natives could draw upon in their attempt to survive in the modern environs.

Those who chose to remain in the Native community quickly discovered that they were not immune to the modernization process that was sweeping Canada. Furthermore, their lives were taken over by the creation of federal and provincial departments such as Indian and Northern Affairs, which had the single mandate of focusing on Native issues. The continued enforcement of the provisions within various federal and provincial legislation, e.g., the Indian Act, insured that few Natives would be isolated from their impact. Major social, political, and ideological changes were forced upon Native communities. Traditional Native institutional structures would be destroyed or substantially modified. The government implemented social control strategies and procedures that further restricted the influence of traditional structures in the community. For example, initial government attempts in economic development were limited to exploiting Natives and their resources, hoping that in the process they would assimilate or die out. There were few attempts to provide Natives with the necessary educational, social, or technical skills for them to enter the modern economy or make decisions affecting their community. In short, the bonds linking the individual to his or her society were severely weakened or destroyed.

Confronted with legislation that restricted or controlled their every movement, Native peoples became a dependent nation or culture. As the gap between the Native and the modern economy widened, the dependent relationship deepened. As the dependency increased, there was a weakening of the family, community, and regional bonds, as well as increasing social disorganization in the community. Traditional leaders were unable to make decisions without the prior approval of government officials, and when action was taken, there was no assurance that government officials would continue to support the community leaders. Actions were taken by stakeholders outside the Native community, actions that Natives had no control over (and in many cases did not even know about); these actions influenced both the structure and quality of institutions in the community. For example, educational policies were made between the federal and provincial governments without involving the Native peoples themselves. Government imposed a style of governance upon Native peoples that it deemed advisable for the 'good government' of Natives. Government officials became middlemen between Native communities and the larger economic structure of Canada. Government officials entered the Native community and brought their own special form of ethnocentrism. They dealt with the community (comprised of intertwined kinship networks) and the dominant society's institutional structures. Natives, with their agrarian society based upon a subsistence economy, lacked the necessary knowledge and skills to participate fully in the export and import economies (Zenner 1991). Government officials, developing specific policies, insured that the linkage would not occur.

Natives have refused leadership positions that would require them to deal with two constituencies having very different goals, i.e., government and the community.[19] They have also been aware that when failure occurs, they will be held personally responsible by both constituencies. Natives have taken a strategy appropriate to cultures under siege: resisting change and assimilating slowly when goal objectives are not identical, thus supporting what has been called a separatist complex. As a result, Natives have continued to maintain a segregationist perspective, e.g., low out-marriage rate, to retain loyalty to their original language, although in many cases the language retention rate is very low. They have also continued to maintain a double standard, i.e., what is acceptable behaviour in dealing with non-Natives is not acceptable when dealing with members of one's own group. As Zenner (1991) notes, ideologically these patterns of self-segregation are supported by various belief systems, some of which are mythical, others real. Over time, Native communities have remained static, undeveloped ethnic enclaves defined as pariahs by the dominant society. Subjected to punishment for not accepting the dominant values and norms, Native communities have, until recently, accepted their dependent status and behaved appropriately.

Today, Native leaders are able to participate within their own communities, but only within circumscribed roles, e.g., as band manager. Native leaders must operate within the legislative confines of federal or provincial legislation, e.g., the Indian Act and Métis Act. Native leaders are also aware that at any time the government may remove them from leadership positions by invoking special legislation established to deal with Native peoples. Leadership in the community has emerged only when one of the several factions in the community has amassed enough support from their constituency to take charge. However, little concerted effort is made by the leadership to form coalitions within the community or to develop long-range plans that will benefit all residents.[20] Severe external constraints, such as the lack of technical skills, limitations of government policy, as well as the inability to organize the community as a whole, restricts long-term, holistic planning. For example, the current legislation dealing with Natives has been premised on the assumption that the government knows best. As Ponting (1993) points out, Native communities are often marked with negativism, fatalism, scepticism, alienation, and a dependency mentality. Together these attributes militate against the success of political and economic development ventures. He argues that before substantial social organizational efforts can take place in Native communities, the victims of physical abuse, psychological manipulation, and coercive tutelage will need to be dealt with. Sensitive counselling programs are needed to relieve the victims of 'that enormous emotional baggage and all its destructive, alienating, crippling, potential' (Ponting 1993:95).

Over the years, the federal government has created a large and complex organizational structure to look after Native affairs. At present it employs about 5,000 people, hires nearly 1,000 consultants a year, and has a budget that now exceeds $5 billion annually. Employees of the Department of Indian and Northern Affairs, the agency created to look after Native affairs, are seldom evaluated on whether or not their programs have produced positive results for Native peoples. That is, the failure of a program or policy is not the basis for removing the individual from his or her position in the organization. What is considered more important is insuring that the organization remain free of conflict. Action taken on behalf of the organization that generates conflict between Natives and the organization is far more likely to bring a reprimand.

Because Native peoples are dependent upon the government for considerable financial backing, social control by government departments can be subtly enacted, e.g., contracts can be given or withdrawn, projects can be created or removed, programs can be implemented or denied. The government's monopoly over Native affairs means that Native peoples are totally dependent upon the government for economic ventures.[21] In addition, a lack of economic well-being limits the members' ability to engage in long-term planning. For example, the income distribution of Natives in the labour force clearly demonstrates that there are few social groups in our society with less income.[22] Their extremely disadvantaged position in Canadian society has led Native peoples to accept minority (inferior) status, and reduced the collective and individual self-esteem and belief that they need to plan strategies to escape from their disprivileged state. This internalization of inferior status is supported by institutional arrangements established by the dominant society and has led to social behaviours that are not acceptable to the larger society. Figure 13.5 outlines the centrality of networks in the linkage of structural variables to the occurrence of deviant behaviour.

CONCLUSION

Most Native communities do not exist primarily as the result of efforts undertaken by Aboriginal peoples. Rather, these communities have been placed on lands set aside by the government; this policy of relocation created the least disruption in the process of colonial settlement, while at the same time it allowed government officials to monitor Native actions. Native communities are encapsulated political systems embedded in a larger sociopolitical institutional order that includes both government and non-governmental agencies. Hence, Aboriginal communities of today are primarily a result of government planning and restrictions. This is not to suggest that Natives do not have a strong attachment to the land, but it is not the residential community per se that evokes strong linkages. Natives find that there is little about the community that exists because of their own efforts. Housing is provided by the government, educational institutions were (until recently) operated by religious organizations, few businesses exist in Native communities, and outsiders remain in control over most internal domestic social policies, e.g., expenditures of monies and planning strategies. Almost all actions taken on the reserve are subject to approval by various federal or provincial legislation.

Native community formation and survival requires that the problems facing the community be dealt with. Opportunities for community development must be sought and exploited. As Breton (1991) points out, community governance involves formulating policy with regard to opportunities and establishing structures that will take advantage of those opportunities. As such, goal achievement requires the investment of time, energy, finances, and the support of the community. Incentives are needed to encourage people to invest their resources (Knoke 1988). Because of historical and structural factors operating on the reserve, there is no sense of obligation towards the community and its members.[23]

Natives have been forced to give up their traditional values and norms and accept new perspectives without having had the opportunity to revise and gradually adapt non-Native values and integrate them into their existing culture. Older Natives still accept their traditional cultural values and norms. They were raised in the traditional culture and complied with its values. Their actions confirm the legitimacy of these traditional values. However, they have been forced to accept the dominance of new values introduced by the dominant group. This disjuncture in Native communities between the old and the new has also made the elders of Native communities redundant, or at least non-influential. In most societies, the older generation socializes the young. In the present case, the older generation has not given up its traditional values, nor has it internalized the new. The older generation occupies a marginal position and has no authority to carry out and support socialization efforts. The younger generation is subjected to the new dominant values, which define proper and acceptable behaviour, yet this generation finds itself living day to day in a community that has many residents who adhere to the old cultural ways. The socialization process has not come from the family or community but from outsiders such as church officials, educators, government officials, and business entrepreneurs. This has precipitated considerable confusion among the younger people as they try to determine which route to follow.[24] As Suttles (1968) pointed out in his analysis of Black communities, 'defeated neighbourhoods' were unable to participate fully in their own governance, in part because of the stigma of being Black. In addition, residents retreated from most forms of public participation. Finally these types of communities were subject to external agents' decisions, which were antithetical to the goals of the community. These factors are remarkably characteristic of Native communities today.

Unable to plan for themselves and control their destinies (either as individuals or as a community), Native peoples have turned inward in their quest to give meaning and structure to their lives. Families were the basis for enclosure, but this soon fell to the individual as the family, clan, and tribe were unable to provide structure and meaning for the individual. As a result, there is an extreme sense of anomie in most Native communities. Community norms and values are no longer benchmarks that determine the behaviour of individuals, and, given the marginal state in which Natives exist, social costs for engaging in deviant behaviour are minimal. There is no way to reconcile the community goals with those of the individual because the community is factionalized and does not have a clear sense of the goals it wishes to achieve nor a demarcation of the hierarchy of goals identified. Furthermore, there are few socializing agents in the community that can provide direction for the younger generation to link the goals of the community with those of the individual in an attempt to give meaning to their lives.

The result of the extreme social disorganization within Native communities today has led to both a lack of social control and social direction. A new socially constructed world has to be created in order to generate order for individuals and groups so that life makes sense. People operating within this anomic structural system are unable to achieve long-term goals. Furthermore, when it is possible to do so, they are unable to find the structural conditions that will facilitate those goals. Faced with this highly unstructured, uncontrollable environment, Native peoples have adopted a lifestyle that combines the traditional values and norms with those of the modern society, feeling free to manipulate the structure and their behaviour when it is to their advantage. These seemingly 'free-floating' values have created an environment in which Native peoples engage in behaviour not understood by members of the mainstream society, nor is it predictable or sanctioned by either culture but defined as deviant by the dominant structure. Until Natives are able to anchor their behaviour in one cultural ethos, they will continue to engage in behaviour that will be defined as bizarre, unacceptable, and deviant by the dominant society.

NOTES

1. We use the term Native as a generic term referring to individuals who share cultural and racial attributes of Aboriginal Canadians. Thus, for the purposes of this paper, we will not use specific legal terms denoting a subgroup of Natives. For example, the term Indian refers to those individuals who are identified through the Indian Act. Other specific references such as First Nation, Métis, Inuit, Inuvialuit, Treaty, Blood, and Innu denote an identified group and will not be used unless the reference is specific.

2. We realize that groups in dominant positions define deviant behaviour, and that the definitions of deviant behaviour change over time.

3. Few Native communities today are prepared to accept those who are 'two-spirited' (androgynous) as individuals holding special powers worthy of acknowledging.

4. For example, Natives were not baptized and were thus under the influence of 'original sin'. Others claimed they were descendants of Ham and were cursed by God, thus explaining their deviant behaviour.
5. Less than a generation ago, most of the Native population was living a subsistence way of life. They were a hunting and gathering population, although some were agriculturalists in various parts of Canada. Nevertheless, their level of development was commensurate with the technology they had available.
6. This chapter takes the position that there are individual explanations for some cases of deviant behaviour. For example, people who are mentally ill or have defective genes are likely to demonstrate deviant behaviours. The structural conditions surrounding them are irrelevant to their behaviour. However, this type of behaviour is minimal and does not account for most of the deviant behaviour identified.
7. The first time a Native served on a Canadian jury was in 1972.
8. There is some evidence that government officials believed Natives would die out as a people within a generation, thus resolving many of the anticipated social issues confronting them at the time.
9. The dominant society, believing its culture and world view were correct, could not see the benefit of Natives retaining their culture.
10. Early eighteenth-century ideology viewed Indians as non-human and thus the locus of cause was within the individual, not the Indian culture.
11. It would not be until 1950 that these laws were removed from the statutes of Canada.
12. There are four levels of social organization in traditional Native culture that need to be noted when analysing the organizational functioning of Native communities: the individual, the family, the clan, and the nation.
13. Chapman et al. (1991) note that there are different but related variations of the Medicine Wheel for different Native groups.
14. Tagaki and Platt (1978) have argued that isolation of ethnic communities, where members of the community are continually exposed to norms that encourage criminal behaviour, is a cause of deviance.
15. Shaw and Mckay (1929) argued that the cultural transmission allowed deviant behaviour (culture) to be passed from one generation to another.
16. People such as Natives may also carry other stigma besides racial attributes, which expose them to prejudice and discrimination. For example, most Natives have an accent. Blacks in the United States have identified this as a limiting stigma in their struggle to integrate into the mainstream society.
17. The costs and rewards will be culture-specific, which means that

choices made by Natives, using their cost-reward matrix, may be quite different from those made by members of the dominant society.

18. People placed in this situation will be defined by the larger society as placing themselves in a context that does not allow access to legitimate actions. Alternatively, they will be defined as having some deficit that prevents them from accessing legitimate actions.

19. In the 1950s and 1960s, emerging Native leaders were co-opted into larger government institutions. The impact of such a social control strategy was to remove emerging human resources from the Native community and allow for continued external control.

20. Of course one must remember that Natives are limited in their planning options because of the policy and fiscal restraints under which they operate.

21. While funds can be raised from private industry, governmental legislation imposes such restrictions on the linkages that most industries find the proposals submitted by Natives as unattractive. For example, bands are unable to sign agreements with private companies. Tax arrangements prevent industries from moving into Native communities to carry out industrial developments.

22. Sixty per cent of the potential labour force (fifteen to sixty-four years) are not in the active labour force. In addition, many of those in the active labour force are only part-time. The result is that nearly 80 per cent of the income taken in by Natives is 'unearned' income; that is, it comes from social programs—old age pension, social welfare benefits, and veteran payments.

23. The linkage between individual and collective identity within the Native community has not been established. Thus an individual's fate is not defined as a function of community activities.

24. In the classic Mertonian sense, younger Native people are exposed to the rewards of participating in the larger urban, capitalist economy, while at the same time thwarted from attaining those goals.

FURTHER READINGS

Mallea, P. 1994. *Aboriginal Law: Apartheid in Canada?* Brandon, Manitoba: Bearspaw Publishing.

McCaskill, D. 1992. 'When Cultures Meet'. In *Aboriginal People and Canadian Criminal Justice*, edited by R. Silverman and M. Nielsen, 218–34. Toronto: Butterworths.

Richardson, B. 1993. *People of Terra Nullius.* Vancouver: Douglas & McIntyre.

Royal Commission on Aboriginal Peoples. 1993. *Partners in Confederation: Aboriginal Peoples, Self-Government, and the Constitution.* Ottawa: Minister of Supply and Services.

Wotherspoon, T., and V. Satzewich. 1993. *First Nations: Race, Class, and Gender Relations.* Toronto: Nelson Canada.

REFERENCES

Bailey, F. 1970. *Strategems and Spoils: A Social Anthropology of Politics.* Oxford: Basil Blackwell.

Black, D. 1976. *The Behaviour of Law.* New York: Academic Press.

Blau, J., and P. Blau. 1982. 'The Cost of Inequality: Metropolitan Structure and Violent Crime'. *American Sociological Review* 47:114–29.

Breton, R. 1991. *The Governance of Ethnic Communities.* New York: Greenwood Press.

Chapman, I., et al. 1991. 'Management in Contemporary Aboriginal Organizations'. *The Canadian Journal of Native Studies* XI, no. 2:333–49.

Cohen, A. 1955. *Delinquent Boys: The Culture of the Gang.* Glencoe: Free Press.

Cohen, L., and R. Machalek. 1988. 'A General Theory of Expropriative Crime: An Evolutionary Ecological Approach'. *American Journal of Sociology* 94, no. 3:465–501.

Cullen, F. 1984. *Rethinking Crime and Deviance Theory: The Emergence of a Structuring Tradition.* Totowa: Rowman and Allanheld.

Durkheim, E. 1933. *The Division of Labour in Society,* translated by G. Simpson. New York: Free Press.

Dyck, N. 1991. 'What Is the Indian "Problem"?' St John's: Institute of Social and Economic Research, Memorial University of Newfoundland.

Erickson, K. 1966. *Wayward Puritans.* New York: Wiley.

Heitgerd, J.L., and R.J. Bursik, Jr. 1992. 'Extracommunity Dynamics and the Ecology of Delinquency'. *American Journal of Sociology* 97, no. 3:775–87.

Keon-Cohen, B. 1982. 'Native Justice in Australia, Canada and the U.S.A.: A Comparative Analysis'. *Canadian Legal Aid Bulletin, Special Issue, Part II* 2, no. 3:187–258.

Knoke, D. 1988. 'Incentives in Collective Action Organizations'. *American Sociological Review* 53:311–29.

Kobrin, S. 1951. 'The Conflict of Values in Delinquency Areas'. *American Sociological Review* 16:653–61.

Krohn, M. 1986. 'The Web of Conformity: A Network Approach to the Explanation of Delinquent Behavior'. *Social Problems* 33:81–93.

Law Reform Commission of Canada. 1991. *Aboriginal Peoples and Criminal Justice: Equality, Respect and the Search for Justice.* Ottawa: Law Reform Commission of Canada.

Lynch, M., and W. Groves. 1989. *Radical Criminology*, 2nd ed. New York: Harrow and Heston.

Matsueda, R. 1992. 'Reflected Appraisals, Parental Labeling, and Delinquency: Specifying a Symbolic Interactionism Theory'. *American Journal of Sociology* 97, no. 6:1577–1611.

Merry, S. 1982. 'The Social Organization of Mediation in Non-Industrial Societies: Implications for Informal Community Justice in America'. In *The Politics of Informal Justice*, edited by R. Abel, 143–65. Toronto: Academic Press.

Merton, R. 1938. 'Social Structure and Anomie'. *American Sociological Review* 3:672–82.

Moss, W., and E. Gardner-O'Toole. 1991. 'Aboriginal People: History of Discriminatory Laws'. Ottawa: Research Branch, Library of Parliament.

Nagey, N., G. Larcque, and C. McBride. 1989. 'Highlights of Aboriginal Conditions, 1981–2001'. Ottawa: Indian and Northern Affairs, Minister of Supply and Services.

Native Counselling Services of Alberta. 1982. 'Native People and the Criminal Justice System: The Role of the Native Court Worker'. *Canadian Legal Aid Bulletin*, Special Issue, Part I:55–63.

Nielsen, M. 1992. 'Criminal Justice and Native Self-Government'. In *Aboriginal Peoples*, edited by R. Silverman and M. Nielsen, 243–58. Vancouver: Butterworths Canada Ltd.

Ponting, J. 1993. 'Crisis and Response: Challenges of the 1990's in Alberta Indian Affairs'. In *Alberta into the 21st Century*, edited by J. Frideres and R. Gibbins, 89–104. Calgary: University of Calgary.

Rainwater, L. 1970. *Behind Ghetto Walls: Black Families in a Federal Slum*. Chicago: Aldine.

Sampson, R., and W. Groves. 1989. 'Community Structure and Crime: Testing Social Disorganization Theory'. *American Journal of Sociology* 94, no. 4:774–802.

Shaw, C., and H. McKay. 1929. *Delinquency Areas*. Chicago: University of Chicago Press.

Skogan, W. 1986. 'Fear of Crime and Neighborhood Change'. In *Communities and Crime*, edited by A.J. Reiss, Jr, and M. Tonry, 203–29. Chicago: University of Chicago Press.

Steffensmeier, D., et al. 1989. 'Age and the Distribution of Crime'. *American Journal of Sociology* 94, no. 4:803–31.

Stinchcombe, A. 1968. *Constructing Social Theories*. New York: Harcourt Brace & World.

Suttles, G. 1968. *The Social Order of the Slum*. Chicago, University of Chicago Press.

_____. 1972. *The Social Construction of Communities*. Chicago: University of Chicago Press.

Tagaki, P., and T. Platt. 1978. 'Behind the Gilded Ghetto: An Analysis of Race, Class and Crime in Chinatown'. *Crime and Social Justice* 9:2–25.

Vila, B., and L. Cohen. 1993. 'Crime as Strategy: Testing and Evolutionary Ecological Theory of Expropriative Crime'. *American Journal of Sociology* 98, no. 4:873–912.

Wilson, R. 1992. *Compliance Ideologies: Rethinking Political Culture*. Cambridge: Cambridge University Press.

Zenner, W. 1991. *Minorities in the Middle*. New York: State University of New York Press.

—14—

Youth Culture, Racism, and Alienation:
The Control of Youth

Thomas Fleming

INTRODUCTION

> Why are today's youth so angry? That's what one of the angry victims in
> yesterday's brawl ... demanded to know ... 'There was real disrespect, an out-
> and-out loathing towards the police. Who are these kids? What have they
> experienced, what [sic] they got to be so angry about' (*Toronto Star*, 2 June
> 1992, A6)?

On 1 June 1992, armed teenage gangs wielding baseball bats converged on
Toronto's Centre Island. Police estimated that 2,500 students travelled to
the island a mile across Lake Ontario from the site of the Skydome. Eight
people, including two police officers, had to be hospitalized for their injuries
and eight people were arrested after a 'word-of-mouth high school party on
the Toronto Islands erupted into four hours of violent skirmishes' (*Toronto
Star*, 2 June 1992, A1). Student witnesses blamed the incident on four youth
gangs: The LA Boys, The Christie Boys, The Fred Hamiltons, and
McCormack Boys. Five months later, over fifty high school students from
two Toronto schools gathered to have a fight. The police were called and
dispelled the crowd before violence ensued. Two shotguns were removed
from students' bags.

Expressions of youthful discontent have been a common feature of Western culture since the end of the Second World War. Unlike British, German, and American youths, until very recently English-Canadian adolescents have not demonstrated collective forms of social disruption, violence,
and criminality that warranted intense public, police, and media scrutiny
evident in other modern capitalist societies. In Canada, youthful rebellion
has historically centred largely, but not exclusively, on the emulation of
'styles' borrowed from British and American pop rock (Brake 1985), sports
teams, and, in a few cases, from 'cult' organizations. As these incidents

indicate, there has been an intensification of organized youth violence in Canada since the late 1980s. This chapter explores the phenomena of collective forms of youth violence ranging from swarming, runs, and wildings to the emergence of 'super gangs'. In order to develop a descriptive analysis of the cultural significance of these emerging forms of youthful protest, disaffiliation, alienation, and rebellion, analysis must be directed to wider sources of political and economic dissent in our society. Specific attention is directed towards race and racism within Canada as a predetermination of youth alienation and rebellion.

Swarming is a highly visible and media-focused form of youthful deviance that involves organized violence, intimidation, and criminality. Swarming first surfaced as part of the punk rock musical revolution in the 1970s. British and American 'punks' derived their name and rock style from their disdain for the established hierarchy of rock and roll, largely composed of 1960s groups, which had continued to dominate popular rock forms despite their immense fame and wealth. The punks wanted music that was not so élitist, so any young person could dream of escaping working-class culture to become a rock icon, which they deemed to be an integral part of rock's legacy. The 'super groups' of the time: Led Zeppelin and Supertramp, to name two, did not represent a voice for the young, disaffiliated, and increasingly unemployable youth. In England in 1975, The Sex Pistols, as well as groups like The Clash, began, in concert with their followers, to define the essential elements of the punk repertoire, which included such gear as leather jackets, black stove-pipe jeans, diaper-pin ear and nose rings, and brightly dyed hair. Female punks dress in what Brake (1985:176–7) describes as 'reappropriated Hollywood ideologies of femininity ... They parody its Aryan make-up ideals, mocking its expensively coiffed hairdos with greasy, spiked hair and exchanging its precarious high heels for strapping steel-toed boots.' Music and performance were to be reduced to their essential elements, and cheap instruments and lack of virtuosic skills were extolled as virtues. The performance, with its focus upon audience participation, borrowed elements of the earlier mod musical movement in Britain, which encouraged dancing in crowds. According to Michael Brake, 'Punks celebrated chaos, linked to the surreal and to situationalism making public the perverse elements of sexuality such as bondage or fetishism ... Dances were the robot, the pogo and the pose ... fanzines were deliberately anti-professional, rejecting the expensive glossy magazines ... The punks wore clothes which were the sartorial equivalents of swear words, and they swore as they dressed ...' (Brake 1985:78).

The roots of swarming, then, developed as part of the cultural expression of British youths during the 1970s and 1980s. But why did violence become part of this expression? During the 1970s Britain experienced large waves of immigration from India and the British colonies, coupled with rising levels of unemployment under successive Labour governments. This caused wide-spread youth unemployment. Also, school leaving at fourteen years of age was a common feature of British school life. Unfortunately, for the first time in postwar Britain, young men and women with this low level of educational achievement were no longer assured of relatively easy access to employment. Many service-sector jobs were filled by immigrants anxious to succeed in Britain. Under Margaret Thatcher's government, which took office in fall 1979, the economic hardships on the working class began to increase at an astounding rate as state-owned and state-run industries like the mines, auto works, and power suppliers began to revert to private ownership or close altogether. In this atmosphere racist propaganda groups such as the National Front began to exploit the anger of British youths by pointing to immigrants as the cause of their miseries. Out of this increasingly violent atmosphere of confrontation and clashes emerged an evolved form of 'working-class warrior,' the skinhead. The skinheads were a forms of visible vanguard, the outcropping of youthful resentment of immigration. This anger was reflected in the film, *My Beautiful Launderette*, where local youths brutally batter the Pakistani owner of a launderette.

Throughout the 1970s, youths' anger was expressed increasingly in racist terms in the form of marches against immigration and for a homogenized White Britain and in brutal attacks on immigrants. This is now being repeated in Germany where neo-Nazi youths have repeatedly attacked refugee camps in a country with one of the most liberal sets of refugee laws in the world. Skinheads reflected the new racism of Britain in the 1980s. In two well-publicized incidents, dozens of soccer fans lost their lives in Spain and in England after rioting started by skinheads, who also happen to be soccer fans. In 1981, riots swept over Britain in Liverpool's Toxteth district and in Birmingham, and Brixton, all areas hard hit by unemployment and where long-term, working-class White Britons clashed with more recent Black, Indian, and Pakistani residents.

Although this chapter does not present a detailed analysis of female involvement in youth gangs, it should be noted that women do participate in punk and skinhead youth gangs. While their actions are typically subordinated to male members, in interaction with non-members they can and do assume leadership roles. It is important to emphasize that within all youth subcultures, there are varying degrees of commitment. For example, Brake notes the critical distinction between those who 'dress punk' as opposed to 'being punk'. The Canadian skinhead subculture has British origins. Violence as a part of this movement is comprehensible only if one realizes that the skinhead movement was never a solely music-driven development in popular culture but had its roots in political expression of dissatisfaction with immigration and unemployment in Europe during the 1970s. In Canada, while some segments of the skinhead subculture have retained racist ideologies, other segments have developed very strong antiracist views. In Canada both punk and heavy metal subcultures have directed their anger at 'yuppies' who had achieved financial success, which was denied to the young people of Generation X.

Swarming first emerged in Toronto, Canada's largest metropolitan area (with a population of slightly more than 2.3 million) in 1989. 'From a dozen to over thirty youths would surround a male and demand their leather jackets, shoes and money at risk of personal assault if they did not comply' (Barber 1989:19). The incidents occurred in the downtown Toronto shopping and business core, and the Metropolitan Toronto police engaged in intensive surveillance to control the phenomenon so business and tourism would not be threatened. Nevertheless, swarming was imitated in other cities and in other parts of Toronto, and there were various victims of swarming in the months that followed.

> In addition to the innumerable teenagers who lost expensive jackets and jewelry, some of last spring's victims included a whole family of Dutch tourists, assaulted and robbed in broad daylight outside the Eaton Centre; an eighty-year-old woman who suffered a broken hip during a swarming at the same location; a teacher pummelled by four youths in the hallway of a north Toronto junior high school; a blind boy beaten and stomped at a crosswalk on Gerrard Street East, and a mentally handicapped boy who suffered the same treatment on Dundas Street ... a fifteen-year-old boy hit across the nose with a broom handle in the Donlands subway station and kicked by six assailants onto the track as a train approached the station (Barber 1989:19).

Social psychologists maintain that swarming may be youths' collective effort to escape boredom, seek thrills, and exercise power over their victims because of their sense of absolute powerlessness in their own lives. In these cases, the attacks were intended to humiliate the victims and challenge the legitimacy of the relations of production in Canadian society. It signalled that some youths were not content to stand by and watch others prosper while they were left behind. Disenchanted youths were ready and willing to take signs of prosperity away from the visibly well-heeled, attack the disabled, the elderly, and the vulnerable, leaving doubts about the police's ability to control youth violence. While reported swarmings number probably under a dozen reported incidents, they attracted not only considerable media, public, and political attention but were also the object of intense police attention.

RUNS AND WILDINGS: SPONTANEOUS AND PLANNED RAMPAGES

Runs and wildings are other forms of spontaneous and organized collective behaviour involving youths. They first appeared in 1990 and are worthy of detailed sociological analysis. Runs first surfaced in 1989 at Toronto's Canadian National Exhibition. On the last day of the national fair, a large group of youths ran through the fairgrounds, pushing people over and 'ripping off' prizes from the fair booths. The unexpected act caught law enforcement off guard. The youths quickly dispersed after a few minutes. A more sinister form of run occurred in 1991 when a group of armed youths ran through a local flea market in the city of Scarborough. In this case, a mob of fourteen to seventeen year olds charged through the premises and smashed display cases with baseball bats. Jewellery and goods valued at over $100,000 was stolen. In the previous month, police in Toronto were forced to close the prestigious Eaton Centre in the downtown core when 100 teens ran through the mall and looted a store of most of its merchandise (Orwen 1991:A2).

Two types of runs have evolved in Canada. First, there are those that arise out of situational exigencies, and might be said to be a form of political protest; youths' economic deprivation is exacerbated by others' spending frenzy at carnival activities such as at the CNE. In such situations, the displacement of youths from the mainstream of economic relations is accentuated, and these situations provide a backdrop and a stimulus for riotous behaviour. These spontaneous runs do not produce the kind of violence or theft involved in swarms, gang behaviours, or more organized runs. The second form of run, typified by the one that occurred in Scarborough, is an organized and deliberate crime. It is divorced from political protest. Organized runs masquerade as youthful rebellion, but are actually a cover for theft and violence. The perpetrators use the run to obtain profit under the guise of youthful exuberance or rebellion.

The term wilding arose out of a night of terror in New York's Central Park. A young woman jogging through the park was savagely attacked by a group of young men, who took turns brutally raping and beating her severely, leaving her for dead. Wildings are a form of gang-rape and violence directed towards female victims. The phenomenon is not exclusively American. A 1990 case in Toronto involved a group of teenagers at a party who, finding a female in an intoxicated state, gang-raped her. A wilding is intentional and connotes the viciousness and savagery that characterizes these attacks, which normally occur in secure surroundings, such as private premises, or in parks at night where no one is likely to enter. There are, one suspects, many similar incidents that occur as a by-product of gang violence. Dietz (1983) found that felons committing robbery and other violent crimes in Detroit also often engaged in sexual assaults. Sociologists have struggled to explain the origins of 'mindless violence'. One of the common factors in extreme violence, according to Elliott Leyton (1986), is the perpetrators' feeling that they have been denied access to a middle-class existence. Our society sets up normative expectations for its citizens, i.e., if one works hard enough one will succeed, etc., but many, of course, are denied these rewards. There are limited rewards in our society and thus limited means for many to express their personal value. If we as a society value success above all, then those who are unsuccessful must constantly suffer the pains associated with failure. One should not use such explanations to excuse or condone such violent actions, but one should also be aware of their influence in classism, racism, and sexism.

GANG BEHAVIOUR

Most of our knowledge of youth gangs has evolved from American studies of large gangs, such as those that have a long history, often spanning several generations in major American cities like Los Angeles, Chicago, and New York. Sociologists argue that gangs have evolved as a social protest against barriers to social advancement. Like Merton's (1968) innovators, gang members sought ways to escape the abject poverty and violence in the barrios, ghettoes, and slums of America's inner city. In the 1950s, gangs in LA resembled those portrayed in West Side Story: 'It had to do with hanging out with your buddies, not firing high-tech weaponry' (Bing 1991:80). In 1990, however, over 140 children were murdered in Detroit. Some victims were murdered for their shoes or jackets, or were the victims of random drive-by shootings in which the assailant fires randomly at passersby. The hopelessness that many residents of LA's Southside feel is hauntingly reflected in movies like *Boyz in the Hood* or *Grand Canyon* in which a mother is confronted by an insurance salesman through her heavily grated front door, urging her to buy life insurance for her children so that she will be able to afford to bury them when, with certainty, they fall victims to violence.

The Bloods and the Crips are two long-standing gangs in the Los Angeles area. Both gangs have several hundred members and survive by engaging in a variety of criminal behaviours: drug peddling (particularly of crack cocaine), theft, mugging, auto theft, assault, and murder. Gangs are well organized to control the drug trade in their 'hoods', and enforce ownership of their turf with violence and intimidation. Turfs are marked with gang letters spray-painted onto any available surface, and members of other gangs entering illegally are fair game for assault or death. Drive-by shootings are common and police patrols are infrequent in these areas, so a sense of lawlessness and vigilantism prevails. Consider, for example, the reasons given by some convicted gang members as to why they would take a human life: revenge, because the victim said something wrong, because 'he look at me funny', because 'he gave me no respect', because 'he is a disgrace, he a buster', for money, so he or she can be 'jacked' (ripped off) for dope, and finally, 'for the fuck of it'.

While Canada has not experienced these 'supergangs' (Zevitz and Takata 1992:98), there is no doubt that there is considerable gang activity in our urban areas and that youth gangs have become a disturbing problem for

large Canadian cities. Few communities have been immune from gang disturbances, crimes, and quasi-criminal activities. While police youth workers
acknowledge that gangs have been a problem in cities since the 1980s, the
problem has been the focus of media attention only in 1990 (*Globe and Mail*,
6 November 1990:A10). In Toronto, gangs with the names of The Un-
touchables, The Markham Massive, and A Bunch of Fucking Goofs are
associated with gang activities similar to but of a less serious nature than that
of their LA counterparts. Their criminal activities include drug use and
sales, assaults, swarming, 'hangin', and accosting or threatening citizens when
they pass gang members.

The JTP Boys (Jack Town Posse) is a five-member posse of White youths
who spend their leisure time 'hangin' out with large numbers of poor youths.
'Hangin' is loitering in malls, doughnut shops, parking lots, and on select street
corners. The JTP Boys fit well into Miller's tenets of working-class culture and
life. They spend much of their time attempting to overcome the boredom from
economic marginalization. Excitement and its creation are paramount in their
collective activities. For the JTP Boys, excitement is swarming younger males for
troop jackets. Nightly activities are vandalism, writing graffiti on public spaces,
intimidating people on the street or in malls, or shoplifting.

The subject of gang behaviour has held considerable fascination for sociologists of the postworld war period. Fowler has argued that the factors that
draw members to gangs can be summarized as follows. Inner-city gangs are
formed out of dissatisfaction with the existing power structure. Prospective
gang members are usually disenchanted with the educational system, have
been given little guidance or encouragement, or can see no future for themselves as academics. Youths may join gangs for identity, recognition, or to
attain status and respect. Some perceive themselves as warriors or soldiers
defending their neighbourhood, while others may join for protection from
rival gangs or to seek a sense of family and cohesiveness.

For groups of poor youths like the JTP Boys, identity is established initially not by wearing certain clothing and accessories but by the group planning and execution of a criminal or deviant act. In the end, the troop jacket
represents more than a symbol of economic status and identification with a
youth trend. Its deeper significance is in the method by which it was obtained and the bonds forged by the collective action. This production and
expression of group loyalty shares much in common with other gang affiliations explored later in this chapter.

Violent youth crime in Canadian cities has been rising over the past
decade. Part of the explanation for Canadian gangs, which are not organized
in the way American gangs are, lies in their members' sense of powerlessness. 'As individuals', a probation officer commented, 'these guys are insignificant. They're nothings.' Attending school is the limit of the JTP Boys'
commitment to society: 'We go to school to keep our parents off our backs.'

Thompson (1970) and Wolf (1991) have offered a similar analysis of more formalized gang membership in their respective analyses of The Hell's Angels Motorcycle Club and a Canadian biker gang. Street gangs are a recent phenomenon in Canada and have developed both informal and formal groupings that I will explore later.

ASIAN YOUTH GANGS: RETREATING FROM THE DOMINANT CULTURE

Two groups in Vancouver, The Red Eagles and The Alley Boys (or Gum Wah), and The Posse in Toronto draw their membership from the Asian and Black communities respectively for the same reasons that other working-class gangs do and engage in the same activities, including drug sales, extortion, violence, assaults, and even suspected homicides. Brake argues that being 'black and poor' is a 'profoundly different experience from being white and poor' (Brake 1985:122). The experience of many new Asian and Caribbean and West Indian refugees and immigrants to Canadian society can be characterized as one of 'multiple marginality'. This was a concept originally developed by Vigil (1988) to explain the phenomenon of Chicano youth gang membership. Moving between extremely different cultures with highly disparate social, educational, familial, language, and cultural expectations is the source of multiple interrelated stresses and pressures for young people. It has been argued by various authors that ghetto life is set in the context of racism. The institutions of society reinforce these social relations. Black people relate to White people through experiences mediated by racism. Racism also guarantees a subordinate position for Hispanic people from a culture of Indian-Spanish descent, and for Native Americans and Native Canadians. Like White youths, Black youths experience structural problems generationally, but race remains the primary mode through which these problems are experienced. As such, race also gives them a comprehension and consciousness that enable them to deal with their exploitation. This may take the form of political consciousness, but it may revert to primitive rebellion, refusing dead-end work, dropping out of school, hustling, and engaging in crime (Brake 1985:121–2). The economic marginalization of many of these immigrant groups and the problems associated with the education system can be effective roadblocks to attaining culturally prescribed goals of material success. Hence, having perceived that they will be unable to achieve status through culturally approved means, youths turn to gangs to acquire money and status without the necessary requisites of hard work and education. Their paths circumvent concepts of the work ethic and existing relations of production. Gang membership also provides a means to attack the dominant culture and its members.

Research on Asian gangs in the United States and police bureau data from Canada indicate clearly that the means to achieving these goals is comprised of traditional criminal pursuits associated with organized crime: drug running, sales of sex, and violence. Extortion and protection are two further forms of violence for profit (Dietz 1983) that are regularly practised by Asian gangs. There are four types of extortion, according to Chin (1991:136–42). First, the most prevalent is simple extortion for monetary gain. New store owners are often approached for *li shi* or 'lucky money'. Later the gang members return to inform the owners that these payments will have to continue. Chin (1991:140–1) relates some of the techniques used by gangs to extract compliance. A group of youths may enter a restaurant during the lunch or dinner hour and occupy a number of tables. They tell the manager they are waiting for friends. They sit for hours, and act in a rowdy fashion to intimidate customers. They may fight with each other, smash the dishes, or insist on remaining in the restaurant after closing hours. Young men may go into a restaurant and order the finest dishes on the menu. When they leave, they write 'Shadows' or 'Dragons' on the back of the bill and do not pay. Other members may pose as concerned customers, berate their fellow gang members, and offer protection to the restaurant owner. This playing off of good guys versus bad guys is referred to as *hei bai lian* ('black and white faces').

Symbolic extortion is used to demonstrate control or power over an area or an individual. Victims are typically store owners, restaurateurs, and small-business people who give heavy discounts, free food, and cigarettes to gang members. In extortion for revenge, victims are beaten up, robbed, or even murdered if they do not comply with the extortion threats. In instrumental extortion, the intent is to force the victim to withdraw from a business venture or to settle personal conflicts (often a gambling debt). Many businesses simply close under the constant threats of intimidation and extortion on an almost daily basis.

RACISM, ECONOMIC CRISIS, AND THE STATE

The problem with youth gangs, according to Fowler (1989:9) and other sociological researchers, is 'one that, if unchecked, quickly escalates into very serious trouble'. The prevalence and escalation of youth gang violence throughout the 1980s led to the establishment of two forms of policing response in Canada: the national gang unit was formed within the RCMP and focused on organized crime activities, and the local police established gang and Asian crime units in Vancouver and Toronto. This chapter describes the character and evolution of youthful collective deviance in contemporary Canadian society set within a historical framework informed by popular culture. The goal has been to challenge traditional explanations for gang involvement (the search for identity or excitement in an otherwise boring and limited existence) by examining two additional factors—the real oppression, both social structural and racial—that mark youths' lives. For youths in a position of structural and racial inequality, gang membership may offer a means for self-fulfilment and an escape from poverty and prejudice.

In 1992, Toronto experienced two major riots by youths. The *Toronto Star* reported that 1,000 young people cut 'a path of destruction' through the heart of Toronto's retail district. The riot started after a demonstration on racial discrimination in the wake of the acquittal of police involved in the Rodney King beating. The rally was to be followed by a march to Yonge Street. It was reported that the demonstration had 'switched focus' due to the police shooting of a '22 year old suspected drug dealer, who was black' the preceding day. The organizer of the protest, Dare Meade, was reported as yelling 'No justice, no peace' (*Toronto Star*, 5 May 1992:A1). In a similar vein, Black activist Dudley Laws commented, 'If the blood of our people continues to run like streams along the countryside, then the blood of others will run like rivers.' The rioters looted and caused damage for five hours on Yonge Street and hurled several fire-bombs. Police authorities and politicians tried to downplay the expression of racial disharmony by blaming the riot on 'hell raisers' and 'hooligans'. Arrests and subsequent prosecutions were few in number. Indeed, only seventy-five people were arrested, twenty-eight of whom were charged for breach of the peace, a non-criminal charge. This was in the wake of reported damages exceeding $250,000 and the theft of $122,000 in property. Only seven prosecutions had been reported by the end of summer 1992. Media attention focused upon the marginality of rioters, citing the case of a young male who had arrived in Toronto from Nova Scotia the day before the riot. He was portrayed as one of a group of 'career criminals exploiting a peaceful demonstration by a black community group' (*Toronto Star*, 23 June 1992:A1).

This explanation of the situation, while offering political reassurance about the peaceability of Black protesters, does not explain the riot, which involved over 1,000 people. The group rioted for over five hours! Surely one cannot be expected to believe that all 1,000 were career criminals who happened to converge on Yonge Street at the same time to take advantage of a Black protest? I believe the riot reflected the disenchantment of marginalized youths, both Black and White, in Canadian society. The disenchantment lies in the country's failure to provide work for a growing number of unemployed, of the increasing use of police force to handle social problems, and of the relegation of many tens of thousands of young people to a life of dependency (O'Reilly-Fleming 1993). It is no surprise that homeless youths (numbering more than 10,000 in the Toronto area) express anger and hostility towards a society that has abandoned them. Nor is it surprising that many of the reported looters were either people with no fixed address or were from the poor areas of the city. The racial disharmony was not lost on politicians in the Rae government, who invited Steven Lewis to prepare a report on racism in Ontario. Lewis stated that anti-Black racism was systemic, and that young Blacks were 'unemployed in excessive numbers' and were either inappropriately screened or were dropping out of the educational system. He found that Blacks were shunted into small, ghettolike areas where depression and hopelessness abound. They were mistrustful of the police, deeply concerned for the safety of their children, and found the criminal justice system racist.

In conclusion, the police's ability to control collective youth violence has not been impressive to date except in very temporary or limited forms. Traditional techniques that have largely failed include exerting extensive police control in public settings, jailing gang leaders (who are immediately replaced), using informant networks, and using Mafia-style intelligence units to ascertain group intentions and anticipate or control criminality. The potential for escalating and exacerbating trouble is confirmed by increasing gang membership and their involvement in violent behaviours. Certainly one has to agree with Fowler (1989:8) that early intervention with youngsters is a more effective use of our societal resources than attempting to change the behaviours of confirmed gang members. Any effort would involve all three levels of government as well as local community agencies, businesses, individuals, and educators in providing meaningful programs for those in the pre-gang, ten to twelve year age range. Athletic, creative arts, music, computer, and other programs could provide children with an opportunity to benefit from positive reinforcement. In the wake of the Lewis report, special attention has to be given to involving minorities in the delivery and implementation of these programs if they are to reach adolescents in Canadian inner cities. Community groups on drug use, alcohol, sexual issues, crime, policing, and the legal system could provide a direct method of combating youth alienation and dissatisfaction. Collective youth violence is a relatively new phenomenon in Canadian society, but there are disturbing signs that it is growing and becoming increasingly serious. Solutions to these problems lie not in the exertion of increased control but in giving greater attention to the political, economic, and social factors that produce this form of mass criminality. As this chapter has shown, the police are ineffective in dealing with the increasing numbers of disaffiliated youth who have now learned, in the wake of the Yonge riots and the Centre Island riots, that there is power in numbers and relative immunity from social control efforts.

NOTES

1. I would like to thank my anonymous source from probation who provided interview material on the JTP Boys. All names were changed to provide anonymity. I am a former resident of East Toronto and attended Monarch Park High School.

2. Police youth bureau data courtesy of Barry Clark, executive director, John Howard Society, Windsor/Essex County.

FURTHER READINGS

Department of the Solicitor General. 1993. *Youth Violence and Youth Gangs: Responding to Community Concerns*. Ottawa: Department of the Solicitor General.

Matthews, F. 1993. *Youth Gangs on Yough Gangs*. Ottawa: Department of the Solicitor General.

Spergel, I.A. 1995. *The Youth Gang Problem: A Community Approach*. New York: Oxford University Press.

Visano, L.A. 1987. *This Idle Trade*. Concord: Vitasana.

REFERENCES

Barak, G. 1989. 'Newsmaking Criminology'. *Crime and Social Justice* 2:34–69.

Barber, J. 1989. 'The Swarm'. *Toronto Magazine* (May):19–42.

Bing, L. 1991. *Do or Die*. New York: HarperCollins.

Brake, M. 1985. *The Sociology of Youth Culture and Youth Subcultures*. London: Routledge and Kegan Paul.

Buford, B. 1991. *With the Thugs*. London: Octopus.

Chin, K.L. 1991. 'Chinese Gangs and Extortion'. In *Gangs in America*, edited by J.D. Vigil. New York: Praeger.

Cloward, R.A., and L. Ohlin. 1960. *Delinquency and Opportunity*. New York: Free Press.

Cohen, A.K. 1955. *Delinquent Boys*. New York: Free Press.

Cohen, S. 1973. *Folk Devils and Moral Panics*. London: Penguin.

Dietz, M.L. 1983. *Killing for Profit*. Chicago: Nelson Hall.

Downes, D. 1966. *The Delinquent Solution*. London: Routledge and Kegan Paul.

Ericson, R., et al. 1987. *Visualizing Deviance*. Toronto: University of Toronto Press.

Fleming, T. 1983. 'Mad Dogs, Beasts and Raving Nutters: The Presentation of the Mentally Disabled in the British Press'. In *Deviant Designations: Crime, Law and Deviance in Canada*, edited by T. Fleming and L. Visano, 153–85. Toronto: Butterworths.

Fowler, K. 1989. 'Youth Gangs: Criminals, Thrillseekers or the New Voice of Anarchy?' *The RCMP Gazette* 51, no. 7 and 8:6–9.

Hagedorn, J. 1988. *People and Folks*. Chicago: Lakeview Press.

Huff, R. 1989. 'Youth Gangs and Public Policy'. *Crime and Delinquency* 35:524–37.

Johnstone, J.W. 1983. 'Recruitment to a Youth Gang'. *Youth and Society* 14:281–300.

Klapp, O. 1970. *The Collective Search for Identity*. Toronto: McClelland and Stewart.

Klein, M. 1971. *Street Gangs and Street Workers*. Englewood Cliffs: Prentice-Hall.

Leyton, E. 1979. *The Myth of Delinquency: An Anatomy of Juvenile Nihilism*. Toronto: McClelland and Stewart.

_____. 1986. *Hunting Humans: The Rise of the Modern Multiple Murderer*. Toronto: McClelland and Stewart.

Lewis, S. 1992. *Racism in Ontario*. Toronto: Government Printers.

Maxson, C., et al. 1985. 'Differences Between Gang and Non-gang Homicides'. *Criminology* 23:209–22.

Merton, R. 1968. *Social Theory and Social Structure*. New York: Macmillan.

Miller, W.B. 1981. *Crime by Youth Gangs and Groups in the United States*. Office of Juvenile Justice and Delinquency Prevention, US Department of Justice. Washington, DC: US Government Printing Office.

Moore, J. 1978. *Homeboys: Gangs, Drugs and Prison in the Barrios of Los Angeles*. Philadelphia: Temple University Press.

Murdock, G., and R. McCron. 1973. 'Scoobies, Skins and Contemporary Pop'. *New Society* 23, no. 247.

O'Reilly-Fleming, T. 1993. *Down and Out in Canada: Homeless Canadians*. Toronto: Canadian Scholars.

Orwen, P. 1991. 'Gangs, New Rules Pose Threat to Malls'. *Toronto Star* (4 April):A2.

Smith, L.S. 1978. 'Sexist Assumptions and Female Delinquency'. In *Women, Sexuality and Social Control*, edited by C. Smart and B. Smart. London: Routledge and Kegan Paul.

Sugarman, B. 1967. 'Involvement in Youth Culture, Academic Achievement and Conformity in School'. *British Journal of Sociology* (June):151–64.

Thompson, H.S. 1970. *The Hell's Angeles: A Strange and Terrible Saga*. New York: Ballantine.

Vigil, J.D. 1988. *Barrio Gangs*. Austin: University of Texas Press.

West, G. 1984. *Young Offenders and the State*. Toronto: Butterworths.

Wilson, D. 1978. 'Sexual Codes and Conduct: A Study of Teenage Girls'. In *Women, Sexuality and Social Control*, edited by C. Smart and B. Smart. London: Routledge and Kegan Paul.

Wolf, D. 1991. *The Rebels: A Brotherhood of Outlaw Bikers*. Toronto: University of Toronto Press.

Yablonsky, L. 1963. *The Violent Gang*. New York: Macmillan.

Zevitz, R.G., and S. Takata. 1992. 'Metropolitan Gang Influence and the Emergence of Group Delinquency in a Regional Community'. *Journal of Criminal Justice* 20:93–106.

Part V

Education and Social Control

Studies of the historical construction of social order have documented the emergence of new social institutions, such as the police, an organized judiciary, prisons, poorhouses, schools, and asylums in the late nineteenth century. The social control function of these institutions is now being recognized. According to some, the compulsory education of children in the late nineteenth century was the pinnacle of social control. 'Supervised by its trusty teacher, surrounded by its playground wall, the school was to raise a new race of working people—respectful, cheerful, hardworking, loyal, pacific and religious' (Johnson 1977:91). This final section on the network of social control institutions will discuss the institution of education and the mechanisms by which Canadian children and adolescents are educated through the formal and hidden curriculum in our schools. This conceptualization of the education system as the locus of social control can also enable us to analyse the process whereby class and gender resistance can occur. We can see how opposition, rebellion, and resistance are produced in the everyday world of the classroom and the postsecondary institution.

In Chapter 15, Wotherspoon asks us to consider the system of formal education that specifies rather inflexible duties and obligations for teacher, students, and school administrators. For instance, the classroom is based on formidable rules of control that dictate when students may talk, when they may stand, and even when they may use the washroom. The presumption in the education system is that these rules of control must be maintained before teaching and learning can occur. This chapter on the 'Hidden Curriculum' examines the intentions of such a system by questioning whether the standards of conduct and evaluation are applied universally and fairly, whether all students benefit equally, and whether the standards of conduct and control originate with the more privileged and powerful sectors in society. Ultimately, the chapter addresses the ability of the hidden curriculum to shape educational practices and to determine individual success or failure.

In 'Campus Sex Crime, Journalism, and Social Control', Linda Mahood also asks questions about the hidden curriculum, in this case, in the sexist and homophobic climate of the university campus. Mahood argues that discussions about sexual harassment and sexual violence on Canadian university campuses in the popular press and TV have gone a long way to create increasing social recognition of sexual harassment as detrimental to the individual and society. She asks questions about the meanings of the most notorious incidents ascribed by the various 'witnesses' who are asked to comment in the press. By critically examining the role the media play in the construction of campus sex crimes as a 'special case' of sexual assault and exploring how campus date-rape protesters are treated, Mahood argues that the publicity given to sex crime functions as a warning to those young women who venture into a man's world. The caution is that without protection, a young woman is unable to avoid danger—or to even recognize the danger she is in. Such narratives of sexual danger might be really just another form of social control.

In 'Deviance and Discipline in the Classroom', Randle W. Nelsen examines what happens to female minority (African American, Asian, Aboriginal) and working-class students. He claims that the hidden curriculum grounded in White, middle-class notions about gender, ethnicity, and social class results in the construction of both 'deviance' and 'normalcy' within and outside of schools. The general public frequently perceives the resistance by those students who are defined as 'deviant' as examples of what is wrong with today's schools. By focusing on the social construction of 'deviance' and 'normalcy' via a description of the typical school day and weekend activities of a hypothetical, suburban high school student, Nelsen makes some interesting observations about student resistance to schooling as well as the school authorities' responses to this behaviour.

REFERENCE

Johnson, R. 1977. 'Educating the Educators: "Experts" and the State, 1933-9'. In *Social Control in Nineteenth-Century Britain*, edited by A.P. Donajrodski, 77–107. London: Croom Helm.

—15—

The Hidden Curriculum

Terry Wotherspoon

Discipline and control are central features of formal education. Formal regulations and legislation outline duties and obligations, such as compulsory attendance, that must be adhered to by pupils, teachers, and other school system officials. Students learn early that school rules are paramount; they must sit, stand, talk, keep quiet, eat, change activities, and go to the bathroom according to someone else's schedules and directions rather than when they feel like it. Teachers recognize that they must establish control before they can deal with curricular content and, moreover, that they cannot simply teach what they want to, whenever they want.

There is a general expectation among educational participants that these disciplinary procedures and control measures are essential for education's success as a public good. In a liberal democratic society, formal schooling is valued for giving people opportunities for socio-economic advancement and meaningful participation in social activities. With relatively few exceptions, parents send their children to school not only because they have to, but because they choose to.

Viewed more critically, however, several key questions must be raised about the nature and organization of formal education systems. On what basis are criteria for discipline and control established? Whose standards of success and failure, and proper and improper behaviour, are employed? How fair are these standards and the outcomes of their application? Who benefits and loses in the process? By posing these questions, we begin to draw attention to the complex interplay that connects the ideological and substantive, and overt and covert, dimensions of educational practices and structures. This chapter examines the relationships among these factors, paying particular attention to the role that the 'hidden curriculum' plays in shaping educational practices and outcomes.

THE HIDDEN CURRICULUM

Writers who analyse education systems frequently make a distinction between the formal curriculum and the hidden curriculum. The former refers to the visible, structured aspects of schooling that are offered to students in regular lessons, school activities, and learning materials. The hidden curriculum, by contrast, consists of the informal messages that students receive as a consequence of their everyday experiences in schools. The know-how that students gain about social expectations, interpersonal relationships, authority structures, and school rules and procedures are all part of the hidden curriculum, as are various other mechanisms within schooling that contribute to the perpetuation of social inequalities (Lynch 1989; McLaren 1989: 183–4). What students learn in schools, both explicitly and implicitly, extends far beyond what is officially taught to them. More important, education in its various guises has a contradictory significance for the learner, the school system, and the interplay between schooling and other social structures.

It is sometimes difficult to discern the boundaries between the formal and hidden curricula. Some writers (e.g., McLaren 1989) argue that the hidden curriculum is the result of the unintended consequences of schooling. In practice, though, the hidden curriculum produces both anticipated and unanticipated outcomes. When students are graded on an assignment, for example, they are being evaluated, in accordance with explicit school expectations, on their knowledge about some aspects of the formal curriculum. In the process, however, they also gain important information about such things as how to read and respond to the expectations of specific teachers, how to study for the test rather than to apply their learnings in a broader way, how to rank themselves in relation to other people and groups, and how to anticipate and deal with success or failure.

A question of greater significance concerns the implications of what is transmitted in the hidden curriculum. Structural functionalist analysis, represented by writers like Durkheim (1977), Parsons (1959), Jackson (1968), and Dreeben (1968) contend that schooling, in both its formal and informal manifestations, provides opportunities for students to internalize learned behaviours that are essential for their postschool social life. While functionalists acknowledge that both the formal and informal dimensions of schooling contribute to differential chances of success and failure among the school population, they present social inequalities, along with people's abilities to adapt to unequal socio-economic outcomes, as necessary for the maintenance of a stable social order. Neo-Marxist critics, by contrast, highlight the contradictions between the visible and the hidden dimensions of schooling. Bowles and Gintis (1976), for example, emphasize that the democratic aims of opportunity and equality in education are undermined by the ways in which schools effectively restrict those opportunities and select people for unequal positions within class society. Other writers point out the importance of additional dimensions besides class in educational inequality. Feminist analysis stresses that school curricula and organizational practices contribute both explicitly and implicitly to the subordination of women's experiences and opportunities relative to those of men (Deem 1978; Smith 1991). Similar observations are made of the ways in which educational processes have silenced the voices and perpetuated the oppression of Blacks, Aboriginal peoples, and other racial minorities (Bolaria and Li 1988; Fine 1989). A more fundamental critique of formal education's contribution to social divisions is offered by Foucault (1977, 1979), who argues that schools are part of a wider, integrated network of control in society. For Foucault, all human subjects in advanced societies are regulated by elaborate structures of power and discipline, most predominantly in institutions like schools, prisons, asylums, and workplaces.

Recent analysis of the hidden curriculum, commonly posed in terms of social and educational reproduction, has tended to focus on a number of points of departure arising from critiques of the literature summarized in the previous paragraph. Two issues in particular—the role of the state, and the significance of various forms of struggle and resistance—are most pertinent in this regard (Aronowitz and Giroux 1985; Carnoy and Levin 1985; Lynch 1989; McLaren 1989; Weiler 1988). The first issue emerges from the recognition that educational processes and changes do not operate merely in an abstract way but rather are social practices organized by and through the state. The analysis of what happens in schools can only be understood with reference to the material context and concrete policies regarding schooling. This is related to the second concern, whereby these policies and practices are shaped by and give rise to distinct alignments among various social groups. In the process, qualities like deviance and failure, which are often assumed to be characteristics of individuals, are produced within the framework of social relations, which includes educational relations.

Education often appears to be neutral, but it is affected at every level by different visions about what schools should be, what they are, and how they operate. Under these circumstances, we must recognize that what happens in schools does not always correspond with what is formally planned or with what is intended by any particular interest or group. While policy makers, educational administrators, teachers, students, parents, and other community members may share certain general expectations about the education system, varied participation within the system is likely to yield diverse perceptions and experiences. At the same time, as the critical literature on reproduction and the hidden curriculum makes clear, inequalities in both the structure of opportunity and the distribution of power produce distinct advantages for dominant social interests relative to subordinate groups, whether defined in terms of class, gender, race, or other significant social characteristics (Apple 1986; Carnoy and Levin 1985; Wotherspoon 1991). Viewed as sites organized around social reproduction, schools are characterized by possible contestation over educational practices. Both formal and hidden curricula are subject to change, leaving open the possibility that shifts will occur in the boundaries between what is formally planned and what is not.

The remainder of this chapter explores the nature of the hidden curriculum as a mechanism for social control through its changing relationship with the formal curriculum. These relations are discussed with reference to the major characteristics of public education systems in Canada. The variable nature of the hidden curriculum and its implications for educational practices is outlined briefly through reference to two early periods of educational growth: the promotion of educational objectives that accompanied the rise of mass public schooling in the last half of the nineteenth century, and the use of ideologies of science and professionalism to justify the extension and diversification of formal education in the early twentieth century. The chapter concludes with a discussion of the contradictions inherent in educational expansion following the Second World War.

MASS PUBLIC SCHOOLING AND THE SHAPING OF A NATION

Mass public schooling, from the outset, was an active rather than a passive venture. Its objectives were linked solidly to the goals of political and economic leaders, who sought to mould the character of a new nation. Nineteenth-century North America provided a context in which boundary consolidation, state formation, and eventual industrialization were core features of capitalist expansion. In the midst of these transformations, social reformers placed demands for a state-supported system of mass education at the centre of their political agenda for a stable social order. Prominent educational promoters like Egerton Ryerson in Upper Canada and John Jessop in British Columbia extolled the virtues of a system of common secular schooling that would elevate people, and thereby society, to high levels of civic and intellectual virtue. In order to accomplish those ends, mass public schooling from its inception has been as concerned with regulating character formation among its pupils as with transmitting skills and knowledge to them.

Nineteenth-century school promoters stressed the importance of schooling for the inculcation of proper habits, cleanliness, obedience, and high moral standards (Corrigan, Curtis, and Lanning 1987; McDonald 1978; Prentice 1977; Wotherspoon 1993). Using forums like annual school reports, speeches, and newspaper editorials, educational reformers made continual reference to the need for schooling to provide all children with proper guidance to achieve responsible citizenship. The expectations of students, to be both conveyed and exemplified by teachers, were many, including, in the words of Upper Canada school officials in 1853, cultivation of 'the principles of piety, justice, and a sacred regard to truth, love of their country, humanity and universal benevolence, sobriety, industry, frugality, chastity, moderation and temperance, and those other virtues which are the ornament of society, and on which a free constitution of government is founded' (Upper Canada 1853:170–1). Schools, in other words, were to control and shape the entire person into a new subject, who in turn was a cornerstone for the new nation.

Two factors in these early school reform movements are of significance to an analysis of the hidden curriculum. First, the prominence given to moral and personal discipline within the schooling enterprise reveals that these features were public and intended, within selected parameters, rather than hidden and unintended. The elements that constituted 'proper' subjectivity and morality were encoded into early school legislation and regulations, and references were made to them repeatedly in public documents such as the annual reports of school superintendents and inspectors. Reporting on 'the moral discipline', for instance, Ontario school inspector James McBrien wrote in 1886 that 'In this respect our progress is highly satisfactory to all who are really patriotic', adding that 'the sovereign principle of the whole school discipline' must be founded upon the recognition that 'a direct appeal to [children's] conscience, through their intelligence, is required, and in cultivating its moral aptitude by rendering the right visible to their understanding' (Canada 1886:122).

Although these statements were formally available to all citizens, in practice they were directed towards legislators and public officials whose class, gender, and racial characteristics (literate, petit bourgeois White males) were not representative of the general population. Such social realities constitute the basis for the second feature of early school reform, which concerns the rhetoric of common public schooling. The school promoters' language seductively held out promises of equality that could not be accomplished in practice. For the school reformers, free access to schooling, public participation, and the cultivation of common values were framed within a conception of democracy that was severely restricted, given real constraints on wage labour and other socio-economic opportunities. Schooling was a device to build and stabilize, not radically alter, the bourgeois state and its capitalist foundations. Formal education was premised upon notions of the common good that transcended particular class alignments and other bases of social fragmentation. In an introduction to the revised elementary school course of studies for New Brunswick, Chief Superintendent of Education Theodore Rand wrote in 1880 that,

> The public school is primarily an agency for the general education of all classes of youth. It is a common school, furnishing a common education useful alike to rich and poor, high and low. This primary function of the public school is of the highest practical importance and value. Its comprehensive aim

is to prepare the child to discharge the duties and meet the obligations of coming manhood, including his relations to the family, society, and the State,—relations involving the highest and most important activities of civilized life. The public school assumes that every child that crosses its threshold to receive instruction is to reach mature life and engage in manly duties, and that his first and highest need is to have the elements of manhood within him developed, quickened, energized, and rightly directed (New Brunswick 1881).

In a similar manner, in an address to the Ontario Educational Association in 1898, James G. Hume (1898:233) observes that, in school, the child 'learns the lesson of self-control, self-expression and self-development in devotion to the claims of truth, which is higher than selfishness, higher than mere likings, aversions and individual waywardness and caprice'. Under such conditions, the ideal citizen was to be 'responsible' in a way that did not challenge the existing social and economic order. As McDonald (1978:98) observes, 'The great task of the school, then, was not only to direct intellectual behaviour, but also moral and social behaviour. The safety of the state depended on the "safe" citizen. The ideal state was one in which there was order, stability, and loyalty.'

The notion of cultivating a 'safe' and loyal citizenry is central to the development of formal education. To a large extent, schools have been concerned with reconciling demands for unity within a diverse population. Common or public schooling became important in the nineteenth century precisely because it could stand as a basis from which to cultivate allegiance to the state or the public interest. Although founded upon principles of Christian morality, public schooling was to be secular rather than subject to the influence of particular denominational dogmas. As a state institution, free schooling could counteract the stifling effects of illiteracy and ignorance as well as the fragmenting impact of private education intended to serve narrow constituencies. Organized within the public domain, schooling could be managed by a hierarchy of officials who monitored school activities but who at the same time remained politically and administratively responsible. In the words of the Sicotte Committee on education in Lower Canada, 'Surveillance ought to exist everywhere, and on the spot' (Legislative Assembly of Canada 1852–3). Public schooling, once it was extended to everyone, would, more than was possible within any other institutional setting, bring together boys and girls of many diverse class, racial, ethnic, and regional backgrounds.

Claims to such unity, and adherence to a higher order, privileged particular sets of values and interests to the detriment of others. School promoters could speak confidently about the virtues of public education because they had a sympathetic audience of people who shared their class and political interests. The labouring masses and opponents of public schooling, by contrast, could be portrayed in condescending and patronizing terms as uncivilized and unrefined, and therefore in need of moral and intellectual guidance (Corrigan, Curtis, and Lanning 1987). Excluded from regular channels of bourgeois political discourse, they were the objects rather than the subjects of educational policy making and schooling practice. The hidden curriculum, in this context, did not operate so much as an unintended or obscured mechanism of control. Rather, its effectiveness lay in its ability to secure the legitimacy of the social structure through the organization of the schooling system.

HIDDEN FEATURES OF THE CURRICULUM: SCIENCE AND EDUCATIONAL EXPANSION

In the late nineteenth and early twentieth centuries, the size and diversity of school clientele expanded amidst population expansion, particularly in urban areas, and industrialization. In the process, schools were subjected to several conflicting pressures. School enrolments were boosted, taking on a new character through increased immigration, settlement, and stabilization of families. Nationally, public elementary and secondary school enrolment nearly doubled, from 943,000 in 1890 to over 1.8 million in 1920, while the percentage of average daily attendance in schools rose from 62.2 per cent of total enrolment to 72.7 per cent over the same period (Leacy 1983:W67–8). Industrial growth altered the social and economic life of large segments of the Canadian population, with shifting patterns of employment and altered work processes demanding new household divisions of labour and child care arrangements.

Formal schooling was increasingly regarded as an agency through which to accommodate social stability amidst the changed relationships within and among industry, community, and household. New demands were placed upon the curriculum to provide skills and knowledge appropriate to the requirements of an industrial society. More important, however, the realm of the hidden curriculum expanded to incorporate disciplinary control that extended beyond schooling.

The success of schooling began to be linked with the cultivation of ties with and discipline over parents. Compulsory attendance legislation insured that parents would be held responsible for sending their children to school. School administrators encouraged teachers to give homework assignments to pupils so that parents would be aware of and become involved in school lessons. Parental visitations, home and school associations, and other social liaisons were promoted by education officials to insure that community members would be committed to the goals and practices of the education system.

One of the most powerful tools that educators employed to promote the notion that schooling was superior to home and family influences was the use of ideologies of science and professionalism. Curricular planning and pedagogical practice were to be oriented to elevating individual capacities to their fullest potential. Behavioural science advanced in the service of these ends, premised upon the notion that child development and learning behaviour were complex processes that could only be revealed by systematic analysis. The supposition that only knowledge that had a scientific basis was valid created a separation between two realms in which research findings were given precedence over commonsense perceptions. Scientific knowledge was the domain of the trained professional, not something that was accessible to the layperson. Educational organization and delivery, in other words, were represented by educational authorities as matters that were too important to risk being left to the haphazard discretion of untrained employees.

It was crucial, if the goals to advance science and professionalism in education were to be fulfilled, for schools to be staffed with a complement of appropriately trained teachers. By the early years of the twentieth century, most jurisdictions across Canada increased the qualifications for teacher certification and required beginning teachers to attend a minimum of several weeks at Normal Schools to learn about the art and craft of teaching. Educational administrators stressed the necessity of such training both for its practical importance and the confidence that it would inspire in teachers to demonstrate their professional credibility. As the principal of the Vancouver Normal School emphasized in 1905, the trained teacher 'may train parents by assuming that they are anxious to have their children do the right thing in all matters', and must 'never allow parents to dictate to teacher on professional matters' (BCTF 1926:29). Subsequent modifications in teacher education extended the rational or scientific basis of teaching and classroom management by the introduction of training in psychology and child development, the application of scientific management to curriculum design and classroom organizational principles, and reliance upon standardized testing to measure pupil intelligence and achievement (Johnson 1964; Muir 1968).

These initiatives to professionalize teaching and organize schooling according to scientific principles were not always successful. Teachers, regardless of how they were trained, tended to retain considerable autonomy in their classrooms. The hiring of teachers and the acquisition of school resources were often governed more by immediate needs and inadequate funding than by adherence to any grander objectives. Classrooms were frequently staffed with unqualified or underqualified teachers, and teachers, both through their own professional organizations and in more informal ways, frequently resisted the imposition of rules and regulations by school administrators (Danylewycz, Light, and Prentice 1991; Warburton 1986).

Regardless of their success, struggles for the professionalization of teaching and the establishment of a scientific base within schooling had a significant and contradictory impact on the hidden curriculum. The planning process and the principles that underlay it assumed a growing importance in relation to the classroom. The means to accomplish social control were increasingly centralized in the hands of professionals and managers, whose legitimacy depended upon their claims to and ability to mystify scientific expertise. Lasch (1977:15) argues that, 'Educators, psychiatrists, social workers, and penologists saw themselves as doctors to a sick society, and they demanded the broadest possible delegation of medical authority in order to heal it.' Whereas school reformers in the nineteenth century were able to present their visions of schooling in a direct manner, at least to state officials and teachers, the discourse of science mediated the messages that were transmitted through the schooling process. Educational processes were no longer concerned primarily with direct inputs such as 'the teacher' and 'the lesson'. Instead, emphasis was placed on the rational organization of schooling through lesson planning and systematic classroom management. The extension of training and professional status made teachers accomplices in these endeavours, at the same time as teaching itself was subject to technical reorganization as an input into an ever more complex school bureaucracy.

Driven by the logic of bureaucratic organization and scientific knowledge, schools placed increasing emphasis upon norms of achievement and proper conduct. School rules and evaluation procedures, under the guise of a scientific basis, could be applied universally to all pupils, thereby providing an apparently objective mechanism for differentiating between 'good' students (high achievers who engaged in behaviour that conformed to school rules) and failures and 'deviants'. In addition, consistent with the medical analogy observed by Lasch, the mandate of schools now extended beyond simply sorting and preparing students in a general way to managing and correcting deviant behaviour. Schools became a vital social agency for insuring that human resources were nurtured to their fullest potential. The schools, facilitated by the work of teachers, became parents and police officers charged with the duty to send well-regulated, properly functioning young citizens into the labour force and other social institutions.

THE HIDDEN CONTRADICTIONS OF DEMOCRATIC EDUCATION

Several changes to schooling throughout the twentieth century have altered both the appearance and the character of formal education in many ways. These have included shifts towards larger comprehensive and centralized schools; more curricular subjects and extracurricular activities; the introduction of alternative supervisory, pedagogical, and disciplinary techniques; and the involvement of community and parental resources as well as professionals other than teachers in the schools. As the curriculum has become more diverse than ever before, the range of educational activities has achieved greater prominence and visibility. Schooling has become public in the dual sense that it is widely accessible to the general population and that school-based practices are open to scrutiny and input through democratic participation. However, in common with nineteenth-century school reforms, contemporary educational reform is guided by formal notions of equity and democratic participation that are not realized in a substantive sense. Through both overt control structures and features of the hidden curriculum, there are still limits to the extent to which members of different social groups are able to benefit equally from educational expansion.

One area of educational change in which there is substantial overlap between the formal and hidden curricula is the practice of streaming. Students are channelled both formally and informally into distinct ability groups and learning programs. Streaming practices range from organizing students within a classroom into working groups according to their observed achievement and pace of learning, dividing pupils within a single grade or level in larger schools into streamed forms or classes, and separating students (especially at the high school level) into schools that specialize in vocational, technical, or academic programs. Streaming arrangements appear to satisfy two of the main objectives of liberal democratic education: equal opportunity and recognition of individual differences. Each educational stream or group increases the availability of educational services with an array of programs tailored to meet the varied requirements and interests of individual pupils. It seems unfair and wasteful, for example, for a student planning a career in the automotive industry to have to take classes oriented to university preparation.

In practice, however, streaming has many contradictory and unequal consequences (Curtis, Livingstone, and Smaller 1992). Since the Second World War, Canadians overall, and members of minority groups in particular, have experienced steadily increasing levels of educational attainment and higher rates of enrolment in postsecondary educational institutions. While these trends suggest that there has been a democratization of education, there are still serious inequalities in access to and completion of educational programs among major social groups (Wotherspoon 1991). Women, for example, have made significant inroads into non-traditional areas of study, notably constituting a majority of recent graduates of university programs, but they are still concentrated in educational programs that lead to relatively unrewarding career prospects or are related to traditional women's pursuits arising from domestic work and child care (Gaskell and McLaren 1992). With a few exceptions, racial minorities, especially Aboriginal peoples, also have lower than average levels of educational attainment and are underrepresented in important postsecondary educational programs (Li 1988; Satzewich and Wotherspoon 1993).

Inequalities in educational outcomes are the consequence of a complex set of factors, including variations in school funding and resources as well as individual factors and structural inequalities that transcend schooling. They are, though, at least partially enhanced and reinforced through common practices in the classroom. Teachers attempt to control the flow of activities and information, often in ways that privilege some learners over others. Teachers' actions, in turn, are embedded within a framework of regulations and curricular guidelines that shape what is regarded as acceptable in the classroom.

Emphasis on these curricular and participatory aspects of education draws our attention to the everyday details of schooling activities, which, nonetheless, cannot be made sense of without exploring deeper connections between the hidden and visible curricula. Four interrelated factors in particular are important in this regard: (1) the compartmentalization of knowledge, (2) the assessment of the individual, (3) the notion of cultural capital, and (4) the exclusion of spheres of activity from classroom discourse.

First, while schools are overtly concerned with the transmission of knowledge, we must ask crucial questions about the nature of that knowledge. Curricula that emphasize the presentation of factual information as opposed to material that represents particular values tend to be based upon uncritical examinations of what we assume facts to be and how the material was selected. Critical analyses of the curriculum, notably by writers who concerned themselves in the 1970s and early 1980s with what they called 'the new sociology of education', have drawn attention to the ways in which the curriculum distinguishes between school knowledge regarded as valid or legitimate and that which is not recognized as such (see, e.g., Gorbutt 1972; Whitty 1985; Young 1971). All science, for example, emerges from particular assumptions about the nature of the world and how we come to know that world. Curricula, in this regard, can never be neutral or inevitable. Instead, they are constructed by a conscious selection of alternative images, ideas, and resources. Moreover, as presented to the student, the various elements of the curriculum tend to be fragmented into discrete subjects represented by distinct blocks of time and, commonly, space. Consequently, students experience these representations in different ways, depending in part on their pre-existing knowledge and the skills that they acquire in the schooling process to manage the everyday realities of formal education.

This cultural capital, or sensitivity towards what is important and the know-how to manoeuvre successfully through the routine demands of schools and other social institutions, is an important feature of the hidden curriculum. School-based activities commonly proceed from an assumption that such knowledge is common-sensory, something that we all possess or have the means to acquire. In fact, however, as a significant body of literature attests, both the presuppositions behind and the content of cultural capital serve the interests of the dominant classes in reproducing unequal class, gender, and racial structures (Apple 1986; Bernstein 1977; Bourdieu and Passeron 1977). Schooling is about form as well as content. Schools validate particular kinds of experience, relegating alternative ways of knowing and doing things to the margins. Reminiscent of nineteenth-century reformers' concerns about the nurturing of proper habit, what counts is often not so much what is accomplished as the way in which it is accomplished.

By emphasizing both achievement and process, schools send contradictory messages to students. Students must learn to operate at both levels. Formal evaluation and reporting procedures come to be expected as part of the curriculum as methods of ranking and charting student progress. Students may variously resist or accept their relative standings, but they know that grades count as indicators of success or failure. At the same time, an emphasis on form and process opens up all dimensions of the individual to external scrutiny and assessment. Not just performance on specific activities such as an examination or written assignment, but the whole personality, from social interaction to personal habits and hygiene, becomes subject to evaluation. Within what Bernstein (1977) calls 'invisible pedagogies', or relatively unstructured teacher-supervised educational practices, several dimensions of the learner's behaviour are exposed without explicit awareness of how he or she is being evaluated. Therefore, steps in the direction of what appear to be progressive educational innovations may potentially extend control over the individual. This process, in comparison with evaluation based upon more readily apparent or universalistic standards, may help to explain parents' uneasiness in situations where formal grades have been replaced by anecdotal observations on student report cards. There is also, as proponents of the cultural capital thesis stress, a built-in bias because students from White, middle-class families are likely to be better equipped than students from other backgrounds for learning and evaluative situations organized around invisible pedagogies.

The curriculum, in these respects, is as important for what it excludes as for the elements it contains. Formal curriculum guidelines, the texts and materials employed in the classroom, and the organization of classroom activities all contribute to what, at best, is a partial representation of reality and, at worst, shuts out or undermines important knowledge bases. Only over the past two decades have educators become sensitized, for instance, to the racial and gender stereotypes that pervade textbooks and learning resources. School curricula frequently have ignored the contributions of women, Blacks, Aboriginal peoples, and the labouring classes to history and literature. Even recent attempts to redress these shortcomings through initiatives such as multiculturalism and cultural sensitivity training have often been patronizing and even racist through narrow, decontextualized images that tend to treat culture as static traditions rather than as diverse, changing modes of adaptation.

Social and cultural vantage points that do not meet established school norms are also undermined by routine classroom practices. Teachers commonly adopt many different strategies under the guise of 'sticking to the curriculum' or maintaining classroom order that regulate the exchange of information within the learning process. Students learn to recognize, from both overt and subtle cues, that official curricula and school structures count more than information that may be of direct interest or relevance to them. Fine (1989) refers to the practice of 'silencing', whereby discussion about matters that are critical of official educational ideologies is 'subverted, appropriated, and exported'. There is a systematic denial of opportunities, especially for minority students, to assess their place in school and its relation to the general social world. Insights that could potentially become critical and liberating are lost to a likely future of continued subordination.

Formal education, in this sense, tends not to be reflexive since schooling is presented and experienced by its participants as something to do rather than something to look at or analyse in itself. However, the experiential aspects of school are limited even further by supervisory practices and disciplinary procedures that regulate spheres of activity. In the classroom, the hallway, and on the playground, behaviours are channelled into directions regarded officially as legitimate. Classroom discussions, for instance, are expected to be to the point, thereby frequently shutting off opportunities for debate about controversial matters or alternative approaches to a subject (McLaren 1989). Similarly, informal conversation between pupils in and out of the classroom often provides a vital exchange of knowledge and information that tends to be discouraged or discounted in the formal curriculum.

These examples, of course, do not fit every classroom situation. Effective teachers frequently draw out students' conversations to clarify the linkages between pupils' social realities and more formal learning objectives. Schools also produce experiences through field trips, artistic presentations, and audio-visual aids that students might not otherwise encounter. Nonetheless, even these activities are often part of a process whereby schools co-opt or appropriate elements from particular environments to repackage them for pupils in forms deemed socially responsible by educators and curriculum planners.

STUDENT RESISTANCE AND THE CONSTRUCTION OF DEVIANCE

This chapter has been concerned primarily with the organization, delivery, and impact of the official and hidden curricula. This concluding section offers a brief commentary on the importance of student reaction and resistance to the social control dimensions of the curriculum.

Student resistances take many forms, ranging from simple withdrawal (as a response to boredom, for example) to defiance and overt rejection of school authority and curricula. The diverse nature and meaning of student resistance are discussed extensively by several writers (see, e.g., Connell et al. 1982; McLaren 1989; McRobbie 1978; Weis 1990; Willis 1977). What is significant from the perspective of an analysis of the hidden curriculum is that social control is not only built into the school curriculum but socially produced within the schooling process through interaction among the various educational participants.

If we assume that formal education is intended to promote personal growth and intellectual development, then we might conclude that schools employ different modes of social control to insure that opportunities for educational benefits are distributed widely and equitably. We have observed, on the other hand, various practices and mechanisms that contribute to the reproduction of social inequalities through the education system. The conditions that foster reproduction, moreover, are problematic as they are open to contestation and change. Student resistance, and the ways in which schools respond to it, constitute part of the contestation process.

The formal curriculum is based upon the expectation that students will conform to official school rules and procedures. As we have seen, adherence to school policies is reinforced at several levels, from teachers' classroom management practices to formal disciplinary action taken or authorized by educational administrators and school boards. The primary goal of these controls is to maintain order in the classroom and school system so as to focus the students' attention on the learning opportunities they are presented with, however unrealistic or irrelevant they may be. Because of this concern for order, a pupil's lack of attentiveness to the curriculum, either by withdrawing or engaging in alternative activities, tends to be regarded by teachers and educational authorities as a failure within the individual student rather than as a symptom of inadequacy within the school itself. The deviant, maladjusted, or learning-disabled student, not the lived circumstances that produced particular activities as rational responses, becomes the focus of official educational problem solving.

As sites that contribute to the accomplishment of social control, schools are not oriented in a strict sense with the achievement of conformity. Instead, schools operate in a contradictory way to produce conditions that foster both social harmony and social diversity. Formal education provides opportunities for participation and socio-economic advancement, but it does so in such a way as to reproduce fundamental social inequalities. The formal curriculum announces publicly the divergent school objectives, which in turn are managed (sometimes in concert with, and at other times in contrast to) the stated school aims. These contradictions are experienced and responded to by students in different ways, often to the detriment of learners from disadvantaged or marginalized backgrounds.

FURTHER READINGS

Apple, M.W. 1986. *Teachers and Texts: A Political Economy of Class and Gender Relations in Education*. New York: Routledge and Kegan Paul.

Gaskell, J., and A. McLaren, eds. 1991. *Women and Education*, 2nd ed. Calgary: Detselig Enterprises.

Lynch, K., 1989. *The Hidden Curriculum: Reproduction in Education, an Appraisal*. London: The Falmer Press.

McLaren, P. 1989. *Life in Schools: An Introduction to Critical Pedagogy in the Foundations of Education*. Toronto: Irwin Publishing.

Weis, L. 1990. *Working Class Without Work: High School Students in a De-industrializing Economy*. New York: Routledge and Kegan Paul.

REFERENCES

Apple, M.W. 1986. *Teachers and Texts: A Political Economy of Class and Gender Relations in Education*. New York: Routledge and Kegan Paul.

Aronowitz, S., and H. Giroux. 1985. *Education under Siege: The Conservative, Liberal and Radical Debate over Schooling*. South Hadley, Mass.: Bergin & Garvey.

Bernstein, B. 1977. 'Class and Pedagogies: Visible and Invisible'. In *Power and Ideology in Education*, edited by J. Karabel and A.H. Halsey, 511–34. New York: Oxford University Press.

Bolaria, S., B. Singh, and P.S. Li, eds. 1988. *Racial Oppression in Canada*, 2nd ed. Toronto: Garamond Press.

Bourdieu, P., and J.C. Passeron. 1977. *Reproduction in Education, Society, and Culture*. Beverly Hills: Sage Publications.

Bowles, S., and H. Gintis. 1976. *Schooling in Capitalist America: Educational Reform and the Contradictions of Economic Life*. New York: Basic Books.

BCTF (BC Teachers' Federation). 1926. 'Voices from the Past'. *The B.C. Teacher* 6, no. 4:27–33.

Canada. 1886. 'Extract from Report of James McBrien'. Canada *Sessional Papers* 5 A1886:122–3.

Carnoy, M., and H.M. Levin. 1985. *Schooling and Work in the Democratic State*. Stanford: Stanford University Press.

Connell, R.W., et al. 1982. *Making the Difference: Schools, Families and Social Division*. Sydney: George Allen & Unwin.

Corrigan, P., B. Curtis, and R. Lanning. 1987. 'The Political Space of Schooling'. In *The Political Economy of Canadian Schooling*, edited by T. Wotherspoon, 21–43. Toronto: Methuen.

Curtis, B., D.W. Livingstone, and H. Smaller. 1992. *Stacking the Deck: The Streaming of Working-Class Kids in Ontario Schools*. Toronto: Our Schools/Our Selves Education Foundation.

Danylewycz, M., B. Light, and A. Prentice. 1991. 'The Evolution of the Sexual Division of Labor in Teaching: A Nineteenth-Century Ontario and Quebec Case Study'. In *Women and Education*, 2nd ed., edited by J. Gaskell and A. McLaren, 33–60. Calgary: Detselig Enterprises.

Deem, R. 1978. *Women and Schooling*. London: Routledge and Kegan Paul.

Dreeben, R. 1968. *On What Is Learned in School*. Reading, Mass.: Addison-Wesley.

Durkheim, E. 1977. *The Evolution of Educational Thought*. New York: Routledge and Kegan Paul.

Fine, M. 1989. 'Silencing and Nurturing Voice in an Improbable Context: Urban Adolescents in Public School'. In *Critical Pedagogy, the State, and Cultural Struggle*, edited by H.A. Giroux and P. McLaren, 152–73. Albany: State University of New York Press.

Foucault, M. 1977. *Discipline and Punish: The Birth of the Prison*. New York: Pantheon.

———. 1979. *Power, Truth, and Strategy*. Sydney: Feral Publications.

Gaskell, J., and A. McLaren, eds. 1992. *Women and Education*, 2nd ed. Calgary: Detselig Enterprises.

Gorbutt, D. 1972. 'The New Sociology of Education'. *Education for Teaching* 89:3–11.

Hume, J.G. 1898. 'Moral Training in Public Schools'. *Proceedings*, 233–4. Toronto: Ontario Educational Association.

Jackson, P.W. 1968. *Life in Classrooms*. New York: Holt, Rinehart and Winston.

Johnson, F.H. 1964. *A History of Public Education in British Columbia*. Vancouver: University of British Columbia Publications Centre.

Lasch, C. 1977. *Haven in a Heartless World: The Family Besieged*. New York: Basic Books.

Leacy, F.H. 1983. *Historical Statistics of Canada*, 2nd ed. Ottawa: Statistics Canada.

Legislative Assembly of Canada. 1852–3. 'Report of the Select Committee Appointed to Inquire into the State of Education in Lower Canada'. *Journals of the Legislative Assembly of Canada* 1852–3, Appendix J.J.

Li, P.S. 1988. *Ethnic Inequality in a Class Society*. Toronto: Wall & Thompson.

Lynch, K. 1989. *The Hidden Curriculum: Reproduction in Education, an Appraisal*. London: The Falmer Press.

McDonald, N. 1978. 'Egerton Ryerson and the School as an Agent of Political Socialization'. In *Egerton Ryerson and His Times*, edited by N. McDonald and A. Chaiton, 81–106. Toronto: Macmillan.

McLaren, P. 1989. *Life in Schools: An Introduction to Critical Pedagogy in the Foundations of Education*. Toronto: Irwin Publishing.

McRobbie, A. 1978. 'Working Class Girls and the Culture of Femininity'. In *Women Take Issue*, edited by the Centre for Contemporary Cultural Studies Women's Group, 96–108. London: Hutchinson.

Muir, J.D. 1968. *Collective Bargaining by Canadian Public School Teachers*. Task Force on Labour Relations Study no. 21. Ottawa: Information Canada.

New Brunswick. 1881. 'Report of the Chief Superintendent of Education for the Year 1880'. *Journals of the Legislative Assembly of New Brunswick.* Fredericton: Province of New Brunswick.

Parsons, T. 1959. 'The School Class as a Social System: Some of Its Functions'. *Harvard Educational Review* 29, no. 4:297–318.

Prentice, A. 1977. *The School Promoters: Education and Social Class in Mid-Nineteenth Century Upper Canada.* Toronto: McClelland and Stewart.

Satzewich, V., and T. Wotherspoon. 1993. *First Nations: Race, Class and Gender Relations.* Toronto: Nelson.

Smith, D.E. 1991. 'An Analysis of Ideological Structures and How Women Are Excluded: Considerations for Academic Women'. In *Women and Education*, 2nd ed., edited by J. Gaskell and A. McLaren, 233–56. Calgary: Detselig Enterprises.

Upper Canada. 1853. *Annual Report of the Normal, Model, Grammar and Common Schools in Upper Canada for the Year 1853*, Appendix One, Regulations.

Warburton, R. 1986. 'The Class Relations of Public School Teachers in British Columbia'. *The Canadian Review of Sociology and Anthropology* 23, no. 2:210–29.

Weiler, K. 1988. *Women Teaching for Change: Gender, Class & Power.* New York: Bergin & Garvey.

Weis, L. 1990. *Working Class Without Work: High School Students in a De-industrializing Economy.* New York: Routledge and Kegan Paul.

Whitty, G. 1985. *Sociology and School Knowledge: Curriculum Theory, Research and Politics.* London: Methuen.

Willis, P. 1977. *Learning to Labor: How Working Class Kids Get Working Class Jobs.* New York: Columbia University Press.

Wotherspoon, T. 1991. 'Educational Reorganization and Retrenchment'. In *Hitting the Books: The Politics of Educational Retrenchment*, edited by T. Wotherspoon, 15–34. Toronto: Garamond Press.

_____. 1993. 'From Subordinate Partners to Dependent Employees: State Regulation of Public School Teachers in Nineteenth Century British Columbia'. *Labour/Le Travail* 31 (Spring):75–110.

Young, M.F.D. 1971. 'An Approach to the Study of Curricula as Socially Organized Knowledge'. In *Knowledge and Control*, edited by M.F.D. Young, 19–47. London: Collier-Macmillan.

—16—

Campus Sex Crime, Journalism, and Social Control

Linda Mahood

> It was weeks before I could grasp that this man was definitely following me and staring at me ... At first I thought I must be overreacting. But he was always there. I became so uncomfortable that I changed my swim times, first to weekends, then to lunch time. But it wasn't long before he showed up too (*Toronto Star*, 20 Jan. 1990a, F1).

> The [University Sexual Harassment] board is dominated by people identified too closely to the feminist movement and is therefore unable to differentiate between leering at women and looking at them (*Globe and Mail*, 9 Jan. 1990a, A3).

These two quotes illustrate two opposing perceptions of the same incident. The first is a statement by the female engineering student who, in 1990, complained that she was being leered at by a professor at the University of Toronto swimming-pool. The second quote is by the accused sixty-year-old chemical engineering professor, whom journalists nicknamed 'the frogman'. The professor responded that the charge of sexual harassment was ridiculous. He lashed out at the student and called the special university committee appointed to investigate the allegation a 'kangaroo court' (*Globe and Mail*, 9 Jan. 1990a, A3). Three lifeguards testified that the professor's staring was 'obvious, prolonged and troublesome'. They recalled occasions when he 'stared so hard at women walking on the deck that he actually bumped into pillars' (*Toronto Star*, 20 Jan. 1990a, F1). These lifeguards, the aquatics director, and the complainant herself all confronted the professor, but he did not stop. In his defence, a female colleague of the professor testified that she played squash regularly with him and never felt uncomfortable. She 'accused some of the women students who testified against him of being vindictive and heading a witch hunt' (*Globe and Mail*, 9 Jan. 1990a, A3). The sexual harassment committee determined that the act of donning swim goggles and following swimsuit-clad females around the pool constituted 'offensive star-ing' because the behaviour was intimidating and hostile.

Laughable, sad, or frightening, the media reporting of cases such as this has become increasingly common over the past decade, as newspapers, maga-zines, radio, and television talk shows have publicly linked certain time-honoured university traditions, such as Lady Godiva rides and dorm raids, with cases of sexual and gender harassment, physical and sexual violence, and homophobia. This chapter examines the social control implications of one aspect of campus culture, which I shall call 'campus sex crime', as it has been played out in the print media. This will be accomplished through a systematic content analysis of newspaper coverage of sexual assault and ha-rassment cases on Canadian campuses. The goal is to examine two impor-tant questions. First, the question of whether the media plays a role in the construction of campus sex crimes will be raised by examining the sources they use as 'experts' when reporting a case. And second, what are the social control implications for the staff, students, and faculty who work and study at these institutions?

'FRIENDLY' RUBS, PATS, AND HUGS: DEFINING SEXUAL HARASSMENT

Sexual harassment may be seen as a form of sex discrimination, a subtle form that 'demoralizes as well as undermines [a recipient's] attempts for equality and opportunity in work and at school' (McDaniel and van Roosmalen 1991:4). Sexual harassment includes a range of behaviours from sexually suggestive comments to overt demands for sexual favours and forced sexual relations—what generations of students refer to as 'an "A" for a lay'. Monique Frize (1993) argues that while sexual harassment might occur in a single episode, it is more accurately conceptualized as a process. It frequently oc-curs on a 'continuum of intimacy', where a harasser might be warm and empathetic one day and cold and threatening the next. She has identified five types of harassment: sexual, personal, gender, racial, and velvet glove. People who work and study at universities can be victims of any of these. Sexual harassment can include such subtle conduct as 'friendly' rubs, pats, and hugs; dirty jokes and sexual innuendoes; and less subtle forms such as displays of pin-up pornography, leering, and verbal abuse. For instance, many professors have used sexist humour to liven up their lectures; an anatomy professor might end a slide show with a slide of a woman's buttocks with 'the end' inscribed upon it. In 1990, the *Calgary Herald* reported that five professors of medicine had been charged with sexual harassment and gross professional misconduct. An internal investigation found that three of the professors were guilty of 'inappropriate behaviour' and contributing to a 'sexually offensive workplace' (*Calgary Herald*, 30 Aug. 1990c, B1; 12 Sept.

1990e, B1). Two female medical students testified that the professors joked about the size of the female students' breasts, distributed pornographic material, hosted drinking parties in their labs, and used the tub for testing body temperatures as a party toy: 'They filled [the tub] with water and climbed in fully clothed. The breasts of women students thrown into the tub were photographed through their wet clothing and the photos were posted on the lab bulletin board' (*Calgary Herald*, 17 Feb. 1990b, A1). Three male medical students admitted that they too 'felt pressure to participate in sexual games that exploited female students' (*Calgary Herald*, 17 Feb. 1990b, A1).

Personal, gender, and racial harassment are also often linked to lifestyle choices, such as derogatory or degrading sexual remarks directed towards members of one's gender or ethnic group, or one's sexual preference group, for example, singling out women of colour or homosexuals. Velvet-glove harassment is a form of paternalism that suggests women are too delicate and feminine to do 'men's work'. While it appears chivalrous, the result is that women, especially those in traditionally 'male' faculties, are denied work and study-related opportunities, such as field work, that are essential to their preprofessional training and career advancement.

There are certain difficulties in developing a comprehensive definition of sexual harassment. For example, harassing behaviour is not always different from other actions. Depending on the social context and the situation of the people involved, putting one's arm around someone may be perceived as harassment or as a friendly gesture (Hornosty 1986:19). While lustful glances may be naughty and exciting when they are mutual, what distinguishes sexual attraction from harassment is that it is 'one-sided, unwanted and comes with strings attached' (Hornosty 1986:19; *Toronto Star*, 20 Jan. 1990a, F1). In the university environment, it occurs in a context of unequal power and authority and is experienced as a threat to one's work, education, or recreational activities. Sexual harassment can also occur between people of the same status: student-student, faculty-faculty or staff-staff. While sexual harassment complaints are not necessarily gender specific, to date women are considered to be the most vulnerable and 95 per cent of the charges have been laid by women against men (Frize 1993).

In 1982, the Canadian Association of University Teachers drew up guidelines to prohibit sexual harassment. These guidelines, upon which many Canadian universities base their own policies, define sexual harassment broadly in the following way. Sexual advances, requests for sexual favours, and other verbal or physical conduct of a sexual nature constitute sexual harassment when (a) submission to such conduct is made either explicitly or implicitly a term or condition of an individual's employment, academic status, or academic accreditation; (b) submission to or rejection of such conduct by an individual is used as the basis for employment, academic status, or academic accreditation decisions affecting him or her; or (c) such conduct has the purpose or effect of unreasonably interfering with an individual's work or academic performance or creating an intimidating, hostile, or offensive working or academic environment (Hornosty 1986:19).

In sum, sexual harassment is unsolicited, non-reciprocal behaviour that asserts a person's sex role over his or her role as a worker or student. Sexual assault is any unwanted act of a sexual nature. The act of sexual assault ranges from forced kissing to forced intercourse. It is estimated that 68.5 to 83 per cent of women who are sexually assaulted know their assailant. In a 1987 survey of women with disabilities, 67 per cent of those surveyed said they had been physically or sexually assaulted as children. This number is twice as high as that for non-disabled women (Haberman, Sardi, Morton 1992). In Canada sexual assault, sexual assault with a weapon or causing bodily harm, and aggravated sexual assault are criminal offences under sections 271, 272, and 273 of the Criminal Code. They carry maximum penalties of ten years to life imprisonment. Sexual harassment is also illegal and is contrary to the Human Rights Act and should be reported to the Human Rights Commission.

CAMPUS SEX CRIME: A SPECIAL CASE OF SEXUAL ASSAULT

In this research, 'campus sex crime' refers to a continuum of behaviours ranging from the extreme of physical sexual assault and date and acquaintance rape, coercive and non-coercive intimidation through threats and bribery, to verbal and non-verbal insults between students, staff, and faculty on Canadian campuses. Since the late 1980s, several widely publicized cases of sexual and gender harassment and physical and sexual violence on Canadian campuses have propelled the issue of 'campus sex crime' onto the front pages of newspapers and popular magazines, as the following examples illustrate. In 1988, an issue of *Maclean's* magazine reported that on 22 September, a McGill University fraternity called Zita Psi was holding one of its notorious parties. The occasion was in honour of the female rugby team, which was initiating twenty of its rookies. As part of their initiation, the young women were required to obtain male signatures on their stomachs. At 8:00 they arrived at the packed fraternity house, where they were treated to all the beer they could drink. The male rugby team had twenty-five of its own initiates pay a naked visit to the party. Later, a nineteen-year-old initiate of the female team told a reporter that 'she was sexually assaulted by three men while as many as ten others looked on' (*Maclean's*, 31 Oct. 1988, 56).

At Wilfrid Laurier University in late September 1989, the *Toronto Star* reported that first-year male students raided a women's dormitory. The next morning, students arriving for breakfast in the main dining hall were astounded to see walls plastered with crude, hand-painted posters flaunting women's underpants, some of which had been decorated with ketchup and other gunk to represent blood and feces. Each panty was captioned. One example: 'Do you take VISA?' The *Toronto Star* journalist claimed that other insults were 'too gross to be repeated here' (*Toronto Star*, 25 Oct. 1989, cited in Wise Harris 1991:38).

Three months later, on 6 December 1989, a twenty-five-year-old man named Marc Lepine entered L'Ecole Polytechnique de l'Université de Montréal. He entered an engineering class and ordered the women and men to opposite sides of the room. He is reported to have yelled at the female students: 'You're women! You're going to be engineers! You're all a bunch of feminists! I hate feminists!' When he left the classroom, he shot six women dead with his semiautomatic rifle. He then rampaged through other parts of the building, shooting women and screaming. By the time he turned the rifle on himself, fourteen women were dead. Many survivors later re-called that it was the last day of classes before final exams and they initially thought Lepine's hunting gear, rifle, and orders were part of a 'prank'; some even laughed. The contents of a suicide note found on his body was revealed on 25 November 1990 and reprinted in *La Presse*. Lepine wrote:

> ... if I commit suicide today 89-12-06 it is not for economic reasons ... but for political reasons. Because I have decided to send the feminists, who have al-ways ruined my life to their Maker ... I have decided to put an end to those viragos ... Even if the Mad Killer epithet will be attributed to me by the media, I consider myself a rational erudite ... the feminists have always enraged me. They want to keep the advantages of women ... while seizing for themselves those of men (Mallette and Chalouh 1991:180).

Clearly, what we now call the 'Montreal massacre' is an extremely com-plex case of misogyny, but everyday cases of harassment continue on Cana-dian campuses, as the following examples of student-student harassment illustrate. On 11 October 1990 at the University of British Columbia, thirty fraternity brothers from Caribou House gathered in the basement of their residence to write invitations to the women at a co-ed residence called Vanier Place, inviting them to a tug-of-war and dance. As the night of invitation writing and power drinking progressed, 'a competition started to see who could write the "best" invitations. At 4:00 a.m. ten men obtained the front-door key to Vanier Place and delivered the hand-written invita-tions to approximately 300 women. The women awoke the following morn-ing to find that the invitations had been slid under their doors' (*Globe and Mail*, 18 Oct. 1990c, A4; *Vancouver Sun*, 16 Oct. 1990b, A1). The notes included overtures to the women to engage in acts of oral sex and sexual intercourse. For example, 'come to the tug-of-war-we'll f___ the shit out of you', 'we'll crush your cervix to oblivion', 'we'll suck your nipples bloody', and one student counsellor received a note that said, 'What's the best thing about f_____ an advisor? Killing her afterwards and giving her 2 points for screaming' (Hookham and Merriam 1991:58).

One month later, on the other side of the country, journalists from the *Montreal Gazette* reported that at Queen's University, the university student union was sponsoring a date-rape awareness campaign. In addition to guest speakers, posters with the slogan 'No means no' were displayed around the university campus. On 2 November, nine male residents of Gordon House responded to the campaign by constructing posters and banners with slogans of their own, notably: 'No means kick her in the teeth', 'No means on your knees, bitch', 'No means tie her up', 'No means more beer', 'No means she's a dyke'. According to one journalist, 'Obscene and violent messages, displayed in the windows of a men's residence at Queen's University have sparked a heated battle of the sexes' (*Montreal Gazette*, 3 Nov. 1990, cited in Wise Harris 1991:38).

In April of the same year, Celeste Brosseau, a female engineering student and campus activist, was booed off the stage at the University of Alberta. While performing at a 'light-hearted' skit night, male cast members appeared on stage wielding toy guns and members of the audience began to chant 'Shoot the bitch, Shoot the bitch', in reference to Brosseau's feminist activism. A professor who watched the production later told a reporter from the *Globe and Mail* that Brosseau 'should have known better than to take the stage when she knew she was unpopular' (*Globe and Mail* 25 April 1990, A2). In 1991, the *Calgary Herald* reported that twenty-five engineering students at the University of Toronto paraded through campus, passed around a life-size inflatable female doll and forced a beer bottle between its legs. The incident ended with several of the men jumping on the doll, simulating rape (*Calgary Herald*, 14 June 1991a, A1).

JOURNALISTIC IDEOLOGY AND THE CONSTRUCTION OF 'MEANING'

Sophia Voumvakis and Richard Ericson (1984) argue that the journalist as investigative reporter plays a significant role in the selection of cases and the construction of how a case will be reported. Like other professionals, journalists operate within their own occupational culture. Sociologists of the media have identified two major characteristics of the ideological system by which journalists select news items and interpret these events for their readers: background assumptions and professional ethics. Background assumptions are the unconscious part of the news production process. Journalists are the products of their socialization, culture, gender, class, and ethnic background, and are constrained by the larger ideological system they work within. Consequently, their own beliefs and values, including biases, prejudices, and stereotypes, influence their perceptions of what constitutes reportable news. The professional ethics include conceptions of fairness, impartiality, balance, and objectivity. This influences which sources they decide to include or exclude and how they interpret the meaning of the events. Put simply, the goal of the news is to appear as 'factual' as possible, and the news reports deemed most 'factual' are those grounded in the authoritative statement of experts.

The investigative reporter does not simply collect and repeat the facts of a case but plays an important role in shaping events, which influences how the public interprets the event. Debbie Wise Harris argues that the meaning of the event is constructed through the selection of sources—'of who gets to speak' (1991:39). Meanings and interpretation are constructed in part through the selective use and ordering of sources. What emerges is a striking similarity in the range of sources used by journalists. It is argued that the media systematically overemphasize the interpretations of the accredited spokespersons of state organizations, institutions, and certified experts who are asked to comment with an aura of impartiality (Voumvakis and Ericson 1984:30; Stone 1993). According to Howard Becker (1967), 'those at the top have access to a more complete picture of what is going on than anybody else. Members of lower groups will have incomplete information and their view of reality will be partial and distorted in consequence' (Becker 1967:39). As their journalistically interpreted thoughts appear in the media, these 'authorized knowers' symbolically reproduce society's 'hierarchy of credibility' (Becker 1967). Thus people who lack organizational positions of authority or other signs of formal qualifications will not be called upon as sources with frequency or regularity.

The image of objectivity or neutrality in the press has received considerable criticism by sociologists. Media critics argue that you should not believe everything you read in the paper or see on TV. They argue that the mass media do not simply provide information but *shape* and *structure* the meaning and the content of an event, which leads to the exclusion of alternative interpretations and opposing points of view. A good illustration of this argument about the role of the media in defining which social issues will be the subject of public debate is the reporting of ethnic relations. While the media do not necessarily encourage racial prejudice, the coverage of ethnic relations in the press tends to be disproportionately unfavourable. For example, in his analysis of the press coverage of the seventy-eight day stand-off between the Canadian army and Mohawk Warriors at the Kanesatake Reserve near Oka, Quebec, in the spring of 1992, Thomas O'Reilly-Fleming suggests that in order to subvert public sympathy away from the Mohawks, the press supported the federal government's view that the Mohawk leaders were part of an organized crime syndicate or mafia, 'criminals' who were involved in 'the sale of cut-rate gas and cigarettes on Canadian reserves, and in disputes at Akwesasne over legalized gambling' (O'Reilly-Fleming 1994:236). By characterizing them as criminals and terrorists, press coverage diverted attention from the fact that the Mohawks were involved in land claim negotiations with the federal government and struggling to gain sovereignty and protect the rights of their people.

Research in the area of gender and the media has concluded that while women appear in a minority of crime reports, they feature in the majority of cases as victims of crime. In a study of the press reports of violence against women in Toronto in 1982, Voumvakis and Ericson concluded that the press attributed the cause of attacks against women in the city, in significant proportions, to the victim's own actions. For instance, the victims were walking alone in unsafe places, or working unconventional shifts, or had failed to heed police warnings about provocative dress and dangerous strangers, or because they had not taken appropriate self-defence or personal safety measures. In sum, 'if the victim had taken care not to place herself in perilous circumstances she could have avoided victimization' (Voumvakis and Ericson 1984:47). The result is a 'blaming the victim' analysis, which emphasizes that it is the 'victim's responsibility' to recommend solutions for controlling a social problem. The remainder of this chapter will examine the role the press plays in the construction of meaning when violence, harassment, and assault occurs on Canadian campuses.

'BOYS WILL BE BOYS':
MEDIA AND THE SOCIAL CONSTRUCTION OF MEANING

The subject index of the *Canadian News Index* (CNI) between 1985 and May 1992 was used as a basis for selecting items. The survey yielded the titles of fifty-one newspaper stories and eight magazine articles in which incidents of sexual assault and harassment were linked to postsecondary educational institutions. This study is limited to newspapers indexed in the CNI, thus not every case is examined and some cases are cited more than once. Magazines surveyed include *Maclean's, British Columbia Report, Alberta Report, Chatelaine,* and *Canadian Living.* The newspapers surveyed include *Vancouver Sun, Calgary Herald, Winnipeg Free Press, Globe and Mail, Toronto Star, Montreal Gazette,* and *Halifax Chronicle Herald.* The news items include cases of gender harassment of students by professors, gender harassment of female students by male students, sexual assault of students by students, press releases about research on date rape and sexual and gender harassment on Canadian university campuses, and police reports of cases under investigation. Through the use of content analysis, a total of 388 sources quoted in the fifty-nine news stories and magazine articles were identified.

In order to examine what meaning the sources attributed to the incidents, three major variables were selected for qualitative comparison among the sources quoted. First, the sources were identified according to their position within a university or college. For example, were they students, staff, or administrators? Second, the sources were then ranked on the basis of their access to information about the specific case. For example, were they complainants, witnesses, or investigators? Finally, the attributions made by the source were textually analysed and coded. For example, how did they attribute responsibility, culpability, or blame for the incident? What was their awareness of the systemic problem of sexual assault, sexism, and homophobia on campuses?

The sources were then divided into eight categories: the participants (complainants and respondents), benign administration (presidents, academic vice presidents, deans, heads of departments), support staff (dormitory staff, student health staff, security), feminist bureaucracy (sexual harassment officers, employment equity officers, status of women administrators), campus community (supportive and unsupportive female and male students, faculty and staff), off-campus experts (researchers, politicians, criminal justice system workers), and, finally, the journalists who interpret the meaning of the events.

The sources were then ranked on the basis of their access to information or involvement in the case. Level One sources are the participants. They have the most information about the case. Level Two sources are the administrators and support staff who had access, by virtue of their employment in the university, to reports or files and testimony collected by the police or grievance officer. Level Three sources are members of the campus community who had little direct knowledge of the case apart from the gossip-mill, but are frequently recruited as sources by journalists. Level Four sources are the off-campus experts who have a professional interest in sex crime or harassment issues. Level Five sources are the off-campus journalists who play an important role in selecting sources and constructing the story for campus dwellers and the general community.

In order to examine how these events are explained when they occur on campuses, we must return to our consideration of the professional ethics of journalism, or the need for a balanced view of the story and how this goal comes into conflict with the internal organization of the university. G. Tuchman (1978) developed the concept of the 'strategic ritual of objectivity' to describe how the journalist attempts to provide a balanced view of the story by presenting opposing viewpoints. In cases of sex crime on university campuses, this proves to be more difficult than reporting on sexual assault cases among the general public for a number of reasons. Most university sexual harassment policies have confidentiality clauses that require universities to protect the identities of the complainants and respondents in sexual harassment cases. A *Calgary Herald* columnist complained that it was very difficult to get at the truth due to 'the elaborate contractual cobwebs that enmesh these places' (*Calgary Herald*, 12 Sept. 1990f, A5). Another journalist complained that university policy is more rigid than the federal Young Offender's Act, which at least permits the details of a case involving juveniles to be reported, provided neither names nor revealing details are disclosed.

Thus, unlike reporting on sexual assault cases before the criminal court where court reporters rely on a network of police and court informants,

TABLE 16.1

News Sources, 1985 and May 1992

	Stories	Magazines	Total Cases
Level One:			
Participants	39 (15%)	23 (19%)	62 (16%)
Level Two:			
Benign Administration	35 (13%)	6 (5%)	41 (11%)
Support Staff	10 (4%)	2 (5%)	12 (2%)
Feminist Bureaucracy	23 (9%)	12 (10%)	35 (9%)
			88 (23%)
Level Three:			
Unsupportive	32 (12%)	39 (49%)	71 (18%)
Supportive	32 (12%)	21 (17%)	53 (14%)
			124 (32%)
Level Four:			
Off-Campus 'Experts'*	43 (16%)	12 (10%)	55 (14%)
Level Five:			
Journalists	51 (19%)	8 (7%)	59 (15%)
Total	265	123	388

* Less than 3 per cent of these sources were police or criminal justice system professionals

journalists who report on campus cases have limited access to information unless someone violates confidentiality clauses. Generally, those with most access to the information about the case are prohibited from speaking to journalists. Consequently, the sources with the most information about the case are obviously the participants and the investigators, as Table 16.1 indicates, though they make up only 16 per cent of the sources.

The *in loco parentis* position of North American universities is apparent in its handling of sexual harassment cases. According to one journalist, university administrators are analogous to benevolent but neglectful father figures. It was his perception that an unspoken understanding 'exists that sexual abuse on campus is not a problem for society at large to solve but for the campus family to solve, the not-yet-adult society of the school, with its own special code of behavior' (Weiss 1991:62). According to one university president, 'There is a considerable gap between what the Criminal Code covers and what we need ... We have accepted the fact that we need to regulate the internal community of the university ... We certainly don't think we can let the law deal with all cases' (*Globe and Mail*, 9 Feb. 1993, A6). Thus campus sex crimes can be regarded as a 'special case' of sexual and gender harassment. In other words, if a group of men broke into a woman's apartment and stole items of clothing or vandalized her property, when caught they would be charged with break and entry and theft. However, when this happens on campus, the crime is called a 'panty-raid' and the thieves are called 'pranksters'.

Recent media attention on sex crimes on Canadian campuses has been a great source of embarrassment for university administration. Just when the 'ivory tower' is being attacked as a redundant and ineffectual institution, media attention on sexual harassment and assault by staff, faculty, and students is one more unwelcome public relations problem for the administration. Clearly reluctant experts, only 11 per cent of the journalists' sources were actually administrators. Over the past decade, university administrations have responded to growing concerns about sexual and gender discrimination and harassment, or what we call 'climate issues', by establishing what Veronica Strong-Boag calls 'feminist bureaucracies' (quoted in *British Columbia Report* 1991:32), which constitute 9 per cent of the sources. To this troubled family is brought the healing touch of the feminist bureaucracy. Like wives in 'traditional marriages', their role is tension management to 'soothe and smooth'. In many institutions, however, they lack the authority to do much more.

The feminist bureaucracy is expected to control the damage to the university's public image, so through their press releases, the administration publicly passes responsibility for the incident over to the feminist bureaucracy. Joyce Nelson (1989) argues that press releases help corporations control how an event will be reported:

> What the press release does is establish lines of control regarding information. It initiates the news-making process, and sets ideal boundaries around what is to be known by emphasizing some information and leaving out other information. An enterprising reporter can follow up a press release, asking further questions ... but often, given the constraints of news deadlines ... this isn't done (Nelson 1989:43-4).

Carefully crafted press releases enable university administrators generally to handle negative publicity associated with some cases by showcasing their own recent initiatives to stamp out visible sexism in the hope of diverting attention from the case. Three of the most popular strategies have been appointing a presidential adviser on issues of women and gender, establishing women's studies research centres and women's studies programs, and establishing student-run women's centres. The resulting illusion is that the situation is under control and, depending on the nature of the case, a clever administration can actually use the media as a public relations opportunity to promote its commitment to equity policies or to showcase the activities of its beefed-up feminist bureaucracy and generate interest in new gender-sensitive courses advertised in the university calendar.

The double-edged responsibility of the feminist bureaucracy is to interpret events in a way that supports the institution's view of itself as a responsible corporate citizen without revealing the identity of the offender/respondent or the limitations of university policy regarding the charges or the limitations of the feminist bureaucracy's own power, which may make it difficult for them to get justice for the complainant. Clearly, many sexual harassment officers have refused to support their institution's claim that they are responsible corporate citizens. For example, one 'anonymous' sexual harassment officer confided to a *Chatelaine* reporter: 'This university is more interested in protecting its own reputation than in protecting students.' Another stated: 'Most of the top administrators are men, and they don't understand what it's like to feel vulnerable and often don't believe a woman who says she's been assaulted' (*Chatelaine*, August 1991, 78).

Table 16.1 indicates that 39 per cent of the sources quoted belonged to Level One and Level Two sources; that is, people whose positions in the university prohibited them from giving information that might facilitate the journalist's investigation. The potential for Level One and Level Two sources to be of use to the journalist is quickly depleted. In their pursuit of the 'strategic ritual of objectivity', the journalist turns to the third and fourth level, or individuals with no direct knowledge of the case, or no contact or official affiliation with the institution. Nevertheless, their comments, insights, and analyses comprise 61 per cent of the comments identified in this study. The heavy reliance on third and fourth level sources contributes to the social construction of campus sex crimes as 'special cases' of sexual assault because a significant majority of the sources quoted do not have access to information about the case, and would be likely to be regarded as inappropriate sources if they were not members of the university or college community or if the incident had occurred off-campus.

The off-campus experts category includes members of Parliament, sexual assault centre staff, white-ribbon campaign spokespeople, a president of the Canadian Engineering Association, a vice-president of Ontario Hydro, spokespeople for the National Action Council on the Status of Women, and various family members and friends of the complainants and respondents (only 3 per cent were criminal justice system officials). The sources in this category have differing levels of access to information on the case, and although many were not involved with the university, they were asked by reporters to comment on the case.

In their study of press reports on violence against women, Voumvakis and Ericson (1984) noted that many special interest groups used the 'moral panic' about sexual assault for their own purposes, such as demanding more funding for their projects or more business for their industries. Politicians frequently get publicity by attaching their names to controversial social issues. The same trend has been observed in this study of campus sex crime.

Level Three sources are composed of the general campus community (Table 16.2). As such, they are supposed to represent the campus version of the 'person on the street' or the 'vox pop' response. Following Voumvakis and Ericson (1984), Level Three sources were divided on the basis of how they attributed blame or responsibility for the incident. For example, did they perceive the incident as the fault of the complainant (blaming the victim) or in the context of systemic discrimination against women and gays?

TABLE 16.2

Level Three: Campus Community

Supportive—43%		
	Females	57%
	Males	43%
Unsupportive—57%		
	Females	37%
	Males	63%

THE SUPPORTIVE COMMUNITY

Forty-three per cent of the supportive statements allegedly came from female and male students, staff, and professors. They are considered to be supportive because they were sympathetic and sensitive to issues involving campus safety and gender discrimination, and violence against women, and they do not repeat myths about sexual assault victims. As one-first year student, a victim of date rape in her freshman year, told a *Maclean's* reporter:

> Frosh think they're invincible ... You never think that anything will happen to you. And I was definitely one of those people. Date rape happened to other women, women who drank and went out with the wrong guys ... I had done nothing ... I hadn't kissed him. I hadn't held his hand. I did resist, and I said 'no' in no uncertain terms. But he just kept forcing me, and I was afraid of being hurt. Then, I gave in almost to avoid embarrassing us both ... I'm sure he didn't think he was raping me ... I'm sure he thought, 'She'll have a nice happy glow on her face when it's all over, just like Vivien Leigh in *Gone With the Wind* ... So many women have told me about experiences that were classic date rape and acquaintance rape, but they won't identify them as such. And I know a lot of men who feel they have forced women into sexual activity that they didn't want (*Maclean's*, 9 Nov. 1992a, 45).

The content analysis revealed that 43 per cent of the supportive comments were made by men. On campuses across Canada, groups of male faculty and students have organized seminars and workshops to teach men about the impact of violence upon themselves and on women. Men's comments range from empathetic comments — like 'I feel so awful for girls nowadays' and 'Some guys just don't understand what date rape actually is or how aggressive behaviour makes women feel' — to activism. But men's activism in support of women has met the same forms of resistance as women's activism. One male student workshop organizer explained it this way in *Chatelaine*: 'Certain guys call us fags and man-haters, and perceive this sort of group effort to talk about how we can change as an attack on men' (*Chatelaine*, Aug. 1991, 78). Fear of harassment on the basis of sexual orientation is also a real concern for gay and lesbian students and staff on Canadian campuses. A campus security officer at the University of Alberta recalled this incident: 'a student who acknowledged that he was homosexual was seized by other students in one of the university residences and left tied to a chair with a sign attached. "They grabbed him, pulled his pants down to his knees, bent him across a chair and tied him to it ... There was a sign. I think it said something like, 'I'm gay, use me'"' (*Globe and Mail*, 25 April 1990b, A2).

THE UNSUPPORTIVE COMMUNITY

Fifty-seven per cent of the comments were alleged to have come from both female and male students, faculty, and staff whose attitudes reveal a lack of support for either the plight of the complainant, a lack of awareness of the issue of sexist and homophobic violence, and a lack of interest in efforts to be educated about the issue. For example, a male student who was at Queen's during the 'No means no' campaign told a reporter from *Maclean's*:

> We were fresh out of high school, expecting all this sexual freedom ... And then we got bombarded by all this 'No means no' stuff ... [the signs ... were a good joke]. Then ... everything got too serious ... the issue has been overblown. There is so much denial ... When is 'no' a little 'no' and when is it a capital 'No'? To make it into a stereotype, it's the girl's role to say no, and the guy's role to get into her pants. She says no, and you kiss her back a little harder. You go slower and faster. With 'No means no' you can't even play the game (*Maclean's*, 9 Nov. 1992a, 44).

Another male student whom a *Chatelaine* reporter interviewed at an acquaintance rape seminar at the University of Toronto in 1991 summed up the problem this way: 'If a woman wears a tight dress, she knows what she's getting into and what she's asking for ... It's not a Utopian world. Don't wear something sexy if you don't want a guy to get the impression you want to have sex' (*Chatelaine*, Aug. 1991, 35).

Female and male sources also spoke in support of offenders, even after they were found guilty. In defence of colleagues charged with creating a 'sexually offensive workplace', twenty-one female medical students, technicians, assistants, and faculty circulated a petition defending their workplace and the character of their male colleagues, which they published in the *Calgary Herald*. They argued that their work environment was friendly and supportive:

> Most of us have either worked in or are currently associated with the allegedly 'sexually offensive' environment and feel there is no justification for this label ... We rate the environment in the faculty of medicine as demanding yet supportive. We find the emotional milieu relaxed, friendly and non-intimidating, students are treated equitably as junior colleagues ... We feel the complaints in this case have capitalized on the media interest in this subject and the university's vulnerability to 'bad publicity' to further their case ... The faculty of medicine's reputation has been damaged ... As women our reputations have been especially hurt ... We are concerned that people will believe that women in the faculty of medicine earn their degrees for nonacademic reasons. There have been insinuations that any female students who succeeded did so by participating in 'sex games' with male faculty members ... We are distressed by these insinuations and by suggestions that if we do not feel sexually harassed that is simply because we are 'coping' with a sexist environment. This conclusion is sexist and degrading ... (*Calgary Herald*, 12 Sept. 1990f, A5).

They were referring, of course, to the practice of some medical faculty's use of a body temperature tub as a party toy, and the habit of posting on the bulletin board photographs of female students' breasts under wet clothes. In the gender harassment case, where Celeste Brosseau was booed off the stage at the engineering skit-night, a professor who was not actually present that evening told the task force set up after the incident that what happened to the female student was not sexism.

> 'The anger directed at one female engineering student on skit night was no more severe—possibly less so—than that directed at perceived male traitors from time to time' at the university. He also stated that female speakers at the University of Alberta have been guilty of their own 'anti-male diatribes ... For the sake of those who don't care about harm to men, however, let me also point out that hatred has a way of being returned ... It would not surprise me if one of the demons that tortured Marc Lepine was the steady torrent of abuse directed at men in general by too many feminists' (*Globe and Mail*, 25 April 1990b, A2).

SOCIAL CONTROL IMPLICATIONS: LABELLED 'TROUBLEMAKERS'

Level Five includes the journalists. In many ways the voice of the journalists is the loudest. Journalists select the sources that support their view of the event, rank the responses, and interpret the meaning of the attributions made. Like other professionals, journalists are the product of their socialization and are consciously or unconsciously influenced by cultural biases and prejudices. This is evident in the press coverage of campus sex crimes. For example, Susan McDaniel and Erica van Roosmalen observed that while student groups have been demanding that professors be sanctioned for using sexist jokes as teaching methods, 'similar jokes were made by journalists in Canada about the leering professor with goggles in the University of Toronto pool' (McDaniel and van Roosmalen 1991:5).

According to a feminist columnist for the *Toronto Star*, 'when it comes to questioning male sexual privileges, or asking that a woman's experience be given serious and equal consideration, most of the mainstream media are— alas—willfully, complacently, blind and deaf' (*Toronto Star*, 20 Jan. 1990a, F1). Journalists who see campus sex crimes as 'isolated' incidents will select sources and quote research data that support this non-feminist view. For example, Lepine's suicide note, like a press release, was designed to control the interpretation of the event. He knew his actions would be reported in the press, and he wanted it to be clear that he was not crazy, that the femicide he committed was a 'political act'. Nevertheless, the initial press coverage described Lepine's violence as the isolated actions of a madman. Mallette and Chalouh (1991) argue that the mainstream press 'scrambled to ignore or downplay the significance of the victims being women and the analyses of feminists was ignored or ridiculed or rejected with hostility' (Mallette and Chalouh 1991:1). A recent study of press coverage of violence against women supports the argument that on the whole, feminists' views are absent from press coverage, but Sharon Stone insists that there are 'openings where feminists could achieve a significant amount of access to the press to express their views' (Stone 1993:377).

Journalists are careful to stress in their articles that in contrast to feminists, most women are not troubled by sexist comments. A female engineering student interviewed by a *Calgary Herald* reporter said that, 'if you are going into a male dominated industry you have to learn to live with men' while 'her friends nodded in agreement' (*Calgary Herald*, 12 Jan. 1990a, A7). In contrast to 'feminist' Celeste Brosseau who was reduced to tears, the other female engineering students 'who appeared in skits endured crude chants from men urging them to bare their breasts. But none seemed bothered by the remarks' (*Calgary Herald*, 12 Jan. 1990a, A7). While investigating the threatening and obscene tug-of-war invitations at the University of British Columbia, one journalist suggested that the majority of note recipients, whom the journalists described as 'generally sympathetic to the men', were undisturbed by the content of the notes. 'It's hard on the guys', one woman allegedly stated. 'I don't think the guys should be evicted from residence. They didn't sexually attack us, they verbally attacked us ... If they get kicked out, or get a sex assault on their record, it ruins their life' (*Vancouver Sun*, 16 Oct. 1990b, A2).

> ... Many of the young women offered rationales for what their fellow students had done. They were drunk after the regular Wednesday drinking night at the

Pit; they were in a group and 'this is normal for guys when they get together in a group like this.' 'There is so much pressure in those [boys'] dormitories to conform' (*Vancouver Sun*, 16 Oct. 1990b, A2).

The meaning constructed by the media coverage of campus sex crimes is that 'normal' women react to sexual and gender harassment with grace, dignity, and, best of all, with humour, like the Queen's women students who responded to the 'No means tie her up' posters with signs of their own, notably, 'No means too small'. McDaniel and van Roosmalen argue, however, that humour serves to excuse, rationalize, and even support harassment (McDaniel and van Roosmalen 1991:5).

Sexual harassment is a power issue, and press coverage can result in a 'textual silencing' of complainants, taking away their power by denying any real harm, trivializing the incident, portraying them as overreacting feminists, or emphasizing their victim status and helplessness. This has serious social control implications for all victims of sexual harassment and assault. The statements made by complainants give the clear impression that women who speak out against sexual harassment and discrimination are not well treated by those whose authority and privilege they threaten. This is indeed the lesson the woman who 'blew the whistle on ... the former frogman of Hart House' would learn when the professor whom she charged with sexual harassment violated agreed-upon confidentiality rules and publicly named her and her place of work in the press. As one columnist pointed out, she became 'the butt of merciless media ridicule'. She told him as tears of outrage welled in her eyes, 'I was determined to fight dirt with dignity' (*Toronto Star*, 20 Jan. 1990a, F1).

Moreover, complainants seldom feel that they have received justice. One of the 'bitter' complainants who charged five medical professors with sexual harassment at the University of Calgary told a *Calgary Herald* reporter that the light reprimand the professors received 'is simply a signal to professors that their behaviour, even at the highest levels, is approved of and to students that it is futile to go through the internal system to get justice' (*Calgary Herald*, 2 Aug. 1990c, B1). The other complainant said, 'In spite of all the problems I have encountered it has been infinitely better to be a complainant than a silent victim' (*Calgary Herald*, 12 Sept. 1990e, B1). However, we also learn that these women were forced to leave the university and 'fear they have been blacklisted in the medical community because they have been labelled "troublemakers"' (*Calgary Herald*, 2 Aug. 1990c, B1).

Wise Harris (1991) argues that gender bias and the goal of journalistic balance combine to create a 'politics of overreaction'. She argues that the juxtaposition of opposite reactions to the same event gives the impression that campus feminists have blown everything out of proportion, that feminist thought-police are limiting freedom of choice and freedom of expression and, most seriously, of spoiling everyone's fun! One female fourth-year nursing student told a *Maclean's* reporter that she had to lie on the ground while a male student did push-ups on top of her during her Queen's initiation in the late 1980s. She complained:

> Frosh week is so lame now ... We were just killing ourselves laughing ... Mind you, the guy was really cute. But if I were to say something like that on campus now, they'd massacre me. They'd say, 'You're looking at women as mattresses' (*Maclean's*, 9 Nov. 1992a, 45).

This genre of press coverage fuels the postfeminist discourses on violence against women at Canadian universities by distinguishing feminists from regular women. 'The strategy of divide and rule is used again to mark out feminists as extremists who are against the interests of "ordinary", "normal" women.' According to Wise Harris:

> Within the post-feminism that pervades the discourses on violence against women at universities, is the notion that women and men are engaged in a 'battle' or 'war' of the sexes. This is a false symmetry of power ... This notion of a 'level playing field' is used continually in the public discourse about the threats of violence by men to women on university campuses (Wise Harris 1991:40).

CONCLUSION

> 'People who care about me have told me not to talk to the media or anyone' (Celeste Brosseau, *Globe and Mail*, 25 April 1990b, A3).

In the current discourse about sex crimes on Canadian campuses, as it is played out in the popular press and on TV, a number of experts have emerged, each claiming the right to speak 'the truth' on behalf of victims and assailants. Across the country, lecherous professors, fraternity brothers, and the postfeminist sisterhood face off against the new feminist bureaucracies and the mobilized and politically conscious student body, while somewhere in the background, the benign administrators and the complainants themselves run interference. While sexual assault and harassment are not new, these experts are in the sense that problems of sexual violence and abuse on campus have now been named (since 1976), and there is a growing societal recognition of their detrimental effects on the individual and society.

Consider these headlines: 'Rape on campus: Is your daughter in danger?' 'Leers from professor, jeers from the media', 'Abusive prof got off scot-free', 'Campuses "hunting grounds" for sexual assaults'. I have called these incidents 'campus sex crimes' because the media coverage has created a new genre of pulp crime fiction, which portrays the campus, the library, the computer labs, and co-ed dorms as the locus of 'sexual danger' where no one is safe. Is this what we want? Carol Smart argues that 'fear of rape keeps women off the streets. Keeps women home. Keeps women passive and modest for fear of being thought provocative' (Smart and Smart 1978:100). What constitutes social control is the fact that internalization, through constant socialization, of the 'possibility' of sexual assault or sexual harassment causes women to censor themselves and their activities in the hope of keeping themselves safe. It has been argued that press coverage of violence against women on campus contributes to social control because it represents a vehicle for keeping women in 'their place'. When the women are students, staff, and faculty, and the locus of the crime is their place of work and study, the regulatory regime they are expected to follow is very clear. Women who step out of line are vulnerable to sexual assault and harassment. Those who dare to complain about it are held up for scrutiny, may be lampooned in the press, and seldom get the retribution or satisfaction they deserve.

FURTHER READINGS

Kitzinger, C., and A. Tom, eds. 1996. *Sexual Harassment: Contemporary Feminist Perspectives*. London: Open University Press.

McDaniel, S., and E. van Roosmalen. 1991. 'Sexual Harassment in Canadian Academe: Explorations of Power and Privilege'. *Atlantis* 17:3–18.

Renner, K., C. Wackett, and S. Ganderton. 1988. 'The "Social" Nature of Sexual Assault'. *Canadian Psychology* 29:163–73.

Wise Harris, D. 1991. 'Keeping Women in Our Place: Violence at Canadian Universities'. *Canadian Woman Studies* 11:37–41.

Wright, D.B., and L. Weiner. 1984. *The Lecherous Professor: Sexual Harassment on Campus*. Boston: Beacon Press.

REFERENCES

Alberta Report. 1992. 'Four Hundred U of C Faculty Sexist Pigs?' (17 August):24, 25.

Becker, H. 1967. 'Whose Side Are We On?' *Social Problems* 14:239–47.

British Columbia Report. 1991. 'UBC's Feminist Bureaucracy' (19 August): 32–3.

Calgary Herald. 1990a. 'Female Engineer Jeered' (12 January):A7.

_____. 1990b. 'U of C Probes Prof's Conduct' (17 February):A1.

_____. 1990c. 'Sexual Harassment Profs Keep Jobs' (2 August):B1.

_____. 1990d. 'U of C Dogged by Sex Scandal' (30 August):B1.

_____. 1990e. 'Rally on Campus Uncovers Differing Harassment View' (12 September):B1.

_____. 1990f. 'Every Story Has a Number of Different Sides' (12 September):A5.

_____. 1991a. 'Harassment Continuing on Campuses' (14 June):A1.

_____. 1991b. '46 Campus Cases, "Just the Tip of the Ice-berg"' (26 November):B1.

_____. 1992. 'One in Seven Assaulted' (11 November):B5.

Chatelaine. 1991. 'Rape on Campus: Is Your Daughter in Danger?' (August):33–5, 76–8.

Frize, M. 1993. 'Eradicating Sexual Harassment in Higher Education'. Paper presented at Canadian Association Against Sexual Harassment in Higher Education Conference, Ottawa, November.

Globe and Mail. 1990a. 'Professor Seeks Review of Ogling Conviction' (9 January):A3.

_____. 1990b. 'University Fights Outbreak of Sexism "Virus"' (25 April):A1, A13.

_____. 1990c. 'Brothers No More at UBC' (18 October):A4.

_____. 1990d. 'When Sexism Stalks the Campus' (27 November):A21.

_____. 1990e. 'Student Raped, Beaten within Sight of Campus' (2 December):A1, A2.

_____. 1993. 'Campus Date Abuse Spurs Debate' (9 February):A6.

Halifax Chronicle Herald. 1991a. 'UCCB Sex Scandal May Lead to Disciplinary Action' (12 October):A1, A2.

_____. 1991b. 'UCCB Student Defends Her Story' (18 October):A1, A2.

_____. 1991c. 'UCCB to Set Up Abuse Committee' (25 October):A3.

_____. 1991d. 'MP Wants University Heads to Deal with Date Rape Issue' (4 December):A6.

Haberman, M., L. Sardi, and M. Morton. 1992. *Sexual Violence on Campus: From Personal to Political Action.* Toronto: Ryerson.

Hookham, L., and N. Merriam. 1991. 'The Caribou House Incident: Sexual Harassment of UBC Women'. *Canadian Woman Studies/Les cahiers de la femme* 12, no. 1:58–9.

Hornosty, J. 1986. 'Sexual Harassment: It's Everyone's Business'. *CAUT Bulletin* (November):19–20.

Maclean's. 1988. 'Rape on Campus: Wild Parties and Fears About Walking Alone'(31 October):56.

_____. 1992a. 'Campus Confidential' (9 November):43–6.

_____. 1992b. 'Taking a Campus Pulse' (9 November):38, 41.

Mallette, L., and M. Chalouh. 1991. *The Montreal Massacre.* Charlottetown: Gynergy Books.

McDaniel, S., and E. van Roosmalen. 1991. 'Sexual Harassment in Canadian Academe: Explorations of Power and Privilege'. *Atlantis* 17:3–18.

Montreal Gazette. 1989. 'Campus "Date Rape" All Too Common Study Suggests' (10 November):A8.

Nelson, J. 1989. *Sultans of Sleaze: Public Relations and the Media.* Toronto: Between the Lines.

O'Reilly-Fleming, T. 1994. 'The Mohawk-Canada Crisis: Native Peoples, Criminalization and the Justice System'. In *Reading Racism and the Criminal Justice System,* edited by D. Baker, 233–42. Toronto: Canadian Scholars' Press.

Smart, C., and B. Smart. 1978. 'Accounting for Rape: Reality and Myth in Press Reporting'. In *Women, Sexuality and Social Control*, edited by C. Smart and B. Smart, 89–103. London: Routledge and Kegan Paul.

Stone, S. 1993. 'Getting the Message Out: Feminists, the Press and Violence Against Women'. *Canadian Review of Sociology and Anthropology* 30:377–400.

Toronto Star. 1990a. 'Leers from Professor, Jeers from the Media' (20 January):F1.

———. 1990b. 'Is Life on Campus REALLY SAFE?' (8 September):D1.

———. 1991a. 'We Should Have Been Warned' (27 May):B1, B3.

———. 1991b. 'Betrayal Is Worst Aspect of Date Rape, Studies Show' (7 October):B1.

Tuchman, G. 1978. *Making the News: A Study in the Construction of Reality*. New York: Free Press.

Voumvakis, S., and R. Ericson. 1984. 'News Accounts of Attacks on Women: Comparison of Three Toronto Newspapers'. Toronto: Centre of Criminology.

Vancouver Sun. 1990a. 'UBC Adds Sexism Course for Engineering Students' (24 August):B3.

———. 1990b. 'UBC Harassment Investigated' (16 October):A1, A2.

———. 1990c. 'UBC Women Reluctant to Complain Officially' (17 October):B1, B2.

———. 1991a. 'Steps Taken to Counter Problem' (18 January):C11.

———. 1991b. 'When No Means No' (18 January):C11.

Weiss, P. 'The Second Revolution: Sexual Politics on Campus'. *Harper's* (April):58–62, 64–72.

Winnipeg Free Press. 1991. 'Campus "Hunting Grounds" for Sexual Assaults, Crown Says' (24 December):A10.

Wise Harris, D. 1991. 'Keeping Women in Our Place: Violence at Canadian Universities'. *Canadian Woman Studies/Les cahiers de la femme 2*, no. 4:37–41.

—17—

Deviance and Discipline in the Classroom

Randle W. Nelsen

In this chapter education in schools is discussed as a standardization of particular social and cultural norms. A hidden curriculum grounded in gender, ethnicity, and class results in the construction of both deviance and normalcy, within and outside of schools. Thus special attention is paid to analysing what happens to female, 'minority' (African American, Asian, Aboriginal) and working-class students—those students whose backgrounds make it more difficult for them to fit in with prevailing social and cultural norms. Attention is given to the way in which the hidden curriculum, embedded within the power arrangements of the current socio-economic system, is important in creating, disciplining, and controlling school deviants. The resistance of those defined as deviant is analysed as a statement about what is wrong with today's schools, as well as what kind of alternative learning environments might be better suited to meet the needs of most students.

The chapter is organized into six sections. In the first section the focus is on the social construction of, the dialectic between, deviance and normalcy. What could be considered typical school day and weekend activities of a hypothetical, suburban high school student are analysed to illustrate the social construction of reality (see Berger and Luckmann 1966) and to make problematic what Alfred Schutz (1967) talked about as 'the world taken-for-granted'. In the second section, the extent and normalcy of early school leaving or 'the drop-out problem' is reviewed.

A third section focuses on gender, ethnicity, and class as key elements in a hidden curriculum that supports an ideology of meritocracy—an ideology that in turn is supportive of and supported by prevailing socio-economic arrangements. A fourth section completes this discussion of the hidden curriculum by reviewing a fourth key element, technology. Here the focus is upon the electronic technology of television (although brief attention is also given to video games and computers) as a socializing agent in competition with, as well as in helping to shape, the school and its culture.

Sections five and six have to do with student resistance to schooling, as well as the school authorities' responses to it and a conclusion that discusses liberatory alternatives to the present social control emphasis in current schooling. Again, as with deviance and normalcy, emphasis is upon recognizing today's school and proposed changes to it as socially constructed—an order negotiated and reproduced within the power inequities of the larger socio-economic arrangements that shape the school.

THE SOCIAL CONSTRUCTION OF DEVIANCE AND NORMALCY

As the classic French sociologist Emile Durkheim (1895) and countryman Michel Foucault (1977) have convincingly argued, defining which behaviour is 'deviant' or 'criminal' gives important perspective in deciding what is 'normal'. In short, what comes to be defined as deviant depends on a kind of social relativism. As Jack Haas and Bill Shaffir (1974:12), in discussing what they call 'decent citizen deviance', emphasize, 'the matter of who is defined and treated as deviant is not so much determined by what people do as by the social distance between agents of control and deviating persons'.

Focusing upon peer control and the development of subcultures, Howard Becker (1953, 1955) also emphasizes the social and power arrangements connected to deviance labelling. Beginning with the easily observable, sociological truism that different groups judge different actions as deviant, Becker (1963) elaborates by noting that the determination of which behaviours become defined as deviant will vary with regard to time, place of enactment, and what response those observing or aware of the action in question decide to make.

An instructive way to illustrate the social construction of deviance and the part played by gender, ethnicity, socio-economic class, and technological change is to focus on some everyday activities of young people. Taking tests and writing essays, smoking cigarettes, waiting for the weekend to engage in leisure activities such as dancing and playing video games, and returning to school on Monday morning are common occurrences in the daily lives of high school students, but they can tell us much about the dialectic, the interplay, between what we define as deviant and normal. In the discussion that follows, I have constructed a Friday-through-Monday and a weekend scenario for a hypothetical student engaged in the everyday activities mentioned earlier.

Let's say on Friday a multiple-choice test in geography has been scheduled and an essay in social studies is due. Our hypothetical high school student is pressed for time, so she gets together with three classmates she trusts and who know how to study in order to divide up the four chapters of material upon which they will be examined, each student being responsible for one chapter. Then at the examination they employ the 'stick-shift' technique, a strategy for getting the upper-hand on multiple choice tests. Once the examination begins, the student who is responsible for the relevant material or who knows the answer to a particular question places her or his foot at one of the five positions of a car's gear shift. For example, if the correct answer is A, then the student would place her foot where first gear would be on a stick-shift and so on, A through E. This strategy, along with many others, according to a brief write-up in *Harper's* (April 1992:20), are in a book written and published by a Rutgers University junior named Michael Moore, who writes that cheating is the 'easiest and most surefire way of achieving great grades, a diploma, and ultimately a good job'. His book, *Cheating 101: The Benefits and Fundamentals of Earning an Easy 'A'*, is basically a how-to-manual, quite different from such modern-day classics as Becker et al.'s (1968) *Making the Grade* and Van den Berghe's (1970) *Academic Gamesmanship*. The normalcy of cheating, as illustrated by the stick-shift technique, is attested to by the more than 6,000 copies of Moore's book, which was sold for $7 through mail-order advertisements placed in student newspapers at more than 400 campuses across the United States.

Obviously, the question as to what constitutes academic cheating or plagiarism continues to be raised and is one that has a variety of answers. Later in the day our hypothetical student turns in her social studies essay, which she bought ready-made from a term paper company (more on this later). Certainly academics (see Birenbaum 1992; Fletcher 1991), journalists (see *Chronicle-Journal*, 29 Dec. 1991b, A6), and other professionals as role models for students often provide students with mixed signals and a confusing set of normative definitions. The sources of our ideas, an area of specialization that sociologists call the sociology of knowledge, are often elusive. It just may be that 'there is nothing (or little) new under the sun' and most creative work is just a recombination of already existing ideas. Certainly, many believe that ideas often seem to be 'stolen', with the theft covered by footnoting, directly quoting, and so-called 'responsible paraphrasing'. As turn-of-the-century writer Wilson Mizner, often quoted by cynics, put it, 'When you steal from one author it's plagiarism. If you steal from many, it's research' (quoted in *Chronicle-Journal*, 29 Dec. 1991b, A6). But what is it when you buy a whole paper written by another or others and pass it off as your own work?

Most observers today would probably still call this plagarism and label it deviance. However, there are some groups of people who are developing new norms grounded upon the view that the whole school certification process is basically a sham (or a 'scam'), and they argue that this term paper 'contracting out' is acceptable. One should remember that norms, sociologically viewed, are relativistic or situationally specific and based upon social

agreement. It is equally important to remember that these normative definitions change over time.

Take, for example, our student's smoking of a cigarette between her
geography and social studies classes. On the one hand, what she is doing
could be considered quite normal for her gender and age group. Recently, as
Joan Baril (1992:10) has reported, Canada became the first country in the
Western world where women smokers outnumber men smokers, in large
part the successful result of a massive advertising campaign that links cigarette smoking to the beauty myth (Wolf 1991)—a myth that keeps the so-
called 'ideal' woman thin, if not at the anorexic and underweight level. Thus
it is not surprising that in 1985, a greater percentage of women than men
aged fifteen to nineteen smoked regularly. However, between 1978–9 and
1985, the proportion of both sexes aged fifteen to nineteen who smoked
regularly decreased by 13 per cent, an even greater decline than the 7 per
cent decrease in daily cigarette smokers for the Canadian population as a
whole (see McKie 1990:87–8). With these figures, as well as recent ordi-
nances prohibiting smoking in public places in mind, our student smoker
might be considered deviant.

Our hypothetical student decides to go out dancing on Friday night with
her boyfriend. They visit a downtown club to participate in a new dance
craze called 'moshing'. According to observers, young people punch, kick,
and slam each other into walls and seem to love it. An offshoot of early
1980s' slam dancing, moshing has been popular in metropolitan centres such
as Toronto, New York, and Seattle for a number of years. An organizer of
mosh parties in Edmonton claims moshing is a physical but not violent
dance that allows kids to vent their frustrations: 'It's part of a new revival of
youth culture. It's representative of an alternative lifestyle ... I guess it's a
protest against anything that's established' (*Chronicle-Journal*, 15 June 1992c,
16). In the same newspaper article, a mosher echoes this view, saying that he
moshes because 'it goes against the mainstream'. Again the questions concerning normalcy, deviance, and the connections between the two are raised.

Does moshing go against the mainstream any more than the Charleston
did in the 1920s, the twist in the 1960s, and so on? Are our student and her
boyfriend being deviant as they jump around the dance floor in a circle with
other moshers, flailing arms, kicking legs, belly flopping into the crowd, and
bashing friends? Or are they simply being normal teenagers enjoying the
latest dance craze? One thing is pretty certain: within this social context,
they are unlikely to be arrested and punished by the authorities for assault
and battery.

Our student spends much of the rest of a rainy weekend in front of the
television and a friend's computer, absorbed in video games. As Eugene F.
Provenzo, Jr (1991:52) makes clear in his recent book, *Video Kids*, these
games 'have a history of being sexist and racist' and they reflect themes of

violence and destruction. One can argue that violence and destruction in the service of control and power are largely masculine fantasies (see the Zimbardo quote in Provenzo 1991:50). It can be further argued that these fantasies are the major organizing themes of our culture, and since most video games tend to feed into and reinforce these fantasies, our student's fascination with these games might be considered normal. Certainly Thomas W. Malone's (1981) finding that the most important reason for a game's popularity among students has to do with whether it has a specific and clear goal is not surprising and to be expected in a society that is increasingly goal-oriented in leisure and work. In brief, there are solid consumer data for the appeal of video game play as a kind of norm among a sizeable percentage of the teenage population (see Provenzo 1991:8–23, 28–43).

Part of this boom in video game popularity has to do with the promise of wider accessibility for both teenagers and their elders to 'virtual reality'. The new computer technology associated with virtual-reality systems has moved beyond devices like the Power Glove and U-Force to the manufacture of specially designed clothing that links the computer to the user. According to observers, a virtual-reality user who wears a helmet fitted with earphones and a wraparound viewing screen can, with simple head movements, be initiated into the wonders of space exploration, take a guided tour of the surface of Mars or of Great Britain—all without leaving the comfort of an easy chair in his or her living-room (see *Chronicle-Journal*, 5 Jan. 1992a, A2). Of course, the technological construction of these computer-based microworlds, as C.A. Bowers (1980) and others have pointed out, is not only radically changing our patterns of communication but also restructuring and reorganizing knowledge—redefining and transforming our culture. At the very least, the changes brought about by computer technology eventually should force us to reflect upon the connections between virtual reality and the reality outside the microworlds. With regard to our video game-playing student, all of this should again raise questions as to what gets defined and enforced as normal or deviant.

The weekend is over, it's Monday morning, and our hypothetical student heads back to school. Attending compulsory schooling Monday through Friday may seem normal or customary now. However, the last 125–40 years of compulsory schooling in Canada, until very recently (the 1950s), was resisted by both the wealthy and the increasingly affluent working and middle classes (see Curtis 1988; Prentice 1977; Schecter 1977). On this day, our Canadian student's school entry is uneventful; however, if she lived in the poor inner-city neighbourhoods of Washington, DC, New York City, or other American metropolitan centres, she might have to pass through a metal detector at the school's entrance (see *Maclean's*, 16 March 1992, 30). Given time, this search for handguns, brass knuckles, knives, and so on may be deemed necessary in the suburban school attended by our student, and the procedure might come to be viewed, just as it is now viewed in airports and inner-city schools, as part of a normal day.

EARLY SCHOOL LEAVING OR 'THE DROP-OUT PROBLEM'

Many students, unlike our hypothetical student, do not return to school on Monday morning—in fact, an increasing number of early leavers are not returning on Tuesday through Friday mornings either. While I do not like the term 'drop-out' because of its many negative connotations and because of data supporting my view that some who are so labelled are doing activities more challenging and exciting than school, the statistics of the so-called 'drop-out problem' can be sobering. Not only are observers urging, for good reasons, earlier scrutiny of potential 'at risk' students starting in the elementary years (see Ensminger and Slusarcick 1992; Hanson et al. 1991) but this kind of attention is also now being extended to Canada's university students (Tausig 1991:48).

With reference to high school students, the *Ontario Study of the Relevance of Education and the Isssue of Dropouts*, commonly known as the Radwanski Report (Radwanski 1987:67), defines a drop-out as '*any student who leaves school before having obtained his or her Secondary School Graduation Diploma (SSGD)*. In practical terms, that means any student who leaves high school before having successfully completed Grade 12.' Radwanski (1987:68–70) calculates that the drop-out rate in Ontario as of the mid-1980s is somewhere between 31 and 33 per cent. The latest figures from Statistics Canada are the same. They show that 30 to 33 per cent of students leave high school before successfully completing Grade 12 (see *Chronicle-Journal*, 8 Sept. 1991a, A7).

These statistics are corroborated by other Canadian studies undertaken by some school boards and districts. In the Ontario city of Hamilton, for example, 34.5 per cent of those students enrolled in secondary schools as of September 1985 had 'retired' by September 1986. These 'retirements' were predominant among general level (as opposed to advanced level) students, with four out of every five early leavers coming from general level programs.

Figures on early school leavers in the United States are similar to those in Canada. Gary R. Wehlage and Robert A. Rutter (1987:70) provide what is probably a conservative estimate of 25–7 per cent of American adolescents who fail to graduate from high school. They also ask readers to develop a historical perspective, keeping in mind that it was only until the 1950s that the drop-out rate for males fell below 50 per cent. The rate continued to drop until the mid- to late 1960s when it started to rise again. They cite California statistics as an example, a state where in 1967 only 12 per cent left before high school graduation, but where this figure rose to 17, 20, and 22 per cent respectively by 1970, 1972, and 1976.

None of these state/province, national, or even city averages take into account gender, ethnicity, and socio-economic class (key elements in the hidden curriculum) to explain inner-city early school leaving rates that approach and surpass 50 per cent. When the application of technology is added to these other elements, one might even be able to explain why Statistics Canada reports that over 30 per cent of recent early leavers had A or B grade averages when they left (see *Globe and Mail*, 17 Dec. 1991, A10), as well as why Jonathan Kozol (1986:3–12) cites an equal or higher percentage of potential buyers of his *Illiterate America* as being unable to read the words he writes, even though many hold high school diplomas. In brief, whether or not they leave school early, students who are either illiterate and/or aliterate, those immersed in today's electronic culture, seem to be quickly becoming the norm.

THREE KEY ELEMENTS IN THE HIDDEN CURRICULUM AND THE IDEOLOGY OF MERITOCRACY

Gender, ethnicity, and class differences are important in explaining today's student as 'a product' of present-day schooling. Each of these elements is reviewed to show how it supports the ideology of meritocracy—a part of the ideological foundation of the current socio-economic arrangements of monopoly capitalism.

Gender

The newspaper (*Chronicle-Journal*, 5 Feb. 1992b, 20) reports that a year after the Iraqi occupation of 1991, Kuwaiti women active in the resistance turned their attention to fighting another campaign—a campaign for the right to vote. Kuwait lags behind the Arab countries of Egypt, Algeria, Libya, and Syria, where women have already attained this right. However, when Kuwaiti women turn to Saudi Arabia, where women cannot drive an automobile and must be fully veiled in public, *they* see a 'backward' nation. Even if women in Kuwait are eventually successful in acquiring the vote, they would still have to trace their ancestry in Kuwait back to 1920 in order to be eligible to vote (a requirement presently met by the 90,000 eligible male voters in a country with a total population of 1.2 million).

While Saudi women must be fully veiled in public, many women in Canada and the United States are afraid to appear in public alone. As a teenager in Montreal, recalling the 1989 tragedy at l'Ecole Polytechnique of the University of Montreal where fourteen women were murdered, put it: 'Girls can't even walk on the streets after school. We always have to have someone with us. We always have to be afraid. We can't go anywhere by ourselves' (Bula 1991:A18).

At Canadian universities women are reporting sexual harassment by males as 'the norm' (see Pyke 1991:13–18). Incidents range from sexual staring and remarks to sexual advances and assaults. Incidents seem to be unrelated to age, marital status, or graduate program, but Morris (1989), surveying women graduate students at the University of Western Ontario, found that doctoral students were more likely than students at the master's level to report more of these types of harassment. Could it be that sexual harassment is more 'the norm' as one progresses through the ranks of formal schooling?

One norm that is certainly emphasized in universities and other schools is what Belenky et al. (1986) have described as 'procedural knowledge'. This kind of knowledge, often labelled 'separate knowing', is characterized by an emphasis upon prediction, mastery, control, evaluation, impersonality, and distance; it contrasts markedly with 'connected knowing' as a procedure in which the emphasis is upon the qualities of understanding, caring, empathy, acceptance, and first-hand experience (the characteristics of both knowings taken from Pyke 1991:19). Feminist scholars (see, for example, Abramson 1975; Belenky et al. 1986; Fee 1986; Rosser 1990) continue to argue that most women prefer to construct their knowledge of the world in this connected knowing way as opposed to the separate knowing, 'malestream' manner (see O'Brien 1981, 1988). They argue that women's ways of knowing are different—different from the way or mode of knowing emphasized and rewarded in schools. If they are correct, is it possible that the reluctance of female high school students to take advanced courses in mathematics and science (see Mura et al. 1987) and in computers (see Chiareli 1989 and Collis 1987) is *not* related to their ability as a group but rather to low self-confidence and interest levels resulting from the way in which these subjects are introduced and taught in schools (see Lewington 1992)?

Ethnicity

If you are both female and Aboriginal, you might be less concerned with getting through math, science, and/or computer courses than just getting through, period. Suicide rates among Aboriginal or First Nations peoples are six times the Canadian national average, as well as being significantly higher here than among First Nations peoples in the United States (Shkilnyk 1985:235). The rate is higher for the young, especially for girls and young women.

The rates of suicide and attempted suicide among females are extremely high. Grassy Narrows, an Ojibway community near Kenora in northwestern Ontario, offers a depressingly instructive example. According to Shkilnyk (1985:16), who reviewed data from the Ontario Provincial Police for the period June 1977 to May 1978, twenty-three out of twenty-eight reported suicide attempts (or 82 per cent of all attempts) were made by females.

In brief, to be Aboriginal and young, whether female or male, is to live with a significant likelihood that you will attempt or succeed in killing yourself or become a victim in violent incidents and accidents. For those who escape this violence, it is unlikely that they will reach high school, let alone graduate. When Shkilnyk gathered her data in the late 1970s in Grassy Narrows, somewhere between 40 and 50 per cent of all students had left school by grades four and five. Further, 'in 1977–78, of the sixty-nine young people in the fifteen to nineteen age-group, only nine were enrolled in high school, and four of these dropped out by the end of the first quarter' (Shkilnyk 1985:35). Today the situation is only marginally better and Aboriginal young people continue to have very significant school drop-out rates (see Frideres 1987; Randhawa 1991). Likewise, both Black Canadians (*Our Schools/Our Selves* 1991) and African Americans (see Stark 1992:483) are groups fighting high drop-out rates.

As with Aboriginals who leave the reserve for school and then return as 'cultural apples' (red on the outside and white on the inside), many Black Canadians and African Americans find themselves dealing with 'the oreo question' of how to make it through the White-dominated school system while maintaining ties to their culture and local community. As Rutgers' Fordham and Berkeley's Ogbu describe the problem, 'what appears to have emerged in some segments of the black community is a kind of cultural orientation which defines academic learning as "acting white", and academic success as the prerogative of white Americans' (quoted in D'Souza 1992:235). Again, what is the norm or customary varies greatly, and in many Black communities, to drop out or leave school early may be more normal or usual, and less deviant, than to stay in school.

A statistic that might help the reader in thinking about normalcy and deviance is provided by Estrich (1989:24) when she notes that African Americans account for about 12 per cent of the United States population and nearly 50 per cent of its prison population. Is prison for African Americans deviant or normal? This same 11 to 12 per cent receives slightly more than 2 per cent of all PhD degrees awarded in the United States, with about half of these in recent years being granted in the field of education (see D'Souza 1992:167–8). Perhaps this concentration in a single field, an area of study that is also very popular among Aboriginals, can be explained by the difficulties African Americans experience in a White-dominated educational system. Or perhaps African Americans are simply abnormally overinterested in the school (and the prison) as an institution.

Recent statistics indicate that some of the most well-known and prestigious universities and colleges in the United States are very interested in African Americans and other minority students, making repeated attempts to entice them to attend. 'At Ivy league colleges, which are among the most competitive in the nation, incoming freshmen [*sic*] have average grade scores close to 4.0 (all As) and average SATs (Scholastic Aptitude Test scores) of

1,250 to 1,300 (out of a possible 1,600). According to admissions officials, however, several of these schools admit black, Hispanic, and American Indian students with grade averages as low as 2.5 and SAT aggregates "in the 700 to 800 range"' (D'Souza 1992:3). Roughly the same pattern can also be found at state schools that are, for the most part, publicly financed.

To be of Asian background can and often does lead to a story with a different ending. While African Americans are literally being recruited for admission to élite universities, the cream of the crop among Asian Americans are finding that an exclusionary system of minority quotas based upon new admission criteria often excludes them. Thus D'Souza (1992:3) found that at the University of California at Berkeley, Asian Americans are up to twenty times (or 2,000 per cent) less likely to be accepted for admission than African American and Hispanic students with the same academic qualifications. And this is happening even though Asians, when compared to White, Hispanic, and African American students as distinct groups, score a good deal higher on the standard admission criteria of high school GPA (grade point average) and SAT results.

Obviously, some are more equal than others and admissions policies based upon quota systems at Berkeley and elsewhere are once again raising personal and individualized questions about the extent of structural and institutionalized racism and the connections or dialectic between the two. Racism re-emerges when the principle of 'merit' admissions gives way to that of quotas based upon proportional representation or diversity, and so do sexism and élitism. Class, gender, and ethnic backgrounds all become important as educators in a supposedly meritocratic society struggle anew with the question of what exactly constitutes merit. For many, 'merit', as determined by the numerical criteria of GPAs and SAT scores, is simply a synonym for privilege.

Class, the Hidden Curriculum, and the Meritocracy

Merit is not only mediated and partially determined by ethnicity and gender but is also most significantly affected by socio-economic class (see McLaren 1989, especially 8–10, 151; Turrittin 1986, especially 432). As the following discussion of testing, tracking, and term paper companies should make clear, social class background or privilege hides behind the official ideology of merit as the foundation for what school observers have called 'the hidden curriculum'. This curriculum, which is not acknowledged or made public by school officials, teaches the hierarchical bureaucratic order expected at the workplace—the designation of experts and subordinates, the social organization of a teacher-centred classroom, and so on. This hidden curriculum, as many argue (for example, see Rosenthal and Jacobson 1968), is far more important than the publicly acknowledged curriculum in selecting, sorting, and classifying students for 'success' in school and job placement.

The matter of testing is illustrative. Over the past thirty-five years, arguments have moved from a general statement critical of *The Tyranny of Testing* (Hoffman [1962] 1978) to much more specific charges concerning the class and cultural biases of the most well-known standardized tests. The general argument is that the class, culture, ethnic, and gender biases of standardized testing not only undermine so-called meritocratic and egalitarian criteria but also the intelligence and school aspirations of those marginal students who do not fit the middle-class, White, and male orientation of today's schools. Recently, Crouse and Trusheim (1988), Greene (1988), Weiss et al. (1989), and Fallows (1980) have all been critical of the content of the SATs and the manner in which they are used by university and college admissions officers; the results are reproducing class, ethnic, and gender inequities rather than solving them. Most recently, Evangelauf (1990) has broadened this emphasis upon 'cultural capital' differences and the ways in which standardized tests like SATS exacerbate them with a general discussion of how reliance upon multiple-choice testing continues to harm minorities and hamper reform.

Moving from testing to 'tracking' or 'streaming' in schools, one can see the same hidden curriculum at work. Evidence gathered by Jeannie Oakes (1985) and Glenna Colclough and E.M. Beck (1986) summarizes what continues to be a heated discussion on this matter. It shows that tracking students into so-called ability groups perpetuates social class inequalities, further disadvantaging the already disadvantaged. In Peter McLaren's (1989:9) words, 'tracking fosters the *illusion* of meritocratic competition while in reality functioning as a "ranking" system that legitimates differences based on race, gender, and social power and locks students into positions of limited opportunity.'

Finally, a few remarks on term paper companies may be instructive, showing how students' use of their services supports the hidden curriculum in a manner that promotes meritocratic ideology. For the past twenty-five years, these companies have served the needs of students required to research and write term papers or essays. Some students want only a bibliography, some want annotated summaries of research relevant to their topics, some want particular sections of the paper to be written for them, and others want the entire essay researched and written for them. All students, of course, would prefer that their professors remain unaware of their having contracted out their school assignments.

As a graduate student in the early 1970s, I was able to win the trust of enough students to do an informal survey and found that among those who wanted the whole essay done for them, a student's chances of getting caught or continuing undetected had much to do with class background and money. Those who could afford only the least expensive model received a term paper that had been used several times before, increasing their risk of being detected as 'cheaters' and exposing them to the harsh sanctions of school authorities. Students who could afford more expensive models, of course, minimized their risks as the price went up. At the top, the wealthiest students received 'original', made-to-order works rather than reprints, with virtually no attendant risks. In brief, whether you decide to cheat or play it straight, the hidden curriculum and its most fundamental building-block, socio-economic class background, are paramount in determining whether or not you are seen as 'meritorious'. As a former colleague in the history department used to jokingly advise, advice I routinely pass on to my students, 'Choose your parents well.'

TECHNOLOGY AND THE HIDDEN CURRICULUM

It is not mere happenstance that authors writing about schools and childhood also often write about television. In Canada this is true of Joyce Nelson (1987, 1988) as well as Morris Wolfe (1985), and of Neil Postman (1982, 1985) and Marie Winn (1978, 1983) in the United States.

Postman provides us with a theory explaining why childhood is disappearing. It is a theory formulated out of 'a series of conjectures about how media of communication affect the socialization process; in particular, how the printing press created childhood and how the electronic media are "disappearing" it' (Postman 1982:xii). Postman shows how the invention and diffusion of the printing press restored adult literacy, education in age-segregated schools, and a sense of adult shame necessary for the reintroduction of childhood—something that had disappeared with the collapse of the Roman empire and the descent into the Dark Ages and then the Middle Ages.

During the Enlightenment, an age of print-connected literacy, this concept of childhood as a necessary social and intellectual category was rediscovered. In turn, schools once again became necessary when an increasingly sharp division between readers and non-readers made print literacy synonymous with adulthood, a status to be earned in school by learning to read. As stages of childhood were matched with a sequenced curriculum reserved exclusively for children, children became further separated from adults with regard to dress, games, language, and literature. Part of the adult world involved a sense of shame related to adult secrets, which Postman (1982:48) relates to the self-control (the contemplative quietness, immobility, and regulation of bodily functions) necessary to become a reader—an adult: 'Print gave us the disembodied mind, but it left us with the problem of how to control the rest of us. Shame was the mechanism by which such control would be managed.'

Postman (1982) goes on to explain the current disappearance of childhood as the result of electronic media, which is fast destroying the print culture that formerly connected literacy, schools, and the separation of child-hood from adulthood. He convincingly argues that television, which he calls 'the total disclosure medium', destroys shame and the adult secrets that accompany it, as well as the focus upon acquiring print literacy as the mea-sure of adulthood. Thus the age of electronic media threatens to leave school instruction behind as an antiquated irrelevancy. Postman elaborates this the-sis, showing how television helps merge and mix childhood and adulthood by encouraging children to become more like their parents, the ever-more childlike adults.

Winn (1983) shares Postman's concerns. She discusses the increasing similarity between today's adultlike children and childlike adults by illustrat-ing how television helps move children 'from protection to preparation'. In brief, she shows how today's television-age children are quickly losing their childhood and also warns, along with David Elkind (1981, 1984, 1987) and others, of the dire consequences. Winn (1983) is especially concerned with what is happening to children's play within the current electronic environ-ment. Writing about 'the end of play', she compares and contrasts video games with marbles while examining what she refers to as 'out-of-control television' viewing and its effects. The sedating effect of this kind of viewing is contrasted with the spontaneous activity of the childhood games it has replaced. Rapidly disappearing are both the idea and the parent-supported reality of childhood as a special and protected condition, for accompanying out-of-control television are 'out-of-control parents' and parenting—'adults whose mounting divorce rate and two-career families put them mostly out of the picture, pardon the pun, for most of their children' (Nelsen 1985a:308).

Winn's argument, like Postman's, goes beyond and is not simply re-stricted to out-of-control television. Rather, their arguments in significant ways turn on the reality that the mere presence of television in the home has altered traditional parent-child relationships. In so arguing, they both follow and owe much to the work of Canadian scholars Harold Innis (1972) and Marshall McLuhan (1964).

McLuhan's popularization of the phrases 'the medium is the message' and 'the medium is the massage' (McLuhan and Fiore 1967) is viewed here as simply an elaboration of Innis's emphasis upon the non-neutrality of communications technology; or, put another way, this phrase refers to the realization that changes in the technology of communications media alter the things thought about, thought with, and the area in which thoughts develop. The work of Innis and McLuhan draws our attention to the ways in which the structure of our interests is changed by the technology of the communications medium in question. In brief, each medium has a form or mould, the structural limitations of which change us to correspond to and fit within it.

In Canada, as in the United States, this has meant schools are patterned ever more closely after television's present-time orientation. Schools are patterned after television news programming, with preference given to the brevity of non-contradictory and discontinuous, fast-paced information over the more lengthy development of stories grounded in a kind of knowledge where perspective is developed—where one is encouraged to see both the contradictions and implications of the present within its historical context. These are schools where the joy in this kind of serious knowledge discovery is no longer often expected or desired by either teachers or students, and where whatever playfulness remains in childhood is quickly being replaced by the entertainment jolts of what Wolfe (1985) has described as 'the TV wasteland' centred in the United States.

Yet, what else might we reasonably expect? Recent surveys show that most Canadians and Americans watch, conservatively estimated, about four hours a day of television, and that conversation between parents and children is all but absent, save for 'don't' and 'do' directives. In our culture, as Postman (1985) points out, public discourse has given way to show business. Certainly, our culture's increasing preoccupation with the jolts of entertainment television has had a marked impact upon the way both teachers and students perceive their own and each other's roles and, consequently, upon the way they interact. Good teaching increasingly has come to be defined in many quarters in terms of its entertainment value. In short, social contexts, school and others, are both changed by and change the ways in which a given technology is appreciated and used.

Elsewhere I (Nelsen 1991:137–50) have analysed our latest technology fixation, the computer, raising the question of whether the production and widespread use of computers is a technology from which we can expect fundamental social change in the most disastrous inequalities and continuing structural problems created by current socio-economic arrangements. Or is the social context created by widespread computer use more likely to encourage a passiveness and an acquired inability, already promoted by out-of-control television viewing, to bring about fundamental social change?

My answers temper the salutory messages of those advocating the wonders of the personal computer. I (Nelsen 1991), along with Postman (1992), argue that the computer, like television, comes with a point of view or a hidden curriculum embedded in the form of the medium itself and in the structure of power relations governing its production and distribution. The manufacturers of both computer hardware and the programmed-learning packages that accompany it are some of our largest corporate monopolies—IBM-type corporations, whose stake in the prevailing economic, status, and knowledge inequities both reifies and reproduces the current class, ethnic, and gender biases of the hidden curriculum, both within and outside the classroom. In a sentence, whatever liberating potential widespread computer use may have is at best muted and often altogether lost.

In sum, the reality of both computer and television use is currently increasing homogenized programming for mass audiences who, like the producers, are ever more pacified by a learning-as-product mentality. This mentality forecloses viewing and developing learning as an active, dynamic process. Some students, frequently labelled 'deviant', are in some measure resisting this mentality by doing something other than simply being caught up in passive support of the main technological drift. Thus it is especially important to listen to the dissenting voices in our schools—the students who are resisting, saying no to current school arrangements.

STUDENT RESISTANCE AND THE RESPONSE OF AUTHORITIES

Student Resistance
Elsewhere (see Nelsen 1985b or 1991:10–40) I have traced the connections between compulsory schooling, boredom, and the deviance of school vandals, school skippers, and early school leavers. I argue that authorities should treat the actions of these 'deviants' (those who make public the school-is-boring and growing-up-is-absurd reality of their everyday experience by 'voting with their feet') not as an excuse for punishment but as a serious statement about what is wrong with today's schools. The forced socialization of schooling standardizes emotions as well as analytic perceptions and, in so doing, often diminishes or eliminates potentially important differences for the sake of moulding students to professionalized bureaucratic routines.

With regard to this moulding, this shaping, one should ask to what extent does compliance with the norms and rituals of school mean that students have to change identities central to their psychosocial make-up—identities related to the fit between their backgrounds and the school's hidden curriculum with regard to socio-economic class, ethnicity, and gender. Success in school depends to a large extent upon knowledge of and compliance with the hidden curriculum, and mastering this curriculum has much to do with cultural capital, which refers to the general cultural background, knowledge, skills, predispositions, and disposition passed on from one generation to the next. As Henry Giroux (1983; Aronowitz and Giroux 1985), drawing upon the work of French sociologist Pierre Bourdieu (1986), Basil Bernstein (1971–5), and others has pointed out, the school systematically depreciates the cultural capital of students from 'disadvantaged' backgrounds—students whose values, ways of acting (mannerisms), language practices, and so on do not match those of the dominant culture. Viewed from this perspective, psychologizing or individualizing student failure is, as McLaren (1989:221) insightfully notes, yet another part of the hidden curriculum: 'In effect,

psychologizing school failure indicts the student while simultaneously protecting the social environment from sustained criticism.' Viewed within the
cultural capital argument, then, academic performance does not represent
individual competence or ability; rather, it represents the school's position
within the larger structure of prevailing socio-economic arrangements.

In order not to be misunderstood in my interpretation of the cultural
capital thesis, here are a few words of clarification. I am not subscribing to
a static or mechanical theory of cultural reproduction through schooling.
I focus upon making class, ethnic, and gender-based distinctions in cultural
capital not simply to note difference but to note and examine opposition. I
join Giroux, Michael Apple (1982), and others in viewing schools as partially
autonomous sites of struggle over social relations and their meaning—sites
where the dynamics of everyday interaction create potential for fundamental
social change. In a word, some students often, and almost all students sometimes, *resist* the authority of the school to mould them.

A literature has developed during the past fifteen years, with most of the
data gathered using participant-observation techniques, analysing the reality
that students play a significant role in negotiating the order of the school
(Beynon 1984; Furlong 1984; Martin 1976; Woods 1984). Paul Willis (1977),
Paul Corrigan (1979), and Robert Everhart (1983) have shown how boys
from the working class limit output and encourage group cohesion by emphasizing the practicality of doing rather than theorizing, and by developing a distinctive form of language together with a sophisticated repertoire
of physically intimidating humour or practical jokes. What these 'lads' are
doing is using the cultural capital provided by their backgrounds to develop
an oppositional or counterschool culture to gain some student control over
the work process as defined by school authorities.

John Ogbu (1986) has added to this research, which emphasizes class
background as the major variable by focusing upon the cultural capital of
ethnicity. He argues that the resistance of Black students in the United
States is part of a 'folk system' that cannot be fully explained by their subordinate economic status. Ogbu shows how the ethnic background of African
Americans pressures them to not 'act White' by not speaking standard English, not being on time, not working overly hard to get good grades, and so
on. The work of J. Rick Ponting and Roger Gibbins (1980) and others can
be used to make a similar argument for Aboriginal youths in Canada and the
United States. Here one could supplement Ogbu's list with the disinclina-
tion, language problems notwithstanding, of Aboriginal students to speak up
in class (their cultures often emphasize the wisdom gained in remaining
silent), as well as their reluctance to make eye contact during discussions and
oral presentations (such contact is usually interpreted as a sign of disrespect
in their cultures). These are but two of many examples of Aboriginal cultural

traits devalued by the school culture as it represents the dominant cultural ethos or character.

Finally, not only is the culture of the school middle class and White, it is also, in emulating the governing class that controls it, patterned along hierarchical lines and male-dominated (patriarchal). Angela McRobbie (1978, 1980) has insightfully shown how girls, in asserting their definitions of 'femaleness' by the way they dress and comport themselves, defy 'the good girl' image prized by school authorities. Their grown-up woman, a kind of sexual or sexy, resistance is often accompanied by the 'bein' tough' stance taken by boys who resist. However, it should be well emphasized, as McRobbie's work elaborates, that the resistance of girls is quite different from that of boys. Their resistance must be viewed within the sexism of the larger society in which school education for girls continues to be thought of as a kind of frill—a time-serving social preparation for girls while they wait to be further exploited in the world of domesticity and/or in the female job ghettos of the paid labour market.

Authority Response

Authorities' response to student resistance varies somewhat as disciplinary techniques and philosophies change over time and from one place to another, but the goal continues to be social control. While sitting in the corner wearing a dunce cap and bending over to the tune of a teacher's paddle are punishments no longer endured by today's recalcitrant students, teachers still keep children after school, force students to write many repetitions of 'thou shalt not' on the blackboard, and assign extra homework. Added to this list of 'negatives' is a kind of isolation known as 'in-school suspension'. More popular as control mechanisms are the 'positive reinforcement' techniques involving systems of merit points, which students can use in exchange for special privileges and consumer goods, and the increasingly popular video game-playing time awarded to students for good behaviour, finishing work on schedule, good quality of work, and so on.

Paddling, strapping, and other forms of corporal punishment are no longer everyday occurrences in our schools. The older 'carrot-and-stick' techniques have given way to a more subtle kind of positive reinforcement couched in the jargon of behaviouristic psychology. Thus when the dictates and social etiquette of bureaucracy fail to co-opt students into the control process as apprentice authority figures active in monitoring their own behaviour, school administrators often turn to consulting psychologists for help in bringing wayward students into line with the school's expectations. And from here, it is but a short step to drugging students into conformity. As I have noted (Nelsen 1991:26–7), 'when the school psychologists need aid they often turn to psychiatrists and other medical doctors who direct pharmacists to provide doses of Ritalin and other amphetamines (and tranquilizers), thereby daily drugging thousands of Canadian and American school children into acceptable classroom behaviour (Gray 1975:423–5; Rapoport 1974:71–4; Repo 1974:75–91).'

When all else fails to change the behaviour of students who resist, authorities lock them up. According to Robert L. Thompson, executive director of the Creighton Centre in Thunder Bay, detaining and jailing youths no longer seems to be viewed as a measure of last resort. He cites recent figures that show that the average daily number of youths in detention in Ontario has risen dramatically—an increase of about 35 per cent from 1986–7 to 1989–90. It is not merely happenstance that as so-called 'target hardening' of schools makes them look more like jails and similar custodial institutions, in-school suspensions (a kind of solitary confinement) and other punishment techniques remind one more and more of the treatment accorded to hardened criminals.

Of course, much of this has to do with the reality that teachers are retained and given permanent job security for their ability to maintain order in the classroom. They are empowered and required by law to do so. While lawyers like Anthony F. Brown (1991:40) note that according to the Criminal Code of Canada, 'everyone who is authorized by law to use force is criminally responsible for any excess thereof' and warn teachers to be aware that many boards of education have banned or severely restricted the use of corporal punishment, the Code continues to read as follows: 'Every school teacher, parent or person standing in the place of a parent is justified in using force by way of correction toward a pupil or child, as the case may be, if the force does not exceed what is reasonable in the circumstances.'

Beyond these legalities governing teacher-student interaction, it is critical to understand that much of the control school authorities feel they must exercise has to do with another legal aspect, the reality that school-aged children are legally compelled to attend school until their sixteenth birthday or to make acceptable alternative (usually home schooling) arrangements. As one of my current students insightfully noted, the unfreedom of such compulsory schooling is often best demonstrated by those labelled deviant who wind up in prison. Moved from the jail-like circumstances of compulsory schooling to real jails, some are able for the first time to see a way out of their 'disadvantaged' position. They are capable of envisioning a more 'advantaged' position for themselves because they now have a choice—ironically, a sort of freedom behind bars—to attend school and to educate themselves. Of course, I offer this insight not to suggest jail either as a means of becoming upwardly mobile in the larger society or as an ideal solution for social problems inextricably connected with and endemic to our present socio-economic structure. Rather, I cite my student's observation to emphasize the importance of doing institutional analysis that is firmly grounded in relations of authority and power.

Despite differences among countries and cultures in their deference to authority (see Friedenberg 1980), schools all over the globe, as institutions of socialization, make similar attempts to discipline and control their student populations. This has something to do not only with teachers standing in place of parents but also with the developing globalized economy and especially, as Jacques Ellul (1964) and Foucault (1977) have eloquently argued, with developments that continue to bureaucratize an increasingly totalitarian environment of administration. In brief, when one talks of student resistance to the forced standardization of their behaviour and the response of school authorities, we are talking of more than simply school deviance. Relations of power are fundamental to this discussion of school as a business bureaucracy, which shapes and controls its participants. It is not by accident that recently the most compelling case against bureaucracy has been made by feminists (see Ferguson 1984), a group conscious of and committed to changing the current power arrangements so oppressive to all women.

Analyses based upon gender and the other critical variables reviewed herein—ethnicity, class, and the application of new technology—should make it clear that the school and the so-called 'deviants' among its student population cannot be fully understood in isolation from the governing class structural arrangements of the larger society. Arrangements of power are critical and elsewhere I (Nelsen 1978:40–66) have detailed the work of three well-known American analysts (Clark, Riesman, and Jencks) who have developed sociologies of education offering ideological support for status quo arrangements. Simultaneously during the 1960s and 1970s, Canadian sociologists, the most prominent being the late John Porter, were developing themes similar to those found in the American sociologies of education and with the same effect—support of the status quo.

In *The Vertical Mosaic*, for example, Porter (1965) describes a Canadian society that is rapidly becoming more meritocratic and postindustrial. Like the Americans, Porter viewed education systems as being relatively autonomous and developed a sociology of education grounded in a pluralistic view of the structure of power—a view that *assumes* a rather wide dispersion of power among a large number of people representing a variety of groups and issues. Such a view is revealed, according to Marilyn Assheton-Smith (1979:45) in her critical review of Porter's education writings, in his 'concern that Canadian academics tend to make their knowledge available to government bureaucracies rather than political parties'. According to Assheton-Smith, Porter was concerned because he felt that this practice by academics would eventually upset the countervailing forces between bureaucratic and political élites, which hold steady the precarious balancing of power. That scientific or expert knowledge might be ideological or that the countervailing forces of an interest group's balance of power might be an illusion maintained by a governing class interested in perpetuating its hidden curriculum of inequalities in schools are complexities that seemed to have escaped both Porter's and the Americans' sociology of education.

Porter, as is the case with the Americans I studied, viewed the schools as supporting the status quo balance of power in a society that was both pluralistic and meritocratic. In performing the twin functions of transmitting values to the young and of sorting/allocating talent, the schools would be reaffirming and supposedly passing on the values of efficiency, liberty, and a democratic equality of opportunity.

It has been a major contention of this chapter that what actually gets passed on to students with the help of this type of mainstream sociology is an ideology and practice of social control as opposed to a more progressive emphasis upon social change. What follows are some ideas that, if implemented, could help us move towards developing educational alternatives to school as social control.

CONCLUSION: A LEARNING ALTERNATIVE TO TODAY'S SCHOOLS

Elsewhere I have argued for the abolition of compulsory schooling and the development of community-based, voluntary learning. I draw upon the work of several analysts (Gayfer 1976; Gittell 1970; Goodman, 1964; Lind 1974; Minzey and LeTarte 1972; Stevens 1974) in stating that 'even when the school system is benevolent, it is in the bureaucratic death-grip of a uniformity of conception from the universities down, that cannot possibly suit the multitude of dispositions and conditions' (Nelsen 1991:30). What is required is decentralization and local empowerment at the community level. These are more than simply my opinions, for they are built upon an analytical foundation grounded in the empirical evidence of research studies.

The three most important findings related to this research indicate the following. First, there is much learning that occurs outside classrooms (see Hamilton 1987:162–4). Second, the size of school and student-adult ratios matter greatly—smaller is indeed more beautiful (see Hamilton 1987:148, 154; McDill, Natriello, and Pallas 1987:125). Third, teachers and counsellors have crucial roles to play in determining what kind of experiences students have in schools (see Lockhart 1991; McDill et al. 1987:125–7; Payne 1989:113–28; Smith 1986).

All of these factors are, of course, interrelated. By their very nature, learning settings outside the traditional classroom push students and other school participants out into the wider community. In this way learning is reconnected within the web of community life, ideally making learning and living seamless or all of one piece. The result is more learner-based, individualized, one-to-one learning situations—moving away from the current overly centralized bureaucratic model towards a more decentralized appren-ticeship-type model. Not only is the structure-content of the curriculum changed to emphasize 'a real world meaning system' (see Farrell 1990:149–63) that starts with the needs of learners where they are, but also a premium is placed upon the diligence and commitment of adults in their roles as teachers and counsellors, the educational decision makers (Cicourel and Kitsuse 1963), to make a difference in the lives of students.

It has been well documented, especially by G.D. Gottfredson and col-leagues (see McDill et al. 1987:144 for citations), that so-called 'alternative schools' with learning environments grounded upon these three findings help potential early school leavers find greater satisfaction in their school experiences. Experiencing alternatives to the 'normal' school, the hostility of so-called 'at risk' students disappears (see Kulka, Mann, and Klingel 1980:59) and so-called 'discipline and drop-out problems' are minimized. This is not surprising to observers like Wehlage and Rutter (1987:81), as the best data available to them 'suggest that school factors related to discipline are signifi-cant in developing a tendency to drop out'. In brief, school policy makers and administrative officials need to appreciate fully the implications of what many school observers and analysts already understand—namely, that the 'deviance' observed among students is in many important ways related to the school context. This is why it is so important to listen to and act upon the concerns voiced by early school leavers and others who are making their school dissatisfactions public.

The work of Apple (1989:205–23), along with that of several other soci-ologists of education, continues to emphasize the correspondence principle—that is, the direct connections between the reality of the larger socio-eco-nomic arrangements surrounding the school and the school in shaping what goes on there. Thus for Apple, a focus on the issue of drop-outs as primarily an educational problem with an educational solution is largely misguided and wrong because such a focus is based on the 'assumption that we will find long-term answers to the dropout dilemma and to the realities of poverty and unemploy-ment by keeping our attention within the school' (Apple 1989:206).

Apple is certainly correct in his analysis of the long-term implications of misguided thinking. As Ivan Illich (1972) argued some twenty-five years ago, we must eventually destroy the monopoly that schools have been given over both learning and certification. It is not enough, however, simply to recog-nize long-term implications and then sit back to await a fundamental change in today's monopoly arrangements. Given persistent and pervasive inequities grounded in gender, ethnicity, and class as well as the endemic problem of school boredom (see, for example, Csikszentmihalyi, Larson, and Prescott 1977; Farrell 1990:106–19), all of us are being called upon in the short term to respond immediately and responsibly.

I have argued here for the development of a sort of movable feast—a decentralized, community-based, and more individually focused alternative

to the present depersonalizing and dehumanizing school bureaucracy. Recent research indicates that not only is this the proper direction in which to
move but also that even more emphasis must be placed upon the important
roles to be played by classroom teachers and school counsellors. David Hanson
and colleagues (1991) emphasize this point while also calling for substantial
reductions in class size to help personalize and humanize learning by lowering the student-adult ratio. In an otherwise sociologically weak and badly
flawed analysis of Ontario's schools, Radwanski (1987) is also able to recognize the critical importance of both small class size and the roles played by
teachers and counsellors. Even he understands that we must begin to give
students back their voices and then listen to what they are saying. In short,
we must dramatically change today's school reality where, to use Michelle
Fine's (1987:99) excellent description, 'For the most part schooling is structured so that student opinions, voices, and critical thoughts remain silenced
... Classrooms are organized more around control than conversation, more
around the authority of teacher than autonomy of students, and more around
competition than collaboration.'

Providing students with opportunities in different types of learning environments to empower them will not be easy. It will take effort on all sides
for, as Steen Esbensen (1991:238–47) has correctly noted, the reinstatement
of student rights in Canada goes well beyond equality issues traditionally put
forward by liberals. It will involve moving beyond our current understanding of conscience as 'a thoroughly private matter' to recover the word's
Latin root, *com & scire*, meaning 'to know together' (see Nelson 1991:8).
This, of course, brings us back to the importance of community and the com-
panion word 'consciousness'—a word that, as Nelson (1991:8) points out, shares
the same Latin root as 'conscious' and 'suggests a dialectic or dynamic interaction among awareness, conscience, and society'. It is in appreciating the
importance of this dialectic that we may begin to rethink the role of today's
schools in the social construction of deviance and normalcy. It can only be
hoped that this rethinking is part of a praxis that will eventually move prevailing socio-economic arrangements and the schools shaped by them away
from their current disciplinarian and prisonlike emphasis on social control
into more freedom-oriented and liberatory learning environments.

FURTHER READINGS

Cayley, D. 1992. *Ivan Illich in Conversation*. Concord, ON: Anansi.
Davies, S. 1994a. 'In Search of Resistance and Rebellion Among High
    School Dropouts'. *The Canadian Journal of Sociology* 19, no. 3:331–50.
_____. 1994b. 'Class Dismissed? Student Opposition in Ontario'. *The
    Canadian Review of Sociology and Anthropology* 31, no. 3:421–44.

_____. 1995. 'Reproduction and Resistance in Canadian High Schools: An Empirical Examination of the Willis Thesis'. *The British Journal of Sociology* 46, no. 4:662–87.

Davis, B. 1990. *What Our High Schools Could Be ...* Toronto: Our Schools/ Our Selves and Garamond.

Foucault, M. 1977. *Discipline and Punish: The Birth of the Prison.* New York: Pantheon.

Gaskell, J. 1992. *Gender Matters: From School to Work in the 1990s.* Toronto: Ontario Institute for Studies in Education.

Gilligan, C. 1982. *In a Different Voice: Psychological Theory and Women's Development.* Cambridge, Mass.: Harvard University Press.

Jacoby, R. 1994. *Dogmatic Wisdom: How the Culture Wars Divert Education and Distract America.* New York: Doubleday.

McKibben, B. 1993. *The Age of Missing Information.* New York: Plume (Penguin).

Muller, J., ed. 1990. *Education for Work, Education as Work: Canada's Changing Community Colleges.* Toronto: Garamond.

Nelsen, R.W., ed. (Forthcoming) *Inside Canadian Universities: Another Day at the Plant.* Kingston, ON: Cedarcreek Publications.

_____. 1991. *Miseducating: Death of the Sensible.* Kingston, ON: Cedarcreek Publications.

Richer, S. 1988. 'Equality to Benefit from Schooling: The Issue of Educational Opportunity'. In *Social Issues: Sociological Views of Canada*, 2nd ed., edited by D. Forcese and S. Richer, 262–86. Scarborough, ON: Prentice-Hall.

Smith, D.E. 1990. *The Conceptual Practices of Power: A Feminist Sociology of Knowledge.* Toronto: University of Toronto Press.

Tanner, J. 1990. 'Reluctant Rebels: A Case Study of Edmonton High School Drop-Outs'. *The Canadian Review of Sociology and Anthropology* 27, no. 1:74–94.

Turkle, S. 1984. *The Second Self: Computers and the Human Spirit.* New York: Simon and Schuster.

Wotherspoon, T., ed. 1991. *Hitting the Books: The Politics of Educational Retrenchment.* Toronto: Garamond.

REFERENCES

Abramson, J. 1975. *The Invisible Woman: Discrimination in the Academic Profession.* San Francisco: Jossey-Bass.

Apple, M.W. 1982. *Education and Power.* Boston: Routledge and Kegan Paul.

_____. 1989. 'American Realities: Poverty, Economy, and Education'. In *Dropouts from School: Issues, Dilemmas, and Solutions*, edited by L. Weis,

E. Farrar, and H.G. Petrie, 205-23. Albany: State University of New York Press.

Aronowitz, S., and H.A. Giroux. 1985. *Education under Siege: The Conservative and Radical Debate over Schooling*. South Hadley, Mass.: Bergin and Garvey.

Assheton-Smith, M. 1979. 'John Porter's Sociology; A Theoretical Basis for Canadian Education'. *Canadian Journal of Education* 4, no. 2:43–54.

Baril, J. 1992. 'Women, Weed & Death'. *Thunder Bay Post* (17 June):10–11.

Becker, H.S. 1953. 'Becoming a Marihuana User'. *American Journal of Sociology* 59:235–42.

_____. 1955. 'Marihuana Use and Social Control'. *Social Problems* 3:35–44.

_____. 1963. *Outsiders: Studies in the Sociology of Deviance*. New York: Free Press.

_____, et al. 1968. *Making the Grade: The Academic Side of College*. New York: Wiley.

Belenky, M.F., et al. 1986. *Women's Ways of Knowing*. New York: Basic.

Berger, P.L., and T. Luckmann. 1966. *The Social Construction of Reality: A Treatise in the Sociology of Knowledge*. Garden City, NY: Doubleday.

Bernstein, B.B. 1971–5. *Class, Codes and Control*, vol. 1–3. London: Routledge and Kegan Paul.

Beynon, J. 1984. '"Sussing Out" Teachers: Pupils as Data Gatherers'. In *Life in School: The Sociology of Pupil Culture*, edited by M. Hammersley and P. Woods, 121–44. Milton Keynes, UK: Open University Press.

Birenbaum, R. 1992. 'Establishing Guidelines for Research Integrity'. *University Affairs* 33:6–9.

Bourdieu, P. 1986. 'Forms of Capital'. In *Handbook of Theory and Research for the Sociology of Education*. New York: Greenwood Press.

Bowers, C.A. 1980. *The Cultural Dimensions of Educational Computing: Understanding the Non-Neutrality of Technology*. New York: Teachers College Press.

Brown, A.F. 1991. *Legal Handbook for School Administrators*, 2nd ed. Scarborough, ON: Thomson.

Bula, F. 1991. '"Girls Can't Even Walk on the Street ... We Always Have to Be Afraid"'. *Montreal Gazette* (7 December):A18.

Chiareli, D.L. 1989. 'Sex and Computers: Equity vs Inequity'. *Comment on Education* 18, no. 3:12–19.

Chronicle-Journal. 1991a. 'Education System Critics Look at Money, Methods: One-third of Canadian Students Don't Finish High School' (8 September):A7.

_____. 1991b. 'Plagiarism' (29 December):A6.

_____. 1992a. 'With Virtual Reality You Can Travel at Home" (5 January):A2.

_____. 1992b. 'Kuwaiti Women Seek Vote' (5 February):20.

_____. 1992c. 'Punches, Kicks Part of Dance Fad' (15 June):16.

Cicourel, A.A., and J.I. Kitsuse. 1963. *The Educational Decision-Makers.* Indianapolis: Bobbs-Merrill.

Colclough, G., and E.M. Beck. 1986. 'The American Educational Structure and the Reproduction of Social Class'. *Sociological Inquiry* 56:456–76.

Collis, B. 1987. 'Adolescent Females and Computers: Real and Perceived Barriers'. In *Women and Education: A Canadian Perspective*, edited by J. Gaskell and A. McLaren, 117–31.

Corrigan, P. 1979. *Schooling the Smash Street Kids.* London: Macmillan.

Crouse, J., and D. Trusheim. 1988. *The Case Against the SAT.* Chicago: University of Chicago Press.

Csikszentmihalyi, M., R. Larson, and S. Prescott. 1977. 'The Ecology of Adolescent Activity and Experience'. *Journal of Youth and Adolescence* 6, no. 3:281–94.

Curtis, B. 1988. *Building the Educational State: Canada West, 1836–1871.* London, ON: Althouse.

D'Souza, D. 1992. *Illiberal Education: The Politics of Race and Sex on Campus.* New York: Vintage Books.

Durkheim, E. 1895. 'Crime et santé social'. *Revue Philosophique* 39:518–23.

Elkind, D. 1981. *The Hurried Child: Growing Up Too Fast Too Soon.* Reading, Mass.: Addison-Wesley.

_____. 1984. *All Grown Up and No Place to Go: Teenagers in Crisis.* Reading, Mass.: Addison-Wesley.

_____. 1987. *Miseducation: Preschoolers at Risk.* New York: Alfred A. Knopf.

Ellul, J. 1964. *The Technological Society.* New York: Random House.

Ensminger, M.E., and A.L. Slusarcick. 1992. 'Paths to High School Graduation or Dropout: A Longitudinal Study of a First-Grade Cohort'. *Sociology of Education* 65 (April):95–113.

Esbensen, S. 1991. 'Student Rights in Canada: Beyond Equality Issues'. In *Social Change and Education in Canada*, edited by R. Ghosh and D. Ray, 238–47. Toronto: Harcourt Brace Jovanovich.

Estrich, S. 1989. 'The Hidden Politics of Race'. *Washington Post Magazine* (23 April):23–4.

Evangelauf, J. 1990. 'Reliance on Multiple-Choice Tests Said to Harm Minorities and Hinder Reform'. *Chronicle of Higher Education* (30 May):A1.

Everhart, R.B. 1983. *Reading, Writing and Resistance: Adolescence and Labor in a Junior High School.* Boston: Routledge and Kegan Paul.

Fallows, J. 1980. 'The Tests and the Brightest'. *The Atlantic* (February):37–48.

Farrell, E. 1990. *Hanging In and Dropping Out: Voices of At-Risk High School Students.* New York: Teachers College Press.

Fee, E. 1986. 'Critiques of Modern Science: The Relationship of Feminism to Other Radical Epistemologies'. In *Feminist Approaches to Science*, edited by R. Bleier. Elmsford, NY: Pergamon.

Ferguson, K.E. 1984. *The Feminist Case Against Bureaucracy*. Philadelphia: Temple University Press.

Fine, M. 1987. 'Why Urban Adolescents Drop Into and Out of Public High School'. In *School Dropouts: Patterns and Policies*, edited by G. Natriello, 89–105. New York: Teachers College Press.

Fletcher, R. 1991. *Science, Ideology, and the Media: The Cyril Burt Scandal*. New Brunswick, NJ: Transaction.

Foucault, M. 1977. *Discipline and Punish: The Birth of the Prison*. Translated by A. Sheridan. New York: Pantheon.

Frideres, J.S. 1987. 'Native People and Canadian Education'. In *The Political Economy of Canadian Schooling*, edited by T. Wotherspoon, 275–89. Toronto: Methuen.

Friedenberg, E.Z. 1980. *Deference to Authority: The Case of Canada*. White Plains, NY: M.E. Sharpe.

Furlong, V.J. 1984. 'Interaction Sets in the Classroom: Towards a Study of Pupil Knowledge'. In *Life in School*, edited by M. Hammersley and P. Woods, 145–60. Milton Keynes, UK: Open University Press.

Gayfer, M. 1976. *Open Doors: A Community School Handbook*. Toronto: Ministry of Education for Ontario.

Giroux, H. 1983. *Theory and Resistance: A Pedagogy for the Opposition*. South Hadley, Mass.: Bergin and Garvey.

Gittell, M. 1970. 'The Balance of Power and the Community School'. In *Community Control of Schools*, edited by H.M. Levin, 115–37. New York: Simon and Schuster.

Globe and Mail. 1991. Toronto (17 December):A10.

Goodman, P. 1964. 'Compulsory Mis-Education'. In *Compulsory Mis-Education and the Community of Scholars*. New York: Alfred A. Knopf and Random House.

Gray, F. 1975. 'Order in the Classroom: Drugging for Deportment'. *The Nation* (1 November):423–5.

Greene, E. 1988. 'SAT Scores Fail to Help Admissions Officers Make Better Decisions, Analysts Contend'. *Chronicle of Higher Education* (27 July):A20.

Haas, J., and B. Shaffir, eds. 1974. *Decency & Deviance: Studies in Deviant Behaviour*. Toronto: McClelland and Stewart.

Hamilton, S.F. 1987. 'Raising Standards and Reducing Dropout Rates'. In *School Dropouts: Patterns and Policies*, edited by G. Natriello, 148–67. New York: Teachers College Press.

Hanson, D., et al. 1991. *A Study of At-Risk High School Youth and Early School Leavers in Five Puget Sound Area School Districts*. Olympia:

Washington State Legislature, Office of State Superintendent of Public Instruction.

Harper's. 1992. (April):20.

Hoffman, B. [1962] 1978. *The Tyranny of Testing*. Westport, CT: Greenwood.

Illich, I. 1972. *Deschooling Society*. New York: Harper and Row.

Innis, H. 1972. *Empire and Communications*. Toronto: University of Toronto Press.

Kozol, J. 1986. *Illiterate America*. New York: New American Library.

Kulka, R.A., D. Mann, and D.M. Klingel. 1980. 'A Person-Environment Fit Model of School Crime and Disruption'. In *Violence and Crime in the Schools*, edited by K. Baker and R.J. Rubel, 49–60. Lexington: D.C. Heath.

Lewington, J. 1992. 'Women Come to Grips with Math Ghost'. *Globe and Mail* (7 May):A10.

Lind, L.J. 1974. *The Learning Machine: A Hard Look at Toronto Schools*. Toronto: House of Anansi.

Lockhart, A. 1991. *Schoolteaching in Canada*. Toronto: University of Toronto Press.

Maclean's. 1992. 'A Blackboard Jungle' (16 March):30.

Malone, T.W. 1981. 'What Makes Computer Games Fun?' BYTE (December):258–77.

Martin, W. 1976. *The Negotiated Order of the School*. Toronto: Macmillan.

McDill, E.L., et al. 1987. 'A Population at Risk: Potential Consequences of Tougher School Standards for Student Dropouts'. In *School Dropouts: Patterns and Policies*, edited by G. Natriello, 106–47. New York: Teachers College Press.

McKie, C. 1990. 'Lifestyle Risks: Smoking and Drinking in Canada'. In *Canadian Social Trends*, edited by C. McKie and K. Thompson, 86–92. Toronto: Thompson.

McLaren, P. 1989. *Life in Schools*. Toronto: Irwin.

McLuhan, M. 1964. *Understanding Media*. Toronto: McGraw-Hill.

_____, and Q. Fiore. 1967. *The Medium Is the Massage*. Toronto: Bantam.

McRobbie, A. 1978. 'Working Class Girls and the Culture of Feminity'. In *Women Take Issue*, edited by Women's Study Group, Centre for Contemporary Cultural Studies. London: Hutchinson.

_____. 1980. 'Settling Accounts with Sub-cultures'. *Screen Education* 34.

Minzey, J.D., and C. LeTarte. 1972. *Community Education: From Program to Process*. Midland, Michigan: Pendell.

Moore, M. (n.d.) *Cheating 101: The Benefits and Fundamentals of Earning an Easy 'A'*. New Brunswick, NJ: self-published.

Morris, R. 1989. 'Safety Problems and Sexual Harassment on Campus'. In *Women in Graduate Studies in Ontario*, edited by C. Filteau. Toronto: Ontario Council on Graduate Studies.

Mura, R., et al. 1987. 'Girls in Science Programs: Two Steps Forward, One Step Back'. In *Women and Education: A Canadian Perspective*, edited by J. Gaskell and A. McLaren, 133–49. Calgary: Detselig.

Nelsen, R.W. 1978. 'The Education-as-Autonomous Argument and Pluralism: The Sociologies of Burton R. Clark, David Riesman, and Christopher Jencks'. In *Reading, Writing, and Riches: Education and the Socio-Economic Order in North America*, edited by R.W. Nelsen and D.A. Nock, 40–66. Kitchener-Toronto: Between the Lines.

_____. 1985a. 'The End of Childhood: Technological Change, Parenting and the School'. *Canadian Review of Sociology and Anthropology* 22 (May):303–10.

_____. 1985b. 'Books, Boredom and Behind Bars: An Explanation of Apathy and Hostility in Our Schools'. *Canadian Journal of Education* 10 (Spring):136–60.

_____. 1991. *Miseducating: Death of the Sensible*. Kingston, ON: Cedarcreek Publications.

Nelson, J. 1987. *The Perfect Machine: TV in the Nuclear Age*. Toronto: Between the Lines.

_____. 1988. *Sultans of Sleaze: Public Relations and the Media*. Toronto: Between the Lines.

_____. 1991. 'Introduction'. In *The Noam Chomsky Lectures: A Play*, edited by D. Brooks and G. Verdecchia, 7–9. Toronto: Coach House Press.

Oakes, J. 1985. *Keeping Track: How Schools Structure Inequality*. New Haven: Yale University Press.

O'Brien, M. 1981. *The Politics of Reproduction*. London: Routledge and Kegan Paul.

_____. 1988. *Reproducing the World: Essays in Feminist Theory*. Boulder: Westview.

Ogbu, J. 1986. 'Class Stratification, Racial Stratification, and Schooling'. In *Race, Class and Schooling*, edited by L. Weis. Buffalo: Special Studies in Comparative Education, Comparative Education Center, Faculty of Educational Studies, State University of New York at Buffalo.

Our Schools/Our Selves. 1991. 'Racism and Education: Fighting Back' 3, no. 21 (December):19–105.

Payne, C. 1989. 'Urban Teachers and Dropout-Prone Students: The Uneasy Partners'. In *Dropouts from School: Issues, Dilemmas, and Solutions*, edited by L. Weis, E. Farrar, and H.G. Petrie, 113–28. Albany: State University of New York Press.

Ponting, J.R., and R. Gibbins. 1980. *Out of Irrelevance: A Socio-Political Introduction to Indian Affairs*. Toronto: Butterworths.

Porter, J. 1965. *The Vertical Mosaic: An Analysis of Social Class and Power in Canada*. Toronto: University of Toronto Press.

Postman, N. 1982. *The Disappearance of Childhood*. New York: Delacorte.
_____. 1985. *Amusing Ourselves to Death: Public Discourse in the Age of Show Business*. New York: Penguin.
_____. 1992. *Technopoly: The Surrender of Culture to Technology*. New York: Alfred A. Knopf.
Prentice, A. 1977. *The School Promoters*. Toronto: McClelland and Stewart.
Provenzo, E.F., Jr. 1991. *Video Kids: Making Sense of Nintendo*. Cambridge, Mass.: Harvard University Press.
Pyke, S.W. 1991. 'Gender Issues in Graduate Education'. The Second Annual Trevor N.S. Lennam Memorial Lecture in Graduate Education, University of Calgary, 27 March.
Radwanski, G. 1987. *Ontario Study of the Relevance of Education, and the Issue of Dropouts*. Toronto: Ministry of Education.
Randhawa, B.S. 1991. 'Inequities in Educational Opportunities and Life Chances'. In *Hitting the Books: The Politics of Educational Retrenchment*, edited by T. Wotherspoon, 139–58. Toronto: Garamond.
Rapoport, R. 1974. 'The Educator as Pusher: Just a Little Pill to Keep the Kids Quiet?' In *The Politics of the Canadian Public School*, edited by G. Martell, 71–4. Toronto: James Lewis and Samuel.
Repo, S. 1974. 'The Educator as Pusher: Drug Control in the Classroom'. In *The Politics of the Canadian Public School*, edited by G. Martell, 75–91. Toronto: James Lewis and Samuel.
Rosenthal, R., and L. Jacobson. 1968. *Pygmalion in the Classroom: Teacher Expectation and Pupils' Intellectual Development*. New York: Holt, Rinehart and Winston.
Rosser, S.R. 1990. *Female-Friendly Science*. Elmsford, NY: Pergamon Press.
Schecter, S. 1977. 'Capitalism, Class, and Educational Reform in Canada'. In *The Canadian State: Political Economy and Political Power*, edited by L. Panitch, 373–416. Toronto: University of Toronto Press.
Schutz, A. 1967. *The Phenomenology of the Social World*. Translated by G. Walsh and F. Lehnert. Evanston, Ill.: Northwestern University Press.
Shkilnyk, A.M. 1985. *A Poison Stronger Than Love: The Destruction of an Ojibwa Community*. New Haven: Yale University Press.
Smith, F. 1986. *Insult to Intelligence: The Bureaucratic Invasion of Our Classrooms*. New York: Arbor House.
Stark, R. 1992. *Sociology*, 4th ed. Belmont, CA: Wadsworth.
Stevens, J. 1974. 'Community Schools'. *Education Canada* 14, no. 4:11–15.
Tausig, C. 1991. 'University Dropouts: "Why Are We Losing So Many?"' *University Affairs* 33 (October):48.
Turrittin, A.H. 1986. 'Inequalities of Social Class'. In *Sociology: An Introduction*, edited by K. Ishwaran, 409–37. Toronto: Addison-Wesley.

Van den Berghe, P. 1970. *Academic Gamesmanship: How to Make a Ph.D. Pay*. Toronto: Abelard-Schuman.

Wehlage, G.G., and R.A. Rutter. 1987. 'Dropping Out: How Much Do Schools Contribute to the Problem'. In *School Dropouts: Patterns and Policies*, edited by G. Natriello, 70–88. New York: Teachers College Press.

Weiss, J., et al. 1989. *Standing Up to the SAT*. New York: Arco Books.

Willis, P.E. 1977. *Learning to Labour: How Working Class Kids Get Working Class Jobs*. Farnborough, UK: Saxon House, Teakfield Limited.

Winn, M. 1978. *The Plug-In Drug*. New York: Viking.

_____. 1983. *Children Without Childhood*. New York: Pantheon.

Wolf, N. 1991. *The Beauty Myth*. New York: Morrow.

Wolfe, M. 1985. *Jolts: The TV Wasteland and the Canadian Oasis*. Toronto: Lorimer.

Woods, P. 1984. 'Negotiating the Demands of Schoolwork'. In *Life in School*, edited by M. Hammersley and P. Woods, 225–37. Milton Keynes, UK: Open University Press.

Contributors

Barry Adam, Department of Sociology, University of Windsor
Marilyn Bicher, Social Science Department, Vanier College
Carolyn Carey, Department of Sociology and St Peter's College, University of Saskatchewan
Patricia Erickson, Addiction Research Foundation, Toronto
Thomas Fleming, Department of Sociology, University of Windsor
Deborah Findlay, Department of Sociology and Social Anthropology, Dalhousie University
Jim Frideres, Department of Sociology, University of Calgary
Ron Hinch, Department of Sociology, University of Guelph
Kathleen Kendall, Department of Sociology, University of Reading, UK
Linda Mahood, Department of History, University of Guelph
Eleanor Maticka-Tyndale, Department of Sociology, University of Windsor
Randle W. Nelsen, Department of Sociology, Lakehead University
Nancy Poon, Department of Criminology, University of Keele, UK
Vic Satzewich, Department of Sociology, McMaster University
Bernard Schissel, Department of Sociology, University of Saskatchewan
Frances M. Shaver, Department of Sociology and Anthropology, Concordia University
Kathy Storrie, Department of Sociology, University of Saskatchewan
Walter Murray Collegiate, Grade Eleven Advanced Studies Class, Saskatoon. Teachers: Shammi Rathwell and Marshall Whelan. Students: Sarah Cox, Lisa Hall, Alan Hiebert, Alison Jeppeson, Chris Kreutzweiser, Carla Morris, Bina Nair, Tan Quach, Nathan Schissel, Jason Smith, Carey Tufts, Cristina Weir, Jennie Wilson.
Terry Wotherspoon, Department of Sociology, University of Saskatchewan
Li Zong, Department of Sociology and St Peter's College, University of Saskatchewan

Index

Aboriginal communities: as defeated neighbourhoods, 313; definition of crime in, 294–5; deviance in, 289–90, 294; education, 291; and federal government, 311–12; housing, 291, 293–4; modernization in, 309–11; quality of life, 291–4; sexual abuse in, 290; substance abuse in, 290–1; suicide in, 290–2, 380; unemployment in, 291; violent death, 290–2

Aboriginal culture: and behaviour, 302; and dominant culture, 299–300; values of, 302–3; wrongdoing in, 294–5

Aboriginal justice system, 295

Aboriginal peoples: admissions to jails, 290–1; cultural traits of students, 388–9; definition of Indian, 277; differences among groups, 276–7; disenfranchisement of, 261, 277; and government, 309–12; history of, 263, 275, 297–300; ideology of racism, 274; relocation of, 312–13; as surplus, 263, 276; and traditional culture, 295; women in prison, 114, 116

abortion, 228, 230; acceptance of by teenagers, 81, 88; rights, 231

abuse. *See* child sexual abuse; male domestic abuse; sexual abuse; substance abuse; wife abuse

Academic Gamesmanship (Van den Berghe), 375

Act for the Gradual Civilization of the Indian Tribes in the Canadas (1857), 277

Act for the Gradual Enfranchisement of Indians, 298

Adam, Barry, 202

Adams, D., 245

addiction: and medical profession, 61; societal response to, 60

Adler, Freda, 103–4

advanced capitalism, and role of women, 111–12

African Americans: drop-out rate, 381; and prison population, 381. *See also* Black communities

Ageton, S.S., 44

AIDS, 227–8; awareness movement, 234; constructing, 232–4; debates over, 202; punitive approach to, 233–4

Akers, P., 205
Alberta: medical coverage in, 157; sterilization in, 141
Alberta Report, 359
alcohol, 66; Quebec culture, 72; societal response to, 59–62; and teenage attitudes, 81–2, 84–5, 87–8, 91–4
alcoholism: and biological research, 8; medical model, 62
Allen Memorial Institute, 144
The Alley Boys (Gum Wah), 327
alternative schools, 393
American Medical Association, 151–2, 153, 178
American Psychiatric Association, 144, 163, 164
Amir, M., 43–4
amniocentesis test, 156
Andre, G., 142
androcentric bias, 243
anger management techniques, 250, 252
anomie, 10–11, 205
Anthias, F., 266, 271, 283
anti-Asiatic riot (1907), 70
antidepressants, 164–5
antidiet, 186–7
antidrug ideology, 71
antifeminism, 230
antihomosexual campaign, 231
antipsychiatry movement, 144–5
Appeals Court: British Columbia, 214; Ontario, 214
appearance norms. *See* body appearance norms
Apple, Michael, 388, 393
Archambault Commission, 113
Asians: and university quota systems, 382; and youth gang members, 327
Assheton-Smith, Marilyn, 391–2
Assiniboine people, 276

Association for Social Knowledge, 231
atavism, notion of, 102, 110

Backhouse, C., 32, 47
Bacon, Francis, 3
Bad Attitude, 236
Badgley Commission, 236
'Bad Trick Sheets', 218
Bandura, A., 9
Banton, Michael, 263, 267–8, 270, 277
Baril, Joan, 376
Baril, M., 36, 39
Barker, M., 267, 283–4
Barnes, B., 241
Barrett, S., 52
Basic Instinct, 235
battered women, feminist approach to, 244–6
battered-women's movement, 247–8
Bear (Engel), 235
Beccaria, Cesare, 4
Beck, E.M., 383
Becker, Howard S., 16, 264, 358, 374, 375
behavioural science, 342
behavioural strategies, deviance, 308–9
behaviourism theory, 9
Belenky, M.F., 380
Bentham, Jeremy, 4
benzodiazepines, 162
Berstein, Basil, 346, 387
Bicher, Marilyn, 127
Bini, Lucio, 138
biodeterminism, 110
biological determinism, and female criminality, 102
biological factors, of mental disorder, 163–4
biological inferiority/superiority theory, 268

Canadian Mental Health Association (CMHA), 161, 169
Canadian National Committee for Mental Hygiene (CNCMH), 141
Canadian National Exhibition, 324
Canadian News Index (CNI), 359
Canadian Urban Victimization Survey. *See* CUVS
cancer, and the Même implant, 191
cannabis, 68; decriminalization of, 66, 70. *See also* marijuana
capitalism: control of body and, 180; division of labour in, 49; and institutions for the mad, 132; and patriarchy, 112; racism as feature of, 269; and socialist feminism, 48; society under, 228
Carey, Carolyn, 26–7
Carlen, P., 107–8
Castles, S., 269
CBC, 231
censorship, 228; and Canada Customs, 235
Centre Island (Toronto), teenage gangs, 320
Cerletti, Ugo, 138
certification, of teachers, 342
Chalouh, M., 367
Chambliss, W.J., 13, 49
Chapman, I., 302
Charter of Rights and Freedoms, 67
Chatelaine, 359, 363, 365
cheating: and school grades, 97–8; and teenage attitudes, 84, 375
Cheating 101: The Benefits and Fundamentals of Earning an Easy 'A' (Moore), 375
Cher (entertainer), 187
Chicago School of Sociology, 12
child-bearing, and role of women, 150–1
childhood, disappearance of, 384–5
child sexual abuse, 38, 236

Chin, K.L., 328
Chinese, attitudes towards, 282–3
Chinese Immigration Act (1923), 283
chorionic villi sampling, 156
Christie, Nils, 70
The Christie Boys, and Centre Island (Toronto), 320
church, as force of social control, 2
CIA, and Canadian psychiatry, 144
Circle, teachings of, 302
Clark, L., 36, 37, 39, 51
The Clash, 321
class: and appearance norms, 176, 184–5, 196; and cosmetic surgery, 190; and dealing with distress, 160–1; and health of women, 150–1; ideology of meritocracy, 382–4; of immigrants, and attitudes towards, 282–3; and knowledge, 242; and prostitution charges, 215–16; and split labour market theory, 269–70; and types of crime, 48; and use of term paper companies, 383–4
classical criminological theory, 11
classical theory, 3–5
client/call-girl relationships, 217
climate, as component of character, 280
climate issues, universities and feminists, 362
cocaine: addictive quality, 65; societal response to, 59, 62, 67–9
codes of conduct, and power, 1
coercive sexuality, 51
cognitive behavioural approach, 250
cognitive development theory, 9
cognitive social learning theory, 249
Cohen, A., 305
Cohen, L., 32, 47
Cohen, S., 143, 248
Colclough, Glenna, 383

Cumberland, F.B., 274
Currie, D., 109
CUVS (Canadian Urban Victimiza-
tion Survey), 34–7, 40, 41

Dalkon Shield, 192
Dalton, K., 103
dangerousness, as social construct,
26
Dans La Rue (Montreal), 218
Darwin, Charles, 6–7
date rape: awareness campaign, 357;
on campuses, 334; and school
grades, 98–9; and teenage attitudes, 84, 93
Davis, Kingsley, 10, 205
decent citizen deviance, 374
DeKeseredy, W.S., 33, 39, 105
Delinquency in Girls (Cowie, Cowie,
and Slater), 103
democratic education, 343–7
Department of Indian and Northern
Affairs, 311
Department of Justice, 38, 204, 214
depression: hospital treatment for,
164–6; social factors in, 163–4
DES hormone, 192
deterrence/cost-benefit principle, 5
deterrence theory, 5, 11
Detroit, 325
deviance, 16; in Aboriginal communities, 289–90; among teenagers,
86–9; behavioural strategies, 308;
biological explanations for, 296;
and community structure, 288;
and hidden curriculum, 373;
implications of term, 1–2; as
lifestyle decision, 2; of prostitution, 204–5; rural versus urban
youths, 79–83; and school
context, 393; and sexuality, 201–2;
social construction of, 374–8;
violent, 98–9

deviant populations, and race, 264
*Diagnostic and Statistical Manual of
Mental Disorders* (American
Psychiatric Association), 163
Dickinson, H.D., 142
Dietz, M.L., 324
differential association theory, 12
differential socialization, 205
Discipline and Punish (Foucault), 17
discourse theory, 17–18
disease, and social norms, 181
disease model, of mental illness, 143
distress, dealing with, 160–1
Domestic Abuse Intervention
Project (Duluth, Minnesota), 253
Dow Corning Corporation, 190–1
Dreeben, R., 336
drug control, 26; and perceived
abuse, 63; and politics, 62–3
drug crisis industry, 65
drugs: and controlling behaviour of
children, 389–90; mythology of,
64; perception of effects, 63–4
drug use: and culture, 63–6; normalcy of, 71; and social controls,
63, 72; and teenage attitudes, 82,
84, 91
D'Souza, D., 382
dualism, of gender, 187
dual systems theory, 48
Durham, Lord, 271–2
Durkheim, Emile, 10, 11, 288–9,
336, 374
Dyck, N., 299
dysfunctionality, and deviance, 289

early school leaving. *See* school
drop-out rate
Eating Disorder Information Centre
(Toronto), 195
eating disorders, 182–9, 194–5
Eaton Centre (Toronto), run in,
324

foetal heart monitors, 158
Fonda, Jane, 187
Food and Drugs Act, 67
food consumption, societal regulation of, 180–1
Fordham (of Rutgers), 381
formal education, 347; curriculum, 333, 336, 338, 348; discipline and control in, 335; and notions of common good, 339
Foucauldianism, 127
Foucault, Michel, 2, 17–18, 132, 248, 337, 374, 391
Fowler, K., 326, 328, 330
France, Anatole, 105
francophone women, in Kingston P4W, 114
Frankfurt School, 14
Fraser Committee (Special Committee on Pornography and Prostitution), 209
Fredericton, 38
The Fred Hamiltons, and Centre Island (Toronto), 320
Fredsburg, Ralph, 237
Freeman, Walter, 139
free will, classical theory of, 3, 5
Freidson, E., 133
French-English relations, as race relations, 271–4
Freud, Sigmund, 8–9, 139–40
Frideres, Jim, 261
Frize, Monique, 353
frogman of Hart House, University of Toronto, 352–3, 367
frustration-aggression hypothesis, 9
functionalism. *See* structural functionalism

gang crime unit, Vancouver, 328
gangs: Asian, 327–8; behaviour of, 325–7; Chicano membership, 327; and group loyalty, 326; male, 8;

membership in, 262; violence, 328; women in, 322
gay liberation movement, 231–2
gays and lesbians, 229, 231–2; fear of sexual harassment, 365
Gebhard, P.H., 42
Geffner, R., 247, 251
gender: and deviance, 83–6; harassment, 354; ideology of meritocracy, 379–80; and psychiatric treatment, 164–6; and street prostitution, 217–18; and treatment for emotional distress, 161–2
gender inequality, and female crime rate, 108
gender role, assumptions early 20th c., 111
general paresis, 136
general practitioners, and emotional distress, 161–2
Generation X, 323
germ theory of disease, 136
Gibbons, Roger, 388
Gintis, H., 336
Giroux, Henry, 387–8
Glad Day Bookstore (Toronto), 236
Globe and Mail, 68, 357, 359
Gottfredson, G.D., 393
Grade Eleven Advanced Program, Walter Murray Collegiate Institute, 78
Gramsci, Antonio, 14–15
Grand Canyon, 325
Grant, A., 159
Grassy Narrows, 380–1
Greek and Roman models, of madness, 130–1
Greene, E., 383
Griffin, S., 37
group composition of Advanced Research, 78–9

group conflict theory, 205
Gunn, R., 36, 40–1, 53
gynaecological surgery, 137

Haas, Jack, 374
Halifax, 35; prison for women, 115;
  prostitution charges, 214
Halifax Chronicle-Herald, 359
Hamilton, 35, 38, 41; early school
  leavers, 378
'hangin', 326
Hanson, David, 394
harm reduction conference, 70
Harper's magazine, 375
Hartmann, H., 48
Harvard, 154
hashish, 66
Health and Welfare Canada, 191;
  Division of Narcotic Control, 61
health care: Medicare, 151; need to
  politicize, 194–7
health fascism, 189
hedonism, 3–4
hegemony: concept of, 15; European, 297–300
heightened surveillance, 248
Heitgerd, J.L., 302
The Hell's Angels Motorcycle Club,
  327
heroin: effects of, 64, 70; societal
  response to, 59, 62, 67
hidden curriculum, 333–8, 342–5;
  and cultural capital, 345–6, 387–
  8; and school deviants, 373; and
  social control, 348; and technology, 384–7
hierarchy of credibility, and the
  media, 358
hierarchy of schools, 389
high school students, drop-out rate,
  378
Hinch, R., 25, 31, 33, 35, 36, 49–50,
  52

Hippocrates, 130
Hirschi, Travis, 5
History of Sexuality (Foucault), 17
HIV transmission, and safer sex
  message, 233–4
Hobbs, A.T., 137
Hoffman, B., 383
Hoffman-Bustamente, D., 103
Holland, infant mortality rate, 155
homeless youths, 329
homophobia, on university campuses, 334, 365
homosexual assault, 29–30
homosexuality, genetic link to, 8
homosexual panic defence, 237
honest-but-mistaken defence, 30,
  50–2
hooks, bell, 196
Hôpital Général, Paris, 132
Hudson's Bay Company, 195–6,
  275–6
Human Rights Act, 355
Hume, James G., 340
humoral theory, 130–1

iatrogenesis, cultural and social,
  156–7
idealist criminology, 105–6
idealist Marxism, 13
ideology: of capitalism, 112; journalistic, 357–9; of meritocracy,
  373, 379–84; of patriarchy, 112;
  of science and professionalism,
  341–2
illegal drugs, and teenage attitudes,
  80, 85. *See also* specific drugs
Illich, Ivan, 393
Illiterate America (Kozol), 379
image, of female body, 128
immigration: and race making, 278–
  83; and youth unemployment,
  321–2
Immigration Act, 141

Wolfgang, M.E., 44
women: and appearance norms,
174–82; assessments of in correctional reports, 110–11; and media
crime reports, 359; and mood–
modifying prescription drugs,
143, 162; and non-violent property crime, 101; in prisons, 26,
101–2, 109–16; targets for
wildings, 324; in university
programs, 344; in youth gangs,
322 Women Against Violence
Against Women, 235
*Women and Mental Health in Canada:
Strategies for Change* (CMHA), 161
Women and the Psychiatric Paradox
(Penfold and Walker), 167
women's movement, 229, 232
Woodsworth, J.S., 279, 280–1, 283
work, as therapy, 135–6
working class: racism, 270; students
in schools, 334; warrior, 322;
women and appearance norms,
176

World Charter for Prostitutes'
Rights, 219
World Health Organization, 159,
178
World Psychiatric Association, 144
Wotherspoon, T., 333
wrongdoing, in Aboriginal culture,
294–5
Wyer, Johann, 131

Young, J., 106
Young Offenders Act, 360; and
labelling theory, 16
youth crime, and justice, 26
youth discontent, 262, 321–2
youth gangs. *See* gangs
youths: in detention, 390; homeless,
329
yuppies, as focus of youth anger, 323
Yuval-Davis, N., 271, 283

Zenner, W., 311
Zita Psi fraternity, 355
Zong, Li, 261